The Collected Works of CHARLES COLSON

The Collected Works of CHARLES COLSON

Loving God

Kingdoms in Conflict

INSPIRATIONAL PRESS

NEW YORK

First Inspirational Press edition published in 1995.

Inspirational Press
A division of Budget Book Service, Inc.
386 Park Avenue South
New York, NY 10016

Inspirational Press is a registered trademark of Budget Book Service, Inc.

Published by arrangement with Zondervan Publishing House.

Library of Congress Catalog Card Number: 95-78590

ISBN: 0-88486-121-X

Printed in the United States of America.

CONTENTS

LOVING GOD

by Charles Colson

To those who introduced me to the love of God, to those
who demonstrated it in their love for me, and to those who
challenged me to love Him in return.
And especially to my co-workers in Prison Fellowship,
who share with me the daily pilgrimage of loving God.

EDITOR'S NOTE

All the stories in this book are true. In some, names have been changed; in others, editorial liberties have been taken to combine certain events for purposes of clarity or illustration. In one case, the use of allegory proved the most effective literary device to make the point. But in all instances the events underlying the stories are true. Background details have been researched as thoroughly as possible, although at times inferences were drawn from the limited facts available. Where that is the case, it is made evident in the text.

CONTENTS

THE HUNGER FOR HOLINESS

THE HOLY NATION

LOVING GOD

STUDY GUIDE

The most pleasurable journey you take is through yourself ... the only sustaining love involvement is with yourself.... When you look back on your life and try to figure out where you've been and where you're going, when you look at your work, your love affairs, your marriages, your children, your pain, your happiness — when you examine all that closely, what you really find out is that the only person you really go to bed with is yourself.... The only thing you have is working to the consummation of your own identity. And that's what I've been trying to do all my life.

Shirley MacLaine[1]

It is vain, O men, that you seek within yourselves the cure for your miseries. All your insight only leads you to the knowledge that it is not in yourselves that you will discover the true and the good.

Blaise Pascal

How It All Began: An Introduction

Two strong forces — one external, one internal — came together to forge my decision and determination to write this book. The external force was the result of what I saw happening in the culture around me over a period of years. The internal force had to do with my own spiritual life. Let me explain.

For a generation, Western society has been obsessed with the search for self. We have turned the age-old philosophical question about the meaning and purpose of life into a modern growth industry. Like Heinz, there are fifty-seven varieties, and then some: biofeedback, Yoga, creative consciousness, EST, awareness workshops, TA — each fad with an avid following until something new comes along.

Popular literature rides the wave with best-selling titles that guarantee success with everything from making money to firming flabby thighs. This not-so-magnificent obsession to "find ourselves" has spawned a whole set of counterfeit values; we worship fame, success, materialism, and celebrity. We want to "live for success" as we "look out for number one," and we don't mind "winning through intimidation."

However, this "self" conscious world is in desperate straits. Each new promise leads only to a frustrating paradox. The 1970s self-fulfillment fads led to self-absorption and isolation, rather than the fuller, liberated lives they predicted. The technology created to lead humanity to this new promised land may instead obliterate us and our planet in a giant mushroom cloud. Three decades of seemingly limitless affluence have succeeded only in sucking our culture dry, leaving it spiritually empty and economically weakened. Our world is filled with self-absorbed, frightened, hollow people.

Amid these debilitating paradoxes of modern life, men and women search for some shred of meaning, some understanding of self. But the obsessive search for self leads only to the narcissistic destruction of what is so avidly sought. Consider the young woman cited in a *Psychology Today* article: her nerves were shot from too many all-night parties and discos, her life an endless round of pot, booze, and sex. When asked, "Why don't you stop?" by her therapist, her startled reply was, "You mean I really don't have to do what I want to do?"

And in the midst of all this we have the church — those who follow Christ. For the church, this ought to be an hour of opportunity. The church alone can provide a moral vision to a wandering people; the church alone can step into the vacuum and demonstrate that there is a sovereign, living God who is the source of Truth.

BUT, the church is in almost as much trouble as the culture, for the church has bought into the same value system: fame, success, materialism, and celebrity. We watch the leading churches and the leading Christians for our cues. We want to emulate the best-known preachers with the biggest sanctuaries and the grandest edifices.

Preoccupation with these values has also perverted the church's message. The assistant to one renowned media pastor, when asked the key to his man's success, replied without hesitation, "We give the people what they want." This heresy is at the root of the most dangerous message preached today: the what's-in-it-for-me gospel.

The "victorious Christian life" has become man's victorious life, not God's. A popular daily devotional quotes Psalm 65:9, "The streams of God are filled with water," and paraphrases it, "I fill my mind to overflowing with thoughts of prosperity and success. I affirm that God is my source and God is unlimited."[2] This is not just a religious adaptation of the look-out-for-number-one, winner-take-all, God-helps-those-who-help-themselves gospel of our culture; it is heresy.

Thus, both the world and the church are groping for answers.

As I saw what was happening around me, I also became aware of something happening inside me. This surfaced a few years ago when I was experiencing one of those periods of spiritual dryness we all encounter. When I told a friend, he suggested I watch a videocassette lecture series by Dr. R. C. Sproul on the holiness of God.

All I knew about Sproul was that he was a theologian, so I wasn't enthusiastic. After all, I reasoned, theology was for people who had time to study, locked in ivory towers far from the battlefields of human need. However, at my friend's urging I finally agreed to watch Sproul's series.

By the end of the sixth lecture I was on my knees, deep in prayer, in awe of God's absolute holiness. It was a life-changing experience as I gained a completely new understanding of the holy God I believe in and worship.

My spiritual drought ended, but this taste of the majesty of God only made me thirst for more of Him. So I gathered up contemporary books on the subject of discipleship—by the armload. Many were excellent, though they often dealt more with evangelism than discipleship; and most seemed concerned with how to get more out of the Christian life. I wanted to know how to put more into it.

One thing all the books dealt with, of course, was God's love for humanity and how He showed that love by the sacrifice of His Son on the cross. The more I read about this, the more I wanted to know about what I had begun to see as the corollary—how I show my love for Him. Somehow that seemed to be the key to putting more into the Christian life.

The greatest commandment of all, Jesus said, is "Love the Lord your God with all your heart and with all your soul and with all your mind."[3] I'd memorized those words but had never really thought about what they meant in practical terms; that is, how to fulfill that command. I wondered if others felt the same way. So I asked a number of more experienced Christians how they loved God.

"Well ... by loving Him," one stammered, then added by way of explanation, "... with all my heart, soul, and mind."

"By maintaining a worshipful heart, offering myself as an acceptable sacrifice," another answered quickly. When I pressed for specifics, he began detailing his devotional reading schedule and prayer life. Halfway through his discourse, he stopped and shrugged. "Let me think about it some more."

Faithful church attendance was a frequent response, and tithing ranked high on the list. Several recited favorite sins they no longer pursued while many tried to explain "loving God" as a feeling in their hearts, as if it were something akin to a romantic encounter. Others looked at me suspiciously, perhaps thinking my query some kind of trick question.

That did it. The cumulative effect of my survey convinced me that most of us, as professing Christians, do not really know how to love God. Not only have we not given thought to what the greatest commandment means in our day-to-day existence, we have not obeyed it. And if this was true for individual believers, what were the ramifications for the church? Perhaps the reason the church was so ineffective in the world was that it had the same needs I did.

Seeing the desperate hunger in the culture, and realizing how much we as the people of God need to love God, the message of this book was urgently pressed upon me. To use a rather strange, but perhaps appropriate, analogy, I saw a need to attempt to do for the gospel what Lenin did for Marx.

Though frequently thought of as an arm-waving, fiery revolutionary, Karl Marx was for most of his life a thinker, a theoretician. There was no great workers' revolution during his lifetime, and after his death in 1883, Marxism seemed destined to take its place as just another philosophy spawned by the fertile minds of the nineteenth century. Indeed, it probably would have, were it not for Lenin, a young Russian who voraciously devoured the ideas of Engels and Marx and became a Marxist in 1889.

Three years later, Lenin published *What Is To Be Done?* in which he spelled out the absolute of action, of taking Marx's theories and applying them to life. That book and Lenin's tireless labor inspired a handful of professional revolutionaries who within a few years turned Russia upside down. Lenin's passionate singlemindedness, his absolute commitment and application of Marx's principles changed not only his own country, but today, less than a hundred years later, has enslaved over half the world.

My question then, for individual believers and thus the church, is this: do we view our faith as a magnificent philosophy or a living truth; as an abstract, sometimes academic theory or a living Person for whom we are prepared to lay down our lives? The most destructive and tyrannical movements of the twentieth century, Communism and Nazism, have resulted from fanatics singlemindedly applying fallible philosophies. What would happen if we were actually to apply God's truth for the glory of His kingdom?

The result would be a world turned upside down, revolutionized by the power of God working through individual Christians and the church as a whole.

But we will only be weak and stumbling believers and a crippled church unless and until we truly apply God's Word — that is, until we truly love Him and act on that love.

Thus, forces internal and external have compelled me to write this book. As mentioned, the search leading to the discoveries recounted herein was sparked by the teaching of Dr. R. C. Sproul, now my dear friend and tutor. But my decision to begin writing came as the result of a visit to one of the squalid places where I spend so much of my life.

Delaware Prison, Easter morning, 1980 . . . one of the most important mornings of my life. . . .

OBEDIENCE

Only he who believes is obedient;
only he who is obedient believes.

Dietrich Bonhoeffer

1

Prologue: Paradox

It was a glorious Easter Sunday, the spring sun sparkling and warm, the air fresh and sweet. Too nice a day to spend in prison, but that's where I was bound.

As I approached the sprawling complex of brick buildings surrounded by barbed wire fences, I remembered my first visit here nine months earlier. As in most states, Delaware's institutions were dangerously overcrowded. The legislature, though unwilling to allocate needed funds, was carping mercilessly at corrections officials. To help make his own assessment of the situation, Governor DuPont had asked me to report on conditions at Delaware State Prison.

On that steamy August day I had visited every corner of the complex. I had walked through dormitories so jammed with sweaty bodies that the air was difficult to breathe. I had seen the psycho ward where a man writhed convulsively against the chains around his bloodied wrists and ankles. Immune to sedation, without restraints he would have destroyed himself. I had continued on to the "hole," stopping to talk with each man isolated there in solitary lockup.

One, who introduced himself as Sam Casalvera, had been sentenced to life without parole. Sam was tough, his huge, muscled arms testifying to hours of weight lifting. His defiant gaze told me prison — even solitary confinement — had not broken his spirit.

Sam was the exception. By the end of the tour I was overwhelmed, as I am in so many prisons, by the sight and stench of death. It was reflected in the inmates' eyes, in their head-bowed shuffle, in their endless staring at nothing through hand-clutched bars. The suicidal patient chained in the psychiatric unit was perhaps the most rational of all, I thought ironically; he was merely struggling to bring his body and spirit to the same point.

I asked the young chaplain if I could meet with the Christian inmates. We gathered in a small conference room off the warden's office. Of the eight prisoners present, all were lifers, seven were black.* These strong, earnest men were a dramatic contrast with what I had just seen. Joyous about their faith, they had resolute assurance that Jesus was alive and real, even in the midst of the human hopelessness of prison. We prayed together, holding hands around the table, and then I promised I'd be back.

A few months later we sent a Prison Fellowship seminar team into the Delaware prison. With the help of twenty volunteer laypeople from the nearby community, our two staff members (one an ex-con himself) conducted thirty-two hours of teaching. More than one hundred men signed up for that first in-prison seminar, and before the week was over, seventy-five met Christ. That made the week memorable, as did another unusual incident.

One study session was interrupted when two guards burst into the room, clamped handcuffs on a frightened young inmate, and hustled him out of the room to a waiting van. Those in the seminar, who knew only that he was being taken to court, prayed fervently.

Arriving in the courtroom, the inmate stood shaking before a stern-faced judge. "Young man," the judge said somberly, "I've been examining your records." He paused, then looked up. "And I've decided to reduce your sentence to time served. You're a free man.

"Good luck," he concluded, nodding at the speechless prisoner and rapping his gavel.

"Thank you, your Honor," the inmate choked; then, more loudly, "but sir, if it's all the same to you, could I stay in prison the rest of this week? I'd like to finish the Prison Fellowship seminar."

The judge, shocked, muttered something about working it out. The

*It was not surprising to find only eight Christians in a prison population of eight hundred. About 1 percent is the ratio we often find when we begin ministry in an institution.

man was returned to the seminar's expectant group of believers where there was much celebration.

During the months following I received a series of exciting reports about the Christian fellowship continuing to grow in Delaware. As spring approached, I knew I wanted to spend Easter with these brothers.

Now as I arrived at the front gate on Easter morning, I was met by the corrections commissioner, more than seventy-five Prison Fellowship volunteers, several judges including a justice of the state supreme court, and a bevy of other state officials. We were quickly escorted around the metal detectors and processing rooms — none of the usual search routines this morning.

The Christian inmates, more than one hundred in number at this point, had gotten permission to host a breakfast for us. As we were served in the mess hall, I took a perverse pleasure in watching the justice turn away from the dried-out porridge and sausages of dubious origin.

One of our enthusiastic hosts rapped his spoon against a cup, and when the group quieted he announced that an inmate, Sam Casalvera, would read a poem composed for the occasion — and dedicated to Chuck Colson.

Sam rose, wearing the broadest grin I'd ever seen; it was obvious he was not the same rebellious convict I'd met in solitary nine months earlier. I didn't need to ask what had happened.

Sam cleared his throat and began reading:

> I heard you were coming to worship once more
> With souls who were floundering when you came before.

He hesitated, took a deep breath, and continued.

> We had direction but needed a push
> You made us a promise and also a wish.

Sam paused to take a wrinkled cloth from his pocket and dab his eyes.

> Your promise was kept — Prison Fellowship you sent.
> Whatever I write can't tell you what it meant.
> Some who attended made your wish come true.
> They gave their life to Jesus, as you did too.

Men and women in prison don't cry. It's a sign of weakness, and weakness can be dangerous in prison. But Sam could not control his emotions. Tears flowed down his cheeks and his broad shoulders heaved.

I rose and walked to the front of the hall, put my arm around his shoulders, and took the paper from him. For a moment I thought I would dissolve along with Sam, but somehow I was able to read the remaining lines of his poem. I've loved poetry all my life and treasure many classics, but none have affected me as deeply as Sam Casalvera's earnest stanzas.

After breakfast our inmate hosts escorted us out of the mess hall and on a long procession to the chapel on the other side of the prison. As we began to cross the compound, I squinted through the bright sunlight and stopped short at the scene ahead. A crowd of prisoners surrounded the chapel, some carrying placards. In two hundred prison visits I'd never seen anything like it. Instinctively I reviewed the possibilities: a riot brewing; a demonstration against prison conditions; Muslim inmates protesting our presence?

A few steps further and I could make out, to my amazement and relief, the crude lettering on the signs: COME TO THE CHAPEL, read one. JESUS SETS THE PRISONERS FREE! was another.

Just as people in prison don't cry, neither do they call attention to their faith. To do so invites scorn, ridicule, or worse. But this group of Christians was parading the compound, advertising chapel!

Their daring had broken barriers. Men were gathering from all over the prison. The chapel was packed. And because three hundred prisoners were in solitary lockup, the Christian brothers had mounted four speakers on the chapel roof so the service could be heard throughout the prison. (Judging by the size of the amplifiers, it could also be heard by neighbors for miles around.)

The prison choir began the service. Their task was to warm up the crowd, and they were a roaring success. Even the supreme court justice, sandwiched between two muscular convicts in the front row, loosened up. Struggling at first to maintain his dignity, he gradually began tapping his foot and soon was grinning and clapping with the rest.

As I sat on the platform, waiting my turn at the pulpit, my mind began to drift back in time . . . to scholarships and honors earned, cases argued and won, great decisions made from lofty government offices. My life had been the perfect success story, the great American dream fulfilled. But all at once I realized that it was *not* my success God had used to enable me to help those in this prison, or in hundreds of others just like it. My life of success was not what made this morning so glorious — all my achievements meant nothing in God's economy. No, the real legacy of my life was my biggest failure — that I was an ex-convict. My greatest humiliation — being sent to prison — was the beginning of God's greatest use of my life; He chose the one experience in which I could not glory for *His* glory.

Confronted with this staggering truth, I discovered in those few moments in the prison chapel that my world was turned upside down. I understood with a jolt that I had been looking at life backward. But now I could see: only when I lost everything I thought made Chuck Colson a great guy had I found the true self God intended me to be and the true purpose of my life.

It is not what we do that matters, *but what a sovereign God chooses to do through us*. God doesn't want our success; He wants us. He doesn't demand our achievements; He demands our obedience. The kingdom of God is a kingdom of paradox, where through the ugly defeat of a cross, a holy God is utterly glorified. Victory comes through defeat; healing through brokenness; finding self through losing self.

Of course, our success-mad, egocentric culture cannot grasp that crucial truth. It is understandable only when the false values that obsess us are stripped away, sometimes in the midst of our most abject failures. Surely that was so in my life, and it was so in the life of a man by the name of Boris Kornfeld.

Kornfeld was a Russian doctor. What we know about him can only be pieced together from scanty records and accounts of one who knew him. But what emerges is a classic illustration of the principles of the kingdom of paradox, an example that has been a source of continuing inspiration to me. Let me tell you his remarkable story.

2

A Russian Doctor

No reporters have visited the prison camps of Soviet Russia, unless they have gone as prisoners. So to this day we have little information about the millions who have lived, suffered, and died there, especially during Stalin's reign of terror. Most will remain nameless for all time, remembered only in the hearts of those who knew and loved them. But from time to time, scraps of information have filtered out about a few. One of those few was Boris Nicholayevich Kornfeld.

Kornfeld was a medical doctor. From this we can guess a little about his background, for in post-revolutionary Russia such education never went to families tied in any way to czarist Russia. Probably his parents were socialists who had fastened their hopes on the Revolution. They were also Jews, but almost certainly not Jews still hoping for the Messiah, for the name Boris and the patronymic Nicholayevich indicate they had taken Russian names in some past generation. Probably Kornfeld's forebears were *Haskalah*, so-called "enlightened Jews," who accepted the philosophy of rationalism, cultivated a knowledge of the natural sciences, and devoted themselves to the arts. In language, dress, and social habits they tried to make themselves as much like their Russian neighbors as possible.

It was natural for such Jews to support Lenin's revolution, for the czars' vicious anti-Semitism had made life almost unendurable for the prior two hundred years. Socialism promised something much better for them than "Christian" Russia. "Christian" Russia had slaughtered Jews; perhaps atheistic Russia would save them.

Obviously Kornfeld had followed in his parents' footsteps, believing in Communism as the path of historical necessity, for political prisoners at that time were not citizens opposed to Communism or wanting the Czar's return. Such people were simply shot. Political prisoners were believers in the Revolution, socialists or communists who had, nevertheless, not kept their allegiance to Stalin's leadership pure.

We do not know what crime Dr. Kornfeld committed, only that it was a political crime. Perhaps he dared one day to suggest to a friend that their leader, Stalin, was fallible; or maybe he was simply accused of harboring such thoughts. It took no more than that to become a prisoner in the Russia of the early 1950s; many died for less. At any rate, Kornfeld was imprisoned in a concentration camp for political subversives at Ekibastuz.

Ironically, a few years behind barbed wire was a good cure for Communism. The senseless brutality, the waste of lives, the trivialities called criminal charges made men like Kornfeld doubt the glories of the system. Stripped of all past associations, of all that had kept them busy and secure, behind the wire prisoners had time to think. In such a place, thoughtful men like Boris Kornfeld found themselves reevaluating beliefs they had held since childhood.

So it was that this Russian doctor abandoned all his socialistic ideals. In fact, he went further than that. He did something that would have horrified his forebears.

Boris Kornfeld became a Christian.

While few Jews anywhere in the world find it easy to accept Jesus Christ as the true Messiah, a Russian Jew would find it even more difficult. For two centuries these Jews had known implacable hatred from the people who, they were told, were the most Christian of all. Each move the Jews made to reconcile themselves or accommodate themselves to the Russians was met by new inventions of hatred and persecution, as when the head of the governing body of the Russian Orthodox Church said he hoped that, as a result of the Russian pogroms, "one-third of the Jews will convert, one-third will die, and one-third will flee the country."

Yet following the Revolution a strange alignment occurred. Joseph Stalin demanded undivided, unquestioning loyalty to his government; but both Jews and Christians knew their ultimate loyalty was to God. Consequently people of both faiths suffered for their beliefs and frequently in the same camps.

Thus it was that Boris Kornfeld came in contact with a devout Christian, a well-educated and kind fellow prisoner who spoke of a Jewish Messiah who had come to keep the promises the Lord had made to Israel. This Christian — whose name we do not know — pointed out that Jesus had spoken almost solely to Jewish people and proclaimed that He came to the Jews first. That was consistent with God's special concern for the Jew, the chosen ones; and, he explained, the Bible promised that a new kingdom of peace would come. This man often recited aloud the Lord's Prayer, and Kornfeld heard in those simple words a strange ring of truth.

The camp had stripped Kornfeld of everything, including his belief in salvation through socialism. Now this man offered him hope — but in what a form!

To accept Jesus Christ — to become one of those who had always persecuted his people — seemed a betrayal of his family, of all who had been before him. Kornfeld knew the Jews had suffered innocently. Jews were innocent in the days of the Cossacks! Innocent in the days of the czars! And he himself was innocent of betraying Stalin; he had been imprisoned unjustly.

But Kornfeld pondered what the Christian prisoner had told him. In one commodity, time, the doctor was rich.

Unexpectedly, he began to see the powerful parallels between the Jews and this Jesus. It had always been a scandal that God should entrust Himself in a unique way to one people, the Jews. Despite centuries of persecution, their very existence in the midst of those who sought to destroy them was a sign of a Power greater than that of their oppressors. It was the same with Jesus — that God would present Himself in the form of a man had always confounded the wisdom of the world. To the proud and powerful, Jesus stood as a Sign, exposing their own limitations and sin. So they had to kill Him, just as those in power had to kill the Jews, in order to maintain their delusions of omnipotence. Thus, Stalin, the new god-head of the brave new world of the Revolution, had to persecute both Jew and Christian. Each stood as living proof of his blasphemous pretensions to power.

Only in the gulag could Boris Kornfeld begin to see such a truth. And the more he reflected upon it, the more it began to change him within.

Though a prisoner, Kornfeld lived in better conditions than most behind the wire. Other prisoners were expendable, but doctors were scarce in the remote, isolated camps. The authorities could not afford to lose a physician, for guards as well as prisoners needed medical attention. And no prison officer wanted to end up in the hands of a doctor he had cruelly abused.

Kornfeld's resistance to the Christian message might have begun to weaken while he was in surgery, perhaps while working on one of those guards he had learned to loathe. The man had been knifed and an artery cut. While suturing the blood vessel, the doctor thought of tying the thread in such a way that it would reopen shortly after surgery. The guard would die quickly and no one would be the wiser.

The process of taking this particular form of vengeance gave rein to the burning hatred Kornfeld had for the guard and all like him. How he despised his persecutors! He could gladly slaughter them all!

And at that point, Boris Kornfeld became appalled by the hatred and violence he saw in his own heart. Yes, he was a victim of hatred as his ancestors had been. But that hatred had spawned an insatiable hatred of his own. What a deadly predicament! He was trapped by the very evil he despised. What freedom could he ever know with his soul imprisoned by this murderous hate? It made the whole world a concentration camp.

As Kornfeld began to retie the sutures properly, he found himself, almost unconsciously, repeating the words he had heard from his fellow prisoner. "Forgive us our trespasses, as we forgive those who trespass against us." Strange words in the mouth of a Jew. Yet he could not help praying them. Having seen his own evil heart, he had to pray for cleansing. And he had to pray to a God who had suffered, as he had: Jesus.

For some time, Boris Kornfeld simply continued praying the Lord's Prayer while he carried out his backbreaking, hopeless tasks as a camp doctor. Backbreaking because there were always far too many patients. Hopeless because the camp was designed to kill men. He stood ineffectively against the tide of death gaining on each prisoner: disease, cold, overwork, beatings, malnutrition.

Doctors in the camp's medical section were also asked to sign decrees for imprisonment in the punishment block. Any prisoner whom the authorities did not like or wanted out of the way was sent to this block — solitary confinement in a tiny, dark, cold, torture chamber of a cell. A doctor's signature on the forms certified that a prisoner was strong and healthy enough to withstand the punishment. This was, of course, a lie. Few emerged alive.

Like all the other doctors, Kornfeld had signed his share of forms. What was the difference? The authorities did not need the signatures anyway; they had many other ways of "legalizing" punishment. And a doctor who did not cooperate would not last long, even though doctors were scarce. But shortly after he began to pray for forgiveness, Dr. Kornfeld stopped authorizing the punishment; he refused to sign the forms. Though he had signed hundreds of them, now he couldn't. Whatever had happened inside him would not permit him to do it.

This rebellion was bad enough, but Kornfeld did not stop there. He turned in an orderly.

The orderlies were drawn from a group of prisoners who cooperated with the authorities. As a reward for their cooperation, they were given jobs within the camp which were less than a death sentence. They became the cooks, bakers, clerks, and hospital orderlies. The other prisoners hated them almost more than they hated the guards, for these prisoners were traitors; they could never be trusted. They stole food from the other prisoners and would gladly kill anyone who tried to report them or give them trouble. Besides, the guards turned a blind eye to their abuses of power. People died in the camps every day; the authorities needed these quislings to keep the system running smoothly.

While making his rounds one day, Kornfeld came to one of his many patients suffering from pellagra, an all-too-common disease in the camps. Malnutrition induced pellagra which, perversely, made digestion nearly impossible. Victims literally starved to death.

This man's body showed the ravages of the disease. His face had become dark, one deep bruise. The skin was peeling off his hands; they had to be bandaged to staunch the incessant bleeding. Kornfeld had been giving the patient chalk, good white bread, and herring to stop the diarrhea and get nutrients into his blood, but the man was too far gone. When the doctor asked the dying patient his name, the man could not even remember it.

Just after leaving this patient, Kornfeld came upon a hulking orderly bent over the remains of a loaf of white bread meant for the pellagra patients. The man looked up shamelessly, his cheeks stuffed with food. Kornfeld had known about the stealing, had known it was one reason his patients did not recover, but his vivid memory of the dying man pierced him now. He could not shrug his shoulders and go on.

Of course he could not blame the deaths simply on the theft of food. There were countless other reasons why his patients did not recover. The hospital stank of excrement and lacked proper facilities and supplies. He had to perform surgery under conditions so primitive that often operations were little more than mercy killings. It was preposterous to stand on principle in the situation, particularly when he knew what the orderly might do to him in return. But the doctor had to be obedient to what he now believed. Once again the change in his life was making a difference.

When Kornfeld reported the orderly to the commandant, the officer found his complaint very curious. There had been a recent rash of murders in the camp; each victim had been a "stoolie." It was foolish — dangerously so at this time — to complain about anyone. But the commandant put the orderly in the punishment block for three days, taking the complaint with a perverse satisfaction. Kornfeld's refusal to sign the punishment forms was becoming a nuisance; this would save the commandant some trouble. The doctor had arranged his own execution.

Boris Kornfeld was not an especially brave man. He knew his life would be in danger as soon as the orderly was released from the cell block. Sleeping in the barracks, controlled at night by the camp-chosen prisoners, would mean certain death. So the doctor began staying in the hospital, catching sleep when and where he could, living in a strange twilight world where any moment might be his last.

But, paradoxically, along with this anxiety came tremendous freedom. Having accepted the possibility of death, Boris Kornfeld was now free to live. He signed no more papers or documents sending men to their deaths. He no longer turned his eyes from cruelty or shrugged his shoulders when he saw injustice. He said what he wanted and did what he could. And soon he realized that the anger and hatred and violence in his own soul had vanished. He wondered whether there lived another man in Russia who knew such freedom!

Now Boris Kornfeld wanted to tell someone about his discovery, about this new life of obedience and freedom. The Christian who had talked to him about Jesus had been transferred to another camp, so the doctor waited for the right person and the right moment.

One gray afternoon he examined a patient who had just been operated on for cancer of the intestines. This young man with a melon-shaped head and a hurt, little-boy expression touched the soul of the doctor. The man's eyes were sorrowful and suspicious and his face deeply etched by the years he had already spent in the camps, reflecting a depth of spiritual misery and emptiness Kornfeld had rarely seen.

So the doctor began to talk to the patient, describing what had happened to him. Once the tale began to spill out, Kornfeld could not stop.

The patient missed the first part of the story, for he was drifting in and out of the anesthesia's influence, but the doctor's ardor caught his concentration and held it, though he was shaking with fever. All through the afternoon and late into the night, the doctor talked, describing his conversion to Christ and his new-found freedom.

Very late, with the perimeter lights in the camp glazing the window-panes, Kornfeld confessed to the patient: "On the whole, you know, I have become convinced that there is no punishment that comes to us in this life on earth which is undeserved. Superficially, it can have nothing to do with what we are guilty of in actual fact, but if you go over your life with a fine-tooth comb and ponder it deeply, you will always be able to hunt down that transgression of yours for which you have now received this blow."

Imagine! The persecuted Jew who once believed himself totally innocent now saying that every man deserved his suffering, whatever it was.

The patient knew he was listening to an incredible confession. Though the pain from his operation was severe, his stomach a heavy, expansive agony of molten lead, he hung on the doctor's words until he fell asleep.

The young patient awoke early the next morning to the sound of running feet and a commotion in the area of the operating room. His first thought was of the doctor, but his new friend did not come. Then the whispers of a fellow patient told him of Kornfeld's fate.

During the night, while the doctor slept, someone had crept up beside him and dealt him eight blows on the head with a plasterer's mallet. And though his fellow doctors worked valiantly to save him, in the morning the orderlies carried him out, a still, broken form.

But Kornfeld's testimony did not die.

The patient pondered the doctor's last, impassioned words. As a result, he, too, became a Christian. He survived that prison camp and went on to tell the world what he had learned there.

The patient's name was Alexander Solzhenitsyn.

3

Faith and Obedience

Boris Kornfeld is the great paradox personified. A Jew who betrayed the faith of his fathers. A doctor whose years of training were senselessly wasted. A political idealist whose utopian vision led only to a barren Siberian prison. A prisoner who gave up his life for nothing more than a loaf of stolen bread. In every one of these areas, Boris Kornfeld was a failure — at least in the world's system of values. Yet God took that failure of a man and through his singleminded obedience used him to lead to Christ another who would go on to become a prophetic voice and one of the world's most influential writers.

For Kornfeld's words did their convincing, convicting work, touching what Solzhenitsyn later called "a sensitive chord." That was his moment of spiritual awakening; "God of the universe, I believe You again! Though I renounced You, You will be with me," he cried out.[1] It was a spiritual transfusion — life taken from one man and pumped into another for God's sovereign purpose.

And in his conversion Solzhenitsyn saw clearly the kingdom paradox. For in the emptiness of that Russian gulag, he perceived what pleasure-seeking millions in the abundance of Western life cannot. He wrote later, "the meaning of earthly existence lies, not as we have grown used to thinking, in prospering, but in the development of the soul."[2]

Kornfeld's brief Christian life was lived in circumscribed circumstances, almost in isolation. In many ways it would seem that his decision not to sign the medical forms, his reporting of the corrupt guard, even his few hours of testimony to a perhaps terminally ill patient were futile, would gain him nothing but that which came in the end — a brutal death at the hands of his captors. Yet Kornfeld's faith was strong, sure, and sincere. And somehow his fellow Christian and the Holy Spirit had communicated one fact to him: what God demanded of him was obedience, no matter what. Singleminded obedience in faith.

And that lesson of the Russian doctor's life was my lesson at Delaware: what God wants from His people is obedience, no matter what the circumstances, no matter how unknown the outcome.

It has always been this way. God calling His people to obedience and giving them at best a glimpse of the outcome of their effort.

Most of the great figures of the Old Testament died without ever seeing the fulfillment of the promises they relied upon.[3] Paul expended himself building the early church, but as his life drew to a close he could see only a string of tiny outposts along the Mediterranean, many weakened by fleshly indulgence or divided over doctrinal disputes.

In more recent times, the great colonial pastor Cotton Mather prayed for revival several hours each day for twenty years; the Great Awakening began the year he died. The British Empire finally abolished slavery as the Christian parliamentarian and abolitionist leader William Wilberforce lay on his deathbed, exhausted from his nearly fifty-year campaign against the practice of human bondage. Few were the converts during Hudson Taylor's lifelong mission work in the Orient; but today millions of Chinese embrace the faith he so patiently planted and tended.

Some might think this divine pattern cruel, but I am convinced there is a sovereign wisdom to it. Knowing how susceptible we are to success's siren call, God does not allow us to see, and therefore glory in, what is done through us. The very nature of the obedience He demands is that it be given without regard to circumstances or results.

A scriptural analogy of the unquestioning obedience God expects is found in Jesus' healing of the centurion's servant.[4] Matthew and Luke tell how the officer came to Christ on behalf of his paralyzed servant; when Jesus offered to go home with him, the centurion quickly replied that he knew Christ need only give the command and the man would be healed. The centurion understood about such things because when he ordered his troops to go, they went; in the same way he perceived Jesus' authority as that of a military commander to whom one gives unquestioning allegiance. Joyful to discover such faith, Jesus not only healed the servant, but used the centurion as an example of faith in His comments to the crowd.

The Bible makes clear, and experiences such as Kornfeld's confirm, that unquestioning acceptance of and obedience to Jesus' authority is the foundation of the Christian life. Everything else rests upon this. It also provides the key to understanding what is for many the great mystery of Christianity: faith.

Saving faith — that by which we are justified, made right with God — is a gift of God; and, yes, it involves a rational process as well since it comes from hearing the Word of God (more on that in later chapters). "All right," the struggling Christian may say, "but practically speaking, how does my faith become real? How do I get that vibrant, strong faith of Christian maturity?"

That's where obedience comes in. For maturing faith — faith which deepens and grows as we live our Christian life — is not just knowledge, but knowledge acted upon. It is not just belief, but belief lived out — practiced. James said we are to be doers of the Word, not just hearers. Dietrich Bonhoeffer, the German pastor martyred in a Nazi concentration camp, succinctly stated this crucial interrelationship: "Only he who believes is obedient; only he who is obedient believes."

This may sound like a circular proposition, but many things are — in truth and in practice. Think of learning how to swim. We are told what to do. We gingerly enter the water, launch out, and promptly forget everything we've been told. We flail about, splashing frantically, gasping and sinking. Finally, usually at the point of utter despair, we capture for a moment the sensation of staying afloat. Realizing it is possible, we remember our instructions and begin to follow them. They work. Like learning to balance a bicycle or mastering a foreign language, faith is a state of mind that grows out of our actions, just as it also governs them.

So obedience is the key to real faith — the unshakable kind of faith so powerfully illustrated by Job's life. Job lost his home, his family (except for a nagging wife), his health, even his hope. The advice of friends was no help. No matter where he turned, he could find no answers to his plight. Eventually he stood alone. But though it appeared God had abandoned him, Job clung to the assurance that *God is who He is*. Job confirmed his obedience with those classic words of faith: "Though he slay me, yet will I trust in him."[5]

This is real faith: believing and acting obediently regardless of circumstances or contrary evidence. After all, if faith depended on visible evidence, it wouldn't be faith. "We walk by faith, not by sight," the apostle Paul wrote.

It is absurd for Christians to constantly seek new demonstrations of God's power, to expect a miraculous answer to every need, from curing ingrown toenails to finding parking spaces; this only leads to faith in miracles rather than the Maker.

True faith depends not upon mysterious signs, celestial fireworks, or grandiose dispensations from a God who is seen as a rich, benevolent uncle; true faith, as Job understood, rests on the assurance that *God is who He is*. Indeed, on that we must be willing to stake our very lives.

There was a time when eleven men did just that. They staked their lives on obedience to their leader, even when doing so was contrary to all human wisdom. That act of obedience produced a faith that emboldened them to stand against the world and, in their lifetimes, change it forever.

Forty days after His resurrection, Jesus summoned His disciples to meet Him on the Mount of Olives. Imagine their excitement, believing as they apparently did that this very day their Master would establish His kingdom on earth and fulfill the great promise the Jews had clung to through centuries of suffering and exile. Christ would be king, not just of Israel but of the whole world. And they would be at His side, judging the nations, reckoning accounts, rewarding the righteous. Centuries of injustice would be set straight. These eleven men, most of them uneducated fishermen, had gambled their lives on Jesus; had lost everything at the Crucifixion; had seen their hope revived in the Resurrection; and this day would see the Jesus they had trusted ruling the earth. How their hearts must have raced in anticipation as they scampered through the streets of Jerusalem and up the gentle slope of the mountain.

Then the breathless majesty of the moment was upon them; their beloved Jesus was waiting for them, looking searchingly into each of their eyes. His mere presence produced such awe that one by one they dropped to their knees. This was the Coronation.

Finally one of them burst out with the question they all wanted to ask: "Lord, are you at this time going to restore the kingdom to Israel?"[6]

Jesus was sharp, rebuking in His reply. "It is not for you to know the times or dates the Father has set by his own authority." He had already commanded them to wait in Jerusalem; now He told them that a power would come to them there. "And you will be my witnesses in Jerusalem, and in all Judea and Samaria, and to the ends of the earth."[7]

Then it was as if the universe breathed, putting a sea of space between Him and them. Before they could protest, He was gone, ascended into a cloud.

It is difficult to even imagine the wild emotions those eleven men must have experienced at that moment. Holy awe? Terrifying fear? And what initial disappointment! They were left alone, outcasts in their own land. They had few human resources. And on top of all that, they had been commanded to go back and wait — the hardest thing of all for strong-willed men to do.

Knowing how very human they were and where each had come from, we can surmise the options they must have considered: Philip, the timid one, would want to hide in the hills; James and John would want to quickly spread the word; Simon the Zealot would want to organize a guerrilla campaign; others would see their hope in moves such as seizing control of government — the same options so many believers today find so appealing.

But Jesus had ordered them to go to Jerusalem and *wait*. Wait for what? Contrary as it must have been to their every instinct, "wait" is precisely what they did. They obeyed and, hard though it is to understand, did so with "great joy."

For ten days they waited — 120 of them in all, gathered together, of one mind and continually in prayer. They waited. And then it came.

With the force of a thousand tornadoes the power promised rested on them and the Holy Spirit empowered these ordinary men to do the work of God. Each of the eleven became a giant of faith. As a result, within a century half the then-known world came to Christ.

The disciples' decision to obey Jesus after the Ascension proved a pivot point of history. The world was never the same again.

The disciples' realization that Christ is who He says He is compelled them to obedience. That is the historic reality of Christianity.

Understanding this is crucial, for it distinguishes Christianity from all other religions. The Christian faith rests not merely upon great teachings or philosophies, not upon the charisma of a leader, not upon the success in raising moral values, not upon the skill or eloquence or good works of its advocates. If it did, it would have no more claim to authority than the sayings of Confucius or Mao or Buddha or Mohammed or any of a thousand cults. Christianity rests on historic truth. Jesus lived, died, and rose from the dead to be Lord of all — not just in theory or fable, but in fact.

With that understood, Christianity must evoke from the believer the same response it drew from the first disciples: a passionate desire to obey and please God — a willingly entered-into discipline. That is the beginning of true discipleship. *That is the beginning of loving God.*

For the disciples it was clear-cut; Jesus audibly instructed them to return to Jerusalem and wait. But how do we know what we are to do? Such clear instructions do not usually come with our conversion; no voice from heaven gives us marching orders. So where do we turn to find them?

A lawyer, a Pharisee attempting to trick Jesus, put a similar question to the Master centuries ago. "Teacher," he said, "which is the greatest commandment in the Law?"[8] Christ's response has been engraved in the memories of believers ever since: "Love the Lord your God with all your heart and with all your soul and with all your mind. This is the first and greatest commandment."

"But how do we love the Lord?" we ask. Jesus answered this in a discussion with His disciples: "If you love me, you will obey what I command"[9] Or, as the apostle John wrote later, "This is the love of God, that we keep his commandments."[10]

And that leads us to just one place: the Holy Bible. To obey His commandments, we must know His commandments. That means we must know and obey the Scriptures, the key to loving God and the starting point for life's most exciting journey.

But be warned: Unless you are prepared to have your comfortable notions uprooted, you may want to stop reading right now.

A few years ago a magazine article about my prison ministry concluded that "prison radicalized the life of Chuck Colson." It is understandable that the reporter might have thought that, but it is simply not so. I could have left prison and forgotten it; I wanted to in fact. But while every human instinct said, "Put it out of your mind forever," the Bible kept revealing to me God's compassion for the hurting and suffering and oppressed; His insistent Word demanded that I care as He does.

What "radicalized" me was not prison, but taking to heart the truths revealed in Scripture. For it was the Bible that confronted me with a new awareness of my sin and need for repentance; it was the Bible that caused me to hunger for righteousness and seek holiness; and it was the Bible that called me into fellowship with the suffering. It is the Bible that continues to challenge my life today.

That is radical stuff. It is irresistibly convicting. It is the power of God's Word and it is, all by itself, life-changing. Certainly this was the case for a young man whose experience and life have taught me so much — perhaps because I can identify with him so clearly.

Wise in the ways of the world, powerful, steeped in the good life, he was to all appearances successful and satisfied with himself and his life — at thirty-one a young man on the move. Yet his life, too, was changed — radically — by the Word of God.

THE WORD OF GOD

We owe to Scripture the same reverence which we owe to God.

John Calvin

Divine inspiration not only is essentially incompatible with error but excludes and rejects it as absolutely and necessarily as it is impossible that God Himself, the supreme Truth, can utter that which is not true.

Pope Leo XIII

4

Take Up and Read

The Mediterranean sky curved hot and clear over the terrace of the home of Aurelius Augustinus outside Milan, Italy. Beyond the garden wall, acres of fruit trees carpeted the valley, rising to meet the soft green vineyard-covered hillsides. Within the wall, Augustine and his best friend, his student Alypius, sat with the visitor Ponticianus. Though his chest ached, his busy schedule pulled at him, and his mind was thoroughly unsettled, Augustine was taking time to speak with this important government official.

Brilliant, learned, and handsome, Augustine held one of the most enviable professorships in the city. When he spoke, the words of this professor of rhetoric crashed like thunder. When he argued, he was overwhelmingly persuasive. Few felt themselves his equal.

As the three men exchanged polite conversation, Augustine's mother appeared frequently, ostensibly offering refreshments and other hospitable overtures; in reality she was hovering, keeping a close eye on her son.

Monica was a protective mother, strong-minded, practical, utterly determined that her beloved son become a Christian. She prayed for him daily and had since he was a small boy. But while Augustine loved his mother, he paid no attention to her.

Monica had hardly let her son out of her sight since she was widowed in North Africa while Augustine was a teenager. He had had to trick her to come to Italy alone, lying about his departure so he and his mistress and their illegitimate child could sail off without her. But before long Monica had followed him to Milan. She had even succeeded in getting him engaged to a good Christian girl and in sending away his mistress of fifteen years. But his fiancee was very young and his marriage two years off; so Augustine was again sleeping with a woman. Sex was necessary to him, he said, for he had no power to resist his natural desires.

Monica could not understand her son's strange ideas about right and wrong. He indulged in such licentiousness without, apparently, a pang of conscience, but lamented the time when he had stolen fruit from a neighbor's pear tree with a gang of youthful rowdies. Augustine dwelt on this mere childish prank as though it were the great evil of his life while practicing habits much more sinful in his mother's eyes.

Yet she had never stopped hoping for his conversion, and lately her hope had been stronger than ever. Augustine had recently broken with his religion, a strange cult following the teachings of a Persian named Mani who claimed that powers of darkness controlled every physical being. Augustine had quit astrology, too, and had been going to church. Perhaps the bishop was right, Monica thought.

She had visited an African bishop many years earlier, pleading with him to talk with her son. But the churchman refused, telling her that Augustine was not ready to talk.

"Let him be," the bishop had advised. "Only pray to the Lord on his behalf." The bishop knew Manicheanism well; he believed someone as bright as Augustine would see its nonsense eventually.

Monica was not put off so easily, however. She had wept uncontrollably, begging the bishop to speak to her son. Finally, losing patience, he told her to leave. But she had taken his parting words, "It is impossible for the son of such tears to perish," as a promise from heaven and had often reminded Augustine of them, triumphantly.

But Augustine could not become a Christian just to please his mother.

In the garden, Augustine's visitor, idly looking about him as he contemplated his departure, picked up a book lying on a small table nearby. A puzzled smile crossed his face.

"The apostle Paul," he said. "Are you reading this, Augustine?"

His host nodded. "Not only am I reading it. I have been wearing it out. And wearing myself out trying to grasp the meaning of the Christian faith." He looked around, making sure his mother was not lurking within earshot.

"Did you know I am a Christian?" Ponticianus smiled hesitantly.

Augustine and Alypius nodded. They had heard this rumor.

"But I thought this would be one of your philosophical books," Ponticianus said. "I never dreamed I would find *you* reading the Bible."

"The philosophers have helped me understand the Bible," Augustine admitted. He explained that until recently he had believed that only what he could see, measure, rationally and systematically prove could be real. The idea of an invisible, spiritual God seemed just talk. But studying Plato and his followers had convinced him that the real things were invisible, spiritual.

"This has helped me a great deal." Augustine was candid to a fault. Yet he watched Ponticianus carefully, his posture tense. "But there is a major difference. To follow Plato, one merely thinks like Plato. To follow Christ is something much more. You must put your whole life into it and leave behind whatever hinders you from following Him. I don't know what it is exactly that enables a man to give himself to God — to commit himself to a life of sacrifice and faith. That's more than adopting a particular point of view, isn't it?"

Ponticianus nodded, as did Alypius. Alypius, younger than Augustine, practically worshiped the scholar.

Wrapped in his own thoughts, Augustine went on speaking, almost as though working out a problem for himself. "Plato takes you up on a high mountain peak where you can see the land of peace. But you do not know how to get there. There must be a highway leading straight to that land, but you can't find it." He shook his head wearily.

Augustine had few illusions about himself. He knew how easily his mind fell into habits and was chained by them. His women. His pride. I *am utterly depraved*, he thought, *and the mind alone is no match for the seduction of evil pleasure*.[1]

As Augustine spoke, Ponticianus had grown excited. Now he jumped up, paced briskly in front of his host for a moment, then whirled to point a finger at him.

"Have you heard of Antony?"

"Well," Augustine drew back a bit, startled at his visitor's abruptness, "I do know several Antonys, but none worth mentioning in the context of this discussion."

"No—no—Antony the monastic—the one Athanasius wrote the biography of. Many Christians have been greatly influenced by it." To Ponticianus's astonishment, neither of his listeners had heard of this Antony.

"I must tell you then. . . . Antony was a rich young fellow, born into a Christian family in Egypt. His parents died when he was just entering his teens; their large estate fell to him. He grew up fast, carrying that responsibility. He had all the money in the world and all the cares, too.

"In church one Sunday the Scripture reading came from Christ's reply to the rich young ruler: 'If you want to be perfect, go, sell your possessions and give to the poor, and you will have treasure in heaven. Then come, follow me.'

"Something in that familiar passage hit Antony. It was as though Jesus had given those words directly to him, personally, that very moment. Antony didn't even wait for the service to end. He rushed out of the church and set about preparing his records so that his property could be sold and the profit distributed to the poor.

"From that day, Antony devoted his life to prayer. He went to live in a hut on the edge of town, farming to keep himself alive. Fifteen years later he moved into the desert. He wanted to show that the power of God would supply living water in an arid land, that from little or nothing He could bring forth the fruits of the Spirit."

Ponticianus then dramatically described the miracles of Antony's life, telling how though he sought complete obscurity, he became famous, even living in the desert. People traveled great distances to meet with him. And as a result of his example, small groups of men and women began to form communes devoted to prayer.

"To me, Antony is a sign that God will meet us wherever we are," Ponticianus concluded, looking directly into Augustine's eyes, "even in the wasteland of our lives."

Augustine now rose to stand beside his guest, placing his hand briefly on his forearm. He was clearly moved. "I can hardly believe I've never heard of him," he said. "Nor any of his followers. Are there any in Italy?"

"In Italy?" Ponticianus was astonished. "Why, right here in Milan there is a small community of such men. They live outside the city walls. Ambrose has charge of them."

"Ambrose!" He was the pastor whose preaching Augustine had been hearing, originally out of curiosity about the man's style, for Augustine had a professional interest in any good speaker. But Ambrose's substance had made a deeper impact than his style. *Because of him*, Augustine mused, *I have grown interested in the Scriptures again.*

Augustine had first tried reading the Scriptures while a teenager, but was not impressed. At the time he had been in love with beautiful language, and the language of Scripture had seemed dull and plain, far inferior to that of the great Roman writers. But years had passed since then. Great rhetorical flourishes seemed less important than they once did. *Under Ambrose's influence, the simplicity of Scripture has begun to sound like the simplicity of profundity.*

Already Augustine was ready to concede that what the sacred writings said was true. But he could not do anything halfway. He knew the truth of Scripture demanded a commitment to Christ; and commitment to Christ meant total change. He would have to give up misusing sex. More, he would have to give up all his dreams of success and glory. He would have to please God and not the world around him. *Part of me wants to,* he said to himself; *part is unable to.*

Ponticianus interrupted Augustine's thoughts. "When I think of Antony, of his immediate obedience to the Word of God that morning, of what he left without looking back, I am moved to tears." He reached out to grasp his host strongly by both shoulders. "When God calls someone, Augustine, nothing on earth can stop him."

Outwardly Augustine carried on politely, thanking Ponticianus for coming, saying his farewells. Inwardly his disturbed thoughts traveled elsewhere. After his guest left, he paced across the terrace, lashing himself mentally.

As Ponticianus spoke, you turned me back upon myself, O Lord. You took me from behind my own back, where I had placed myself because I did not wish to look upon myself. You stood me face to face with myself so that I might see how foul I am, how deformed and defiled, how covered with stains and sores. I looked and was filled with horror, but there was no place for me to flee to get away from myself.

He thought back bitterly to the day twelve years before when, after reading Cicero, he had decided to dedicate his life to search for wisdom — to prefer to know the truth over any other pleasure in life. But he only talked about it; he never did it. He drifted along in life, living for success and anything that made him happy for a few hours.

You know, O Lord, how during my university days at Carthage I found myself in the midst of a hissing cauldron of lust. I was in love with the idea of love. Although

*my real need was for you, I placed my hopes in what was merely human and often
enough in the bestial as well.*

*Still, I thought of myself as a fine fellow. You know, O Lord, how I grew proud
in the imagination of my heart. . . .*

*When I thought of my Christian upbringing and determined to read the Scrip-
tures, inflamed with self-esteem I judged them but a hash of outmoded Jewish superstition and historical inaccuracies.*

Augustine had been frustrated with himself before, but never to this
point.

*I remember how one day you made me realize how utterly wretched I was. I was
preparing a speech in praise of the emperor, intending that it should include a great
many lies, which would certainly be applauded by an audience that knew well enough
how far from the truth they were. I was greatly preoccupied by this task. As I walked
along one of the streets in Milan, I noticed a beggar who must, I suppose, somehow
have had his fill of food and drink since he was laughing and joking. Sadly I turned
to my companions and spoke to them of all the pain and trouble which is caused by
our own folly. My ambitions had placed a load of misery on my shoulders, and the
further I carried it the heavier it became, but the only purpose of all the efforts we
made was to reach the goal of purposeful happiness. This beggar had already reached
it ahead of us.*

Perhaps I shall never reach it.

Alypius looked in astonishment at his friend. He had heard Augustine talk about his misery, of course, but now he seemed to be in true
anguish. His face was flushed, his eyes darting frantically.

"What is the trouble with us?" Augustine asked aloud in a strangled
voice. "What is this? What did *you* hear? The uneducated rise and take
heaven by storm and we, with all our erudition but empty of heart, see
how we wallow in flesh and blood. Are we ashamed to follow them? Isn't
it shameful for us not to follow them?" He could not continue, but turned
and ran into the garden beyond the wall.

Really alarmed now, Alypius followed his mentor closely, afraid of
what Augustine might do to himself. He also had to know how this
struggle would end, for whatever Augustine became, he wanted to become also.

Getting as far from the house as he could in the little garden, Augustine slumped onto a bench, his body showing the struggle within.
Scarcely conscious of what he was doing, he tore at his hair, slapped his
forehead, locked his fingers together and clasped his knees.

*I know I have a will, as surely as I know there is life in me. When I choose to
do something or not to do it, I am certain that it is my own self making this act of*

will. But I see now that evil comes from the perversion of the will when it turns aside from you, O God. I can say with your apostle, the good I would I do not.

You have raised me up so that I can now see you must be there to be perceived, but I confess that my eyes are still too weak. The thought of you fills me with love, yes, but also with dread. I realize that I am far from you.

Augustine continued to think of his life — his hopes for a good position, a comfortable home, for admiration and fame as a thinker and writer. He thought of the women in his life and something whispered, "From the moment you decide, this thing and that will never be allowed to you, forever and ever." His habits spoke up insistently, "Do you think you can live without us?"

So he sat in the garden, his friend nearby, utterly silent in the stillness of the summer heat. Only inside did the storm rage. Misery heaped up, until finally it seemed his chest would burst. He threw himself under a fig tree, sobbing, unable to stop.

O Lord, how long? Will I never cease setting my heart on shadows and following a lie? How long, O Lord? Will you be angry forever? How long? How long? Tomorrow and tomorrow? Why not now? Why not in this very hour an end to my uncleanness?

Then . . . a voice.

He heard a voice. . . .

A childish, piping voice so high-pitched he could not tell whether it was male or female.

The voice seemed to come from a nearby house.

It chanted tunelessly, over and over . . . "Take up and read. Take up and read. Take up and read."

What did the words mean? Were they part of some children's game?

"Take up and read. Take up and read."

Were the words for him?

"Alypius, do you hear that?" he called. His friend stared back in silence.

"Read what?" Augustine shouted into the sky.

The letters of the apostle Paul were nearby. They had, in fact, started the conversation about Antony. Like Antony, was he hearing God's words to him? Was he to take up the Scriptures and read?

Augustine ran and snatched up the book Ponticianus had noticed and began reading the page to which the book was open — Romans 13. The words burned into his mind: "Not in orgies and drunkenness, not in sexual immorality and debauchery, not in dissension and jealousy. Rather clothe yourselves with the Lord Jesus Christ, and do not think about how to gratify the desires of the sinful nature."

Instantly, as if before a peaceful light streaming into his heart, dark shadows of doubt fled. The man of unconquerable will was conquered by words from a book he had once dismissed as a mere fable lacking in clarity and grace of expression. Those words suddenly revealed that which he had so long vainly sought. Now he knew with assurance he had confronted truth. Those very words, "clothe yourself with the Lord Jesus Christ," had settled it; whatever it cost, he would give his life to Christ.

Putting his finger in the book to mark the spot, Augustine told Alypius what had happened inside him. Thrilled at his friend's joy, Alypius said he would join him. He, too, would follow Christ. The two then called Augustine's mother.

Monica's joy was even greater: "Praise God," she said, "who is able to do above that which we ask or think." Shortly thereafter, she and Augustine enjoyed together a great mystical vision. Nine days later, Monica, her lifelong prayers answered, passed peacefully from this world.

"Take up and read." For the next forty-four years Augustine did just that. He read the Scriptures to work out his own salvation and then read and interpreted them to settle complex theological disputes within the early church. His classic defense of the authority of Scripture laid the foundation for Christians of every age thereafter. No serious Bible student has been able to ignore Augustine's monumental contribution to the church's understanding of the Old and New Testaments. His life and thought drew on the "the revered pen of God's Spirit."

Prior to his conversion Augustine thought the Scriptures a collection of texts that must be interpreted and revised in comparison to the "advanced wisdom" of the philosophers. But in the garden he saw that the Scriptures were not just words to be interpreted; they were words that interpreted their reader. Through Scripture, God spoke personally and inerrantly to him. And as God's voice, Scripture knew infinitely more about Augustine than Augustine knew about Scripture.

Immediately after his conversion, Augustine began to write freely, quickly completing several books. His autobiographical Confessions, replete with quotes and paraphrases from Scripture, has provided intellectual challenge and spiritual illumination to Christians for centuries.

Augustine went on to become the Bishop of Hippo, one of the most influential men in his world, while the seemingly eternal Roman Empire fell apart. In response he wrote his masterpiece, The City of God, which gave Christians new hope and direction in the midst of turmoil and despair. Some say he almost singlehandedly rescued the gospel from the ruins of the Empire.

All this began when God, through a child's voice, said to him, "Take up and read." Obedient, Augustine found words that exposed his dilemma with a brilliant light and told him plainly what he had to do.

5

Just Another Book?

Augustine's story captures my imagination. Here was a great scholar who had studied and understood the Greek philosophers and read widely in the classics, a genius teaching at a leading university; yet this man of great intellect and compelling personality was utterly transformed by the Word of God. What power those Scriptures hold!

The Bible — banned, burned, beloved. More widely read, more frequently attacked than any other book in history. Generations of intellectuals have attempted to discredit it; dictators of every age have outlawed it and executed those who read it. Yet soldiers carry it into battle believing it more powerful than their weapons. Fragments of it smuggled into solitary prison cells have transformed ruthless killers into gentle saints.[1] Pieced-together scraps of Scripture have converted whole villages of pagan Indians.[2]

Yearly, the Bible outsells every best-seller. Five hundred million copies were published last year alone.[3] Portions have been translated into more than 1800 languages and even carried to the moon.

Literary classics endure the centuries. Philosophers mold the thoughts of generations unborn. Modern media shape current culture. Yet nothing has affected the rise and fall of civilization, the character of cultures, the structure of governments, and the lives of the inhabitants of this planet as profoundly as the words of the Bible.

"My word that goes out from my mouth ... will not return to me empty, but will accomplish what I desire and achieve the purpose for which I sent it," said the Lord through the prophet Isaiah. Even those who are hostile to the Word sense its inherent power, as I discovered during a fascinating encounter with one of today's most renowned atheists.

In 1978 British interviewer David Frost invited me to a televised debate with Madelyn Murray O'Hair. The show was to be taped before a live New York audience and then broadcast nationwide on NBC.

Before the taping I studied transcripts of Mrs. O'Hair's past encounters with believers to familiarize myself with her methods and material. I learned that during her debates she would appear to quote the Bible at length to support her militant anti-Christian views. But, in fact, she craftily used passages out of context and subtly rearranged words to change their meaning. In light of this, though I knew it would arouse her ire, I decided to take my Bible to the debate.

From the opening round Mrs. O'Hair was true to form, angrily spitting invectives at Christians in general and me in particular. When I was speaking and she was off-camera, she contorted her face and made obnoxious gestures in a coarse effort to distract me. Aggressively interrupting, glibly misquoting Scripture, she scored her blows early, to the crowd's delight.

I kept my Bible unobtrusively at my side, but when she shouted, "The Bible teaches you to kill," I leaned across a startled David Frost and thrust it at her. "Wait a minute!" I demanded. "You know this book, Mrs. O'Hair. Find where it says that. Read it to me."

She blanched, for a moment groped for words, then drew back in her chair shaking her head furiously. I thrust the leather-covered book toward her once more. She recoiled again. Even in the heat of the moment I was struck by her absolute refusal to touch the Bible.

With that, the tide of the confrontation was turned, and she seemed subdued and on the defensive thereafter.*

After the taping I once more asked Mrs. O'Hair to find the passages she had referred to, but she still refused to take the Bible in her hands. Of course, if she was determined to remain an atheist, Mrs. O'Hair was correct not to draw too close, for the holy Sword might pierce her heart.

Just another book? Hardly. The Bible's power rests upon the fact that it is the reliable, errorless, and infallible Word of God. And if that

---

*For reasons unknown to me, this debate was never aired by NBC.

is true — as the Scriptures claim it is — then it has authority over the life of every believer. On this assertion the Christian faith stands or falls, for if the Bible is faulty, so is our faith.

I confess that for a long time I struggled with this central proposition of the faith, that the Bible is the infallible Word of God simply because it says it is. My lawyer's mind demanded evidence, something more than just this bold self-definition, which seemed at best a tautology.

So if the Christian faith — my faith — depended on the truth or falsehood of this argument, it was imperative that I examine it more closely.

The first thing I realized was that the Bible's claims about itself really only raise the questions. Without such prompting, it would never occur to us that a book written thousands of years ago might be absolutely authoritative for our lives. We would treat it like any other book of philosophy or religion. Take it or leave it. Or take part of it, discard the rest. But a book presenting itself as the Word of God, without error? That bold claim forces the question: is it or isn't it?

The next step was to find an authority to answer the question. As a believer, I had to turn to the One in whom I believe, Jesus Himself. Christ plainly asserted the authority and infallibility of Scripture. Consider just a few examples:

When He began His ministry, Christ used Scripture to announce His commission. "The Spirit of the Lord is on me, because he has anointed me to preach good news to the poor. He has sent me to proclaim freedom for the prisoners and recovery of sight for the blind, to release the oppressed, to proclaim the year of the Lord's favor," He read from the scroll of Isaiah.[4] Indeed He repeatedly cited the Old Testament Scriptures as the authority for His work and the verification of His person.[5] He used the Word as His sole defense against Satan and He asked His Father to sanctify His disciples in the truth ("Thy Word is truth").[6]

Jesus rested His entire ministry and His authority upon His delegation from God and the revelation of God in Scripture: "All authority in heaven and on earth has been given to me."[7] So if we claim faith in Jesus, we must take His word for the authority of Scripture; it was His authority for His authority.

As I considered that fact, I realized it solved one problem and led to another. We depend on Scripture for the fact that Jesus said these things; but how do we know He really said them? How do we know His words and the events of His life are accurately recorded in the Bible?

Because this is so crucial, no question has been more exhaustively and critically examined through the centuries. My own study brought me to these basic conclusions.

The men who penned the New Testament were Hebrews, and scholars agree that the Hebrews were meticulous in precise and literal transcriptions. What was said or done had to be recorded in painstaking and faithful detail; if there was any doubt on a particular event or detail, it was not included.

Moreover, the gospel accounts were written by contemporaries of Jesus who had firsthand knowledge of His life and the events of the early church (unlike, for example, Buddhist literature which was developed two centuries after Buddha's death). "We proclaim to you *what we have seen and heard*," said the apostles.[8]

And external evidence continues to add historical verification. New archeological discoveries in the field of biblical studies have added weight to the evidence that the Gospels were written by contemporaries of Jesus. For example, at one point critics attributed the Gospel of John to the late second century and considered it possibly a romanticized fable about a simple Galilean peasant "deified" long after his death. However, a recently discovered early papyrus on which John 18 was written was scientifically determined to have been written *no later than* 125 A.D.[†]

Critical historical issues are not all neatly resolved, of course, and probably never will be. Yet it is an underreported fact that the more evidence is uncovered, the more scholars agree (even those who don't consider Jesus' deity) that the New Testament is a reliable accounting of what the writers saw and heard.

This led me to the final challenge of the proposition: *granted*, Jesus used Scripture as His authority and said it was to be ours; *granted*, what He said was accurately recorded; but how do we know He was right? In short, how do we know that Christ's view of the Scriptures is true?

Well, if Jesus is God and perfect man, as He claims, He cannot be mistaken in what He teaches and He cannot lie. An infallible God cannot err; a holy God cannot deceive; a perfect teacher cannot be mistaken. So He is either telling the truth, or He is *not* who He says He is.

Therefore, if Christ's divinity and perfect humanity are established, we know that His view of the Scriptures as infallible and authoritative is true. The real proof of the Scriptures' authenticity, then, turns on the

†Since this fragment is a copy, the original must have been earlier and indeed contemporaneous with the rise of the early church.

proof of Christ's authenticity. And resolving Christ's authenticity is the key to breaking the otherwise circular argument that the Bible says Jesus is the Son of God and Jesus says the Bible is true. But what proves Christ's authenticity?

It is the fact that He was bodily raised from the grave. The historical truth of His victory over death and His consequent eternal kingship over the world affirms Jesus' claim to be God. The Resurrection establishes Christ's authority and thus validates His teachings about the Bible and Himself. Paul minces no words about this: "If Christ has not been raised, your faith is futile."[9]

Some might think Paul rash for staking the case for Christianity on the bodily resurrection, but the apostle made his bold assertion for two reasons.

First, Paul was absolutely certain about Christ's resurrection. He had encountered Jesus face to face on the road to Damascus and had talked both with the apostles who were with Jesus and with many of the five hundred eyewitnesses who saw the resurrected Lord.

Second, Paul was simply being honest. For if Christ was not bodily raised from the dead — if He had remained dead — then He was not God and could not have the authority He claimed. And if that were true, Christianity was a cruel hoax.

In the final analysis the question is simply this: if we believe the Scripture narrative was faithfully recorded, *how can we know the Scripture writers were telling the truth when they asserted that Jesus rose from the dead?*

My answer came from an unlikely source: the Watergate cover-up.

6

Watergate and the Resurrection

Saturday, June 17, 1972, was warm and oppressively humid, typical of summer in Washington D.C. As Special Counsel to the President of the United States I was on call day and night, leaving little time for myself or my family. But this Saturday we were enjoying a rare, uninterrupted family day at our suburban McLean home. The President had just returned from the triumph of his presidency, the Moscow summit, and was resting in his Florida hideaway.

Patty and the kids were stretched out by the pool, and I was starting up the grill for a cookout, when the phone with the direct line to the White House switchboard rang. It was John Ehrlichman, one of the President's senior assistants; without explanation he brusquely asked what seemed like a ridiculous question: "Where is your friend Howard Hunt?"

Hunt was a shadowy ex-CIA agent I'd known casually and had recommended for a minor White House job investigating leaks of government documents. But it had been months since I'd seen him or heard from him. So I pressed Ehrlichman: what in the world was so important about Howard Hunt's whereabouts to interrupt my quiet Saturday afternoon?

It was then I learned for the first time that a group of ex-Cuban freedom fighters had been arrested while breaking into the Democratic

61

National Committee offices. One of the men had had a piece of paper in his pocket with Hunt's name on it. I can still remember my distracted thoughts as I hung up the phone. *Hunt's no amateur. He wouldn't get involved in a common burglary. Yet if he had been ... I know him ... my name could be dragged in.* Then I shrugged and dismissed these foreboding thoughts, went back to the pool and steamy sunshine and grilled some hamburgers.

That was how Watergate began for me.

During the following weeks I was comforted by my belief that no one in the White House or the Nixon campaign would be so stupid as to think they could find anything of value at the headquarters of a bankrupt party being ignored by its own candidates. This was no moral judgment, just practical politics. Even as the burglars' connection to Howard Hunt and his compatriot G. Gordon Liddy was uncovered, that was dismissed; both men had been part-time White House consultants but had been removed from the rolls months earlier.

Though a burglary under D.C. law, the break-in was really nothing more than campaign spying, I thought — like stealing the signals out of the other team's huddle. Certainly it was nothing much more than things I had done or others had done to me in my twenty years of political campaigns. (It was not until two years later, the summer of 1974, when the infamous "smoking gun" tape was released, that the world as well as some of us on the inside learned that in the early days after the break-in the President was involved in attempting to sidetrack the FBI's investigation; that would later become *the* cover-up.)

In light of what happened later it sounds naïve, but at the time I believed nothing more was at stake than surviving the political brick-throwing through the November elections. The whole affair would then be neatly buried beneath the electoral landslide and we would get on with the more important business of governing the country. Or so I thought.

In the post-election euphoria that November no one paid much attention to Watergate. I recall only occasional discussions about it with the President, who was consumed with the frustrating negotiations to end the war in Vietnam. Henry Kissinger was shuttling back and forth to the Paris peace talks. Bob Haldeman, Chief of Staff, and John Ehrlichman were busy reorganizing the bureaucracy for the second term. John Mitchell, former Attorney General and campaign manager, had moved back to his lucrative law firm in New York. And I was packing up my office, preparing to return to my own Washington law practice.

Then in January, 1973, Watergate, at least from my perspective, began to take on new implications. Howard Hunt, fearing imprisonment, sent his lawyer to see me. As the attorney demanded assurance of clemency for Hunt (which I refused to give him), I learned for the first time that the Watergate burglars were being given funds for support and legal fees. This was dangerous business, and I told Haldeman so later.

"Come on, Chuck," he laughed, looking unusually mellow as the winter sunlight flooded through the tall office windows behind him. "There's nothing wrong with raising a defense fund. Angela Davis* did it. Why not us?"

I stared at Bob, wondering whether he was putting on an act for my benefit or whether he really believed that. I concluded that he was sincere, and looking back, I now realize that as a practicing Christian Scientist, Haldeman would not allow himself to think or see anything wrong. Ehrlichman, also a devout Christian Scientist, likewise seemed to ignore or deny the problems associated with Watergate.

But Haldeman and Ehrlichman were not the only ones doing this. Judging from the memoirs of the others, written over the succeeding decade, only the President's young counsel John Dean acknowledged that he had any real apprehension before January, 1973. He also said he shared his concerns with no one.

How could so many lawyers — Ehrlichman, Mitchell, Krogh, Dean, Nixon, and Colson, to mention only a few — have been so oblivious to what later became so obvious? What deadly blindness it proved to be.[†]

Following the visit of Hunt's lawyer, I consulted my law partner, Dave Shapiro, a two-fisted trial veteran who had scrapped his way up from the streets of Brooklyn. Together we broke out the law books. It was then, late January, 1973, as we reviewed the tight columns of fine print in the criminal statutes, that I began for the first time to understand the possible criminal implications for the White House.

---

*A celebrated Communist activist accused of murder.

[†]I think there are two reasons for this. First, by definition a conspiracy is the sum total of a lot of bits and pieces; the individuals involved often see only their own particular bits and pieces, rarely the entire mosaic. Second, the only exposure to criminal law that 98 percent of all attorneys have is one course in law school and occasional court-assigned criminal cases, usually quickly settled by out-of-court plea bargains — a remarkable commentary on the American judicial system. The closest most lawyers come to the drama of courtroom confrontation is watching Perry Mason with the rest of the populace on late-night television. My first experience with the obstruction of justice statutes was when I was prosecuted — and sent to prison — under one.

So in mid-February, with the Vietnam War finally over, I summoned up the courage to confront the President. It was during our last meeting in the Oval Office before I returned to my private law practice that, at an opportune moment, I gave President Nixon the painful advice, "Whoever did order Watergate, let it out . . . let's get rid of it now. Take our losses."[‡]

The President had been leaning back in his chair, legs crossed and feet propped up on his massive mahogany desk. The words were barely out of my mouth when he dropped his feet and came straight up in his chair. "Well, who do you think did this? . . . Mitchell? Magruder?"[§] He was angry, righteously so I supposed, that I would suggest putting the finger on a loyal aide. He was also, I still believe today, oblivious of the possible criminal implications, even as the net was being drawn increasingly tighter around us all.

According to the exhaustive records compiled from tape recordings, mountains of documents, endless Congressional hearings, and massive volumes of testimony, the first serious Oval Office discussion of likely criminal involvement took place the morning of March 21; that was the fateful meeting when John Dean warned the President of the "cancer on his presidency."

Later on March 21 (the specific dates are important) Haldeman called Mitchell in New York and Mitchell, in turn, told Jeb Magruder, his campaign assistant, he would "assist" him if he went to jail. That was also the day $75,000 in additional money was dispatched to Hunt for "lawyer's fees." The President conferred again with Haldeman and Ehrlichman and Dean. And that same evening the President, without disclosing anything that had gone on that busy day, called me at home for a thirty-one minute conversation.

Though I had officially left his staff, it was not surprising to receive a call from the President; he had told me he wanted to continue to call on me for advice. What was surprising was the President's impatient, almost distracted voice. I had spent countless hours across a desk from him or on the phone and could almost always read his mood. When big issues were on his mind, like Vietnam bombings or dealings with China, the President was remarkably cool. When little things came to his attention, like sniping in the press, he seemed the most unnerved.

[‡]From official White House transcripts of February 13, 1973, released by Watergate Special Prosecutor.

[§]Same source as above.

The evening of March 21 he quickly dispensed with small talk and plunged into Watergate.

"What's your judgment as to what ... what ought to be done now ... whether, uh, there should be, uh, a uh, report made or something, you know, or just hunker down and take it or what?"

The official transcripts show my reply. "The problem I foresee in this is not what has happened so far — that is, the mystery of the Watergate. I don't know whether somebody else higher up in the Committee for the Re-election is gonna get named or not but, uh, to me that isn't of very great consequence to the country if it happens. The thing that worries me is that, is the possibility of somebody, uh, charging an obstruction of justice problem — in other words that the subsequent actions would worry me more than anything."

I then went on to suggest that the President remove Dean and appoint an independent Special Counsel to handle Watergate for him. Though I wasn't aware then of earlier meetings with Dean and the others, it was, as hindsight confirms, good advice. But those chilling words "obstruction of justice" must have made the President's day. No wonder he didn't call me again for two weeks! ‖

After March 21 everything changed — it was all downhill, and fast. Conversations grew thick and heavy the next week: talk of perjury, "stonewalling," obstruction of justice, the kind of stuff that gives grown men weak knees and sweaty palms.

On March 23 Judge Sirica released a letter from one of the Watergate burglars who had made a deal; he would tell all in exchange for a lighter sentence. That afternoon Haldeman called me with a series of questions: Had I promised clemency to Howard Hunt? Had I urged the campaign people to get intelligence on the Democrats? Bob's voice was cool, as always, but from the way he repeated my answers, I was certain someone else was in the room with him — the President. His questions also revealed what was happening behind the massive iron gates of 1600 Pennsylvania Avenue. The occupants were stocking the bunkers for what they now realized would be a bloody siege. Increasingly distrustful of my colleagues and sensing that all was not well, I dictated a memorandum of our conversation as soon as I hung up the phone.

Thinly disguised panic began to sweep the plush offices of the

‖Transcript of recorded conversation not introduced in Watergate trial and not made public until 1981.

stately old building that houses the most influential and powerful men in the world. Events escalated so fast there was no way to keep track of them. As the press bannered allegations that campaign officials had ordered the break-in, Dean rushed off to Camp David to write a "report."

On March 26 the grand jury reconvened to hear new charges from one of the original burglars. That same day Dean called Magruder and taped his conversation.

On March 27 Haldeman and Ehrlichman discussed the crisis for two and a half hours with the President. Also, Mitchell met with Magruder to discuss clemency, while Mitchell's wife, Martha, made one of her legendary calls to the *New York Times*, charging that someone was trying to make a "goat" out of her husband.

While at Camp David on March 25, John Dean had secretly contacted an old law school classmate for advice on the best criminal lawyer he could hire. Five days later he retained a tough ex-Kennedy administration prosecutor, Charles Schaeffer. Then on April 8,1973, Dean met with Watergate prosecutors to bargain his testimony for immunity and save his own hide, as he acknowledged with refreshing candor in his memoirs.[1]

Within hours the cover-up collapsed. Magruder, already in contact with the prosecutors, began negotiations in earnest. Dave Shapiro, sensing it was now "every man for himself," coaxed me into taking a lie detector test to establish my innocence, then gave the results to the *New York Times*. The prosecutors called me; I offered to testify.

The White House was like a front-line command post under heavy shelling. Though men like Ehrlichman and Haldeman put on a brave front, they trusted no one and were taping every phone conversation.

Daily headlines fed the public fresh tidbits, mostly from stories leaked by aides or their lawyers seeking to clear their skirts or entice the prosecutors into a better deal. Meanwhile, the prosecutors were so busy with White House officials offering testimony that they couldn't handle the traffic in and out of their offices. Suddenly Watergate was a three-ring circus.

History reveals that after the criminal investigation of the White House began — as it did with Dean's April 8 meeting with the prosecutors — the end of Mr. Nixon's presidency was only a matter of time. The cover-up was discovered — and doomed — and this is why the dates are so important. For though the cover-up technically dated back to the June, 1972, break-in, the serious cover-up — the part everyone knew or should have known was criminal — really began March 21, 1973. And it ended April 8, 1973.

With the most powerful office in the world at stake, a small band of hand-picked loyalists, no more than ten of us, could not hold a conspiracy together for more than two weeks.

Think of what was at stake: Each of us involved — Ehrlichman, Haldeman, Mitchell, and the rest — believed passionately in President Nixon. To enter government service for him we had sacrificed very lucrative private law practices and other endeavors; we had sacrificed our family lives and privacy; we had invested our whole lives in the work, twenty-four hours a day if necessary. Only a few months earlier the President had been re-elected in an historic landslide victory; the ugly Asian war was finally over; we were riding the crest in every way.

Think of the power at our fingertips: a mere command from one of us could mobilize generals and cabinet officers, even armies; we could hire or fire personnel and manage billions in agency budgets.

Think of the privileges: a call to the military aide's office would produce a limousine or jet airplane; the National Gallery delivered classic paintings to adorn our office walls; red-jacketed stewards stood in waiting to serve food and drink twenty-four hours a day; private phones appeared wherever we traveled; secret service men were always within sight — as many as we wanted.

Yet even the prospect of jeopardizing the President we'd worked so hard to elect, of losing the prestige, power, and personal luxury of our offices was not enough incentive to make this group of men contain a lie. Nor, as I reflect today, was the pressure really all that great; at that point there had certainly been moral failures, criminal violations, even perjury by some. There was certain to be keen embarrassment; at the worst, some might go to prison, though that possibility was by no means certain. But no one was in grave danger; *no one's life was at stake.*

Yet after just a few weeks the natural human instinct for self-preservation was so overwhelming that the conspirators, one by one, deserted their leader, walked away from their cause, turned their backs on the power, prestige, and privileges.

So what does all this have to do with the resurrection of Jesus Christ? Simply this:

Modern criticism of the historic truth of Christianity boils down to three propositions: first, that the disciples were mistaken; or second, that the disciples knowingly perpetrated a myth, intended as a symbol; or third, the eleven disciples conceived a "Passover plot" — spirited the body of Christ out of the tomb and disposed of it neatly — and to their dying breaths maintained conspiratorial silence.

Let's consider each.

The first is the shakiest. After all, a man being raised from the dead is a rather mind-boggling event — not the kind of thing people are likely to be vague or indecisive about. The Scriptures state very honestly that the disciples were so staggered by Jesus' reappearance that at least one demanded the tangible proof of fingering the wounds in His hands and side. Jesus knew human nature, knew they needed physical evidence. Luke says, "He showed himself to these men and gave many convincing proofs that he was alive. He appeared to them over a period of forty days. . .".[2] The records of the event, written independently by various eyewitness reporters, belie the possibility that the disciples were mistaken.

But could it have been a myth? This second theory seems plausible at first since it was customary in the first century to convey religious truths through symbols. But this assumes that all the disciples understood that they were using a symbolic device. Even a cursory reading of the Gospels reveals not allegory or fable, but a straightforward, narrative account. Moreover, Paul, an intimate associate of the original disciples, shatters the myth theory altogether when he argues that if Jesus was not *actually* resurrected, Christianity is a hoax, a sham.[3] Nothing in Paul's writings remotely suggests mythology.

The myth theory is even more untenable than the mistake theory. So if one is to assail the historicity of the Resurrection and therefore the deity of Christ, one must conclude that there was a conspiracy — a cover-up if you will — by eleven men with the complicity of up to five hundred others. To subscribe to this argument, one must also be ready to believe that each disciple was willing to be ostracized by friends and family, live in daily fear of death, endure prisons, live penniless and hungry, sacrifice family, be tortured without mercy, and ultimately die — all without ever once renouncing that Jesus had risen from the dead!

This is why the Watergate experience is so instructive for me. If John Dean and the rest of us were so panic-stricken, not by the prospect of beatings and execution, but by political disgrace and a possible prison term, one can only speculate about the emotions of the disciples. Unlike the men in the White House, the disciples were powerless people, abandoned by their leader, homeless in a conquered land. Yet they clung tenaciously to their enormously offensive story that their leader had risen from His ignoble death and was alive — and was *the* Lord.

The Watergate cover-up reveals, I think, the true nature of humanity. None of the memoirs suggest that anyone went to the prosecutor's office out of such noble notions as putting the Constitution above the President, or bringing rascals to justice, or even moral indignation. Instead, the writings of those involved are consistent recitations of the frailty of man. Even political zealots at the pinnacle of power will save their own necks in the crunch, though it may be at the expense of the one they profess to serve so zealously.

Is it really likely, then, that a deliberate cover-up, a plot to perpetuate a lie about the Resurrection, could have survived the violent persecution of the apostles, the scrutiny of early church councils, the horrendous purge of the first-century believers who were cast by the thousands to the lions for refusing to renounce the Lordship of Christ? Is it not probable that at least one of the apostles would have renounced Christ before being beheaded or stoned? Is it not likely that some "smoking gun" document might have been produced exposing the "Passover plot"? Surely one of the conspirators would have made a deal with the authorities (government and Sanhedrin probably would have welcomed such a soul with open arms and pocketbooks!).

Blaise Pascal, the extraordinary mathematician, scientist, inventor, and logician of the seventeenth century, was convinced of the truth of Christ by examination of the historical record. In his classic *Pensees*, Pascal wrote: "The hypothesis that the apostles were knaves is quite absurd. Follow it out to the end and imagine these twelve [sic] men meeting after Jesus' death and conspiring to say that he had risen from the dead. This means attacking all the powers that be. *The human heart is singularly susceptible to fickleness, to change, to promises, to bribery.* One of them had only to deny his story under these inducements, or still more because of possible imprisonment, torture and death, and they would all have been lost."[4]

As Pascal correctly observes, man in his normal state will renounce his beliefs just as readily as Peter renounced Jesus *before* the Resurrection. But as the same Peter discovered *after* the Resurrection, there is a power beyond man that causes him to forsake all. It is the power of the God who revealed Himself in the person of Jesus Christ.

Take it from one who was inside the Watergate web looking out, who saw firsthand how vulnerable a cover-up is: Nothing less than a witness as awesome as the resurrected Christ could have caused those men to maintain to their dying whispers that Jesus is alive and Lord.

This weight of evidence tells me the apostles were indeed telling the truth: Jesus did rise bodily from the grave; He is who He says He is. Thus, He speaks with the absolute authority of the all-powerful God. And that fact breaks what might otherwise be considered a circular argument.

Thus we can arrive at some crucial conclusions about Holy Scripture:

(1) The Bible is the Word of God. For the Son of God who speaks with absolute authority did not use the Scriptures as pious sayings or as a guide for the fulfilling Christian life. He regarded Scripture as the *revelation* of God Himself.

(2) Jesus entrusted His own life to the Scriptures, relying on them totally. He submitted to the *authority* of Scripture.

(3) Examining Jesus' stand on Scripture throughout His ministry, it is clear that He believed the Word infallible and *inerrant* — that is, reliable and without error.[5]

How can we who purport to follow Him do any differently?

7

Believing God

As an attorney, I have always believed strongly in the importance of precedents; that's how lawsuits are decided — on the basis of what courts have decided in the past, the body of common law developed over the years through careful deliberation. So naturally as I examined the case for the authority of Scripture, I looked to the evidence of the centuries. There I found a consistent flow subscribing to the authority and infallibility of the Word from Jesus Himself down through the early church and throughout church history.

St. Paul, the first church theologian, resoundingly affirmed the truth of Scripture.[1] Irenaeus, brilliant second century apologist whose writings stemmed the early tides of heresy, argued that the Scriptures were "perfect since they were spoken by the Word of God.[2] Augustine wrote, "I have learned to hold the Scriptures alone inerrant."[3]

In the sixteenth century, Luther spoke movingly of the Word of God as "greater than Heaven and earth, yea, greater than death and Hell, for it forms part of the Power of God and endures everlastingly."[4] His fellow reformer John Calvin argued that that which distinguishes Christianity is the knowledge that God has spoken to us and so "we owe to the Scriptures the same reverence which we owe to God."[5]

Jonathan Edwards, second president of Princeton University, ardently defended these views, as did John Wesley, Thomas Aquinas, Charles Haddon Spurgeon, and the other great names of the church too numerous to recount. The Roman Catholic position has been unwavering; a 1943 encyclical sums up its classical view: "Divine inspiration 'not only is essentially incompatible with error but excludes and rejects it as absolutely and necessarily as it is impossible that God Himself, the supreme Truth, can utter that which is not true. This is the ancient and constant faith of the Church.' "[6] In this encyclical on promoting biblical studies, Pope Pius XII begins by calling Scripture "heaven-sent treasure."[7]

If Jesus, the Head of our church, and the weight of precedents point so clearly to a wholehearted acceptance of and subscription to the Scriptures, why does twentieth century culture manifest a steady decline in biblical belief? Gallup reports that in 1963, 65 percent of all Americans believed the Bible to be infallible; that number dropped to 37 percent in 1982.[8] Why?

I believe it is because the prevailing attitudes of the culture have thoroughly infiltrated the ranks of faith and belief. The relativism of the modern mind-set is loathe to subscribe to the absolute authority of anything, and that attitude has seeped into *our* perspective, resulting in a barrage of questions, attacks, and rewrites of the Scriptures.

So, though evangelicals say they hold fast to their orthodoxy, in truth they are succumbing to relativism and modern cynicism. It is no wonder really, for millions sit in church pews Sunday after Sunday never bothering to think about what they believe or why; thus they are easy prey for the trendy clichés that dismiss Scripture as the "legends" of *unenlightened* ancients. (How semantics influence our values! Words like "progressive" can reverse the rules of logic. That is, the longer historical evidence persists, the less reliable it becomes; the newer the conclusion, the less proven by history, the more "progressive" and, presumably, more appealing it is.)

In such a climate, commonly voiced objections insidiously become accepted as facts that no one bothers to challenge. And if many were honest they would have to admit that these objections also provide a convenient rationalization for not picking up a Bible and wrestling with its hard and convicting truths.

What are some of these objections?

One we often hear is "*The Bible is unbelievable.*" The parting of the Red Sea, the raising of Lazarus, the visitation of angels and the like confound our natural senses and reason. Of course they do. They are *supernatural.*

But that is the essence of what God is — super-natural. Beyond the natural senses.

If there is no supernatural, there is no God.

Second: *"The Scriptures don't really matter."* Going to services, being faithful to family, and operating ethically in one's dealings — these are the "Christian" standards, reason many churchgoers. After all, God knows we are doing our best.

This is an echo of a widespread belief in our country — a form of civil religion — that says it doesn't matter what you believe so long as you believe in something. This kind of thinking, by doing away with individual responsibility, ignores a central truth of our Judeo-Christian foundation.

Third: *"It's out-of date."* The events in Scripture took place thousands of years ago when shepherds tended flocks and primitive tribal customs prevailed. Times change, says this modern relativist; ancient ritual is irrelevant to today's morality.

Yes, the biblical account deals with ancient times, for ancient Israel was the particular place God chose to covenant with His people and some 1,200 years later to enter time and space through Jesus Christ. But God's truth is eternal.

Time passes. Customs change. Truth remains. Absolute objective truth can never depend on custom, common perceptions, or changing trends, and it remains true whether believed or not.

Though it is sometimes difficult to understand the cultural backdrop of the biblical drama, the play remains unchanged.

Fourth: *We live under the new covenant so we needn't bother to read the archaic, outdated laws of the Old Testament."*

It is impossible to appreciate Jesus apart from the historical context in which He lived. Without understanding the Old Testament covenants between God and His chosen people and humanity's consistent failure to adhere to them, God's grace and the supreme atonement of the cross lose their significance. The Old Testament, as well, is indispensable in teaching us about the character of God and the promises fulfilled in Christ.

Fifth: *"The red letters count more than the black."* An astonishing number of Christians accept Jesus' teachings as the Word of God but reject the writings of "Paul and all the others" as human opinions.

But where do we find Christ's words? He didn't write them down Himself. His words are reported by the Gospel writers. So is Luke more believable than Paul? We have no indication that Luke met Jesus face to face, but we know Paul did. In a court of law, therefore, Luke's red letters would be hearsay; Paul's black letters direct evidence.

Ultimately, if we believe all Scripture is inspired by God,[9] all must be given equal weight.

Sixth: *"There are so many contradictions and different interpretations that I can't accept the Bible as literally true."*

Confusion over how to read, interpret, and understand the Bible is the single greatest cause of biblical illiteracy and skepticism.

Though it is unique, in a structural sense the Bible must be read like any other book: metaphor is metaphor, poetry is poetry, parables are parables. Scripture must be read in context and according to its literary genre (the technique of communication the author selected).

Remember, too, that any author writes so his readers can understand. When critics attack the literal truthfulness of Scripture by citing language like "the sun rose," they are ignoring basic rules of literary communication. Of course, the sun does not rise; the writer is simply communicating in terms he and his contemporaries understand. (Even in our enlightened age, of course, TV weather forecasters still give the times each day for *sunrise* and *sunset*.)

By applying the basic rules of logical interpretation, examining historical narratives in the light of didactic teaching, taking the explicit over the implicit, we can clear up much of the ruckus over the Bible's seeming contradictions.*

And seventh: *"I just don't get anything out of the Bible."*

These critics expect the Bible to be the ultimate quick-fix, self-fulfillment manual, in the same category as all the how-to books crowding our bookstore shelves, intended to fulfill our every need and desire. Of course, we find spiritual fulfillment in reading the Scriptures, but the holy Word of God is intended to do much more than that: it is to satisfy the believer's deepest hunger for knowledge about acceptable living and service for his sovereign King.

Objections like the above reveal why the family Bible is more often used to adorn coffee tables or press flowers than it is to feed souls and discipline lives. They also reveal why Christians do not know how to love God. For we should read God's Word not for what we can get out of it,

---

*It is not my purpose to examine the issues of interpretation and study of Scripture in depth. But because of the importance of this issue, I strongly recommend further reading on the subject in such highly readable and instructive sources as *Knowing Scripture* by R. C. Sproul (Inter-Varsity Press, 1977).

not for what it will do for us, but for what it will teach us to do for our God.

"Your word is truth," Jesus said.[10] Nothing less than knowledge of that truth is demanded of Christ's disciples. That knowledge comes only from fervent study of truth, that is, study of His Word. This is indispensable to genuine discipleship. It *is indispensable to loving God.*

But perhaps the real reason we do not pursue that radical discipleship rooted in the Word of God is that we have not recognized the clear choice before us. Perhaps we believe *in* God — as 96 percent of all Americans say they do — but we do not *believe God,* that is, obey His Word. That choice is most clearly illustrated for us in the sharp contrasts of two biblical accounts: first Eve in the Garden of Eden and then Christ in the wilderness of Judea. Consider the responses of each when confronted with Satan's challenge regarding the Word of God.

Satan came to Eve as a serpent, asking with beguiling innocence, "Did God really say, 'You must not eat from any tree in the garden?'"[†]

If Eve answered yes, she would be lying; God hadn't forbidden *all* the trees. But a straight no wouldn't be truthful either. So, unaware of the trap being set, Eve replied, "We may eat fruit from the trees in the garden, but God did say, you must not eat fruit from the tree that is in the middle of the garden, and *you must not touch it* or you will die."[11] (In her answer Eve demonstrated that she knew God's Word, though she elaborated by adding the words, "You must not touch it." Adding to Scripture is as dangerous as taking away from it — and this perhaps was part of Eve's undoing.)

"You will not surely die," the serpent reassured her. Surely a loving God would not mean anything so cruel as that. No, the beguiler continued, "God knows that when you eat of it your eyes will be opened, and you will be *like* God, knowing good and evil."

What an irresistible proposition — as it is today. After all, Eve was made in God's image; shouldn't she know what He knew? And be *like* Him? The serpent was simply helping her interpret what God had meant to say in the first place.

So Eve succumbed, probably believing she was doing the right thing. Adam immediately joined her. And this temptation has plagued humanity ever since: the desire *to be like God.* Simply put, it is humanism, man's

---

[†]Before the Fall, the serpent was a crafty but engaging creature, not the slithering reptile he became after God's curse was put on him.

ultimate arrogance — his pretension that he can be his own Lord. And it began in the Garden.

Satan continued enticing humanity with that same lure, as the history of the Old Testament bears witness. And seventy-five generations later the beguiler appeared to Jesus Christ with the same temptation.

The Devil's first challenge was simple: "If you are the Son of God, tell this stone to become bread." (A minor thing for One who would later multiply a few loaves and fish to feed five thousand.) But Jesus understood this was not only a challenge to His authority, but a temptation to choose the material over the spiritual. So He relied solely on the Word of God, answering: "It is written: 'Man does not live on bread alone.' "[12]

A pause ... and then a second attack: the tempter offered Christ the kingdoms of this world. (This temptation has caused power-hungry men from Alexander to Hitler to cut a bloody swath through history.) But again Jesus answered from the Word of God: "It is written: 'Worship the Lord your God and serve him only.' "[13]

Finally, the Devil played his trump. "If you are the Son of God," prove it. "Throw yourself down from here." Then Satan quoted from Psalm 91: "He will command his angels concerning you to guard you carefully." But once again Christ stood on the firm foundation of the Word. Unlike Eve, He quoted Scripture precisely: "It says: 'Do not put the Lord your God to the test.' "[14]

These two great confrontations with Satan present us with the clear contrast. Eve knew what God said, but when put to the test, she disobeyed His Word. Her disobedience caused the fall of humanity.

Jesus also knew what God said. Put to the test, He obeyed and trusted His whole life to the Word. His obedience — even unto the death of the cross — is the way of our redemption from the Fall.

If presented with the choice, to be like Eve or be like Jesus, most of us would hasten to line up with Christ. We Christians are usually quick to say we want to "be like Jesus." But if we are honest about what those familiar Sunday school words really mean, we'll see they compel us to adopt His attitudes; and that means belief *in*, and submission to, the Scriptures. Instead, we find a thousand ways to resist their truth, to rationalize their calling on our lives. For deep inside we know that obedience to the Scriptures without concern for consequences is penetrating and painful. It requires us to die to self and follow Christ. It demands that we recognize the sin in our lives and that we acknowledge and repent of that sin.

This is the first major intersection on the spiritual pilgrimage. Many prefer to turn off at this point, or think they can live the Christian life on their own terms — that is, without the conversion in attitude and action that must follow the conversion of heart.

I do not think anyone illustrates this better than the man in the next chapter, an infamous character of a generation ago.

I first heard about Mickey Cohen from the chairman of Prison Fellowship, George Wilson. George, for years the manager of Billy Graham's business operations, had gotten to know Cohen in the 1950s when the man attended some of Billy Graham's first crusade meetings.

After George had told me about a hilarious episode involving himself and Cohen, I was prompted to read more about the man in old newspaper accounts, in Cohen's autobiography, and in the accounts of another person you'll meet in the story, Jim Vaus. As I did this minor investigation into the life of a rather flamboyant character, and later as I began gathering material for this book, it struck me that Mickey Cohen's story pathetically but perfectly illustrates what genuine repentance means and how impossible it is to love God without it.

SIN AND REPENTANCE

We are not sinners because we sin;
we sin because we are sinners.

R. C. Sproul

8

A *Christian Gangster?*

Most of the nightclubbers turned to look when the troupe entered the Starlight Room of the Ambassador Hotel. Comedian Buddy Lester paused in his act as tough-looking bodyguards and extravagantly dressed women swirled about a short, pudgy man whose thick, inverted-v eyebrows accented big brown eyes.

As the party snaked its way through the round tables, jeweled hands reached out from all sides to welcome the newcomer. Though attired in a pearl gray, custom-made suit and exuding expensive cologne, the figure was not imposing. Apparently his presence was, for the maître d' seated the patron with reverence, bowed, and personally brought hot towels with which the man wiped his face and hands thoroughly, meticulously, as though trying to erase the oily handshakes he had just endured.

Later, oblivious to the sycophants smoking and drinking around him, the abstimous figure held court for stars and would-be stars. As he sipped his ginger ale and scanned the room for friends he might have missed on his way in, Jimmy Durante, Sammy Davis, Jr., and Humphrey Bogart made their way over to share a few laughs. Others, their faces not so readily recognizable, approached the table with a whispered question or pressed a folded note into a bodyguard's hand.

The Hollywood of the late 1940s was a tinsel town at the height of its glamour. Movies like "12 O'Clock High," "Sunset Boulevard," and "All About Eve" were rolling out of its mammoth production studios. Film stars were larger than life, their furs, jewels, and limousines the props for roles they played to the hilt — even when they left the set. Gossip columns linked starlets and mobsters, movie moguls and politicians' daughters. Celebrities measured their status by the number of morning headlines devoted to their exploits the night before.

And within this gilded world ruled a short figure with a receding hairline and an abrupt New York accent. An unlikely king, he could cause a sensation even at the celebrity-packed Starlight Room.

Myer Harris Cohen, known to friends and ememies alike as Mickey, mobster and "number-one bad boy" of Los Angeles, had invented his own role in life and written the script to please himself. Born poor in New York City, he had once been a New Jersey punk and strong-arm man. Later he moved to the West Coast and became a self-styled gangster in the tradition of Al Capone, whose work he greatly admired. Cohen was tough to the core, with an immense ego and an innate sense of self-preservation. Contracts were repeatedly put out on his life; his home was bombed; his car machine-gunned.

By 1949, Cohen was top man in the Los Angeles underworld, handling half a million dollars every day from his gambling casinos, floating crap games, private gambling clubs, legalized poker games, and the biggest nonsyndicate bookie business west of Chicago. He had a luxurious home, a glamorous wife, and entertained lavishly for his friends. Nothing happened in that glittering town without his say-so, for Cohen's charisma was power not glamour. Yet he had the charm of a kid brother who wanted nothing so much as to be liked.

People first drawn to Cohen because of his power were surprised when they became his friends; ruthless as he was at running the rackets, Mickey was equally generous and kind to those he cared for.

But Cohen had won his power with muscle — physical and financial — and he retained it with those same forces. Anyone behind the scenes knew this all too well. . . .

The director in the control booth adjusted his headset as he told his assistant to switch to camera two. Pressing the microphone closer to his lips, he spoke to one of the cameramen out on the floor of the television studio. "Now, Jim. Close in. There. That's great. Hold that tight head shot."

Beyond the window of the monitoring booth a heavy gray-haired man in sheriff's uniform sat at the polished desk on the cramped set. Red and blue bunting draped a screen behind him; an American flag stood on a platform to his left. The desk hid the ample paunch straining the buttons of his stiff gray shirt, but the glaring lights reflected off the sweat beading his high, balding forehead. He was obviously concentrating on keeping his gaze direct and obeying the director's orders to "pretend you're talking to your neighbor over the back fence."

"Most of you folks feel the same way I do about Los Angeles," he was saying. "It's the nearest thing to paradise on God's earth. But a great big ol' snake has got hisself coiled around this city. And that snake's name is Organized Crime. In my first term I went after him, like I said I would. Today we're right to the place where we can almost lop that varmit's head right off. We just need to get rid of its number one man. So if you elect me next Tuesday, the first thing I'll do is rid us forever of the chief of the underworld out here — Mickey Cohen."

In the booth the director smirked and the sound engineer chuckled, looking down at the two men lingering at the edge of the set beyond the bright circle of light trained on the sheriff. The director's assistant, clipboard in hand, ventured toward the figures in the shadows and spoke to the shorter of the two.

"You planning on going on the lam, Mickey?"

"Sure. Getting Tumbleweed elected ain't been no joyride. I deserve a vacation."

The sweating sheriff Mickey Cohen had in his pocket had denounced him convincingly, just as he had been instructed. The broadcast would be worth the price Cohen had paid for it.

This kind of drama was all in a day's work for Mickey Cohen. Unfortunately, many of his other scenarios were more sinister. One of these, a "piece of work" he undertook in 1949, would cause the first crack in his power base.

It revolved around Alfred Pearson, owner of an L.A. radio repair shop. Pearson was a skinflint who enjoyed nothing more than a good lawsuit followed by a foreclosure. He had filed several nuisance suits against the city of Los Angeles, and in one case had succeeded in attaching the $4,000 home of a widow named Elsie Philips over a $9.00 repair bill she owed him. As time went on, the mayor of L.A. decided the well-publicized case reflected badly on his city and that he had had quite enough of Alfred Pearson. So Mayor Fletcher Brown instructed the chief executive for the police commission and another of his political lieutenants to contact Mickey Cohen about the matter.*

Mickey, who hated Pearson's cruelty to the poor, graciously offered to have him "knocked in," but the mayor didn't want Pearson dead, just beaten within an inch of his life. Mickey thought this an inefficient way to do business, but the police commissioner promised him that there wouldn't be a cop within miles of Pearson's store on a certain Saturday between noon and one o'clock; Mickey and his boys could "run down this deal" on Pearson in good style. Since he enjoyed playing Robin Hood, Mickey agreed. (He later bought Philips' home back for her when it was suggested this would look good for his image.)

Mickey and his associates arrived at the radio shop at the appointed day and hour. Mickey went in alone first. The shopkeeper was working in the back of the store behind a locked iron screen that separated the repair shop from the showroom where new television sets and radios were displayed. Mickey politely asked the man to come talk with him, but Pearson refused to come out from behind the screen.

Cohen left, waited fifteen minutes, and sent in an associate — a small man with a pencil behind his ear, posing as a reporter. When the little guy succeeded in enticing Pearson out of his stronghold, the others moved in.

With baseball bats and tire irons, Cohen's boys methodically broke Pearson's arms and legs and cracked open his skull. Taking their time about it, they delivered blow after blow with a calm recital of the man's lawsuits. Pearson screamed for help, cursed, and practically tore his store apart trying to get away.

The noise attracted the neighbors; soon some three hundred bystanders were assembled in front of the store, but no one intervened in the shopkeeper's behalf. Instead, they cheered Cohen and his boys on as if they were a liberating army.

However, someone unacquainted with Pearson's business practices came along at the end of the beating, saw the bleeding man crawling out of the store, and raced off to get the police. Cohen, of course, had left the scene by this time.

Two rookie cops apprehended Mickey's boys a few blocks from the store, ordered them out of the car, and lined them up on the sidewalk.

---

*This version of the Pearson incident is taken from Cohen's autobiography.

Finding the bloodied irons and bats and learning from the license plate that the car had been stolen, the cops thought they had made the biggest bust since Dillinger. Cruiser sirens wailing, they hustled the men off to the Wilshire police station.

While the cops had been frisking the men on the sidewalk, an amateur photographer happened by, clicked the shutter, and took the photos to the L.A. *Times*. A seasoned police reporter took one look at the pictures and jubilantly recognized the men as hoods in the upper echelon of Cohen's organization.

Meanwhile, Mickey was at Slapsie Maxie's, a club he was using as his floating office. When he heard of the arrest, he called the captain of the Wilshire station and got his men released. It wasn't much of a problem since the captain was on his payroll, but the professional in Mickey disapproved of any job done badly.

To his detriment Mickey found out just how bad it was. The *Times* printed the photo and the story broke, implicating him and the police and forcing the authorities to arrest and indict him.

At the trial, the jury brought in a verdict of "not guilty," but the Pearson incident had given Mickey the kind of publicity he didn't want — and it would return to haunt him.[†]

Late one night in that same year, 1949, Cohen received a phone call from one of his employees, a man named Jim Vaus. Vaus was an electronics wizard, one of the original wire-tappers. He had first worked for the police in criminal investigations, then for Hollywood stars seeking evidence in divorce proceedings, and finally for Cohen and other underworld figures. Even so valued an employee as Vaus wouldn't have dared call Cohen that late at night unless what he had on his mind was urgent. The gangster invited Jim and his wife, Alice, to come to his home in Brentwood immediately.

In Cohen's living room, Jim Vaus explained that he had attended something called a Billy Graham Crusade in downtown L.A. and had become a Christian. Mickey was Jewish and considered all Gentiles Christians. He said he didn't understand what Vaus was talking about. Jim

---

[†]Tried a number of times for murder, armed robbery, and assault, Mickey Cohen was never convicted of a violent crime.

explained that becoming a Christian involved a personal commitment to Jesus Christ as Savior and Lord.

Mickey paused, then smiled indulgently. "That's good to hear, Jim. As far as I'm concerned, this little Jew's in your corner 100 percent. All I'd like ya to promise me is that I don't want to ever hear ya turned back."

"Well, I'm giving up everything," Vaus said.

Mickey didn't know what "everything" meant. Jim Vaus's renunciation of his criminal life forced him to come up against — or, as they would say, double-cross — other underworld figures not as understanding as Mickey. For example, Vaus was due to fly to St. Louis that week for a piece of work that was to expand a horse-race betting scam that had already netted bushels of gambling money for Jim and several underworld partners. When Jim called his St. Louis associates, told them about his conversion and that he wasn't coming, they assured him they would be . . . coming for him.

One day, as expected, the musclemen came. They told Vaus it was time to settle the score and that they expected him to come quietly. Jim knew they had been ordered either to cripple him for life or kill him. He stood on his porch steps and for forty-five minutes told them what had happened to him, how Jesus Christ had transformed his life. At the end of his account, the hoods turned and walked away. They never came back.

Mickey's strange "good boy" streak was revealed as he backed Vaus's decision for Christ by releasing him from his "employment." Of course, his motives were mixed as usual. Cohen loved nothing more than associating with famous people, and the young evangelist Billy Graham was becoming a hot item in the local papers. Radio star Stuart Hamblen, a cowboy with a reputation as a rounder and hard drinker, had made a decision for Christ at the crusade and immediately broadcast the news of his reformation to his huge radio following. As a result of this and other celebrity conversions, the young Graham was on his way to becoming a celebrity himself. Mickey asked Vaus if he would introduce him to "that guy who's converting all those famous folks."

Through a series of circumstances, Mickey did meet Graham. Intrigued, the gangster agreed to hear the evangelist preach at a private meeting of a group of Hollywood people that included Stuart and Suzy Hamblen as well as western stars Roy Rogers and Dale Evans. Unsure of what to expect, Mickey didn't want his attendance publicized — an unusual desire on his part. So elaborate arrangements were made to get him to the meeting without an accompanying bevy of reporters.

First, the Hamblens drove Graham and his associate George Wilson to a designated street corner in the lower reaches of Hollywood. Billy remained in the car; George Wilson stepped out and waited on the sidewalk. A dark green Cadillac, of the vintage when Cadillacs resembled the swan boats in an amusement park Tunnel of Love, rolled up to the curb. The door opened and Wilson got in the back seat. There Mickey Cohen greeted him cordially.

Next, Cohen leaned forward and whispered in the driver's ear. The man got out, walked up to Hamblen's car and spoke with him. George could see them both gesturing, their voices low. Then Mickey's driver returned and repositioned himself behind the wheel. Suddenly both cars exploded into action, screeching away from the curb and swinging on two wheels around the first hairpin turn. A group of reporters had gotten wind of Cohen's plans and the little man was determined to shake them.

Stuart Hamblen more than obliged, relishing the high-speed chase, deliberately choosing a route that sent both cars charging up and flying over steep hills and roaring down to bottom out on stomach-churning flats.

George Wilson, a man of determinedly even temperament, tried to keep his gaze on the road as the car careened through the Hollywood hills, but his eye was caught by a giant pastel Kleenex box on the back seat between himself and Cohen. Surely no gangster used pink tissues, he thought. He had seen machine guns in violin cases in the movies; perhaps underworld types in real life used Kleenex boxes for smaller weapons . . . like handguns. Inching away from the box, Wilson fixed his eyes on the dubious comfort of the flying landscape.

After fifteen minutes of creative aerial driving, the two cars finally lost the pack of reporters and arrived at the home of Holmy Hills, a producer. Mickey, who had noticed that the ride hadn't fazed Graham's man — though Wilson did seem to have an aversion to Kleenex — determined to stick next to such a cool guy during the course of the meeting.

Fifty or sixty people crowded together on chairs and the floor to hear Billy Graham. After the tall young preacher finished his gospel message, J. Edwin Orr, another evangelist, got up to give an invitation. He also invited people who were simply interested in learning more about Christianity to raise their hands; he wanted to give them copies of the Gospel of John.

Mickey whispered to his new friend, George Wilson, that he would like a copy. George insisted that if Mickey wanted one he would have to raise his own hand. Impressed by what he had learned about Christianity that night, the gangster did so.

Jim Vaus's conversion led him to make restitution for the crimes he had committed. He had stolen $15,000 worth of electronic equipment from the telephone company and a local radio station. He sold his house and automobile in order to pay back the money. When a notice of his actions appeared in the paper, he received a call from Cohen.

"How you going to get around without no car, Jim?" Mickey asked.

"Well, the buses and streetcars are still running."

"Sure, but lookit, let me loan you a car."

"Thanks, Mickey, but no."

"Why not?" his former boss asked.

"I'm working for a new boss now, Mickey. There are new rules. I can't take something that somebody got through crime."

"But whatcha gonna do? You're in a spot. I'm just trying to help you out as a friend."

Vaus told Mickey not to worry about him, that God could supply all his needs. Then he went on to tell what had happened when the St. Louis boys came to call. "If the Lord can do that for me, Mickey, why should I worry about a little thing like money?"

"That's a fabulous come-off, I'll admit," Cohen said slowly. "But if you need me, you don't be stupid ... you call."

As it turned out, Mickey was the one needing help. The Alfred Pearson incident had piqued the federal government's interest in Mickey Cohen, and eventually he was indicted for tax evasion. While the criminal authorities couldn't put Mickey away, the IRS did a thorough job of proving he had spent far more than he had reported as income. In 1951, Cohen was convicted and sentenced to five years in jail.

While in prison, however, Mickey continued to operate, making sure through underworld connections that his obsession with cleanliness was taken into account. Mickey used tissues constantly as a buffer against dirt, dust, and almost the sensation of touch itself. He could not open a door until he had placed a tissue around the knob, nor answer the phone until he had wrapped the receiver in a tissue. In prison Mickey was allowed to shower three or four times a day and was given six rolls of toilet paper daily to use in place of his Kleenex.

When Mickey came out of prison in October of 1955, he no longer had his power in L.A., nor the muscle to regain it. Yet he still yearned for the high life. He glumly concluded, "If I couldn't live my life style, I might as well have been back in the joint." But from then on the IRS kept track of every penny he spent.

Jim Vaus called Mickey shortly after his release and offered his help, including the loan of a car. Recalling Vaus's reply to the same offer a few years earlier, Mickey shot back, "The buses and the streetcars are still running, aren't they?" But Mickey accepted the loan. Vaus also stocked Mickey's apartment with groceries and let him have the run of the office where Vaus now carried on a ministry to young people.

Before Mickey went to prison, Vaus had introduced him to leading Christian layman in Los Angeles, W. C. Jones. Bill Jones was a small, impeccably groomed man with a high forehead, a straight nose, and eyes set to gaze into the distance. Rescued by Christ from addiction to alcohol and gambling, in the past Jones had placed innumerable bets with Mickey's operatives. He was well-qualified to talk with the gangster about Christ's ability to transform lives. Bill Jones took Mickey on as a special project after he came out of prison, devoting hours to cultivating their friendship.

Mickey seemed to be changing. At least he paid more attention to those who truly had his welfare at heart. Also, he had always been oddly charitable, raising money for the Irgun Freedom Fighters in Israel, donating funds to hospitals, sending out Thanksgiving baskets. Now he appeared to see that personal acts of charity could not compensate for a life of crime. He went with his probation officer to speak at camps of delinquent boys about the tragic course they were pursuing.

Seeing this new current within Mickey, and after spending hours with him, Bill Jones urged him to commit his life to Christ. He explained God's plan of salvation, beginning by telling Mickey that God loved him and had a wonderful plan for his life.

Mickey thought that was great.

Then Jones told him that he was sinful, like all mankind, and separated from God.

Mickey had trouble with that one. For one thing, he was a Jew, and a Jew was one of God's chosen people. How could he be separated from the God of the Jews? Besides, he wasn't such a bad guy. "I always strive for the best. Even with my limited education ... I always strive to do things in a professional way ... I mean I have my own principles about things Like when I pulled off a heist, it was a bad reflection upon my own self if anybody just standing around got hurt. I worked clean, see. ... Especially after my Cleveland and Chicago days, I was never a person who would take the life of anybody unless it was absolutely a must. ... No one who knew ever said Mickey Cohen wasn't one of the finest."

Jones said that wasn't quite the point. He moved on to explain about God's provision for man's sin in Jesus Christ and that Mickey had to individually receive Christ as his Savior and Lord so that he might know and experience God's love and plan for his life. Bill quoted Revelation 3:20: "Behold, I stand at the door and knock: if any man hear my voice, and open the door, I will come in to him."

"That means you, too, Mickey," Bill Jones said. "You said that you're not the kind of people that Billy Graham or church folk generally like. But it's not up to them; it's up to Christ, and he says *anyone*."

"So fine," Mickey said. "I'm glad to hear it."

"But you've got to act on it, Mickey," Jones said. "This is called the penitent's prayer. If you'll repeat it after me, you can know right here and now that you will be reborn as a son of God. You will live in heaven forever. You've seen the high life, Mickey, but none of us have seen anything like heaven. So will you pray with me?"

To Bill's surprise and delight, Mickey repeated the prayer.

Had Mickey Cohen, famous Hollywood gangster, really become a Christian?

Bill Jones was convinced Mickey's decision was genuine. What a testimony! As the word spread through the Christian community, there was jubilant response. What a trophy! In a day when the evangelical church was seldom in the news, this was headline stuff.

But Jones also knew that Mickey was badly in need of further instruction about the Christian life. He called Jim Vaus and discussed the possibility of flying Mickey to New York to meet with Billy Graham, who was soon to begin a crusade in Madison Square Garden. Vaus agreed to help pay for Mickey's expenses in New York.

Within a few days Cohen had flown east and moved into the Waldorf-Astoria. Graham met with him and in a marathon session tried to explain the significance of what Mickey had done in his prayer with Bill Jones. Though Mickey was amiable, Graham sensed a wall of inner resistance that could not be scaled.

Nevertheless, Mickey showed up two days later at the Graham Crusade in the Garden, along with several bodyguards and a flock of reporters. Speculation was rife: Would Cohen go forward, making public his commitment?

Mickey tried to get backstage to be photographed with Graham. The evangelist, who spent the time just prior to preaching in prayer and meditation, wisely refused to allow the photographers near him. Mickey was then escorted to an area reserved for special guests.

No matter what Cohen's motives were for attending, he stayed, though obviously displeased with the lack of royal treatment. And he was thoroughly uncomfortable, for the Spirit of God was at work; Graham's message seemed particularly appropriate for the disgruntled gangster with the giant box of Kleenex by his side.

"You and I deserve hell," thundered Graham. "You and I deserve to spend eternity separated from God. . . . Oh, yes, the Scriptures teach that you're a sinner. And so am I. . . .

"You may think you are a good and upright person and that you have done nothing worthy of damnation. You may say, I am honest in my business dealings; I love my kids; I give to the United Way. But there's no middle ground between heaven and hell. You are either on the road to one or the other. . . .

"The Bible shows us the perfect example of a man who wanted to escape his responsibility for his own sinfulness before God—the Roman ruler, Pilate. After Jesus had been tried by the Sanhedrin, he was taken before Pilate. But Pilate was just like you and me; he wanted to remain neutral. He declared Christ innocent, then took a bowl of water and washed his hands in front of the whole multitude. 'I am washing my hands of this just man,' he said. Then he allowed Christ to be lead away and crucified.

"Tradition tells us that Pilate spent the last years of his life up in the mountains of Switzerland, washing his hands constantly. When anyone asked him, 'What are you doing?' he said, 'I am trying to wash the blood stain of Jesus Christ off my hands.' Through all eternity Pilate will try to wash the blood stain off, but he will never be able to do it.

"Tonight you have to make your choice. Every man, every woman, every boy and every girl, you will have to make your choice between pleasure and Christ, amusements and Christ, popularity and Christ, money and Christ. Whatever is keeping you from the kingdom of God, you will have to make a choice tonight, and if you refuse to make the choice, that very act means you have already made it."

For one wild, impetuous, holy moment, Mickey Cohen wanted to take his giant box of Kleenex and fling it away forever. But in the next moment he found himself ripping several tissues out and dabbing at his forehead, his neck, his hands, and wanting to take it on the lam out of there. He endured the rest of the service for the vainglory of leading the reporters outside and having his picture taken under the marquee bearing Billy Graham's name.

After he returned to Los Angeles, Mickey dropped Bill Jones and contacted Jim Vaus less frequently. He began hanging around with his underworld cronies again. This perplexed and upset Jones, who went to Mickey and told him that as a new Christian he ought to be putting as much mileage between himself and his mob connections as possible.

"Jones," Mickey replied, "you never told me that I had to give up my career. You never told me that I had to give up my friends. There are Christian movie stars, Christian athletes, Christian businessmen. So what's the matter with being a Christian gangster?

"If I have to give up all that — if that's Christianity — count me out."

9

Whatever Became of Sin?

Mickey Cohen quietly lived out his last years at his suburban Los Angeles home, dying of cancer on July 29, 1976. Mickey was alone when he stepped from this world. His wife had divorced him years earlier, there were no clamoring crowds of reporters, no dancing girls, no bodyguards. The over-publicized accounts of Mickey's exploits had faded from memory; even his public flirtation with Christianity became a minor story, buried in old newspaper microfilm.

Why Mickey was first drawn to Christianity we will probably never know. Maybe he saw it as a way to gain respectability he could never earn on his own. Maybe he saw a glint of hope — and real power. Whatever it was, the image of Jesus knocking at the door was as compelling to him as it has been to millions through the centuries; and he began to open that door, only to discover that doing so involved a choice. He must surrender himself or close the door. When he finally understood what was demanded of him, what repentance meant, he closed the door. Mickey Cohen could not repent.

Though Cohen's life reads like a movie script, the crucial point of this dramatic story is that, at heart, each one of us is exactly like Mickey Cohen — sinful and struggling with repentance.

Granted, he was flamboyant and neurotic, a gangland figure guilty of every crime in the book. Granted, his guilt made the headlines, his sins were public knowledge (some of us have experienced that, too, though).

But in voicing his comical, outrageous, poignant question "What's the matter with being a Christian gangster?" Cohen was echoing the millions of professing Christians who, though unwilling to admit it, through their very lives pose the same question. Not about being Christian gangsters, but about being Christianized versions of whatever they already are — and are determined to remain. C.S. Lewis called these hybrids "hyphenated Christians."

And, like Mickey, we cannot love God — cannot obey Him — and remain what we are. We must repent.

For most of us, the word "repentance" conjures up images of medieval monks in sackcloth and ashes or Old Testament prophets rending their garments in anguish. Or we see repentance as something someone "really wicked" — like Mickey Cohen — must do to sanitize his corrupt life.

But repentance is much more than self-flagellation, more than regret, more than deep sorrow for past sins; and it applies to everyone. The biblical word for repentance is "metanoia" in the original Greek. *Meta* means "change" and *noia* means "mind," so literally it means "a change of mind." One church scholar describes it as "that mighty change in mind, heart, and life, wrought by the spirit of God."[1]

Thus, repentance is replete with radical implications, for a fundamental change of mind not only turns us from the sinful past, but transforms our life plan, values, ethics, and actions as we begin to see the world through God's eyes rather than ours. That kind of transformation requires the ultimate surrender of self.

The call to repentance — individual and corporate — is one of the most consistent themes of Scripture. The Old Testament contains vivid accounts of kings and prophets, priests and people falling before God to plead for mercy and promising to change. The demand for repentance is clear in God's commands to Moses,[2] and its broken-hearted reality and passion flows through David's eloquent prayer of contrition.[3] It is the consistent refrain of the prophets.[4]

Repentance is the keynote of the New Testament as well. It is John the Baptist's single message: "Repent, for the kingdom of heaven is near."[5] And according to Mark's Gospel, "Repent and believe the good news," were among Jesus' first public words.[6] And His last instructions to His disciples before the Ascension included the directive that "repentance and forgiveness of sins will be preached in his name to all nations."[7] All told, the words "repent" or "repentance" appear more than fifty times in the New Testament.

Repentance is an inescapable consequence of regeneration, an indispensable part of the conversion process that takes place under the convicting power of the Holy Spirit. But repentance is also a continuing state of mind. We are warned, for example, to repent before partaking of communion.[8] Also, believers "prove their repentance by their deeds."[9] Without a continuing repentant attitude — a persistent desire to turn away from our own nature and seek God's nature — Christian growth is impossible. Loving God is impossible.

If all this is true, then, some may ask, why is repentance so seldom preached and so little understood? I believe there are three reasons.

Noted church historian J. Edwin Orr sums up the first: *the appeal of modern evangelism is "not for repentance but for enlistment."*[10] To put it even more bluntly, some evangelists see converts as trophies in a big game hunt and measure their success by numbers; thus, they do not want to frighten off their prey.

One Christian leader, asked why he never mentioned repentance, smiled and replied, "Get 'em first, let them see what Christianity is, and then they'll see their need to repent." Tragically, this attitude pervades the church not only because we're afraid the truth will scare newcomers, but because it might also drive a number of the nodding regulars right out of their comfortable pews.

Repentance can be a threatening message — and rightly so. The Gospel must be the bad news of the conviction of sin before it can be the good news of redemption. Because that message is unpalatable for many middle-class congregations preoccupied with protecting their affluent lifestyles, many pastors endowed with a normal sense of self-preservation tiptoe warily round the subject. And the phenomenal growth of the electronic church has only aggravated this trend, for while the Sunday morning pew-dweller is trapped, unable to escape gracefully when a tough subject like repentance comes up, the TV viewer has only to flip a switch or go out to the refrigerator.

The result of all this is a watered-down message that, in large part, accounts for today's epidemic spread of easy believism, Christianity without cost, or "cheap grace" as German martyr, Dietrich Bonhoeffer, so aptly labeled it a generation ago — grace in which "no contrition is required, still less any real desire to be delivered from sin ... a denial of the living word of God, in fact, a denial of the incarnation."[11]

The second reason repentance is so ignored or misunderstood comes much closer to home, as I have discovered: *often we are simply unwilling or unable to accept the reality of personal sin and therefore to accept our need for repentance.*

We have no difficulty seeing Mickey Cohen's sin, but we would certainly never put ourselves in the same category with this old-style gangster. He probably broke most of the Ten Commandments (and we haven't?). Well, even if we aren't perfect, we're a lot better than Mickey Cohen. After all, nobody's perfect, and God understands we're only human. Most good professors grade on a curve; God probably does, too.

Why is it so hard for us to see our own sin? That it has always been this way is eloquently illustrated by King David.

Soon after he was enthroned, David committed not only the sin of adultery with Bathsheba, but also the sin of murder by having her husband sent to certain death in battle. Though he was described as a man after God's own heart and administered justice and righteousness, David was blind to his own sin. He could not see what he had done until the prophet Nathan, sent by God, described the sin in parable form, attributing it to someone else. Nathan asked David to judge the man, which David did: *death*. Only then did Nathan tell David that it was his own sin.[12] What he was quick to judge in others, David was unable to see in himself.

We are all like David, for in our fallen state we have an infinite capacity for justifying whatever acts we commit. Psychologists call this the "self-serving bias" and confirm the truth of William Saroyan's comment, "every man is a good man in a bad world — as he himself knows."[13]

And this leads us to the third reason for our shallow understanding of repentance: *our culture has written sin out of existence.* Even Christians who should understand the basic truth that *all* are heirs of Adam's fall and thus *all* are sinners are influenced, often blinded, by humanist values.

Humanism began in the Garden when the tempter invited Eve to be "like God." Ever since it has encouraged us to believe what our sinful nature wants us to believe — that we are good, getting better through science and education, and can through our own efforts become perfect, masters of our own fate. We can be our own god.

In recent decades popular political and social beliefs have all but erased the reality of personal sin from our national consciousness. Take, for example, the passionately advanced argument that society, not the individual, is responsible for the evil in our midst: individuals commit crimes because they are forced to, not because they choose to. Poverty, racial oppression, slums, hunger — these are the real culprits; the wrong-doer is in reality the victim. President Lyndon Johnson's attorney general, Ramsey Clark, summed up that viewpoint, asserting that poverty *is* the cause of crime.[14] And President Jimmy Carter, after the power blackout and resulting widespread looting in New York, echoed, "Obviously the number one contributing factor to crime ... is high unemployment among young people, particularly those who are black or Spanish speaking.[15]*

This desire to treat their fellow-man with compassion is commendable. But if carried to the extreme, this attitude destroys individual accountability and encourages the very behavior that is so offensive.

No one political camp has a monopoly on perpetuating this myth. Ronald Reagan, accepting an award from the National Conference of Christians and Jews, repeatedly asserted his belief in the "basic goodness" of man, winding up with a quote from Anne Frank's diary dated July 5, 1944: "In spite of everything, I still believe that people are really good at heart."[16] (What tragic irony!)

Richard Nixon was fond of quoting DeTocqueville: "America is great because she is good and if America ever ceases to be good, America will cease to be great."† (I confess that I, along with millions of others, got goose bumps whenever he used that quote.)

Politicians tell people what they want to hear, and people like to be told they are really "good." So speech lines like these are sure-fire applause-getters. But good politics can make bad theology; and when we begin to believe our own press releases, we become victims of our own delusions.

Whatever became of sin? Karl Menninger's startling book title and theme is the most timely question anyone could ask of the church today.

The answer lies within each of us, but to find it we must come face to face with who we really are. This is a difficult process. That hidden self is buried deep inside our hearts, and, as Jeremiah warned, the human heart is deceitful above all things.[17] Confronting that true self is an excruciating discovery, as I learned in prison after my conversion.

---

*A study conducted a month later by New York City's Criminal Justice Agency, Inc. revealed that 45 percent who were arrested looting had jobs and only 10 percent were on welfare rolls. In most cases people stole things they did not need.

†This quote is often attributed to Alexis DeTocqueville even though the Library of Congress can find no record of it among his works.

10

It Is in Us

Most people make it through life without seeing their sins plastered across banner headlines. Their trangressions remain their own private property. At the most they are shared with a priest or minister, a close friend, or perhaps a prayer group. I have not had that luxury.

Having been at the center of the biggest political upheaval of this century, I've had my sins — real and imagined — spread mercilessly across the front pages around the world, re-enacted in living color on movie and TV screens, and dissected in hundreds of books. As a result, I am often asked which of my Watergate perfidies causes me the greatest remorse.

My invariable reply, "None. My deepest remorse is for the hidden sins of my heart which are far worse," either puzzles or infuriates the media.

But it is an honest answer. My Watergate wrongs could be explained (though not justified) as political zealotry or expedience, misplaced idealism, blind obedience to higher authority, or even capitulation to the natural temptation of the human will, which Nietzsche said seeks power over others above all else. The sins for which I feel the greatest contrition are those sins so perfectly illustrated by an episode from my life thirty years ago, etched in my consciousness as clearly as though it happened yesterday....

I was a brand-new Marine lieutenant, as proud and tough as basic training could make a man. My spit-shined shoes reflected the sun like two mirrors, matched in brilliance only by my polished gold bars.

In the midst of Caribbean maneuvers, our battalion was landed on Vieques Island, a tiny satellite of Puerto Rico. Most of the mountainous little land was a Navy protectorate used for landing and target practice, but on one end a clan of poverty-stricken souls endured the ear-splitting shellings just to eke out a living selling beer and cold drinks to invading Marines.

Before landing, we officers were instructed to buy nothing from these peddlers who, though strictly forbidden to enter the military reservation, invariably did so. The order was given with a sly smile and wink because no one obeyed it.

The second day in the field, I was leading my platoon of forty grimy, sweating riflemen up and over a craggy ridge when just across the next ridge I spotted an old man leading a scrawny donkey nearly collapsing under the load of two huge, obviously ice-filled, canvas sacks.

The scorching midday July sun had us panting, and our canteens were getting low, so I immediately routed my men toward the distant figure. When the men saw the elderly man and his loaded beast, they picked up speed, knowing I would blink at orders and permit them to buy cans of cold drinks. I could hear several digging in their pockets for coins.

When we were but a few yards from the grinning old man, who was undoubtedly congratulating himself on his good fortune and counting up what might be several months' income, I ordered my troops to halt. "Sergeant," I commanded, "take this man prisoner. He is trespassing on government property." The platoon sergeant, a veteran of a dozen or more Vieques landings, stared at me in disbelief. "Go ahead," I barked. The sergeant shook his head, swung about, and, with rifle at the ready, marched toward the old man whose smile suddenly turned to stone.

I commanded my men to "confiscate the contraband." Cheering lustily, they did so. While the sergeant tossed cans of chilled fruit juice from the two bulging sacks, the old man squinted at me with doleful eyes. His sacks emptied, we released our "prisoner." Shoulders hunched, he rode away on his donkey, perhaps grateful we hadn't strapped him to a tree. (Small wonder that years later "independence" movements in Puerto Rico agitated for removal of the U.S. military!)

Technically, of course, I had observed military law. Yet I had not given a fleeting thought to the fact that those satchels of juice might have represented the old man's life savings or that my order could mean an entire family might go hungry for months. Rather, I was smugly satisfied, believing that my men were grateful to me for getting them something cold to drink (which they would have happily purchased) and that I had proven I was tough (though my adversary was defenseless). As for the old man, *well*, I thought, *he got what he deserved for violating government property.*

This incident, though quickly forgotten at the time, was vividly brought to my mind years later, after my conversion, as I sat in prison reading from Augustine's *Confesssions* the well-known story of his youthful escapade stealing pears from a neighbor's tree. Augustine recorded that late one night a group of youngsters went out to "shake down and rob this tree. We took great loads of fruit from it, not for our own eating but rather to throw it to the pigs." He went on to berate himself for the depth of sin this revealed. "The fruit I gathered I threw away, devouring in it only iniquity. There was no other reason, but foul was the evil and I loved it."[1]

Contemporary critics, though generous in their praise of Augustine's literary genius and profound philosophical insights, mock him for his seeming obsession with the pear tree episode. Why would one harmless prank loom so large in the saint's mind? By his own admission he had taken a mistress, fathered a child out of wedlock, and indulged in every fleshly passion. Surely any of these were more serious than stealing pears.

But Augustine saw in the pear incident his true nature and the nature of all mankind: *in each of us there is sin* — not just susceptibility to sin, but *sin itself.* Augustine's love for sensual pleasure could be explained as the natural arousing of his human desires, proving inner weakness or susceptibility to sinning. But he had stolen those pears for the pure enjoyment of stealing (he had an abundance of better pears on his own trees). Augustine knew his act was more than weakness; it was sin itself — sin for the sake of sinning.

Alexander Solzhenitsyn discovered the truth of *this individual and universal human condition* following his remarkable encounter with Boris Kornfeld.

During his pain-wracked days and sleepless nights in the grim prison hospital following his cancer surgery, Solzhenitsyn reviewed the strange turns his life had taken. The words of Dr. Kornfeld had reawakened in him a hunger for the God he had once known and renounced. Thus, even in his agony Solzhenitsyn could rejoice, for he was spiritually reborn. But

Kornfeld's words also made him restless as he tossed about on his narrow cot. The remarkable statement, "No punishment comes to us in this life which is undeserved," lingered in his mind.

It was an unsettling thought coming from a man who had been unjustly imprisoned and from a Jew, whose race had been mercilessly persecuted. The extraordinary words forced Solzhenitsyn to look back on his own life. And so it was that the then-unknown prisoner saw how he really was and could write, "In the intoxication of youthful successes I had felt myself to be infallible and I was therefore cruel. In the surfeit of power I was a murderer and an oppressor. In my most evil moments I was convinced I was doing good."[2]

A bright shaft of light shone into the recesses of his soul, and Solzhenitsyn came face to face with his true self — a sign of genuine conversion.

"And it was only when I lay there on rotting prison straw," he continues, "that I sensed within myself the *first* stirrings of good. Gradually it was disclosed to me that *the line separating good and evil passes not through states, nor between classes, nor between parties either — but right through every human heart — through all human hearts*."[3]

In these few lines Solzhenitsyn captures a truth that has eluded humanity from the beginning. The world is not divided into white hats and black hats; it is not divided into good people and evil people. Rather, good and evil coexist in every human heart.

As I lay in prison and watched the events of my own life — such as the Vieques incident — parade before my eyes, I, too, became aware of this painful reality of the human heart and saw myself: I was a sinner and my sin manifested itself in individual acts of my own making. And worst of all, I had delighted in it.

"Sinner" is not some theological term contrived to explain away the presence of evil in this world; nor is it a cliché conceived by colonial hymn writers or backwoods preachers to frighten recalcitrant congregations.

R.C. Sproul sums it up well: "We are not sinners because we sin; we sin because we are sinners." We are not theoretical sinners or honorary sinners or vicarious sinners. We are sinners indeed and in deed.[4]

Man goes to great lengths to avoid his own responsibility. Many blame Satan for every imaginable evil — but Jesus states clearly that sin is in *us*.[5] Others recoil with horror at the sins of the society around them, smugly satisfied that sinful abominations are not of their doing — not realizing that God holds *us* responsible for acts of omission as well as acts of commission. Still others believe, as did Socrates two thousand years ago, that sin is not man's moral responsibility, but is caused by ignorance. Hegel, whose philosophy so enormously influenced nineteenth and twentieth century thought, argued that man is "evolving" through increasing knowledge to superior moral levels.

But what do we see around us in the last third of this twentieth century that has produced such advances in knowledge, technology, and science? Soaring crime rates. Countless shattered families. A globe scarred by continual wars and oppression. All our knowledge has not ushered in a brave new world. It has simply increased our ability to perpetrate evil. History continues to validate the biblical account that man is by his own nature sinful — indeed, imprisoned by his sin.

And we are not reluctant prisoners. Like Augustine, *we actually delight in sin and evil*. What else explains our secret delight in another's fall? What else accounts for our morbid fascination with violence on television or the bloody carnage of horror films? Alypius, Augustine's friend and student who shared his experience in the garden, learned this lesson well.

Alypius was addicted to his day's popular form of entertainment, the bloody gladiatorial games. Frightened by the grip these had on him, he vowed passionately to break his addiction. After avoiding the games successfully for some time, Alypius one day met several friends who, knowing his weakness, dragged him to the arena. Forced into the crowded coliseum, Alypius determined *he would not watch*. So he hunched in his stone seat, jammed among screaming, frenzied fans, his eyes screwed shut and his hands over his ears.

Suddenly, with a single voice, the crowd sent up the loudest blood-curdling cry of delight he had ever heard. Curiosity gripped him. He opened his eyes in time to see one of the fighters fall, covered with blood. He drank in the insane violence. "And I fell more miserably than that gladiator," he confided to Augustine later.

Though Alypius thought himself above the enjoyment of such bloodshed, his will was no match for the evil thrill it brought. He became "drunk on blood and pleasure," and he was again one with his friends and the evil he abhorred.[6]

Who has not found himself at some point slyly boasting of his sins, as Augustine confessed, to earn the "praise it brought"?[7] So pervasive is the sin in us that we are subject to lonely shame if we cannot share in the sins of our peers.

What causes a man like Alypius to cheer lustily as a gladiator's head is lopped off? Why, in our modern gladiatorial contests played out on a national and international scale, now called war, do we sense a certain spellbinding grandeur in the drama of armies moving across a field of battle?[8] Why do those who find war's allure the most irresistible often become national heroes?[9] (Remember the moment in the movie "Patton" when the legendary general, played by George C. Scott, looked over the field of battle from a command vehicle with undisguised exaltation: "Look," he said to his companion, "could anything be more magnificent? ... I must tell the truth — I love it — God ... I do love it!"[10]) And why does the same bloody thrill grip a movie theater audience when a demon-possessed child gouges out her mother's eyes?*

What is it? Nothing less than the evil within us, the dark side of the line that, Solzhenitsyn wrote, passes through each human heart.

Indeed, that is where the real battle is being fought. It is not between "good" people and "bad" people, like a game of cops and robbers; it is not between "good" governments and "bad," like the U.S. and the Soviet Union. It is not being fought for mere national or international stakes. The war to end all wars is a battle for eternal stakes between spiritual forces — and it is being waged *in* you and *in* me.

When we truly smell the stench of sin within us, it drives us helplessly and irresistibly to despair. *But God* has provided a way for us to be

---

*There are those incurable optimists who argue that man visits his inhumanity on others out of fear and a natural instinct for self-preservation. They say he acts aggressively and violently out of fear that his fellow-man will harm him if he does not act first. But consider this example of man's cruel violence toward helpless animals from an account of the early years of the great naturalist W. H. Hudson: "The native manner of killing a cow or bullock at that time was peculiarly painful....One of the two or three mounted men engaged in the operation would throw his lasso over the horns, and, galloping off, pull the rope taut; a second man would then drop from his horse...and with two lightning-quick blows of his big knife sever the tendons of both hind legs. Instantly the beast would go down on his haunches, and the same man...thrust the long blade into its throat just above the chest, driving it in to the hilt and working it round; then when it was withdrawn a great torrent of blood would pour out from the tortured beast, still standing on his fore-legs, bellowing all the time with agony. At this point the slaughterer would often leap lightly onto its back, stick his spurs in its sides, and, using the flat of his long knife as a whip, pretend to be riding a race, yelling with fiendish glee. The bellowing would subside into deep, awful, sob-like sounds and chokings; then the rider, seeing the animal about to collapse, would fling himself nimbly off" (from *Far Away and Long Ago*, E. P. Dutton and Co., 1924, pp. 41-42).

freed from the evil within: it is through the door of repentance. When we truly comprehend our own nature, repentance is no dry doctrine, no frightening message, no morbid form of self-flagellation. It is, as the early church fathers said, a gift God grants which leads to life.[11] It is the key to the door of liberation, to the only real freedom we can ever know.

Because it does mean freedom, perhaps it is not surprising that people in prison seem to have an easier time understanding repentance than those on the outside. Prisoners are captives in every sense. They have had their most blatant sins exposed in the blinding light of the courtroom and they have been locked into the midst of every form of evil and depravity.

Thus, it is not surprising that I have found the most vivid illustration of repentance in the Bible beginning in a prison cell. . . .

11

Remember Me

By the small square of light from the tiny, high window, the men could tell the sun had risen, but the glimmer barely penetrated the thick darkness of the stone cell where the three prisoners waited.

Since the first hint of dawn they had been standing, pacing, waiting, though each was chained to a guard. The room stunk of urine, but it was not fastidiousness that kept them from sinking to the filthy floor. They simply could not sit; they were waiting to die.

The man called Barabbas leaned lightly against the outer wall under the window. While the other two paced and pulled at their chains, cursing the guards, Barabbas stood still, his head lifted as though listening to some far-off sound. He had not spoken to the other men, even when asked a direct question. But like the others, he was waiting.

Despite his resistance, the guards treated Barabbas with a kind of rough respect; he was an important prisoner, almost a celebrity, the leader of a small band of freedom fighters. The government officials hoped his death today would snuff out the tiresome rebellion.

David, the tall, young prisoner with a long and hungry face, had been watching the still, shadowed figure for some time. Now he gestured toward Barabbas and asked, "What does he hear?"

The third prisoner, a middle-aged man with graying hair and a stoical expression, was called Jacob; he had been a minor lieutenant in Barabbas's insurrectionist band. His answer to David's questions was a shrug of heavy shoulders.

"He hears something," David insisted, tugging nervously at his chain. "Look at the way he's listening."

"Maybe he thinks we're going to be rescued," Jacob grunted with disdain. "Maybe he's waiting for Jerusalem to wake up and come to our rescue — throw off the Romans for good and make him king."

"But you were with him," David said. "You were in the same cause."

"Sure" Jacob confirmed bitterly. "I've always been a fighter. You start young, choose sides, and fight to the finish. And this is the finish. That's life."

David's hunger-thin face tightened with suppressed emotions. "You aren't afraid then?"

Jacob swore. "Of course I'm afraid. Who wants to die? If you know a way out of here, tell me about it. But I've never had any illusions. We had our moments — now they have theirs."

Distant sounds filtered into the silence that followed. David strained to hear. "Sounds like a crowd out there."

"Sure it's a crowd," one of the guards said. "City's packed. It's the Jews' Passover. They're waiting for the good show you're going to put on for them."

But the sounds were more than ordinary street noises. A chant, muffled by the distance and stone walls, rumbled in the background.

"What are they saying?" David asked.

His guard laughed. "They say, 'Dear, generous, Pilate, please release those nice criminals you're about to crucify. They never meant any harm.' " The other two guards joined his mocking laughter, a brief relief from their boring duty.

The chant, whatever it had been, died out. The three men stood, locked together in silent, separate agony. David, like the others, had had his moment before Pilate, had heard the verdict "guilty" and the sentence "death by crucifixion." But it takes time for such words to sink in. Now, the mockery of the guards roused a scream of denial within him. I can't die. I don't deserve to die. This is unfair. There must be a way out. I've always gotten away before. There must a way to escape.

The guards filled the silence with talk about their families, their bad luck in drawing this duty. To David, their words were like the buzzing of the countless flies the sun had awakened.

"Do you regret anything," he asked Jacob. He couldn't stand his own silence and sought the consolation of shared fear.

"Yeah, getting caught."

"No, I mean . . . are you sorry — "

"For what?"

"Well . . . that you didn't lead a more normal life . . . that, well, you've murdered and stolen. Do you regret that — or just getting caught?"

"What about you?" Jacob snapped, refusing the question. "You did the same."

"I never killed anyone!" David cried. "And I only stole what I needed to live. Look at me!" He jerked open his ragged clothing to expose his protruding ribs. "A man has to eat."

"Not when he's dead," Jacob laughed bitterly. "What are you, a slave?"

"I was. But never again."

"Sure. I know the story. Your master was cruel. You ran away. Where from?"

"Cyprus."

"Cyprus, huh. So you lied and got on a ship — bought your passage with money stolen from your master. Right? And somehow got here, half alive. Let me guess the rest. You were begging for food when one of the gangs offered you a living. All you had to do was work as a lookout, warn them when the soldiers were near, carry some messages through the city. No harm in it. Not when you're starving to death. Which gang was it? I know them all."

David did not answer, stunned by the accuracy of the man's words. Before Jacob could continue, they heard the sound of the outer gate opening and footsteps approaching. The guards' voices came clearly through the small grating of the wooden door.

"Did you know they have that fellow Jesus?" one asked.

"The rabbi?"

"Whatever they call him. They arrested him last night. One of his own men turned him in."

"What are they doing with him?"

"The Jews want him crucified. Can you believe it? He's the wrong kind of Jew apparently. They've been shouting it out there in the streets for hours. Couldn't you hear them? 'Crucify him! Crucify him!' "

"So what does Pilate say?"

"He doesn't know what to say. I think this guy has Pilate scared. I was in the hall when they questioned him. This Jesus talked as though

Pilate was on trial. No pleading . . . nothing. I've never seen anyone face Pilate like that. I swear Pilate was spooked."

"What are they charging him with?"

"They say he claims to be the king of the Jews."

"King of the Jews? Who cares?"

The door opened and two soldiers looked into the cell, trying to adjust to the darkness. "Which one's Barabbas?"

Barabbas did not move, gave no indication he had heard his name. His guard rattled the chain between them and laughed, "Here he is. He's waiting to be rescued."

"Well, here we are," one said as they strode over and began unlocking the chain. "We're the rescue party. We'll send you safely to another world."

"Do you want to be king, too, Barabbas?" the other laughed. "Here's your crown." He placed the palm of his hand on the prisoner's forehead and slammed his head against the wall. "Hail to the king!"

David listened to their steps as they pulled Barabbas through the room beyond and out to the courtyard. Almost immediately he heard the whip. At each crack, David flinched.

"Pray they give you a lot, boy," Jacob said quietly. "Pray they whip you half to death. You go quicker on the cross that way."

At the twelfth crack Barabbas' grunts became an unearthly cry, a sob, a scream. They took him up to twenty, then the whip hissed no more.

Heavy footsteps crossed the room outside, the door opened, and Barabbas was dumped face down on the floor. In the light from the doorway David could see that the man's back was raw, bloody meat.

They were unchaining Jacob when he took a sudden kick at one of the soldiers, catching him in the groin. The man doubled over, clutching himself, and the other soldier reflexively hit Jacob across the side of the head with the flat of his sword and sent him spinning to the floor. Cursing, the soldiers dragged Jacob to his feet and held him while their injured companion planted a knee into Jacob's groin once, twice, three times. Then they dragged him out. As the whip cracked, Jacob began screaming.

When the fog cleared from David's head after his turn under the lash, his face was in the foul dirt floor, his nostrils filled with it, his teeth gritty. His thoughts came at him in slow motion, framed in a hazy light. He couldn't remember where he was at first. Somewhere in the distance he could hear a crowd calling, "Barabbas . . . Barabbas. . . ." Why were they calling that name? Raising his head from the floor he came back to his surroundings. Jacob and Barabbas were still there. All the soldiers were gone.

"Why are they calling your name?" David asked Barabbas, his voice thick in his throat.

"I don't know." It was the first David had heard the man speak.

What was it they had chanted earlier? "Crucify him! Crucify him!" Calling for the death of the man named Jesus, the soldiers had said. David knew a little about the one called Jesus of Nazareth. He had seen the man enter the city last week surrounded by a crowd of followers. Everyone had been talking about him then. Some said he could heal diseases, do magical things. David had even heard rumblings that he was Messiah, the leader many Jews had been waiting for to rescue them from the tyranny of Rome.

Suddenly David felt as though he were up in the sky looking down at this cell and the world outside. From this vantage point he saw his own life clearly as it fit in with all the others. His life, so precious, so special to him was repeated a million times over. His desperate hopes, his desire to be free, were as common as cooking pots. *Everyone has dreams* he thought. *Everyone seizes on any hope, no matter how flimsy.* And slowly the heavy weight of life squeezed those hopes dry. Crushed, people cried for the blood of whoever dared to make them hope. The bigger the dream, the fiercer the anger. That was why the guards had singled out Barabbas for their mockery; he had made people hope. *The man called Jesus must be getting it even worse,* David thought.

The door opened and the soldiers entered again, the ones who had dealt with Barabbas. "This is your lucky day, Barabbas. You've been pardoned."

The prisoner sat still, did not acknowledge their presence.

One cuffed him on the side of the head. "C'mon, wake up. Did you hear me? You're off the hook. Get up."

Still Barabbas did not move. "You cannot tempt me to hope," he said without feeling. "I am ready to die. Play your torture games with someone else."

The soldier laughed and poked him in the back with the hilt of his sword. Involuntarily Barabbas opened his mouth to scream, though no sound came. "Get up. You're free. They always release one prisoner on this day of Passover. You're it this year. The people asked for you. Pilate offered them you or Jesus — they chose you. You're a free man."

Meanwhile, other guards were removing the chains from David and Jacob. For a second David thought he, too, had been freed. His heart began beating wildly as the shackles dropped from his wrists. Then he was jerked to his feet and hustled out the door, a guard on each arm. Glancing back in terror, he caught a last glimpse of Barabbas in the dark cell, still crouched on the floor.

Then, blinded by the sudden sunlight, David cried out as a heavy wooden beam was thrust onto his raw shoulders. Hands seized his hands and forced them to grip the rough wood. A heavy palm slapped his face. "This is your cross, slave. Let's go."

When David's eyes grew accustomed to the light, he saw that they were surrounded by a pressing, jostling crowd whose attention was concentrated on another prisoner. Jeering, spitting, shaking their fists, they cursed a man gruesomely beaten. A wreath of wicked thorn branches was embedded into his skull, his head and hair caked with blood from the long, sharp spikes. Dark smudges of blood sponged through the garment stuck to his back.

The man turned his head toward David, and for a moment they stared into each other's eyes. David had never seen such a look — quiet, strong — a look of profound peace in the midst of their shared horror.

David realized he had seen the man before. *That's the man Jesus.* His body seemed shrunken, his shoulders weighted by pain, but his face was marked with quiet, absolute authority. Even now David could see why people had followed this man, why they thought he could save them. He had a presence. *Why is this man being executed?* David wondered. *He has done nothing wrong.*

A guard pushed Jesus into motion, and the condemned men began to stumble forward under their crosses, lurching toward their execution.

To the citizens of Jerusalem the crucifixion of thieves and murderers and insurrectionists was rather commonplace. Today, however, the presence of the man called Jesus added a different note, seemed to bring out more venom from the curious and the idle. Hostile faces jammed every space along the route through the narrow city streets, at the gates in the city wall, and along the dusty road leading to the place of execution, a hill called Golgotha. They all seemed concentrated on Jesus — jeering, spitting.

Jesus was ahead of David, weaving slowly under the weight of the wooden burden, stumbling often. Finally the soldiers, impatient to get on with it, grabbed a startled bystander and made him carry the crossbeam for the Nazarene.

I am really taking my last steps, David thought as the procession paused briefly. *These faces are the last I will ever see. This street is the last I will ever walk. My life is over.* Regret and disbelief piled up and spilled over into his entire being. No. *I cannot die. I don't want to die. I have done nothing wrong. Nothing worse than you who stare at me. You would have done the same in my place. Maybe worse. I don't want to die.*

A row of thick poles rose before them now as they left the city walls behind.

"Put your crosspiece down," a soldier ordered.

In terror David surveyed the crowd that had followed them from the city. It was a strange sampling of society: soldiers, curiosity seekers, officials of the Jewish temple, and an odd little cluster of frightened-looking men and women standing off to one side.

A soldier offered him a cup.

"What is it?" David asked.

"Wine and myrrh. It dulls the pain."

David gulped greedily until the vessel was pulled away and thrust at Jesus, who tasted it and then refused to drink. Jacob drained the remaining liquid.

The soldiers tugged at David's ragged clothing. When he clutched the cloth, without thinking, his hands were pushed away. "You have to strip, slave." In a second he was naked. Nearby, two soldiers were pulling on the ends of the garment they had just taken from Jesus, arguing over it. The commanding officer slapped one of them in the face. "Let go, you fool. You'll tear it. We'll divide things later."

The command came, "Lie down," and hands pushed David to the ground, his shoulders pressed against the rough beam he had carried. "Spread your arms." His right arm was stretched out to full reach and held down. He closed his eyes and felt a sharp prick on his palm. At the same instant he heard a terrible long-drawn scream, and before he had time to wonder whose voice it was, his had joined it as his hand became a fire, pinned to the plank. The soldiers were shouting at him not to move, cursing him; then they had his other hand and that, too, exploded in fire. He filled his lungs with air and screamed.

Now the hands were lifting him up, supporting his legs and lifting his buttocks to rest on a block of wood nailed halfway up the post. They were fastening the crosspiece to the pole with rope. Someone had his feet now, pushing them up so they were bent to the side. Another sharp tip touched his heel — and he was screaming again even before the pain began. With a terrible thud a nail shot through one heel bone and into the other. Hands pressed the fire hard against the post and another hammer blow fastened his feet into place. He emptied his stomach and passed out.

David had too much life in him to stay unconscious for long. The pain that had mercifully sent him into oblivion now cruelly brought him back to consciousness. The fire had spread from his hands and feet throughout his whole body. No description could do justice to such agony.

Yet he could see and hear — and think.

A small crowd was scattered around the crosses. Some, perhaps sickened or fearful, watched from a distance. Others stood close as though to see clearly the expressions on the dying faces. David could hear as they talked among themselves. A few days ago he was mingling with them. Now an invisible curtain closed him from them. *Why don't they help me?* he cried. *Why don't they at least meet my eyes? Why don't they care?*

The pain beyond words was equaled only by his terror of the death he faced and the dying that separated him from every human kindness. Even if he cried out, those people would not hear him. *Oh, God, let me off this cross. Get me out of here. Please.*

They were jeering at Jesus now. The high priest of the Temple, of all people, had started a mocking outcry — "Come down from your cross, king. You saved others; now save yourself."

David looked over at the Nazarene. Only a few feet separated them. Jesus' eyes were staring straight ahead. Again the thought struck: *This man had done nothing wrong. Why is he here?*

A muscle spasm moved David's hand, tore the wound, and the pain stopped all thoughts. He writhed and choked. When the haze cleared for a moment, he looked at Jesus again, drawn by the strength in that compelling face. *What has this man ever done?* But immediately his pain tore him away. *Oh, God, get me out of this,* he cried.

The religious leaders stood in a small huddle a few yards from the crosses, talking together, occasionally making loud comments. Now one of them walked to within a few feet of Jesus' cross and stood staring up at him.

"Come down, Jesus," he said. "Why stay up there and suffer? You are the son of God, aren't you? Well, then, why not come down?" Some of the soldiers laughed at the jest. The priest had probably never spoken to a Roman before, especially not a soldier. Now he did. "Isn't that typical. He saved others, but he can't save himself. He's the king of Israel. So he says! Let him come down from the cross and we will believe in him. He trusts in God. Let God rescue him now if he wants him. He says he is the son of God. Would God forget his son? Ha!"

David caught at the words, "He says he is the son of God." *Did Jesus really say that*? He remembered hearing it from someone. The son of God? Dying? Here? Even Barabbas, with all his big ideas, never claimed to be the son of God.

He moved his head to look at Jesus again. The movement caused excruciating pain: blood slammed through his head and the pressure he applied to his feet to hold his balance caused the nail to tear higher into his flesh.

This time Jesus' eyes looked into his. What made his face so inviting? David had never before seen innocence combined with wisdom. Usually a man was wise from bad experience and therefore hardly innocent — or innocent but foolish and therefore not wise. David turned his eyes away; he could not look at this good man.

That face called up things David did not want to remember. He was a child again with his master's children, playing with them, almost as equals. Until the day his best friend Servius, the master's eldest son, had been separated from him. A teacher had come to instruct Servius, but slaves did not get educated. David had hardened with anger, bitterness, and hatred at losing his friend and being treated as a slave. When Servius had tried, afterward, to make up to him, David had refused to speak to him as a friend. From that moment on he had kept the cautious, distant, polite speech and angry spirit of a slave. On that day his desire to be free had been born.

He had always been proud of that day — looked upon it as the beginning of his manhood. Now, suddenly, looking into the calm, loving face beside him, that bitterness seemed ugly. On that day years ago Servius had become a master and he had hated him for that. Servius had learned to read and he, David, had learned to hate — even his best friend.

There is so much in my life to be ashamed of, he thought, then immediately rejected that thought. No! No! *I have done no wrong, unless it is wrong to want to be free. I do not deserve to die.*

Though it cost him great pain, he moved his head to look at Jesus again. *He said he is the son of God. Why doesn't he say something to those mockers now? Curse them? Why not leave their consciences — if they have any — with his curses. Curse those who curse you.* But the face he looked into was not printed with anger or hatred. The lips moved. David could hear him — he was asking God to forgive them!

David suddenly felt guilty, unclean, naked. *I am ashamed of my life, of the hatred in me,* he thought. Not because he hung there beaten, stripped, and condemned for all to see, but because he felt exposed before some power much greater than any of these who had the power to kill him. Something more painful than the fire consuming his body began to burn within his soul.

The soldiers had taken up the jeering theme of the priests. Bored, waiting out their duty, they were amused by the thought of a Jewish king. One of them bowed repeatedly before the center cross. "If you are the king, save yourself."

"And save us!" The angry, desperate sound came not from the lazy, teasing soldiers. It was Jacob's voice. "Aren't you the Christ? Save yourself and us."

The soldiers had flogged Jacob without mercy; they had given him what he wanted. Now he hung limp, nearer death than the other two. But anger dies last. If Jesus would not go out cursing, Jacob would. Now he turned his anger on one as helpless as he.

Jacob's snarling touched a nerve in David. This man with the quiet face was innocent. How could Jacob — how could he, himself — begin to compare himself with Jesus? They were guilty. This man ... David burst forth at Jacob, his lungs heaving, his voice choked, "Aren't you afraid of God? Since you are under the same sentence? You and I deserve our punishment. We earned our death. But this man has done nothing wrong." The words hung in the air. The effort of speaking was agony, but Jacob's mocking cry had turned the last resisting bolt in David's soul. *This man must be the king he says he is.* And though he could barely gather strength or breath, David whispered what his heart was crying, "Jesus, remember me ... remember me when you come into your kingdom."

And as though he had been waiting for that very plea, Jesus replied, "I tell you the truth, today you will be with me in paradise."

I *am dying*, David thought as the air grew black, but as he tried to focus he realized the darkness was not in his eyes. The sky was growing darker and darker, as though the air was filled with a thick, heavy dust. The sun disappeared. The crowd had become silent — even the soldiers.

It took concentration to suffer this death, to even draw a breath. Spasms of pain tore at David's wounds. But even as the very atmosphere reflected his nightmare of pain, he thought about the last words he had spoken to Jesus and of the promise received in return. He had felt compelled to cry out, believing that somehow Jesus could save him.

Yet how could Jesus save him? Clearly Jesus was dying, too. He was not escaping the cross. Yet he had promised, "Today you will be with me in paradise." *His kingdom must be of another world*, the type of world David had ceased to hope for long ago. And if that were true, how could he serve this king? He had nothing left but dying.

The darkness grew deeper, the human figures shadowy. Jesus twitched in the spasm leading to death. He made no cry, but spoke a few words to a woman standing beneath him, weeping, and the man she clung to, apparently one of his followers. Then he cried out words David could not understand. The soldiers ran to place a sponge to his lips. Then another loud cry: "Father, into your hands I commit my spirit!" And he slumped limp against his impaling bonds. The darkness became thicker ... the ground shook ... the crowd fled ....

David was alone. Utterly alone. Jesus was dead. All he had to hold onto in this endless dying was a promise that he was going to the same place Jesus had gone. But now he knew how to die. He had heard Jesus' last words.

Sounds filtered to him — soldiers talking. The priests wanted the bodies down by sunset. They were asking the soldiers to break the legs so the men would die immediately. Hearing the brutal discussion going on before him, David thought again how cruelly men treat each other. But then came a new thought: *If I was in their position, I'd be doing the same thing*. There was only one person he could not picture acting out that brutality — and he was the son of God.

Barely able to see now, David watched the hazy form of a soldier take a large iron ax and walk to Jacob's cross. With a powerful blow he hit the man's shin with the flat side. Jacob did not scream, just wriggled like a dying creature. The ax fell on the other leg.

The soldier surveyed his work, seemed satisfied, turned and walked toward David.

David looked full into the soldier's face just below him. As the ax lifted, he closed his eyes and whispered, "Jesus, into your hands I commit my spirit."

12

We Were There

Golgotha — what a grim set on which to play out the crucial act in the drama of redemption. Golgotha — from the Aramaic meaning "skull" and the Hebrew implying "a skull-like mound" — was well-named in light of the bloody business conducted there. The rocky hilltop was chosen as an execution site because of its location near the heavily traveled highway outside the walls of Jerusalem. This assured that people passing by would witness the terrible spectacle of crucifixion, for the authorities believed (even as many so vainly believe today) that public violence would discourage individual violence.

There was a large supporting cast playing out that pivotal day of history, all manner of humanity: the spectators, the scoffers, the soldiers, the mourners. But the central drama of Golgotha was played out upon the crosses themselves.

"Are you not the Christ? Save yourself and us," cried the one I have called Jacob, angry to the end. He might even have believed that the limp figure beside him was the son of God. But so what? If He couldn't save Himself, He certainly couldn't save anyone else.

The other thief, the one I call David, convicted by the Holy Spirit, realized that he deserved to die. Like Boris Kornfeld, David understood that no matter what he had done or not done, no matter what the circumstances, "no punishment comes to us in this life on earth which is undeserved."

And therein lies the crucial distinction between the two thieves. It had nothing to do with their crimes, their moral values, the relative goodness or badness of their lives. In fact Scripture suggests the irrelevance of these criteria by the stark lack of detail describing their lives. The distinction was that David recognized his own sin. His reply to Jacob, "We are punished justly, for we are getting what our deeds deserve. But this man has done nothing wrong,"[1] is one of the purest expressions of repentance in all Scripture. And his words "Remember me," are the classic statement of faith. With such simplicity and power this man repented and believed and died trusting in Christ.

How absurd David's words, "we are getting what we deserve," must have sounded to Jacob. Deserve? Deserve death? For doing what everyone else did in one way or another? He was no worse or better than anybody else, including the ghouls watching him die.

As I consider this scene, I am reminded of the haunting old spiritual, "Were you there when they crucified my Lord?" I have always understood this refrain in the classic theological sense that we were all there—we were all guilty of putting Jesus to death because of our fallen nature and our need of the atonement His death made. But as I began looking more closely at the crucifixion scene itself and the responses of the two thieves, I did feel cause to "tremble, tremble, tremble." For those two men who actually died alongside my Savior are representative of all mankind. We either recognize our sinful selves, our sentence of death, and our deserving of that sentence, which leads us to repent and believe—or we curse God and die.

But Jacob provides another illustration of the sin that is within us. For if there is anything worse than our sin, it is our infinite capacity to rationalize it away. The Bible tells us this is a fearsome thing. During the period of the divided kingdom, Ahab, described as the most corrupt in a long line of corrupt leaders, became king of Israel. And he "considered it trivial to commit the sins" of his predecessors.[2] This man who angered God more than all the evil kings considered his sins *trivial*.

Ahab was not unique. So powerful is the human tendency to trivialize sin that only the Holy Spirit can open our eyes. As John and other writers of Scripture point out, the Spirit must convict us of our sinful nature.[3] I remember this vividly from my own conversion.

I wasn't sure what caused me to visit my old friend Tom Phillips that August night in 1973. I had been impressed by what he told me about his conversion to Christ and by his demeanor; I wished I had what he did. So I suppose I was seeking spiritual answers, but not for any escape from my sin. For despite the daily bombardment of Watergate charges, I saw nothing particularly wrong with myself. I knew what I had done was at least no different than what everyone else had done. Right and wrong were not determined by absolute standards, but were relative to people and situations. People in politics played dirty; it was all part of the game.

But that night when I left my friend and sat alone in my car, my own sin — not just Watergate, but the evil deep within — was thrust before me by the conviction of the Holy Spirit, forcefully and painfully. For the first time in my life I felt unclean. Yet I could not turn away. I was as helpless as the thief nailed to that cross, and what I saw within me was so ugly I could do nothing but cry out to God for help.

Without the conviction of the Holy Spirit and the repentance that must follow, there is no way out of our predicament. We have the capacity to change anything about our lives — jobs, homes, cars, even spouses — but we cannot change our own sinful nature.

An episode involving one of Prison Fellowship's seminar instructors, Randy Nabors, illustrates just how true this is.

Randy was conducting an in-prison seminar in a sprawling southern penitentiary. Located in a remote rural area, the prison provided a handsome Victorian guesthouse for those staying overnight on official business. Late one evening when Randy was in his room engrossed in his notes for the next day's lecture, a state-employed psychiatrist, at the prison for one of his routine visits, knocked at his door.

Soon the frustrated doctor was describing his day's cases. "I'll tell you, Reverend, I can cure somebody's madness, but I can't do anything about his badness," he moaned after describing an especially difficult encounter. "Psychiatry, properly administered, can turn a schizophrenic bank robber into a mentally healthy bank robber; a good teacher can turn an illiterate criminal into an educated criminal. But they are still bank robbers and criminals!"

The doctor seemed near the point of despair. The sultry July evening conspired to add to his discomfort. Pulling a chair next to Randy and wiping his brow with an already soggy handkerchief, the psychiatrist recounted a session that day with a man who, while high on angel dust, had murdered his own child.

"He tells me he's depressed," the doctor was almost shouting. "Of course he's depressed! Who wouldn't be? But if I had done that, I hope I'd have more courage and do the only honorable thing — kill myself, too." He quickly put his hand up, palm outstretched, and added, "Wait a minute. Of course I didn't tell my patient that." Then he settled back into his chair with a long sigh.

As Randy Nabors witnessed to the doctor that night, the man admitted that there must be an answer to the dilemma of evil within, because he had seen lives changed among the Christian inmates. But, he added sadly, he had not experienced it himself.

Weary and frustrated prison psychiatrists are not the only ones who cry out in despair over the human condition. Years after his personal encounter with Christ, the apostle Paul posed the eternal question: "What a wretched man I am! Who will rescue me from this body of death?"[4] He saw that moral precepts could not free him; in fact, paradoxically, they made matters worse while convicting him. "I would not have known what it was to covet if the law had not said, 'Do not covet.' But sin, seizing the opportunity afforded by the commandment, produced in me every kind of covetous desire."[5]

What a desperate plight. Trapped in and by our own sin. Thankfully, there is an an answer to the wrenching dilemma. Paul described it in the next chapter of his letter to the Romans: "There is now no condemnation for those who are in Christ Jesus. . . . For what the law was powerless to do in that it was weakened by the sinful nature, God did by sending his own Son . . . to be a sin offering."[6] That took place that momentous day on Golgotha nearly 2,000 years ago.

And how is all this part of loving God? Well, when we see the reality of our sin, when we come face to face with it and look into the raging fires of hell itself, and when we then repent and believe and are delivered from that plight, our entire being is filled with unspeakable gratitude to the God who sent His Son to that cross for us.

We must express that gratitude. But how? Simply stated: by living the way He commands. By obedience. That is what the Scriptures mean by holiness or sanctification — believers are set apart for holy living. Therefore, holiness is the only possible response to God's grace. Holy living is loving God.

However, as I began to learn not long after my conversion, and as everyone who has tried to live a holy life knows, holiness is the toughest, most demanding, vocation in the world.

THE HUNGER FOR HOLINESS

Our progress in holiness depends on God and ourselves — on God's grace and on our will to be holy.

Mother Teresa

13

Be Holy Because I Am Holy

The Anacostia section of Washington, D.C. sits on a bluff overlooking the capital city. Just across the river from the imposing Capitol itself, Anacostia — a ghetto of hunger, crime, drugs, and hopelessness — might as well be a continent away. None of Washington's celebrities and power brokers, nor the reporters who track them, cross that natural divide.

However, one balmy June morning in 1981 proved the exception. Black limousines and television camera trucks lined the curb in front of the old red brick Assumption Catholic Church in the heart of Anacostia.

Soon after the cameras and reporters were in place, a small group of nuns and priests arrived, clustered about a wisp of a woman in a white muslin sari. The tiny figure moved with unusual grace up the steps of the church, waving at a cluster of children nearby and brushing past the reporters crowding the doorway.

This celebrity who somehow managed to understate her own arrival, an attitude unheard of in a city that thrives on pomp and protocol, was a seventy-year-old Albanian nun named Teresa Bojaxhiu — better known as Mother Teresa. As 1979 Nobel Prize winner and a world-famous figure, she could have commanded an airport welcome by a host of government bigwigs, addressed a joint session of Congress, or attracted thousands at one of the city's great cathedrals. Instead, she went as inconspicuously as possible to a troubled and neglected corner of the city to establish an outpost for nine of her Sisters of Charity.

Since Mother Teresa wouldn't come to them, the power brokers had come to her. The mayor and city officials trailed the press into the stark church hall with its chipped and cracked plaster walls. The press, which cultivates its irreverence for politicians, were more restrained with this little woman from the streets of Calcutta. Still, she had to dodge the boom mikes coming at her like spears.

"What do you hope to accomplish here?" someone shouted.

"The joy of loving and being loved," she smiled, her eyes sparkling in the face of camera lights.

"That takes a lot of money doesn't it?" another reporter threw out the obvious question. Everything in Washington costs money; and the more it costs, the more important it is.

Mother Teresa shook her head. "No, it takes a lot of sacrifice."[1]

The press was bewildered. Everyone who comes to Washington has grand plans, usually involving the creation of agencies with armies of bureaucrats. That's what the city is for: setting agendas, passing laws, organizing departments — and trumpeting it all to the press. But this woman with her leathery, wrinkled face talked about "sharing suffering" and "caring that people can live and die with dignity."

No grandiose scheme, her message: Do something for someone else ... for the sick, unwanted, crippled, heartbroken, aged, or alone. Strange words indeed for Washington's sophisticated commentators who left the conference shaking their heads.

Like them, the world cannot understand the source of Mother Teresa's power. Though her words sound naive, something extraordinary happens wherever she goes. For *what* Mother Teresa does, whether in Washington or Calcutta, is what the Bible calls "religion ... pure and faultless."[2] But *why* she does it is our point here.

A few years ago a brother in the order came to her complaining about a superior whose rules, he felt, were interfering with his ministry. "My vocation is to work for lepers," he told Mother Teresa. "I want to spend myself for the lepers."

She stared at him a moment, then smiled. "Brother," she said gently, "your vocation is not to work for lepers, your vocation is to belong to Jesus."[3]

Mother Teresa is not in love with a cause, noble as her cause is. Rather, she loves God and is dedicated to living His life, not her own. This is holiness. It is the complete surrender of self in obedience to the will and service of God. Or as Mother Teresa sums it up, complete "acceptance of the will of God."[4]

Mother Teresa's definition may sound rather nebulous to many Christians who have from childhood associated holiness with a long string of dos and don'ts. But seeing holiness only as rule-keeping breeds serious problems: first, it limits the scope of true biblical holiness, which must affect every aspect of our lives. Second, even though the rules may be biblically based, we often end up obeying the rules rather than obeying God; concern with the letter of the law can cause us to lose its spirit.[5] Third, emphasis on rule-keeping deludes us into thinking *we* can be holy through our efforts. But there can be no holiness apart from the work of the Holy Spirit — in quickening us through the conviction of sin and bringing us by grace to Christ, and in sanctifying us — for it is grace that causes us to even *want* to be holy. And finally, our pious efforts can become ego-gratifying, as if holy living were some kind of spiritual beauty contest. Such self-centered spirituality in turn leads to self-righteousness — the very opposite of the selflessness of true holiness.

No, holiness is much more than a set of rules against sin. Holiness must be seen as the opposite of sin. Sin, as the Westminster Confession defines it, is "any want of conformity to, or transgression of, the law of God." Holiness, then, is the opposite: "conformity to the character of God and obedience to the will of God"[6] (precisely Mother Teresa's point to the recalcitrant brother). Conforming to the character of God — separating ourselves from sin and cleaving to Him — is the *essence* of biblical holiness, and it is the foundational covenant, a central theme running throughout Scripture.

The earliest call to holiness came soon after Moses had led Israel out of Egypt and through the parted waters of the Red Sea. Safe at last from the Egyptian army, this unruly horde of humanity — 600,000 men accompanied by women and children — camped at the foot of Mount Sinai. There, God called Moses to the mountaintop and instructed him in the laws by which His chosen people were now to live. These laws ranged from the all-encompassing Ten Commandments (the first four of which demand unconditional, reverent worship of a holy God) to such detailed ordinances as the means of restitution for stolen animals.[7]

When the Israelites accepted God's covenant with the words, "Everything the Lord has said we will do ... we will obey,"[8] God again called Moses to the mountaintop where He made one of the most remarkable promises in the Bible: "I will consecrate the Tent of Meeting and the altar and ... I will dwell among the Israelites."[9] What a staggering thought!

The sovereign God of the universe promised to pitch His tent, *actually* to dwell in the midst of His chosen people.

Many are tempted to skip over these chapters of Exodus and Leviticus that describe in such detail the construction of the tabernacle, the forms of worship and the like. Altars and acacia wood and cubits sound irrelevant today, superseded by the atonement of Christ. But this is a perfect example of the necessity of taking the Word of God in its entirety. For the prescriptions for the place wherein God was to dwell and be worshiped reveal the very character of God Himself.

The tabernacle reflects a holy God, a God set apart, unique, utterly unstained by the sin of the world. No wonder God specified rules of cleanliness for those who worshiped there. It was not because He had some obsession with personal hygiene, but because in every way possible His people were to be clean, set apart — holy — as they entered to worship in the place where He, a holy God, *actually* dwelt.

This is indeed the very heart of the relationship God demands with His people, expressed in the covenant: "I am the Lord your God; consecrate yourselves and *be holy because* I *am holy.*"[10] Understanding this basic covenant, the character of God, and what He expects is essential to understanding the New Covenant. For the character of God has not changed, nor has His expectation of holiness from His people.

In fact, the same remarkable promise that God made to Moses — that He would *pitch His tent* and dwell in the midst of His people — is a central theme throughout Scripture. In the familiar passage of John's gospel, "The Word became flesh, and *dwelt* among us,"[11] the Greek word for *dwelt* literally means to "pitch a tent." So now, through Christ, God comes to "pitch His tent" among His people. And to carry the theme to its conclusion, John, in describing his apocalyptic vision of the new heaven and new earth, writes, "The tabernacle of God is among men, and He shall dwell among them, and they shall be His people."[12] Again the word *dwell* is literally translated to "pitch a tent."

Thus, from Exodus to Revelation we find the identical imagery, a holy God "pitching His tent" among His people: first in the tabernacle, then in Christ and Christ in us, and ultimately in His kingdom.

Salvation, therefore, is not simply a matter of being separated from our past and freed from our bondage to sin; salvation means also that we are joined to a holy God. By pitching His tent in our midst, God identifies with His people through His very presence. The reality of a "God who is here" — personal and in our midst — is an extraordinary assurance, one which distinguishes the Judeo-Christian faith from all other religions.

But God demands something in return for His presence. He demands that we identify with Him — that we be holy because He is holy.

Holiness is not an option. God will not tolerate our indifference to His central command.* It is the central covenant and command of Scripture, the "cardinal point on which the whole of Christianity turns," William Wilberforce wrote.[13] It is not just for well-known saints like Mother Teresa, but for every believer.

What does this mean for us, then, in the real world in which we live every day?

---

*Moses and Aaron were not permitted to lead the Israelites into the Promised Land because they failed to treat God as holy (Numbers 20:12). Then a long succession of kings failed to respect God's holiness and the Israelites ended up in captivity again.

14

The Everyday Business of Holiness

When we think of holiness, great saints of the past like Francis of Assisi or George Müller spring to mind — or contemporary giants of the faith like Mother Teresa. But holiness is not the private preserve of an elite corps of martyrs, mystics, and Nobel prize winners. Holiness is the everyday business of every Christian. It evidences itself in the decisions we make and the things we do, hour by hour, day by day.

The following few examples, drawn from the lives of Christians I've encountered in recent years, might help make the point.

It was a quiet December evening on Ward C43, the oncology unit at Georgetown University Hospital. Many of the rooms around the central nurses' station were dark and empty, but in Room 11 a man lay critically ill.

The patient was Jack Swigert, the man who had piloted the Apollo 13 lunar mission in 1970 and was now Congressman-elect from Colorado's 6th Congressional District. Cancer, the great leveler, now waged its deadly assault on his body.

With the dying man was a tall, quiet visitor, sitting in the spot he had occupied almost every night since Swigert had been admitted. Though Bill Armstrong, U.S. Senator from Colorado and chairman of the Senate subcommittee handling Washington's hottest issue, social security, was one of the busiest and most powerful men in Washington, he was not visiting this room night after night as a powerful politician. He was here as a deeply committed Christian and as Jack Swigert's friend, fulfilling a responsibility he would not delegate or shirk, much as he disliked hospitals.

This night Bill leaned over the bed and spoke quietly to his friend. "Jack, you're going to be all right. God loves you. I love you. You're surrounded by friends who are praying for you. You're going to be all right." The only response was Jack's tortured and uneven breathing.

Bill pulled his chair closer to the bed and opened his Bible. "Psalm 23," he began to read in a steady voice. "The Lord is my shepherd, I shall not want. . . ."

Time passed. "Psalm 150," Bill began, then his skin prickled. Jack's ragged breathing had stopped. He leaned down over the bed, then called for help. As he watched the nurse examining Jack, Bill knew there was nothing more he could do. His friend was dead.

Politicians are busy people, especially Senate committee chairmen. Yet it never occurred to Bill Armstrong that he was too busy to be at the hospital. Nothing dramatic or heroic about his decision — just a friend doing what he could.

Holiness is obeying God — loving one another as He loved us.

When Orv Krieger, a hotel broker with a friendly midwesterner's grin, received a call about a choice piece of property for sale in Spokane, Washington, he was thrilled. He knew the 140-unit Holiday Inn — minutes from the airport and perched on thirteen acres of firry hillside overlooking the city — was a buy, despite its multi-million-dollar price tag. So instead of listing it for sale to someone else, Orv took the plunge and bought it himself.

Only one problem. The Inn's restaurant was the big money maker, and no wonder — the bar grossed an average of $10,000 a month. But Orv wasn't going to keep the bar. Not that he wanted to impose his own views on others, but as a Christian he chose not to run a business subsidized by alcohol sales.

The motel manager argued that if guests couldn't get a drink at the

Inn they'd be out the door to a competitor in a flash. He also gave Orv some convincing statistics that showed the motel couldn't make it without the bar. Orv listened politely — and closed the bar. He must stick to his convictions. The manager promptly quit.

Orv continued with his plans. He remodeled the hotel lobby and replaced the bar area with a cozy coffee shop brimming with greenery. In his first five years of business, food sales went up 20 percent, room bookings up 30 percent. Still, profits aren't what they could be. If the bar were open, the hotel would be a real money machine.

But, as Orv says, his grin as big as ever, "Beliefs aren't worth much if a fella's not ready to live by them."

Holiness is obeying God — even when it's against our own interests.

When she arrives at the prison gate each weekday at noon, the guards wave her through. Prison officials stop to ask how her kids are doing or about her work at the office. After all, Joyce Page is family; she's been spending her lunch hour at the St. Louis County Correctional Institution just about every weekday since 1979.

Joyce began going to the prison with her supervisor, also a Christian concerned for prisoners. When the supervisor was transferred, Joyce continued by herself, leaving her office alone with a peanut butter sandwich while other secretaries bustled off in clusters for the cafeteria.

Each day Joyce meets with a different group of inmates, from the men in isolation and maximum security to a small group of women prisoners. "What we do is up to them," she says. "Sometimes we have a worship service, or a time of testimony and singing, or in-depth Bible study and discussion. It depends on their needs."

When she slips back to her desk at one o'clock, one of her co-workers is usually already bemoaning her lunchtime excesses and loudly proclaiming that she really will have the diet plate tomorrow. Joyce laughs to herself. She knows exactly what she'll have for lunch tomorrow — another peanut butter sandwich at the wheel of her car on the way to prison.

For many, meeting with inmates every day in the middle of a hectic work schedule would be an unthinkable chore. Joyce, in her matter-of-fact way, sees it differently. "For me it's a real answer to prayer," she says. "You see, I don't have time to go *after* work — I have six kids of my own that I'm raising by myself."

Holiness is obeying God — sharing His love, even when it is inconvenient.

No one in his right mind would pick the village of Duvalierville on the island of Haiti as the location for a factory, especially if he lived in North Carolina. But retired businessmen Kenneth Hooker and Donald Adcox did just that.

It all began in the mid-1970s when Donald Adcox was contacted by a Haitian pastor for help; the pastor had found Adcox's name in a magazine article about Christian laymen. As a result, Donald and several other Christian businessmen visited Haiti and were appalled at what they found. Entire villages subsisted in huts with barely enough to eat; disease was rampant and medical care scarce.

Don enlisted the help of his long-time associate, Ken Hooker, and some other businessmen. Government aid, they discovered, was a slow and cumbersome process and might never reach those it was intended to help. And they realized that the people in Haiti wanted opportunity more than welfare. So they linked up with the pastor of the Duvalierville church and got to work.

Along with two other Christian businessmen, Robert Vickery and Don Crace, Ken and Don bought a small rug factory in Pennsylvania and shipped the machinery and supplies to Haiti to set up the plant. This completed, they brought two young leaders, chosen by the Haitian church, to North Carolina for training.

Today the Duvalierville plant is the center of a thriving community of a thousand people. The church consists of six hundred people, and the church school enrolls seven hundred children. Don, Ken, and others have helped the Haitians build a clinic and guesthouse on the factory grounds and are setting up a program for Christian doctors and dentists from the States to donate their services.

The busy factory is a tangible encouragement, and the villagers' pride in their plant comes from a sense of ownership, for the plant *does* belong to them. Don and Ken and the other businessmen who participated quietly gave the business to the church a few years ago.

The establishment of the Haitian plant has also brought new hope to another unlikely place — North Carolina prisons. When Don and Ken set up a prototype factory to learn the rug business, they needed a few people to run it. Ken had been volunteering with Prison Fellowship for several years, so he and Don began hiring prisoners on work release to run the rug-braiding machines. In fact, several inmates had their sentences shortened because they had the promise of a steady job. The factory isn't large, employing only three or four at a time, but a nearby plant has followed their example by providing work for prisoners on work release and for ex-offenders.

Meanwhile, Ken Hooker and Don Adcox are busy cooking up other ideas to expand the Haitian ministry and are working with Christian laypeople in other projects. They still claim they're retired, but the past few years have been their busiest.

"We try to put people and available resources together," Ken says. "We just do what we can," adds Donald.

Holiness is obeying God — finding ways to help those in need.

Heroism is an extraordinary feat of the flesh; holiness is an ordinary act of the the spirit. One may bring personal glory; the other *always* gives God the glory.

These illustrations can be helpful as practical examples, but the sure standard for holiness is Scripture. There God makes clear what He means by holy living or, as theologians call it, the process of sanctification.

The Ten Commandments, from which all other commandments flow, are the beginning; they apply today as much as they did when God engraved them on tablets of stone for Moses. Next, the life of Jesus provides holiness in the flesh; in His persevering self-denial, His unqualified obedience of the Father's will, and the fullness of the Holy Spirit in His daily life, Jesus remains our example.

Then Paul gives explicit guidelines. Consider just this sampling of injunctions:

Lay aside falsehood and speak the truth.
Do not let the sun go down on your anger.
Let him who steals, steal no longer but work.
Let no unwholesome word come from your mouth.
Be rid of bitterness and wrath and malice.
Be kind to each other, forgiving.
Walk in love.
Be careful so you will not even be accused of immorality, greed, or any impurity.
Engage not in silly or coarse or filthy talk.
Do not practice idolatry in any form nor associate with those who do.
Abstain from sexual immorality and conquer lustful passions.
Do not lead weaker brethren to sin.[1]

In Galatians 5, Paul gives a summary of the fruit of the Spirit along with the contrary sins of the flesh. What a check list!

Love	Immorality
Joy	Impurity
Peace	Sensuality
Patience	Idolatry
Kindness	Sorcery
Goodness	Strife
Faithfulness	Outbursts of anger
Gentleness	Drunkenness
Self-control	Jealousy

The apostle's picture of life by the Spirit versus desires of the sinful nature is graphic. Having set forth the contrast, he exhorts the faithful not to "become weary in doing good. A man reaps what he sows."[2]

The quest for holiness, then, should begin with a search of the Scriptures. (The few verses above are but samples of the rich treasure that awaits.) We next begin applying what we find, seeking His will for our lives. As the nineteenth-century Scottish theologian John Brown put it: "*Holiness* does not consist in mystic speculations, enthusiastic fervors, or uncommanded austerities; it *consists in thinking as God thinks and willing as God wills.*"[3]

That thinking and willing is a process requiring discipline and perseverance and is a joint effort: God's and ours. On the one hand, the Holy Spirit convicts of sin and sanctifies.[4] But that doesn't mean that we can sit back, relax, and leave the driving to God. God expects — demands — that we do our part. As Mother Teresa says, "Our progress in holiness depends on God and ourselves — on God's grace and on our will to be holy."[5]

Understanding this joint responsibility makes clear what is otherwise one of the most troublesome areas for many Christians, found in Paul's letter to the church at Rome where on one hand he says we are dead to sin and in the next verse exhorts us not to let sin reign in our mortal bodies.[6]

Why should we turn away from sin that is already dead? The answer to this seeming contradiction underscores the joint responsibility for sanctification. We are dead to sin because Christ died to sin for us. He settled the ultimate victory. But as we live day by day, sin still remains a constant reality. Though God gives us the will to be holy, the daily fight requires continuing effort on our part.

In his marvelous book, *Pursuit of Holiness*, Jerry Bridges likens this to nations at war: one defeats the other, as at Calvary Christ defeated Satan. But the losing army, though vanquished, then takes to the hills and fights on as a guerrilla movement. Fighting off sin, he says, is like beating back continuing guerrilla attacks.[7]

Holy living demands constant examination of our actions and motives. But in doing so we must guard against the tendency to focus totally on self, which is easy to do — especially as the culture's egocentric values invade the church. In fact, this self-indulgent character of our times is a major reason the topic of true holiness is so neglected today by Christian teachers, leaders, writers, and speakers. We have, perhaps unconsciously, substituted a secularized self-centered message in its place. For when we speak of "victory" in the Christian life, we all-too-often mean personal victory — how God will conquer sin *for us* (at least those sins we'd like to be rid of — those extra ten pounds, that annoying habit, maybe a quick temper). This reflects not only egocentricity but an incorrect view of sin.

Sin is not simply the wrong we do our neighbor when we cheat him, or the wrong we do ourselves when we abuse our bodies. Sin, all sin, is a root rebellion and offense against God, what R.C. Sproul calls "cosmic treason."

We must understand that our goal as believers is to seek what we can do to please God, not what He can do for us. Personal victories may come, but they are a result, not the object. True Christian maturity — holiness, sanctification — is God-centered. So-called "victorious Christian living" is self-centered. Jerry Bridges puts it well:

> It is time for us Christians to face up to our responsibility for holiness. Too often we say we are "defeated" by this or that sin. No, we are not defeated; we are simply disobedient. It might be well if we stopped using the terms "victory" and "defeat" to describe our progress in holiness. Rather we should use the terms "obedience" and "disobedience."[8]

So we have come full circle — back to where we started. The Christian life begins with obedience, depends on obedience, and results in obedience. We can't escape it. The orders from our commander-in-chief are plain: "Whoever has my commandments and obeys them, he is the one who loves me."[9]

Loving God — really loving Him — means living out His commands no matter what the cost.

A young woman in a surburban Washington church recently demonstrated this truth.

No one was surprised when Patti Awan stood during the informal praise time at the Sunday evening service. A young Sunday school teacher with an air of quiet maturity, she had given birth to a healthy son a few months earlier, a first child for her and her husband Javy. The congregation settled back for a report of the baby's progress and his parents' thanksgiving. They were totally unprepared for what followed.

Hanging onto the podium before her, Patti began. "Four years ago this week, a young girl sat crying on the floor of a New Jersey apartment, devastated by the news of a lab report. Unmarried and alone, she had just learned she was pregnant."

The congregation grew completely quiet; Patti's tear-choked voice indicated just who that young woman was.

"I considered myself a Christian at the time," she continued. "But I had found out about Christ while in the drug scene. After I learned about Him, I knew I wanted to commit myself to Him, but I couldn't give up my old friends or my old habits. So I was drifitng between two worlds — in one still smoking dope every day and sleeping with the man who lived in the apartment below mine; in the other, going to church, witnessing to others, and working with the church youth group.

"But being pregnant ripped through the hypocrisy of my double life. I had been meaning to 'get right with God,' but I kept slipping back. Now I couldn't live a nice, clean Christian life like all those church people.

"I felt the only answer was to wipe the slate clean. I would get an abortion; no one in the church would ever know.

"The clinic scheduled an abortion date. I was terrified, but my boyfriend was adamant. My sister was furious with me for being so stupid as to get pregnant. Finally, in desperation I wrote my parents. They were staunch Catholics, and I knew they would support me if I decided to have the baby. My mother called me: 'If you don't get an abortion, I don't want to see you while you're pregnant. Your life will be ruined and you'll deserve it.'

"I had always been desperately dependent on other people. But I knew this was one decision I had to make alone. I was looking out my bedroom window one night when I thought clearly for the first time in weeks. I realized I either believed this Christianity or I didn't believe it. And if I believed in Christ, then I couldn't do this. *God is real*, I thought, *even if I've never lived like He is.*

"That decision was a point of no return. I put my faith in the God of the Bible, not the God I had made up in my head. I was still everything I never wanted to be — pregnant, alone, deserted by family, and rejected by the one I had loved. Yet for the first time in my life I was really peaceful, because I knew for the first time I was being obedient.

"When I went to an obstetrician and told him of my decision to have the baby and why I had made that choice, he refused to charge me for the pre-natal care and delivery. I confessed my double life to the church, and through the support of Christians was able to move away from my old friends to an apartment of my own. I began going to a Christian counseling agency and felt God leading me to give the baby up for adoption.

"I had a beautiful baby girl and named her Sarah. She was placed with a childless Christian couple, and we all felt God's hand in the decision.

"And so that's why I praise God this evening. I thought in the depths of my despair that my life was ruined, but I knew I had to at least be obedient in taking responsibility for my sin. But today, because of that very despair and obedience, I have what I never thought I could — a godly husband and now a baby of our own. But what matters more than anything is that I have what I was searching for so desperately before — peace with God."

Holiness is obeying God.

15

And His Righteousness

William Wilberforce, eighteenth century slave trade abolitionist, wrote in his diary: "God Almighty has set before me two great objects, the suppression of the slave trade and the reformation of manners." The latter did not refer to table etiquette, of course, but to the moral standards of professing Christians.

Wilberforce believed holy living, what he called the "reformation of manners," would inevitably foster righteousness in the land and end the injustice of slavery; conversely, the end of slavery would uplift the moral character of the nation.

That is precisely what happened. Slavery was abolished as a great spiritual awakening swept England clean of its indulgent apostasy.[1]

If only that lesson of interdependence could be learned today! Churches, particularly evangelical ones, are packed with people attempting to practice personal piety, to establish moral lifestyles, and "to witness." Yet they seem oblivious to the need to work for those same standards in their society and world. At times the church seems schizophrenic: pious and righteously aroused in the safety of pews and prayer groups, but indifferent in the world outside.

From the beginning God made plain the standard He demands of His people. Following His commission to Moses that Israel was to be a "kingdom of priests and a holy nation,"[2] God carefully prescribed the just way the affairs of this nation were to be managed. Exodus 21 through 23 set forth standards for justice for individuals, personal injury claims, rights of private property, restitution, and care for the poor, orphaned, widowed, and foreign.

For God holds man responsible not only for his individual sins but for the corporate sins of society. Wrongs such as aggression, inflation, injustice, racism, and economic oppression are manifestations of man's sin just as much as our individual transgressions. The great impersonal entity called "society" is not responsible for these sins — we are. These conditions grieve the heart of God, and He clearly calls us to account for them and to repent.*

In Leviticus, Numbers, and Deuteronomy the pattern for God's people is established: repentance and restitution prescribed for offenses against God and society; cities of refuge ordered to protect those who had committed manslaughter; strict safeguards for imposition of capital punishment.†

God's command is clear: "Follow justice and justice alone, so that you may live and possess the land."[3] Centuries later when Saul was removed from the throne of Israel, God chose a man "after his own heart" the young David, to be the king who "administered justice and righteousness for all his people."[4]

Following David came his son Solomon whose wisdom has become a political cliche. At every swearing in, from county dog-catcher to president, someone ritualistically prays that the newly elected one be endowed with "the wisdom of Solomon." Unfortunately, few bother to look up the source of their quote. If they did, they would probably be startled to find that when God asked Solomon what one thing he wanted, the young man replied, "Give your servant a discerning heart to govern your

*Examples of responsibility and repentance for corporate sins are found throughout Scripture. Moses often went before God in earnest repentance for the sins of his people. Moses might have counted himself blameless; after all, he had told the people the right thing to do. They were the rebels. Yet Moses repented for the corporate sins of his people. See also Nehemiah 1:6. Throughout the prophetic literature, there is consistent call by God for His people to repent for the sins of their nation.

†Many Christians cite Genesis 9:6 as the biblical justification for capital punishment but fail to cite the protection for the accused that God *also* demanded — such as two eyewitnesses, and the requirement that an accuser participate in the execution (Deuteronomy 17:6-7). Nothing comparable to those biblical safeguards can be found today in any of the state statutes that call for the death penalty.

people and to distinguish between right and wrong."[5] God was so pleased with Solomon's request — not for himself, but in order to dispense justice to others — that He rewarded him with wisdom never given before or since.

However, following this bright spot the record descends into one of shameful apostasy. King after king committed idolatry and did evil in the sight of God. Judah was divided from Israel, and both became weaker as justice disappeared.

Since the kings could not be trusted to do justice, God raised up a new breed of servant: the prophets. The line began with Elijah and Elisha, through the great evangelical prophet Isaiah, to Jeremiah and Ezekiel.[6] Each repeated the same three-pronged message: condemnation of unrighteous kings and people; a call to justice and holy living; and the promise of miraculous intervention of God in history to bring judgment to the wicked and blessing to the obedient.

Significantly, justice is seen not through the eyes of the powerful but through the eyes of the powerless. (In fact, many of the prophets were men God raised up from among the peasant class.) The moral worth of a society, the prophets declared, is measured not by life in the palace but by life in the streets. For the former to prosper at the expense of the latter violates God's standard for the humanity He created in His image. *To know the all-powerful God, one must know the powerless.*[7]

The angriest judgments come from the lips of the men we call the Minor Prophets. One of these, the prophet Amos, brought a message that was particularly devastating to the powerful elite of Israel. Every time I read and study Amos, I am chilled by some parallels with today's culture; it is a book with special and powerful insights for twentieth century Christians, for it reveals a view of God's justice that today's society often ignores to its peril.

Amos was a shepherd living in the rugged terrain south of Jerusalem. One day while about the regular duties of sheep-tending, he was dramatically confronted by a vision of God's fearsome judgment. Knowing this vision was from God, Amos left his flock to deliver the stinging rebuke to Israel.

He was received as a pariah — an occupational hazard for prophets. For like a doctor ripping gauze bandages off a putrid sore, Amos laid bare Israel's ugliest sins, including pagan rituals and immoral sexual practices such as temple prostitution.[8]

Blatant as these sins were, Amos exposed something even more offensive. Under Jewish law, a man's coat might be held as collateral for his debts during the day when the temperature was usually warm, but had to be returned in the evening for protection against the cold night air. However, the wealthy were ignoring this and were keeping the pledged coats. And heaping sin upon sin, they were then using the coats as bedding for sex acts in the temple, thus desecrating the temple twice: by sexual immorality and by flounting God's law intended to protect the poor.

Amos also exposed the practice of selling wheat on the Sabbath, cheating with dishonest scales, and selling the refuse of wheat remaining after the harvest which under Jewish law was to be left at the edges of the field for the poor.[9] This was God's welfare plan, but the Jews had become so greedy profiting at the expense of the poor and powerless that they were depriving them of the crumbs needed to stay alive.‡

Amos pronounced God's judgment upon Israel because "they sell the righteous for money and the needy for a pair of sandals," a reference to the common practice of the wealthy who could bribe judges with as little as the price of a poor man's sandals.

Greed had replaced justice, money had triumphed over mercy, and the judicial system was merely a pawn of power and privilege used to oppress the very people it was intended to protect. The righteousness of God was no longer the standard in the land.

And so, speaking through Amos, God demanded that the nation repent. "Hate evil, love good; maintain justice in the courts."[10] And then, in one of the grandest declarations of Scripture, he thundered, "Let justice roll down like waters and righteousness like an ever-flowing stream."[11]

Let those who believe that "God helps those who help themselves" read Amos. The Bible teaches exactly the opposite of that hallowed American maxim: God cares *especially* for those who can't help themselves — the poor and needy, the forgotten and helpless. Amos warned that the nation whose vested interests manipulated power structures for their own gain, at the expense of the poor, must face the judgment of an angry God.

That's why a leading Christian lawyer, Jay Poppinga, writes: "When

---

‡It should be noted that God does not attack the rich for being rich but rather for being unjust in the use of their riches. For example, all these offenses cited had to do with profit, but there's nothing wrong with making a profit — elsewhere it can be argued the Bible legitimizes it. But profit must be made honestly and in accordance with God's standards. The problem here was the method and the motive. Materialism had become Israel's god.

we speak of justice in the biblical sense we. . . . are talking about meeting need wherever it exists and particularly where it exists most helplessly."[12]

Some will say, however, that these standards for corporate holiness are no longer in force. Applicable to Old Testament times, yes. In force today, no.

That is tempting to believe — tempting, but not biblical. For while it is true we now live under grace since Jesus came to fulfill the law, Jesus did not repeal the law.[13] A perfect, just God cannot change His perfect standards of justice.

Jesus' first sermon reflects this: Walking into the synagogue, He picked up the parchment with the words of the prophet Isaiah and read:

> The Spirit of the Lord is on me,
>   because he has anointed me
>   to preach good news to the poor.
> He has sent me to proclaim freedom for the
>   prisoners
>   and recovery of sight for the blind,
>   to release the oppressed,
>   to proclaim the year of the Lord's favor.[14]

Jesus put down the scroll and said, "Today this scripture is fulfilled in your hearing."[15]

Jesus went on to demonstrate in His ministry a deep compassion for the suffering and forgotten. He fed the hungry, healed the lame, gave sight to the blind. He was concerned not only with saving man from hell in the next world, but delivering him from the hellishness of this one. Thus, the Son reflected the Father's passion for mercy and justice. And His message of social justice was just as unsettling and convicting as it was in the time of Amos — and as it is today.

Consider just one of Jesus' last admonitions to His disciples and to us. The setting is the Mount of Olives and Jesus is giving His followers a glimpse of the future — His eventual return and the faithfulness expected of them in the meantime. Then He describes the final judgment before the throne of the Lord, where with a wave of His hand the righteous and unrighteous will be separated. With terrifying finality, Jesus says, the unrighteous will hear God's final judgment: "I was hungry and you gave me nothing to eat, I was thirsty and you gave me nothing to drink, I was a stranger and you did not invite me in, I needed clothes and you did not clothe me, I was sick and in prison and you did not look after me."[16]

This is not hellfire and brimstone evangelism. This is justice. And, yes, this is love as well. God loves us so much that He holds us accountable; for by judging us according to how well we live out His holy standards of justice and righteousness, He ascribes meaning to our daily actions. He ensures that what we do matters.

So Christianity is not just a high-sounding ritual we perform on Sunday mornings. Christianity is abiding by biblical standards of personal holiness and in turn seeking to bring holiness into the society in which we live. And that's why Jesus called us "salt and light."[17] It is what He meant in the magnificent words of the Sermon on the Mount: "Seek ye first the kingdom of God, *and* his righteousness."[18] (Too many Christians glibly quote the first part of this verse, "seek ye first the kingdom of God," forgetting the demanding command to which Jesus gives equal emphasis, "*and* his righteousness.")

The path of personal holiness can be a tough one, but hacking out a holy pathway in society brings us face to face with the cost of discipleship. It means making moral judgments by God's standard's not man's, sometimes pitting the believer against the state. That can raise sticky questions in a democracy where, as Supreme Court Justice Oliver Wendell Holmes put it, "Truth is the majority vote of that nation that could lick all others."[19]

As a politician I not only believed that, but fervently worked for it; and in the Korean War I would have laid down my life in its defense. But that is not the way of the kingdom of God. Because something is legal does not make it right. Nor can the will of the majority be confused with the will of God. They may be very different; in fact, they often are.

Let me tell you what happened to a judge who found himself caught between this government of man and the justice of God. . . .

16

Contra Mundum

The handcuffs chafing Fred Palmer's arms had rubbed his wrists raw. Heavy chains connected the cuffs to a steel belt circling his waist. The dark holding cell, into which he was packed along with twelve other men waiting to be sentenced, stank from the heat of unwashed bodies despite the cold February wind outside.

When the electronic lock clicked and the heavy cell door swung open, armed officers herded Fred and a few others toward a barred elevator. After a short wait, they pressed together into the tiny cage to be transported up two flights. The guards then took them to a small, bleak room where they were to wait until called into the courtroom as each of their cases came up.

Fred Palmer leaned against the wall. He was a rather short man, in his mid-twenties, with thick dark hair, blue eyes, and a muscular build. He carried himself well, though now the chains held his aching arms in a supplicant position. Not that pleading would do any good, he thought. He had heard about the man he would face in the courtroom. Bontrager. The hanging judge.

Down the hall from the courtroom Judge William Bontrager, his long frame stretched in a reclining leather swivel chair and his booted feet propped on a gleaming walnut desk, stared at the snow-covered trees outside his corner office. At thirty-six his face was unlined, his crew cut sandy. His brown eyes focused intently on whatever had his attention, and at the moment his attention was on the morning's court schedule and the men to be sentenced. *Fred Palmer*, he thought as he inhaled deeply on a cigarette, *that's the case.*

He got up, took the black robe from the closet, slipped the garment over his head, and took a final drag before crushing the cigarette out in a heavy marble ashtray. Then Judge William D. Bontrager, Superior Court 2, Elkhart, Indiana, went to take his place at the bench.

It was a modern courtroom, especially for Elkhart. Built only ten years before, it was carpeted, had recessed lighting, a sophisticated sound system, and polished walnut furniture. The judge's elevated platform had the witness stand, attorneys' tables, and jury box all in sight, designed so the man presiding could exercise control over his courtroom without turning his head.

And Bill Bontrager was in control, though he never used his gavel. His deep voice carried through the sensitive sound system with an intensity and authority commanding respect.

Today the courtroom was nearly empty, with just a few relatives and observers dotted throughout the public seating area. But one row, right in the middle, was full. These people waited with a common expectancy, for they were the victims of one of the men to be sentenced, Fred Palmer.

Randy Brown sat in the center of that row. He and his wife had been on their honeymoon when Palmer broke into their small house and stole all their wedding presents. They had come home to find a window smashed, wrapping paper strewn everywhere, and their gifts gone. Even thinking of the mess made bile rise in Randy's throat. He couldn't wait to see justice done.

Finally a deputy sheriff escorted Fred Palmer into the courtroom where he took a seat beside his attorney. When Fred looked back to the spectator section, he could see his wife Loretta, her face tight with anxiety. *She looks like I feel*, he thought. *She must have left Jamie with a babysitter.* Then he turned back and lifted his head toward the unsmiling, robed figure at the front of the room.

Judge Bontrager looked piercingly at the young defendant, then picked up the pre-sentence report. Harry Fred Palmer, age twenty-five, involved in drugs and alcohol; charged with house burglary; arrested, pled guilty, confessed to eleven similar crimes. At the time of arrest, mid-September, 1977, Palmer's offense drew a mandatory sentence of ten to twenty years. However, Indiana legislators had recently passed a new penal code designating a lesser penalty for this particular crime and giving the judge discretion in sentencing; unfortunately for Palmer the new code did not take effect until October 1, eighteen days after his arrest. Therefore, he must be sentenced under the old statute to no less than ten years imprisonment.

Fred's prior offenses included marijuana possession, auto theft, possession of stolen property, but all except one of public drunkenness were committed after returning from service in Vietnam. Bontrager had looked over the impressive list of entries in the report pertaining to Palmer's war record: Bronze Star, National Defense Ribbon, Air Medal, Vietnam Service Medal, Vietnam Campaign Medal, Honorable Discharge.

It was also noted that Palmer had a young wife, Loretta, and a one-year-old daughter, Jamie, and that the defendant said he had committed his life to Jesus Christ while sitting in the Elkhart County Jail for five-and-a-half months awaiting trial. Bontrager had taken somewhat passing note of the last item. A lot of cons claimed jailhouse conversions. Only time would tell whether Palmer's was sincere.

Now the judge cleared his throat and leaned on one elbow into the microphone. His index finger jabbed the air as he spoke.

"Mr. Palmer," he thundered, "you are aware that under Indiana state law you must be sentenced according to the mandatory strictures of the old penal code, since your crime was committed before the new code went into effect. And you are aware that the penalty of no less than a ten and no more than a twenty year sentence is, under Indiana law, not suspendable. And perhaps you know that the victims of your burglaries have written letters to this court suggesting that the maximum penalty of twenty years will not be long enough to keep you off the streets of Elkhart."

There was a heavy pause of anticipation as Bontrager launched into his sentencing. "It is the opinion of this court, however, that fixed sentences themselves do not deter crime; what deters crime is that which the offender himself perceives as punishment. I am aware, of course, that you have spent five-and-a-half months in the Elkhart County Security Center, Mr. Palmer — but that is not sufficient punishment. It is the opinion of this court that what you would most likely perceive as punishment is a solid dose of maximum security incarceration.

"I am also aware, Mr. Palmer, that you claim a religious change of heart. If true, it is that which will sustain you as you are exposed to what we call the therapeutic shock value of the hellholes of the Indiana state prison system."

The words slowly tumbled through Fred Palmer's mind. He turned his head sharply to see Loretta's face completely white, her dark eyes panic-stricken. But something told him to hold on; this judge wasn't finished with him yet.

Bontrager paused, looking at the row of victims. His voice grew softer and his face, if possible, sterner.

"However, this court recognizes that the Indiana State Constitution is unique in that its penal code is founded on a principle of reformation, and not vindictive punishment. So this court is going one step further and declaring the mandatory and non-suspendable ten-to-twenty-year sentence in violation of that Indiana constitution. For to send Fred Palmer — in light of his individual case, post-Vietnam syndrome, and never having been in prison before — to a ten-year sentence in a maximum security prison would in fact be vindictive, cruel and unusual punishment that would ruin him unavoidably for life.

"Therefore, in the interest of society, as well as Mr. Palmer, this court holds that he serve 205 days in a state maximum security facility — one year, less the 160 days already served — that he then be released and make all reasonable restitution to his victims, engage in drug and alcohol therapy as needed, and remain on probation for a five-year period."

The judge leaned toward Palmer and added a final word: "Further, Mr. Palmer, as those who have spent time in my courtroom can tell you, I do not give people a second chance."

The victims, subdued while the judge spoke, now erupted. Their anger was no longer focused on Palmer, but on the judge. Bontrager looked calmly over the sputtering row of enraged spectators as the deputy sheriff approached to escort Fred Palmer back to the cell. Palmer shot a quick glance at his wife, noticing that her shock had been replaced by a glimmer of hope. On his way through the side door, he looked up at the young judge whose face was as hard as ever, but who somehow also seemed to flash him a look of challenge.

Bill Bontrager's decision to overturn an Indiana mandatory sentencing law surprised no one who knew him. Though he had been a judge for only slightly more than a year, that year had been marked by his aggressive, often controversial style. He was restless, idealistic, driven.

He came by this naturally. His father, prominent in state Republican politics, had been a stern, hard-working attorney who ruled his three sons with an iron will. He had favored black suits and crisp white shirts, perhaps because of his upbringing among the Amish "plain people." A self-made man who studied law by correspondence, the senior Bontrager had reached his political summit as the Republican nominee for the U.S. Senate, running on the same ticket that Barry Goldwater led to defeat in 1964. If by national standards he never reached great recognition (though a stand he took in the state legislature was written up in a 1954 *Readers' Digest*), in Indiana his name meant hard work, strong principles, and stubborn independence.

To his middle son, Bill, he was a pair of eyeglasses behind a news-paper, or an incensed listener to evening news broadcasts, too busy to show much interest in or warmth toward his sons. As Bontrager remem-bered years later, "In one sense I idolized my father and doted upon the possibility of a compliment or the acknowledgment of my existence. In another sense I hated him with everything I had, and hated myself more for allowing him to totally dominate my life.

"But my father taught me that morality is an absolute and not situational; he taught me that a man must be true to God, the Creator; he taught me that the rules we must live by can be found only in the Bible; he taught me to have the courage of my convictions and the willingness to speak them regardless of the personal cost. Unfortunately, he did not teach me to be tactful."

Reacting to this domineering presence, teen-age Bill Bontrager swore four oaths, meant to make him as unlike his father as possible. He vowed he would never be an attorney, he would never return to Elkhart, he would never enter politics, and he would be a better father and husband than his father had been.

The first oath was kept through one year of college. Bill had planned to be an engineer. Then, without really understanding why, he decided to leave Purdue and study pre-law at the University of Colorado. Perhaps because, as his Aunt Grace pointed out, all lawyers were frustrated actors, and Bill certainly had a flair for the dramatic. He also loved the Rocky Mountains which seemed to offer a size and scale to match his own ambitions and drive. While there he began to wear cowboy boots and string ties, a style as unlike Elkhart (and his father) as possible.

One Saturday afternoon in 1960 while handing our Nixon/Lodge stickers to football fans before the game, he noticed a tiny girl with a wide smile, also dispensing Nixon buttons. Her name was Ellen, and she was a freshman. Five months later they were married. Nine months after that they had their first child. With a family to support, Bill had to work every kind of menial job to pay his way through school.

His second vow — never to return to Elkhart — went out the window when he graduated from law school. He had accepted a position as a law clerk in the Supreme Court of Idaho. Then on New Year's Eve, having drunk a good quantity of rum-laced eggnog, he roared into a fierce confrontation with his father over why he was not returning to Elkhart. Typically, his dad couldn't simply ask him to come home because he wanted him in his law office, for that would show warmth and love; he had to argue on principle. But ten days later Bill called Idaho and told them he wasn't coming, then called home and asked for a job in his father's firm.

Bill and Ellen settled into Elkhart, and over the next ten years life flowed somewhat predictably. Bill's caseload was steady and their income good, giving them a new home in a pleasant suburb.

Bill's third vow — to stay out of politics — lasted four years. He decided to run for the state House of Representatives, but his father talked him out of it. Four years later, after his father's death, Bill ran for the state senate and lost. But his involvement in Republican politics won him an appointment by the governor to the State Board of Corrections, which recommended policy for prisons. Bill knew nothing about prisons, but dug into the job with his usual fervor, studying the subject, visiting prisons, and gradually developing a philosophy about corrections and criminal justice.

He was, however, more interested in politics than in prisons and spent most evenings in political or community meetings. Thus, his fourth vow to be a better father and husband than his own father nagged at him, for he spent little time at home with his wife and children.

Bill Bontrager knew about the God who made the heavens and the earth, who was all-powerful and had given an exacting standard of justice for men to live by. He knew nothing about a God who loved, who could weep, who sought intimacy with His human children. God was, in short, made in the image of his father; Bill respected and feared Him but could never come close to Him.

Ellen had even less background in the Christian faith. However, she became involved with a group of women who gathered weekly to study the Bible. Bill noticed that she began to change. She quit drinking, and she took considerably more interest in church. She even managed to drag him in occasionally. Bill was pleased that she had found an outlet that kept her busy and happy, but had no interest himself. Nothing was further from his mind than his need for God.

Then tragedy struck. The Bontragers' sons, Danny and Richard, were playing in the garage with a chemistry set when their concoction exploded. Flames enveloped ten-year-old Richard's face, chest, and right leg, covering him with third-degree burns. After several days, visitors could be admitted to his hospital room only if they removed clothing, scrubbed down completely, and suited up in surgical garb and facial masks. In spite of this laborious process, usually taking at least half an hour, one visitor came every day: Rev. Fred Finks, pastor of Winding Waters Brethren Church in the Bontrager's neighborhood. Fred would sit working puzzles with Richard day after day; also, each day he would ask a riddle and come with the answer the next. Richard looked forward to the minister's visits almost more than his parents'.

During his son's recovery, Bill found in Fred Finks, and in his congregation, religion that was more than moral principles; it was life lived compassionately with strength and joy. That attracted him.

Perhaps that explains why one day in early 1976 Bill took the highly unusual step of stopping by the pastor's office in the middle of the afternoon to seek some personal advice about a judgeship in Elkhart's Superior Court 2 that would soon be available. Several colleagues had suggested that Bill run for the office.

At first the idea seemed ludicrous. Not yet thirty-five, Bill was already earning much more than a superior court judge. Moreover, he had good political opportunities ahead. But as he thought about it, the idea became more appealing.

Rev. Finks listened to Bill's pros and cons, but gave little advice. He simply told Bontrager to discuss it with his wife and pray for guidance from God. Bill went home, talked it over with Ellen, but didn't bother to pray. He announced his candidacy.

As a Republican in Elkhart County with the name of Bontrager, he knew he could not lose. He was right.

January, 1977, found Bill Bontrager, thirty-five years old with the crew cut he had worn all his life and the cowboy boots and string ties he had worn since his Colorado days, residing in the plush judge's chambers of Superior Court 2, County Court Building, Elkhart, Indiana. Un-knowingly, it seemed he had been heading toward this vocation all his life. Here he found the natural outlet for his training and talents, and an arena in which to exercise his beliefs about law, order, justice, absolute morality, and individual accountability. He couldn't help thinking that his dad would finally be proud.

Bill had thought a judge's hours would leave much-needed time for his family (that fourth vow again), and that had been part of the post's attraction. But the caseload increased dramatically from month to month and his passionate involvement made the choice between family and work more difficult. Soon he was spending twelve and fourteen-hour days in the courthouse, coming home late and exhausted.

One October weekend Ellen planned to attend a conference at the Winding Waters church. Bill didn't intend to go; praying and sharing feelings with a group of church folk wasn't his idea of relaxation. But that Friday night his juvenile court cases, which ordinarily went to 8:00 P.M., wound up early at 6:30. So he stopped by the church to explain to Ellen that he was going home to fix himself dinner, stare at the TV set, and fall into the sack. As he walked around looking for his wife, different members kept greeting him so warmly that he got talked into staying. At first he merely listened. Then, to his amazement, he found himself sharing his own struggles. At last, as he said later, "I split open like an overripe tomato," and for the third time in his life wept openly.

That night Bill Bontrager realized he needed more than iron prin-ciples. He needed Jesus. So he opened his heart to Christ and remarkable joy and peace flooded over him. He felt drained of everything rotten and filled with the Spirit of God. Judge William Bontrager had become a Christian..

This new life in Christ did not change Judge Bontrager's view of the law; nor did he surrender to the Lordship of Christ at that time. It did, however, strengthen his sense of compassion. His image of a judge was not a blind official mechanically weighing evidence, but a sensitive, open-eyed justice applying the law to individual cases, aware of the entire legal system and people caught in it. He also believed that his role involved more than meting out penalites.

With these principles, he attacked the criminal justice system in Elkhart with all his energy, though not always with tact. He soon offended people in the Probation Department, the Prosecutor's Office, the Welfare Department, the Juvenile Court, the County Council and County Commissioners, and the Elkhart school system — the many agencies that try to help troubled families. He demanded that these agencies change their procedures, and some slowly did. When he came to the bench, many trials were taking place eighteen months after the crime committed; he cut that time to under five months. For the first time in many years the juvenile arrest rate fell, at least partly because Judge Bontrager insisted that school truancy not be ignored but treated as a serious problem.

But mandatory sentences were a growing part of the legal system, and he had no power to change that. While he had a reputation as a tough, no-nonsense judge, Bill believed that mandatory sentencing destroyed the concept of individual justice. For instance, anyone convicted of two felonies had to serve at least two years in prison. In general, that sounded reasonable. But the way the law was stated, that meant that someone convicted of two shoplifting offenses twenty years apart would have to go to prison for two years; the judge had no discretion to consider the particular crime and the individual. Knowing the prisons as he did, Bontrager did not take two years inside lightly. He believed there was no more certain way to ruin a person's life, for most who went in for more than a year came out embittered, hardened, and violent criminals. So he was just waiting for an opportunity to challenge the mandatory sentencing laws and in February, 1978, Fred Palmer's case presented that opportunity. But when Bontrager sentenced Palmer to only one year, he also knew he was confronting the plain language of the law; and he knew the prosecuting attorney would take the case to the Indiana Supreme Court. Bontrager hoped his boldness would encourage the Supreme Court to uphold a person's right to be treated as an individual under the law.

When Fred Palmer left the courtroom that February day after sentencing, he was whisked by police van to the Indiana Reception and Diagnostic Center for processing where he found himself in line behind a kid who confided his panic at the prospect of prison. Fred felt much of the same terror, but he believed the same God who had entered his life in the Elkhart County Jail would be with him in prison. Concerned for the terrified boy, Fred prayed, Lord, send me where this guy ahead of me goes. He strained forward and heard the choice offered the young prisoner: Michigan City or Indiana State Reformatory at Pendleton — equally tough joints, equally crowded. He heard the kid opt for Michigan City, so when the officer in charge asked Fred's preference, after filling out the necessary forms, Fred said, "Michigan City."

Palmer's time in prison was tough, but he studied his Bible, got involved with Christian volunteers through Prison Fellowship, and stayed in touch with the young man he had followed there. Through Fred's ministry that young man, along with many other prisoners, became a Christian.

Seven months later, Fred was released and went home to Loretta and Jamie in Bristol, Indiana. He got involved in a solid church fellowship, found a job, and scheduled appointments with his victims to pay them back for the money and goods he had stolen. Most were eager to confront him, but as they met the new Fred Palmer, they, too, were changed.

Randy Brown was particularly anxious to face Palmer, for he had watched in helpless rage as Palmer got off with a mere year of time. At least this victim-restitution program offered a chance to meet Palmer face to face and tell the worthless con what Randy thought of him.

But the Fred Palmer he confronted was no monster. Fred asked the Browns' forgiveness, told them about his time in Vietnam, his struggles with alochol, the needs of his wife and child at the time of his crimes. Now he wanted to make restitution.

Randy found him "a guy just like me." And he was ready to pay them back, not knowing what kind of revenge they might want. That took guts. Randy watched from inside while Fred began by chopping firewood on their lot. Soon he was out the door giving Fred a hand.*

The year following the Palmer decision was fairly uneventful for Bill Bontrager. His work load increased, as did his crusade to reform the system. He and Ellen and the boys went camping and spent a lot of time together at church. Bill even began teaching Sunday school.

Usually he prepared his Sunday school lesson on Saturday evening,

*An additional interesting result of the restitution made by Fred Palmer: Another of his victims was Randy Yohn, who was also present at Fred's trial because he was a deputy sheriff. As a result of his meeting Fred Palmer during the restitution time, Yohn realized that there was a "better way" than prison. He later became chairman of the Victim-Offender Reconciliation Advisory Board.

but one week he chose to begin on Sunday afternoon right after church. He read through Amos, the short Old Testament book they were to study. It meant nothing to him — just a dry, dusty sermon preached to an insignificant nation almost three thousand years ago. The study guide didn't help either. So Bill kept picking the Bible up at odd moments during the week, trying to get a meaningful lesson out of it before the next Sunday.

Then early one evening as he sat in his chambers with the words of Amos before him, the pages suddenly came alive with a howl of rage against the injustices in the courts and palaces of Amos's land. Bill grabbed the pen he had parked behind his ear and began scribbling on a legal pad. Soon the long yellow sheets were filled with his own paraphrases of the Lord's words to Amos:

> I demand righteousness and a right relationship with you. I demand justice and a compassionate integrity toward all. I demand that you stick by My standards and insist that you do the right thing toward others for the right reasons. The picture of Me that you make in your own mind so that you feel complacent and secure is idolatry. You think justice blind, but My justice is open-eyed. It passionately seeks out wrong and tries to right it. It is dedicated to other people's needs, and especially the needs of those less able to care for themselves.

His heart racing with exhilaration, Bill threw down his pen, leaned back and lit a cigarette. *What I've been fumbling around trying to say all my life is right here,* he thought. *It's really what God says . . .' let justice roll down . . .* In his own small way in the Palmer case he had been trying to do his part to uphold God's standards of justice, even though it meant opposition to the laws of the state.

As the events of the next three years crashed about him, Bill Bontrager returned often to Amos. The words of the ancient peasant prophet became his own — as did the howl of rage.

The wheels of justice in America grind slowly. A year passed. Palmer was out of prison, establishing a credible new life, and most people had forgotten the case. But Bill Bontrager still waited, knowing that the Supreme Court of Indiana would either overturn the sentencing law or overturn his decision.

Then on Friday, March 23, 1979, his secretary, Eloise, brought in the day's mail with a bulky brief from the state supreme court on top. It confirmed his worst fears: the court had not only reversed his decision but ordered him to send Fred Palmer back to prison for the remainder of his ten to twenty year mandatory sentence.

In the outer office, Eloise jumped as she heard the judge's fist crash down on his desk. Coffee cups and ashtrays rattled as he stormed around like an enraged bull. "That does it," she heard him utter in increasing volume. "THAT DOES IT!"

Bill Bontrager was hurt and angry. He did not like to be told he was wrong. But his reaction was more than hurt pride. He was infuriated at the tyranny of a mechanical court. A group of men in Indianapolis who had never met Fred Palmer were willing to mete out their version of justice and ruin Palmer's life to satisfy the letter of a law no longer even on the books, and furthermore, without considering the rehabilitation that had taken place in Palmer's life. To Bontrager that was not justice.

Bontrager reached for the phone and called Fred at his trailer home in Bristol. Fred was speechless. He could not believe the news. "I served my sentence," he kept saying. "I'm paying my victims back. Why in the world would the court want to send me back to prison?"

"Don't worry," Bontrager assured him. "We're going to fight this."

With those words, Bontrager crossed a line, though he did not realize it at the time. He was no longer an impartial judge dispensing justice; he had joined Fred Palmer's side.

Bontrager made the twenty-minute drive home in half the usual time. He was taking a troop of Boy Scouts to Ohio for the weekend and hadn't packed yet. He slammed into the house, up the stairs to the bedroom, and began flinging jeans, shirts, and boots into an old suitcase, shouting his news to Ellen who stood in the doorway.

"That does it!" he said for the umpteenth time that day. "The Supreme Court wants to send Fred back to prison! I'm resigning my judgeship!" Socks flew through the air from the dresser to the suitcase. "I've called a press conference for Monday morning," he continued. "I want you to be there. I can't continue in this kind of a system."

Bill slammed the suitcase shut and bounded down the stairs, Ellen behind him, "Bye," he yelled. "Handle any calls. Okay?"

On Monday morning the Elkhart courthouse was humming. Clusters of curious secretaries and court clerks gossiped excitedly; attorneys paced the second floor hall like expectant fathers. Inside Judge Bontrager's office, klieg lights, TV cameras, microphones, and reporters from newspaper, radio, and TV jammed the overheated room.

Bontrager sat at his desk, fingers interlaced behind his head. On a small couch nearby Ellen sat with a young couple.

Bontrager told the press that he was going to resign his judgeship. He described the Palmer case and said he could not in conscience send Fred Palmer back to prison.

"When God's law and man's law come into conflict," he said, "we must choose God's law. Christ cared for the individual. So must we." He paused. "If I have to be true to something, I will be true to God and not the law." The man who in the past could not, like his father, show emotion had gravel in his voice and bit his cheek to stifle his tears.

The reporters knew they had a great story: small-town Republican judge throwing his career away because of concern for an individual abused by the system. What a "one man standing alone" headline.

For Bontrager it was not that simple. Still angry, still hurt, he knew his flair for drama was playing on his passion for justice. His motives were mixed up just as this case was mixed up. But he was certain of one thing: while the news media would focus on Bontrager and the Supreme Court and the wording of the law, somebody ought to be caring about Fred Palmer and his family. In all the legal maneuverings, lives were at stake.

Bontrager stood and walked over to the couch, took a seat beside his wife, and put his arm around the young man seated there. "This is Fred Palmer," he said, "I wanted you all to meet him. He is the story, not me. Bill Bontrager will survive; I'm not the one going back to those prison hellholes."

By evening the story was a major item on the local news. By the next day, it was national. Calls came from across the nation, even across the ocean. But friends in Elkhart hounded Bill for a different purpose. They didn't want him to quit. Even some of the folks he had offended asked him to stay on, trying to convince him that he could do more to fight injustice as a judge than he could through the dramatic gesture of resigning.

So after two weeks of turmoil, Bill announced he would stay. That decision made, he launched himself back into his work the way he always had — long hours, heavy caseload. But he did not stop thinking about the Palmer case. He investigated legal strategy Fred could use to avoid returning to prison. After all, the man had served his sentence. If the

Supreme Court said he, the judge, had mistakenly judged the case, why should Palmer suffer for it?

In June, the Supreme Court's decision was made official. Palmer was to appear in court immediately to be sent back to prison. Bontrager ordered him in, but then granted delays to his lawyer. Then he went further. He began to work with Palmer's lawyer, guiding his legal strategy and helping him gather evidence about the Indiana prisons Palmer would be sent to. This move took Bill beyond acceptable standards of judicial involvement in a case.

The prosecuting attorney burst into Bill's office one day, shut the door, and told him in no uncertain terms that he was a flaming idiot. He was risking contempt of the Indiana Supreme Court and was too emotionally involved in the case.

"It isn't too difficult to see that you are wrong when someone hits you between the eyes with a four-by-four," Bontrager confessed later.

So Bill removed himself from the case and a local attorney, Richard Sproull, was selected as Special Judge. He made a decision that Palmer would have to be sent back to prison but then ruled that such punishment would be manifestly unjust and cruel. He was practically inviting another appeal of Palmer's sentence, and Palmer's lawyer made it. Palmer stayed out of prison while the case went back to the Supreme Court.

The wheels of justice rolled on for two more years while the court made a full investigation of the case. Fred Palmer continued to grow as a Christian and as a responsible father and husband and continued meeting with his victims and making restitution. He and Loretta also were expecting a second child.

Bontrager also grew as a Christian during this time, often returning to the Book of Amos. He regretted stepping over his bounds in the Palmer case, but believed that the Indiana Supreme Court would overlook his exuberance in light of the right judgment he had made. He told Palmer not to worry; the court would never send him back to prison.

On January 30, 1981, a Friday evening, Bill and Ellen and the boys were eating a late dinner and discussing plans for an upcoming ski trip when the phone rang. Ellen reached to answer it, then handed the receiver across the table to Bill.

Bill took the phone; it was the prosecuting attorney in the Palmer case. He listened for a moment, made no response, and hung up, his face drained of color.

As Ellen and the kids watched, wondering what had happened, the doorbell rang. Ellen opened the front door to an abashed state trooper and escorted him to the dinner table.

"I'm really sorry to have to give you this, Judge," said the officer, handing Bill a stiff sheet of paper. The document confirmed what the attorney had called to tell him: the Indiana Supreme Court had dismissed Fred Palmer's case, ordered Palmer back to prison, and charged both Judge William Bontrager and Special Judge Richard Sproull with criminal contempt of court.

Bill was dumbfounded, to say the least. The Supreme Court had caught him in a vise. The legal battles for Fred Palmer were over; his own were just beginning. But the hardest thing facing him at that moment was how in the world he was going to call Fred and tell him he would have to go back to prison. He had reassured Fred a hundred times that justice would be done.

He could not sleep, and early the next morning made the dreaded call.

The phone rang several times in the Palmers' trailer. Fred was still asleep, Loretta was in the shower, and Jamie was watching cartoons on TV. Still half asleep, Fred picked up the bedroom phone and heard Jamie pick up the kitchen extension at the same time.

His voice choked with tears, Bill did not mince words. "Fred," he said, "the Supreme Court's made a decision. They dismissed your appeal — and they've ordered you back to prison."

Fred felt his stomach turn over, then realized that his little girl had heard Bill's words, for she had dropped the extension and was screaming hysterically.

"Wait," Fred shouted into the phone. "Bill, hold on." He ran to the kitchen and picked up his daughter, trying to quiet her. He began praying out loud and gradually her sobs ceased. By this time Loretta was out of the shower, tears streaming down her face as she heard the news.

Jamie eventually lifted her head from Fred's soggy shoulder. "It's going to be all right, daddy," she said. "Jesus told me so."

When Fred got back to the phone, Bill continued, "Fred, you need to turn yourself in."

"I'll be there," Fred replied. "Give me until six o'clock this evening. I need to help my family get ready."

When they had hung up, a shaking Fred called some friends. Within an hour the small trailer was full of people from church. They prayed, sang, read Scripture, and cried.

At 5:30 that afternoon Fred Palmer walked into the Elkhart County Jail and turned himself in.

A week later Fred Palmer appeared in court for final sentencing. The courtroom was packed with members of the press, members of the Palmers' and Brontragers' churches, friends, and supporters. Several of the victims, including Randy Brown and Randy Yohn were again in court — this time on Fred's behalf. Ellen and Loretta sat together, their faces, like many others, wet with tears.

The proceedings were brief. Fred was led in from the holding cell in chains. Bontrager didn't allow himself to say much, knowing he would break down. He simply read out the sentence — no less than ten and no more than twenty years — enacting the will of the state. Then the guards took Palmer away, back to prison for at least nine more years.

Ellen went out to meet Fred in the back hallway as he was being led away. The man in chains and the wife of the judge stood quietly holding hands. "It's okay," Fred said. "Tell Bill I understand."

A month later, February, 1981, the Supreme Court of Indiana found Judge William Bontrager in contempt of court. They sentenced him to thirty days in prison and fined him $500, then suspended his prison sentence. They also ordered a complete investigation of his four years as a judge, with a possibility of removing him from the bench and taking away his license to practice law. By November, 1981, ten charges had been filed against him.

For Bill and his family, 1981 was agony. He continued to serve as a judge while the legal threat and mounting legal costs hung over him. Besides the contempt finding, a computer error in his pay cost him $700 a month in income; Ellen injured her knee and spent the year in physical therapy; Richard had unsuccessful skin-graft surgery.

Bill contemplated resigning several times, but decided to let the legal battle run its course, whatever the outcome. His sons also urged him to stay and fight, for they, too, had learned the need to stand on principles.

Ironically, the very system he had tried to change was now bearing coldly and mechanically down on him, threatening to take away his livelihood and his sense of worth.

His reputation was shot. He had been a promising politician, a successful lawyer. Now gossip pictured him as a troublemaker, a man with unquenchable thirst for drama, a maverick who loved to make waves and tilt with windmills. He could see a kernel of truth in the gossip, too; he had made mistakes, big mistakes. Had he ultimately helped the cause of justice or harmed it? Had he helped Fred Palmer or hurt him? He was uncertain. All he knew for sure was that his current dilemma had come about because he had cared about Harry Fred Palmer, cared that he be treated justly under the law, and believed that was how God meant him to feel. By the letter of the law, however, he had cared too much.

The Bontrager case ended unexpectedly and rather undramatically. While the charges stood before the Supreme Court, an unrelated controversy grew in the juvenile courts. Bontrager foresaw a fight that could only hurt the reputation of the court. Rather than fight and see the court harmed, he resigned in December, 1981. His staff wept at the news. The Supreme Court dropped their charges.

Fred Palmer served twenty more months of his sentence before being released by a special clemency order of Governor Robert Orr. After an additional six months in a work-release center, Palmer finally returned home.

"Sometimes in prison," he says, "people would ask me, 'If God's so good, why did He send you back to prison?' and I would tell them, 'God didn't send me back here. He allowed men to send me back to tell people like you about Jesus Christ.'

"Since I came to Christ," he continues, "I view all those things from a different perspective. God is sovereign. When I was in prison, I was still living within my Father's house. Prison had nothing to do with rehabilitating me. It was the Word of God that did that."

Bill Bontrager operates a struggling law practice from a small house in Elkhart. Business is scarce and reporters don't come around any more. They have moved on to other stories.

Bill often feels he is wasting his time. Once he was Judge Bontrager, sweeping the courts clean, making justice just. Now many in Elkhart think of him only as a chapter in history. And yet he still sometimes daydreams of different outcomes. He ponders his own mistakes, his personal shortcomings, and he surely does not think of himself as a saint or a martyr.

Bill sees his own experiences as part of God's plan: "I met and accepted Christ in 1977, but I continued in control of my own destiny. It wasn't until November, 1981, after becoming an emotional wreck, that I let go and turned the future over to Him. I surrendered myself. Since then He has continued to teach me submission and patience, the need to study His Word and seek Him in prayer. He has removed much of my anger; in short, I am at peace today, *knowing Him* — and that makes me count as gain all that the world might count as loss."

His court reporter, Zo Ann Myers, thinks she understands Bill's decisions: "He became a Christian while on the bench, you know, and that made it harder for him. He was a judge who had compassion. I've seen him rule on a juvenile case, then rip off his robes and run out to the hall and put his arm around the kid as he was being led away. 'I care about you,' he would say. And they knew he did. Sometimes he would get choked up during a case, right there in the courtroom.

"He stood on his convictions. When he felt the legal system was at odds with God's law, he knew he had to obey God. And he loved his job. But near the end, when he was so emotionally drained from the whole thing, I heard him say many times, 'I've just got to do what I know to be right, even if I lose my job over it.' "

Which he did.

So whatever you think of Bill Bontrager and his stand, however you sum up his passionate personality and the mistakes he made, what he did remains clear: he saw something he believed was wrong under God's standards and he did something about it. He took the risk of action.

And he paid dearly for that action. Obedience to God does not always mean a happy ending. But why should we think it would?

17

The Radical Christian

Whenever old-timers — lawyers, court officials, and reporters — gather around the Elkhart County Court house, it is not unusual for the conversation to turn to Bill Bontrager. Some understand what he did; others still can't, and wonder why the judge got so worked up over "the kid who just got what he had coming." Old political cronies have the hardest time, for they can't figure out why a conservative Republican would go against his fellow conservatives on the State Supreme Court. "Bontrager," one office holder shrugs, sighing in resignation, "well, he's just gone radical, that's all."

Gone radical. What a great term for it. Unfortunately, "radical" has taken on unpleasant, even nasty connotations in modern times. It suggests something un-American, like the violent protesters of the 1960s who blew up campus buildings, or fiery-eyed extremists of the right. But the word "radical" comes from the Latin *radix* meaning "the root" or "the fundamental." So it simply means going back to the original source or "getting to the root of things."

Indeed, in a world where values are being shaped by the fleeting fantasies of secular humanism, it is radical to stand for the fundamental truth of God, to go to the "root," the Word of God.

Believers today have many ancestral radicals in their family tree. In fact, the kingdom of God is full of them.

John Wesley passionately argued that there could be "no holiness but social holiness . . . [and] to turn [Christianity] into a solitary religion is to destroy it."[1] Wesley was branded a radical for his famed St. Mary's speech, an angry, but accurate denunciation of his fellow Oxford faculty members for their weak-kneed faith (he was never invited to speak there again). Later he captured the essence of radical holiness when he wrote: "Making an open stand against all the ungodliness and unrighteousness, which overspreads our land as a flood, is one of the noblest ways of confessing Christ in the face of His enemies."[2]

Anyone who has read my books or heard me speak knows the profound impact William Wilberforce has had on my Christian life. That's why I refer so consistently to his radical stand for Christ in his culture and why I quote so often from a letter written by John Wesley to Wilberforce — then a recent convert. Wesley, who was to die only days later, commissioned Wilberforce to lead the radical campaign against slavery. I've carried this excerpt from Wesley's letter in my Bible for the past seven years:

> Unless the Divine Power has raised you up to be as Athanasius, *contra mundum*, I see not how you can go through your glorious enterprise in opposing that execrable villainy which is the scandal of religion, of England, and of human nature. Unless God has raised you up for this very thing, you will be worn out by the opposition of men and devils, but if God be for you, who can be against you? Are all of them together stronger than God? Oh, be not weary in well doing. Go on, in the name of God and in the power of His might, till even American slavery, the vilest that ever saw the sun, shall, vanish away before it.[3]

Wilberforce took his stand, at first but a single, lonely voice against a business that was the mainstay of the lucrative West Indies trade, employing some 5,500 sailors and 160 ships worth 6,000,000 pounds sterling a year. For twenty years the radical Wilberforce, later joined by a small group of Christian friends known as the Clapham Sect, fought the economic and political might of the British Empire. In the end, righteousness prevailed, and for the next half century a mighty revival swept across England and the Western world.

Contra mundum. Against the world. Radicals.

Certainly that describes believers like Dietrich Bonhoeffer and other German Christians who had the audacity to stand against Hitler and his super-race monstrosity, and whose stand led many of them to imprisonment and death. And certainly it describes Bill Bontrager.

Radical stands do, however, lead us into the briar patch of thorny questions about the Christian's role in government and politics.

First comes the issue of civil disobedience.

The Bontrager case suggests that Christians must disobey their government when it directs them contrary to God's law. Yet Scripture plainly commands us to obey civil laws and to be in subjection to governing authorities.[4] Isn't this a clear conflict?

No. But to resolve it requires understanding a major biblical purpose of government. The origin of government goes back to humanity's first sin, when to keep rebellious Adam and Eve away from the Tree of Life, God stationed an angel with flaming sword at the entrance to the Garden; this was, so to speak, the first cop on the beat. Thereafter the Bible makes clear that government was established as God's means for restraining man's sin.* God's people are enjoined to submit to those in authority not because governments are inherently sanctified, but because the alternative is anarchy. In its sinfulness, humanity would quickly destroy itself.

Government, then, is biblically ordained for the purpose of preserving order, but, as Francis Schaeffer writes, "God has ordained the State as a *delegated* authority; it is not autonomous."[5] So when government violates what God clearly commands, it exceeds its authority. At that point, the Christian is no longer bound to be in submission, but can be compelled to open and active disobedience. Dr. Carl Henry sums up the Christian duty: "If a government puts itself above the norms of civilized society, it can be disobeyed and challenged in view of the revealed will of God; if it otherwise requires what conscience disallows, one should inform government and be ready to take the consequences."

John Knox, the great Scottish lawyer and theologian, advocated Christian revolution under such circumstances — to the shock of the Christian world of the sixteenth century.[6]

Furthermore, the Bible provides clear precedence for civil disobedience. Moses' parents are cited approvingly for their decision to hide their child from Egyptian officials, as are Daniel and his friends for their

---

*Avaricious as it is by nature, government has today strayed far from its biblical purposes; it is hard to imagine how subsidizing college professors or controlling tobacco crops, laudable though such ventures may seem, can be considered as necessary for preserving order and maintaining justice. So the Christian, when weighing his biblical responsibility toward governments, may draw ethical distinctions between a government's exercise of a clear biblical mandate and the exercise of some illegitimate function.

refusal to bow before the statue of Nebuchadnezzar. In the days following Pentecost, Peter and John defied the orders of the Sanhedrin, the Jewish governing body, who ordered the disciples to stop speaking of Jesus.[7]

Most cases are not this clear-cut, of course, and therefore the Christian's response can never be made lightly or automatically. Only after seeking every other remedy, after prayer, consultation with Christian brothers and sisters, and a thorough search of Scripture should civil disobedience be employed.

The second thorny question is whether men and women who seek to be faithful to Christ can serve in public office.

My answer is yes. For if Christ is not only truth, but *the* truth of life and all creation, then Christians belong in the political arena, just as they belong in all legitimate fields and activities, that "the blessings of God might show forth in every area of life," to quote the great Puritan pastor Cotton Mather. Indeed, it is the Christian's duty to see that God's standards of righteousness are upheld in the governing process. This may be accomplished from within the structures themselves or from the outside by organizing public pressure to influence the system.

Or, it may have to be done as Bontrager did by taking a stand in open defiance of the system.

This, then, leads us to the third and perhaps the thorniest question: can Christians be vigorous advocates for justice and morality without destroying the separation of church and state?

The New Testament is clear: there is to be no merger of church and state until Christ returns and the kingdoms of this world become "the kingdom of our Lord and of his Christ."[8] As Schaeffer writes, we must not "confuse the Kingdom of God with our country . . . or wrap Christianity in our national flag."[9]

Yet Christians sometimes do just that, using God to sanctify their own political prejudices, becoming arrogant and divisive in equating their favorite form of government or their political hobbyhorse with Christianity.

Politicians are willing partners in this process, all too often deftly turning the tables so that the religious leader who thinks he is influencing the government may suddenly discover he's the one being manipulated — for the politician's gain. (As one whose job it was to woo religious leaders for the Nixon White House, I can testify that they are no more immune than anyone else to the blandishments of power.)

Or as one clear-sighted writer warns: "History has shown that when society embraces religion, religion usually hugs back. Accommodation is often followed by assimilation and amalgamation. We accept some popularity and, craving more, we discard the convictions we have that might be unpopular ... our identity as Christians is threatened."[10]

The key to answering this question is to understand that the Christian's goal is not power, but justice. We are to seek to make the institutions of power just, without being corrupted by the process necessary to do this. It requires a delicate balance, and Deity is our role model:

> God in His sheer power could have crushed Satan in his revolt by the use of that sufficient power. But because of God's character, justice came before the use of power alone. Therefore Christ died that justice, rooted in what God is, would be the solution. ... Christ's example, because of who He is, is our standard, our rule, our measure. Therefore power is not first, but justice is first in society and law.[11]

But, some say, it's just common sense that to be in a position to exercise justice one must acquire power first. How often that rationale has been used to justify the most awful abuses committed in the name of religion. Though it is one of the most baffling paradoxes of the Christian faith, often precisely the opposite seems true. Malcolm Muggeridge helps explain it: "It is in the breakdown of power rather than in its triumph that men may discern its true nature and in an awareness of their own inadequacy when confronted with such a breakdown that they can best understand who and what they are."[12]

Bontrager learned that lesson. So did I ... in prison.

All my life I sought wealth, success, and fame because they were the keys — or so I thought — to security and power. I was influenced, like most children of the Great Depression, by memories of breadlines and parents worrying whether there would be enough money for food and rent. The vision of the American dream drove this immigrant's grandson, and I believed with determination and hard work I could make it to the top. Money and property were the keys to the kingdom where I could lock the door against want, fear, and insecurity.

Law school only deepened my convictions about the importance of private property. (In the post-war era, property courses in law school outnumbered courses about individual rights by at least 4 to 1; there were, incidentally, no courses on ethics.)

Then, I discovered that practicing law was like most businesses: the most desirable clients were those able to pay the most. So I began to spend my time almost exclusively with corporate executives or individuals with resources. (Like 98 percent of all lawyers, my only brush with criminal law or the poor and disadvantaged were those dreaded occasions — once or twice a year at most — when my number was called in one of the local courts and I was assigned an indigent client.)

I became convinced that law — justice, that is — functioned to protect the individual's property and to act as the ultimate arbitrator in a mercantile society. Thus I saw my mission to be one of using my persuasive abilities in Congress or in the courts on behalf of those whose economic interests I represented (and by whom, not incidentally, I was very well paid). Justice was, in short, the sum of the rules and policies I tried to shape.

When I moved into politics, my task was not really any different, except that my clients became the politicians I served, the political convictions I had formed, the party platform, and those whose campaign contributions or influence could get them through the imposing security of the White House gates. (I used to scoff at the protesters who couldn't get through those gates. "Law is not made in the streets but in the halls of government," was a favorite expression. A nice way of saying that justice was determined by those of us who controlled the levers of political power.)

Ultimately, of course, I saw justice as the instrument for removing from society, and punishing, those who refused or were unable to live by the rules people like myself made. To be sure I had fundamental convictions about individual liberty and, as a student of Locke and Jefferson, believed deeply in man's inalienable rights and the preservation of individual freedoms. But my basis for judgment (as well as the causes and individuals I fought for) was almost entirely subjective, hence dangerously vulnerable to every whim and passion. The brighter I became, the more dangerous I was; the more power I acquired, the more power acquired me.

I was blind. Indeed, only in the "breakdown of power" did I finally understand both it and myself. For my view of life was through such narrow openings as the elegantly draped windows of the White House, and my vistas were of lush green lawns, manicured bushes, and proud edifices housing the corridors of power. But looking at the world from the underside through the bars of a dark prison cage and the barbed wire of forced confinement, I could, for the first time, really *see*.

Lying on the next cot, three feet away in the crowded, noisy dormitory, was a former small-town bank president doing three years for a first offense conviction of $3,000 tax fraud. So deep were the wounds of years of fruitless appeals that his face was drawn and gaunt. He was the first flesh-and-blood casualty I met of the great economic wars I had fought. *Maybe*, I thought, *he ran afoul of one of those quirks or loopholes I'd engineered in the Internal Revenue Code.* (Prison was full of people prosecuted under laws I had written or enforced; that's why my life was threatened during those first days in prison.)

Next I encountered a man in his twenties whose face reflected perpetual pain. A filling station owner, he was doing six months for having cashed a customer's $84.00 check which later proved to be stolen. First offense, too. His harsh sentence was the result of some ambitious prosecutor making a name for himself and a judge with a mean streak and a reputation for impulsiveness.

A moon-faced black lad with doleful eyes came to talk with me, insisting he did not know what his sentence was. Certain he was playing dumb to win my sympathy and legal assistance, I brushed him aside. Some days later, to my astonishment, I discovered he was sincere. A court-appointed lawyer had given him twenty minutes, persuaded him to plead guilty to a charge of knowingly purchasing stolen property, and marched him terrified and handcuffed before a judge who mumbled something about four years and cracked the gavel with that sound no defendant ever forgets. This young man, who had never been in jail before, had spent the next thirty days fending for his life, crouched in the corner of a holding cell in a Tennessee jail. For weeks after arriving at our prison he cowered like a dog who had been beaten.

These men were not exceptions. Most of those in prison with me were poor; or if they had had any money, it had been wiped out by their enormous trial costs. Though folklore has it that minimum security prisons, like the one I was in, are full of wealthy "white-collar criminals" doing a few months of "easy" time, I met but a handful who could have afforded to hire me as their lawyer only a year earlier.

So it was there, surrounded by such despair and suffering, that I began to see through the eyes of the powerless. I began to understand why God views society not through the princes of power, but through the eyes of the sick and needy, the oppressed and downtrodden. I began to realize why in demanding justice God spoke not through easily corrupted kings, but through peasant prophets who in their own powerlessness could see and communicate God's perspective. As a result, I learned to say with Solzhenitsyn, "bless you, prison" for coming into my life. For only in the breakdown of my own worldly power did I see what power is, what it had done to me, and what it had done through me to others. I learned that power did not equal justice.

But the Christian who breaks radically with the power of the world is far from powerless — another kingdom paradox. For example, some might think that in surrendering the power of his judgeship, Bill Bontrager forfeited any chance to influence the justice system in his state. But the verdict on that is not in yet, and reform efforts are actively underway in Indiana. At the very least, his move revealed a system of injustice to eyes that might never otherwise have seen it. In my own life it is certainly clear that my powerlessness has been used by God to influence the criminal justice system far more than anything I did from my office of worldly power.

If we would love God, we must love His justice and act upon it. Then, taking a holy, radical stand — *contra mundum* if need be — we surrender the illusion of power and find it replaced by True Power. That was certainly one of Alexander Solzhenitsyn's greatest discoveries in the Soviet gulag.

Like other prisoners, Solzhenitsyn worked in the fields, his days a pattern of backbreaking labor and slow starvation. One day the hopelessness became too much to bear. Solzhenitsyn felt no purpose in fighting on; his life would make no ultimate difference. Laying his shovel down, he walked slowly to a crude work-site bench. He knew at any moment a guard would order him up and, when he failed to respond, bludgeon him to death, probably with his own shovel. He'd seen it happen many times.

As he sat waiting, head down, he felt a presence. Slowly he lifted his eyes. Next to him sat an old man with a wrinkled, utterly expressionless face. Hunched over, the man drew a stick through the sand at Solzhenitsyn's feet, deliberately tracing out the sign of the cross.

As Solzhenitsyn stared at that rough outline, his entire perspective shifted. He knew he was merely one man against the all-powerful Soviet empire. Yet in that moment, he also knew that the hope of all mankind was represented by that simple cross — and through its power, anything was possible. Solzhenitsyn slowly got up, picked up his shovel, and went back to work — not knowing that his writings on truth and freedom would one day enflame the whole world.

Such is the power God's truth affords one man willing to stand against seemingly hopeless odds. Such is the power of the cross.

THE HOLY NATION

They love one another. They never fail to help widows; they save orphans from those who would hurt them. If they have something they give freely to the man who has nothing; if they see a stranger, they take him home, and are happy, as though he were a real brother. They don't consider themselves brothers in the usual sense, but brothers instead through the Spirit, in God.

Aristides describing Christians
to the Emperor Hadrian

18

The Holy Nation

At the height of the energy crisis in 1977, the governor of Virginia ordered energy use restricted in non-essential buildings. No one seemed particularly surprised that churches headed his list. In the eyes of the world, as well as many church-goers, the church is only a building, and an expensive, under-used one at that; except for a few hours on Sunday and an occasional mid-week service or function, the building sits empty. So why use scarce resources to heat it?

These same people consider the church just another institution with its own bureaucracy, run by ministers and priests who, like lawyers and doctors, are members of a profession (though not so well-paid). And while this parochial institution fulfills a worthwhile social and inspirational function, rather like an arts society or civic club, most people could get along fine without it.

In many ways, of course, the church has allowed itself to become what the world says it is. (This seems to be a common human bent — to become what others consider us to be.) But that sad fact has not dulled or changed God's definition of, and intention for, His church. For biblically the church is an *organism* not an organization — a *movement*, not a monument. It is not a part of the community; it is a whole new community. It is not an orderly gathering; it is a new order with new values, often in sharp conflict with the values of the surrounding society.

The church does not draw people in; it sends them out. It does not settle into a comfortable niche, taking its place alongside the Rotary, the Elks, and the country club. Rather, the church is to make society uncomfortable. Like yeast, it unsettles the mass around it, changing it from within. Like salt, it flavors and preserves that into which it vanishes.

But as yeast is made up of many particles and salt composed of multiplied grains, so the church is many individual believers. For God has given us each other; we do not live the Christian life alone. We do not love God alone.

To believe Jesus means we follow Him and join what He called the "kingdom of God" which He said was "at hand."[1] This is a "new commitment ... a new companionship, a new community established by conversion."[2]

Consider how Aristides described the Christians to the Roman Emperor Hadrian:

> They love one another. They never fail to help widows; they save orphans from those who would hurt them. If they have something they give freely to the man who has nothing; if they see a stranger, they take him home, and are happy, as though he were a real brother. They don't consider themselves brothers in the usual sense, but brothers instead through the Spirit, in God.[3]

Aristides was describing the kingdom of God made visible by believers.

Paradoxically, it was Peter, the most Jewish and parochial of all the apostles — the one who argued with Paul over circumcision and who was reluctant to preach the Good News to the Gentiles at Caesarea — who grasped most clearly this vision of a new kingdom. He addressed the young church, made up of believers of every country, race, and language of the then-known world as "a holy nation."[4]

This was no catchy phrase Peter thought up to describe the church; he took the words from the Scriptures — from the words God spoke to Moses when He called the Israelites to be His "holy nation."[5] In those days God literally pitched His tent and lived among His people. Now the kingdom is evidenced through those in whom Christ dwells. As John Calvin said, it is the first duty of the Christian to make the invisible Kingdom visible.

Can it happen? Can we be not only a holy people but a holy nation? Yes, we *must* be. But to do so requires an understanding and practice of certain truths — what might be considered basic principles for the church. I have found some of these best illustrated by a church in what might at first seem an unlikely place — Seoul, Korea.

The Republic of Korea, a country of 37,000,000 people, is predominantly Buddhist; there are only 7,000,000 Christians, of which perhaps 2,000,000 are evangelical. Yet I was astonished during my first visit to Seoul in 1981 to see signs of Christian influence everywhere: thriving churches, Christian values, and complete openness to the Gospel. I was given access to the prisons, even those with political prisoners, preaching three times to packed prison halls, where many inmates made profession of faith. I was permitted to meet with American inmates held on Korean charges and was even allowed unmonitored visits with leaders of dissident groups.

The highlight of the trip was a Sunday morning service at the Full Gospel Church in Seoul — again to my astonishment. I was wary. I had read about this church's phenomenal growth from a tiny mission with a handful of members in the early 1960s to the largest congregation in the world twenty years later — over 150,000 members.

I have never believed growth should be the prime goal of the church and certainly not proof of its spirituality. So I mumbled a bit to myself about super-hype when I arrived and saw the mobs being herded in and out, buses lined up for blocks, TV cameras and technicians everywhere. *They must not preach the Gospel* I thought, judging that only Madison Avenue and Hollywood transplanted to Seoul could do this — not the Holy Spirit. I was also apprehensive because I'd heard the crowd was even more demonstrative than most Pentecostal churches in the U.S. I like amen corners, but....

Though I've spoken to large crowds many times, it was electrifying to look out over the more than 10,000 people packed wall-to-wall and be told there were 15,000 more in overflow halls watching on closed-circuit television. And this was only one of six Sunday services!

As I began to preach, the Senior Pastor Cho at my side translating rapidly, I sensed a genuine warmth radiating from the congregation, a powerful surge of the Spirit. My speaking became effortless. The language barrier, often evident through even the best interpreters, vanished as the pastor and I developed immediate rapport. And though I couldn't understand the words during the rest of the service, there was excitement and, to my delight, real reverence. It was a holy time.

Afterward, I met with Pastor Cho in his study. A pale and slender man, the pastor seemed shy and withdrawn until he began to speak; then there was a fire about him.

"Fantastic church you lead, Pastor," I said.

"Oh, no," he waved aside the compliment. "This is not the church.

This is only where we all come together once a week. The church is in the home — 10,000 cell groups which meet regularly all around this city."

My mistake was a natural one. I figured a church so phenomenally successful must be the result of the leader's charisma and personality, for so often our American churches and parachurch movements grow because of the personality of the pastor or leader. This pattern is merely another Christian adaptation of the celebrity cultism of our society.

But a charismatic leader is not the secret of the vitality and size of the Full Gospel Church in Seoul. Cho *is* dynamic and brilliant; but the growth of the church resulted from his brokenness, not his strength. Cho has been ill most of his life, has had TB diagnosed in its terminal stages, has suffered a nervous breakdown from fatigue, and has had repeated severe ulcer attacks. The cell concept was developed as necessity because Cho was so weak he couldn't manage the church; thus, he commissioned elders to take responsibility for the people in each of their neighborhoods. (Breaking customs deeply rooted in his Oriental culture, Pastor Cho named many women to head cell groups.)

Those cell groups, really home churches, evangelized their neighborhoods, provided a way neighbors could help each other, encouraged spiritual discipline, and began to mushroom.[6]

I silently chastised myself for my judgmental attitude as Pastor Cho told me that though he had a carefully organized system for maintaining appropriate pastoral authority and providing structured sermons and teaching materials for the groups, from 1964 to 1973 he never once totalled the membership of the church. When he finally discovered that through the quiet evangelization of the home church the membership had jumped during that time from 8,000 to 23,000, Cho was stunned.

This raises what I believe is the first principle for the church: *the body of believers called the church is to grow from the inside out in response to the Spirit.* Built that way, the church prevails against anything.

Ever aware that an army of North Korean divisions is poised at the DMZ, twenty-six kilometers north of Seoul, Pastor Cho is quick to point out that he could be arrested, the church doors barred, his staff removed overnight, and the church would still grow. (That's exactly what happened in China, where the church multiplied several times over during the dark years of the cultural revolution and the great purges.)

What would happen if your pastor was removed and your church building closed or destroyed? Most churches are totally dependent on the pastor and church staff. Youth for Christ president, Jay Kesler, sometimes quips, "The western church is like a pro football game on Sunday afternoon: 100,000 people sitting in the stands watching 22 men knock their brains out on the field." Take away the 22 and there is no game.

Cho has not allowed that to happen in Seoul. He believes God at one point ordered him "to let my people grow," so he has taken his mission "to equip the lay people, so the lay people can carry out the ministry both inside and outside the church."[7]

Beloved pastor and Chaplain of the Senate, Dick Halverson, agrees that "equipping the saints" — which of course means all believers — is the central thrust of any pastor's calling. "Nowhere in the Bible," he writes, "is the world exhorted to 'come to church.' But the church's mandate is clear: she must go to the world ... the work of ministry belongs to the one in the pew, not the one in the pulpit." So, he says, the church comes together on Sunday mornings principally to be prepared to carry out its ministry the rest of the week in every walk of life.[8]

And that is the second principle for the church: *it must equip the laity to take the church into the world.*

If practiced, this principle would cure the schizophrenia so many Christians have. Ask a church layman, "What is your ministry?" and the reply is invariably the same: "Oh, I'm a computer programmer by day, but every Thursday night I work with the Gideons. That's my ministry." Halverson calls this a false dichotomy between the sacred and the secular. The believer's ministry is being Christ's person right where he or she is, in the marketplace or the home, every moment of every day. This is part of the everyday business of holiness. This is the very nature of loving God.

The church in Korea has problems, of course — and in some cases the criticism that it is in an unholy league with the government may be valid. Despite this, its people are characterized by an intense commitment to spiritual discipline. Many of the cell groups from Cho's church and prayer groups from other churches meet in the early morning hours for Bible study and prayer. Few serious Korean Christians would begin their day without a devotional time. Because of the pervasiveness of this commitment, many employers permit prayer and study groups to meet in factories and office buildings during lunch breaks.

The Full Gospel Church has a retreat center called Prayer Mountain where on any given day a thousand or more believers may be found kneeling on straw mats in tiny caves hollowed out of a mountainside. The overflow fills one of the center's large halls. Workers will often take the first half of their two-week vacation at this place for fasting and prayer.

Is it any wonder that though outnumbered 5 to 1 by Buddhists, the Christian church is the most powerful influence in the Korean culture? While in sad contrast, the Christian church in America, outnumbering other religions 10 to 1, is far from the dominant influence in our culture.

The third key principle for the church, then is *spiritual discipline — fervent prayer and serious study of God's Word*. This is the life or death principle, for churches that neglect the Word and the prayer life quickly wither. But churches that exercise spiritual discipline can be mightily used.

The great revivals have been born in times when Christians were intent on prayer. The lay revival of 1858, which affected the Western world for half a century, began when businessman Jeremiah Lanphier started a weekly prayer meeting with a handful of people in a small room of the Old North Dutch Church in New York City. The group grew, then meetings were held daily. Several churches followed the pattern, and soon all public meeting places in the city were regularly packed. Within a few months 10,000 people gathered daily at noon for open prayer meetings in New York streets. In two years, 2,000,000 converts entered American churches.

Like flood waters, the revival spread through the Hudson River Valley and on to Chicago, where Dwight Moody was just beginning his work with young people. Then it jumped the Atlantic to Ireland, Scotland, England, Wales, and danced like fire across much of Europe, then to South Africa and India. There was no elaborate evangelistic organization. Communication was slow; word had to spread from one prayer cell to the next, from church to church, from city to city. It was movement inspired by the fervor of thousands of Christian laypeople.

Similar evidence can be found about the other mighty spiritual movements of recent centuries.

This evidence also makes clear that revivals are not confined geographically. For the church of Jesus Christ is not American or Korean or English or Dutch. It is one church, one body, one holy nation transcending man's arbitrary geographic and political boundaries.

This leads us to the fourth key principle for the church: *as one holy nation, we must break free of any provincialism and work for unity in Christ*.

Before my conversion, I confess, some ugly prejudices lurked in the darker corners of my heart, particularly toward those nations which America had fought against in the wars of this century. But in my travels as a believer among fellow believers of other races and nationalities, the Lord has given me some of His richest fellowship in those very countries. The Holy Spirit can break down every barrier.

Thus, what happens in the church on the remotest continent is as important as the life of our local congregation. The rest of the world is as far away as the nearest fund-starved ghetto church in our town or as close as the underground cell in China.

"If one part suffers, every part suffers with it."[9] The great exodus to the suburbs in the last three decades makes this scriptural truth especially urgent in America. Thriving new middle-class congregations now ring center-city ghettos where the older, almost-abandoned churches are starving to death. Like an army retreating from the battlefield, prosperous suburban congregations have left the wounded to die in the core of great metropolitan areas — both physically and spiritually.*

Congregations that continue to look inward will find their field of vision ever-narrowing. Those that recognize, as Peter did, that the church of Christ is one holy nation will discover unimagined spiritual treasure.

Eastminster Presbyterian Church in Wichita, Kansas, has experienced this. Though pastored by a gifted minister, Frank Kik, responsibility for the church is shared by strong laypeople and the saints are being well-equipped. Christian scholars from around the country frequently lecture there; laypeople are involved in serious theological study; many in the church are involved in prayer groups; and the congregation actively supports overseas missions and mercy ministries around the country.

All this is, I believe, the direct result of the conscious decision at Eastminster to break from its natural provincialism and put the unity of the holy nation principle into practice.

During 1975 the church, then 850 members, had raised $500,000 for an addition to its always-crowded sanctuary. The architect's drawings were nearly completed and the members were excited about the imminent construction.

Then a missions conference was held at the church, and a missionary from Guatemala showed slides of the terrible devastation from the massive earthquake which had hit that country two weeks earlier. Villages were totally wiped out; everything was in rubble, including what had once been small but growing mission churches.

---

*One simple solution to this problem would be for each suburban church to adopt one center-city church, sharing resources and teaching. The impact can be dramatic and the giving church is greatly blessed. A fine Christian movement known as STEP is dedicated to this vision: STEP Foundation, 2429 Martin Luther King Blvd., Dallas, TX 75215 (214-421-9210). Prison Fellowship is also working to mobilize inter-city communities, matching need with resources. Contact Prison Fellowship, Community Mobilization, P.O. Box 17500, Washington, D.C. 20041.

When the slide presentation was over, there was a long, uncomfortable silence, as if each member had been seized with the same thought. One man spoke for everyone: "All of this has gone on and here we are planning to spend half a million dollars on a new building."

Another added in hushed tones, "How can we build a Cadillac when our brothers and sisters in Guatemala haven't even got a Volkswagen?"

Eastminster scrapped its plans and drawings, scaled down its expansion to $100,000 for a multi-purpose fellowship hall, and voted that the remaining $400,000 be sent to Guatemala along with a credit line for $500,000. Pastor Kik and two elders traveled to Guatemala to oversee the building of twenty-six village churches and twenty-eight parsonages.

But the requirement for individual cells within God's holy nation goes far beyong sharing financial resources; the church is called to give itself, to share in the hunger and pain of those in need.[10]

Jesus Himself shared the pain of the needy; He suffered for the entire world. As God's visible presence in the world today, should not His people also participate in the suffering of the world?

Most emphatically, yes. Not until we go where need is and share in the suffering of the poor, alienated, isolated, and downtrodden will the holy nation of God's people also become the loving nation.

As a small group of Christians in Jefferson City, Missouri, illustrates, this is indeed how the church loves God.

19

Shared Suffering

The shadow people made no noise in Jefferson City. They appeared for a day or two, spent little money, then drifted away. They slept under bridges, on park benches, in empty parking lots; in fact, they slept anywhere they could.

While the citizens of Jefferson City knew about these shadows, they didn't think much about them, for they had no real link to the "normal" life of this city in the middle of Missouri in the middle of the Midwest.

Jeff City is a state capital of neat shops, quiet streets, area universities. The shining legislature building, modeled after the U.S. Capitol, sits on a high bluff overlooking the Missouri River. The town of 35,000 is sprinkled with churches.

But if you follow East High Street for a few blocks from downtown, then turn left, you come face to face with a high, gray wall spiked with guard towers. This wall encloses the forty-seven acres of the Missouri State Penitentiary; along with the three other prisons in Jefferson City, this maximum security facility holds half of Missouri's prison population.

Most of these prisoners never see a visitor. They are lost to the world, hidden from sight and memory. The few whose families do visit have the best chance of staying out of prison once they're released. So prison authorities encourage visitation.

The shadow people were the wives, children, girlfriends, parents — the families who did come to visit. They came from St. Louis and Kansas City, miles away, or from smaller towns scattered across the state. Most of them lived on welfare checks, and if they used up their meager funds just getting to Jeff City, they certainly couldn't afford to pay for lodging.

So those who managed to come invented ways to pass the night. Like the woman who took the last possible Greyhound from Kansas City so she arrived at Jefferson City's grimy bus station at two in the morning. She then carried her six-month-old baby a few blocks to a downtown hotel, sneaked through the lobby into a rest room, wedged herself and her baby into a toilet stall, and passed the hours until eight in the morning when the prison opened for visitors. As long as she kept the baby quiet, nobody bothered her, and she felt safe. As safe as a shadow.

Others were not so safe — like the two women who, with their two small children, timed their drive from a tiny upstate town so they arrived a little after nightfall. They then drove to one of the area's many bridges — four rivers converge in Jeff City — and pulled under the shelter of the arches. Out of sight of the highway, with all four doors locked, they felt fairly secure. But they took turns sleeping in two-hour shifts, just in case.

For the most part, the shadow people weren't molested. But they felt thoroughly unwelcome in a strange city, without a place to sleep, a warm meal, or a place to shower and change clothes. They felt they were being punished along with their imprisoned loved ones.

But shadows aren't really invisible, and someone had begun to notice them as more than a nuisance or necessary evil. A group of concerned individuals from some of the area churches and civic organizations began wondering what they could do to help these obviously needy people. A study group began meeting once a month to discuss the problem, but a year passed without action.

Meanwhile, another group — Prison Fellowship volunteers already involved working with prisoners — was talking about the biblical mandate to help "the strangers among us" and were concerned about Jeff City's shadow people. So they began inviting inmates' families to their homes. It was a start, but soon proved inadequate for the need; there were just too many visitors.

Then one volunteer, Janice Webb, began to get big ideas. A Baptist laywoman active with Prison Fellowship for several years, Janice had learned about a West Virginia hospitality house for inmates' families. Used to mobilizing people for action, Janice thought, "Why couldn't a house like that work in Jefferson City?"

About the same time, Sister Ruth Heaney, a nun who served on a criminal justice commission and was also in the civic study group, contacted Janice Webb. In Sister Ruth's opinion, Janice was "the only logical person to get the job done."

In May, 1980, the two women formed the Agape House Board, deciding on a name before they had any place to put it: *Agape* because they wanted to "show the unconditional, caring love of Jesus"; and *House* because they wanted a "place that would show that love."

The board was made up of Catholics, Presbyterians, Episcopalians, Methodists, and Baptists; they united to attack the problem with gusto. Gusto was all they had at the time, for as Janice wryly recalls, "We didn't have a nickel in the bank; the whole thing was a venture of faith."

But faith along with enthusiasm got the job done. First they stumbled across an old rooming house just two blocks from the Missouri State Penitentiary; the place had nearly a dozen bedrooms, three kitchens, and a price tag of $46,000. In just six weeks the board raised the $5,000 down payment and a Christian attorney donated his legal services to manage the transaction.

The board members and their churches and families moved into the musty old house like a liberating army — hammering, sawing, painting, patching, cleaning. Five churches divided up the upstairs bedrooms. The Presbyterians' fresh wallpaper and rocking chair in one were rivaled by the Methodists' respackled ceiling, bright trim, and dried flower arrangements in another.

Downstairs, Sister Ruth coaxed hanging plants into life to fill a bright bay window. The long stairwell was festooned with big banners brightly decorated with Scripture verses; a huge family Bible graced the foyer sideboard. Two youths from an area Catholic high school arrived one Saturday armed with a rug shampooer that attacked the acres of ancient carpet. A group of fourth graders sent freshly baked cookies to treat the troops. And one small church made a particularly significant contribution — a continuing supply of toilet paper for Agape House.

But the board knew that creating their house of love was more than just a matter of appearance. Scripture verses on the walls would not bring Scripture alive. The home would live up to its name only if the people who ran it lived up to its name.

Sister Ruth Heaney was willing to serve as the first assistant manager, and for the crucial role of house manager the board found Mildred Taylor, a small, quiet, thoroughly Southern Baptist lady waiting at her home in South Carolina for God's call to service. She was ready for whatever He had for her in Missouri.

On November 2, 1980, Mildred Taylor welcomed the first guests to Agape House, warmly offering them New Testaments along with clean sheets and towels and room keys. The charge was $3.00 a night — if they could afford it. If not, they could stay for free.

Without money, detailed studies, proposals, conferences, or government grants, the people of God reached out to the poor and those in prison. Though initially skeptical, most of the citizens of Jefferson City were happy about the house. And soon the word began to spread to the people who were no longer shadows.

New smells filled the old rooming house: fresh paint, beans or macaroni or hot dogs cooking on the kitchen stove; cigarette smoke and nail polish. New sounds filled it, too: women talking, laughing, crying; children playing and giggling.

And at night the murmur of conversation could be heard in the small apartment at the back of the big house. For from the beginning, manager Mildred Taylor made it clear to guests that the door to her quarters was always open. As the months passed, increasing numbers sought her out for a cup of tea and a quiet chat.

One weekend guest who tapped on Mildred's door was a young mother visiting her son at one of the prisons. Sara didn't talk much, but seemed comforted just to sit with Mildred. As she prepared to leave on Sunday afternoon, Sara stopped at Mildred's apartment to give her a hug. "Thank you for having me here," she said. "You can't know how much this house means."

A few days later, Mildred received the following letter from Sara:

Dear Sister Mildred,
I told you how much staying at your house meant to me, but I did not tell you the most important thing. I read the Bible you gave me the very first night but was too sick and heavy-eyed to finish. I had been trying to reaffirm my faith for months. The next night I had $13 left to get home on and I saw that Shirley there was in greater need than I was so I gave her half of it because I knew God would provide. . . . Well, I went to bed feeling good that I could, with God's help, do something for someone. I read more of the Bible and got to the page where you say the prayer to get saved, and I prayed and was washed clean of my sins! I prayed a lot before I went to sleep.

Then the next day I told the Lord how sick and tired I was, and if it was His will that I might have a dry road home so it would not take me six hours. Before I went a mile the rain had stopped and I had sun all the way. I sang and praised God all the way home. The country had never looked so good.

Mildred Taylor eventually returned to South Carolina, hoping to start a ministry like Agape House in her hometown of Columbia. Because of her heavy workload with the Justice Commission, Sister Ruth also left, but remained on the board. They have been replaced by Marietta Borden, a lay volunteer with the Southern Baptist Home Mission Board, and Lunette Bouknight, a former nun who spent thirty-eight years in a Catholic convent.

When Marietta was called to come to Agape House, she left her home in New York and drove straight to Missouri with $500 in her pocket and everything she owned packed in her car.

Lunette first came to the house when her life-long friend Mildred was still there — to help for a month. "I got hooked," she explains. "I knew I could stay in the convent and save my soul. But if I wanted to do the perfect will of God, I knew I'd have to come out and minister to His people."

Lunette and Marietta share the house's small apartment and nearly everything else. They rise every morning at five to pray and study the Bible — first individually, then together. The rest of the day they respond to the needs around them — gathering soiled linens, emptying garbage, cleaning bathrooms, keeping finances straight, buying supplies, and registering guests. And they keep their apartment door open, just as Mildred Taylor did.

"We're in the business of planting seeds," Lu will say. "We don't know when a lot of them will be harvested, but that's God's business. We just do what we can."

Lu and Marietta don't see many dramatic conversions, and not everyone who comes to Agape recognizes their sacrifice and love for what it is. Some take the house simply as a cheap place to sleep. They pay — sometimes — and leave. Others wonder what the angle is, but accept the clean, warm comfort.

No matter, Lu and Marietta and all the others involved in the Agape House ministry want to provide love and care, not to calculate results. They are loving God.

The following vignette tells it all:

Sherry, a tall young woman with thick red hair and a serious manner, first heard about Agape House from her husband Al. She was getting ready to leave the prison visiting room early so she could catch the bus back to St. Louis before dark, when he mentioned a rooming house he had heard about from some other inmates whose wives and girlfriends had stayed there. "It's sort of a rooming house, but cleaner, with kitchen privileges," he said.

So Sherry walked over to the house, and though the place was just about full, the ladies in charge made a place for her. Now she was here for her third weekend and it seemed like home. Lu and Marietta welcomed her warmly, asked about Al, and bustled around with clean sheets and a readiness to talk and laugh. Sherry had put her things in a room upstairs, made up her bed, then started her dinner. She was sitting with a group at the big dining room table, engrossed in writing her nightly letter to Al while the others ate and chattered, when Jane's shrill voice called to her from the kitchen.

"Sherry," Jane screeched, "you'd best get out here and turn the heat down on them beans if you're serious 'bout eatin' 'em."

Sherry flicked her hair out of her eyes, threw down her pen, and got up from the table. Jane was right; the pork and beans were stuck to the bottom of the pan, but she was so hungry she didn't care. She ladled the unburnt beans onto a large plastic plate from the cupboard, grabbed her Pepsi from the refrigerator, and rejoined the group in the dining room.

Patty, her blond hair coiled on bright pink curlers, was telling a story while she finished applying the dark red polish to her pointed fingernails. Marcia held her daughter on her lap and spooned carrots and mashed potatoes into the small mouth, while next to her Brenda plaited little LaVon's wiry black hair.

Sherry finished her beans, pushed the plate away, and lighted a cigarette. *You'd think this was Saturday night at a neighborhood gathering if you didn't know every last person here has a husband or father two blocks away locked up in the state pen*, she laughed to herself. And even these women were a tough bunch. Patty had served a couple prison terms and now tended bar at a beer joint in Kansas City. Her husband was a lifer. Marcia's son was in for dope. Sherry didn't know much about Brenda yet, for in the prison visiting room the blacks and whites kept pretty much apart. But she might find out more later that night when she shared a room with Brenda and her little girl.

Sherry watched Marietta come through the room carrying clean sheets and stop to compliment Patty on her neat nail-polish job. Sherry couldn't figure out what made these two ladies tick; she knew they were religious, of course. There were Bible verses everywhere, and they gave paperback New Testaments to everyone who came in. She hadn't looked at hers yet. With all the other things going on in her life she wasn't getting involved in religion. Not now anyway.

I do know one thing, though, she mused as she crushed out her cigarette. *If God is real and He is good, He must be something like these ladies at Agape House.*

20

The Church on the Front Lines

Agape House wonderfully illustrates the description once given the church by Archbishop of Canterbury and Bible commentator, William Temple: "the only cooperative society in the world that exists for the benefits of its non-members."* Too often, though, the church's strategy for reaching those who "don't belong" is exactly backward. Priority goes to constructing an attractive edifice in a location near a growing suburb and as far from crime-infested downtown as possible. Next come the committees organizing concerts, covered-dish suppers, Bible studies, slide shows, and the like. Then, with fresh welcome mat at the door, the members enthusiastically wait for all the lost and needy souls to come and join them.

Of course they never do. What the church attracts are the neighbors who are bored with their old church anyway, or those looking for a group

*An unexpected affirmation for the Agape House staff and board came in April, 1982, when President Reagan singled out Agape House as an example for the nation. Addressing a White House gathering of 150 religious leaders, the President commended the House as a prime example of volunteerism at work and captured the spirit of the Agape ministry when he summed up, "They provided bed and bath, but something deeper — the certainty that someone cares."

with a bit more "status." The folks "out there" have no interest in the handsome sanctuary and progressive programs and wouldn't feel comfortable inside no matter what wonderful attractions were offered. (And probably the church members wouldn't feel comfortable if they did come.)

The cultural barriers in our American society are imposing. Millions live in conditions unimaginable to the typical white, middle-class American congregation. The family in the ghetto, for example, lives a day at a time, often one welfare check away from disaster; and odds are it's a one-parent family with one or more of its members victims of one of the plagues epidemic in America's inner cities — child abuse, alcoholism, drug addiction, prostitution.

But when the church fails to break the barrier, both sides lose. Those who need the gospel message of hope and the reality of love, don't get it; and the isolated church keeps evangelizing the same people over and over until its only mission finally is to entertain itself.

Isn't it interesting that Jesus didn't set up an office in the temple and wait for people to come to Him for counseling? Instead, He went to them — to the homes of the most notorious sinners, to the places where he would most likely encounter the handicapped and sick, the needy, the outcasts of society.

I am not naive enough to think the church can bridge the cultural chasms overnight. But I do know we can come out of our safe sanctuaries and move alongside those in need and begin to demonstrate some caring concern. Our presence in a place of need is more powerful than a thousand sermons. *Being there* is our witness. And until we are, our orthodoxy and doctrine are mere words; our liturgies and gospel choruses ring hollow.

Agape House and ministries like it are taking the gospel to people wherever they are, meeting them at their point of need as Jesus taught us to do. As we love God through our love for others, seemingly insurmountable barriers fall before us, as I saw dramatically demonstrated during my first visit to the Indiana Penitentiary in 1981.

After speaking to more than two hundred inmates in the auditorium for a Prison Fellowship seminar,[†] I asked the warden to let us visit death

---

†We constantly encounter cultural obstacles in prison, too. For example, we draw twice as many inmates if we meet in the auditorium or mess hall instead of the chapel. Some of it is peer pressure, of course, and fear of being tagged "religious." But much of it is the association of the chapel with an "insensitive" church.

row. I knew things were tense there because Stephen Judy had just been executed (electrocuted). But I wanted to see two Christian inmates with whom I'd been corresponding. The warden agreed and invited a group of our volunteers to come along as well. So about twenty of us made our way through the maze of concrete cellblocks to the double set of barred doors that led into the most despairing of all places — death row — the end of the line where men live for years from appeal to appeal. The only way out is a new trial or death.

The warden opened the individual cell doors, and one by one the men drifted out, slowly mixing with our volunteers and gathering in a circle on the walkway.

I was especially glad to meet Richard Moore, whose wife had written me such moving letters, and James Brewer, a young black man who, though seriously ill with a kidney disease, was a powerful witness to the others on death row. Whether his death would come swiftly by several thousand volts of electricity or slowly by uremic poisoning, James was at perfect peace with God and his warm smile showed it.

Nancy Honeytree, the talented gospel singer who often goes with us into the prisons, played her guitar and sang a few songs. I spoke briefly. Then we all joined hands and sang "Amazing Grace." (Nowhere do the words of that hymn have richer meaning than among a group of society's despised outcasts condemned to die for the most awful crimes.)

My schedule was extremely tight, so after we finished "Amazing Grace" we said our good-byes and began filing out. We were crowded into the caged area between the two massive gates when we noticed one volunteer had stayed back and was with James Brewer in his cell. I went to get the man because the warden could not operate the gates until we had all cleared out.

"I'm sorry, we have to leave," I said, looking nervously at my watch, knowing a plane stood waiting at a nearby airstrip to fly me to Indianapolis to meet with Governor Orr. The volunteer, a short white man in his early fifties, was standing shoulder to shoulder with Brewer. The prisoner was holding his Bible open while the older man appeared to be reading a verse.

"Oh, yes," the volunteer looked up. "Give us just a minute, please. This is important," he added softly.

"No, I'm sorry," I snapped. "I can't keep the governor waiting. We must go."

"I understand," the man said, still speaking softly, "but this is important. You see, I'm Judge Clement. I'm the man who sentenced James here to die. But now he's my brother and we want a minute to pray together."

I stood frozen in the cell doorway. It didn't matter who I kept waiting. Before me were two men: one was powerless, the other powerful; one was black, the other white; one had sentenced the other to death. Anywhere other than the kingdom of God, that inmate might have killed that judge with his bare hands — or wanted to anyway. Now they were one, their faces reflecting an indescribable expression of love as they prayed together.

Though he could hardly speak, on the way out of the prison Judge Clement told me he had been praying for Brewer every day since he had sentenced him four years earlier.

After we left the prison, the judge cancelled his court calendar for the next morning and spent the day in the Prison Fellowship seminar. His testimony — and the story of his meeting with Brewer, which quickly spread through the prison grapevine — brought dozens of men to Christ.

Taking the gospel to people wherever they are — death row, the ghetto, or next door — *is frontline evangelism.* Frontline love. *It is our one hope for breaking down barriers and for restoring the sense of community, of caring for one another,* that our decadent, impersonalized culture has sucked out of us. It is the most urgent challenge for the holy nation, the fifth and perhaps most important principle.

One other story from our ministry underscores this point.

In November, 1981, Prison Fellowship brought to Atlanta, Georgia, six inmates from Florida's Eglin Prison. The six were on two-week furlough and stayed in the homes of Fellowship volunteers. (Significantly, none of the families who agreed to take inmates into their homes asked the color of their skin or the nature of the crimes of which they had been convicted. Two of the men were black, two were white, and two were Hispanic.)

Each morning the six men gathered with Fellowship instructors in a small room at the Georgia Avenue Presbyterian Church, a red brick Victorian structure that only a generation ago towered over the quiet tree-lined streets of the Grant Park area; now the old church was nearly abandoned, a victim of Atlanta's sprawling urban decay.

After their Bible study the men descended upon the homes of two elderly widows in the neighborhood. Crawling in the mud underneath the small frame houses, they put in insulation; they did weatherstripping, caulking, and painting. Their work was part of our community service project program, initiated to show that non-violent inmates could be used to perform worthwhile community projects rather than sitting in a prison cell at a cost of $17,000 per year per inmate to the taxpayer. For we believe restitution, not prison, is the biblical prescribed form of punishment for these kinds of offenses.[‡]

The program was a great success and without incident. Two widows' homes were winterized for a fraction of the estimated cost of $20,000 and without government red-tape and bureaucratic bungling.[§] But the real significance of the project went far beyond a demonstration of a useful alternative to prison. The real story is what happened in the lives of the people and the community. . . .

One of the widows, Roxie Vaughn, eighty-three years old and blind, was elated when informed that her tiny two-room house had been chosen for the project; the thin, shingle-covered walls barely kept out the chilling winter winds, and each month half of her social security check went to pay for fuel for the one space heater in her living room.

But, when Roxie learned the work was to be done by six inmates, she was terrified; her home had been broken into four times in the prior two years. One can only try to imagine what fear that would mean for an elderly blind woman living alone. However, she finally agreed to have the men come.

By the second day, Roxie had invited the men in for cookies and milk. Then they began to pray together each day. And before the first week was over, Roxie and the six men were fast friends. An Atlanta TV crew, having heard about the project, captured an unforgettable scene:

[‡]See Exodus 21. The Bible continually mandates restitution for property offenses. The Old Testament contains repeated references; and in the New Testament is found the example of Zacchaeus giving back fourfold what he had wrongly taken. Nowhere in Scripture are prisons instituted as punishment for crimes. They are referred to as places for detaining people and for political purposes. The use of prisons for rehabilitation or punishment following conviction is a very recent invention, the result of Quaker-initiated reforms two centuries ago. The word "penitentiary" comes from the Quaker idea that the criminal needed to be penitent and repent and reform themselves. The first state prison in America was the Walnut Street Jail in Philadelphia, Pennsylvania, opened in 1790.

[§]The program drew national attention and has been duplicated many times since. For further information contact: Justice Fellowship, P.O. Box 17500, Washington, D.C., 20041.

Roxie playing her small electric organ with the six convicts standing behind her, singing. The song? "Amazing Grace," of course.

Georgia Avenue Church hosted the closing services from which the men were to be returned to prison. People came from all over Atlanta, black and white, rich and poor, famous and forgotten. Folks were there from the twelve churches of different denominations and four local Christian groups that had sponsored the project with Prison Fellowship, most of them working together for the first time. The gathering was like a fresh breeze blowing through the musty, dark sanctuary.

There were some tears. The youngsters of one host family kept saying, "Mommy, don't let Bob go back to prison." And when the men told the congregation what the two weeks had meant to them and when the widows were introduced and some of the volunteers spoke, eyes throughout the audience were wet.

The dilapidated, neglected old church seemed to stand tall against the gray November sky that Saturday afternoon, as if swelling with pride and joy because at last it was doing what it was meant to do.

It is the nature of man to organize. Probably since the Tower of Babel we have been setting up hierarchies, organizational flow charts, orders of authority, and all the other structural schemes dreamed up through the ages. The more advanced the civilization, the more refined the organizational schemes.

However, though structures are essential to hold society together, they are there to serve, not be served. The marvels of modern technology have produced a sophistication in systems and structures that encourages what Jacques Ellul, the French historian, calls the "political illusion," the misguided belief that all problems can be solved by structures — namely, institutions.[1] So for each new problem, a new institution is created.

Unfortunately this mentality has invaded the church, and we treat it as a structure (and just another one of many in society at that) dependent on charts and manuals and plans and computer print-outs.

But the true church is not held together by any structure man creates; it is not an organization. It is alive, its life breathed into it by a sovereign God. Its heart beats with God's heart. It is one with Him and moves as His Spirit moves — where He chooses and often against the designs of man.

The life function of this living organism is to love the God who created it — to care for others out of obedience to Christ, to heal those who hurt, to take away fear, to restore community, to belong to one another, to proclaim the Good News while living it out. The church is the invisible made visible.

I witnessed this when I was in prison. A few of us began meeting each night to pray, read the Bible, and support each other. From that grew a Bible study. Others became involved, men gave their lives to Christ, and attendance in the prison chapel increased. This was not the clever strategy of men, but the Spirit of God at work — and in a place where faith and religion are mocked, believers sometimes persecuted.

My experience pales beside that of the believers in my next story. But perhaps because of my prison experience, and the evidence of the power of the Spirit, without human intervention, I have been inspired by this group of men who found that, indeed, the gates of hell itself cannot prevail against His church....

21

This Is My Body

This was Captain Jeff Powell's forty-second career mission, He was flying about thirty miles southeast of Hanoi in an F-105 Thunderchief, a supersonic aircraft carrying almost half its weight in munitions. His target was a bridge, a vital North Vietnamese supply line between the Haiphong harbor and the Ho Chi Minh Trail.

Powell let down through a 10,000-foot cloud ceiling, sighted the objective, did a roll-in, and released his stores. Half the cement span distintegrated. When he tried to pull out of the maneuver, the controls wouldn't respond.

This isn't possible, he thought. I *didn't hear anything*.

The sky around him turned a bright white as the fuel tank under the left wing exploded. He was forced to eject before he could radio anyone.

A month later, stripped of his survival gear, blindfolded, trussed with wire, Jeff Powell was being marched through the jungles and rural villages of North Vietnam by night, his captors traveling under cover of darkness to avoid being spotted by American bombers or rescue planes. At one point, nauseous and feverish, he was hung from a banana tree in a large village as the star attraction in a circus of mockery. He was stoned and urinated on by the villagers. Later propaganda movies and photographs were taken of him being marched under the gun-toting guard of a little girl dressed in pajamas.[1]

THE GULF OF TONKIN, ONE MONTH LATER . . .

Captain Terry Jones had survived the destruction of his F-4 Phantom II by a surface-to-air missile, ejecting only after trying every emergency procedure to regain control of his plane. As he floated downward he knew that his only injury was a cut on the arm, but he was terrified. Beneath him, excited villagers and militiamen were gathering in a rice paddy. Some brandished what looked like sticks or machetes; others carried guns.

As Jones looked upward at his parachute and the sky, he wondered, *Did the flight leader see me go down?* Below him, the shouts grew louder.

Six weeks later, Terry Jones was in a bamboo cage in the jungle, lying on his stomach with his feet in wooden stocks, his arms tied behind him with wet ropes. Following this torturous confinement he was taken to a temple near a rice paddy where he was turned over to a North Vietnamese officer who had with him another American pilot dressed in native garb. Jones' countryman had obviously been on the road longer than he — was heavily bearded and emaciated.* The officer told the two prisoners that they would be taken to Hanoi and that if they tried to communicate with each other, they would be executed.

HANOI, THE SAME YEAR . . .

Thus Jeff Powell and Terry Jones, and many others like them, came together to a place the American airmen called the Hanoi Hilton. It was a triangular building the size of a city block, surrounded by a dry moat and twenty-foot walls studded with sharp hunks of glass and topped with electrified barbed wire. The prison had been built by the French during their occupation of Vietnam; there was still a guillotine in the basement.

On the streets surrounding the prison, bicycles darted back and forth and truck horns blared. Inside, from the cellblock called Heartbreak, a prisoner in solitary confinement could be heard crying, "Oh God!" Because he would not give his captors information beyond his name, rank, serial number, and date of birth, he had been bent over backwards

---

*At that point, Captain Powell weighed about 110 pounds and Captain Jones had already lost about forty pounds.

and tied so that his spine threatened to snap like a dry stick at any moment.

Jeff and Terry both went through Heartbreak — everybody did — were classified, then moved to another area of the Hilton. Some prisoners were sent to outlying prison camps. The frequency and severity of the torture depended on a prisoner's rank and the quality of information he could give the enemy.

ALONE, 1966–1970 . . .

Major James Kasler arrived at the Hilton with a broken thighbone sticking into his groin. He was beaten from 6:00 A.M. to 10:00 P.M., each hour, for days on end. His head was smashed and his buttocks ripped to hamburger with fan belts. His mouth was so badly bruised that he could not open it, and one of his eardrums was ruptured. But Kalser found that when he recited the Lord's Prayer, concentrating intently upon it, he was able to block out the pain for a time.

Norman McDaniel knew that it was 5:30 A.M. because the morning gong had sounded and the camp's p.a. system was blaring the "voice of Vietnam" broadcast, nicknamed Hanoi Hannah by the Americans. McDaniel folded his mosquito netting and blotted out the propaganda with a verse he remembered from his youth: "Lo, I am with you always, even unto the end of the world."

Captain James Ray, shot down on Mother's Day, 1966, had been in solitary confinement for two years. Each day's menu consisted of two servings of pumpkin soup with a lump of pig fat in it. He shared his cell with ants, lizards, mosquitoes, and flies. It would have been easy to lose his faith, but sometimes, mysteriously, he felt he was not alone. His family and the people in his church back home in Texas were praying for him.

THE BODY INVISIBLE . . .

From inside his cell at Heartbreak, Howard Rutledge could hear the guard walking through the corridor and methodically unlocking the thick teak doors of the cells. Rutledge counted to three, and then it was his turn. The key turned and the door swung open. Rutledge knelt down, as if to genuflect in front of his captor, and grasped the two bowls of rations that were placed on the grimy cement floor in front of him. After receiving the food, he stood at attention in front of the guard; he would be punished if he did not. When the door closed, a waft of air bearing the odor of excrement took away what appetite he had. He sat on his cement-slab bed and kept one hand over his bowl of sewer greens to keep the cockroaches out of it. When he chewed on the hard bread, bits of sand imbedded in the dough crunched between his teeth.

The guard came to the door again and the first of Rutledge's two daily meals was finished. A gong sounded, signaling that it was time to lie down for two hours. Periodically a guard pacing the corridor would open the Judas hole in the cell door to make certain he was prone. He dozed until another gong sounded, the one that forbade him to lie down; now he had to stand or sit for seven more hours.

Rutledge heard a soft whistle from the cell across from his. It was Harry Jenkins whistling "Mary Had a Little Lamb," the signal that he wished to communicate.

Rutledge placed his bare feet on the cement slabs on either side of his cell and boosted himself up to the metal-barred window above the door.

"Howard," Jenkins whispered.

"I'm here," whispered Rutledge.

"I remembered another story," said Jenkins quickly.

"What is it?"

"Ruth and Naomi. How Naomi lost everything she had — her husband, her sons, and her land."

"I remember some of it."

"Ruth was Naomi's daughter-in-law. Ruth was faithful to Naomi and stayed with her. They went to a foreign land."

"What happened?" Rutledge asked.

"I can't remember that."

A prisoner in a neighboring cell coughed, signaling that a guard was near. Rutledge climbed down from his perch.

He paced his cell, thinking of Jenkins' story. He tried to remember the name of the person who had helped Ruth and Naomi. Three hours later he was still going over the story in his mind. He had learned it in Sunday school when he was ten. He meditated on the story throughout the second and final meal of the day — seaweed soup and sowbelly fat.

"Hanoi Hannah" crackled to life on the loudspeakers at 8:30 P.M. for a bedtime propaganda story which lasted half an hour. When it was over, Rutledge climbed up to the opening again and whispered, "Jenkins."

A pause. Then, "What?"

"Boaz."

"I know. I just remembered."

Gradually communications between the prisoners improved. They made up a code based on Morse Code and communicated that way, with their ears to the walls and their bodies wrapped in blankets — if they had them — to keep the noise levels down. The alphabet was translated into a 5x5 dot matrix in which each letter was represented by the placement of vertical and horizontal wall taps. Once a prisoner knew the code, he was "on line." Via this network, the men recalled and taught each other Scripture and learned the names and serial numbers of every prisoner in the cellblock. They learned who had been transferred and who was being tortured; in this way they shared each other's pain.

On Sunday morning, when the guards gave them a chance, the senior officers in each cellblock thumped on the wall five times, alerting the prisoners in solitary as well as those who had cellmates, that it was time to worship. This signal was "church call."

Each man recited to himself the Lord's Prayer or the 23rd or 100th psalm. Then they had silent hymns and private prayers.

A new prisoner was stuck in solitary at the end of the building. Each morning he ran in place to keep in shape, shaking the entire structure. After the new man was taught the tap code, he began running in an odd, jerky way. Seven men at the other end of the cellblock deciphered the jogger's message: "I will lift up mine eyes to the hills from whence cometh my help. I will lift up mine eyes. . . ."

THE BODY VISIBLE . . .

After an unsuccessful American rescue attempt on November 21, 1970, the North Vietnamese decided for security reasons to move all the airmen in the outlying camps back to the Hanoi Hilton with the other prisoners. To make room for the influx, new cells were partitioned off; men were moved out of solitary into large, open, bay-typed cells that could accommodate forty, fifty, and sixty prisoners. The new cellblock was named Camp Unity. Unliked the cells in Heartbreak, the cells in Camp Unity had huge, high, barred windows that let in rivers of daylight.

Conditions improved somewhat. Occasionally the prisoners were let out for reasons other than interrogation or torture. Sometimes they did chores — anything was a relief to the boredom; they emptied the two-gallon toilet bucket, washed dishes and cleaned the courtyard. If they bathed or washed their own clothes, they usually had to use sewage.

For years these prisoners had asked for a Bible. Not until December, 1970, did they even see one. Then the English-speaking interrogator brought one into cell 4 and the men gathered around. Jeff Powell read the Christmas story aloud, then several psalms, then the Sermon on the Mount. The men were not sure how long they would have the Bible or whether they would ever see it again, so James Ray turned to 1 Corinthians 13 and memorized the chapter. The Bible was in the cell for two hours.

On the condition that the prisoners follow an approved format, the North Vietnamese allowed as many as twenty men at a time to gather for formal church services. This had to take place out in the courtyard, behind bamboo screens which obstructed their view of the other cells. There they worshiped while the English-speaking interrogator monitored everything they said and did.

On more than one occasion, the prisoners digressed from the "format" by reciting Scripture that had not been previously approved by the interrogator. When this happened, he pushed into the circle shaking his head furiously, and thrust the men back into their cells.

One Sunday morning James Ray called the men to order by leading them in singing the Doxology. He prayed, "We thank You, Lord, for Your protection and mercy. For bringing us together." Eight of the men then assembled in front of the group and sang, "Holy, holy, holy, Lord God almighty, early in the morning, my song shall rise to Thee."

The prisoners' obvious determination to worship caused repeated confrontations with their captors.

For example, a guard would hear the men singing hymns in their cell and would run for the English-speaking interrogator, who would order, "No political meetings."

"It isn't political."

"There are too many of you. You cannot hold a political meeting."

"Join us. Find out. This isn't a political meeting."

"We will throw you in solitary if you continue."

"Join us and see. This isn't a political meeting."

"No."

Eventually, despite solitary confinement, threats of torture, and harrassment, the captives wore down their captors and more freedom was given to those in Camp Unity.

In the spring of 1971 the North Vietnamese permitted three prisoners to copy the Bible for one hour a week. James Ray was one of the three. He sat on a wooden chair at a wooden table and began copying the Sermon on the Mount. The guard standing close by, watching, repeatedly placed his elbow on the verse Ray was trying to copy. When the guard moved his elbow, Ray wrote so fast his hand cramped. When the guard wasn't holding his elbow on the page, sometimes for up to fifteen minutes at a time, he was trying to distract Ray with inane questions. During the five weeks the program lasted, James Ray managed to copy much more than the Sermon on the Mount.

Each day when he brought the precious words back to the cell, Ray's cellmates recopied the words in the crude fashion they had devised for other writing: on toilet-paper rations with brick-dust ink and quill pens. They recopied the verses because each week Ray had to return his previous week's copy before he could transcribe more. The verses were also immediately memorized by different prisoners.

EASTER SUNDAY, 1971 . . .

Captain Tom Curtis woke up early and studied the notes and verses that he and James Ray had assembled the previous evening. Curtis looked at the roomful of sleeping prisoners around him. Twenty-eight men. All of them flyers. How had they managed to survive in this place?

The morning gong sounded just as sunlight struck the western wall of the cell. Several of the men limped or stretched painfully while getting up. Old wounds had not healed.

At about ten o'clock Curtis stood in front of the drab eastern wall and called the service to order. The men gathered in a semi-circle before him. It was Easter Sunday.

A quartet sang "The Old Rugged Cross" and then everyone joined in "Amazing Grace." Curtis recited the version of the passion of Christ that the men had patched together from somewhat faulty memories. "And when they had bound Him, they led Him away and delivered Him to Pontius Pilate. And they stripped Him and put a crown of thorns on His head, and spit on Him and hit Him. And they said, 'Crucify him.'"

As he listened to the familiar words, Curtis thought of the experiences they all had shared: being bound, chained, spit upon, whipped, lashed to trees, stoned. . . .

Then someone handed Curtis several pieces of bread that had been saved from their previous day's rations. "And He took the bread, and when He had given thanks, He broke it and gave it to His disciples, saying, 'Take, eat, this is My body that is broken for you. Do this in remembrance of Me.' "

The bread was passed and quietly eaten.

Then Curtis repeated the verses about the cup — "This is My blood shed for you."

These men know about blood, Curtis thought. Their own blood flowing from open wounds, from lacerations and ruptured eardrums, from torn-out fingernails — blood that seeped through every makeshift bandage. Now they thought about Christ's blood shed for them.

The cup of carefully saved seaweed soup was passed. Someone quietly hummed "Amazing Grace."

As Curtis brought the cup to his lips, he began to weep. He wondered if they had any right to identify their suffering with Christ's. But then wasn't their presence in this place, alive against all odds, a sign of Christ's continuing presence with them? He remembered that Christ had said He would found His church and the gates of hell would not prevail against it. They were part of that church, a part of the broken body of Christ in every way.

Yes, Christ had prevailed; for here they were, worshiping Him in the jungles of a world gone mad. Relying on Him, they had nothing less than the privilege of showing the Lord's death, burial, and resurrection — His presence, the church — in what otherwise was a living hell.

LOVING GOD

For whoever wants to save his life will lose it, but
whoever loses his life for me will find it.

Jesus, to His disciples

22

Life and Death

And so the church of Jesus Christ is vital and alive and changing the world — wherever individual believers obey Him, live out His Word, and love Him, whether it be in the Hanoi Hilton or in a dreary Georgia nursing home where I met a remarkable woman....

I had first heard about Myrtie Howell from an inmate in a New Hampshire prison when he wrote to ask those of us at Prison Fellowship headquarters to join in prayers for her health. The Fellowship had matched this man and Mrs. Howell up as pen pals, something we do with thousands of inmates and volunteers.

"Please pray for Grandma Howell," pleaded his childlike scrawl, "cause she's sick and may be going to die. Nobody has ever loved me like she has. I just wait for her letters, they means so much."

Our office staff began praying for Mrs. Howell. Then some months later, I received a letter from the woman herself reporting on the inmates she was corresponding with and telling me how each one was doing, about their morale and their problems.

She concluded: "Writing to inmates has filled my last days with joy." That was a cheerful thought. But then she added the ominous request that I come to speak at her funeral. She had instructed her pastor to notify me when the day came. "It won't help me," she wrote, "but it will wake up my church to the need of taking part in prison ministry."

I wrote back to Mrs. Howell, reminding her that the days of our lives are numbered by, and known only to, the Lord. Therefore I didn't feel I could make a commitment to preach at her funeral since nobody knew the date. . . . To say the least, it was a most awkward letter.

Over the next year, Myrtie's letters kept coming — always upbeat and usually enclosing what was literally her widow's mite (once she simply endorsed over a $67.90 U.S. Treasurer's check that was her supplemental income). In each letter she reported on "her boys" and frequently asked for more names to add to her correspondence list. At one point we tallied that she was actually writing to seventeen inmates. No small task for a ninety-one-year-old woman.

No small task for anyone, for just the thought of writing to prisoners scares most people, including Christians, half to death. They have visions of dangerous criminals getting their names and addresses and, once out of prison, tracking them down for nefarious purposes. Why was this elderly, obviously frail, woman different? Why, at ninety-one, did she care at all, yet alone so much?

I thought I might get my answer when a Prison Fellowship seminar and community rally was scheduled for Columbus, Georgia, in June, 1981. Columbus was Myrtie's home town. So I wrote and invited her to attend the rally. She replied immediately, explaining that since her hip had never healed from a fall, she couldn't move without a walker and wouldn't dare attempt a crowded auditorium.

"But," she wrote, "I have a great desire to meet you and I am claiming Psalm 37:4."* I stuck the letter in my briefcase without looking up the Scripture and kicked myself for being so insensitive as to suggest she attend a big public rally.

The day of the seminar and rally was a full schedule, as always, but that morning I knew I had to make time for one more thing. I just had to meet Myrtie Howell, this woman whose letters could call forth such concern from incarcerated men she had never met.

When I tracked her down, I found that Myrtie lived in an old soot-covered brick high-rise in downtown Columbus, an apartment building converted a few years earlier into a home for the aged. Inside, the lobby resembled the waiting room of a hospital, except more depressing. There were no ringing words of encouragement to break the tension of the place, no reassuring banter, no youthful voices, no hopeful expressions.

*"Delight yourself in the Lord and he will give you the desires of your heart."

Instead, I saw rows of wheelchairs lined in front of a blaring television set; bodies hunched about on pea-soup green plastic couches and overstuffed chairs with worn upholstery patterns long since erased. The sit-com soundtrack bounced harshly off garish yellow walls. Most of those turned to the set were either dozing or staring blankly. Others thumbed idly through magazines or watched the lobby door like sentries at their post. I felt chilled just walking across the lobby.

After signing in at the front desk, I rode the elevator to Myrtie's floor. The hallway was carpeted with a rippling, colorless, thread-bare strip that had seen years of scuffling footsteps.

At her door I knocked. "Come in, come in," a firm, strong voice shouted.

As I opened the unlocked door, I was greeted by a broad, welcoming smile as Myrtie leaned back in her rocker in satisfaction, her white fleecy hair neatly parted at the side. Her blue eyes sparkled behind thick, black-rimmed spectacles and her cheeks glowed with life. *This woman is not preparing to die*, I thought.

"S'cuse me for not getting up," she said, gesturing toward the walker alongside her chair. "Oh, I don't believe you are really here . . . I just don't believe it. It's so . . . the Lord does give us the desires of our heart." She kept grinning and rocking and I just had to lean over and hug her, experiencing that familiar affinity believers so often have on first meeting.

I took the armchair opposite her with its doily-decorated arms. Myrtie's apartment had one window and was no larger than a modest hotel room. It contained a bed, a 12-inch television set, a dresser, a mirror, the two chairs we sat in, and a fragile desk crowded with Bibles and commentaries and piled high with correspondence. Photographs lined the edges of the mirror hanging just above the desk. I'd seen cells with more amenities.

Unlike her surroundings, Myrtie looked almost regal, her hands folded in her lap and her shoulders proud beneath her shawl.

I started to thank her for her faithful ministry, but before I could finish my first sentence, Myrtie waved her hand, started grinning again, and interrupted with a protest.

"Oh, no, you've helped me. These last years have been the most fulfilling of my whole life. I thank you — and most of all I thank Jesus," the last word pronounced with great reverence.

And I knew that Myrtie, despite living alone in this dreary place, crippled and in continuous pain, really did mean what she said. I was already sensing a spiritual depth to this woman that I'd not often encountered. I asked her to tell me about her life and her spiritual journey.

Born in Texas in 1890, Myrtie was brought to Columbus, Georgia, at the age of three; at ten she went to work in the mill for ten cents a day.

"We was raised poor," she said, explaining that she had had only one year of schooling. Her parents gave her little in the way of religious education, but from the age of ten on she knew there was a God, felt He had His hand on her, and knew she would "do best to obey Him." At the age of sixteen she joined a Christian church.

Married at seventeen, she had her first child the next year and two more in rapid succession. Her middle child, a son, died at the age of two. Indeed, the deaths of her closest relatives proved the crucible for Myrtie's faith. During the late 1930s, Myrtie's mother and her husband's father lived with them. In mid-December of 1939, Myrtie's mother died. Then in mid-January Myrtie's husband was killed in an accident; two weeks later her father-in-law died as well.

Tears brimmed in Myrtie's eyes she recalled to me, "I felt like Job. I just felt like old Satan had a conversation with the Lord and said if the Lord would just let him get that Myrtie he'd make her give the Lord up. But it only made me lean more closer, more to Him."

The death of her husband resulted in the loss of her home also, and Myrtie had to go back to work to support herself. At first she did "practical work," piece work from the mill, and then "for two years I run a dress shop. And then I run a little cafe. I always been doin' somethin' to take care of myself. I didn't want to get on with the children or nothin' like that." So Myrtie worked until her advanced age and declining health forced her to move into, as she put it, "this old folk's home."

The death of her youngest son, her "baby boy," the declining health of her oldest, and her own move into the home sent Myrtie into a spiritual depression. So many of her loved ones had died and she "couldn't do" for those who remained; she felt she had nothing left to live for. She wanted to die.

"Lord, what more can I do for You?" she prayed with all her heart one day. "If You're ready for me, I'm ready to come. I want to die. Take me."

"I knew I was dying," she continued. "But then He spoke to me as clear as be: WRITE TO PRISONERS. Three words: WRITE TO PRISONERS. Imagine that! I want to die, figure I'm about to, and the Lord say, 'Okay now, Myrtie, you go back and write to prisoners.'

"He couldn't of spoke to me any clearer if'n He'd been standing before me. And I was afraid at first. I said, 'Lord, me write to prisoners? I ain't got no education, had to teach myself to read and write. And I don't know nuthin' bout prisons.'

"But there wasn't no doubt. I would have squirmed out of His hand if I hadn't obeyed. I had to."

Myrtie's call became even more miraculous to my mind when she told me that at the time she'd never heard of Prison Fellowship or any other prison ministry. She had never given such a task the merest thought.

But she was faithful to God's command and acted on the best plan she could think of. She knew there was a penitentiary in Atlanta, so she wrote there, the envelope addressed simply, "Atlanta Penitentiary, Atlanta, Georgia." Inside her message read:

> Dear Inmate,
> I am a Grandmother who love and care for you who are in a place you had not plans to be.
> My love and sympathy goes out to you. I am willing to be a friend to you in correspondent.
> If you like to hear from me, write me. I will answer every letter you write.
>
> A Christian friend,
> Grandmother Howell

The letter must have been passed on to the prison chaplain, for Myrtie received eight names of prisoners to whom she was invited to write. Chaplain Ray, who carries on an extensive prison ministry, sent her additional names, as did Prison Fellowship when we were put in contact with her.

Myrtie has subsequently corresponded with hundreds of inmates, up to forty at a time, becoming a one-woman ministry reaching into prisons all over America.

Her strategy is simple: "When I get a letter, I read it, and when I answer it, I pray: 'Lord, You know what You want me to say. Now say it through me.' And you'd be surprised sometimes at the letters He writes!

"His Spirit works. I obey. I don't put anything in there that I feel's of self, of flesh. As He gives me, I write it.

"But the real blessings, they're in the answers," she said, reaching over to the stack of letters piled on her desk, within arm's reach of her chair. "Just look at these," she said, grinning and handing me a packet. As I scanned the pages, phrases leaped out at me:

> Dear Grandmother . . . was very happy to get your letter . . . the guys kidded me when they said I had a letter . . . I didn't believe them,

but it was true ... I don't have anyone to care about me but the Lord and you ... I'm in the hole now, that's why I can write letters ... Why am I so afraid, grandmother? Why doesn't God answer my prayers about this? ... I am really glad to know that there is someone out there who cares ... I will remember you in my prayers every night starting now and for the rest of my life ... please write back soon ... love, Joe ... in the love of Jesus, David. ...

One letter, signed "Granddaughter Janice," read:

Dear Grandmother,

I received your letter and it made me sad when you wrote that you think you may not be alive much longer. I thought that I would wait and come to see you and then tell you all you have meant to me, but now I've changed my mind. I'm going to tell you now.

You've given me all the love and concern and care that I've missed for years and my whole outlook on life has changed. You've made me realize that life is worth living and that it's not all bad. You claim it's all God's doing but I think you deserve the credit.

I didn't think I was capable of feeling love for anyone again but I know I love you as my very own precious grandmother.

"Bless you, Myrtie," I said, putting the stack of letters back on the desk.

"Oh, the Lord has just blessed me so wonderful, Mr. Colson. I've had the greatest time of my life since I've been writing to prisoners.

"And you know, once I turned over my life to Him — I mean, really did it — He took care of all my needs. Things go right before I even think about 'em."

After I asked about the Bible commentaries on her desk, Myrtie told me how she spends her days. She said she doesn't "do much of anything" but write to prisoners, read and study the Bible, pray, watch a few religious programs on TV and "be carried" to and from the common dining room where she takes her meals. Myrtie insisted that time passed faster and more joyously for her now than it ever did before.

As our time together drew to a close, Myrtie gave me a final bit of advice: "So, now, Mr. Colson, you just keep remembering the Lord don't need no quitters. Once in a while old Satan tells me I'm getting too old, don't remember things good ... had to agree with him there. ... But we mustn't listen to him. First thing you know he'll turn us around every which way. So I just keep remembering what the Lord told me and I can't quit," quickly adding with an admonitary gesture toward me, "and neither can you."

With that, Myrtie Howell gave me her wonderful grin again, exuding the joy of life lived to the fullest.

We prayed together, hugged one more time, and I promised we'd see each other again, holding to that marvelous thought C.S. Lewis was so fond of: Christians never have to say good-by.

Two Prison Fellowship volunteers were waiting at the desk downstairs to take me to my next meeting. As we reached the front door, I felt compelled to turn and take one more look at that lobby. No, the scene hadn't changed.

Keeping my voice low, I said, "Look at that. Nothing left — "

"But to wait for the bodies to be carried out," one of my companions added, his expression quickly turning somber as he realized his bad joke was no joke at all.

All at once I was overwhelmed by the sad scene before me — the mirthless pit of depression, despair, emptiness. There was no joy in any of their expressions. Instead, their sunken eyes seemed to reflect a raging anger: anger that their families had left them there; anger that fate had dealt them cruel blows; anger that their minds were weak and their bones brittle; anger that their favorite TV program was interrupted or that someone else was served ahead of them at lunch. And jealously, too, that someone less deserving than themselves might survive and watch them being carried off through that lobby door — unless, that is, they could hold on long enough to relish the sight of that someone being carried out first.

My heart ached for these pathetic figures, clinging so desperately to something they never had, seeking to save a life that for so many had been only a cruel hoax: seventy or eighty or ninety years of joy, defeat, pain, and pleasure and then just sitting, waiting, for darkness to come. Waiting. Waiting — for this meaningless existence to end. And what was beyond? Nothing? Or more of this hell? If there is no God, or if He can't be known, then why live at all?

Meanwhile, upstairs, sat Myrtie Howell with her wide ninety-one-year old grin of joy and triumph. Ready to live. Ready to die. By now she was probably back at her desk WRITING TO PRISONERS!

But Myrtie, too, had known the hell this world can be. She had known loneliness, pain, being unloved, loss of home and family, drudgery of menial tasks to survive.

The difference was that Myrtie had recognized the vanity and purposelessness of life without God; the emptiness of life lived for self. She understood the futility of being unable to answer the questions: why was I born? why have I lived? where am I going? So she had cried out to God to lead her out of that hell in the only way anyone has ever escaped — by giving up her life to gain His life. Yes, Myrtie long ago had learned life's central paradox.

I turned away from that dreary lobby and passed through the doors into the warm June day. The air was fresh, clean, and I took several deep breaths to clear my head. But I could not clear away the memories of that day — nor would the passage of time. For in that Georgia nursing home God gave me an unforgettable vision of heaven and hell. The heaven of life with God. The hell of life without Him.

And God gave me the final link in my search to learn what loving God really means: Myrtie Howell. To believe, to repent, to obey, to be holy, to bind up the brokenhearted, and to serve.

Myrtie Howell knew all about *loving* God.

In the Arena: An Allegory

Late one spring evening I was in my library thumbing through the final draft of this manuscript. After months of work I was at last satisfied with the flow of logic and principles in the book; and I was especially happy with the concluding chapter. Myrtie Howell surely exemplified what *Loving God* is all about, a fitting end to a well-ordered book.

Occupied with my thoughts, I leaned back in my worn leather desk chair, hands clasped behind my head, and thought about the people whose stories I'd told. Scenes from my own life passed through my mind as well as I reflected on my spiritual pilgrimage, my beginnings, my journey thus far.

I don't know how long my thoughts drifted, but my reverie was suddenly interrupted by the shrill ring of the desk telephone. The caller was Dave Chapman, an old friend living in another state. Dave brushed aside my greetings and announced he was in town, at the airport, with several hours to spare before he had to catch a late flight out to the West Coast. He insisted he had to see me.

Within twenty minutes I heard a car pull into the driveway, then the slam of a door and the jab of the doorbell.

Dave looked the same as ever — sandy-haired, deeply tanned, with the kind of boyish good looks that can see a man from thirty to sixty without much change. He was dressed in his usual style, too—light oatmeal suit, oxford-cloth shirt, silk tie, and tasseled loafers.

I escorted Dave into my library and gave him the straight-backed, maple chair across the desk from me. He said he'd only stay for a few minutes, but that chair would help him keep his word.

"Okay, Dave, what's going on?" I asked, fighting the urge to yawn. I didn't bother clearing away the mound of paper between us, the cleanly typed final chapters of *Loving God*.

Dave started like a fighter coming out of his corner at the sound of the bell. He was so excited his sentences collided into one another; and he kept thrusting his index finger down on my desktop as he made his points, as a skilled lawyer might do on the mahogany rail of the jury box.

The Dave Chapman I'd known casually was a calm, successful businessman, not the kind of person to get so worked up. Conservative, perhaps a bit uptight, but certainly not a dynamo. What could have happened to change him so? He was animated, alive, with a self-assurance that was remarkable—despite the personal dilemma he was telling me about that now threatened his business, the political power he'd recently acquired, his friends, and everything he had considered important. His voice was strong, his eyes determined. I was mesmerized.

"Wait a minute. Slow down." I exclaimed, coming straight up in my chair. "I want the whole story, beginning to end. Take your time but tell it all."

And for the next two hours I listened, enthralled, as Dave Chapman related the remarkable events of his life over the last few years. When he finished, explaining his dilemma, Dave leaned as far back as the straight-backed chair would allow and waited for my response. But all I could do was stare at the mounds of paper on my desk.

"Well, what do you think?" he finally asked.

"What do I think? You want to know what I think?" I exclaimed. "I think you've just rewritten the ending of my book!"

For, of course, he had. As much as I wanted to leave my book with its orderly flow of logic and theological soundness, concluding with the poignant but triumphant story of Myrtie Howell, life isn't like a book. Life isn't logical or sensible or orderly. Life is a mess most of the time. And theology must be lived in the midst of that mess.

Authors can write books about God and man, but for all their illustrations and interpretations, it is no more than opinion from the bleachers unless it is lived. And life is not lived in the bleachers, but on the muddy fields by human beings who get bloody and bruised and who contend for the score to their last gasp.

So I decided to end this book with Dave Chapman.

Dave is nobody special. Well, actually that's not true. He's me; he's you; he's dozens of people you and I know—no hero or saint in the world's terms, no spiritual expert. Dave Chapman's story is our story; his struggles and decisions confront each of us every day. So I tell you his story—as I remember it—as he told it to me as the hours passed and that spring twilight darkened into night. I don't know whether Dave ever caught his plane that night. As a matter of fact, I haven't seen him since.

Dave's story began on a warm summer evening in 1979....

He was late coming home. Though Dave owned his own accounting firm representing several of the largest businesses in the state, it really didn't require his working day and night any longer. But these gatherings of his wife's were getting harder to take, so he took refuge in working late.

Dave's wife, Kay, had become a Christian several years before. After that she had been out to evangelize her entire social circle, and had hit upon the scheme of bringing leading Christian speakers to address small dinner parties once every three months. These evenings had proved so successful that her pastor had asked whether Kay's parties might be intergrated into the outreach program of Calvary Church. Since Kay was running out of people to invite anyway—all of her social contacts had "been won or run" as Dave expressed it—she agreed, and now gave quarterly Thursday evening punch-and-cookie receptions for a revolving guest list provided by the church. The speaker then remained as the Chapmans' house guest for the weekend while giving seminars at the church.

As Dave came in late this particular Thursday evening, the speaker, a Dr. Jack Newman, well-known theologian, had already held the fifty guests spellbound for an hour talking about the historical background of the writing of the Gospels. The group was well into refreshments and conversation.

Dave greeted people superficially as he wended his way from kitchen to dining room, grabbed a tumbler of iced tea, and retreated to a hassock at the far end of the living room. Between sips, he watched the star of the evening surrounded by a semi-circle of admirers.

Jack Newman was tall and lean with a long, dark-complexioned face and black hair graying at the temples. His eyes were large and deeply set and his Roman nose gave an edge to his profile that suggested intelligence and wit. Somehow, his comfortable posture threw the gestures and mannerisms of those around him into high relief.

Dave became aware of how wide Lucy opened her mouth when she let out her whooping laugh; how craven Stan appeared, unable to stand still and meet the man's eyes; how uneasy others seemed as they posed and waited to impress with their questions. Every craning neck and twisted body tightened Dave's own shoulder muscles; he wished they would all clear out of his house.

Much later, when the guests were gone, Kay had shown Dr. Newman his room and then gone on to the master bedroom to collapse; Dave, too restless to sleep, sat comfortably on a chaise lounge out on the screened-in back porch, a plate of left-over cookies at hand.

To his surprise, he heard footsteps and Dr. Newman stepped onto the slate paving stones from the wide open doorway of the family room.

"Need a break of fresh air after all that, Doctor?" Dave asked.

"Yes, it's a beautiful night and I spotted this porch earlier this evening," Newman replied. "I've always felt a bit deprived that our place doesn't have one." Newman had taken off his coat and tie, as Dave had, and his white shirt, with sleeves rolled back against his forearms, stood out sharply in the darkness.

"Have a seat, Doctor. After a long day, I always feel like I can finally breathe out here." Dave gestured to the wicker chair separated from his by a small glass-topped table. Newman hiked his gray slacks at the knees and sank gratefully into the comfortable cushions. The two men sat for a few moments listening to the loud green whine of the crickets.

"You don't find the church people easy to take, do you?" Newman asked.

"No," Dave said, drawing the word out. "Not always. But that's not why I wasn't here for your lecture tonight. A client had me hung up at the office. I really am sorry. Everyone said you were great."

"I was watching you with your guests tonight after you came in," Newman said, ignoring Dave's excuse. "You looked off in the distance, as if you were listening to music somewhere in the background. And you were at the same time really looking everyone over. What was going through your mind?"

"I guess I was just watching them in relationship to you. They're such a bunch of turkeys sometimes."

"You looked like something was wrong. I told myself that if I got the chance, I'd try to talk to you. Care to tell me about it?"

"Well, I didn't know it was so obvious," Dave chuckled rather forcedly. "Sure, I'll tell you about it. With your experience in the church and all, maybe you'll understand. Which would be a good thing, because I sure don't. I just know that every time I'm around those people it puts me in a bad mood."

"What kind of bad mood?" Newman asked.

"I don't know if I can describe it. It's sort of what you said — about listening to background music. I have a hard time feeling involved with what's going on around me. I mean I feel that way all the time."

"I've felt like that, Dave," said Newman.

"You have?"

"Sure. Everyone has. We don't all go through it the same way, but sooner or later most people feel that sense of meaninglessness at some point in their life."

"Well, it always gets worse when I'm around church people," Dave said. "It even makes me wonder about the whole business. Christianity, I mean. Maybe it doesn't work. For me."

"You say that as if I might be offended."

"Why not. You've given your life to it. And here I'm telling you I think it might be a dry run."

"If it were, do you think I would prefer you not to try and tell me?"

That struck Dave. He thought of religious people as those not quite willing or able to look at life realistically. Newman seemed different — unintimidated—a quality Dave always looked for in business associates. He liked a man who didn't panic.

"How did you become a Christian, Dave?" Newman asked. "Your wife said you both came into the church a few years ago."

"Yeah, Kay's in the church all right. She wakes up in the morning, sings the doxology in the shower, then runs off to a Bible study, to some save-the-savages guild, to choir practice, to something that ought to be called Protestants for Prudery, and even attends a Christian exercise class called Praise-R-Cize, if you can believe! And seminars! I'm sure your talks are worthwhile, but after 'life together,' 'family life,' and 'body life,' Kay doesn't have time for our life."

"But what about you, Dave," Newman pressed. "You must have thought Christianity was true at one time."

"I don't know any more. I guess I did. If you want my testimony — well, it's nothing real spectacular. Remember, about the time Carter was elected president, when being born-again was the big thing? Well, Kay got caught up in it — was off every night to a revival service or a prayer meeting. She started talking about the devil and hell or she'd write little sayings on the kitchen blackboard. I'd even find the Bible on my desk opened to a certain page. I'll be honest, for a while she was driving me right up the wall.

"Then I met this fellow at the club. Like me, he had worked his way to the top. He gambled and belted his booze with the best of them. But one day I noticed he wasn't at the card tables any more. And soon his whole attitude changed. He had been a bundle of nerves; now he seemed calm, peaceful. And he started drinking ginger ale, for heaven's sake.

"So I asked him what had happened and he said, 'I've accepted Jesus Christ and committed my life to Him.' I felt like I'd been hit with a brick — that was the type of jargon Kay used all the time.

"I didn't want any of that God talk, not at the country club, too. But I did respect his decision and thought he seemed sincere. Months went by. Kay eased up a little, and I didn't mind so much when she shoved an occasional book my way. I'm not much of a reader, but I got so hooked on one that I stayed up two nights running to finish it. I went and saw my friend from the club and we talked until two in the morning. He talked about Christ in terms I could understand. He told me about his own relationship with a God who could be known. We prayed together, and then I went home.

"But I couldn't sleep, even after a couple quick nightcaps. It was a night like this — warm, but with a fresh breeze, so I came out here to the porch and stared out into the darkness, up at the stars. And that moment I knew, as I never had before, that there is a God. And I prayed the prayer my friend had given me.

"I guess I expected to hear the angels kicking up a ruckus, the divine cannons going off, but nothing much happened — except gradually over the next few weeks I began to feel different. I found it easy to lay off the martinis at lunch. And I completely lost my desire to gamble. You preachers would say I was 'delivered' from those things, I guess.

"When I told my friend what had happened, he had me in a weekly prayer group meeting at the bank before I knew what had happened. Of course Kay was overjoyed when I told her. We both joined Calvary Church and started getting involved. In fact, they asked me to head a couple committees the moment I was baptized.

"But it's like a love affair that ran its course. Now I don't know if I ever really felt the love of God. I don't mean I'm drinking again or anything. I just don't feel anything. I wonder if it's possible to know God at all."

Dave had been staring out through the screen as he talked. Now he turned slowly and looked at his guest. "I'm not even sure I know what it means to have faith, if I ever did."

"Faith is believing and acting—acting in obedience to the commands of Christ—even though you can't see what's going to happen," Newman replied.

"That's the kind of simplistic answer you guys give that really stymies me. I'm not breaking any commandments. So what's wrong with me?"

"Are you sure?"

"Well, all right. I don't mean that I've stopped sinning totally, but God knows we can't be perfect in this life. I mean I've honestly tried to do everything the church asks. What more should I do?"

"I don't mean to be simple with you, Dave, but Jesus spelled that out pretty clearly: 'Love the Lord with all your heart, mind, and soul, and your neighbor as yourself.' "

"Well," Dave said slowly, "I try to do that. I mean I go to church and all that stuff—don't we do that because we love God? And nobody really knows how to carry out that 'neighbor' stuff—we've talked about that in church discussions quite a bit. You know, the Good Samaritan bit and all. So where does that leave me?"

Newman sat quietly for a few moments, elbows on knees, hands clasped. "Dave, the fact that you're struggling with all that is actually a good sign. It means you really do want to love God."

"Come off it. You don't have to say that. I hate this business where Christians always feel obliged to be encouraging."

"Let me ask you this, then. Do you love your wife?"

"Yes, very much. You don't stay married these days if you don't."

"There ever come a time after you'd been married a while when you wondered whether you loved her at all?"

"Oh, sure. That's normal."

"What changed things?"

"I don't know—just time mostly."

"But you stayed faithful to your vows and to her, despite how you felt, right?"

"Yes. I've been lucky—never been tempted much."

"I mean more than that," Newman said. "I mean you tried to love Kay as much as you could, despite your feelings."

"Well, sure. It wasn't always easy though."

"Right," said Newman. "Now what you need to learn is how to do the same thing with Christ. You promised Him something—to commit your life to Him and love and obey Him. So you do that no matter how you feel. And the longer and more you do that—obey Him—then you'll begin to feel your love for Him and His love in return. Just like you did with Kay."

"But where do I start, when I'm not even sure I believe it will work?"

"The apostle John says 'This is the love of God, that we keep His commandments.' Straightforward, isn't it? But you can't obey them if you don't know them. So the place to start is in His book, the Bible, by studying."

"Bible study is hard for me," Dave said. "Things always seem to crowd it out."

"You can make the time if you really want to," Newman said firmly. "You will never know what God wants unless you seriously study His Word. But when you begin to do what He tells you there, you'll feel His love."

Dave Chapman had no idea where that simple thought would lead him, but Newman's words were so direct that Dave felt a glint of hope, and he determined to get back to Bible study. For several weeks he got up thirty minutes early every morning to do it. He automatically felt virtuous, even though he rarely could concentrate on the text. His mind turned involuntarily to the work day ahead. Also, most of the study plans Newman had recommended seemed too strenuous—after all, he was new at this. So he chose what he liked to think of as his "target method." He read a favorite passage, such as the Sermon on the Mount and 1 Corinthians 13, and then made forays backward and forward, hoping eventually to hit the whole Bible in sort of overlapping circles of reading.

But he didn't seem to get anywhere. Sleeping in seemed more and more attractive. So he began studying after work. But his powers of concentration were even worse then. He would start to read, and the quiet of his office would entice his tired mind into reveries.

He tried attending the church men's study group that met every Friday morning for breakfast. But when there wasn't a genius like Newman around, Dave's natural inclination to resist instruction took over. He knew his attitude was rotten, but he couldn't keep himself from wondering just where Stan or Bill got off in their pseudo-exposition of the apostle Paul. Besides, they were always dragging in some guest to give his testimony, like the one who told about his sordid life of wine and women and the subsequent collapse of his successful business. Then one day he read a book by some born-again football jock, turned his life over to Jesus, and presto, praise the Lord, he stopped drinking and chasing around. And presto, his business was booming like never before. Instant pudding religion, Dave called it. All alike, all blah.

Then came one of those days. First he spilled egg on his shirt at breakfast, had words with Kay about the laundry's uneven use of starch, discovered that Kay's car which he had to use was almost out of gas, had words with her about that—the woman avoided gas stations like the plague—and got to work a half hour late. When he walked in, his secretary greeted him with the news that the controller of his biggest account, Fairway, had just called and *demanded* that Dave return his call the moment he walked in. Dave would have yelled at his secretary about putting the man off, but he saw the call had upset her already, and she wasn't the kind to be easily ruffled.

Dave went in and sat behind his oval rosewood desk and did a deep breathing exercise he had read about—supposed to calm you down. Then he placed the call. He was put directly through to Fairway's president, rather than the controller. Dave had never heard anyone so angry in his life.

One of Dave's brightest young associates, Brad Pelouze, had without telling anyone disallowed certain assets of a company Fairway had acquired. On the final audit, inventory was adjusted down by $100,000— on the surface not that big a deal. But the net effect had been to reduce the earnings per share of Fairway just below the magic $10 needed for Fairway's underwriters to issue a new stock offering. Fairway would have to wait another year to raise the $7,000,000 it wanted for new acquisitions.

Fairway's president was in an unforgiving frame of mind. "Don't worry about making it up to me," he said in reply to Dave's entreaties. "You're not going to be able to make it up to me. You're not going to be in business that long."

Pelouze had made a dumb mistake, no doubt about that. He had been overly conservative and then had failed to tell the company's controller what he had done. Management didn't discover the adjustment until papers were filed with the Securities Commission for the stock offering, too late to change it. Worst of all, Pelouze had neglected to consult the accountant's bible, the "generally accepted accounting prin-

ciples" published by the American Institute of CPAs. If he had, he would
have discovered he didn't have to make the adjustment.

A short time later Pelouze, a slightly built young man, sat before
Dave. His face ashen, he glanced up once or twice at Dave, then gazed
out the open window as though realizing that his next place of employment lay somewhere out there.

Dave did not spare him. After the introductory lashings, he became
bitterly vindictive. He flipped open his desk copy of the AICPA Professional Standards of Accounting. "See this," Dave said. "Do you see this?
You don't have to go to Duke for eight years, Mr. Pelouze, to read this.
Any schoolboy can read it. But you seem to be one of those educated
beyond your intelligence."

Much later, driving home after work, Dave's neck and shoulders
played back every tense moment of that day. Worse, his mind accompanied it with vivid instant replays of his scene with Brad Pelouze. He
wished he could go back and do the scene again. Then, suddenly, his
vindictive words became a different script: "You call yourself a Christian,
Chapman, and you don't even know the Bible?" He remembered the
effort he had expended absorbing and digesting AICPA. His "target
method" wouldn't have worked with that. He wouldn't have had a chance
of passing his CPA exams if he had studied with that approach. He
realized he was treating the Bible like some magazine just flipping through,
reading here and there as impulse moved him. He wanted spectacular
results in his Christian life, but put in thoroughly mediocre effort. He
would have to change or give it up.

The Pelouze incident prompted Dave to begin studying the Scriptures with dedication. Morning was the logical and best time for him to
do this, so he arose one hour early and spent time carefully going over
and thinking through the chapter each day. He devoted two nights a
week to Design for Discipleship, a systematic Bible study course from
the Navigators that Newman had recommended.

As part of his regimen, Dave also read three psalms each morning.
But he began to discover that he only liked parts of the psalms; there
were huge areas he had totally neglected — never even read. When he
began to delve into those portions he got his first big shock: whoever
had written these nice "praise songs" had been a shrewd and intelligent
man; they appealed to the mind as much as the heart. When he came

across his first command in the psalms, he got his second shock: a commandment in the psalms? But there it was, as plain as day, and he could not think of a single thing he had ever done in his life to obey it: "How long will you defend the unjust . . . ? Defend the cause of the weak and fatherless; maintain the rights of the poor and oppressed. Rescue the weak and needy; deliver them from the hand of the wicked" (Psalm 82:2-4).

Those were sentiments Dave identified with bleeding-heart liberals, those he had always characterized as standing "with both feet planted firmly in the air." But he couldn't escape the fact that this Scripture said that God condemns those who did not do this.

Though uncomfortable, Dave could not see how he was supposed to obey this commandment. It did not fit into the modern scheme of things. No "poor" asked for an accountant's help. He didn't even know any poor people. And how could he defend anyone's cause? He wasn't a judge or a lawyer.

Then he began to notice that the psalms were full of comments about the rich and the poor. In fact, according to the psalms, how one treated the poor determined, at least in part, whether one was a righteous person or a wicked one.

Dave already gave quite generously to the church and to Christian causes. Having served as church treasurer, he knew he probably gave more than anyone at the church. But this did not seem quite the point of the psalms. Genuinely perplexed, Dave found himself sometimes annoyed with the message he got from his Bible studies.

Though the message upset him, he now understood it was true. He had read a little pamphlet Newman had written several years earlier, and the theologian's argument had convinced him. He realized the Bible was from God — His Word — and was absolutely true. It made him all the more uncomfortable.

At about this same time, Dave noticed that a man in his company was performing poorly. Jim Rutledge had spent most of his working life with Dave's company, punching adding machines and calculators, recording figures in a ledger sheet. Jim had always seemed content to plod along, even while coworkers started under his trainership eventually were promoted past him. But in recent months Jim had missed many days of work, and when he did show, his work was slow and full of errors.

So Dave made some discreet inquiries, then set an appointment with Rutledge. In past years, finding what he had, he might have simply fired the man, but the psalms and Rutledge's long history with the company prompted Dave to think of ways to help.

Jim Rutledge entered Dave's office like a man coming to his execution. His eyes were glazed and veined, his color pasty.

"Have a seat, Jim," Dave gestured, and his employee sank into one of the wingbacked armchairs facing Dave's large desk. Rutledge took off his glasses and pocketed them, as if the action would make him invisible.

"Jim, I've called you in because, very honestly, I have been disappointed with your work lately — and we go back a long ways together." Dave then went on to enumerate some of his findings, as Jim sat quietly, not refuting him nor meeting his eyes.

Finally, "Look, Jim," Dave said, "I know you have a drinking problem. I've had my own suspicions. I've confirmed it with others, including your family."

Rutledge looked up, startled, his eyes showing a spark of denial, but Dave continued before he had a chance to speak. "I'm not giving you an option on this, Jim. You're going to enter a rehabilitation program. You need help."

"I'll hand in my resignation right now, then, Dave," Rutledge said. "You don't know what that costs. Four thousand a month, minimum — my wife looked into it once. I don't have that kind of money."

"I'll take care of the bill," Dave said. "It would be far more costly for me to waste your experience here."

Rutledge gasped, tried to speak, but Dave cut him short, his tone more personal. "I know something of what you're going through, Jim. I had a little battle with it myself. It will be tough, but you can lick it. I know you can. The place I've picked comes highly recommended."

"How long?" Jim's hands trembled as he lit a cigarette.

"A month. Two, if necessary." Dave paused a moment. "Will your wife and family be okay?"

"They'll be fine. You don't know ... Jean will be so relieved. How she's held on this year ... I kept waiting for her to leave me."

"Well, the arrangements are made, and my secretary has all the information. See her and then go home and tell your family. You're due at the clinic by tomorrow at 5:00 P.M."

Rutledge switched his cigarette to his left hand, stood, and grasped Dave's outstretched hand. Tears started to his eyes, and he turned and left the office quickly.

Dave basked in the glow of that conversation on his way home that night. Then, he began having second thoughts about the money. The company's medical insurance didn't cover a dry-out farm. He had half planned to take it out of his own pocket, but now he wondered if that was a wise plan.

Then he hit upon a solution. He personally owned the building his accounting firm occupied; the firm paid him rent. It had been a good tax device over the years. So he'd just increase the rent again, and he'd pay Rutledge's bill; in effect, the company would foot the bill. The rent was already high, and each time he increased it he was cutting into the company's profit-sharing plan, but he's managed okay with moves like this in the past.

How many times? a voice asked. *You've used this gambit so often that your profit-sharing plan is more theory than practice.* A few of the more senior associates already knew enough to grumble out loud about it — and they didn't know the half. In the past he would have brushed his conscience aside, but this time he could not.

He had planned to tell Kay what he had done for Rutledge, but found that the glow of his good deeds had died. So he sat through dinner in a moody silence. All evening he tried to rationalize his way out of the predicament. After all, what he had done to the profit-sharing was nothing extraordinary; as an accountant he knew enough to justify it to the IRS and all that. But the thoughts would not go away: in a perfectly legal way, he had stolen from his employees.

The next morning Dave skipped his psalms' reading, thinking he wasn't up for any references to the poor for a while, and went straight to where he was studying the Gospel of Luke in the nineteenth chapter. His reading began with the story of Zacchaeus, a wealthy tax collector. He remembered the story from Sunday school days because they had sung a song about Zacchaeus climbing into a tree in order to see Jesus. Today he read how Jesus invited Himself home with Zacchaeus and how people began to mutter about His associating with such a sinner.

But Sunday school had not prepared Dave for what he read next. "Zacchaeus stood up and said to the Lord, 'Look, Lord! Here and now I give half of my possessions to the poor, and if I have cheated anybody out of anything, I will pay back four times the amount.'

"Jesus said to him, 'Today salvation has come to this house.' "

Dave slammed the Bible shut as though it had bitten him. He sat for a moment with his hands in his lap, looking straight ahead. Then, reluctantly, he opened the Bible, found his place, and read the passage again.

The meaning was perfectly clear: he should not merely pay Rutledge's expenses; he should make restitution for the money he had, in a sense, stolen from his associates. He immediately began calculating what this would cost him. He had a Mercedes on order; he could not possibly afford it if he did this. Just last week he had given Kay the go-ahead on looking for a Florida condo; he would have to tell her to hold off and he would have to explain why. He had never explained much about their finances to Kay, period. He hated to have to begin with a confession.

Dave had not known what hysteria lay just under his calm surface. He had not realized how much security he found in a comfortable bank balance, how profoundly superstitious he was about money. Giving the money back went against every fiscal bone in his body. He saw himself becoming easy pickings for every cause in the world. He saw himself dying penniless, with no legacy for his children. Rack and ruin, soup lines, and people jumping from tall buildings flashed before him.

The next day he went back to his normal reading of the psalms, although a bit grimly, beginning to feel the Bible was not such a friendly book after all. In Psalm 37:25 he found a sly dig at his hysteria: "I was young and now I am old, yet I have never seen the righteous forsaken or their children begging bread. They are always generous and lend freely; their children will be blessed."

This was true, of course. Neither he nor Kay nor the children were likely to become beggars because he boosted the profit-sharing plan back up where it was meant to be. But the thought turned a crucial screw in Dave's mind. He began to see the religious dimension in the talk about the poor. For the rich depended on their wealth for security; the righteous were free to be generous, because their security was in God. As long as he hung onto his bank account as an insurance policy, he could never trust God wholly and would never fully experience God's blessings.

He had to do what was right in the Lord's eyes, no matter what the results might be for him or his family.

Dave made restitution, not only putting a healthy dent in his personal fortune, but causing him embarrassment and humiliation as well. He wondered sometimes whether he was losing his grip and knew some of his old friends thought so. But there was an end to what he had to do, and it had not thrust him into poverty. He felt a new sense of freedom and knew he had changed in a way he would have once thought impossible.

Kay was happy, too, and he had not expected that. He felt guilty punishing her for his own personal moral crusades. But when he hesitantly explained what he had done and his thinking about it all, she had looked at him with her wide, dark eyes and said, "Oh, Dave, I'm so proud of you."

They had been like honeymooners since.

In the months that followed, Dave noticed another change in his perspective. He found himself getting angry at the physical and psychological violence in the world. In fact, he became angrier each day.

When he discussed his feelings with Kay, she suggested he call Dr. Newman. Over the phone, Dave brought Newman up to date on what had happened in his life.

"So things seemed to be shaping up a bit in my life, and now I find myself unsettled again — and about things I am helpless to control. I mean before I always read the *Wall Street Journal* and avoided all that sob-sister stuff and sensationalism that makes headlines in the dailies. Who needs it! But lately I can't help myself. I seem compelled to know what's going on in the world, and then I read about drunk drivers, and abortion clinics doing a landslide business, and unemployed men and women committing suicide, and street crimes, and drug busts, and I can't say 'Thank God, it has never touched me or mine' anymore. I am disturbed about it all — and angry. But it seems so futile to stew over it."

Newman didn't really comment much except to say, "Just think about all you have told me, Dave, and all you are becoming aware of. Something very special is coming your way. It usually does at this stage in one's spiritual growth. Keep your eyes open. And check out Luke 19."

"You mean about Zacchaeus. I didn't mention it, but that's what triggered — "

"No, I mean the passage where Jesus comments on Jerusalem."

When he got off the phone, Dave found the passage. It was after Jesus' Palm Sunday entry into the city. "As he approached Jerusalem and saw the city, he wept over it and said, 'If you, even you, had only known on this day what would bring you peace — but now it is hidden from your eyes.'"

Tears filled Dave's eyes, and he recalled the many Old Testament passages he had read about Jehovah's anger. The God of the Old Testament and Jesus Christ were one, of course — the Father's anger and the Son's tears were one.

Suddenly Dave understood. He was angry at the world because he was beginning to see the world from God's perspective. He had always looked at it solely through the eyes of self-interest, self-preservation. But God's point of view demanded justice for everyone, for society. Dave had feared God's justice, His judgment on his own life, and still did. But that fear seemed insignificant before the vista of a world so rebellious against God.

Dave thought back to the first command he had read in the psalms and the one he had still not, despite his restitution, begun to obey: "Defend the cause of the weak and fatherless; maintain the rights of the poor and oppressed." *Sometime*, he thought, *a chance will come to do that. Don't let me miss it.*

Six months later an unusual speaker turned up at Dave's morning Bible group at the bank. Keith Marks was still in his twenties, with a leather jacket and thick reddish hair curling over his collar, a former convict and presently the state director of Prison Fellowship. Dave, of course, was familiar with Prison Fellowship and had been a heavy donor for several years — but he had never really thought much about prisons. Marks quoted familiar statistics about increasing crime in America and said that the expense of building enough prisons for all these criminals would require an impossible amount of money. Marks said the alternative was to take "nonviolent" criminals out of the prisons and into halfway houses where they would participate in rehabilitation programs and be required to make restitution to their victims.

While the subject was of interest to Dave, Marks' suggestion seemed utterly fanciful. Someone who could break into another man's home was not a Boy Scout; he was a criminal. How could you count on such a person to make restitution?

After the presentation, Dave asked Keith Marks this very question. Keith knew enough to turn away such wrath with a gentle reply; he suggested that Dave accompany him to the Tuesday night Bible study that Prison Fellowship conducted at the state penitentiary. It was only a twenty-minute drive from Dave's office.

Dave started to put him off, then thought. *Why not?*

The prison was a surreal and hostile world. Dave was unnerved by the clanging double bars, the stench of urine, cigarettes, and disinfectant, the suspicious, hardened faces of the guards, the burning lights from the tower. Later, back at home, he could still hear the echoing clicks of his own heels on those bare corridors.

But something beyond the prison itself got to Dave Chapman that night — nearly made him lose control. It was something in the Bible study itself that triggered his emotions. Dave and Keith had sat in a circle with the men in an ancient classroom, and each of the gray-uniformed prisoners had introduced themselves to Dave. *They each had a name.* Someone, some mother or father full of pride had called one "Richard," another "Julio," another. ... *They each had a name.* Dave sat with them, thinking about that simple fact for the rest of the evening.

Dave went back the next Tuesday night and the next and. ... Marks did not ask him to lead the Bible study, so he merely went, watched, and studied and listened to the men. Most of them looked like the kind of fellows he had parted company with back in high school when he had started college prep course; they were like the rough, coarse, ready-to-fight guys who ended up in auto shop until they quit school.

But these men soon became individuals with names and personalities. Dino looked as though he had been strung out on heroin for seven years, which he had, but he was one of the funniest people Dave had ever met. An older man with a quiet voice, almost an undifferentiated hum, became quite special to Dave. Though quiet, Fitzgerald was not shy and took to hanging around Dave for the few minutes they had after the meeting, gradually revealing his story. He had been an inventor, a rock climber, and a top engineer with Boeing. Dave checked him out and found Fitzgerald was telling the truth. He was in prison for tax evasion to the tune of $2,000, an unbelievably paltry sum to Dave, who had miscalculated by that margin dozens of times on his clients' returns.

Fitzgerald was the victim of a crazy system. Dino, on the other hand, had victimized himself; he was a confirmed needle freak and shot up anything he could get his hands on, even in prison.

Dave also met men who had been incredibly transformed by their conversions to Christ. One, Louis Lincoln, a giant black man with a mohawk haircut, was in for murder, but Dave honestly wouldn't have hesitated to recommend him as a babysitter. Louis was a lifer without parole, yet enjoyed life in a way that made Dave want to weep for his own lack of gratitude to God.

One big, gangly kid with pumpkin-colored freckles caught Dave's attention because he was so defenseless and woebegone. Dave learned that Rick's grandparents had raised him after his mother decided he cluttered up her life. After dropping out of high school, he had worked at a gas station for a year and was now in prison for breaking and entering homes to steal television sets and stereos.

Dave's heart went out to Rick and as he talked with him every week, he gradually succeeded in inspiring the young man to get his high school equivalency certificate while in prison and learn as much about carpentry as possible in the prison's woodworking shop.

Rick did make progress, though at an agonizingly slow rate. At least, it seemed slow to Dave. Actually in nine months Rick was remarkably transformed. As the time of release approached, however, Rick seemed to retreat, worried about the world he would face.

Dave thought Rick might be all right if he could get a stable job and have a few people to turn to for help in the first months after prison, so he talked with Keith Marks. Keith suggested that Dave ask his pastor whether Calvary Church might "adopt" Rick — help him find a job, a place to stay, and provide a circle of Christian friends.

The pastor sold the idea to the church board and most of the members took it up with surprising excitement. With their help, Rick struggled through the crisis of release and began to stabilize his life.

On the first anniversary of his release, Rick choked out his testimony at the Sunday evening service. The elder who had expressed the most doubts about the program came to Dave and asked whether he could come along on the next visit to prison.

Dave was flying high, emotionally and spiritually. Unknown to him, however, events were shaping that would put his faith to its greatest test.

The first of these events began in the form of a public honor the next spring which gave Dave as much satisfaction as seeing Rick's success. After receiving the news on the telephone, he did an impromptu jig before rushing to tell Kay. The public announcement was made in one of the smaller meeting rooms of the downtown Holiday Inn. Kay, their son Doug and Christine, who had come home from college for the occasion, were there. So were a dozen members of the press along with camera crew from the local TV station.

The governor, a Republican running for his second term, stood at the podium and announced that Dave Chapman would be the chairman of his re-election campaign's finance committee. Dave had known the governor for years, had audited the books for his textile firm.

In his acknowledgment speech Dave said they expected to raise two million dollars and that the governor should be re-elected because he was restoring fiscal responsibility in the state capitol.

At home later, watching the news, Dave saw why he was the finance man and the governor was the governor. "I tried so hard to sound responsible that I come off like some dull dim-wit," he grumbled to Kay. She teased him that he was already getting ambitious, trying to outshine the governor. They laughed and hugged and Kay said how proud she was of him. All things considered, Dave could have died that night a most happy man.

The governor beat back minor primary opposition, and they began to gear up for the election. The battle with his Democratic challenger promised to be tough, but he led in the polls and had good organization. The money was coming in; Dave was doing his job well. So much so that he wondered whether the governor might offer him an appointment in his administration. Anyway, he was certain all this would be good for his business.

Dave kept up his prison visits throughout the campaign. However, the penitentiary was not the same institution he had first visited two years before. The prison population had been growing at 12 percent a year and the facility had become crowded to the breaking point. The gymnasium had been pressed into service as a dormitory and certain hallways were cordoned off and used in the same manner. At last even the prison chapel was converted to a dormitory.

Places in training programs and workshops were at a premium. Only the best-behaved got them. The most alienated and violent prisoners sat in their cells all day, brooding and becoming more and more angry.

Dave could feel the tension each time he entered the prison doors. And he saw it in the eyes of the prisoners. In the Bible study the men lacked concentration; they wanted to talk about prison conditions. But such talk, if allowed to continue, would lead the prison authorities to stop the study because it was getting "too political."

He could not blame the men for feeling as they did, so Dave spoke to the warden one day about the conditions. The warden politely pointed out that he had no control over overcrowding; the courts sentenced them and he had to imprison them. "And a firm hand is the only way to deal with tensions like this," he said.

Despite that firm hand, trouble began to brew. Each week it seemed the men had a new protest to tell Dave about. One day it was a sit-down in the prison compound; another time ten prisoners had begun a hunger strike, producing a list of demands.

As Dave talked to Fitzgerald after one of the Bible studies, the man slipped him a piece of paper.

"What's this?" Dave asked.

"Those are the demands," Fitzgerald said softly. "I thought maybe you could telephone a newspaper and give them the dope."

"Well, I'll have to think about it," Dave said. Later, he decided that bringing in the media would do more harm than good. Dave had never approved of strikes. On the other hand, he understood the prisoners' frustration. The warden's only response to their demands was to lock up those who led the protests; he put them in segregated cells until they learned to "behave" themselves. The segregation unit, where prisoners paced like caged animals and were allowed out only three times a week to shower, could break anyone down.

What can be done? Dave could not see an answer short of massive interest on the part of the legislature — and that seemed unimaginable. Prison reformers didn't usually get re-elected.

Then one Sunday night Keith Marks called Dave to tell him the Tuesday study had been cancelled by the warden. "He said the protests have reached a serious stage," Keith told Dave. "The whole segregation unit is on a hunger strike, throwing their food into the corridor."

"And they've got Louis locked up now," Marks added.

"What did Louis do?" Dave was shocked.

"I'm not sure what he did, if anything. They're putting anybody who breathes loudly in segregation right now. The warden is determined to stamp this thing out. So there'll be no more Bible studies for a while. The warden thinks they got too political."

"Can I still visit the men?" Dave asked.

"Yeah, visiting is okay. Just no meetings of any kind."

"The more Dave thought about Louis in the segregation unit, the more it bothered him. The unit was meant for violent, dangerous offenders. By locking up such prisoners, the rest of the men were protected. Or so the original justification went. But, in fact, the segregation unit was used as punishment for anyone the guards thought out of line. Some of the guards, Dave knew, would rather herd docile half-numbed sheep from one pen to the next rather than cope with human beings with emotions. *They mean to break Louis's spirit,* he thought. *To break his spirit —* what horrifying language about a human being.

Dave brought his troubled thoughts up to Kay as they lay in bed and again at the breakfast table. He grew so frustrated and angry as he talked that she suggested he call Dr. Newman.

"You want me to get into more trouble?" he asked her.

"Why do you say that?"

"Every time I talk to that guy he thinks up some new scheme for messing up my life."

"Dave, you know that's not true," Kay smiled. "He never tells you what to do."

"No, but I always seem to end up doing what he wants anyway."

Nevertheless, he called Dr. Newman and discussed the situation. As it happened, the theologian was planning to be in town the coming weekend and said he'd like Dave to give him a tour of the prison if possible. Dave was fairly sure that as a long-time, trusted volunteer he could get Newman inside. In fact, he looked forward to being Newman's tour guide and teacher for once.

Dave watched Newman carefully, remembering his own shocked re-action to his first visit. Newman listened to what Dave said but gave few clues to what he was thinking or feeling. He asked few questions.

Dave himself felt the tension as they walked along the maze of concrete corridors in the main prison facility. When they passed the cells, men who knew Dave eagerly came to the bars to shake hands. Several men asked whether he knew that Louis was in the segregation unit.

After they had toured the workshops, the schoolrooms, the chapel-cum-dorm, Dave told Newman that he wanted to see Louis. "Besides, I want you to see the center of this tension."

The segregation unit was a prison within a prison, with its own small, walled-in exercise compound. A guard accompanied them. When they reached the barred gate, it slid open and they walked inside and stopped. The gate slammed into place behind them; when it was fastened shut, the door ahead of them clicked open and they walked into the unit.

The stench struck them like a wall. Solid, putrid, it was the stench of human excrement, urine, choking cigarette smoke, and sweat. Prison always smelled, and the segregation was the worst because the prisoners couldn't get outside. But this was the worst Dave had ever encountered.

When they turned the corner, he saw why. The dimly lit corridor was blocked with refuse.

On their left was a high wall with thick glazed glass windows at the top. The brilliant lights flooding the exercise yard shone through, creating an eerie matrix of light and shadow. On their right was a wall of steel bars enclosing cement cellblocks. In between, on the corridor floor, lay a stinking mess covered with flies. Some of it was recognizable as food. Some of it was feces. Some had been thrown up against the windows, still clinging there. A motion on the floor caught Dave's eye. It was a rat, gobbling into the awful stuff. His stomach flip-flopped.

"Why don't you clean this up?" he asked the guard.

"They threw it out there," the guard answered. "Let them clean it up."

"But they can't clean it up. You only let them out for showers a couple times a week, right?"

The guard shrugged. "Warden says when they act like human beings, we'll treat them like human beings."

Dave and Newman picked their way down the line of cells, gingerly avoiding the most obvious piles of filth. Most of the men lay on their bunks, smoking, staring up at the ceiling or at some invisible point in space. When they spotted Dave and Newman, they got up as if in a daze, came over to the bars and stretched their hands through for a shake. "Hey, man, thanks for coming." "Hey what you doin' in here? Don't you know this is for animals?"

The light from the compound was too bright to permit restful sleep at night, while during the day the cells were too dim to read. Dave wondered how anyone could stand it. And coupled with the stench — so rancid and strong it hurt his sinuses.

They stopped at the cell of a young man with long, straight black hair with a sharp, protruding nose. Dave introduced him to Newman as "Ray."

"Ray is an Apache," Dave said, "and proud of it, right Ray?"

Ray merely nodded. His eyes were two seeds possessed by distant thoughts.

"Hey, Ray, where's your brother?" Dave asked. "I didn't see him."

A line of hurt glimmered over the prisoner's features, then after a silent moment he said, "Man, I know you mean well. Didn't they tell you about Hubert?"

"No, they didn't."

"Man, I thought that was why you came. You know, Hubert's gone. He hung himself. Right down here, man, just down there in the fourth cell." Ray leaned out and pointed down the corridor in the direction from which they had come.

Dave stood in stunned silence as Ray continued. "Dave, did you say this man is a doctor? I mean, can he get some sleeping pills? I just can't sleep. If I could sleep I think I would be okay. But I can't even close my eyes. I asked the guards for pills, but they say I have to wait until the doctor comes next week."

Dave told him that Newman was not a medical doctor, but promised to see whether he could help get some sleeping pills for Ray. He said some words he hoped were encouraging, then offered to pray for Ray. He and Newman both put a hand through the bars to hold one of Ray's arms while Dave prayed briefly.

Ray stood with head lowered, like an animal waiting for a blow to the head. He stayed that way even after the prayer ended. Dave shook his arm slightly to get his attention.

"We'll be back soon, Ray. I'll pray for you."

They went on in silence, placing their feet carefully, until they found Louis. Newman shook Louis's hand, then stepped back while Dave talked with him. Louis seemed his normal, hearty self as they talked, then — "Dave, I think we better put this rap on hold. The professor ... you'd better get him out of here."

Dave turned to look at Newman. His complexion was gray, his eyes unfocused, and his head was tilted toward the floor. Dave grabbed his arm, and as they turned back the way they had come, Louis let out a hearty laugh. "Hey, Dave, see if you can get one of the maids to come down and clean up a little. They try, you know, but they're nearsighted and they miss things, man!" His booming laughter echoed off the high concrete ceiling.

Newman made it out just in time to avoid being sick, but bent over clutching his knees for several minutes and gulping in air. "I'm sorry, Dave," he said when he stood upright. "That smell — "

The guard had let them out into the central compound so Newman could get some fresh air. Gigantic walls surrounded them and from above them powerful lights beamed down on every inch of cracked concrete. The only hint of life was a scum of grass trying to push through those cracks. At one end of the concrete stood a basketball standard without a net.

"So this is where they exercise?" Newman asked, looking around.

"Well, yes, they get to come out once a day. Not the guys in seg-regation, you understand. But the others. They don't exercise much, though. There are over two thousand prisoners here — makes for rather large teams." Dave gestured toward the bare basketball standard.

"What do they do, then?"

Dave shrugged. "Most of them just stroll around. Some are physical fitness fanatics and work out as best they can. This is also where they do their drug deals. Let me show you something." Dave led Newman to a corner of the compound and into a shadow created by the angle at which two buildings in the quadrant intercepted each other.

"They can't be seen here. The men tell me there's always some place like this in every prison — a dark spot the guards can't see from the walls ... look!" Dave knelt down and pointed at the concrete. "Blood stains. This is also where they beat each other, and this is where the rapes often occur." Newman knelt beside Dave and stared at the spot as Dave said, "You can't wash the blood out of the concrete."

Newman put out his finger and gingerly touched the spot, then jerked his hand back. "That's fresh blood," he said. "Look."

It was just a dark spot, for in the artificial spotlight that reflected into the shadowed area there was no color, only grays and blacks.

"Maybe from a rape," Dave said under his breath. Looking around he saw other spots like it. It did look like fresh blood.

As Dave watched, Newman stood and walked away quickly, reached the wall of the compound and touched it with one outstretched palm, then slowly turned and walked back. Dave's already knotted stomach twisted tighter with premonition.

"What are you going to do about this?" he finally asked.

"About what?" Dave asked. "About the rape? I can't do anything. I don't know what happened here, or to whom. And the guards don't care. They figure the prisoners have to take out their aggression somewhere so it might as well be on each other. Better that than on them."

"No, I don't mean that," Newman said quietly. "I mean the condi-tions here. We wouldn't treat a dog the way these men are being treated."

Dave shrugged. "I agree. But what can I do? I've talked to the warden and he brushed me off."

"You're getting pretty high up in the governor's campaign. You must have some influence with him."

Dave shrugged again. "Not too much influence, really. I did talk to him about it, though. It's hard to get even ten minutes, but I finally did.

He says he has in mind a blue-ribbon committee after the election. He says we can't really do anything until after the election."

"That's not going to accomplish anything," Newman said. It was the only time Dave had seen disgust on his face.

"No, it probably won't. I told him I'd like to be on the committee, but I don't expect it to do great things. The public just doesn't care. They don't care and so the politicians don't care. What's in it for them? In fact, any politician who focuses on such an unpopular subject usually washes out his chances for re-election."

"What if you made it a public issue?" asked Newman. "Now, I mean. Wouldn't the governor have to do something if you put him on the spot? His own finance man? Before the election?"

Dave was suddenly at a complete loss for words. Across his mind flashed the memory of his television appearance when the governor named him to his position; he saw himself as dull, stodgy, painfully straight. He could not imagine himself in the role of public advocate.

"I'm doing my part already, Doctor Newman," he said at last, feeling panic creep up his neck. "I'm not a politician. I'm an accountant. I can't go on TV and put the governor on the spot. I'm an accountant."

"But you're also someone who knows this prison. You know it as well as any other single individual. And you know something is wrong here."

"Look, not only would the governor drop me. So would my clients. No one wants Ralph Nader to handle their books."

"So you just forget about these men? You save your own skin and let them rot and die in there." Newman's voice was no longer calm.

"Come on," Dave said shortly. "We've got to go." The theologian's disapproval was too much for him. "Talking won't do any good. We've got to leave here. The guard's going to get antsy."

"Just give me a couple more minutes, Dave," Newman said. "I want to tell you something, and I want to tell you here under these lights, surrounded by these walls, standing by this blood. Then we'll go and I'll shut up."

Dave hesitated, looking around nervously as Newman began his story. . . .

"In the fourth century there lived an Asiatic monk who had spent most of his life in a remote community of prayer, raising vegetables for the cloister kitchen. When he was not tending his garden spot, he was fulfilling his vocation of study and prayer.

"Then one day this monk named Telemachus felt that the Lord wanted him to go to Rome, the capital of the world — the busiest, wealthiest, biggest city in the world. Telemachus had no idea why he should go there, and he was terrified at the thought. But as he prayed, God's directive became clear.

"How bewildered the little monk must have been as he set out on the long journey, on foot, over dusty roads westward, everything he owned on his back. Why was he going? He didn't know. What would he find there? He had no idea. But obediently, he went.

"Telemachus arrived in Rome during the holiday festival. You may know that the Roman rulers kept the ghettos quiet in those days by providing free bread and special entertainment called circuses. At the time Telemachus arrived the city was also bustling with excitement over the recent Roman victory over the Goths. In the midst of this jubilant commotion, the monk looked for clues as to why God had brought him there, for he had no other guidance, not even a superior in a religious order to contact.

"*Perhaps,* he thought, *it is not sheer coincidence that I have arrived at this festival time. Perhaps God has some special role for me to play.*

"So Telemachus let the crowds guide him, and the stream of humanity soon led him into the Coliseum where the gladiator contests were to be staged. He could hear the cries of the animals in their cages beneath the floor of the great arena and the clamor of the contestants preparing to do battle.

"The gladiators marched into the arena, saluted the emperor, and shouted, 'We who are about to die salute thee.' Telemachus shuddered. He had never heard of gladiator games before, but had a premonition of awful violence.

"The crowd had come to cheer men who, for no reason other than amusement, would murder each other. Human lives were offered for entertainment. As the monk realized what was going to happen, he realized he could not sit still and watch such savagery. Neither could he leave and forget. He jumped to the top of the perimeter wall and cried, 'In the name of Christ, forbear!'

"The fighting began, of course. No one paid the slightest heed to the puny voice. So Telemachus pattered down the stone steps and leapt onto the sandy floor of the arena. He made a comic figure — a scrawny man in a monk's habit dashing back and forth between muscular, armed athletes. One gladiator sent him sprawling with a blow from his shield directing him back to his seat. It was a rough gesture, though almost a kind one. The crowd roared.

"But Telemachus refused to stop. He rushed into the way of those trying to fight, shouting again, 'In the name of Christ, forbear!' The crowd began to laugh and cheer him on, perhaps thinking him part of the entertainment.

"Then his movement blocked the vision of one of the contestants; the gladiator saw a blow coming just in time. Furious now, the crowd began to cry for the interloper's blood.

"Run him through," they screamed.

"The gladiator he had blocked raised his sword and with a flash of steel struck Telemachus, slashing down across his chest and into his stomach. The little monk gasped once more, 'In the name of Christ, forbear.'

"Then a strange thing occurred. As the two gladiators and the crowd focused on the still form on the suddenly crimson sand, the arena grew deathly quiet. In the silence, someone in the top tier got up and walked out. Another followed. All over the arena, spectators began to leave, until the huge stadium was emptied.

"There were other forces at work, of course, but that innocent figure lying in the pool of blood crystallized the opposition, and that was the last gladiatorial contest in the Roman Coliseum. Never again did men kill each other for the crowds' entertainment in the Roman arena."

Dave leaned against the compound wall and stared at the cracked concrete floor as Newman finished his story. *The Romans killed men for fun,* he thought. *We destroy them ... for what? ... punishment? ... under the guise of rehabilitation? ... our own ambitions? ... our fear? ... our obscene unconcern?* He thought of Ray, locked in there beneath the shadow of his brother's noose; what was served by such suffering? He thought of Louis, of Fitzgerald, of Rick — they all had faces, they all had names. They were human beings.

Dave looked up at the row after row of windows. He watched the searchlights play on them. They were like an amphitheater of eyes — eyes that chose not to see the circus here in the center of the prison.

"All right," he said quietly to Newman. "I don't know where this will lead me, but I'll do what you want me to do."

Newman shook his head. "No, Dave, I'm not telling you what to do. I don't have the answers."

That made him angry. "Come off it! If you haven't been telling me what to do, what have you been doing? You want me to get on TV, make speeches, holler, jump on the wall and yell, 'In the name of Christ, stop!' "

"No, Dave. I want you to do what God tells you to do. I pushed you only because I don't want you to shrug it off — but knowing you, you can't."

Dave Chapman looked around again. The concrete underfoot held no answers, only the pool of blood. The sky beyond the floodlights was as black as a cavern. He would hear no voices. He had never heard voices. The prompting he had gotten as Newman spoke terrified him. It ran against every cautious, conservative fiber in his accountant's body. It threatened to destroy everything he had built in his business and in his position with the governor. But Newman was right. He could not shrug it off. He had come too far.

He had to get out of here and read the Bible and pray and look for direction. At that moment, oddly, he thought of that psalm David had written out of his years of experience: "I was young, and now I am old, yet I have never seen the righteous forsaken or their children begging bread." And that triggered thoughts of all that had brought him to this spot: of the summer evening on the porch when he had first met Newman, of his firing Pelouze for his mistakes on the Fairway account, of the restitution he had made to his employees, of his growing involvement with Rick and the other men here ... and finally, he remembered the first command he had found in the psalms, the one he was still not sure he could claim to have obeyed:

> Defend the cause of the weak and fatherless;
> Maintain the rights of the poor and oppressed.
> Rescue the weak and needy;
> Deliver them from the hand of the wicked.

Newman had turned and was walking toward the doorway, and Dave Chapman stared at his back as he walked away.

What am I going to do? he groaned.

He did not know.

With Gratitude

The point is made in the section on the church that the Christian life cannot be lived alone. To follow Christ is to become part of a new community. The same may be said about writing a book on the Christian life. It can never be written in a vacuum; the author is inevitably influenced by the lives and writings of others. A book, therefore, is a synthesis of shared experiences — and that is certainly so in this case. *Loving God* draws on the teaching and lives of so many, past and present. Its preparation was very much a team effort.

My dear friend R.C. Sproul opened for me a whole new vision of the majesty of the God we serve, awakening in me a continuing desire for deeper knowledge. So I'm deeply grateful to R.C., not only for that inspiration, for his magnificent books and tapes, but for his encouragement — and his critique of this manuscript as well.

I've been privileged, too, to learn from some of the great scholars of our time. Richard Lovelace of Gordon Conwell Seminary patiently tutored me in the early days of my faith. My times of fellowship with Carl Henry, who has the rare combination of genius and humility, Francis Schaeffer, Jim Houston, John Stott, Vernon Grounds, Dick Halverson, and others have enriched me immeasurably. And I have been blessed to study and worship under two excellent pastors: Neal Jones of my own church, Columbia Baptist in Falls Church, Virginia, and Dr. Charles Webster of Moorings Presbyterian Church in Naples, Florida.

In writing the manuscript, I have been assisted from the beginning by Ellen Santilli, a gifted young writer on the Prison Fellowship staff. Ellen did much of the research, and with a skilled reporter's nose dug out the material for the chapters on Agape House and Judge Bontrager. Ellen's assistance was invaluable both in drafting some material herself and editing much of mine.

Two other writers helped with portions of the book. One was Harold Fickett, whose gift for storytelling first attracted me when I read his marvelously entertaining collection of short stories, *Mrs. Sunday's Problem*. Harold helped with research and drafts of several stories. He and his research assistant, David Voth, were responsible for the powerful story of the church in the Hanoi Hilton.

The second was Tim Stafford. Early in 1983, as the publisher's deadline loomed ominously near and ministry responsibilities were heavily upon me, Tim stepped in to help with the final writing phases. His work, particularly in the crucifixion chapter, was truly inspired.

But the premier member of the team was Zondervan editor, Judith Markham. Judith shepherded this book from the raw and rough outline through the rigors of four drafts to the final product. Her editing was inspired. She never once lost her patience (no small feat for anyone who has to cope with authors), humored me until she got what she knew all along was right, and was not content with less than our best effort. But it was an absolute delight to work with her; I've never met anyone who could be so demanding in such a nice way.

As with my first two books, I complete this task with a renewed appreciation of family and friends. Patty was typist, proofreader, critic, and silent sufferer during the long hours I spent locked away in my library. Patty's partnership in my books, ministry, and life is one of God's choicest gifts to me.

So, too, my co-workers at Prison Fellowship have given me wonderful support. Gordon Loux, who manages the ministry, has over the years become not only a beloved friend but a partner for me in every sense. Senior vice-presidents Ralph Veerman and John O'Grady shouldered part of my burdens as well as their own to give me time to write. I'm especially grateful to my secretary, Nancy Niemeyer, for keeping day-to-day matters under control while I was writing, as well as for typing large parts of the manuscript along with Gordon's secretary, Janie Perdew. And special thanks as well to Jeanne Moody for her careful research and fact checking, and to Anita Moreland for reading the manuscript.

I am most grateful to the several friends who read and critiqued the manuscript: first, an author I enormously respect, Philip Yancey, who gave tremendous guidance; Mary Babcock, a close friend in Miami; Charlotte Cauwels, a Prison Fellowship instructor and wife of board member Dave Cauwels; Len LeSourd, my dear friend and editor of my prior two books; Carl Henry; David McKenna, president of Asbury Theological Seminary; Elizabeth Sherrill, the gifted author who not only critiqued but also blue-penciled a few chapters as she did for *Born Again* and *Life Sentence*; and Art Lindsley, who not only critiqued the book from a theological perspective but prepared the companion study guide as well.

As I write this, it is exactly ten years since I visited my dear friend, Tom Phillips, as the Watergate scandal exploded across the nation's press. Though I felt an awful deadness inside, I didn't think I was searching spiritually. But while Tom's explanation that he had "accepted Jesus Christ" shocked and baffled me, it also made me curious. He was at peace with himself, something I surely wasn't.

Tom explained it all to me that sultry August night. I couldn't show too much interest, of course—I was senior partner of a powerful Washington law firm, friend of the President. But as I left Tom's house, I discovered I couldn't get my keys into the car ignition. I couldn't see them—the White House "hatchet man," as the newspapers called me, the ex-Marine infantry captain was crying too hard. That night I was confronted with my own sin—not just Watergate's dirty tricks, but the sin deep within me, the hidden evil that lives in every human heart. It was painful, and I could not escape. I cried out to God and found myself driven irresistibly into His waiting arms. That was the night I gave my life to Jesus Christ and began the greatest adventure of my life.

A lot of skeptics thought it wouldn't last, that it was just a ploy for sympathy, a foxhole conversion. I don't blame them. If the tables were turned, I'd have thought the same thing.

But not once in these ten years have I doubted that Jesus Christ lives. There is nothing of which I am more certain. And not once would I have turned the clock back. My lowest days as a Christian (and there were low ones—seven months' worth of them in prison, to be exact) have been more fulfilling and rewarding than all the days of glory in the White House.

The years before conversion were death; the years since have been life and the adventure of loving God, the purpose of that life.

And so with each passing day, my gratitude to God for what He did for me — at Calvary and that night in my friend's driveway — grows deeper and deeper.

So, too, does my gratitude for those who have helped me along the way. To Tom Phillips who introduced me to the love of God; to Doug Coe, Al Quie, Harold Hughes, Graham Purcell, and Fred Rhodes who demonstrated that love; to those whose writing and teaching have challenged me; to a loving, supportive family, to Gordon Loux and my colleagues at Prison Fellowship who live it out with me in the dark holes of prison; and to the thousands of others who have prayed for me and written to me, I am deeply and eternally grateful.

CHARLES W. COLSON
June 1, 1983
P.O. Box 17500
Washington, D.C., 20041

Special Acknowledgments

I am grateful for these materials and interviews extensively relied upon in certain chapters of the book.

Chapters 2-3: Alexander Solzhenitsyn, *Gulag Archipelago*, Harper and Row, 1975. See Part IV, Chapter 1, The Ascent.

Chapter 4: *Confessions of St. Augustine*, Translation by John K. Ryan, Doubleday, 1960.

Chapter 5: John W. Montgomery, ed., *God's Inerrant Word: An International Symposium on the Trustworthiness of Scripture*, Bethany House, 1974. See essay by R. C. Sproul.

James Montgomery Boice, ed., *Does Inerrancy Matter?* publication of ICBI, 1979.

R. C. Sproul, *Knowing Scripture*, IVP, 1977.

Chapter 8: Curtis Mitchell, *Billy Graham: Saint or Sinner*, Revell, 1979.

Mickey Cohen, In My Own Words: The Underworld Autobiography of Michael Mickey Cohen, as told to John Peer Nugent, Englewood Cliffs, N.J.: Prentice-Hall, 1975.

We are grateful for the interviews provided by Jim Vaus, J. Edwin Orr, George Wilson, Suzy Hamblen, and Charette Kvernstoen of *Decision Magazine*.

Chapters 9-10: Foy Valentine, *What Do You Do After You Say Amen*, Word, 1980.

Theodore Plantinga, *Learning to Live With Evil*, Eerdmans, 1982 (For one of the few books dealing with the nature and origins of sin and evil — and an excellent one at that — I'm especially grateful to Professor Plantinga.)

Chapter 14: Jerry Bridges, *Pursuit of Holiness*, Nav Press, 1982 (I am deeply indebted to Jerry Bridges; his very readable book on holiness was not only an invaluable reference for this book, but greatly helped my own understanding.)

William Wilberforce, *Real Christianity*, modern edition edited by Professor James Houston, Multnomah Press, 1982.

I am grateful to Senator William Armstrong for his willingness to allow me to tell the story of his bedside vigil with a dying friend. With customary modesty, Bill said he saw nothing special in what he did; he had not even told his own staff about his experience. I am also grateful to Orv Krieger, Ken Hooker, Donald Adcox, Joyce Page, and Patti Awan for sharing their stories.

Chapter 16: Special thanks are in order for Bill Bontrager who opened his files and unselfishly gave many hours to interviews. Various movie producers have expressed an interest in purchasing the Bontrager story; in spite of the fact that its telling here might hurt Bill's chances to sell rights to others, he graciously agreed to our using it. We are grateful to Harry Fred Palmer as well for his cooperation.

Chapter 17: Francis Schaeffer, *Christian Manifesto*, Crossway, 1981.

The story about Alexander Solzhenitsyn and the old man who made the sign of the cross was first told by Solzhenitsyn to a small group of Christian leaders and later recounted by Billy Graham in his New Year's telecast, 1977. It has been retold subsequently, most publicly by Senator Jesse Helms (R-NC).

Chapter 18: Special thanks to Paul Cho and his books.

Chapter 21: We are especially grateful to ex-POWs Norman McDaniel and James Ray for extensive interviews; in addition Howard Rutledge's book, *In the Presence of Mine Enemies*, Revell, 1973, was extremely helpful.

Epilogue: The story of Telemachus is found in Leslie D. Weatherhead's *It Happened in Palestine*, London: Hodder & Stoughton, 1936.

Notes

HOW IT ALL BEGAN

1. Shirley MacLaine, *Washington Post* Interview, 1977.
2. *Daily Word* (October 1982), 19.
3. Matthew 22:37-38; Mark 12:28-31; Luke 10:25-28.

Chapter 3. FAITH AND OBEDIENCE

1. Alexander Solzhenitsyn, *Gulag Archipelago* II (New York: Harper and Row, 1974), 613-15.
2. Ibid., 613.
3. See Hebrews 11, the chapter often called the Hall of Fame of the Faithful, especially verse 39.
4. Matthew 8; Luke 7.
5. Job 13:15 KJV.
6. Acts 1:6 NIV.
7. Acts 1:7 NIV.
8. Matthew 22:36 NIV.
9. John 14:15 NIV.
10. 1 John 5:3 KJV.

Chapter 4. TAKE UP AND READ

1. Italicized portions of this chapter are slightly paraphrased from *The Confessions of St. Augustine*, translated by John K. Ryan (New York: Doubleday, 1960).

Chapter 5. JUST ANOTHER BOOK?

1. "Luke and the Iron Man" (American Bible Society, December 1976).
2. From an interview with Gonzalo Ba'ez Carrago, *Christianity Today* (5 March 1982).

3. Richard C. Halverson, *The Timelessness of Jesus Christ* (Ventura, Calif.: Regal Books, 1982), 46-7.

4. Luke 4:18-19 NIV.

5. John 5:39.

6. Matthew 4; Luke 4: Luke 24:25-27; Deuteronomy 8:3; 6:16; 6:13; John 17:17 KJV.

7. Matthew 28:18 NIV.

8. 1 John 1:3 NIV; Luke 1:1-4.

9. 1 Corinthians 15:17 NIV.

Chapter 6. WATERGATE AND THE RESURRECTION

1. John Dean, *Blind Ambition* (New York: Simon and Schuster, 1976), 233.

2. Acts 1:3 NIV.

3. 1 Corinthians 15.

4. Blaise Pascal, *Pensees*, translated by A.J. Krailsheimer (New York: Penguin Classics, 1966), 125.

5. Matthew 5:18; John 17:17.

Chapter 7. BELIEVING GOD

1. 2 Timothy 3:16; 4:2-3.

2. John Walvoord, *Inspiration and Interpretation* (Grand Rapids: Eerdmans, 1957), 18.

3. Letter to Jerome, quoted in James Boice, *Does Inerrancy Matter* (ICBF Foundation Series).

4. Martin Luther, *Table Talk*, quoted in above work.

5. Ibid.

6. "Divino Afflante Spiritu," September 30, 1943, from *The Papal Encyclicals 1939-1958* (McGrath Publishing Co., 1981).

7. In the sixteenth century at the fourth session of the Council of Trent, the Roman Catholic church adopted the view that "These truths and rules are contained in written book and unwritten traditions, which received by the apostles from the mouth of Christ himself or from the apostles themselves, the Holy Ghost dictating, having come down to us." In 1950, Pope Pius XII reaffirmed the total inspiration of Scripture and criticized those who would pervert the belief that God is the author of holy Scripture. This was Humani Generis 1950, and in that critique of liberal exegesis the pope embraced three of the encyclicals: Providentissiumus Deus issued by Leo XIII in 1893 in which it was stated: "There is no error whatsoever in reference to Scripture; Spiritus Paraclitus 1920; and Divino Afflante Spiritu 1943.

8. *Emerging Trends* (Princeton Religious Research Center, December 1982), 4:10.

9. 2 Timothy 3:16.

10. John 17:17 KJV.

11. Genesis 3:3 NIV.

12. Luke 4:3-4 NIV.

13. Luke 4:8; Deuteronomy 6:13 NIV.

14. Luke 4:9-12 NIV.

Chapter 9. WHATEVER BECAME OF SIN?

1. Richard Trench, Archbishop of Dublin.

2. Leviticus 26:40-41.

3. Psalm 51.

4. See Ezekiel 18:19-22, 30-32 and the entire prophetic literature from Isaiah to Malachi.

5. Matthew 3:3 NIV.

6. Mark 1:14 NIV.

7. Mark 24:47 NIV.

8. 1 Corinthians 11:27.
9. Acts 26:20 NIV.
10. J. Edwin Orr, "The First Word of the Gospel" (an unpublished essay), 1980.
11. Dietrich Bonhoeffer, *Cost of Discipleship* (New York: Macmillan, 1963), 45-6.
12. 2 Samuel 11 — 12:13.
13. David Myers, *The Inflated Self* (New York: Seabury Press, 1980).
14. Ramsey Clark, *Crime in America* (New York: Simon and Schuster, 1970).
15. Jimmy Carter, "Interview with the National Black Network," *Weekly Compilation of Presidential Documents*, July, 1977.
16. National Conference of Christians and Jews, New York City, 23 March 1982.
17. Jeremiah 17:9 NIV.

Chapter 10. IT IS IN US

1. *The Confessions of* St. Augustine, translated by John K. Ryan (New York: Doubleday, 1960), 69-72.
2. Alexandr I. Solzhenitsyn, *The Gulag Archipelago* 1918-1956, translated from the Russian by Thomas P. Whitney (New York: Harper and Row, 1975), 612.
3. Ibid.
4. Romans 3:23; 3:10.
5. Matthew 15:18-20; Mark 7:20-23.
6. *Confessions*, 144.
7. Ibid., 68.
8. J. Glen Gray, *The Warriors: Reflections on Men in Battle* (New York: Harper and Row, 1973).
9. Theodore Plantinga, *Learning to Live with Evil* (Grand Rapids: Eerdmans, 1982), see ch. 11.
10. From the shooting script of "Patton" (Los Angeles: American Film Institute Library).
11. Acts 11:18.

Chapter 12. WE WERE THERE

1. Luke 23:41 NIV.
2. 1 Kings 16:31 NASB.
3. John 16:8.
4. Romans 7:24 NIV.
5. Romans 7:7-8 NIV.
6. "Romans 8:1-3 NIV.

Chapter 13. BE HOLY BECAUSE I AM HOLY

1. Phyllis Theroux, "Amazing Grace," *Washington Post Magazine*, October 18, 1981, 38.
2. James 1:27 NIV.
3. Kathryn Spink, *The Miracle of Love* (New York: Harper and Row, 1981), 66.
4. Ibid., 157.
5. Luke 18:9-14.
6. Jerry Bridges, *Pursuit of Holiness* (Colorado Springs: NAV Press, 1982), 72.
7. Exodus 20 — 23.
8. Exodus 24:3,7 NIV.
9. Exodus 29:44-45 NIV.
10. Leviticus 12:44. The Greek word in Scripture is *Hagios* meaning "set apart, unique, different, above the ordinary."
11. John 1:14 NASB.
12. Revelation 21:3 NASB.

13. William Wilberforce, *Real Christianity*, edited by James H. Houston (Portland, Or.: Multnomah, 1982), 87. Also, see ch. 15, note 1.

Chapter 14. THE EVERYDAY BUSINESS OF HOLINESS

1. Ephesians 4:24-32; Colossians 3:12-13; Ephesians 5:1-21; 1 Thessalonians 4:3-7; 1 Corinthians 6:9-10; Galatians 6:2; 1 Corinthians 6:12; 8:9-13; 10:31.
2. Galatians 6:9,7 NIV.
3. John Brown, *Expository Discourses on 1 Peter* (1848) reprint edition (Edinburgh: Banner of Truth Trust), 1:106.
4. John 14:26; 17:17; Romans 8:9-11; 1 Corinthians 2:12-13; 6:11; 1 Thessalonians 4:7-8.
5. Malcolm Muggeridge, *Something Beautiful for God* (New York: Harper and Row, 1971), 66.
6. Romans 6:2, 11 – 12.
7. Bridges, *Pursuit of Holiness*.
8. Ibid., 84.
9. John 14:21 NIV.

Chapter 15. AND HIS RIGHTEOUSNESS

1. Wilberforce later wrote a biting and prophetic book challenging the church on the issue. It was first published in the early nineteenth century and entitled A *Practical View of the Prevailing Religious Systems of Professed Christians, in the Higher and Middle Classes in This Country, Contracted with Real Christianity*. It is now available in a modern edition as edited by James Houston (See ch. 13, note 13). This is highly recommended reading, for Wilberforce wrote the prophetic insight not only for the England of his time, but for today, especially for the church in America.
2. Exodus 19:6 NIV.
3. Deuteronomy 16:20.
4. 2 Samuel 8:15.
5. 1 Kings 3:9 NIV.
6. Isaiah foretold the One who would ultimately bring "justice in the earth," the Messiah, the perfect image of holiness and justice. See Isaiah 42:3-7.
7. Jeremiah 22:13, 16 KJV.
8. Amos 2:7-8.
9. Amos 8:5-6.
10. Amos 5:14.
11. Amos 5:24 NASB.
12. *Freedom and Faith*, edited by Lynn Buzzard (Westchester, Ill.: Crossway Books, 1982), 161.
13. Matthew 5:17.
14. Luke 4:18-19 NIV; see also, Isaiah 61:1-2.
15. Luke 4:20-21 NIV.
16. Matthew 25:42-43 NW.
17. Matthew 5:13-16.
18. Matthew 6:33 KJV.
19. *Freedom and Faith*, 73.

Chapter 17. THE RADICAL CHRISTIAN

1. Garth Lean, *Strangely Warmed* (Wheaton: Tyndale, 1979), 62.
2. Howard Snyder, *The Radical Wesley* (Downers Groave, Ill.: Inter-Varsity Press, 1980), 86-7.
3. *The Letters of the Rev. John Wesley*, A.M., edited by John Telford (London: The Epworth Press, 1931).

4. Romans 13:1-2; 1 Peter 2:13-14.

5. Francis Schaeffer, *Christian Manifesto* (Westchester, Ill.: Crossway Books, 1981), 91.

6. "A godly warning or admonition to the faithful in London, Newcastle, and Berwich," *Works of John Knox*, collected and edited by David Laing. Edinburgh: Woodrow Society 1836-1848. (Reprinted in New York: AMS Press, 1966), 6 vols.

7. Hebrews 11:23; Daniel 3; Acts 4:18-20.

8. Revelation 11:15 NIV.

9. Schaeffer, *Manifesto*, 121.

10. Jon Johnston, *Will Evangelicalism Survive Its Own Popularity?* (Grand Rapids: Zondervan, 1980).

11. Schaeffer, *Manifesto*, 28.

12. Malcolm Muggeridge, *The End of Christendom* (Grand Rapids: Eerdmans, 1980), 23.

Chapter 18. THE HOLY NATION

1. Mark 1:15.

2. Jim Wallis, *Call to Conversion* (New York: Harper and Row, 1981).

3. Ibid.

3. Ibid.

4. 1 Peter 2:9.

5. Exodus 19:6.

6. Inspired by the New Testament example of the early church.

7. Paul Yonggi Cho with Harold Hostetter, *Successful Home Cell Groups* (Plainfield, N.J.: Logos International, 1981), 16.

8. Halverson, *Timelessness of Jesus Christ*, 104.

9. 1 Corinthians 12:26 NIV.

10. In Philippians 3:10 Paul wrote that he longed for the "fellowship of suffering," for then in a real sense he was sharing in the suffering of Christ.

Chapter 20. THE CHURCH ON THE FRONT LINES

1. Jacques Ellul, *The Political Illusion*, tr. from the French by Konrad Keller (New York: Vintage Books, 1972).

Chapter 21. THIS IS MY BODY

1. This chapter is a composite drawn both from documentation of events that happened to American POWs in Vietnam and from interviews with James Ray and Norman McDaniel. While some names are fictitious, the incidents are not.

KINGDOMS IN CONFLICT

by Charles Colson
with Ellen Santilli Vaughn

To those who serve in "the little platoons"
around the world, faithfully evidencing
the love and justice of the Kingdom of God
in the midst of the kingdoms of this world.

CONTENTS

PART IV: PRESENCE OF THE KINGDOM

Prologue

General Brent Slocum's T-shirt stuck to his sweaty back and powerful, heaving shoulders as he grinned at his twenty-nine-year-old opponent. His adjutant's urgent breathing filled the small handball court.

"Gonna make it through the last point, Rob?" the general asked. It was a pleasure, at fifty-four, to whip a younger man.

Suddenly there was a pounding on the door. "General," another aide shouted from outside. "Command Center on the line, sir."

Slocum hesitated. He wanted to finish the game. The pounding resumed.

"All right, Sloan," the general bawled. "I heard you. Those boys better have something worth my time." Someone was forever using the channels. He wondered whether anybody could get through if a real emergency command—like war—was needed.

The youthful voice on the other end of the mobile communications line was shaking, probably scared half to death to be speaking to the chairman of the Joint Chiefs of Staff. "It's the White House signal agency calling, sir. Shall I patch it in?"

"Of course," Slocum grunted. Almost instantly he heard a second voice, crisp and precise.

"General Slocum, POTUS has asked you to come immediately, sir. The diplomatic entrance. Enter through the south gate. Can I give an affirmative, sir?"

"Of course," he grunted again, then tossed the receiver in his aide's direction as he headed for the locker room. The White House? Six in the morning? Why on earth do they use an acronym for every last living thing in this city, Slocum grumbled to himself, including the President of the United States?

Eight minutes later he strode in full-dress uniform toward his waiting car. From Fort Myer to the White House was a ten-minute drive without traffic. His driver, the Army's best, had practiced many times. Fortunately, the city was just coming to life. Most of the streets were gray and deserted.

The general sat back as his limousine raced toward its destination, his thoughts swirling. He had seen the president only a few times since becoming chairman in January. Never had he entered the White House outside regular hours. Something hot was up. He ran through the possibilities.

It might be Mexico. The Sandinista-backed guerrillas had killed thirty-three in a bomb blast in Acapulco last Friday. Slocum still didn't have an op. plan ready to seal the border; he'd be in trouble if the old man wanted that.

The Middle East? That very morning, before leaving for the handball court, Slocum had glanced over a report of two new Soviet divisions moving into Iran.

Or perhaps, though less likely, it was Britain. Nobody had anticipated the vehemence of the Kinnock government when they discovered two Poseidon subs in their waters in violation of Britain's nuclear-free policy.

Go to the Residence, he had been ordered. Whatever it was, it was important.

The blue-jacketed White House policeman saluted and waved the general's car through the heavy black-steel gates and up the long curved driveway that cut across the South Lawn of the White House. Slocum counted five limousines, all larger than his, at the door. The secretary of defense . . . the secretary of state. . . . Getting out of the car, he stood for a moment and gazed up at the light scum of late snow clinging to the gutters of the Residence. *This could be war*, he thought.

"Right this way, sir," announced a young marine. He steered the general through the oval-shaped Diplomatic Receiving Room and up the flight of marble steps to the Great Center Hall. From there the general followed him toward another flight of stairs carpeted in thick red pile. They led, he knew, to the family quarters, although he had never been above the first floor.

At the head of the stairs stood a secret-service agent, a plug in one ear. He glanced at the general and then seemed to look through him.

The agent's suit sagged as though he'd worn it for a week. It annoyed Slocum. After a life in the military, sloppy civilian dress was difficult to accept.

His marine escort clicked his heels softly and announced, "The Lincoln Sitting Room, sir." He nodded to the door of the study directly off the president's bedroom. The secret-service agent leaned to one side and swung the door open, never taking his eyes off the stairway.

Larry Parrish, the sandy-haired, ivy-league White House chief of staff, was the only one to nod at Slocum as he entered. The others were preoccupied in knots of uneasy conversation. Parrish waved the general into a hard-backed antique chair, then caught President Hopkins's eye.

"Everyone's here," he said.

The small room, which had once served Abraham Lincoln as an office, was crowded with antiques; this morning it seemed even more crowded by the egos of the handful of powerful men the president had summoned. Parrish had taken their measure long ago, however, and he somehow managed to make these egos work together for whatever goals the president chose. He knew people, he knew the system, and he had a finely tuned political sense for what would fly on the 6:00 o'clock news. "I'm a technician," he would say with a smile when pressed about his role in the government. He thought of that now as he surveyed the men before him.

Though the general was the most recent of the president's top appointments, Parrish had known Brent Slocum through a decade of Washington receptions. The general was the best sort of military man: politically unimaginative, but quick to seize the main issues. Neither a paper pusher nor a cowboy, he had just the kind of solid, capable confidence to command any situation.

Seated next to Slocum was Alexander Hartwell, the secretary of defense, revered as the nastiest infighter in Washington's brutal bureaucracy. Parrish had often thought he was glad Hartwell was *their* s.o.b. He would make a formidable enemy.

A veteran of twenty years in the House, Hartwell had worked the deals reconciling the Christian right to the Republican hard-liners that laid the foundation for Hopkins's election. For his reward Hartwell had demanded and been given Defense. He sometimes acted, however, as if he had been given the White House. Parrish worked hard to stay one jump ahead of Hartwell—and to remind him who was president.

Next to Hartwell was Secretary of State Henry Lovelace. Parrish suspected Henry was out of his depth, and so did a lot of other people who referred to him privately as Secretary Love. Lovelace owed his job to his friendship with the president, dating back to college days. The president was comfortable with him, and his weaknesses were compensated for by the strength of Alan Davies, the national security advisor. It was doubtful anyway whether Davies could have worked with a strong counterpart at State.

Davies, whose wispy appearance, blank stare, and ubiquitous bow tie belied his power, crouched in the room's one overstuffed chair. He always reminded Parrish of a time bomb, staring and ticking. Davies read everything and forgot nothing. The president had come to rely on him during his fourteen months in the White House. Almost dangerously so, Parrish thought.

Finally, slumped on a rosewood chair purchased by Mary Todd Lincoln, was the professorial attorney general, Hyman Levin. How the man could talk! He kept the right-wingers happy, crusading with the vigor of the recently converted. Fortunately, though, he was a realist who knew how to talk on one line and compromise on another.

Any one of the five men, with the possible exception of Lovelace, would have dominated another setting. But bluster as they would, in the end they did the president's bidding.

How Hopkins managed this trick Parrish had not quite figured out. Part of it, he sometimes mused, was physical. The president looked like the president: tall, with a magnificent silver mane, a jutting jaw that suggested strength to men, and sparkling blue eyes that charmed women. And he sounded like God Almighty, his thunderclap voice rising out of some lower register.

Mostly, though, Parrish had begun to believe that the president dominated them by sheer goodness. After surviving decades of politics, Parrish didn't believe goodness had anything to do with effective leadership. But Hopkins was different. He radiated something that made you feel morally small after being around him.

Despite these natural assets, Shelby Hopkins had come late to political life. For over twenty years he had been a professor of history and later academic dean at Baylor University. He had entered the political arena in the eighties when evangelical Christians came out of nowhere to become a major force in national politics.

Hopkins had been nominated to run for governor of Texas chiefly because Republican political consultants thought he looked and sounded good on television. To the surprise of many, he had governed imaginatively and circumspectly, coming to national prominence through his handling of the Dallas AIDS riots, which had put him on the network news every night for two weeks. When the Republican hard-liners patched things up with the Christian right after the big split in 1992, Hopkins was a natural candidate for president.

Parrish's thoughts were interrupted now as the president looked up from some papers, smiled briefly, and looked at each of the men. "Gentlemen, let's get started. Sorry to call you in so early this morning. I appreciate your promptness." There was just a trace of Texas in his voice.

"I've asked you here to the Residence because if we were seen at this hour in the west wing, the press would be onto things in nothing flat. We can't have that.

"We seem to have a little trouble brewing in Israel. You all know that the Knesset has been paralyzed for some time, with neither the Likud nor the Labor parties able to get a stable majority to form a government."

Hopkins held up the black-leather notebook engraved with gold letters, *For the President's eyes only*, and continued.

"But this morning's intelligence summary suggests that the logjam is breaking. Both parties have been bargaining with small fringe parties, as you know. Our sources say that the Likud party is very close to striking a deal with the Tehiya party. In fact, since it's midafternoon in Israel now, they may have already reached an agreement. I talked this over with Alan earlier this morning and decided we'd better get to work on it right away."

Parrish scribbled notes furiously. This was the first indication of what had stirred the president. Was it truly an emergency? The difference between the two chief Israeli parties appeared minuscule, especially in their attitudes toward the Arab world. So far as the U.S. was concerned, it made little difference which actually gained power.

At the president's invitation Alan Davies leaned forward and, consulting a red notebook that looked like the president's but without the lettering, told them more than anyone could possibly want to know at 6:30 in the morning about the tiny fanatical religious party known as Tehiya.

The leader was Yosef Tzuria, an Albanian refugee who favored driving all Arabs out of the occupied territories. Tzuria also believed that God had given Israel title to all land west of the Euphrates River—territory inconveniently known as Iraq, Lebanon, and Syria. But—Parrish almost missed the emphasis because of Davies's monotone—Tzuria's big scheme was religious. He wanted to blow up the Dome of the Rock, the sacred Muslim shrine in Jerusalem, and build a temple in its place.

Davies concluded his briefing with a quote from Tzuria: "'We must establish a permanent place of prayer on the mount. It is a desecration of God to enter the mount under the authority of an Arab guard.'

"I might add," Davies said dryly, "that they're quite serious. They're being bankrolled by some big industrialists in Israel, along with a fundamentalist group in Texas, which, we gather, has handed them at least twenty-five million dollars. They've got men in training." A trace of a smile curved his lips. "Not only commandos, but priests. They're in training to perform Jewish sacrificial rites."

Priests? Sacrificial rites? Parrish searched the faces of the other men. Did they understand the significance here? He didn't. Nor could he decipher the strange, excited light in the president's eyes.

"I hate to sound uninformed," Parrish said finally, "but so what?"

"So what?" the president echoed slowly. "So what? This could mean war!"

"The Likud party isn't going to let some marginal crowd of fanatics carry them into war," Parrish said. "Anyway, it sounds to me like their big thing is religion, not politics."

"Yes, that's right, Larry," the president said, nodding his silvery head. "That's just the problem. They take the Old Testament prophecies very seriously. And on the question of whether Likud would allow them to carry the nation into the war, that's why I called you together. This morning's briefing says, and Alan tells me the sources are impeccable, that Tzuria and the Likud leader, Moshe Arens, are in negotiations right now. And Arens has tentatively agreed to look the other way when Tzuria's commandos blow up the Dome of the Rock. What they've yet to agree on is whether Arens will promise to declare Israeli sovereignty over the whole Temple Mount. It looks as though it could actually happen. The Jewish Temple could be rebuilt."

"And that would mean war," added Attorney General Levin. "The Arabs are very religious too, you know—they have always said they are prepared to die before any Jew will pray on the Mount."

Parrish shifted uncomfortably. His own Episcopalian background differed considerably from the president's Southern Baptist roots, and though this had never created any strain between them, Parrish felt out of his depth when it came to the finer nuances of the religious world.

"I'm sorry, Mr. President," he said apologetically. "Maybe everyone else understands this, but I'm not with it. Could you bear with me here until someone explains about the Temple? I must have missed that briefing." He saw to his relief that at least Hartwell and Slocum were in the same boat he was, for Slocum nodded at his request and Hartwell was wearing a tight, bemused smile.

"Maybe I can get Hyman to brief us on that, Larry. He was quite a Levitical scholar up at Yale, you know. Now since his conversion he knows even more than he used to. Explain it, will you Hy?" The president and his attorney general grinned at each other.

This suggestion did not set Parrish at ease. He knew of Levin's conversion to Christianity, but what in heaven's name was a Levitical scholar? And the glances exchanged by Levin and the president, as if they shared some secret fraternity ritual, made him feel like an outsider.

Levin had a high choirboy voice and held his chin up slightly when he talked. He loved the chance to lecture.

"I suppose you know, Larry, that the ancient Israelites worshiped in a Temple built by Solomon in Jerusalem. By the time of King Hezekiah, in 715 B.C., worship was allowed nowhere else. That Temple was destroyed, however, by Babylonian armies in 586 B.C. Then came the Babylonian captivity, after which the returning Jews built a second Temple. That was later replaced by an elaborate monument for King Herod." Levin grinned. "You have heard of King Herod?"

Parrish nodded.

"Good," continued Levin in a high, ironic tone. "But the main fact you need to know is that in A.D. 70 the Jews revolted against Rome, and the Romans retaliated by destroying their Temple. It was never rebuilt. The Muslims erected a mosque over the ruins centuries later. During the Crusades the Christians gained control and turned it into a church, but in recent centuries it has reverted to the Arabs. Today it is the Dome of the Rock, one of the holiest Muslim shrines. They would view its desecration as an unspeakable outrage.

"Now that, Larry, poses quite a problem. Because the devout Jew cannot just forget the Temple. They consider the site sacred. The Temple originally built there contained the Holy of Holies where no one could set foot—except the high priest, once a year—without desecrating God's holy name. So the Muslim control of that spot is . . . a desecration of all that is sacred to them."

"So somebody gets desecrated no matter what," Parrish interjected.

"Very good, Larry. Furthermore, the Jew cannot fulfill the Old Testament sacrificial laws unless a Temple is rebuilt on that site. Promises of Messiah's return to a new Temple are found in Scripture; there and only there does He wish to make His residence. So for the devout Jew a rebuilt Temple is more important than the renewal of the state of Israel."

"But . . . they have synagogues," Parrish said.

"A synagogue is not the Temple. A synagogue is a house of prayer. But you cannot do the blood sacrifices there."

Parrish's face twisted into a combination of pain and disbelief. "Blood sacrifices?"

"Yes, a sheep, a goat, a bull. Killed on the altar and burned on the perpetual fire."

"What in the world—"

"There is one more thing I should add," Levin interrupted him. "To the devout Christian who pays attention to prophecy, the rebuilding of the ancient Temple will set the stage for the last great act of history. It will signal Armageddon. That explains why Christian groups are funding the Tehiya. The Temple will pave the way for Christ's triumphant return."

Levin leaned back, pleased with his presentation. The president looked inquiringly at Parrish.

"Does it make sense now, Larry? Obviously, while these reports are frightening, there's some excitement that comes with them too. You can't help but wonder if these could be events we've all waited for."

Parrish felt a sudden tightening in his stomach as he remembered former President Frank's charges in the '96 campaign that Hopkins would try to make Bible prophecy self-fulfilling and bring on Armageddon. Never before had it crossed Parrish's mind that those accusations were anything but hysteria.

Brent Slocum struggled to accommodate his six-foot-three frame to the undersized antique chair. His head was spinning, particularly with the attorney general's last words. He had visited Israel several times, but to observe Israeli defenses on the Golan Heights, not mosques in Jerusalem. He was a man of war, comfortable talking about supply operations and air support. Not Armageddon.

He glanced at Hartwell. He knew that behind his narrowed eyes and high forehead the secretary of defense was computing fast. Slocum didn't particularly like Hartwell, but he did expect him to talk in terms that made some sense.

Hartwell didn't disappoint him. "So the gist of it is, Mr. President, Armageddon or no Armageddon, we need to head off this deal. It's explosive. Why would Arens even entertain it? He must know all this better than we do."

Davies leaned forward and answered before Hopkins could respond.

"Arens is an old fool," he said flatly. "He'd do anything to regain power. And this issue, strange as it sounds to us, is really quite popular within certain powerful segments of the Israeli population."

"Not with Arens!" Slocum blurted. "I know the man. He doesn't have a religious bone in his body."

"Right," Davies said. "But he's a politician who knows how to play religious issues."

"If he's a politician," Hartwell sneered, "then he ought to know that Israel's existence depends on the good opinion of the United States. If this cockamamy scheme is as serious as you seem to think, then why don't we get him on the phone and tell him to forget it? No ifs, ands, or buts."

"Now hold on," Secretary Lovelace interjected. "That's no way to treat our ally."

"What if he says no?" Parrish asked, looking up from his note taking. "Could you back it up?"

"With a bullet, if necessary," Hartwell said. "We have agents who would find it a pleasure."

Hopkins shook his head violently, and Parrish quickly interjected, "Such matters are never discussed in the president's presence."

Slocum grabbed onto a possibility that made some sense to him. "I can have the Delta Force in the area ready to go in twelve hours, sir."

"Hold on, now," said Parrish. "If I understand it correctly, the question isn't military in nature. We could drop an atom bomb on Jerusalem, if it came to that. The question is, could we back it up politically? Do you really think we can dictate policy to Israel, our only reliable ally in the Middle East? You think the Israel lobby would give us room to maneuver? And Arens knows just how much leeway we have."

"Come off it, Larry," said Hartwell. "We can make Arens come around if we're willing to get rough."

President Hopkins had moved from his chair to the window overlooking the South Lawn, but hadn't said a word. It was unusual for him not to take part in the discussion; he enjoyed a spirited debate. But this morning he seemed far away, his eyes fixed on some distant point.

"Gentlemen," he said finally, "we must keep in mind the very real possibility that this situation is beyond us all." The words hung suspended in the air for a long, awkward moment. Only Levin nodded.

Hartwell shook his head with annoyance and reflexively reached into his jacket pocket for a cigarette. Then he remembered that no one smoked in the White House anymore.

"Mr. President," he said angrily, "whatever cosmic forces may be involved here, Tzuria must be stopped. There's nothing more dangerous than allowing religious fanaticism to replace reasoned political judgment."

"Are you talking about me or Tzuria?" the president asked coldly. Being called a religious zealot during the campaign had stung Hopkins. He had run on the platform "Return America to God" and left no doubt where he stood, but the fanatic label always annoyed him.

"No, Mr. President, of course not. I'm talking about Tzuria. He's the menace."

"Good," said Hopkins, putting on his half-circle reading glasses and picking up a well-worn brown-leather Bible from a table beside Davies's chair. "At the risk of appearing fanatical, I'd like to read you all a passage from Ezekiel. It was written five centuries before the birth of Christ." He flipped a few pages until he located his text. "Listen to this: 'My dwelling place will be with them; I will be their God, and they will be my people. Then the nations will know that I the Lord make Israel holy, *when my sanctuary is among them forever.*'

"Ezekiel tells us that Gog, the nation that will lead all the other powers of darkness against Israel, will come out of the north. Biblical scholars have been saying for generations that Gog must be Russia. What other powerful nation is to the north of Israel? None. But it didn't seem to make sense before the Russian revolution, when Russia was a Christian country. Now that Russia has become communistic and atheistic, it does. Now that Russia has set itself against God, it fits the description of Gog perfectly."

President Hopkins put down the Bible, removed his glasses, and ran a hand through his hair. He stared into the eyes of each man one by one. Slocum felt self-conscious. Parrish, who usually had his head down, taking notes, stared back up at Hopkins.

"I ran my campaign on the Bible," Hopkins said, "and I intend to run this nation on the Bible. Let's keep in mind while we make our plans that God has already made His."

Then the president smiled and broke the tension. "Now let's get down to business. We've talked enough. You know the situation. I want strategy options out of all of you by noon. Keep the subject as mysterious as possible to your aides. I don't want any leaks. Repeat—*no* leaks."

Turning to Parrish, he asked, "Larry, one key question. Is there any hint of this in the press? Do they know about the Arens-Tzuria deal at all?"

"Not to my knowledge," said Parrish. "I'll check, but I don't think there's been anything in the wind."

"Good," the president said tersely. "In fact, just to be sure we keep it that way, steer them a little. Put out a story, Larry. Something from, you know, 'informed sources.' Say there will be a labor–left-wing coalition. Or whatever you think is best. We must buy some time here."

The president sat down, took off his watch, and wound it. "Anything else?" he asked. There was no response. "Then at the risk of again appearing to be a religious zealot, may I suggest that before you leave to prepare your recommendations, we invoke God's blessings upon us and upon this nation. Henry, will you lead us in prayer?"

Slocum watched in horror as the secretary of state stood up, turned around, and knelt before his chair. The president and Parrish followed suit. So did Levin. Davies, with an annoyed look on his face, got slowly onto his knees.

Brave enough to have won a Silver Star in Vietnam, Slocum was not sure he had the courage for this. He looked over at Hartwell who sat obstinately in his chair, his eyes on the floor, his chin on his fist.

But Slocum was a soldier, and a soldier followed his commander-in-chief. Awkward though it felt, he turned his long body around and knelt.

Secretary Lovelace began to pray in a deep, passionate voice. "We humble ourselves before You, the one true God, who governs the affairs of this beloved nation. We serve You only because You have granted us this privilege and authority, and so we ask You, dear Father, to lead us. We seek Your will. Whatever all this means, give us the eyes to see and the ears to hear. Have it Your way, not ours, and forgive us the sin that would make us blind to Your truth. . . ."

8:45 A.M., THE WHITE HOUSE

Each day at 8:00 A.M. the senior aides to the president gathered around a giant mahogany table in the Roosevelt Room, the windowless conference chamber just across from the Oval Office. This morning Parrish's eyes had been drawn to the famous painting on the north wall, Teddy Roosevelt charging up San Juan Hill. The chief of staff had sighed inwardly, wondering exactly what they were charging into with the Israel situation.

Now, over an hour later, Parrish sat, hardly listening, as several self-important aides held forth on a variety of matters—the latest nomination to the Supreme Court; the plan to abolish the Department of Education; and the drive in the Senate for welfare reform. At the moment James Shepherd, head of the Budget Office, was off on his usual tirade about agencies refusing to cooperate with the 10-percent across-the-board budget cut.

A master at disguising his true feelings behind an impassive mask, Parrish stared soberly at Shepherd as his mind churned. One mishandled crisis, especially in Israel, could destroy a popular president's ratings overnight. And as volatile as the Middle East was, one incident there could escalate into a major situation. As concerned as he was about that, however, he was more concerned about another matter. He was beginning to worry about the president.

Parrish had joined Hopkins's team late in the campaign after backing another candidate. Nevertheless, until this morning he felt he knew the president better than his own brother. He still remembered that first interview during the campaign when Hopkins had been feeling out possible talent for his team; within thirty minutes the two men had been talking with the freedom of old acquaintances.

Once in the White House, they enjoyed complete rapport on political matters. Perhaps, Parrish was prepared to admit, that had been easy because so many events had broken in their favor. Oil prices had dropped, curbing the runaway inflation of the early nineties. A cure for AIDS had been announced, without warning, and had given the nation a huge psychological lift. Still, it seemed that the two men understood each other's intentions intuitively through a peculiar type of political telepathy.

Parrish at first thought he might be uncomfortable with Hopkins's up-front religiosity, but he wasn't. Hopkins was so decent and open. He was a good man. *You don't meet many people like that,* Parrish often thought, *especially not in Washington.* Yet there was nothing holier-than-thou about the president. A less sincere man would never have gotten away with such White House piety.

Even the daily prayer and Bible readings at staff meetings had been accepted respectfully. Parrish himself had opened his morning's session with a reading from Psalm 90. The practice had grown out of the president's acceptance speech at the Dallas convention when he had pledged to 100 million Americans watching on TV that he would begin every day on his knees and require the same of his key advisors.

It was a popular promise. People had been fed up with the waves of change sweeping the nation in the early nineties. Not only was prayer outlawed in schools, but in all public places, before football games and commencements, and in all public buildings. Even the Senate chaplaincy had been abandoned. A series of ACLU-sponsored cases had reshaped American geography: Bethlehem, Pennsylvania, was forced to change its name, as was Corpus Christi, Texas. St. Louis was narrowly spared by a five-four decision that held that the word *saint* no longer held a specifically sacred connotation. America's population was declining due to soaring abortions. Drug dealers' armed gangs controlled many public schools.

Hopkins had stood rock-solid against all that, and on that basis he had been elected. But now, for the first time, Parrish was not so sure about the president's motives. He didn't understand the currents moving in Hopkins's mind on the Israeli situation. He had left the president just an hour before, staring into the big brown Bible open before him. Parrish told himself that it was perfectly reasonable for a president to draw strength from the Bible at such a time. What bothered him was that Hopkins didn't seem to be reading his Bible for strength. He seemed to be looking for directions.

10:00 A.M., THE PENTAGON

Once General Brent Slocum was back at the Pentagon, the praying and Bible reading seemed so distant and strange that he almost wondered whether he had imagined the scene at the White House. Relieved to be in familiar territory among a group of uniformed brass, he watched the secretary of defense pace back and forth behind his desk like the pendulum of a tightly wound clock swinging in double time. Shirtsleeves rolled up, tie loosened, collar open, Hartwell punctuated his lecture with readings from intelligence reports clutched in his left hand. His right hand held a cigarette, which he rubbed out whenever it burned down to a stub, only to light another. Ashes floated like dirty snow onto the navy-blue carpet, the desk, and Hartwell's beautifully tailored pants.

He talked as quickly as he walked, a practice he had developed during his twenty years as a congressman.

This former representative from Wisconsin was the unlikeliest member of the cabinet, as profane as the president was pious. A party loyalist since the early sixties, he had stuck staunchly with the party regulars when they fought off the Christian New Right's attempt to take over the precinct caucuses in 1988. But that fight led to the Christian walkout from the '92 convention and their running their own candidate in the general election. As a result of the split, the Democrats won in a record landslide.

The Republican recovery owed much to Hartwell. Always a realist, he had worked tirelessly for a reconciliation before the 1996 election, even to the renaming of the party. Though the words almost choked him, Alexander Hartwell now belonged to the Christian Republican party.

These were not traits to endear Hartwell to a man like Slocum, who distrusted politicians. But the secretary of defense had other more attractive qualities. He was a formidable debater, quick with the facts or, if necessary, his mesmeric personality. He knew how the government worked—and had it down cold—and could store more facts about the budget in his head than an IBM computer.

Now he was jabbing his cigarette in the air like a weapon, lecturing them on the immediate action required. "Arens must be ordered to drop Tzuria like a piece of pork. If not, we will withdraw all support, military or otherwise. The subject is nonnegotiable." Stopping his pacing for a moment, he glared at his audience. "Anybody disagree?"

Slocum shook his head and the others followed suit. Hartwell made sense. They should do all they could to persuade Arens to desist.

General Curt Oliver of Central Intelligence, who sat beside Slocum, had delivered actual transcripts of the Arens-Tzuria meetings. They showed Arens as depressingly querulous and erratic, while Tzuria had the constancy of a hungry predator. Tzuria offered to deliver the votes the Likud needed to form a government, but there was a price. Arens must look the other way when the commandos took out the Dome of the Rock; then he must claim Israeli sovereignty over the site. Tzuria would do the rest. They would move so fast the Arabs wouldn't have time to react. Marble slabs had been precut. The Temple could be up within thirty days. The Soviets, Tzuria argued, would hold back since the rock was strategically worthless.

By now Slocum understood what had earlier sounded like an old adventure movie. On reaching his Pentagon office after the early White House meeting, he had called in a young captain who he knew to be highly religious. "What do you know about the Temple Mount?" Slocum had asked. Captain Bryce had confirmed just what President Hopkins had said, and more. The Temple must be rebuilt within the next generation, according to prophecy, Bryce said. As far as he knew, all born-again Christians believed it because the Bible taught it.

Hartwell was waiting for some verbal response. Slocum cleared his throat. "Mr. Secretary, I confirm your objectives. But I think we need to optionalize contingencies. What if Arens refuses to listen to us? What then? This thing could slip out of gear in a hurry."

"Refuse to listen?" Hartwell snapped. "Come off it, General. Absolutely not. We own him. Three of his Knesset members work for us. Oliver here signs their paychecks." Hartwell gestured toward the deputy director of the CIA. "We say the word, and Arens and his nasty little party dry up and disappear."

"Yes, sir," Slocum said. "I'm sure that's right. However, it seems optimal to prepare for all contingencies. People do strange things when religion gets involved. Also Arens might think he can call our bluff. He knows that this administration will never abandon Israel."

Hartwell flushed. He took a long drag on his cigarette. "General," he said scornfully, "I think I know where this administration stands. The abandonment of Israel is not at stake. The abandonment of Moshe Arens is more to the point."

"Yes, sir," said Slocum. "But the Israelis have been known to confuse the two. And they have a track record of maximizing independence. I'd propose we optionalize the possibility—however infinitesimal—that they ignore our counsel."

Hartwell fumed, stared at Slocum, blew smoke. He detested Slocum's Pentagonese but knew the general was right. The president's loyalty to Israel was a matter of faith, and the Israelis would play that for all they could.

"What do you propose then, General?" Hartwell asked, lighting another cigarette and leaning on the back of his overstuffed, shiny-blue leather desk chair.

"The marines, sir. We have an LPH with the Sixth Fleet that could be off the coast in a little under twenty-four hours. It's up to T/O requirements—and ready . . . one battalion . . . good troops. We'd be able to put twenty choppers with six hundred men into Jerusalem thirty minutes after lift-off. The Israelis wouldn't know how to react, especially if we told them we were on an antiterrorist maneuver. It's now 7:00 P.M. in Tel Aviv. My men could have the Dome of the Rock sealed by this time tomorrow."

Hartwell smiled but didn't interrupt.

"Of course, sir," Slocum continued. "I don't have an op. plan approved by the chiefs. We haven't even contemplated . . . that is, no one ever figured on defending a mosque in Jerusalem."

"Wasn't part of the war games, eh General?" Hartwell burst into laughter, which started a coughing spasm. His assistant, Frank Flaherty, was instantly out of his seat, slapping his boss on the back.

"You've got to quit smoking," Flaherty said mechanically. He'd been saying it for nearly twenty years.

Drying his eyes with a rumpled handkerchief, Hartwell said, "Sorry, General. Just the thought of American marines—probably Christians—defending an Arab mosque against our closest allies, the Jews—" With that he started laughing and coughing again. "Hopkins'll have kittens."

Slocum's military operation was both bold and simple, and thus likely to succeed. Nobody had a better idea, and they kicked it around, discussing logistics. But their conversation lacked energy, drifting to a halt whenever they moved from the military to the political situation. None of them could imagine the president authorizing the marines to invade Jerusalem.

As he thought of this ridiculous limitation on his power, Alexander Hartwell gradually warmed into a fury. He slammed his fist on the desk, jumped to his feet, and began to pace again.

"Something has to move him," he muttered. "Something has to make it too hot for him. Not State. The little pip-squeaks there will be wringing their hands all through afternoon tea. Nobody has the guts for this kind of crisis. Congress'll go berserk."

The others stopped talking, watching Hartwell pace from one end of the room to the other.

Suddenly he whirled around and stabbed a finger at the general. "Slocum, what did you make of Parrish? Where is he in all this?"

"Sir?"

"Could we use Parrish? He seems to know the inside of the president's skull. Do you think he'd work with us?"

Slocum found the very idea of outflanking the president offensive. "Parrish is the president's man. He might agree with us, but I don't believe he'd scheme against his own boss."

Hartwell scowled but passed over the implicit warning. "You're right, I suppose. But we need some way . . ." He paused, his gaze fixed on the vivid colors of his desk pad, etched with the giant seal of the secretary of defense.

A smile twitched the corners of his lips. He muttered, "Of course, of course. Why hasn't anyone thought of this until now? Yes, we'll have to." He looked up at his assistant. "Frank, that's it."

After twenty years Flaherty knew enough to say, "Yes, sir."

"Get the story to the press. Leak it fast, and make sure they go after it full speed ahead. But be careful." He grinned widely. "If Hopkins ever found out it would be my—that is, all of our necks, right on the chopping block."

Slocum sat stiffly, as though coming to attention. "Sir, the president gave us strict instructions not to allow this story out."

"Yes, he did, didn't he, General? That's why I want it kept in this room. If it gets out who's responsible, you'll go down with me. Clear enough?" He was on his feet, leaning across the desk, staring directly at Slocum; then he sat down slowly. "General, I appreciate that this may go against your grain. But this is a case when following protocol may not be in the best interest of the commanding officer. When the enemy's aiming a gun at your commander's head, you just shove him into a foxhole. You don't wait to say, 'sir!' Am I right?"

"Yes, sir," Slocum said grudgingly.

"That's all we're gonna do," said Hartwell with a smile. "Give our commander a little shove into the foxhole. You see?"

Slocum said nothing.

Hartwell was on his feet again, pacing behind his desk, his attention back to the leak. "I can't believe this story hasn't broken yet anyway. Well, no . . . it's a religious thing, so the press probably wouldn't even understand. And the Israelis know how to keep things quiet. I wish we did as well."

He pointed a nicotine-stained finger at his assistant. "Okay, Frank, move on it. Call Stuart or Marvin. No, they're too well plugged in. Call Nolan. He'll buy it in a minute. And let it all out: 'Arens is dealing with the Devil . . . would constitute the worst offense against Arab rights in thirty years of occupation . . . fanatical religious elements are gaining control of Israeli foreign policy.' Just make sure we're well under cover—'informed sources,' you know. Once we point the press in the right direction, they'll scare themselves half to death without our help. But it needs to move fast."

"Yes, sir." Flaherty never looked up from his notes.

"But the Arabs will be tipped off too," General Oliver added. "And that may force Arens's hand. Tzuria may strike before the marines are in position."

"No, no. Think it through, gentlemen. The Israelis can't move except by surprise. This'll create confusion for them, and it'll force Hopkins to intervene. Otherwise he'd appear weak." Hartwell licked his lips. He was obviously pleased with himself.

"General." He wheeled around and jabbed his finger at Slocum. "Order the marines to head due east, full steam ahead. Put the Sixth Fleet on standby alert, and have your battle plan ready to issue as soon as possible. That means in the next hour."

Hartwell took one long satisfied look at the military men arrayed before him and chuckled. 'From the Halls of Montezuma to the Dome of the Rock, eh? All right. Get to it."

Slocum felt a sudden sense of exhilaration as he marched out of the secretary's spacious office. He couldn't quite remember feeling the same way in years. Not since Vietnam when he had led his troops through a particularly bloody firefight. His two waiting aides with braided epaulets draped from their shoulders joined him, and the three men walked briskly to the escalators that would take them down to the War Room in the Pentagon basement. Devising strategy in international affairs was heady business. Someday this would all be in the history books, no doubt. Slocum tightened his lips, thrust his shoulders back, and began walking faster.

LATE AFTERNOON, THE WHITE HOUSE PRESS ROOM

At 2:30 in the afternoon Hartwell's leak exploded in the middle of an otherwise routine Washington day. First, Nolan was on Cable News with the bizarre story. Then the wire services ran their versions, crediting "informed sources," that U.S. policymakers were working day and night to head off a militant Tehiya party takeover of the Israeli government; intelligence experts considered war in the Middle East a real possibility.

A separate story, pulled up on short notice out of the files, told the history and objectives of the Tehiya party, including their financial links to American groups who shared their belief that these were the "last days" and that the Arab-Israeli standoff would be broken only by violent confrontation. The Tehiya rallying cry was "they must go," referring to the Arabs.

Reporters began to congregate in the White House Press Room, first reading the story on computer monitors in the little cubicles lining the back of the room, then rushing to phone their editors.

By 3:00 P.M. the Associated Press cited unconfirmed reports that the U.S. Sixth Fleet had been ordered to the eastern Mediterranean. The Pentagon press office issued a flat denial. But only a half hour later there were reports from naval headquarters in Naples, Italy, that all leaves had been cancelled.

That triggered a flood of dispatches from Middle East correspondents eager to catch up. These included wild and vitriolic quotations from various leaders of the Tehiya; of the Waqf, the Jordanian-backed Muslim group that controlled the Temple Mount; and others.

At 4:15, ABC broke into daytime programming with a brief report. The other networks were on the air by 4:25.

The Christian Broadcasting Company interrupted its regular programming for what they called their "Last Things Report." This included continuous live satellite coverage of the Dome of the Rock, using the site as the backdrop for their news set. The host, an Australian named Sydney Halford, interviewed several Bible scholars, evangelists, and a retired Navy admiral. The White House and Pentagon telephone numbers flashed across the screen at five-minute intervals, and Halford urged everyone who wanted to hasten the return of Christ to call and express unqualified support for Israel.

By 5:00 P.M. the White House switchboard was overloaded, and the signal agency was called in to help.

As the network evening-news deadline drew near, Press Secretary Dolores Lawrence pleaded with Larry Parrish for some kind of release. The White House Press Room was like a den of underfed animals, she said. Parrish told her tersely to stick with "no comment." Finally, after she had interrupted him three times, Parrish checked with the president and then sent Davies down with a written statement reaffirming the government's faith in Israel's democratic processes and stating that no unusual maneuvers were being called for or contemplated.

5:00 P.M., THE OVAL OFFICE

It was clear to Larry Parrish that Hopkins was angry and flustered. An ordinary observer would not have recognized this; Hopkins had his reading glasses on and was perusing reports as though he were reading birthday cards. But his chief of staff had learned the signs. When the president was angry, he would take off his watch, chafe the inside of his wrist, and then put the watch back on—sometimes four or five times in a row. Today his watch was on and off incessantly.

"Larry," the president said in a voice that should have been accompanied by lightning bolts, "I want to know who did it. You find out. I don't care what means you have to take. Well, you know what I mean. I don't want Nixon's plumbers or Reagan's polygraphs. Nothing dirty, understand. But spare no effort. This kind of thing can destroy us. It has us up against the wall right now."

"Yes, sir," Parrish said.

The president took off his glasses, tossed them onto the desk, and rubbed his hands through his hair. "I don't know, Larry. What do we do next? Wait and see what Arens says to Ambassador Walker? This is the first time I've really felt what I've read so often of other presidents: to have the responsibility for the world and yet so little power to do anything. I don't think I've ever prayed like I have today."

"You have the option papers from Hartwell and Davies, sir," Parrish said crisply. "They both want to see you, quite urgently. They're rather insistent. Also, Dolores is begging you to make a statement."

The president was silent for a moment, then said softly, "Larry, I read those option papers. And frankly, I just couldn't believe it. I ran on a platform of military strength, it's true, but not against our allies. And certainly not against Israel. I don't know what's gotten into those men. I can't see any point in talking to them right now. It'd just disturb me."

The president flipped through a few of the reports on his desk, indicating that the subject was closed for the moment. "Did you see this report on phone traffic between Jerusalem and the U.S.? It says a lot of money—millions—is being offered to Tzuria. From Arizona, Texas, California, Florida, Alaska mainly. Some from people we know: the Temple Foundation, the international Christian embassy, the Thromos, the Merchessens. But what I found interesting is that a lot of money is coming from the oil men, especially in Alaska."

"Davies has a theory on that, Mr. President," Parrish said. "He thinks some of the big oil companies would like nothing better than an Arab-Israeli war to send oil prices soaring again. The oil crowd could be stirring this thing up."

Hopkins peered over his reading glasses. "Yes, yes, I suppose. We'll watch that. You call Hy Levin and tell him to alert the FBI. Christians and Zionists have pure motives, but those oil boys, well, that's another story." Then Hopkins gestured with his left hand, as if he were brushing away an annoying insect, and reached across the desk for his Bible. Parrish had never seen Hopkins so preoccupied.

"You know, Larry, I never thought of it before, but isn't there a prophecy of that in Luke? Yes. Here. Listen to this. 'It was the same in the days of Lot. People were eating and drinking, buying and selling, planting and building. But the day Lot left Sodom, fire and sulfur rained down from heaven and destroyed them all. It will be just like this on the day the Son of Man is revealed.' That's Luke 17:28. You see, people will keep right on doing business up to the very moment of Christ's return."

The president smiled, the first break in his gloom all afternoon. "Can you imagine the looks on the faces of those oil boys?"

The president paused, looking up as though he were trying to see through the ceiling. "You know, Larry, I can't help thinking—this really could be *the time*. The generation that saw the Jews return to their homeland is about to pass. It almost has to happen soon. All that is left is for the Temple to be built. That's the last big sign before—"

Parrish stood to his feet as though facing a firing squad. "Mr. President, I feel it's my duty to beg you not to pursue such thoughts. The people of the United States didn't elect you to be their . . ." Parrish groped for the right term. "To be their crystal-ball gazer. They elected you to protect and defend the Constitution of the United States."

Hopkins looked at Parrish, deep disappointment in his eyes. "Larry, you sound like somebody from the *Washington Post*. I made my position perfectly clear during the campaign. Didn't we say we would seek God's will? That God is the ultimate defender of this nation and its Constitution? That's why we were elected."

"Sir, I understand that. But you're the president, and as such, you have clear duties. You took an oath of office—"

Hopkins cut him off. "Larry, you called me a crystal-ball gazer. But that's the farthest thing from what I'm doing. Don't you believe that Ezekiel was a prophet inspired by God? We can't just close our ears to those words and pretend they're irrelevant to this situation."

"No, sir. But when you're in this room, you represent all the people—Christian, Jew, Muslim, atheist. You can't let one view of Bible prophecy influence you. Your job is to protect the nation—and everyone's religious views. I mean, we're talking about war and peace, Mr. President, not church."

The president took off his watch. "Larry, I'm truly disappointed. It sounds to me like you've been blinded by people who want to keep God out of anything that truly matters. The way separation of church and state has been used is just a cover-up for secularization. I'm not trying to impose *my* view on anyone. It's not *my* view, Larry. It's what God has to say so clearly in the Bible. I do want to bring the wisdom of God into the conduct of our affairs. And if the wisdom of the Bible doesn't have anything to say about Israel, I guess I don't know a thing about the Bible."

Parrish was about to respond, but the president's phone beeped gently and a light flashed. Hopkins punched the speaker button hard.

"Sir," said his secretary's gentle voice, "Mr. Davies insists he must see you right away."

*   *   *

Alan Davies strode into the office two minutes later, his normally bland face glistening with perspiration, his bow tie askew. The president seemed glad for an excuse to break off the discussion with Parrish.

"What happened to you, Alan?" the president said jovially.

"Those vultures." Davies gestured in the direction of the Press Room. "They're after red meat. I couldn't get out. They were clawing me with questions."

"Tell me about it," the president said dryly. "And if you have any information about who leaked this business, I want to know."

"Yes, Mr. President," said Davies. "That's not my concern at the moment, however." He pulled a Queen Anne side chair up to the president's massive mahogany desk and began talking even before he sat down. "Ambassador Walker visited Arens an hour ago at his residence, conveyed your concern, and got no satisfactory response. Nothing. The old coot just sat there and said, 'You tell your president that Israel has never had a better friend than Shelby Hopkins.' That's the same thing they've been telling every president since Truman. Now, Mr. President, we need a tough note from you that I can telefax to Tel Aviv. It can be handed to Arens at 8:00 A.M. their time. I have a draft here, sir."

Hopkins put on his reading glasses and took the sheet from Davies. His lips hardened as he quickly scanned it.

"Paragraph three will have to go. I will not threaten any kind of military action against Israel." Hopkins swept his pen angrily across the center of the page.

"You must, sir. It's all they'll listen to," Davies insisted.

"That goes against my deepest convictions." Hopkins glared over his glasses. "And this could be leaked and destroy my credibility. Furthermore, it's unnecessary. Moshe Arens is a friend and a reasonable man."

Davies started to protest, but Hopkins held up his left index finger and kept scratching on the paper, mumbling to himself as he wrote. "There. That's more like it." He leaned back and read through his revisions, then spun the piece of paper across the polished desktop.

"Will that do, Alan?"

Parrish knew Davies was steaming. Hopkins wrote well, often

drafting his own speeches, but Davies wasn't looking for subtlety. He wanted a sledgehammer.

Davies also knew, however, how far Hopkins could be pushed. He shrugged slightly. "It may work, Mr. President. I'll have it typed up and returned at once for your signature." He inserted the paper into a green folder and left immediately.

"Larry," the president said, "I want you to handle Hartwell and Slocum for me. Tell them I've read their papers and I'm weighing the whole thing. Hold their hands a little and let them know they're important. Tell them . . . tell them I fully understand their feelings about Tzuria.

"Call me if anything important happens tonight. But only important matters, please. I'll trust your judgment. I'm going to be in the Lincoln sitting room after dinner. I want time to think and pray some more . . . and I may call Dean Roberts."

"Who's that, sir?"

"Dean Roberts? He's a great old man I've known for many years, a theologian of sorts. He's been president of the Mid-South Seminary for decades. A real saint. I've looked to him for wisdom often when I've been at my wits' end. When my oldest daughter was divorced, I must have called him a dozen times."

As Parrish began gathering up his papers, the president said, "Larry, I'm sorry I lost my temper with you. This has been a trying day, but that's no excuse."

"No problem, Mr. President. I probably had it coming."

"Oh, and one more thing, Larry. When you talk to Hartwell, see if you can find out where this leak came from."

7:00 P.M., THE WHITE HOUSE SITUATION ROOM

Parrish had a strong suspicion who had leaked the story, but he needed to confirm it and find out whether any other secrets were about to hit the fan. He descended the narrow staircase in the West Wing, moved past the basement security desk, then followed the long corridor toward the White House staff dining room. Beyond that he came to an unmarked door and entered the Situation Room, the Security Council nerve center.

Designed for use in World War II, the Situation Room bore little resemblance to its Hollywood counterparts. There were no flashing lights or electronic displays. It was merely a large room with open-office furnishings, strangely silent except for the gentle, steady hum of computers. Men and women moved about in tightly controlled frenzy, transporting the paper that continuously spit from printers.

Parrish entered the nondescript conference room in the center. On one wall was a blackboard, on another a global map, and on a third, a giant video screen used for conferences with the national military command center in the Pentagon. Parrish had chosen to talk to Hartwell and Slocum from here because if was absolutely secure. Soviet listening devices at their hilltop embassy in Washington could pick up most transmissions in the city, but this room was surrounded by an impenetrable electronic shield.

At precisely 7:00 Hartwell and Slocum appeared, full size, on the video screen. With stereo sound, the simulation was so real that participants soon forgot they were five miles apart. A puff of smoke trailing from Hartwell's mouth drifted lazily across the screen. When he realized the video was on, he stared directly at Parrish.

"I don't want to talk with you," he snapped. "I want to talk to the president. We need action. Tell him I must talk to him. We have critical new intelligence."

Parrish deliberately spoke in a soft tone, almost too soft to hear. "The president understands the situation fully. He asked me to update *you*. He wants you to be fully informed at all times of *our* initiatives." He paused to let that sink in and then continued. "A very strong note signed by the president will be delivered to Arens first thing in the morning. We believe that once he realizes our displeasure, he'll reject Tzuria's offer."

"What're you guys smoking over there?" Hartwell exploded. "That's bull and you know it, Parrish. Words aren't going to stop Arens. We need action."

Parrish calculated quickly and decided to risk a slight evasion. "We'll know what we need soon. It's 4:00 A.M. in Jerusalem. In a few hours we'll have Arens's response. We can then proceed to other options as necessary." Hartwell began to interrupt, but Parrish raised his voice just enough to continue. "The president has read your option paper and has it fully in mind."

"What's that mean?" Hartwell asked sarcastically. "He's thinking about it? Don't run that White House we-know-it-all stuff at me, Parrish. Come tomorrow, we'll be in a dogfight. I guarantee it. You tell the president the task force'll be sixty miles off the coast, the Second Battalion Eighth Marines ready to go by tomorrow morning, seventeen hundred hours Jerusalem time."

"And we have an airtight op. plan," Slocum added. "We can secure the Temple Mount in thirty minutes from lift-off."

Parrish deliberately looked down at his fingernails until he had his anger under control. "Who authorized that?" he asked softly but forcefully.

"No authorization was necessary," Hartwell said. "Those are routine precautions—"

"Routine, my foot," Parrish snapped. "Hartwell, I know what you're up to. The president doesn't . . . yet. I haven't told him. But you should know you can't keep secrets from me."

"What are you talking about, Larry?"

"You know what I'm talking about. The leak. What a clumsy move." Watching closely, Parrish thought he saw Slocum flinch.

"Are you accusing me of leaking sensitive military secrets? Because if so—"

"Not me, Al." Parrish raised his hands in a gesture of peace. He knew Hartwell would like nothing better than a shouting match that blurred the issue. "No accusations here. Just mind me from now on. And listen to what I'm saying. You don't get your way with this president by pushing him into a corner. He'll push you right back. This leak has made a bad situation worse. It's distracting him. And it's fired up his fundamentalist brothers too. They've been calling him all day. So don't try anything with those ships and guns. I'm giving you the word right now: the policy of the United States government is that we will not interfere in the domestic affairs of our ally, the sovereign state of Israel. Period. Until you hear differently from here."

Hartwell blew a cloud of smoke over his right shoulder. "I know all that stuff the State Department puts out. By tomorrow the president will be more than grateful that we're ready for action when we have to be. So remember that, Larry, when tomorrow morning comes.

"Now look," Hartwell continued, narrowing his brown eyes slightly. "We've got something new. If the president won't talk to me, you better get this to him. You know we have a man in Arens's inner circle. And we now have absolute intelligence that the decision is made. There will be a deal; Arens will go along fully with Tzuria. And Arens doesn't for a moment believe that Hopkins will lift a finger. In fact, he believes that Hopkins is sympathetic with them." He paused, waiting for a reaction.

"Go on," Parrish said.

"So they'll move on the mosque. We don't know when, but soon. The Arabs will respond. Their honor's at stake. And the Russians, God forbid, may come in. I insist that you inform the president of this. As commander-in-chief, he must know."

"You're saying," Parrish repeated after taking a deep breath, "that the Arens-Tzuria deal is confirmed. You expect the mosque to be invaded shortly. Is that correct?"

"That's it."

"I'll inform him immediately," Parrish said. "I'll phone him from here. Call Alan Davies if anything changes." He punched a button and the screen went blank.

Parrish wanted to get outdoors and clear his head with some fresh air; he wanted to see his wife and kids. He had eaten only a sandwich for lunch—hours ago—yet he felt uncomfortably bloated. He reached for a telephone, but the operator couldn't put his call through. The president was still on the phone with Dean Roberts, she explained.

7:25 P.M., THE LINCOLN SITTING ROOM

"Dean, slow down, if you don't mind. I'm taking notes." The president was seated in a yellow brocade easy chair with the phone cradled against his ear. An open Bible lay on the table next to him.

"The first principle, if I might summarize, is that we must stand with the Jews. Genesis 12:3 . . . yes, yes . . ." He scribbled a sentence on a yellow legal pad propped against his right knee. "And it doesn't matter whether the Israeli government truly believes or whether they're nonbelieving militant nationalists. The point is that Israel today is the biblical nation to which Jesus returns."

At that point the door swung open. The Secret Service would admit only his wife or Parrish without advance permission, so Hopkins scarcely looked up.

"And point two, God has been kind to America because America has been kind to the Jews." The president motioned for Parrish to sit down. "And you say it is clear in Ezekiel and Daniel that the attack will come on Israel from Russia."

Parrish stared at the deep pile carpet. His stomach was beginning to churn. This conversation on top of the information Hartwell had just given him was making the ache in his stomach a dull, dead weight.

"So you believe the 1967 war was a signal—of sorts, that is—that God was declaring Israel's military victory over Jerusalem? I see. I see. I hadn't really thought about that before." Again Hopkins motioned for Parrish to sit down.

"Then point number four is that the Jews must redeem the land. Is that the word, Dean? Redeem? . . . I see . . . I see. So rebuilding the Temple would be the final step, along with preaching the gospel to all the world. . . . Well, we are certainly doing that with all our satellites and radio antennas."

He was writing furiously now. "Yes. . . . Oh, I think I know all that pretty well. The rapture and the tribulation . . . and yes, right, Armageddon. Which would be just about the end of the story, right? I mean as far as *these* events are concerned." Hopkins was beaming, nodding his head at Parrish. "Well, Dean, I can't tell you how much this has helped me. I'm familiar with all this from my own reading and Bible study, of course, but you've given me a succinct summary. This puts it together step by step. . . . Yes, Dean, you do that. Pray that God will give me wisdom. . . . I understand. Yes, call me if you have any leading of any kind. God bless you, Dean."

Parrish wished he could disappear before the president put down the receiver.

"That was my old friend, Dean Roberts," the president explained. "A brilliant mind. At eighty-three he's still razor sharp."

"Yes, sir," Parrish said.

The enthusiasm on Hopkins's face drained away slowly as he confronted his aide's grim expression. "Larry, don't 'yessir' me. Say what's on your mind."

"I don't know what's on my mind, Mr. President. Frankly, sir, you're scaring me to death."

"You mean that, don't you, Larry?" The president stood, half turned away, then whirled back to face him. "I didn't think anything could ruffle you. Tell me why."

"I don't know how to explain it, if you can't see it for yourself, sir," Parrish replied. "You're responsible for hundreds of millions of lives, including mine, including my wife and kids. And you seem to be guiding us by some obscure, kooky theory about the end of the world."

"What if the obscure, kooky theory happens to be true?"

"I'm happy to leave that decision up to God. The end of the world is His business. Our business here in the White House is to *prevent* the end of the world."

"Well, according to my theology, Larry, the end of the world—"

Parrish interrupted, something he never would have done had he not been deeply distressed. "Your theology is irrelevant right now! You weren't elected to be the nation's theologian."

Hopkins was visibly shocked by his aide's words. He turned and walked over to the window and looked out across the South Lawn at the

Washington monument, floodlit against the darkened sky. "Larry, you remember what I said in the campaign: 'America needs a president who will speak for God as well as for the American people'? The people voted for me and for that. So maybe in a sense they did elect me their theologian."

"You know better than that, sir. Not five percent of them know what the word *theology* means. They elected you because you were moral and upright, have one wife, nice kids, and speak soothingly on TV. And they were fed up to here with anti-family, anti-God, anti-everything except the orca whale. So they decided to trust you, Shelby." Parrish had never before called the president by his first name. "They trust you. You can't betray them."

"But I only avoid that if I keep trust with God."

"Then keep us out of a war! Surely God did not put you here to cheer on the Israelis while they blunder into World War Three. Hartwell has information that Tzuria and Arens have reached an agreement. If we don't stop them with our marines, they'll destroy the mosque, probably within the next twenty-four hours. We have to move militarily or there'll be war."

"No," Hopkins said vehemently. "I will not lift a hand against God's chosen people."

"Then you shouldn't have taken that oath last year, Mr. President. You didn't promise you'd defend us against anybody but God's chosen people. You said you'd defend the Constitution—period. And by the way," Parrish said, looking at his watch, "the fleet will be off the coast of Israel in about twelve hours."

"Who ordered that?" Hopkins demanded, taking off his watch to chafe the inside of his wrist.

"Hartwell said it was a routine precaution."

"Routine, my foot."

"That's what I said. But at least it keeps your options open."

Hopkins accepted that with a grunt and dropped into the yellow chair again, stretching out his legs and running his fingers through his hair. "By the way, did you learn anything about the leak?"

Parrish hesitated. "Nothing solid, sir. But I suspect Hartwell was behind it."

The president accepted that too with a grunt, his mind obviously elsewhere. Parrish wondered whether he should leave.

"The truth is, Larry, I'm not sure what to think," Hopkins said gloomily. "You're talking political sense. And my Christian friends are talking another kind of sense. It's almost as though two worlds are colliding here, and I'm in the middle. I wouldn't say this to anyone but you, but maybe I just don't belong in this place."

For the first time, Parrish saw a hint of weakness in Hopkins's eyes, an almost pleading look.

"Larry . . ." The president's voice was tentative, hesitant. "Larry, how did we ever get into this mess?"

He sat forward, took a deep breath as if drawing on hidden reserves, and smiled. "Well, I guess we've done what we can for tonight. Arens will get my letter shortly. And the fleet, you say, is moving. Why don't you go home and spend some time with your family, Larry. It's been a long, frustrating day. Let's pray tomorrow is better."

3:00 A.M., GEORGETOWN

The phone woke Parrish—the special secure phone. It rang five times while he tried to straighten the confusing shapes in his head; he was always slow to awaken. Finally his wife sat up in bed and turned on the light.

"Why don't you answer it?" she asked.

He picked up the receiver and heard Alan Davies's monotone. "Larry, the Soviets have put their Middle East forces on alert." He sounded as though he were reporting the daily amount of rainfall. "We received the first reports half an hour ago. I waited for confirmation before I called you."

"Thanks, Alan. What do you suggest?"

"The problem is to know what they're thinking. My best guess is that they're responding to our ships heading toward Israel. They've probably misinterpreted that as a sign of hostility."

By this time Parrish had fumbled a small notepad out of a drawer and was scribbling notes. His heart was pounding, and he had to force the edge out of his voice. The two men talked tersely for five minutes about possible options. When they finished, Parrish called the president.

Hopkins answered on the first ring; his voice sounded fresh and awake.

"Mr. President," Parrish began, "I must inform you that the Soviets have put their Middle East forces on alert," He waited through the silence, suddenly remembering that Hopkins had assigned the Soviets a role in biblical prophecy. Was the president hearing echoes of eternity in the news?

But the response was commonplace. "What are the Russians up to, then?"

"That's guesswork at this point, Mr. President. Davies's guess is that they've misinterpreted our fleet's movement toward Israel."

"Well, then, the first thing to do is to set their ambassador at ease, don't you think? Have Davies call their ambassador and tell him that our movements ought not to be misinterpreted as aggressive. Don't you think that's a good idea?"

"Yes, sir, I do. In fact, that was one thing Davies suggested."

"Then let's do it. What else did Davies have in mind?"

"He thought we should put our forces on alert in response. Just in case the Soviets have something aggressive in mind themselves. We want to be ready to respond."

"Yes, we surely do," the president said. "But might that too be misunderstood by the Soviets?"

"It could be," Parrish admitted. "We could cover that in our call too."

"Which assumes, doesn't it, that they believe what we say. Which, if they trust us as much as we trust them, isn't very likely. But we can't be caught with our pants down. Let's go on alert. And have Davies get on that call immediately. Anything else, Larry?"

"No, sir."

"No word on a response from Arens, is there?"

"Nothing so far."

"Well, let's all meet at 6:00 A.M. Make it the Oval Office—it doesn't matter now. Hartwell, Slocum, Lovelace, Davies, you, and me. . . . Larry, are you still scared? I've been praying for you and your family."

"Thank you, sir. No, I guess I'm not scared," he lied.

"Well, good. The Lord has been speaking to me, telling me there is no need to be afraid. When this is all over, we're going to praise Him for the magnificent wonders He has wrought. Be of good courage. That's the Lord's message to us both."

7:15 A.M., THE OVAL OFFICE

Alexander Hartwell stood before the president's desk and pounded on it with his fist. The cigarette in his hand trailed ashes across the carpet—the first cigarette in the Oval Office in fourteen months, Parrish thought as he watched in horrified astonishment.

"Mr. President!" Hartwell was almost shouting. "The marines are ready. They'll be in the air within sixty seconds if you say the word. I'm telling you, our information is absolutely certain. Tzuria has the okay from Arens. He'll move on the mosque if we don't get there first. And the Soviets have their blood up. You've got to move!" Hartwell punctuated his last words with two desk-shuddering blows.

The president stood to majestic height. "Hartwell, that's enough," he said in a splendid, controlled bass. "Go sit down. You've had your say."

To Parrish's surprise, Hartwell obeyed. As he sat down, he glanced at his cigarette as though surprised to find it in his hand. Parrish picked up a cup and saucer, and shoved it toward him. Hartwell ground out the cigarette.

"Now I'd like to hear what the rest of you think," the president said, sitting down again. "Come along," he urged, as his invitation was greeted by silence. "What are our options?"

Lovelace finally spoke. "Mr. President, I think the reason we're all sitting here like slugs is we've probably said what we have to say."

It was the first time Parrish had ever heard Lovelace say anything in one sentence. And Lovelace was right. They had been in the Oval Office since sunrise; they had talked themselves out. Everyone except Lovelace favored immediate military action, reasoning that there was no point in having a CIA if they couldn't trust information it said was firm. Lovelace wanted to wait for a definite response from Arens. But the president's note had been given to the Israeli leader almost eight hours before, and there was still no reply. Arens was holed up in his office and had put off the American ambassador repeatedly.

"Nobody wants to say anything else? That's amazing, isn't it? Who would have thought it? Silence from this group." Hopkins smiled wanly. "I'll tell you what I've decided then. I can't in conscience move our troops, with all the risks that entails, until I've heard from Arens. If he won't talk to our ambassador, I guess he'll have to talk to me. Alan, get Arens on the phone for me."

Hartwell exploded again, jumping to his feet. "That'll take time, and we don't have time. Let's at least get our men in the air. We can always recall them."

"No, no, I'm not ready to raise a hand against Israel," the president said decisively.

Davies got up and walked briskly out of the room.

Then the president began to talk, the music of Texas in his voice, something that happened when he reached for his full eloquence. Using his big hands like a television evangelist, he tried pulling his listeners into his point of view, changing the shape of things by massaging the air. He took them back to the Christian Republican convention, recalling his acceptance speech and his promise to undergird his government in prayer. He told of the campaign, of the statement they had repeated from one end of the country to the other.

It is the plight of politicians, Parrish thought, to believe that words still make a difference when events are racing past them. Speeches like this one had gotten Hopkins to the White House. No wonder, when he didn't know what to do, he talked.

The president spoke of the meaning of Israel, how it embodied the hopes the Jews kept through the millennia. He quoted the Bible from memory. He recited America's enduring commitments, suggesting that America's great blessings were linked to its protection of the Jews. On and on and on he went. He could not seem to stop.

Suddenly the door burst open. "Mr. President," Davies announced, "the Dome of the Rock has been destroyed. One minute ago Israeli commandos blew it up!"

Hopkins, interrupted midsentence, stood with mouth open. Hartwell began to swear.

After a brief, stunned silence, Slocum asked, "Any casualties?"

"Definitely. Hundreds of worshipers were in and around the mosque. There were Arab militants all around it too. How many, we don't know yet. Israeli troops are trying to seal the area."

Parrish stood and walked to a wall cabinet. He opened the doors, switched on the large television set inside, and flipped across several channels. The morning talk shows were blathering on, still unaware of the event. But the picture on the Christian Broadcasting Company channel looked like something straight out of hell. Two broadcasting voices were talking on top of each other. The picture seemed out of focus or full of dust.

"That's the mosque," President Hopkins said in a low voice.

Out of the dust appeared two tiny blurred objects. The camera zoomed in on them. They were trucks. When they stopped, small dark particles seemed to scatter from them.

"They're deploying their men," said Slocum. "Throwing up a perimeter, I would guess."

"Extraordinary," murmured Lovelace. "I assume this is live?"

"Alan," said the president softly, "you weren't able to get Arens on the telephone?"

"No, sir."

They watched the picture for another minute. No more movement was discernible. Both broadcasting voices had stopped; the background sound was now a choir singing "The Battle Hymn of the Republic."

"What do you suggest we do, Alan?" the president asked.

Parrish thought he saw just a flicker of the earlier how-did-we-get-into-this-mess look cross Hopkins's grim face.

"I think we'd better try to get General Secretary Kalganov on the telephone," Davies said.

The president nodded and turned to his desk.*

---

*Although this story is fictional, certain quotations attributed to Israeli and U.S. political and religious leaders have been taken from actual public statements; material regarding the takeover of the Temple Mount is also taken from public records.

PART I

NEED
FOR THE KINGDOM

1

Kingdoms in Conflict

Men never do evil so completely and cheerfully as when they do it from religious conviction.

—*Blaise Pascal*

Without Christian culture and Christian hope, the modern world would come to resemble a half-derelict fun-fair, gone nasty and poverty-racked, one enormous Atlantic City.

—*Russell Kirk*

"**H**ow did we get into this mess?" Our fictional president's anguished query echoes a cry heard across our country. For while this story of a decent, moral leader who lets the world slip to the brink of Armageddon would have seemed outrageous fiction just a few years ago, for millions today a similar scenario looms as a terrifying possibility. Equally disturbing to many is the realization that if this nightmare came true, millions of others would welcome it as a long-awaited consummation of human history.

These tensions run deep. On one side are those who believe that religion provides the details for political agenda. On the other are those who see any religious involvement in the public arena as dangerous. Not since the Crusades have religious passions and prejudices posed such a worldwide threat—if not through a religious zealot or confused idealist whose finger is on the nuclear trigger, then certainly by destroying the tolerance and trust essential for maintaining peace and concord among peoples.

Middle East terrorists, many religiously motivated, have spread panic throughout Europe and the United States. Ireland, Sri Lanka, India, and Indonesia are grim examples of nations deeply torn by sectarian strife. Jews, Muslims, and Christians alike endure horrendous persecution under oppressive Marxist regimes. In the West, church-state confrontations are multiplying. As one prominent sociologist observed, this strife "has little to do with whether the state espouses a leftist or rightist political philosophy";[1] the fires rage amid a variety of political systems.

Diverse as they may seem, these tensions all arise from one basic cause: confusion and conflict over the respective spheres of the religious and the political. What Augustine called the City of God and the city of man are locked in a worldwide, frequently bitter struggle for influence and power.

Nowhere has this conflict been more hotly debated than in America. Throughout most of its history, the U.S. has enjoyed uncommon harmony between church and state. The role of each was regarded as essential, with religion providing the moral foundation upon which democratic institutions could function. As recently as 1954 the Supreme Court explicitly rejected the contention that government should be neutral toward religion. Justice William O. Douglas stated that "we are a religious people whose institutions presuppose a Supreme Being."[2] But only nine years later, barbed wire was flung up on the "wall of separation" between the two as the court reversed itself in its landmark school-prayer decision. Though the expulsion of formal prayer from the schoolroom did not impede people's ability to talk to God wherever they wished, the decision reflected the shifting public consensus about the role of religiously based values in public life. It set off major tremors along long-dormant fault lines in America's political landscape.

At the same time the works of such writers as Camus and Sartre were enjoying enormous popularity on American college campuses. These existentialists argued that since there is no God, life has no intrinsic meaning. Meaning and purpose must be boldly created through an individual's actions, whatever they may be.

This relativistic view of truth perpetuated a subculture whose password was "do your own thing"—which for many meant a comfort-able spiral of easy sex and hard drugs. Personal autonomy was elevated at the expense of community responsibility. Even as many pursued these new freedoms in search of fresh utopias, some acknowledged the void left by the vacuum of values. Pop icons like Andy Warhol spoke for the mood of a generation: "When I got my first TV set," he said, "I stopped caring so much about having close relationships . . . you can only be hurt if you care a lot."[3]

Liberal theologians eagerly adapted to the powerful trends of the day. Bishop Robinson's book *Honest to God*, published the same year as the school-prayer decision, gave birth to the God Is Dead Movement, popularized on the cover of *Time* magazine.

By the seventies, classical Judeo-Christian values were toppling as the fault line groaned almost daily. Religion was fast becoming an irrelevant, even an unwanted intruder in politics and public affairs. The Supreme Court often practiced what one dissenting justice in the school-prayer case had warned against: a "brooding and pervasive devotion to the secular and a passive or even active hostility to the religious."[4]

Roe v. Wade, the 1973 decision legalizing abortion, was the final blow for traditionalists. Not only was it seen as a rejection of America's commitment to the sanctity of life, but as a repudiation of moral values as a factor in court decisions. For the first time the justices excluded moral and philosophical arguments from their determination.

Roe v. Wade triggered a counterreaction, sending tremors from another direction. Determined to preserve moral values in the public sphere, conservative church members who had long disdained politics began organizing furiously; the Pro-Life Movement spread quickly across the country. By 1976 evangelicals were flexing their muscles behind a "born-again" presidential candidate. In 1979 a group of con-servative Christian leaders met privately in Washington; the result was the Moral Majority and the Christian New Right. Within only six years this movement became one of the most formidable forces in American politics, registering millions of voters, raising vast war chests for select candidates, and crusading for its "moral agenda" with the fervor of old-time, circuit-riding preachers.

In 1984 the fault line broke wide open with a presidential campaign that resembled a holy crusade more than an election.

First, the Democratic candidate for vice-president, Geraldine Ferraro, questioned whether President Reagan was "a good Christian" because of his policies toward the poor.[5] Days later, the Catholic archbishop of New York challenged Mrs. Ferraro's faith because of her support for pro-choice legislation. At the Republican convention President Reagan told 17,000 foot-stomping partisans that "without God democracy will not and cannot long endure."[6] His Democratic challenger, former Vice-President Mondale, said that faith is intensely personal, should never be mixed up with politics, and that Reagan was "trying to transform policy debates into theological disputes."[7] Governor Cuomo of New York gave a widely heralded address at Notre Dame, in which he stated that as a Catholic he could personally oppose abortion, yet support it as governor as a "prudential political judgment," since he was following the will of the majority.[8]

In thousands of precincts across the country, fundamentalist ministers organized voter-registration campaigns, equating conservative political positions with the Christian faith. New Right spokesmen trumpeted the call for God, country, and their hand-picked candidates, and compared abortion clinics to the Nazi holocaust.

Civil libertarians reacted with near hysteria. Some labeled Jerry Falwell an American version of the Ayatollah Khomeni. People of the American Way, a group organized to counter the Moral Majority, launched a slick media campaign attaching the Nazi slur to the religious right.

Never had religion become such a central issue in a presidential campaign; never had the church itself been so dangerously polarized.

The fissures that broke open in 1984 remain wide and deep today. On one side are certain segments of the Christian church, religious conservatives who are determined to regain lost ground and restore traditional values. "America needs a president who will speak for God," proclaimed one leader. Whether out of frustration or sincere theological conviction, the Christian New Right has become politicized, attempting to take dominion over culture through legislation and court decisions.

Those on the other side are no less militant. Believing Christian political activists will cram religious values down the nation's unwilling throat, they heatedly assert that faith is a private matter and has no bearing on public life. The New York Times, for example, accused Ronald Reagan of being "primitive" when he publicly referred to his faith: "You don't have to be a secular humanist to take offense at that display of what, in America, should be private piety."[9]

The real tragedy is that both sides are so deeply entrenched that neither can listen to the other. Invective and name calling have replaced dialogue. Nothing less than obliteration of the enemy will suffice; either Christianize or secularize America. Many citizens feel that they must choose sides; either enlist with Norman Lear and People of the American Way, or join up with the Moral Majority (now the Liberty Federation) and the Christian New Right.

No matter how we got to this point, the fact is that both extremes—those who want to eliminate religion from political life as well as those who want religion to dominate politics—have overreacted and over-reached. Theologian Richard John Neuhaus does not overstate the case when he argues that this confrontation can be "severely damaging, if not fatal, to the American democratic experiment." Furthermore, both exclusivist arguments are wrong.

There is another way, however. It's a path of reason and civility that recognizes the proper and necessary roles of both the political and the religious. Each respective role is, as I hope this book will demon-strate, indispensable to the health of society.

Wise men and women have long recognized the need for the transcendent authority of religion to give society its legitimacy and essential cohesion. One of the most vigorous arguments was made by Cicero, who maintained that religion is "indispensable to private mor-als and public order . . . and no man of sense will attack it."[10] Augustine argued that the essence of public harmony could be found only in justice, the source of which is divine. "In the absence of justice," he asked, "what is sovereignty but organized brigandage?"[11]

In the West the primary civilizing force was Christianity. According to historian Christopher Dawson, Christianity provided a transcendent spiritual end which gave Western culture its dynamic purpose. It fur-nished the soul for Western civilization and provided its moral legiti-mization; or, as was stated somewhat wistfully in the London Times recently, "The firm principles which could mediate between the indi-vidual and society to provide both with a sense of proportion and responsibility in order to inform behavior."[12]

The American experiment in limited government was founded on this essential premise; its success depended on a transcendent refer-ence point and a religious consensus. John Adams wrote, "Our consti-tution was made only for a moral and religious people. It is wholly inadequate for the government of any other."[13] Tocqueville credited much of America's remarkable success to its religious nature; it was later called a nation with "the soul of a church."[14]

Today, increasing numbers of thinkers, even those who reject orthodox faith, agree that a religious-value consensus is essential for justice and concord. Polish dissident Adam Michnik, who describes himself as a "pagan," applauds the church for resisting tyranny. Reli-gion, he says, is "the key source of encouragement for those who seek to broaden civil liberties."[15] To disregard the historic Western consensus about the role of religion in culture is to ignore the foundation of our civilization.

But men and women need more than a religious value system. They need civic structures to prevent chaos and provide order. Religion is not intended or equipped to do this; when it has tried, it has brought grief on itself and the political institutions it has attempted to control. An independent state is crucial to the commonweal.

Both the City of God and the city of man are vital to society—and they must remain in delicate balance. "All human history and culture," one historian observed, "may be viewed as the interplay of the competing values of these . . . two cities";[16] and wherever they are out of balance, the public good suffers.

This is why today's conflict is so dangerous. It would be a Pyrrhic victory indeed should either side win unconditionally. Victory for either would mean defeat for both.

I have brooded over this dilemma since the midseventies. My concerns deepened each year as the conflict intensified between the body politic and the body spiritual. A variety of questions plagued me: To what extent can Christians affect public policy? Is there a responsible Christian political role? In a pluralistic society, is it right to seek to influence or impose Christian values? How are the rights of the nonreligious protected? Are there mutual interests for both the religious and the secular? Is it possible to find common ground? What does the experience of history say to us today? What would God have us understand about this torn and alienated world—or, considering the mess we've made, has He given up on us?

Friends urged me to write on the subject since I've been on both sides—first, as a non-Christian White House official, and now as a concerned Christian citizen. But the task always appeared too daunting. I couldn't sort out all the questions raised in the blistering American debate. Both sides seemed hopelessly intractable.

Oddly enough, it was on a visit to India in the fall of 1985 that I came to the unmistakable conviction that I must write this book.

At a friend's home in New Delhi, I listened to shocking stories of conflict between Indian Christians and their society. One young man who was converted to Christ after reading Christian tracts had been forced to leave his rural village by his outraged family. Another man who had been preaching on the street was cornered and beaten by an angry crowd. Many others, after converting to Christianity, had been tried by civil authorities.

The same day I was in New Delhi, opposition leader Charan Singh called upon Prime Minister Gandhi to "stamp out" all Christian missionaries lest their converts in certain states seek political independence.[17] Why, I wondered, is there such hostility to one faith in this Hindu culture that believes all roads lead to heaven? They should be the most tolerant of all. What is it about the Judeo-Christian message that makes it so offensive? Ironically, the Indians may understand the heart of the gospel—that Christ is King, with all that portends—better than many in the "Christian" West.

Later that day as my flight lifted off for Bombay, I looked down on New Delhi, which was shrouded in a dense smog from the open cooking fires of its crowded streets. Then, as we broke through to the blue sky above, it was as though the clouds surrounding these issues also broke open for me. I began to see the struggle in America—and around the world—more clearly than ever before.

So it was high in the skies between New Delhi and Bombay that I first wrote, "The kingdoms are in conflict, both vying for ultimate allegiance. Not just in America, but around the world. By his nature man is irresistibly religious—and he is political. Unless the two can coexist, mankind will continue in turmoil. Tragically, we have lost sight of both the nature of man and the nature of God and His rule over the world."

To put it simply, humanists—using that term in its best sense—fail to understand humanity and Christians fail to understand the message of Christ.

Men and women have always been spiritual beings. But modern culture, in its zeal to eliminate divisive influences and create a self-sufficient, "enlightened" society, has ignored this fundamental truth. Along with denying God, today's social visionaries have denied man's intrinsic need for God. At the same time, Christianity has become a pale shadow of the radical Kingdom its Founder announced.

The shock waves that threaten the very foundations of our culture today, then, emanate from society's failure to understand man's need for God and the Christians' failure to accurately present Christ's message of the Kingdom of God. So before we can hope to deal with the modern religious-political conflict, we must take what at first may seem to be a digression. But bear with me. For until we understand the true nature of man and the true nature of Christ's message, we cannot hope to understand the story of President Hopkins and why we are in the mess we are in today—or, more importantly, the way out.

The place to begin, then, is with human nature itself. We'll start with a man who embraced the spirit of the twentieth century and lived it to its logical conclusion.

2

After the Feast

Our Nada who art in nada, nada be thy name thy kingdom nada thy will be
nada in nada as it is in nada. Give us this nada our daily nada and nada us our
nada as we nada our nadas and nada us not into nada but deliver us from nada;
pues nada. Hail nothing full of nothing, nothing is with thee.
—"A Clean, Well-Lighted Place"

The last party went on that entire summer. Papa had come to Spain to
relive memories from earlier, happier days. He delighted in the rough
red Spanish wines, the fresh flowers of the countryside, the uproar of
the *fiera*. He ran with the bulls in Pamplona and crisscrossed the country
following his favorite bullfighters, hanging over the edge of the ring in
his *barrera* seat, tanned and squinting in the sun and dust, cheering the
skill of the matadors. He loved the moment of death: the immense bull,
thrusting and dancing with the slim figure of the matador; the glittering
sword raised high in the air above the deadly horns; and finally the
blade plunging deep between the animal's shoulders. Sometimes,
when the bull could not be killed with the sword, the matador used a
short knife, or *puntillo*. "I love to see the puntillo used," Papa would say
happily. "It is exactly like turning off an electric light bulb."[1]

After the bullfights came the midnight feasts with the matadors and a variety of guests. American college coeds who had hesitantly approached Papa for his autograph suddenly found themselves swept into the party, mingling with Hollywood stars and Papa's old friends from the Spanish Civil War. They clustered around him, toasting his health, laughing at his stories.

That summer of 1960 was Papa's last happy time before the depression set in. It was as if he had gathered all his forces—the friends, the wine, the feasts, the women, the bullfights—for one final tribute to the things that had filled his life so well over the years. The highlight was his sixtieth birthday party, a grand event designed to make up for all the birthdays that had slipped by while he was pursuing lions on safari, marlin off Key West, or lime daiquiris at his favorite Havana bar. Even if the passing of years was no great pleasure for Papa, the fact that he had survived to sixty was cause for celebration.

Guests arrived from the corners of Spain, from Paris, Washington, and Venice. The party began at noon on July 21 at a friend's seaside estate in Malaga. Mary, Papa's wife, had imported champagne from Paris, Chinese food from London, a shooting booth from a traveling carnival, fireworks and flamenco dancers from Valencia. An enthusiastic Spanish orchestra played on the balcony.

Papa declared it the best party ever. He danced through the house, a champagne glass in one hand, shotgun in the other. As the evening spilled on, he entertained guests by shooting cigarettes from the pursed—and presumably drunken—lips of two guests, the Maharajah of Cooch Behar and Antonio Ordonez, Spain's premier bullfighter. When the fireworks erupted, cheers resounded through the estate, and Papa led his guests in the *riau-riau*, the festive dance of the bullfights.

Evening spiraled into dawn, and at noon the next day the last guest staggered home. Before going to bed Papa plunged into the ocean, swimming in long, steady strokes parallel to the shore. A friend swam beside him. As they emerged from the water, Papa said with a sigh, "What I enjoyed most is that these old friends still care enough to come so far. The thing about old friends now is that there are so few of them."

Papa had made hundreds of friends over the years, collected everywhere he had lived and worked. He had lost many as well, abruptly cutting ties with those who disappointed him by being weak or dishonest. With his grizzled white beard, barrel chest, and baggy clothes, he was a man's man who in his fame had become almost a caricature of himself: the world traveler equally at home in Spain, France, Italy, Cuba, Idaho; the mighty big-game hunter of African lion, elephant, kudu. He had collected many women as trophies as well and had married four of them.

Papa started collecting adventures early. Born in Illinois in 1899 into a staunchly religious home, he had escaped during World War I to drive ambulances for the Italian Army. He was nineteen and relished the sweat, the blood, the spectacle of it all. Later a critic would write that he had been born twice—once in Oak Park, then born again to the reality of death on the Italian battlefields of Fossalata.

A few days after he volunteered for frontline duty, an Austrian mortar landed almost on top of him. The man it did hit disintegrated. Papa was severely wounded. He felt life begin to slip from his body "like you'd pull a silk handkerchief out of a pocket by one corner."

But he survived, even carrying a wounded comrade to safety, and spent half a year convalescing in Italian hospitals and back home in the States. (As the years went by, his wounds would continue. Plate glass sliced his head in Paris; a car crash crushed him in London; two plane crashes in Africa left him wounded and burned; boating accidents off the coast of Cuba resulted in concussions.)

After recovering from his war wounds, Papa became a journalist, writing crime stories in Chicago and feature stories in Toronto. He married and decided that Paris was the best place to refine his craft. For first and foremost Papa was a writer. Journalism had given him clean declarative sentences and the beginnings of a style; Paris was to provide a feast of experience that would last the rest of his life.

Papa wrote in cafés of the city. Using a stubby pencil and a small notebook, sipping a *café au lait*, he transformed his experiences into stories. When a story was done, he leaned back and splurged on a carafe of crisp white wine and a dozen oysters fresh from the sea, feeling empty and happy as if he had just made love.

Paris in the twenties had become a haven for writers and artists, and Papa was friends with many of them: Pablo Picasso, James Joyce, Gertrude Stein, Ezra Pound, F. Scott Fitzgerald. From these fellow expatriates, Papa learned how to write dialogue and refine his style. Of their philosophy he learned little, for the prevailing mood already matched his own. Papa had long since given up on the orthodox faith taught in his childhood—what he called "that ton of [manure] we are all fed when we are young." God was irrelevant, if He existed at all. The measure of a man's life was what he did—his experiences, actions, his courage in the face of death. Life was a wine glass to be filled to the brim and relished.

Papa's books of short stories and first novel brought him recognition, success, and granted him the freedom to pursue what suited him best: writing hard, loving hard, eating and drinking well, war, the hunt, and the bullfight.

When the writing flourished, he exuded a vitality, a sense of keen enjoyment that others could not help but admire.

But beneath that fulfillment was a vacuum that sometimes sucked him under. All his life Papa suffered bouts of depression—he called it "Black Ass." As long as there was another fiesta, another party, another good day's work ahead of him, the depression eventually lifted.

But in the end, when he had nothing with which to fill his life, it didn't.

By 1961 Papa had high blood pressure and diabetes. He was overweight and tired of dieting. His liver was corroded from alcohol. He was no longer able to function like a man's man. He had mental problems.

After all, Papa told a friend, "What does a man care about? Staying healthy. Working good. Eating and drinking with his friends. Enjoying himself in bed. I haven't any of them—none of them." Maybe the time had come, he thought.

Papa felt he had already died. After watching the failure, years earlier, of a once-great matador, he had said, "The worst death for anyone is to lose the center of his being, the thing he really is. Retirement is the filthiest word in the language. Whether by choice or by fate, to retire from what you do—and what you do makes you what you are—is to back up into the grave."

For even as he had danced with death over the years—he called it "that old whore"—he believed that when it came time to take her upstairs, that was his choice and his right. What else could a man control in his life if not the time and means of his death? His own father had killed himself years earlier.

If God existed, He might be fair reason to reject the whore; but if not, nothing made much difference after all. Papa had given up on God long before. Taking his life would prove he was master of his own fate.

What interested him most was how to do it. Dying, he said, was easy; it meant "no more worries." But a real man would die "intelligently, the way you would sell a position you were defending . . . as expensively as possible, trying to make it the most expensive position ever sold."

Papa woke up early that Sunday morning, put on his red robe, and padded down the carpeted stairway of his Idaho home, which faced the magnificent Sawtooth Mountains. His wife knew he wanted to make his assignation, so she had locked his hunting guns in the basement. But she had left the keys on the window ledge above the kitchen sink. Perhaps she felt she had no real right to keep Papa from his choice.

He got the keys, went down the basement stairs, and unlocked the dark storage room. He chose a custom-made twelve-gauge Boss shotgun, inlaid with silver, which he had used for years to shoot pigeons. It was his favorite gun—not just a firearm, but a near-sacred object. He selected ammunition, locked the door, and climbed back up to the bright living room.

In the front foyer, a five-by-seven entryway walled with oak, he pushed a shell into each barrel and carefully lowered the gun butt to the floor. He stooped slightly, took a deep breath, and placed the cold metal inside his mouth. Then he tripped both triggers.

Thus did Ernest Hemingway give in to death's seduction. His work and his pleasures were gone; his once-full life had emptied. With no God, it was up to him to assert control over the one thing he still could—his own death.

His immediate legacy was the ruin of blood, bones, teeth, and hair that his wife found blasted onto the foyer walls that sunny morning, July 2, 1961. The legacy of his writing and his philosophy lives on.

In one sense Ernest Hemingway is the quintessential twentieth-century man. Born the year before the century began, he experienced its rapid advance of technology and depersonalization, its growing faith in science and government, and its declining belief in orthodox religion.

The week after the shotgun blast heard throughout the literary world, Time magazine reflected,

> Though he was leery of metaphysical systems, Hemingway was really on a metaphysical quest . . . a tenacious observer of the crisis in belief and values which is the central crisis of Western civilization. . . . Hemingway's "ingenuous nihilism" was early set, but . . . [if] life was a short day's journey from nothingness to nothingness, there still had to be some meaning to the "performance en route." In Hemingway's view, the universal moral standard was nonexistent . . . [so] he invented the Code Hero, the code being "what we have instead of God."[2]

Hemingway was never far from his characters. He extended the drama of his books and stories into the stream of his own life—or vice versa: "The characters Hemingway creates drink everything, see everything, feel everything, do everything. Life to them is a chain of varied links, each different, each exciting and uniquely interesting, and the last link is the largest and most interesting of all, the link of death."[3]

And why not? If Hemingway and his existential friends who frequented the cafés of Paris were correct, their code is reasonable and even heroic. If this life is merely a glass to fill, when the glass is emptied, why not smash it against the living-room wall?

As Hemingway's friend Jean-Paul Sartre put it, "On a shattered and deserted stage, without script, director, prompter, or audience, the actor is free to improvise his own part."[4]

This view sounds both reasonable and romantic in literature or discussions in cafés and coffee bars. But the prospect in real life is stark. Among those who "tie a lamp to the masthead and steer by that" when "the stars are quenched in heaven,"[5] few take their existential belief to the ultimate conclusion. For this comfortless doctrine shreds the very fibers and design of the human psyche.

We need more. And most of us—deep down—cannot deny it. There is a core of truth buried in every heart, a truth that we can't escape.

Papa Hemingway thought he had when he consciously resisted it. The man in the next chapter knew he couldn't.

3

Crossing the Rubicon

The heart has its own reasons which Reason does not know; a thousand things declare it. I say the heart loves the universal Being naturally, and itself naturally, according to its obedience to either; and it hardens against one or the other, as it pleases. . . . The heart has reasons which Reason can never know.
—Blaise Pascal

The rumpled middle-aged man checked the lock on the solid-iron security door of his apartment, then headed toward his office at Cable News Network's Beirut Bureau. Cool Mediterranean breezes rippled the dust of the street as he rounded the corner from his cul-de-sac and turned onto Rue Bliss.[1]

The dark expressive eyes held concern. Late last night there had been shooting between rival Muslim and Christian militia along the Green Line, the barrier dividing East from West Beirut. There had also been reports of scattered shooting in the mountains. *I hope the camera crew's okay,* he thought. He had sent them to the front in the south with a local guide.

He was also thinking about yesterday's surprising announcement. The leaders of Lebanon's major political factions had agreed to meet the following Monday in Switzerland for a reconciliation conference. *Doubt if it'll make any difference,* he thought. *Reconciliation seems out of the question here.* Even the American-sponsored peace treaty between Lebanon and Israel was in danger of being cancelled. Syria was making headway in forcing Lebanon to end the agreement designed to keep the PLO out of an already chaotic Lebanon.

The light tap on his shoulder startled him. He turned and a short bearded man in his early twenties pushed a green handgun into his stomach, propelling him toward a small gray car pulling up to the curb. The back door gaped open. He didn't struggle when his assailant shoved him into the back seat and jumped in behind him.

"Close eyes. Close eyes," the man shouted, waving the revolver as the car sped away. "You see, I kill."

Life in Beirut before that clear March morning in 1984 had been exhilarating for Jerry Levin and his wife Sis. They had seen his assignment as Middle East bureau chief as a new adventure and had not been disappointed. Though the fifty-one-year-old newsman regularly put in fourteen- and fifteen-hour days reporting on the political situation, he relished the challenge of trying to unravel the enigma of Lebanon.

For her part, Sis had willingly interrupted her classes at the University of Chicago's divinity school and enrolled in the Near East School of Theology in Beirut. Typical of her enthusiasm, she had plunged into Arabic lessons, found the local Episcopal church, and made friends with the neighbors in their apartment building. Sis had already received several elegant invitations for teas and soirees, all neatly lettered with the disarming clause, "situation permitting."

Once the seaside Paris of the Mediterranean, Beirut was now a maze of gun emplacements, armed checkpoints, and patrolling militiamen. The civil war that began in 1975, the Israeli invasion of 1982, and the increasingly provocative rule by the Christian minority that had spurred the Shiite Muslim and Druze takeover of West Beirut just a few weeks earlier had all created chaos. No individual or military presence had been strong, willing, or able enough to impose order. Bombings, political assassinations, and kidnappings were the norm.

Jerry Levin was just one more victim.

*　　*　　*

Jerry and his colleagues at CNN had talked about the possibility of kidnapping. You couldn't live in Beirut with its almost daily "situations" without at least having it cross your mind. Now, the gun digging into his back was a sharp reminder that he had underestimated the reality. Jerry Levin was scared.

His captors had blindfolded him, but once they reached their destination, he could vaguely make out the shapes of shadowy figures who shoved guns up under the blindfold. They accused him of being a CIA agent, an Israeli spy, or a defender of the American foreign policy designed to eliminate them and their political goals. After several hours of inquisition they gagged him, wrapped him in heavy packing tape, and threw him in the back of a truck.

Jerry used all his senses to try to track their route. They had left Beirut and were climbing mountain roads that eventually stretched into level highways. They must have driven about two and a half hours. Jerry had studied maps of the area; he guessed they were in the Bekaa Valley, northeast of Beirut, somewhere near its main city, Baalbeck, and that his kidnappers were militant Shiite Muslims who favored the establishment of an Iranian-styled theocratic republic in Lebanon. He was correct on both counts.

When they stopped, he was led into a building and shoved into a room. There they shackled his right arm and leg to a radiator. Then they left. Jerry waited, listened. He was alone.

He lifted his blindfold and blinked, not so much from the light—the blindfold wasn't that impenetrable—as the reality of the situation. The room was tiny and bare except for the narrow foam-rubber mattress he was sitting on. The one small window had been painted over. His arm and leg were secured to the wall by a bicycle-length chain that stretched only enough for him to sit or lie on his left side. He turned and with his free hand carefully scratched a tiny mark on the dingy wall. Day one.

The days passed in a blur of monotony and fear. Once a day his guards led him to the bathroom next door. That was the outer limit of his world for months. Otherwise, he was alone in his small room.

At first Jerry willed himself to think only pleasant thoughts. He blotted out his situation by reliving his first meeting with Sis. He saw her smile at him across the ballroom of an elegant opera party in Alabama. He pictured family and friends. He created long lists of major-league baseball teams and players. It took three days to mentally list every opera he had ever seen—all ninety-eight of them. He envisioned resplendent scenes from his favorites, playing out such roles as Floristan, the political prisoner in Beethoven's *Fidelio*. Chained to the wall in the depths of a dungeon, he sang, "God! This is miserably dark. How horrible the silence, here in my lonely cell." At the end of the aria Floristan's wife, Leonore, came to save him. "I see her. An angel. She leads me to freedom and heavenly life." Jerry imagined Sis rescuing him from his Lebanese prison.

All his escape routes led back to his prison. The labyrinth of his memories could take him only so far. The bicycle chain held him fast to dismal reality.

He lost weight. His back and left shoulder ached from the cramped position. Then the scary thing happened: he began talking to himself. That worried him. *I'm going crazy*, he thought. *But if I don't talk to myself, I'll go crazy anyway*.

What if he talked to someone besides himself? People had been talking to something they called God for several thousand years and hadn't gone crazy. Rabbis did it. Priests did it. Lots of different kinds of people did it. Maybe he could too.

No.

He had no right to talk to God unless he believed in God. He couldn't talk to someone who didn't exist. "If one-millionth of one percent of me doubted, then—I reasoned—I really would not be talking to God; but I would be doing what I was afraid would happen after all—be talking to myself. So I would go crazy anyway."

Jerry had long been an atheist, or perhaps an agnostic. It was a toss-up. His Jewishness was more a cultural than religious force in his life, but he had long since dismissed Christianity as irrelevant. Sis was a Christian, and though he respected the strength of her faith, it held no appeal for him. To him Christianity called up childhood memories of neighbors' rural country churches in Michigan, musty smells, faded lace doilies—a quaint, American-Gothic experience that had little to do with his fast-paced, urbane life. And besides, what about the Christian persecution of Jews, the Inquisition, the atrocities committed in the name of Christ?

Hunched on his foam-rubber mattress, Jerry remembered as best he could the scene from Dostoyevski's *Brothers Karamazov* in which the story is told of a village in Spain during the Inquisition. As he recalled it, Christ Himself returns to the town and begins preaching the gospel. The Grand Inquisitor has Christ thrown into prison, then sentences Him to be burned at the stake. "We can't survive on these teachings," says the Inquisitor. "What you're saying is seditious as far as the church is concerned." Then he pauses and suddenly orders that Jesus be released. "Say all you want," he concludes. "It won't make any difference anyway."

I keep coming back to choices, Jerry thought. Believe God or don't believe. Reject Jesus for His followers' perversions of the faith He taught, or accept Him as the Son of God because of His incredible "extrahuman" life and teachings. Days went by. Jerry's mental struggle continued.

"It was a cosmic Catch-22, definitely not something to be fooled with. Ten days after my meditating began, on April 10, 1984, I approached and then crossed a kind of spiritual Rubicon, a diminishing point in time, a shrinking thousandth, then millionth of a second, on one side of which I did not believe and then on the other side I did."

When he crossed that line, things began to make sense. For example, he had always thought of Jesus' teaching about forgiveness as incredibly tacky, wimpy, and weak-kneed. Now, in his his solitary cell, Jerry saw that "the bully with the gun is the wimp. The man who says go ahead and shoot is not." His first prayer was for Sis and his family. Then these words came out: "God, please forgive men like these—like I'm doing now—because they are in part responsible for bringing me to You and Your Son." He learned to forgive his captors even as he saw more clearly their bitter rage and desperation.

The hostile, bitter men who were holding him had actually done God's work. God had used their bondage to get his attention. *After all,* he thought, *why else would a middle-aged grandfather be sitting in his underwear here in a bare little room in Lebanon, chained to a wall?*

Within a few months Jerry was moved to a different house. There he was allowed to use the bathroom unaccompanied. When he was ready to leave, he had to tie his blindfold back on and knock on the door. Then his captors would lead him back to his room next door.

As the spring and summer passed, he heard the knocks of other hostages being shuffled in and out of the bathroom. The terrorists must have rounded up more Americans for bargaining chips.

In July he understood for the first time why he was a hostage. Looking into the lens of a video camera, he was forced to read a statement written by his captors, appealing to Ted Turner, founder of

Cable News Network, to urge the U.S. government to intercede with the government of Kuwait to free the prisoners there. "My life and freedom," said Jerry's message, depended on the "life and freedom of the prisoners in Kuwait."

The prisoners were seventeen Shiite Muslims convicted of bombing the United States and French embassies in Kuwait in December 1983. Six people had been killed, eighty others wounded. Three of the men had been sentenced to death, the others to long prison terms. Some of Jerry's kidnappers were relatives of these prisoners.

Jerry was certain the U.S. government would never make such a deal. Again he was faced with a choice. Should he try to escape? The youths guarding him had been careless with his chains on several occasions. Would it happen again? He needed to be ready.

The opportunity he had been praying for finally came on February 13, 1985. About midnight he worked his way out of the chain. He tied three thin blankets together and climbed through the window onto the balcony. He then secured the blankets on the railing and lowered himself to the ground. He couldn't let himself even think about the fact that he was free. He zigzagged down the mountain as fast as he could, tripping over loose stones, his heart pounding.

As he neared the bottom, a dog began to bark. The refrain was picked up by dozens of others. Then he heard voices in the dark. He threw himself under a parked truck. Guns fired into the air; lights pointed in his direction. They had caught him.

When he crawled out, however, he saw not his kidnappers, but Syrian soldiers. He began babbling in a mixture of English and French. The soldiers agreed to help, and within thirty-six hours Jerry Levin stepped off an airliner in Frankfurt, West Germany. He walked straight into Sis's waiting arms.

It was then he learned that for eleven and a half months Sis had been practicing what he was just learning. Praying passionately for him, she had traveled to the Middle East with a radical message of forgiveness and reconciliation. Behind the scenes she was helped by Christian, Muslin, and Jewish friends. One Muslim leader in Beirut had told her that never in a thousand years had so many people of different faiths worked together on behalf of one man.

"The irony," says Jerry Levin today, "is that they thought they were working for someone who was a godless man. They could not have known that the skeptic had become a reconciler himself.

"I am convinced now that none of us is ever really godless. I know now that He is always there for us whether or not we are there for Him."

4

Faith and the Evidence

Now it is our preference that decides against Christianity, not arguments.
—*Friedrich Nietzsche*

Experiences like Jerry Levin's are frequently described as foxhole conversions. Maybe so. My own conversion in the midst of Watergate certainly was greeted with skepticism. The cartoonists were busy for months with caricatures of Nixon's tough guy turned to God. But fourteen years later I can write that I, like Malcolm Muggeridge, am more certain of the existence of God than I am of my own.

I understand, however, how people can listen sympathetically to stories like Levin's or mine and still doubt. Just because we need God does not prove He exists. This was, of course, Sigmund Freud's central point: that religion perseveres because people need it. "A theological dogma might be refuted [to a person] a thousand times," he wrote, "provided, however, he had need of it, he again and again accepts it as true."[1]

The influential German philosopher Ludwig Feuerbach believed that God was made in the image of man, a creation of the human mind projecting man into the universe. And Karl Marx saw religion as nothing more than an opiate used by the powerful to tranquilize the exploited masses.

If these arguments are correct, then today's battle over the role of religion relates to the need for a psychological prop. If we create God for our individual needs and to civilize culture, then the secularist is right: religion *is* merely a personal illusion and has no place in political affairs.

But it there is strong objective evidence for the existence of God, if He is not a psychological prop but a fact, then we are dealing with the central truth of human existence. And if that is the case—if He exists— then God's role in human affairs, or religion's role in public life, is indeed the most crucial issue of this or any age.

So while it may seem an intrusion, please join me briefly as I relate a few of the evidences of God's existence and character that I have found convincing. For without such evidence, there is no point in your reading this book—or my writing it.

It was the very question of God's existence that created the most serious stumbling block to my own conversion. That August night in 1973 when my friend Tom Phillips first told me about Christ, I told him that I wanted no part of foxhole religion. And though later I tearfully called out to God, my mind still rebelled. I needed to know: Was this simply an escape from the trouble I was in? Was I having some sort of emotional breakdown? Or could Christianity be real? I needed evidence.

I started with the copy of *Mere Christianity* that Tom had given me. In C. S. Lewis's book I confronted powerful intellectual arguments for the truth of Christianity for the first time in my life.

The existence of God cannot be proved or disproved, of course, but the evidence can be rationally probed and weighed. Lewis does so compellingly, and he cites moral law as a key piece of evidence. Clearly it is not man who has perpetuated the precepts and values that have survived through centuries and across cultures. Indeed, he has done his best to destroy them. The nature of the law restrains man, and thus its very survival presupposes a stronger force behind it—God.

Or consider the most readily observable physical evidence, the nature of the universe. One cannot look at the stars, planets, and galaxies, millions of light years away, all fixed in perfect harmony, without asking who orders them.

For centuries it was accepted that God was behind the universe because otherwise "the origin and purpose of life [would be] inexplicable."[2] This traditional supposition was unchallenged until the eighteenth century's Age of Reason, when enlightenment thinkers announced with relief that the origins of the universe were now scientifically explainable. What we now call the "big bang theory" rendered the God hypothesis unnecessary.

Although this theory has captured the imagination of many, it leaves serious questions unanswered. Who or what made the big bang? What was there before it? And how in the big bang process—a presumably random explosion—did planet earth achieve such a remarkable, finely developed state?* William Paley, the eighteenth-century English clergyman, told what has become a well-known parable on this point. A man walking through a field discovers first a stone, then an ornate gold watch. The stone, the man may reasonably conclude, has simply always been there, a sliver of mineral chipped from the earth by chance. But the watch, which has beauty, design, symmetry, and purpose, did not just happen. It had to have been made by an intelligent, purposeful Creator.

Some have asserted that the universe was self-generated. This violates, however, a primary law of logic: the law of noncontradiction that says the universe cannot be itself *and* the thing it creates at the same time.

Others simply state that the universe itself is self-existent and infinite; it has always been. Yet modern science has discovered no element in the universe that is self-existent.† Granted, the whole can be greater than the sum of the parts, but can it be of a different character altogether? Clearly not.

Nonetheless this is the view widely expressed today, most popularly by Carl Sagan, who proposes that "the Cosmos is all that is or ever was or ever will be."[3] That is simply another way of saying that the universe itself is transcendent. Though Sagan's films and books are widely used in schools as science, his argument is, in fact, only theory. It is also no more than an acknowledgment that we do not know how the universe began.

---

*The big bang thesis is not by itself antithetical to the Christian biblical view. Professor Owen Gingerich, noted Harvard astronomer, frequently lectures on the "strange convergence" between the biblical and modern scientific explanation of the universe's origin. He relates the scientific evidence for the so-called big bang event to the biblical affirmation that the universe flashed instantly into existence in a great showering of light. Gingerich believes, however, that science deals strictly with the question of "how," while the biblical account addresses the equally critical question of "who."

†A tentative theory exists today with respect to quantum physics that may raise questions about this conclusion.

At one point or another even the most obstinate atheist or agnostic must deal with this question of first cause.

During the Watergate scandal, though a new Christian, I approached one of my colleagues to offer spiritual help. "No thanks," he replied. "I'm a rationalist." He tapped his head and said, "It's all in human will. I've thought it all through." He was a confirmed atheist and proud of it.

Since that time I've watched this man not only survive but recover remarkably. He served his prison term without apparent ill-effect, wrote memoirs, built a successful business, and kept his family intact. If anything, he appeared stronger for the ordeal.

Then, a few years ago, I learned that he was reading Christian literature. I wrote to him, and he replied that he was indeed seeking. "I'm now an agnostic," he wrote. "I can no longer be an atheist, for I cannot get by the question of the first cause—that is, how life began. The scientific rationales are simply irrational."

Even if modern scientific theories provided satisfactory explanations for the origin of the universe, however, the question of the origin of man would still be unanswered.

The prevailing view of Sagan and others is that a chance collision of atoms created life; subsequent mutations over thousands of years evolved into the extraordinarily complex creature we know as man.

If this is true, man is nothing more than an accident that started as slime or, as one theologian has put it, we are but grown up germs. Our intuitive moral sense rejects such a trashing of human dignity.

Interestingly enough, even modern scientific research is beginning to question some of its own theories. Given the laws of probability and even allowing for the oldest possible dating of the universe, they ask, has there been enough time for life to begin by random chance and for as utterly complicated a creature as man to evolve?*

---

*A Washington Post article by Eugene F. Mallove, an astronautical engineer, science writer, and Voice of America broadcaster, noted that "some cosmologists are proposing that the universe has been perfectly 'designed' for life in a way that could not have happened 'by chance.'. . . There is an infinity of ways that the universe could have been set up that would have been more 'simple,' with fewer improbable coincidences. . . . Of course in almost any of these 'simpler' universes, the odds for the development of anything as complicated as life—no matter how you imagined it—would be nil." Eugene F. Mallove, "The Universe as Happy Conspiracy: There are Too Many Coincidences for Life to Have Happened by Chance," Washington Post (October 27, 1985), B 1–2.

Actually such odds may indeed be nil. The French mathematician, Lecompte de Nouy, examined the laws of probability for a single molecule of high dissymmetry to be formed by the action of

Weighing the evidence, it is not unfair to suggest that it takes as much faith, if not more, to believe in random chance as it does to believe in a Creator. One can understand why no less a scientist than Albert Einstein, though not of an orthodox faith, felt "rapturous amazement at the harmony of natural law, which reveals an intelligence of such superiority that compared with it all the systematic thinking and acting of human beings is an utterly insignificant reflection." Einstein's belief in the harmony of the universe caused him to conclude, "God does not play dice with the cosmos."[4]

Scientific arguments also fail to take man's basic nature into account: we are imbued with a deep longing for a god. Even an obstinate unbeliever like philosopher Bertrand Russell wrote,

> One is a ghost, floating through the world without any real contact. Even when one feels nearest to other people, something in one seems obstinately to belong to God, and to refuse to enter into any earthly communion—at least that is how I should express it if I thought there was a god. It is odd, isn't it? I care passionately for this world and many things and people in it, and yet . . . what is it all? There *must* be something more important, one feels, though I don't *believe* there is.[5]

When people try to suppress their essential nature, they must either admit the haunting desire for a god, as did Russell, or deal with the inner turmoil through their own means, often with disastrous consequences. Hemingway chose the latter course, as, for that matter, did Marx, Nietzsche, and Freud. Near the end of their lives they were all bitter and lonely men. Nietzsche's insanity, many believe, was due as much to the despair of nihilism as to venereal disease. Freud could not be comforted after his daughter's death, as if he was grieving at the finality of life without God. In his last days Marx was consumed with hatred. All these men were simply reaping the logical consequences of their own philosophies.

But even should we concede that man just happened, and that he

chance. De Nouy found that, on an average, the time needed to form one such molecule of our terrestrial globe would be about 10 to the 243 power billions of years.

"But," continued de Nouy ironically, "let us admit that no matter how small the chance it could happen, one molecule could be created by such astronomical odds of chance. However, one molecule is of no use. Hundreds of millions of identical ones are necessary. Thus we either admit the miracle or doubt the absolute truth of science." Quoted in "Is Science Moving Toward Belief in God?" Paul A. Fisher, *The Wanderer* (November 7, 1985).

creates his own need for God, how do we explain his need for purpose? Consistent evidence points not only to man's deep spiritual longings, but to a purposeful nature in his desire for community, family, and work.

The great Russian novelist Fyodor Dostoyevski said that not to believe in God was to be condemned to a senseless universe. In *The House of the Dead* he wrote that if one wanted to utterly crush a man, one need only give him work of a completely irrational character, as the writer himself had discovered during his ten years in prison. "If he had to move a heap of earth from one place to another and back again—I believe the convict would hang himself . . . preferring rather to die than endure . . . such humiliation, shame and torture."[6]

Some of Hitler's henchmen at a Nazi concentration camp in Hungary must have read Dostoyevski. There, hundreds of Jewish prisoners survived in disease-infested barracks on little food and gruesome, backbreaking work.

Each day the prisoners were marched to the compound's giant factory, where tons of human waste and garbage were distilled into alcohol to be used as a fuel additive. Even worse than the nauseating odor of stewing sludge was the realization that they were fueling the Nazi war machine.

Then one day Allied aircraft blasted the area and destroyed the hated factory. The next morning several hundred inmates were herded to one end of its charred remains. Expecting orders to begin rebuilding, they were startled when the Nazi officer commanded them to shovel sand into carts and drag it to the other end of the plant.

The next day the process was repeated in reverse; they were ordered to move the huge pile of sand back to the other end of the compound. A *mistake has been made*, they thought. *Stupid swine*. Day after day they hauled the same pile of sand from one end of the camp to the other.

And then Dostoyevski's prediction came true. One old man began crying uncontrollably; the guards hauled him away. Another screamed until he was beaten into silence. Then a young man who had survived three years in the camp darted away from the group. The guards shouted for him to stop as he ran toward the electrified fence. The other prisoners cried out, but it was too late; there was a blinding flash and a terrible sizzling noise as smoke puffed from his smoldering flesh.

In the days that followed, dozens of the prisoners went mad and ran from their work, only to be shot by the guards or electrocuted by the fence. The commandant smugly remarked that there soon would be "no more need to use the crematoria."

The gruesome lesson is plain: Men will cling to life with dogged resolve while working meaningfully, even if that work supports their hated captors. But purposeless labor soon snaps the mind.

You might argue that our need to work was acquired over centuries of evolution. But we must do more than work just to survive; we must do work that has a purpose. Evolution cannot explain this. More plausible is the belief of Jews and Christians that man is a reflection of the nature of a purposeful Creator.

But for those who insist that God is created by man, perhaps the most telling argument is to consider the nature and character of the God revealed in the Bible. If we were making up our own god, would we create one with such harsh demands for justice, righteousness, service, and self-sacrifice as we find in the biblical texts? (As someone has said, Moses didn't come down from the mountain with the Ten Suggestions!)

Would Israel's powerful elite have concocted such declarations as, "He defended the cause of the poor and needy . . . Is that not what it means to know me?"[7] Would the pious New Testament religious establishment have created a God who condemned them for their own hypocrisy? Would even a zealous disciple have invented a Messiah who called His followers to sell all, give their possessions to the poor, and follow Him to their deaths? The skeptic who believes the Bible's human authors manufactured their God out of psychological need has not read the Scriptures carefully.

But can we rely on the biblical accounts? you may ask. When I first became a Christian, I certainly raised such questions. In fact, I began to study the Bible with a lawyer's skepticism. I suspected it was a compilation of ancient fables that had endured through the centuries because of its wisdom.

I made some startling discoveries, however. The original documents from which the Scriptures derive were rigorously examined for authenticity by early canonical councils. They demanded eyewitness accounts or apostolic authorship. Today, a growing body of historical evidence affirms the accuracy of the Scriptures. For example, the prophecy recorded in Psalm 22 explicitly details a crucifixion, with its piercing of the hands and feet, disjointing of the bones, dehydration. Crucifixion, however, was a means of execution unknown to Palestine until the Romans introduced it—several hundred years after the Psalms were written. So modern critics concluded the Psalms were written later, such "prophecies" perhaps even recorded after the fact. Then came the discovery of the Dead Sea Scrolls, which made possible the scientific dating of portions of the Psalms to hundreds of years before Christ.*

Modern technology and archeological discoveries are also adding substantial support to the historical authenticity of Scripture.† As historian Paul Johnson has written, "A Christian with faith has nothing to fear from the facts."[8]

But sometimes personal experience offers the most convincing evidence. As I have written elsewhere, it was, ironically, the Watergate cover-up that left me convinced that the biblical accounts of the resurrection of Jesus Christ are historically reliable.

In my Watergate experience I saw the inability of men—powerful, highly motivated professionals—to hold together a conspiracy based on a lie. It was less than three weeks from the time that Mr. Nixon knew all the facts to the time that John Dean went to the prosecutors. Once that happened Mr. Nixon's presidency was doomed. The actual cover-up lasted less than a month. Yet Christ's powerless followers maintained to their grim deaths by execution that they had in fact seen Jesus Christ raised from the dead. There was no conspiracy, no passover plot. Men and women do not give up their comfort—and certainly not their lives—for what they know to be a lie.

Finally, many of the world's greatest philosophers and scientists have gone beyond deductive assent to the confidence that God exists because they have experienced Him. Were Augustine, Aquinas, Luther, Newton, and the great social reformers of the nineteenth century victims of infantile wish fulfillment? Did some psychological whim motivate St. Francis or George Fox to expend their lives in protest against economic elitism? Was Louis Pasteur, who labored against great physical handicaps to achieve scientific breakthroughs to benefit man, simply mistaken in his motivation to do so for the glory of God?

---

*Similarly, modern critics insisted there was no Hittite empire, since the only references to the Hittites were found in the Bible. But earlier this century the great Hittite civilization of ancient Asia Minor was discovered. Today no scholar would deny the authenticity of the Hittite civilization.

†Researchers in Israel, for example, after subjecting the first five books of the Bible to enhaustive computer analysis, came to a different conclusion than expected.

The Torah, or Books of Moses, had long been assumed by skeptics to be the work of multiple authors. But Scripture scholar Moshe Katz and computer expert Menachem Wiener of the Israel Institute of Technology analyzed the book's material through sophisticated computer analysis. They discovered an intricate pattern of significant words concealed in the canon, spelled by letters separated at fixed intervals. Mr. Katz says that the statistical possibilities of such patterns happening by chance would be one to three million. The material suggests a single, inspired author—in fact it could not have been put together by human capabilities at all. Adds Mr. Wiener, "So we need a non-rational explanation. And ours is that the |Torah| was written by God through the hand of Moses." From an Associated Press news story in the *Washington Times* (July 18, 1986), D-5.

What is it that motivates people, both Christian and nonbeliever, to do works of mercy? The goodness of the human heart? Hardly. Man's basic nature, as we shall see in the next chapter, suggests just the reverse. Rather, love for others, like the need for purpose, is implanted in the hearts and minds of men and women—even those who don't acknowledge it—by a loving and purposeful Creator.

Faith requires no surrender of the intellect. It is not blind, unthinking and irrational. Nor is it simply a psychological crutch. For me, the objective evidence for God's existence is more convincing than any case I argued as an attorney.

But most rebellion against God is not intellectual. I have met few genuine atheists who would argue passionately that there can be no God. Instead, the preponderance of objections are moral and personal. Before his eventual conversion, when philosopher Mortimer Adler was pressed on his reluctance to become a Christian, he replied,

> That's a great gulf between the mind and the heart. I was on the edge of becoming a Christian several times, but didn't do it. I said that if one is born a Christian, one can be light-hearted about living up to Christianity, but if one converts by a clear conscious act of will, one had better be prepared to live a truly Christian life. So you ask yourself, are you prepared to give up all your vices and the weaknesses of the flesh?[9]

It is on the moral level that the most intense battle is being fought for the hearts of modern men and women. If Hemingway and the twentieth-century skeptics are right—if God is dead or irrelevant—then the prospect for true harmony and justice is grim.

Sometimes children understand this profound truth better than adults. Several years ago my son Chris and I were discussing the evidences for God. As I argued that if there were no God, it would be impossible to account for moral law, my grandson Charlie, then four, interrupted.

"But Grandpa," he said, "there is a God." I nodded, assuring him I agreed.

"See, if there wasn't a God, Grandpa," he continued, "people couldn't love each other."

Charlie is right. Only the overarching presence and provision of God assures that both Christian and non-Christian enjoy human dignity and a means to escape our naturally sinful condition. Without His presence, we could not long survive together on this planet.

5

Neither Ape nor Angel

They that deny God destroy man's nobility; for certainly, man is akin to the beasts by his body; and if he be not of kin to God by his spirit, he is a base and ignoble creature.

—Francis Bacon

In Aleksandr Solzhenitsyn's masterful novel *The Cancer Ward*, a young, cancerous political prisoner named Oleg finds momentary escape from the hospital's horrors in an attractive nurse, Zoya.[1] One day Oleg volunteers to help Zoya with her reports. Reading from patient records, Oleg notices hardly any deaths in the hospital.

"I see they don't allow them to die here," he says. "They manage to discharge them in time."

"What else can they do?" responds Zoya. "Judge for yourself. If it is obvious a patient is beyond help and there is nothing left for him but to live out the few last weeks or months, why should he take up a bed? . . . People who could be cured are kept waiting. . . ."

Days later, one of Oleg's gravely ill friends is told he is being released from the hospital. The man struggles to dress, weakly bids adieu to his comrades, and sets out for the streets. The best he can hope for is an empty bench where he can lie down and wait to die.

This account may be cruel, but it is not illogical.

The Soviet system is committed to the eradication of any vital practice of religion. God is officially dead there. But the death of God ultimately spells the death of what it means to be truly human. For if worth is not God-given, it must be established by man. And atheistic philosophies, such as the Soviet system, treat man as an object whose value is determined solely by his usefulness to society. Why not, then, subject him to whatever will achieve the government's objectives: oppression, torture, genocide? In utilitarian terms, sending terminal patients out to die is not inhumane, but eminently sensible. Why waste a bed one someone who will not survive?

Now contrast *The Cancer Ward* with the wards of Mother Teresa. For years this faithful nun has provided shelter and help for the homeless, the sick, the poor; for AIDS patients dying in pain, afraid and alone. Sometimes she is criticized: "Why care for those who are doomed anyway?" But she explains, "They are created by God; they deserve to die with dignity." Christianity can never be utilitarian; it holds every human being as precious because human beings are created in the image of God.

To understand the unique nature of this Judeo-Christian view, we need only compare the ancient Hebrew law codes in the Old Testament with, say, the Assyrian laws of Hammurabi, another Middle Eastern legal code from the same period. Historian Paul Johnson has noted that the Assyrian code made the rights of property ultimate, while "the Hebrew [laws] emphasized the essential rights and obligations of man, and their laws were framed with deliberate respect for moral values."[2]

Jesus continued—and expanded—the Old Testament law. He constantly affirmed the dignity and worth of the lowest members of first-century society—women, children, Gentiles, tax-collectors, lepers.

Today's clamor for human rights is ironic. Much of the activism emanates from those who claim no belief in God. But consider what many who have had a major influence on modern thinking believed.

Karl Marx, for example, thought man a victim of economic forces. Sigmund Freud believed all was lost in the dark web of the psyche. B. F. Skinner insisted that freedom was an illusion and dignity a lost cause. More extreme philosophers get downright angry at the snobbery of speciesists—those of us who see man as the highest species—and assert that man enjoys no special standing in the universe. A prominent bioethicist writes:

> We can no longer base our ethics on the idea that human beings are a special form of creation, singled out from all other

animals, and alone possessing an immortal soul. Once the religious mumbo-jumbo has been stripped away, we may continue to see normal members of our species as possessing greater capacities . . . than members of any other species; but we will not regard as sacrosanct the life of each and every member of our species. . . . Species membership alone . . . is not morally relevant.[3]

In this light, human dignity and human rights ar tenuous assertions. If man is merely a fortuitous collection of molecules in a meaningless cosmos, why should he have any inherent rights?

Spinoza once observed that man builds his kingdoms in accord with his concept of God.[4] The rise of atheism in the twentieth century has thus provided unlimited license for tyrants. If there is no morally binding standard above the state, it becomes god and human beings mere beasts of bureaucratic burden. A government cannot be truly just without affirming the intrinsic value of human life.

The Judeo-Christian ethic does more than affirm human dignity, however; it also insists that we are inclined to do evil. Man is more than a beast, but he is not an angel. This dual nature is not properly understood apart from what theologians call *original sin*.

No modern parable portrays man's sinful nature more powerfully than Nobel prize-winning author William Golding's novel *The Lord of the Flies*, in which a planeload of English schoolboys is wrecked on a tropical island.[5] Good British subjects that they are, they attempt to organize themselves into an orderly society while awaiting rescue.

But darker urges soon grip the boys. The veneer of civilization melts away, and many of them revert to savagery, first as a game, then in deadly earnest.

One of them wounds a boar. Suddenly, "the desire to squeeze and hurt was overmastering." Soon the boys are chanting with ritualistic fervor, "Kill the pig! Cut his throat! Bash him in!"

A sow is caught and killed in a primitive sacrifice, the head cut off and placed on a post, allegedly to assuage the "beast" some of the boys have encountered. Great black and iridescent green flies buzz insistently around the severed head. The boys' "chieftain" giggles as he rubs his bloodied hands on the next boy's face.

The young savages soon turn on a fat, asthmatic, bespectacled lad nicknamed Piggy, who retains more civility than they care to have on their island. "Which is better," Piggy asks plaintively as they advance on him, "to have rules and agree, or to hunt and kill?"

Moments later, Piggy is knocked off a cliff. His skull cracks open, his arms and legs twitching. Eventually the pounding waves suck his body into the sea.

Piggy's friend Ralph collapses in a spasm of grief. "With filthy body, matted hair, and unwiped nose, Ralph wept for the end of innocence, the darkness of man's heart, and the fall through the air of the true, wise friend called Piggy."

Later, when the group is rescued, a shocked naval officer asks how such savagery could have happened. "I should have thought that a pack of British boys—you're all British, aren't you?—would have been able to put up a better show than that—I mean . . ."

Civilization, empire, education, all of the trappings of human progress had clothed these young innocents. Now, their faces smeared with blood, their consciences apparently inoperative, they bear the guilt of the death of two playmates.

When William Golding was awarded the Nobel Prize for Literature in 1983, the Swedish Academy declared that his novels "illuminate the human condition in the world today." They reflect as well what Golding described as "an attempt to trace the defects of society back to the defects of human nature. The shape of a society must depend on the ethical nature of the individual and not on any political system, however apparently logical or respectable."[6]

Golding's views sound grimly anachronistic in a culture constantly heralding man's ability to achieve utopia through modern science, education, and technology. This notion was given impetus by, among others, Jean-Jacques Rousseau, the Enlightenment writer who insisted that human misery was rooted in the structures of society. Change the structures and you change the man, he said.

Rousseau looked to primitive human experience as a rosy time of innocence free of socially induced vices. From the beginning of man's history, however, we see not guilelessness, but betrayal and evil. After the account of the Garden of Eden the Bible tells the story of the first four people on the planet—and before long, one of them killed his brother. This first murder was committed long before urban blight and social deprivations. There were—and are—no noble savages.

Human nature has not changed since Cain. This is vividly illustrated in the memoirs of Cuban poet Armando Valladares, *Against All Hope*, in which he recounts his twenty-two-year imprisonment by Fidel Castro for speaking out "against Communism because it went against my religious beliefs and some of my more idealistic notions of the world."[7] For such treason, Valladares was thrown into the man-made hell of a Cuban prison. He was given showers of human urine and excrement by sadistic guards. During an escape attempt he broke three bones in his leg and was captured and brought back to his cell. "Guards . . . stripped us again," he writes.

> They were armed with thick twisted electric cables and truncheons. Suddenly, everything was a whirl—my head spun around in terrible vertigo. . . . The beatings felt as if they were branding me with a red-hot branding iron, but then I suddenly experienced the most intense, unbearable, and brutal pain of my life. One of the guards had jumped with all his weight on my broken, throbbing leg.[8]

One cannot read this and explain the torture, the sadism, and the evil only in terms of godless political systems. The problem is human nature. The only progress between Cain and the Communist jailers of Armando Valladares has been the technological sophistication of cruelty.

Given the wealth of such examples today, why is it so difficult for modern man to acknowledge the inherent evil in the human heart? Why is *sin* an outmoded term, used only by Bible-thumping preachers, born-again zealots, or the titillating covers of paperback thrillers?

English historian Paul Johnson contends that the great obstacle to modern belief in human sin began with the loss of belief in individual responsibility. Coupled with the ascendancy of Freud's theories and Marxist ideologies, collectivism encouraged the belief that "society could be collectively guilty in creating conditions which made crime and vice inevitable. But personal guilt-feelings were an illusion to be dispelled. None of us was individually guilty; we were all guilty."[9]

This misreading of the nature of man, which resulted in the denial of personal responsibility, was institutionalized into various social reforms in the sixties; these contributed markedly to the social pathologies of American inner cities. Charles Murray of the Manhattan Institute for Policy Research has noted: "What many of these reforms shared (in varying ways and degrees) was an assumption that people are not in control of their own behavior and should not properly be held responsible for the consequences of their actions. The economic system is to blame; the social environment is to blame; perhaps accidents and conceivably genetics are to blame."[10]

Any effort to encourage individual initiative and responsibility among America's urban poor was derided as "blaming the victim." Blaming the system rather than the "victim" further eradicated individual responsibility and dignity. As Polish philosopher Leszek Kolakowski wrote: "I remember seeing on American television a young man who was convicted of brutally raping a child, a little girl; his comment was, 'Everybody makes mistakes.' And so, we now know who raped the child; 'everybody,' that is, nobody."[11]

This elimination of individual responsibility has encouraged the corresponding utopian belief in man's collective perfectibility. While Christian teaching emphasizes that each person has worth and responsibility before God, utopianism argues that salvation can only be achieved collectively. Mao Tse-tung could assert, therefore, that "our God is none other than the masses of the Chinese people."[12] And in the name of that god, millions of Chinese people were deprived of their lives.

Utopianism always spells disaster because "the utopian holds that, if the goal is goodness and perfection, then the use of force is justified," as Thomas Molnar writes.[13] In contrast, the Christian realization that perfection eludes us in this life resists the tyranny and bloodshed of the dictator who promises a brave new world.

Thus, twentieth-century men and women have inherited a stark dilemma. With God dead or ill, they are stripped of their source of dignity and reduced to sophisticated beasts. At the same time, society denies individual sin, blaming all social ills on environment, and illogically assumes human perfectibility.

Both propositions run counter to the evidence of history. Man is neither ape nor angel. And as Jerry Levin and countless others have experienced, deep down inside we know we are created. We desperately long to know the Power beyond us and discover a transcendent purpose for living. We long as well to shed the guilt of sin, to be free people, forgiven in the sight of the God we know is there.

Many search for Him through bizarre spiritual journeys, attested to by the popularity of Eastern religions and tabloid psychics, reincarnation, Beverly Hills gurus, crystals, cosmic energy, seaweed, and channeling. Such counterfeits only intensify frustration—and lessen belief in any God at all. And sometimes the end of the journey is gruesome and shocking, like the piles of bodies at Jonestown.

Diverted from the one source that can provide meaning and a sense of worth and responsibility, modern men and women are left to thrash about for themselves. Their frustration inevitably deepens into despair. For some, like Hemingway, who accept the logic of this age, the despair turns to tragedy; for millions of others it fosters a brooding sense of alienation and helplessness.

And so we come full circle, back to where we began. For it is this pervasive sense of impotence that has paved the way for the emergence of political saviors and the all-powerful state that promise salvation through changed structures. Before we discuss our situation today, though, we need to make one more stop. Having looked at the nature of man, we must now look at the nature of the two kingdoms in which he lives.

We can do this by stepping back to a time that bears a striking parallel to our day: Palestine in the first century, where a volatile population eagerly awaited the long-expected political Messiah who would deliver them.

PART II

ARRIVAL
OF THE KINGDOM

6

King Without a Country

My kingdom is not of this world.

—Jesus Christ

Two thousand years ago Palestine was (as it is today) a land in turmoil, its two and a half million inhabitants bitterly divided by religious, cultural, and language barriers. An unlikely mix of Jews, Greeks, and Syrians populated the coastal towns and fertile valleys of the ancient land, and tensions among them often erupted in bloody clashes. Rome did little to discourage this volatile bitterness. As long as the people's passions were spent on each other, they weren't being vented on their conquerors.

Among these disparate groups, the Jews alone had hope for the future, for they clung to the promise that a Messiah, sent from God, would one day come to set them free. According to their Scriptures, this savior would bring swift judgment to Israel's oppressors and triumphantly reestablish the mighty throne of the great King David. "The God of heaven will set up a kingdom that will never be destroyed," the prophecies said.

Some Jews were not content to wait and hope, however. Small

groups of incendiaries, known as Zealots, mapped political strategies for supremacy, including terrorist plots and assassinations. Rome responded with deadly force.

In the midst of this oppression and chaos, a rumor began to spread. It harked back thirty years to a time when stories had circulated about angelic visitations attending the birth of a peasant child named Jesus in the village of Bethlehem. The child had grown up in Nazareth, a dusty stopping place on the caravan route to Damascus, where He had learned the carpentry trade from His father. Now stories about this Jesus were igniting the countryside. Apparently He had abandoned His carpentry tools and was going about preaching a spiritual message and gradually amassing followers. There had even been reports that He had supernatural powers.

Early one Saturday morning Jesus returned to Nazareth to speak in the synagogue. His friends and relatives and neighbors gathered in great excitement. They had watched Him grow to manhood; they knew His parents, Mary and Joseph. So they were astonished at His air of authority as He strode to the center of the crowded stone room and was handed the book of the prophet Isaiah from the Torah shrine. He found the passage He wanted, then read the ancient prophecy: "The Spirit of the Lord is on me, because he has anointed me to preach good news to the poor. He has sent me to proclaim freedom for the prisoners and recovery of sight for the blind, to release the oppressed, to proclaim the year of the Lord's favor."[1]

Jesus handed the Scriptures back to the attendant and stared quietly at the rows of townspeople. "Today," He said slowly, "this scripture is fulfilled in your hearing."

At first there were gasps, then excited murmurings. Was Jesus claiming that their hopes were to be realized? Had the long-dreamed-of day of the Lord—the coming of Messiah—arrived?

Then one of the elders called out sarcastically, "Isn't this Joseph's son?" Others laughed. After all, this young man was merely a hometown boy, a carpenter and the son of a carpenter. What could He know of Messiah?

Jesus knew what they were thinking. "No prophet," He said steadily, "is accepted in his hometown." Then He reminded them of two stories they knew well from their heritage: During a great drought, the prophet Elijah had brought water not to the dying widows of Israel, but to a heathen widow; and his successor Elisha had ignored Jewish lepers and cleansed a Syrian instead.

His words were like a dash of cold water in the faces of the crowd. They expected liberation for the Jews and judgment for all others. Now this arrogant young man was extending the long-awaited promise of their liberation with one hand and insinuating their own judgment with the other.

The crowd surged forward and dragged Jesus out of the building, shoving Him to the brow of the hill on which the synagogue perched. But when they reached the edge, they discovered that in the confusion, Jesus had slipped away.

This humble message at the remote Nazareth synagogue was the inaugural address for Jesus' entire ministry. Through it He formally announced His messiahship and the rule of God in this world. As a result, human history was forever altered.

The Kingdom of God had come.

*   *   *

I've used this message of human liberation from the Gospel of Luke countless times as the centerpiece of my message to prisoners. "He has sent me to proclaim freedom for the prisoners . . . to release the oppressed. . . . " It speaks of men and women set free by the good news of the gospel. Not until I began to research this book did I understand its wider significance.

Of all the Scriptures Jesus might have read, He chose the one that unmistakably announced the coming of the Kingdom of God. Furthermore, the listening Jews understood that in this particular passage of Isaiah, the one speaking *is* the messenger—the Messiah who ushers in the Kingdom era. To those in that synagogue, Jesus' words could only mean that He was claiming to be the Messiah. And if that was true, the Kingdom of Heaven had become a present reality.

One reason I, like many others, missed this deeper meaning of Christ's radical declaration is that I had always read the term *kingdom* metaphorically. Like the Jews in that Nazareth synagogue, most of us think of kingdoms as geographic entities, physical realms with boundaries and defenses and treasuries. But the Kingdom of God is a rule, not a realm. It is the declaration of God's absolute sovereignty, of His total order of life in this world and the next.*

---

*That this Kingdom is not of this world, as Jesus later explained, and that it is spiritual rather than temporal makes it no less authoritative; that it is a rule not a realm makes it no less an actual

Throughout His ministry Jesus repeatedly returned to the Kingdom theme. In the sermon on the Mount, He told His followers to "seek first his kingdom and his righteousness."[2] He consistently defined His work as ushering in the Kingdom of God. Almost all of His parables focused on the Kingdom in one aspect or another, while His miracles authenticated His message. In converting water to wine, calming storms, multiplying loaves and fishes, healing the sick, and raising the dead, Jesus was not working magic to gather crowds; nor was He showing His power to gain credibility. He was demonstrating the reality of His rule. By exercising dominion over every phase of earthly existence, He revealed that in fact the Kingdom of God had come.

The Jews of first-century Palestine missed Christ's message because they, like many today, were conditioned to look for salvation in political solutions. More than anything else they wanted to be set free of Roman rule. They longed for a military messiah who would stamp out their hated oppressors. It is not surprising, then, that support for the Zealots was widespread.

The Zealot political vision was too narrow, however; for Jesus to embrace it would have been to limit the Kingdom of God to Israel. Though, ironically, Jesus was later tried and convicted as a Zealot, He dashed the hopes of those whose narrow political expectations blinded them to His real message.

The same could be said of the Jewish hierarchy. They might have welcomed Jesus because of their messianic expectations. Instead, they jealously guarded their own arrogant, self-righteous interpretation of the Jewish law, as well as the limited autonomy the Romans had given them.

Palestine's factions were embroiled in a struggle over the political and religious future of a limited ethnic group confined and defined by geographic borders. In pointing to a far larger Kingdom, Jesus was a leader without a constituency. Even His closest followers had times of doubt.

Another reason that the Jews missed the full significance of the message of the Kingdom of God was that Jesus spoke about a Kingdom that had come and a Kingdom that was still to come—one Kingdom in two stages. This still confuses people today. Perhaps a contemporary analogy will make it clearer.

---

kingdom, nor its laws less binding than those of nations and states, any more than unseen physical laws are less binding than the laws of legislatures.

Probably the most significant event in Europe during World War II was D-Day, June 6, 1944, when the Allied armies stormed the beaches of Normandy. That attack guaranteed the eventual destruction of the Axis powers in Europe. Though the war continued with seeming uncertainties along the way, the outcome was in fact determined. But it wasn't until May 8, 1945—VE Day—that the results of the forces set in motion eleven months earlier were realized.

We can compare this two-stage process to the strategy of the Kingdom of God.

A holy God would not take dominion over a sinful world. So He first sent His Son, Jesus Christ, to die on the cross to pay the debt for man's sin and thereby provide for men and women to be made holy and fit for God's rule. To extend our war analogy, Christ's death and resurrection—the D-Day of human history—assure His ultimate victory. But we are still on the beaches. The enemy has not yet been vanquished, and the fighting is still ugly. Christ's invasion has assured the ultimate outcome, however—victory for God and His people at some future date.

The second stage, which will take place when Christ returns, will assert God's rule over all the universe; His Kingdom will be visible without imperfection. At that time there will be a final judgment of all people, peace on earth, and the restoration of harmony unknown since Eden.

Many soldiers died to bring about the victory in Europe. But in the Kingdom of God, it was the death of the King that assured the victory. And this leads to the third reason that the Kingdom is often misunderstood: the nature of the King Himself.

What king would ever sacrifice himself for his people? Kings sacrifice their subjects, not themselves. What king would wash his servants' feet, as Jesus did, or freely befriend his lowest subjects? Potentates maintain the mystique of leadership by keeping a distance from those they rule. A certain grandeur seems to robe those who occupy high office.

I vividly recall a glimpse of this from my White House days. One brisk December night as I accompanied the president from the Oval Office in the West Wing of the White House to the Residence, Mr. Nixon was musing about what people wanted in their leaders. He slowed a moment, looking into the distance across the South Lawn, and said, "The people really want a leader a little bigger than themselves, don't they, Chuck?" I agreed. "I mean someone like de Gaulle," he continued. "There's a certain aloofness, a power that's exuded by great men that people feel and want to follow."

Jesus Christ exhibited none of this self-conscious aloofness. He served others first; He spoke to those to whom no one spoke; He dined with the lowest members of society; He touched the untouchables. He had no throne, no crown, no bevy of servants or armored guards. A borrowed manger and a borrowed tomb framed His earthly life.

Kings and presidents and prime ministers surround themselves with minions who rush ahead, swing the doors wide, and stand at attention as they wait for the great to pass. Jesus said that He Himself stands at the door and knocks, patiently waiting to enter our lives.

This was not the kind of messiah the Jews expected. The symbol of the tribe of Judah was a lion, majestic and powerful. The Jews waited for the descendant of this tribe—a man like David, the lion warrior of Judah, to come with chariots and armies. Instead, Christ came as "the Lamb of God." But lambs were for sacrifice. Where was the mighty warrior who would tear Rome to shreds?

Because of the nature of the King and the price He paid for His Kingdom, much is required of its citizens, and Jesus made these demands of the Kingdom clear.

Through the centuries, however, many of His followers have watered down His teaching, stripped away His demands for the building of a righteous society, and preached an insipid religion concerned only with personal benefits. This distorted view portrays Christianity not as the powerful source of spiritual rebirth and the mediating force for justice, mercy, and love in the world, but as the ultimate self-fulfillment plan. The gospel is not a release for the captives, but confidence for the shy. It is the spiritual equivalent of racy sports cars, designer clothes, and Gordon's Gin—a commodity to help one get more out of life.

As we've seen in a previous chapter, many humanists have failed to understand human nature. But many Christians have failed also— failed to understand the utterly radical nature of the central message of Christianity. Other great leaders have expounded creeds, philosophies, and mystical visions. Many are wise and moral, but they are only belief systems: rules to live by, value codes. Men and women require more than rules; they require what Jesus' message of the Kingdom uniquely provides: answers to their most basic needs.

What are these needs?

To know God. "The heart of man is restless until it finds its rest in Thee."[3] With these simple words Augustine expressed man's most primal yearning—the need to know God. In announcing His messiahship Jesus was saying that God's love and just rule had come to earth—in Him. Men and women would thereafter be able to find rest not in a law they could never hope to fulfill, but in the actual person of Jesus Christ.

To find salvation. But how does one come to a personal relationship with this Christ? That is the archetypal question asked by the apostle Paul's jailer: "What must I do to be saved?"[4]

Because we interpret it from our perspective and not God's, salvation has always been misunderstood. The Jew wanted salvation from his oppressor, the Roman centurion. Instead, Christ came to save him from a much greater oppressor—the sin within him.

Sin is essentially rebellion against the rule of God. This is why Jesus coupled the message of the Kingdom with the call to repent and believe. Faith and repentance, the opposite of rebellion, are the necessary human responses to the divine initiative of spiritual rebirth, resulting in salvation.

When Christ first used the term *born again*, it was not the evangelical cliché or secular slur it is today. He used it in a late-night conversation with Nicodemus, a member of the Jewish religious community, telling him it was the key to entering into the Kingdom of God. Imagine the shock of the religious elite when they heard Jesus' words: Salvation was not to be found in proud piety or scrupulous adherence to religious rules, but in a turning from evil and humble faith in One greater than oneself. Just as a person is born physically in a particular nation, so he or she is born spiritually by submitting to God's rule in His holy nation.

To find meaning. This relationship with God meets man's deepest psychological need. As we have already seen, human beings cannot live in a vacuum. We are not a chance collision of atoms in an indifferent universe or islands amid cold currents of modern culture. We each have a personal purpose in history, which is to be found under the purposeful rule of God, as a beloved citizen of His Kingdom.

To find authority. Christianity is more than simply a relationship between man and God, however. The Kingdom of God embraces every aspect of life: ethical, spiritual, and temporal, and it determines the "pattern, purpose and dynamic by which God orders life of the heavenly polis in this world."[5]

In announcing this all-encompassing Kingdom, Jesus was not using a clever metaphor; He was expressing the literal theme of Jewish history—that God was King and the people were His subjects. This tradition dated back to the days of Abraham and the patriarchs, when God made His original covenant with the Jews to be His "holy nation."*

David, the first great king of the Jews, consolidated a visible kingdom for the people of God, but it was to be only a reflection of the ultimate rule of God, their true King. From David, the scepter passed to his son Solomon and on through a succession of rulers, some good, some bad, but all serving as a link between God and His subjects. Later, when the Jews were conquered and sent into exile, prophets promised the coming of Messiah and the eventual establishment of the Kingdom of God. Christ was the fulfillment of that prophecy; He was the final king in David's royal line. But Jesus was not just a king for Israel; He was King for all people.

His message, then, assumes the ultimate authority man requires: God rules every aspect of what He has made. Life, death, relationships, and earthly kingdoms are all in His hands.

This totality of God's authority is a major reason many non-Christians resent Christianity, seeing it as an excuse for religious zealots to try to cram absolute orders from their God down others' throats. But when Christ commanded His followers to "seek first the kingdom of God," He was exhorting them to seek to be ruled by God and gratefully acknowledge His power and authority over them. That means that the Christian's goal is not to strive to rule, but *to be ruled*.

While God's rule *is* authoritarian, it is also *voluntary*. The Good News is that the price has been paid, and His Kingdom is open to all who desire admission.

---

*As R. C. Sproul notes, Americans, steeped in the tradition of democracy, find a monarchy, even with Christ on the throne, an alien concept. We think in terms of human rulers whose limitless lust for power is a constant peril to mankind. But God is not a mirror reflection of human rulers. He is God—and as such, is entitled to rule over all things. His character, as revealed in the Bible and in the person of Christ, reveals absolute justice, mercy, and love. R. C. Sproul, *If There Is a God, Why Are There Atheists?* (Minneapolis: Dimension Books, 1978), 137.

7

Politics of the Kingdom

If the joyful news of the rule of God is proclaimed, if men humble themselves and do justice to its claims, if evil is overcome and men are made free for God, then the Rule of God has already become actual among them, then the Reign of God is "in their midst."

—Hedda Hartl

After a recent lecture on a college campus I was asked, "Mr. Colson, how can you try to live by the Sermon on the Mount and at the same time support the use of military might?"

It's a fair question. Jesus teaches that we should love our enemies, return good for evil. But is this realistic in a world in which evil so often triumphs? Can one forgive seventy times seven and still restrain wrong-doers? Turn the other cheek to terrorism?

These dilemmas lead many to conclude that either Jesus was not speaking literally or if He was, one must live a monastic life to be a Christian. We reach such conclusions, however, because we misunderstand Jesus' teaching about the Kingdom.

When Jesus announced the Kingdom, He did indeed set forth radical standards by which its citizens are to live. He knew such a lifestyle would be both costly and complex, but it would witness the values of God's Kingdom even in the midst of the evil of this world. Christ was not suggesting, however, that the obedient Christian would be able to usher in the Kingdom of God on earth. Only Christ Himself would do that when He returns.

But for this period between the two stages—the announcement of the Kingdom and its final consummation—God has provided structures to restrain the evil of this world. The state is even ordained to wield the sword when necessary; and the Christian is commanded to obey the state and to respect its authority as God's instrument.

The Christian, therefore, follows two commandments: to live by Christ's teaching in the Sermon on the Mount, modeling the values of God's Kingdom—*the one yet to come in its fullness*—and at the same time to support government's role in preserving order as a witness to God's authority over the *present* kingdoms of this world. So while the Christian is not to return evil for evil (he must instead exercise forgiveness, breaking the cycle of evil), he may participate in the God-ordained structure that restrains the evil and chaos of the fallen world by the use of force.

*   *   *

In addition to the state, which preserves order, God has provided two other institutions for the ordering of society: the family for the propagation of life and the church for the proclamation of the Kingdom of God. Each of these three institutions has been established to fulfill a distinct role.

The family is the most basic unit of government. As the first community to which a person is attached and the first authority under which a person learns to live, the family establishes society's most basic values. Paul Johnson observed that the family "is an alternative to the state as a focus of loyalty and thus a humanizing force in society. Unlike the state, it upholds nonmaterial values—makes them paramount indeed."[1]

In most Eastern cultures the family remains the fundamental unit of society. In the West, however, relativism has encouraged the belief that family is a matter of convenience rather than convention. The traditional family has all but disintegrated in the inner city, where more than 50 percent of the children are born out of wedlock. And in the nation as a whole more than half the children are raised in one-parent families where that parent works.[2] Some school textbooks even describe the family as any voluntary grouping of people living together.[3] This attitude is reflected in our laws, our court decisions, our public mores—and in our crime rates.

The widely acclaimed seventeen-year study of Stanton Samenow and Samuel Yochelson concluded that crime is not the result of environment or poverty, but of wrong moral choices.[4] Harvard professors James Wilson and Richard Herrnstein concluded in 1985 that such moral choices are determined by moral conscience, which is shaped early in life and most profoundly by the family. Without the lessons the family alone can teach, commitment to God and duty to fellow man become alien concepts.[5] Little wonder that many of today's youth have been lost to the streets.

Though it is not my purpose here to examine the issue of the modern family, the situation today merits a word of warning. The widespread loss of the God-ordained role of the family leads, as theologian Carl Henry has written, to the "deterioration of society and [the] eventual collapse of the nation."[6] The humanizing force of the family can never be replaced by political or bureaucratic means.

The *state* was instituted by God to restrain sin and promote a just social order. One of the most common misconceptions in Western political thought is that the role of government is determined solely by the will of the people. When Pilate questioned Jesus on the eve of His execution, Christ told the governor that he would not even hold his office or political authority if it had not been granted him by God. The apostle Paul spoke of civil authority as "God's servant, an agent of wrath to bring punishment on the wrongdoer."[7] Peter used similar language, saying that governments were set by God to "punish those who do wrong and to commend those who do right."[8]

Government originated as an ordinance of God. It is, in one sense, God's response to the nature of the people themselves. Man "can adapt himself somehow to anything his imagination can cope with . . . but he cannot deal with chaos."[9] While it cannot redeem the world or be used as a tool to establish the Kingdom of God, civil government does set the boundaries for human behavior. The state is not a remedy for sin, but a means to restrain it. Its limited task is to promote "the good of the community in temporal concerns, the protection of life and property and the preservation of peace and order."[10]

When God established ancient Israel as a nation, His first order of business was the propagation of law, not just for religious purposes, but for the ordering of civil life. Even before the giving of the Ten Commandments there was great need for civil adjudication.

The biblical text records that "Moses took his seat to serve as judge for the people and they stood around him from morning till evening."[11] (Court dockets seemed to have been clogged from the very beginning.) Moses explained that "the people come to me to seek God's will. Whenever they have a dispute, it is brought to me, and I decide between the parties and inform them of God's decrees and laws."[12]

Thus the Israelite involved in a dispute looked not to the whim of a judge or to an arbitrary law but rather to a ruling based on divine laws. The judicial role was not a mechanism to advance the state's perception of social equilibrium, but to discern God's revealed law.

This is the origin of what we call the rule of law; it stands in stark contrast to modern moral relativism. Without transcendent norms, laws are either established by social elites or are merely bargains struck by competing forces in society. In the Judeo-Christian view, law is rooted in moral absolutes that do not vacillate with public taste or the whim of fashion.

Thus rooted, government can perform not only the negative function of restraining evil, but the positive function of promoting a just social order so that people can live in harmony. The apostle Paul had this in mind when he urged his young colleague Timothy to pray "for kings and all those in authority, that we may live peaceful and quiet lives in all godliness and holiness."[13]

In the words of sociologist Robert Nisbet, man is engaged in a continual "quest for community."[14] It is important to remember, however, that the state is not itself that community. Anyone who has ever dealt with a government bureaucracy knows that it is rare enough to get a phone call through, let alone to cultivate warm fuzzy feelings for the mammoth machine of big government.

But the state can protect people's voluntary efforts to shape community by granting equal protection of the law, by upholding principles of justice so the weak and powerless are not exploited, and by guaranteeing liberty and providing security. In this way the government sustains a stable environment in which people can live, producing art, literature, music, and children. Or as C. S. Lewis alluded to it, they can partake of one of the primary benefits of democracy: the simple freedom to enjoy a cup of tea by the fire with one's family.

Christianity teaches, then, that the state serves a divinely appointed and divinely defined task, although it is not in itself divine. Its authority is legitimate, though limited.

The *church* is the community that administers and encourages the worship of God and meets the spiritual needs of God's people, including teaching, offering the sacraments, and the bearing of one another's burdens. "The primary purpose of the church in relation to the world is evangelization,"[15]—that is, to proclaim in word and deed the same gospel that Christ announced.

The church is not the actual Kingdom of God, but is to reflect the love, justice, and righteousness of God's Kingdom within society.* Though the church as a human institution often fails in this high calling, its most potent social weapon is its commitment to live out the Lord's command to love one's neighbor, the law of love. "In essence," writes historian Floyd Filson, "the program of the church disregarded the social divisions of society; it made the church a home for all classes; its democratic basis was a common worship and fellowship and mutual love."[16]

The church's transcendent vision holds the world accountable to something beyond itself. In doing so, its members serve as ambassadors, citizens of the heavenly Kingdom at work in this world. French theologian Jacques Ellul has well summarized the duty of those in the church:

> The Christian who is involved in the material history of this world is involved in it as representing another order, another master (than the "prince of this world"), another claim (than that of the natural heart of man). . . . Thus he must plunge into social and political problems in order to have an influence on the world, not in the hope of making it a paradise, but simply in order to make it tolerable—not in order to diminish the opposition between this world and the Kingdom of God, but simply in order to modify the opposition between the disorder of this world and the order of preservation that God wills for it—not in order to "bring in" the Kingdom of God, but in order that the gospel may be proclaimed, that all men may really hear the good news of salvation through the death and resurrection of Christ.[17]

Thus, the church, while not the Kingdom of God, is to live out the values of the Kingdom of God in this world, resisting the ever-present temptation to usher in the Kingdom of God by political means. Yet this

---

*The church is, as one authority notes, "the community in which through its behavior and mission the reign of God becomes visible, serving as the precursor and avant-garde of the society that will be fulfillment of all hope." Stephen Charles Mott, *Biblical Ethics and Social Change* (New York: Oxford University Press, 1982), 106.

is the temptation to which the church, as we will discuss more thoroughly in later chapters, has most commonly succumbed, and certainly this is its greatest temptation today.

Pope John Paul II may well have had this concern in mind when he addressed Latin American Catholics at Puebla, Mexico, in 1979:

> The gospels make it clear that in Jesus' eyes anything that would distort his mission as servant of the Lord was a temptation. He did not accept the view of those who confuse the things of God with attitudes that are purely political. He rejects unequivocally any recourse to violence. He offers his message of conversion to all, not excluding even the tax collectors. The purpose of his mission embraces far more than political order. It embraces the salvation of the entire person through transforming and peace-giving love.[18]

Unlike the politics of the world, the politics of the Kingdom is the politics of "faith, hope, and love: faith that confesses the Risen Savior, hope that looks for His appearing, love that is inflamed by His sacrifice on the cross."[19] The church "anticipates the form of the world to come and thus it transcends the social and political forms of this world."[20]

While Jesus did not come to establish a political kingdom, the announcement of the Kingdom had profound consequences for the political order.

When Jesus said to Pilate, "My kingdom is not of this earth," Pilate may have breathed a sigh of relief. He should have reconsidered. Which is more threatening to a ruler—an external foe with mighty but visible armies or an eternal king who rules the very souls of men and women? The latter can command the will and affections, demand absolute obedience, impart unlimited power to His subjects, and radically change their values and lives; His followers fear no earthly power and His Kingdom has no end. In the face of such a potentate, any mere political leader must shudder.

This is why the Kingdom of God has had such an astonishing effect upon the most powerful of human empires in every age. It is not a blueprint for some new social order; nor does it merely set the forces of radical cultural change in motion. Rather, God's Kingdom promises radical changes in human personalities.

This is the crucial point. While human politics is based on the premise that society must be changed in order to change people, in the politics of the Kingdom it is people who must be changed in order to change society.

Through men and women who recognize its authority and live by its ethical standards, the Kingdom of God invades the stream of history. It breaks the vicious and otherwise irreversible cycles of violence, injustice, and self-interest. In this way the Kingdom of God equips its citizens, as Augustine said, to be the best citizens in the kingdoms of man.

Such was certainly the case in early nineteenth-century England, when one man dared—against great personal and political odds—to represent the standards of the Kingdom of God for the good of his nation.

8

For the Good of the Nation

Things have come to a pretty pass when religion is allowed to invade public life.
—Lord Melbourne (opposing
abolition of the slave trade)

Scudding clouds obscured the moon as the heavy schooner pitched forward in the dark waters. A lone sailor walked the deck on late watch; at the helm, three others held the wheel against the high seas. Below, the rest of the crew tossed in their hammocks, while in the main cabin the captain dipped his quill in a well of sepia ink and began the day's log. He squinted in the poor light from the tallow candle. ". . . 1787 . . . a fair wind today . . . five hundred miles off the coast of Africa . . . bound due east now for Jamaica with cargo. . . ."

Packed into the dark hold beneath his feet was the ship's cargo— five hundred African men and women layered like fish packed in brine. Barely able to breathe in the air heavy with the stench of human waste and vomit, they lay chest to back, legs drawn into fetal position, feet resting on the heads of those in the next row.

Some had been taken prisoner during tribal wars; some had been jailed as petty criminals; and others had been unsuspecting dinner guests of Englishmen visiting their country. But all had been forcibly enslaved and held in a stockade on the African coast until sold to the highest bidder. That bidder was the captain in the cabin above.

Once purchased they had been branded and rowed to the schooner waiting offshore, their screams and cries ignored by the seamen who hoisted them aboard and chained them in the stinking hold. For the women, however, there was a further torture. The crew, diseased and ill-treated themselves, claimed the one sordid privilege of their trade—the pick of the slave women. Once under way, the ship had become half bedlam, half brothel.

Now, several weeks into the voyage, sixty slaves had already died. Fever had taken some. Others, driven insane by the horror of their lot, had been killed by the crew. Each morning when the lower decks were opened, several dead or near-dead bodies were thrown to the sharks trailing the ship.

The captain cursed as the bodies hit the choppy water. Each body overboard meant lost profits.

For those who survived the hellish three-month journey, an equally gruesome future awaited. They would be auctioned naked in the marketplace to planters who would work them to death on their Caribbean plantations. Never again would these African men and women see their homeland.

Thousands of miles to the north, in a country that profited richly from this human misery, another man sat at his desk. He too gazed into the flickering flame of his lamp, for the early morning darkness still filled his second floor library at Number 4 Old Palace Yard, London. Only his piercing blue eyes reflected the turmoil of his thoughts as he eyed the jumble of pamphlets on his cluttered desk.

He ran his hand through his wavy hair and opened his Bible to begin the day, as was his custom, with Scripture reading and prayer. But his thoughts kept returning to the pamphlets, grisly accounts of human flesh sold like mutton for the profit of his countrymen. No matter how he tried, William Wilberforce could not wipe these scenes from his mind.[1]

*   *   *

William Wilberforce was the only son of prosperous merchant parents. Though an average student at Cambridge, his quick wit had made him a favorite among his fellows, including William Pitt, with whom he shared an interest in politics. Often the two young men had spent their evenings in the gallery of the House of Commons watching the heated debates over the War of Independence in the colonies.

After graduation Wilberforce had run as a conservative for a seat in Parliament from his home county of Hull. Though only twenty-one at the time, the prominence of his family, his speaking ability, and a generous feast he sponsored for voters on election day carried the contest.

The London of 1780, when Wilberforce arrived to take his office, was described as "one vast casino" where the rich counted their profits through a fog of claret. Fortunes were lost and won over gaming tables, and duels of honor were the order of the day. The city's elegant private clubs welcomed young Wilberforce, and he happily concentrated on pursuing both political advancement and social pleasure.

High society revolved around romantic intrigue and adulterous affairs. An upper-class couple might not be seen together in public for weeks during the social season, for no popular hostess would invite a husband and wife to the same event.

The poor, of course, had no such opportunity to escape from one another. Crammed together in shabby dwellings, they were cogs grinding out a living in the Empire's emerging industrial machines. Pale children worked eighteen hours a day in cotton mills or coal mines to bring home a few shillings a month to parents who often wasted it on cheap gin.

Highwaymen were folk heroes. Newgate and other infamous prisons overflowed with debtors, murderers, rapists, and petty thieves—often children. The twelve-year-old who had stolen a loaf of bread might be hanged the same day as a celebrated highwayman, providing public entertainment.

In short, London was a city where unchecked passions and desires ran their course. Few raised their voices in opposition.

So it is not surprising that few argued against one of the nation's most bountiful sources of wealth—the slave trade. In fact, the trade was both a successful business and a national policy. Political alliances revolved around commitments to it. It became known euphemistically as "the institution," the "pillar and support of British plantation industry in the West Indies." In a celebrated case in England's high court only four years earlier, slaves had been deemed "goods and chattels."

Corruption in government was so widespread that few members of Parliament thought twice about accepting bribes for their votes. Planters and other gentlemen involved in the slave trade paid three to five thousand pounds to "buy" boroughs, which sent their representatives to the House of Commons. The same attitude reigned in the House of Lords. Their political influence in Parliament grew until a large bloc was controlled by the vested influence of the slave trade.

The horrors of the trade were remote and unseen, the cotton and sugar profits they yielded very tangible. So most consciences were not troubled about the black men and women suffering far away on the high seas or on remote plantations.

*   *   *

Early in 1784 Wilberforce's friend William Pitt was elected prime minister at the age of twenty-four. This inspired Wilberforce to make a big political gamble. He surrendered his safe seat in Hull and stood for election in Yorkshire, the largest and most influential constituency in the country.

It was a grueling campaign; the outcome was uncertain until the closing day when Wilberforce addressed a large rally. James Boswell, Samuel Johnson's celebrated biographer, stood in the cold rain and watched the young candidate, barely five feet tall, climb onto a table so the wet, bored crowd could see him. The power of his oratory, however, soon gripped them.

"I saw what seemed a mere shrimp mount upon the table," Boswell wrote, "but as I listened the shrimp grew and grew and became a whale."

Wilberforce was elected. As an intimate of the prime minister and as a man respected by both political parties, he seemed destined for power and prominence.

After the election, Wilberforce's mother invited him to take a tour of the Continent with his sister and several cousins. Subsequently, he happened to meet his old schoolmaster from Hull, Isaac Milner, and on impulse asked him to join the traveling party. That invitation was to change Wilberforce's life.

Isaac Milner was a large, jovial man with a mind as robust as his body. Called "an evangelical Dr. Johnson," Milner's forceful personality had contributed to the spread of Christian influence at Cambridge. Not unnaturally, then, he raised the matter of faith and religion to his former pupil as their carriage ran over the rutted roads between Nice and the Swiss Alps.

When Wilberforce treated the subject flippantly, Milner growled at his young companion's derisive wit and declared, "I am no match for you, but if you really want to discuss these subjects seriously, I will gladly enter on them with you." Provoked, Wilberforce eventually agreed to read the Bible.

The summer session of Parliament forced Wilberforce to make a break in his travels, and his visit to the social scene of London revealed subtle changes in his tastes. Parties he had once attended routinely now seemed "indecent." Letters to family and friends indicated his growing distaste for corruption he had scarcely noticed before.

When he and Milner continued their Continental tour in the fall of 1785, Wilberforce was no longer the same frivolous young man. In fact, the rest of the traveling party complained about his preoccupation when he and Milner studied a Greek New Testament in the coach.

Wilberforce returned to London in early November, but his travels had not rested him. Instead, he felt weary and confused. In need of counsel, he sought advice from John Newton.

Son of a sailor, Newton had been impressed into the Royal Navy when he was eleven. He deserted, was caught in West Africa, flogged, and placed into service on a slave ship. Eventually he became involved in the slave trade and in 1750 was given command of his own ship. On one especially stormy passage to the West Indies, however, Newton was converted to faith in Jesus Christ. He renounced slaving and expressed his wonder at the gift of salvation in his famous hymn, "Amazing Grace."

By the time Wilberforce knew of him, Newton was a clergyman in the Church of England, renowned for his outspokenness on spiritual matters. He counseled Wilberforce to follow Christ but not to abandon public office: "The Lord has raised you up to the good of His church and for the good of the nation." Wilberforce heeded his advice.

The responses of his old friends were predictable. Some thought his mind had snapped; others assumed he would now retreat from political life since religion could have little to do with politics. Many, however, were simply bewildered. How could a well-bred, educated young man with so much promise get caught up in a religious exuberance that appealed only to the common masses?

The reaction Wilberforce cared about most, however, was that of his friend Pitt. He wrote to the prime minister, telling him that though he would remain his faithful friend, he could "no more be so much of a party man as before." Pitt's understanding reply revealed the depth of their friendship, but after their first face-to-face discussion, Wilberforce wrote in his diary: "Pitt tried to reason me out of my convictions but soon found himself unable to combat their correctness, if Christianity was true. The fact is, he is so absorbed in politics, that he has never given himself time for due reflection on religion."

*   *   *

Thus Wilberforce arrived at that foggy Sunday morning in 1787 when he sat at his desk and stared out the window at the gray drizzle, thinking about his conversion and his calling. Had God saved him only to rescue his own soul from hell? He could not accept that. He could not be content with the comfort of life at Palace Yard and the stimulating debates of Parliament. If Christianity was true and meaningful, it must go deeper than that. It must not only save but serve. It must bring God's compassion to the oppressed as well as oppose the oppressors. And at the moment, all he could envision were loaded slave ships leaving the sun-baked coasts of Africa.

He turned back to the journal filled with his tiny, cramped writing and dipped his pen in the inkwell. "Almighty God has set before me two great objectives," he wrote, his heart suddenly pumping with passion. "The abolition of the slave trade and the reformation of manners."

With those words, an epic offensive was launched against a society pockmarked by decadence and the barbaric trafficking of human flesh that underwrote those excesses.

"As soon as ever I had arrived thus far in my investigation of the slave trade, so enormous, so dreadful, so irremediable did its wickedness appear that my own mind was completely made up for the abolition. A trade founded in iniquity and carried on as this was must be abolished."

Wilberforce knew the issue had to be faced head-on in Parliament. Throughout the damp fall of 1787 he worked late into the nights on his investigation, joined by others who saw in him a champion for their cause. There was Grenville Sharp, a hook-nosed attorney with a keen mind who was already well-known for his successful court case that had made slavery illegal in England itself—ironic in a time when the country's economic strength depended on slavery abroad. Another was Zachary Macaulay, a quiet, patient researcher who sifted through stacks of evidence to build damning indictments against the trade. A dedicated worker who took pen in hand at four o'clock every morning, he became a walking encyclopedia for the rest of the abolitionists. Whenever Wilberforce needed information, he would look for his quiet, heavy-browed friend and say, "Let us look it up in Macaulay."

Thomas Clarkson was another compatriot. The red-headed clergyman and brilliant essayist with a passion for justice and righteousness was Wilberforce's scout. He conducted exhausting—and dangerous— trips to the African coast. Once, needing some evidence from a particular sailor he knew by sight though not by name, Clarkson questioned dozens of men from slave vessels in port after port until finally, after searching 317 ships, he found his man.

In February 1788, while working with these friends and others, Wilberforce suddenly fell gravely ill. Doctors predicted he would not live more than two weeks. Cheered by this news, the opposition party in Yorkshire made plans to regain his seat in Parliament. Wilberforce, however, recovered. And though not yet well enough to return to Parliament, in March he asked Pitt to introduce the abolition issue in the House for him. On the basis of their friendship, the prime minister agreed.

Lacking Wilberforce's passion but faithfully citing his facts, Pitt moved that a resolution be passed binding the House to discuss the slave trade in the next session. The motion provoked a lukewarm debate and was passed. Those with interest in the trade were not worried about a mere motion to *discuss* abolition.

Then another of Wilberforce's friends, Sir William Dolben, introduced a one-year experimental bill to regulate the number of slaves that could be transported per ship. After several members of Parliament visited a slave ship lying in a London port, the debates grew heated with cries for reform.

Now sensing a threat, the West Indian bloc rose up in opposition. Tales of cruelty in the slave trade were mere fiction, they said; it was the happiest day of an African's life when he was shipped away from the barbarities of his homeland. Besides, warned Lord Penrhyn ominously, the proposed measure would abolish the trade upon which "two thirds of the commerce of this country depends."

Angered by Penrhyn's hyperbole, Pitt himself grew passionate. Threatening to resign unless the bill was carried, he pushed Dolben's regulation through both houses in June of 1788.

The success of Dolben's bill awakened the slave traders to the possibility of real danger. By the time a recovered Wilberforce returned to the legislative scene, they were furious and ready to fight, shocked that politicians had the audacity to press for morally based reforms in the political arena.

"Humanity is a private feeling, not a public principle to act upon," sniffed the Earl of Abingdon.

Lord Melbourne angrily agreed. "Things have come to a pretty pass when religion is allowed to invade public life."

James Boswell, who had initially been astounded by Wilberforce's oratorical prowess, penned a bit of snide verse aptly reflecting the abuse heaped by Wilberforce's enemies:

> Go, W_____with narrow skull,
> Go home and preach away at Hull.
> No longer in the Senate cackle
> In strains that suit the tabernacle;
> I hate your little witling sneer,
> Your pert and self-sufficient leer.
> Mischief to trade sits on your lip,
> Insects will gnaw the noblest ship
> Go, W_____, begone, for shame,
> Thou dwarf with big resounding name.

But Wilberforce and the band of abolitionists knew that a private faith that did not act in the face of oppression was no faith at all.

Wilberforce's first parliamentary speech for abolition shows the passion of his convictions as well as his characteristic humility:

> When I consider the magnitude of the subject which I am to bring before the House—a subject, in which the interest, not of this country, nor of Europe alone, but of the whole world, and of posterity, are involved . . . it is impossible for me not to feel both terrified and concerned at my own inadequacy to such a task. But I march forward with a firmer step in the full assurance that my cause will bear me out . . . the total abolition of the slave trade. . . .
>
> I mean not to accuse anyone, but to take the shame upon myself, in common, indeed, with the whole Parliament of Great Britain, for having suffered this horrid trade to be carried on under their authority. We are all guilty—we ought all to plead guilty, and not to exculpate ourselves by throwing the blame on others.

But the passionate advocacy of Wilberforce, Pitt, and others was not sufficient to deter the interests of commerce in the 1789 session. The House's vote spurred Wilberforce to gather further evidence that could not be ignored. He and his co-workers spent up to ten hours a day reading and abridging factual material, and in early 1791 he again filled the House of Commons with his thundering eloquence. "Never, never will we desist till we . . . extinguish every trace of this bloody traffic, of which our posterity, looking back to the history of these enlightened times, will scarce believe that it has been suffered to exist so long a disgrace and dishonor to this country."

The opposition was equally determined. One member asserted, "Abolition would instantly annihilate a trade, which annually employs upwards of 5,500 sailors, upwards of 160 ships, and whose exports amount to £800,000 sterling; and would undoubtedly bring the West Indies trade to decay, whose exports and imports amount to upwards of £6,000,000 sterling, and which give employment in upwards of 160,000 tons of additional shipping, and sailors in proportion." He paused dramatically, pointed to the gallery where a number of his slave-trading constituents watched, and exclaimed, "These are my masters!"

Another member, citing the positive aspects of the trade, drew a chilling comparison: the slave trade "was not an amiable trade," he admitted, "but neither was the trade of a butcher . . . and yet a mutton chop was, nevertheless, a very good thing."

Incensed, Wilberforce and other abolitionists fought a bitter two-day battle; members shouted and harangued as spectators and press relished the fray. But by the time votes were cast, "commerce clinked its purse," as one observer commented, and Wilberforce was again defeated.

In 1792, when it became apparent that the fight would be long, Henry Thornton suggested to Wilberforce that they gather and work at his home in Clapham, a village four miles south of Westminster; there they would be convenient to Parliament, yet set apart. Thornton's home, Battersea Rise, a Queen Anne house on the grassy Clapham Common, was a lively household. As abolitionist friends came to live or visit, Thornton added extra wings until eventually Battersea Rise had thirty-four bedrooms as well as a large, airy library designed by Prime Minister Pitt. Here, in the heart of the house, many an intense prayer meeting and discussion lasted late into the night as the "cabinet councils" prepared for their parliamentary battles.

Wilberforce took up part-time residence in Thornton's home until his marriage in 1797, at which time he moved to Broomfield, a smaller house on the same property.

As the Clapham community analyzed their battle in 1792, they were painfully aware that many of their colleagues in Parliament were puppets, unable or unwilling to stand against the powerful economic forces of their day. So Wilberforce and his friends decided to go to the people, believing, "It is on the general impression and feeling of the nation we must rely . . . so let the flame be fanned."

The abolitionists distributed thousands of pamphlets detailing the evils of slavery, spoke at public meetings, and circulated petitions. The celebrated poet William Cowper wrote "The Negro's Complaint," a poem that was set to music and sung in many fashionable drawing rooms. Josiah Wedgewood, a master of fine china, designed a cameo that became the equivalent of a modern-day campaign button. It depicted a slave kneeling in bondage, whispering the plea that was to become famous: "Am I not a man and a brother?"

A boycott of slave-grown sugar was organized, a tactic even Wilberforce thought could not work. To his astonishment, it gained a following of some 300,000 people across England. Later in 1792 Wilberforce was able to bring to the House of Commons 519 petitions for the total abolition of the slave trade, signed by thousands of British subjects. This surging tide of public popularity along with Wilberforce's usual impassioned eloquence combined to profoundly disturb the House:

> In the year 1788 in a ship in this trade, 650 persons were on board, out of whom 155 died. In another, 405 were on board, out of whom were lost 200. In another there were on board 402, out of whom 73 died. When captain Wilson was asked the causes of this mortality, he replied that the slaves had a fixed melancholy and dejection; that they wished to die; that they refused all sustenance, till they were beaten in order to compel them to eat; and that when they had been so beaten, they looked in the faces of the whites and said, piteously, "Soon we will be no more."

Even the vested economic interests of the West Indian bloc could not gloss over these appalling facts or ignore the public support the abolitionists were gaining. But again the slavers exercised their political muscle and the House moved that Wilberforce's motion be qualified by the word *gradually*. And so it was carried. Again the traders relaxed, knowing a bill could be indefinitely postponed by that seemingly innocuous word.

Though Wilberforce was wounded by yet another defeat, he had a glimmer of hope. For the first time the House had actually voted for an abolition motion; with the force of the people behind the cause, it would only be a matter of time.

That hope was soon smashed by events across the English Channel. The fall of the Bastille in 1789 had heralded the people's revolution in France. By 1792 all idealism vanished. The September massacres loosed a tide of bloodshed as the mob and the guillotine ruled France.

Fears of a similar revolt abounded in England until any type of public agitation for reform was suspiciously labeled "Jacobinic," after the radicals who had fanned the flames of France's Reign of Terror. This association and the ill-timed slave revolts in the West Indies stemmed the tide of public activism for abolition.

Sensing the shift in the public mood, the House of Commons rejected Wilberforce's motion. The attitude in the House of Lords was summed up by the member who declared flatly, "All abolitionists are Jacobins." Wilberforce saw his hopes wither and his cause lampooned in popular cartoons and ridiculed by critics.

Weary with grief and frustration, he often sat long into the night at his old oak desk, wondering whether he should abandon his hopeless campaign. One night as he sat flipping through his Bible, a letter fluttered from between the pages.

Wilberforce stared at the shaky handwriting. The writer was dead. In fact, this letter was one of the last he had ever written. Wilberforce had read it dozens of times, but never had he needed its message as much as he did now.

> My dear Sir,
>   Unless the Divine power has raised you up to be as Athanasius contra mundum,* I see not how you can go through your glorious enterprise in opposing that execrable villainy, which is the scandal of religion, of England, and of human nature. Unless God has raised you up for this very thing, you will be worn out by the opposition of men and devils, but if God be for you who can be against you? Are all of them together stronger than God? Oh, be not weary of well-doing. Go on in the name of God, and in the power of His might, till even American slavery, the vilest that ever saw the sun, shall vanish away before it. That He that has guided you from your youth up may continue to strengthen in this and all things, is the prayer of,
>
>   Your affectionate servant,
>   John Wesley

"Be not weary of well-doing." Wilberforce took a deep breath, carefully refolded the letter, and blew out the candle. He needed to get to bed; he had a long fight ahead of him.

---

*This Latin phrase, which means "against the world," characterizes anyone who makes an unpopular moral stand against prevailing social opinions. Athanasius (c. A.D. 296–373) was an early church father who opposed many of the heresies of his time.

Wilberforce's resolution returned and for the next several years he doggedly reintroduced, each year, the motion for abolition; and each year Parliament threw it out.

An abrupt reversal came early in 1796 after the fall of Robespierre in France and the resultant swing of public sentiment toward peace. Popular favor again began to swing toward Wilberforce, surprisingly reinforced by a majority vote in the House of Commons for his annual motion for abolition. Victory suddenly seemed within reach.

But the third reading of the bill took place on the night a long-awaited comic opera opened in London. A dozen supporters of abolition, supposing the bill would be voted in this time, skipped Parliament for the opera—and a grieving Wilberforce saw his bill defeated by just four votes.

And so it went—1797, 1798, 1799, 1800, 1801—the years passed with Wilberforce's motions thwarted and sabotaged by political pressures, compromise, personal illness, and the continuing war in France. By 1803, with the threat of imminent invasion by Napoleon's armies, the question of abolition was put aside for the more immediate concern of national security.

During those long years of struggle, however, Wilberforce and his friends never lost sight of their equally pressing objective: "the reformation of manners," or the effort to clean up society's blights. Several years before, backed by Pitt and others, Wilberforce had sent a proposal to King George III that Wilberforce hoped would capture public attention. He asked the king to reissue a "Proclamation for the Encouragement of Piety and Virtue and for the Preventing of Vice, Profaneness and Immorality." On June 1, 1787, the king issued the proclamation, citing his concern at the deluge of "every kind of vice which, to the scandal of our holy religion, and to the evil example of our loving subjects, have broken upon this nation."

Copies of the proclamation were distributed to magistrates in every county. Wilberforce mounted his horse and followed after them, calling on those in government and positions of leadership to set up societies to develop such a moral movement in Britain.

One prominent leader, Lord Fitzwilliam, laughed in Wilberforce's face. Of course there was much debauchery and little religion, he said, but after all, this was inevitable in a rich nation. "The only way to reform morals," he concluded, "is to ruin purses."

In many areas, however, the proclamation was received seriously. Magistrates held meetings to determine how to follow its guidelines, and long-ignored laws were dusted off and enforced.

The years of battle had welded Wilberforce and his Clapham group into a tight working unit; with five of them serving as members of Parliament, they exerted an increasingly strong moral pressure on the political arena of the day. They organized the Society for the Education of Africans, the Society for Bettering the Condition of the Poor, the Society for the Relief of Debtors, which over a five-year period obtained the release of 14,000 people from debtor's prisons. Various members were involved in prison reforms, establishing hospitals for the blind, helping war widows and distressed sailors. Zachary Macaulay, at one time a wealthy man, gave away all he had and died penniless. Derisively labeled "the saints," they bore the name gladly, considering such distinction a welcome reminder of their commitment not to political popularity but to biblical justice and righteousness.

*   *   *

As the abolitionists prepared for their fight in Parliament in 1804, the climate had changed. The scare tactics of Jacobin association would no longer stick, and public sentiment for abolition was growing.

The House of Commons voted for Wilberforce's motion by a majority of 124 to 49, but victory was short-lived. The slave traders were better represented in the House of Lords, which adjourned the bill until the next session.

In 1805 the House of Commons reversed itself, rejecting the bill by seven votes. A well-meaning clerk took Wilberforce aside. "Mr. Wilberforce," he said kindly, "you ought not to expect to carry a measure of this kind. You and I have seen enough of life to know that people are not induced to act upon what affects their interests by any abstract arguments."

Wilberforce stared steely-eyed back at him. "Mr. Hatsell," he replied, "I do expect to carry it, and what is more, I feel assured I shall carry it speedily."

But Wilberforce went home in dismay, his heart torn by the notion of "abstract arguments" when thousands of men and women were suffering in the bonds of slavery. "I never felt so much on any parliamentary occasion," he wrote in his diary. "I could not sleep. . . . The poor Africans rushed into my mind, and the guilt of our wicked land."

Once more he went to Pitt to press for the cause, but his old friend seemed sluggish. Wilberforce pushed harder, reminding him of old promises. The prime minister finally agreed to sign a formal document for the cause, then delayed it for months. It was finally issued in September 1805. Four months later Pitt was dead.

Wilberforce felt his death keenly, sad that he had never seen the conversion of his dear friend. "I have a thousand times wished and hoped that he and I might confer freely on the most important of all subjects," he said. "But now the scene is closed—forever."

William Grenville became prime minister. He and Foreign Secretary Fox were both strong abolitionists. After discussing the matter with Wilberforce, Grenville reversed the pattern of the previous twenty years and introduced the bill into the House of Lords first. A bitter and emotional month-long fight ensued before the bill passed at four o'clock on the morning of February 4, 1807.

On February 22 the second reading was held in the House of Commons. Outside a soft snow fell. Inside candles threw flickering shadows on the cream-colored walls of the long room, filled to capacity but unusually quiet.

Lord Howick opened the debate with a nervous, disjointed speech that reflected the tension in the chambers. Then, one by one, members jumped to their feet to decry the evils of the slave trade and to praise the men who had worked so hard to end it. They hailed Wilberforce and praised the abolitionists.

As the debate came to its climax, Sir Samuel Romilly gave a passionate tribute to Wilberforce and his decades of labor, concluding, "When he should retire into the bosom of his happy and delighted family, when he should lay himself down on his bed, reflecting on the innumerable voices that would be raised in every quarter of the world to bless him; how much more pure and perfect felicity must he enjoy in the consciousness of having preserved so many millions of his fellow-creatures."

Stirred by Romilly's words, the entire House rose, cheering and applauding. Realizing that his long battle had come to an end, Wilberforce sat bent in his chair, his head in his hands, tears streaming down his face.

The motion carried, 283 to 16.

Late that night Wilberforce and his friends burst out of the stuffy chambers and onto the snow-covered streets. They frolicked like schoolboys, clapping one another on the back, their joy spilling over. Later, at Wilberforce's home, the old friends crowded into the library, recalling the weary years of battle and rejoicing for their African brothers and sisters.

Wilberforce, surely the most joyous of all, looked into the lined face of his old friend Henry Thornton. Years of illness, defeat, and ridicule had taken their toll. Yet all of it was worth this moment.

"Well, Henry," Wilberforce said with joy in his eyes, "what do we abolish next?"*

*After the outlawing of the slave trade in 1807, Wilberforce fought another eighteen years for the total emancipation of existing slaves. Despite increasingly poor health, he continued as a leader of the cause in Parliament until his retirement in 1825. He also continued his work for reforms in the prisons, among the poor, and in the workplace. And on July 29, 1833, three days after the Bill for the Abolition of Slavery passed its second reading in the House of Commons, sounding the final death blow for slavery, Wilberforce died. "Thank God," he whispered before he slipped into a final coma, "that I should have lived to witness a day in which England was willing to give twenty millions sterling for the abolition of slavery!"

9

The Cross and the Crown

I die the king's good servant, but God's first.

—Sir Thomas More

If I am faced with the choice between religion and my country . . . . I will choose my fatherland.

—Father Miguel d'Escoto, Nicaraguan Foreign Minister

Wilberforce's dogged campaign to rid the British empire of the slave trade shows what can happen when a citizen of the Kingdom of God challenges corrupt structures within the kingdoms of man. One excellent Wilberforce biography is aptly titled *God's Politician*, and truly he was, holding his country to God's standard of moral accountability.

The kind of conflict that Wilberforce and other activist Christians experience—between their Christian conscience and their political mandates—is unavoidable. Both church and state assert standards and values in society; both seek authority; both compete for allegiance. As members of both the religious and the political spheres, the Christian is bound to face conflict.

The conflict is particularly apparent in the Judeo-Christian tradition because of the assertion that the God of both the Old and New Testament Scriptures is King. That has been an offense to the proud and powerful since the beginning—and the reason Jews and Christians alike have been systematically persecuted.

The tension between the Kingdom of God and the kingdoms of man runs like an unbroken thread through the history of the past two thousand years. It began not long after Christ's birth. Herod, the Roman-appointed king over the Jews and as vicious a tyrant as ever lived, was gripped with fear when the Magi arrived from the East seeking the "King of the Jews." Though not a believer, Herod knew the ancient Jewish prophecies that a child would be born to reign over them, ushering in a Kingdom of peace and might.

Herod called the Magi to his ornate throne room. In what has become common practice in the centuries since, he tried to manipulate the religious leaders for political advantage. He told them to go find this King in Bethlehem so he too could worship Him.

The rest of the story is familiar. The Magi found Jesus but were warned in a dream to avoid Herod and return to the East. Jesus' parents, similarly warned, escaped with their son to Egypt—just ahead of Herod's marauding soldiers who massacred all the male children of Jesus' age in and near Bethlehem.

Herod didn't fear Jesus because he thought He would become a religious or political leader. He had suppressed such opponents before. Herod feared Christ because He represented a Kingdom greater than his own.

Jesus was later executed for this same reason. Though He told Pilate His Kingdom was not of this world, the sign over His cross read "INRE"—King of the Jews. The executioner's sarcasm was doubled-edged.

His followers' faithfulness to Christ's announcement of His Kingdom led to their persecution as well. An enraged mob in Thessalonica threatened Paul and Silas, shouting, "These men who have caused trouble all over the world . . . are all defying Caesar's decrees, saying that there is another king, one called Jesus."[1] During the early centuries Christians were martyred not for religious reasons—Rome, after all, was a land of many gods—but because they refused to worship the emperor. Because they would not say, "We have no king but Caesar," the Roman government saw them as political subversives.

Christians who refused to offer incense before the statue of the emperor were flogged, stoned, imprisoned, condemned to the mines. Later, when Christianity was officially outlawed, they were tortured mercilessly and fed to the lions, to the delight of bloodthirsty crowds.*

With the conversion of Constantine, however, Christianity was legalized in A.D. 313. This marked the end of persecution and ushered in a second phase in church-state relations.† In A.D. 381 Christianity became the official religion of Rome, and in an ironic turnabout, church leaders began exploiting their new-found power. As historian F. F. Bruce has written: "Christian leaders . . . exploit[ed] the influential favor they enjoyed even when it meant subordinating the cause of justice to the apparent interest of their religion . . . they were inclined to allow the secular power too much control in church affairs. . . . Where church leaders were able to exercise political as well as spiritual authority, they did not enjoy any marked immunity from the universally corrupting tendency of power."[2]

Even Augustine, the great church father who provided the classic definition of the roles of the City of God and the city of man, was beguiled by the lure of temporal power; after a wrenching internal struggle he endorsed the suppression of heretics by the state.

Through succeeding centuries the church relied increasingly on the state to punish heresy. By the time of the Byzantine empire in the East, the state had become a theocracy with the church serving as its department of spiritual affairs. In the West both church and state jockeyed for control in an uneasy alliance. In the thirteenth century, for example, Frederick II, king of Sicily, was first excommunicated for not going on a crusade, then excommunicated for going on one without the

---

*In the second half of the second century, Christians were systematically persecuted. This account of a massacre in the Rhone Valley is not atypical: "Many Christians were tortured in the stocks or in cells. Sanctus, a deacon from Vienna, had red-hot plates applied to his testicles—his poor body was one whole wound and bruise having lost the outward form of a man. Christians who were Roman citizens were beheaded. Others were forced through a gauntlet of whips into the amphitheater and then . . . given to the beasts. Severed heads and limbs of Christians were displayed, guarded for six days, then burned, the ashes being thrown into the Rhone. . . . One lady, Blandina, was the worst treated of all, tortured from dawn until evening till her torturers were exhausted and marveled that the breath was still in her body. She was then scourged, roasted in the frying pan and finally put in the basket to be tossed to death by wild bulls." Paul Johnson, *History of Christianity* (New York: Atheneum, 1979) 72–73.

Many Christians went to their death praising their King, and such martyrdom became the church's most potent witness. Pagan Romans were convinced that Christ had taken away their pains. As has often been said, the church was built on the martyrs' blood.

†Historians have questioned Constantine's motives. Some believe it was an effort to save a dying empire, though one contemporary historian has come to a different conclusion. Christianity was practiced only by a small minority. Its universality, the message of Christ Himself, the reliability of written revelation as opposed to myths, began to attract pagan masses. Robin Lane Fox, *Pagans and Christians* (New York: Knopf, 1986).

Pope's permission. The state conquered territory, but the Pope distributed the land to the more faithful crusaders.

The consequences of this alliance were mixed. Certainly Christianity provided a civilizing influence on Western culture through art, music, literature, morality, and ultimately in government. One eminent historian concluded that "society developed only so fast as religion enlarged its sphere."[3] On the darker side, however, the excesses of the politicized church created horrors Augustine could not have imagined.

The church turned to military conquest through a series of "holy wars" that became more racial than religious. Jews, Muslims, and dark-skinned Christians were massacred alike. The goal was not to convert the populace, but to conquer it.

In the twelfth and thirteenth centuries a system was organized for adjudicating heresy. Like many well-intentioned reforms, however, the Inquisition simply produced a new set of horrors. Unrepentant heretics were cast out by a church tribunal, which regularly used torture, and were executed by the state.

The spiritual corruption of the church led to the Reformation of the sixteenth century, which produced several streams of church-state relations. One, believing the state to be essentially coercive and violent, rejected participation in any form of government. A second strand of Reformation thought dictated that the religion of a resident king or prince would be the church of the state. Thus, many kings became their own pope. A third principle encouraged church independence. Scottish church leaders like Samuel Rutherford revived the biblical view that God's law reigns over man and his kingdoms. This profoundly influenced the experiment in constitutional government then beginning in the New World.

A new phase of hostility between church and state began in the eighteenth century when waves of skepticism washed over the continent of Europe. Voltaire, one of the most influential philosophers of the day, was vehemently dedicated to the extirpation of what he called "this infamous superstition."

Religions had been assaulted before but always in the name of other religions. With the French Revolution, Tocqueville noted, "Passionate and persistent efforts were made to wean men away from the faith of their fathers. . . . Irreligion became an all-prevailing passion, fierce, intolerant and predatory."[4] For a time this all-prevailing passion was successful. Wrote Tocqueville: "The total rejection of any religious belief, so contrary to man's natural instincts and so destructive of his peace of mind, came to be regarded by the masses as desirable."[5] The

French Revolution was a conscious effort to replace the Kingdom of God with the kingdoms of man.

But the state must have some moral justification for its authority. Thus France's irreligion was soon replaced by a new faith—man's worship of man.

Against this backdrop Wilberforce and other heirs of John Wesley's Great Awakening in England brought the Christian conscience to bear on a society that was nominally Christian but engaged in vile practices. Their stand strengthened the church in England at the very moment it was under its most vicious assault.

Meanwhile, in the New World a radical experiment opened another chapter in church-state relations. There a group of gentlemen farmers, who were neither naïve about human nature nor pretentious about human society, were drawing up the American Constitution. By refusing to assign redemptive powers to the state or to allow coercive power to the church, the American experiment separated these two institutions for the first time since Constantine.

What might be considered the modern phase in church-state history has emerged in our century. It is an amalgam of elements from the previous eras. The rise of totalitarian regimes has brought back the kind of persecution the church experienced in early Rome; like Herod, modern dictators tolerate no other kings. In the West secularism has aggressively spread irreligion, turning Europe into a post-Christian culture and America into a battleground with orthodox religion in retreat.

Can we conclude from this cursory overview that the church and the state must inevitably be in conflict? To some extent the answer is yes. Dual allegiances always create tension. And in a sinful world the struggle for power, which inevitably corrupts, is unavoidable. When the church isn't being persecuted, it is being corrupted. So as much as anything else, it is man's own nature that has created centuries of conflict.

But every generation has an obligation to seek anew a healthy relationship between church and state. Both are reflections of man's nature; both have a role to play. Christ's teaching clearly delineates these roles.

Jesus was remarkably indifferent to those who held political power. He had no desire to replace Caesar or Pilate with His apostles

Peter or John. He gave civil authority its due, rebuking both the Zealots and Peter for using the sword.

This infuriated the religious right of His day. Eager to discredit Jesus, the Pharisees and Herodians tried trapping Him over the question of allegiance to political authority.

"Tell us," they asked, "is it right to pay taxes to Caesar or not?"

The question put Jesus in the middle: if He said no, He would be a threat to the Roman government; if He said yes, He would lose the respect of the masses who hated the Romans.

Jesus asked them for a coin. It was a Roman denarius, the only coin that could be used to pay the hated yearly poll tax. On one side was the image of the Emperor Tiberius, around which were written the words *Tiberius Caesar Augustus, son of the divine Augustus.*

"Whose portrait is this?" He asked, rubbing His finger over the raised features of the Roman ruler. "And whose inscription?"

"Caesar's," they replied impatiently.

"Give to Caesar what is Caesar's and to God what is God's," replied Jesus, handing the coin back to them. They stared at Him in stunned silence.

Not only had He eluded the trap, but He had put Caesar in his place. Christ might simply have said, "Give to Caesar what is Caesar's." That's all that was at issue. It was Caesar's image on the coin, and Caesar had authority over the state.

What made Him add the second phrase, "Give . . . to God what is God's"?

The answer, I believe, is found on the reverse face of the coin, which showed Tiberius's mother represented as the goddess of peace, along with the words *highest priest.* The blasphemous words commanded the worship of Caesar; they thus exceeded the state's authority.

Jesus' lesson was not lost on the early church. Government is to be respected, and its rule honored. "It is necessary to submit to the authorities," wrote the apostle Paul. "If you owe taxes, pay taxes."[6] But worship is reserved solely for God.

The distinction Christ made is clear; as discussed in chapter 7, both church and state have clear and distinct roles ordained by God. The issue is how to apply these teachings to each institution in today's volatile world.

"Christ did not give the keys of the Kingdom to Caesar nor the sword to Peter," writes a contemporary scholar.[7] In God's provision the state is not to seize authority over ecclesiastical or spiritual matters, nor is the church to seek authority over political matters. Yet the constant temptation of each is to encroach upon the other.

Governments, with rare exceptions, seek to expand their power beyond the mandate to restrain evil, preserve order, and promote justice. Most often they do this by venturing into religious or moral areas. The reason is twofold: the state needs religious legitimization for its policies and an independent church is the one structure that rivals the state's claim for ultimate allegiance.

A contemporary example, though admittedly extreme, is the Soviet Union and its Act of 1918 on separation of church and state. This sounds benign enough, but what the Soviets decreed, reinforced in the 1929 law and in subsequent constitutions, is that churches may conduct worship services when licensed by the government but may not give to the poor, carry on education, or teach religion outside of church. State publishing houses in turn cannot publish religious literature; schools cannot teach religion but must actively teach atheism; and the government has embarked on a campaign to discourage orthodox religious participation and aggressively promote atheism.[8]

So while the edifice of the church is retained, it is a hollow structure; the work of the people of God, which is the true church, is forbidden. Yet in officially promoting atheism, the state is offering its own substitute religion to legitimate its own structure.*

Encroachment upon faith in the West is usually not as dramatic as it has been in modern totalitarian states. It begins in minor ways, such as a county zoning commission barring Bible studies in homes, suppers in church basements, or religious activities on public property. And even when it appears that the state is accommodating religious viewpoints, its action may well be a Trojan horse. Though my opinion is perhaps a minority one, I believe the much-debated issue of prayer in schools is a case in point.

Children or teachers who want to pray in schools should have the same rights of free expression and the same access to public facilities any other group has. But organized prayer, even if voluntary, is another matter. The issue is who does the organizing. If it is the school board, Caesar is being given a spiritual function; admittedly a small crack in the door, but a crack nonetheless. I for one don't want my grandchildren

*Oscar Cullman has written, "According to the Jewish, as to the early Christian, outlook the totalitarian state is precisely the classic form of the Devil's manifestation on earth." Oscar Cullman, *The State in the New Testament* (New York: Scribner's, 1956), 74.

reciting prayers determined by government officials. And in actual practice they would be so watered down as to be of no effect except perhaps to water down my grandchildren's growing faith.

Whenever the state has presumed on God's role, whether in ancient Rome or modern America, the first liberty, freedom of conscience, suffers.

On the other side of the coin, the church, whose principal function is to proclaim the Good News and witness the values of the Kingdom of God, must resist the tempting illusion that it can usher in that Kingdom through political means.* Jesus provided the best example for the church in His wilderness confrontation with Satan when the Devil tempted Jesus to worship him and thus take dominion over the kingdoms of this world.

No small temptation. With that kind of power, Christ could enforce the Sermon on the Mount; love and justice could reign. He might have reasoned that if He didn't accept, someone else would. This rationalization is popular today, right up through the highest councils of government: compromise to stay in power because there you can do more for the common good.

And think of the popularity Jesus could have gained. After all, the people wanted a Messiah who would vanquish their oppressors. But Jesus understood His mission, and it could not be accomplished by taking over the kingdoms of the world in a political coup.

Yet the most consistent heresy of the church has been to succumb to the very temptation Christ explicitly denied. In the Middle Ages this produced bloody crusades and inquisitions; in modern times it has fostered a type of utopianism expressed in a stanza from one of William Blake's most famous poems:

> I will not cease from mental flight,
> Nor shall my sword sleep in my hand,

*James Schall reminds us that "if there is any constant temptation of the history of Christianity, from reaction to Christ's rejection of Jewish zealotism on to current debates about the relation of Marxism to the Kingdom of God, it is the pressure to make religion a formula for refashioning political and economic structures." James Schall, "The Altar as the Throne," in *Churches on the Wrong Road* (Chicago: Regnery/Gateway, 1986), 227.

Till we have built Jerusalem,
In England's green and pleasant land."[9]*

This century's social-gospel movement echoed Blake's sentiments, dissolving Christian orthodoxy into a campaign to eliminate
every social injustice through governmental means. Objectives became political and economic to the detriment of the spiritual. The
reformers' well-intentioned efforts were shattered as social programs
failed to produce the promised utopia, leaving observers to conclude,
"Things are no better. Where is your God now?"

Utopianism is often articulated today in contemporary Christian
circles; it crosses political lines, from the liberation theologians to the
New Right and to the mainline church leaders. As one bishop confided
to Richard Neuhaus, "The mission of the church is to build the kingdom
of God on earth, and the means of the mission is politics."[10]

Such preoccupation with the political diverts the church from its
primary mission. This was evident in the comment of an American lay
missionary who described liberation theology as "a concern for man
and the world as opposed to the concern of the traditional church for
the salvation of man's soul."[11] All Christian political movements run
this risk.

They run another risk too, particularly those on the political right
where many want to impose Christian values on society by force of law.
Some, such as those in the theonomist movement, even want to rein-
state Old Testament civil codes, ignoring Christ's teaching in the parable of the wheat and the tares in which He warns that we live with both
good (the wheat) and evil (the tares), and cannot root out the tares.
Only God is able to do that and He will—when the Kingdom comes in
its final glory.

It is on this point that the church most frequently has stumbled in
its understanding of the Kingdom of God. Oscar Cullman writes: "In the
course of history the church has always assumed a false attitude toward

---

*The problem is, as historian Christopher Dawson observed, "There are quite a number of
different Jerusalems. . . . There is the Muscovite Jerusalem which has no temple, there is Herr
Hitler's Jerusalem which has no Jews, and there is the Jerusalem of the social reformers which is all
suburbs. But none of these are Blake's Jerusalem, still less [the Kingdom of God]." Christopher
Dawson, "Religion and Politics," *Catholicism in Crisis* (June 1985), 8.

All these New Jerusalems are earthly cities established by the will and power of man. And if we
believe that the Kingdom of Heaven can be established by political or economic measures, then
we can hardly object to the claims of such a state to embrace the whole of life and to demand the
total submission of the individual will and conscience.

the state when it has forgotten that the present time is already fulfillment, but not yet consummation."[12]* Even if Christians advocating
dominion gained power, they would be doomed to failure. As Martin
Luther once wrote, "It is out of the question that there should be a
Christian government even over one land . . . since the wicked always outnumber the good. Hence a man who would venture to
govern . . . with the gospel would be like a shepherd who should
place in one fold wolves, lions, eagles and sheep together and let them
freely mingle."[13]

It was perhaps because he realized this truth—that the world
cannot be ruled by spiritual structures and that the church has long
abused power—that John Paul I at his inauguration in 1978 refused to
be crowned with the papal tiara, the vestigial symbol of the claim to
temporal power. John Paul II followed his example. These dramatic
gestures renounced a centuries-old tradition that has contributed to
the darkest moments for the church.

But while the church must avoid utopianism and diversion from its
transcendent mission, it is not to ignore the political scene. To the
contrary, as will be explored in later chapters, its members, who are
also citizens of the world, have a duty, as Carl Henry puts it, "to work
through civil authority for the advancement of justice and human
good." They may provide "critical illumination, personal example and
vocational leadership."[14] Wilberforce is a prime example. There are
proper ways as well for the institutional church to provide society with
its moral vision and hold government to moral account.†

Through the individual Christian's involvement in politics, as we will
discuss later, the standards of civic righteousness can be influenced by

---

*Cullman amplifies his point: "The church's task with regard to the state which is posed for all time
is thus clear. First, it must loyally give the state everything necessary to its existence. It has to
oppose anarchy and all zealotism within its own ranks. Second, it has to fulfill the office of
watchmen over the state. That means it must remain in principle critical towards every state and
be ready to warn it against transgression of its legitimate limits. Third, it must deny to the state
which exceeds its limits, whatever such a state demands that lies within the province of religio-
ideological excess; and in its preaching, the church must courageously describe this excess as
opposition to God." Cullman, The State in the New Testament, 90–91.

†Some Christian traditions similarly believe that they can best model Kingdom values not by
involvement in politics but by the establishment of alternative communities in which they live out
the teachings of the Kingdom. In its proper form, this is not a withdrawal from the world or
abandonment of Christian responsibility; nor is it a privatization of Christian values as with those
who profess to believe but live as if they do not. It is instead a different strategy to the same end
of providing a witness in the kingdoms of man of the values of the Kingdom of God. While I do not
agree with the generally negative view of government held by such groups, I respect the
faithfulness by which they live their convictions.

the standards of righteousness of the Kingdom of God. Such an influence is what theologians call common grace (as distinguished from God's special grace that offers citizenship in the Kingdom of God to all who desire admission). Common grace is God's provision for the welfare of all His created beings, both those who believe in Him and those who don't.

The critical dynamic in the church-state tension is separation of institutional authority. Religion and politics can't be separated—they inevitably overlap—but the institutions of church and state must preserve their separate and distinct roles. In this regard, the American experiment merits closer examination.

America is not the New Jerusalem or a "city upon a hill," though some of its founders harbored that vision. Nor are Americans God's chosen people. The Kingdom of God is universal, bound by neither race nor nation. But Abraham Lincoln used an interesting phrase; Americans, he said, were the "almost chosen people."[15] If there is any justification for that term—not theologically but historically—it is because in the hammering out of a new republic, the combination of wisdom, reason, and providence produced a church-state relationship that uniquely respected the differing roles of each.

The basis of this radical idea came from the partial convergence of at least two conflicting ideologies: confidence in the eighteenth-century Enlightenment belief that both public and private virtue were possible without religion; and a reaction against the excesses of the state church in Europe. The first view was held by the Deists among America's founders, while the second particularly motivated the avowed Christians among them.

These men and women believed that Christ had given the church its own structures and charter, and the state, ordained in God's providence for the maintenance of public order, was not to tamper with it. The church was ordained principally for the conversion of men and women—conversion grounded in individual conscience wrought by the supernatural work of a sovereign God upon the soul. So the state could neither successfully establish nor destroy the church, since it could not rule conscience nor transform people's hearts and souls.*

*The comment of Baptist minister Isaac Backus is representative: "Nothing can be a true religion but a voluntary obedience unto his revealed will, of which each rational soul has an equal right to

Thus two typically mortal enemies, the Enlightenment and the Christian faith, found a patch of common ground on American soil. Both agreed (for different reasons) that the new government should neither establish nor interfere with the church.†It was this reasoning that led to the adoption of the First Amendment, expressly to protect the individual's right to freedom of conscience and expression, and to prevent the establishment of a state church.

But contrary to the belief of many today, this separation of church and state did not mean that America was to be a nation free of religious influence. From the very beginning the American Revolution itself was seen by many as a rebellion fueled by the conviction that man is a creature of God, and his political life is conditioned by that truth. As James Madison insisted, "This duty [homage to the Creator] is precedent, both in order of time and degree of obligation, to the claims of civil society. Before any man can be considered as a member of civil society, he must be considered as a subject of the governor of the universe."[16] A nation under God was no idle phrase.

Nor did the separation of church and state mean religion and politics could be separated or religious values removed from the public arena. For one's political life is an expression of values, and religion, by definition, most profoundly influences values.*

The Founding Fathers were well aware that the form of limited government they were adopting could only succeed if there was an underlying consensus of values shared by the populace. I am always reminded of this when I visit the House of Representatives. A beautiful fresco on the upper walls of the chamber itself contains the portraits of history's great lawmakers. Standing at the speaker's desk and looking straight ahead over the main entrance, one's eyes meet the piercing

judge for himself, every person has an unalienable right to act in all religious affairs according to the full persuasion of his own mind." "A Declaration of the Rights of the Inhabitants of the State of Massachusetts-Bay in New England," in Edwin S. Gaustad, ed., A Documentary History of Religion in America, Vol. I (Grand Rapids, Mich.: Eerdmans, 1982), 268.

†One phrase in James Madison's "Memorial and Remonstrance," presented to the Commonwealth of Virginia in 1785, succinctly sums up the thinking of our Founding Fathers: ". . . that Religion or the duty which we owe to our Creator and the manner of discharging it, can be directed only by reason and conviction, not by force or violence. The Religion then of every man must be left to the conviction and conscience of every man; and it is the right of every man to exercise it as these may dictate." "James Madison's Memorial and Remonstrance, 1785," in Gaustad, ed., A Documentary History of Religion in America: Vol. I, 262.

*The concept of a "wall of separation," a phrase incidentally first used by Jefferson fifteen years after the Constitution was adopted, applied to institutions of church and state, not religious and political values.

eyes of the first figure in the series: Moses, the one who recorded the Law from the original Lawgiver.

John Adams eloquently acknowledged the understanding of our constitutional framers when in 1798 he wrote: "We have no government armed in power capable of contending with human passions unbridled by morality and religion. . . . Our constitution was made only for a moral and religious people. It is wholly inadequate for the government of any other."[17]

Many of these original American visionaries believed that Christian citizens would actively bring their religious values to the public forum. George Washington faintly echoed Augustine when he asserted, "Of all the dispositions and habits which lead to a political prosperity, religion and morality are indispensable supports. In vain would that man claim that tribute of patriotism, who should labor to subvert these great pillars of human happiness."[18]

Thus, when laws were passed reflecting the consensus of Christian values in the land, no one panicked supposing that the Christian religion was being "established" or that a sectarian morality was being imposed on an unwilling people. The point of the First Amendment was that such convictions could only become the law of the land if a majority of citizens could be persuaded (without coercion), whether they shared the religious foundation or not, of the merits of a particular proposition.

Today's widespread relegation of religion to merely something people do only in the privacy of their homes or churches would have been unimaginable to the founders of the republic—even those who personally repudiated orthodox Christian faith. Though America has drifted far from the vision of its founders, this system continues to offer one of the world's most hopeful models in an otherwise contentious history of conflict.

The record of the centuries should not cause despair, however. Tension between church and state is inherent and inevitable. Indeed, it is perhaps the outworking of one of God's great mysteries, part of the dynamic by which He governs His universe. For from the constant tension—the chafing back and forth—a certain equilibrium is achieved.

To maintain this balance the church and the state must fulfill their respective roles. One cannot survive without the other; yet neither can do the work of the other. Both operate under God's rule, each in a different relationship to that rule.

Certainly one thing is clear. When they fail in their appointed tasks—that is, when the church fails to be the visible manifestation of the Kingdom of God and the state fails to maintain justice and concord—civic order collapses. The consequences can be catastrophic, as the tumultuous events described in the next two chapters demonstrate.

PART III

ABSENCE
OF THE KINGDOM

10

Roots of War
(Part I)

In Germany they came first for the Communists, and I didn't speak up because I wasn't a Communist. Then they came for the Jews, and I didn't speak up because I wasn't a Jew. Then they came for the trade unionists, and I didn't speak up because I wasn't a trade unionist. Then they came for the Catholics, and I didn't speak up because I was a Protestant. Then they came for me, and by that time no one was left to speak up.

—Martin Niemoller

One match flared, illuminating a single face above the collar of a brown shirt. He was a middle-aged man with a paunch and a face scarred by innumerable street battles.[1]

The man held the match to a fuel-soaked torch, which leaped into

---

This account is based on historical records and quotations from the major figures. In an effort to recreate the historical environment, however, some dialogue has been invented, along with some minor characters. The main characters, their activities, and their views, are as accurate as it is possible to make them.

flame. Quickly he held the torch to another and then another. In a matter of minutes hundreds were alight, their flickering red glare glazing the street crowded with men dressed in brown shirts and dark pants.

They formed into ranks and began their march through the city. Singing, shouting in triumph, swaggering as though they owned the world, thousands marched, filling the widest streets of Berlin and lighting its ancient walls with their smoking torches. They swept under the Brandenburg Gate and down the Wilhelmstrasse. When they passed the chancellery, they became strangely agitated. The tramping of their steps grew louder and the men strained their necks looking upward.

"Sieg Heil, Sieg Heil." Their cries echoed from the buildings at the sight of their leader.

Above them, at a window, Adolf Hitler fondly looked down. After years in the political wilderness, that very day, January 30, 1933, he had been named Chancellor of Germany.

FEBRUARY 1, 1933, BERLIN

A tall, blond young man, well-dressed and carrying himself with aloof self-confidence, stepped out of the heavy black car that had pulled up in front of the German Broadcasting Company on the busy Potsdamerstrasse. As he entered the building, a younger man in a neat but frayed jacket hustled up to greet him enthusiastically.

"Dr. Bonhoeffer! Please come in. Let me take your coat. It is indeed a pleasure for the former student to welcome his professor. You have your script?"

Dietrich Bonhoeffer tapped his chest. "It is here."

"You have it memorized?" the younger asked, his eyes widening. "Are you sure? This is a live broadcast, you know."

Bonhoeffer's cold, patrician face broke into an amused smile. "No, Herr Schmidt, I have the script here, in my pocket." He reached inside his suitcoat and pulled out a sheaf of typed pages.

"Oh, excuse me, Doctor." Schmidt murmured with a look of embarrassed pleasure. "I know you are brilliant, but . . . one can be too brilliant."

"You know the time limit," the younger man added as he led Bonhoeffer upstairs to the broadcast room. "I'm sure I don't have to tell you it is very strict." Bonhoeffer nodded. He had worked out the length of his speech with his usual precision.

Schmidt took a seat before the microphone and glanced at his watch. "We have a little time," he said. "Would you like to smoke?" Bonhoeffer declined.

Then, with an effort at casualness, Schmidt said, "I hope you won't mind if I say that I was quite surprised at your choice of the subject, 'The Younger Generation's Changed View of the Concept of Führer.' Most of the theologians who come here speak on very dry material. But you have chosen just the topic people want to discuss. Tell me, were you inspired by the parade in the Wilhelmstrasse last night?"

"Inspired?" Bonhoeffer seemed suddenly to notice the younger man. "What do you mean, 'inspired'?"

At this invitation, the words poured out of Schmidt. "People say that Hitler is just one more politician, but I don't think so. Somehow, Dr. Bonhoeffer, I feel he is a different kind of man, a man who knows the soul of Germany. I am sure you must know what I mean. The old people cannot stop living in the past. But they will learn. This man may be the leader we in the younger generation have been seeking. That is what I meant by 'inspired.' That march seemed to signal that he had touched some secret chord in our hearts."

Bonhoeffer appeared aloof, almost bored, when in fact he was intensely interested. "What do you think he will do now that he has power, Herr Schmidt? He has been very evasive in laying out his plans."

"But that is exactly what I mean! He is not just another politician, with one promise or another. He offers himself. We have had so many years of these weak politicians. They act as though Germany's defeat and betrayal is simply a fact that must be accepted. If that is realism, we should get rid of realism! We don't need just another political program; we need a complete transformation of the nation. You can only get that from a leader you trust completely. Our soul was meant to be forced into unity! Don't you think so?"

"I doubt Hitler will last long in power," said Bonhoeffer coolly. "He seems strong because he has not had to be responsible. Now he will have to make the usual compromises." As he spoke, Bonhoeffer fingered a signet ring on his left hand. "Nor, Herr Schmidt, do I completely agree with you about the need for a leader. It is, of course, a very appealing idea. We are so tired of politics. We would naturally like to give it all over to a leader in the way that a child can turn over some difficult struggle to his father. But we cannot just hand over authority to our leaders and consider that the end of our responsibility. I think that is what Herr Hitler would like us to do. But the government can only do, and should only be called on to do certain things. It cannot replace God."

Schmidt was silent for a few moments. When he spoke, he weighed his words carefully. "For years godless Communists have had the run of the streets. You have seen the fights, real battles, as though Berlin were in a war zone. The national economy is devastated. People lack food, jobs. Money has become worthless. Nobody goes to church any more. Now Herr Hitler has at last barred the Communists from meeting, something none of our 'leaders' had the courage to do. He will save us from Bolshevism. This is leadership. This will lead the German people to greatness."

"Be careful that such leadership does not lead you to disaster," Bonhoeffer said quietly.

Schmidt stood up. "Did you bring the extra copy of your script, Dr. Bonhoeffer? I should take it to the director now."

"Why does he need it?"

"It's a new directive. Everything should go across his desk."

Bonhoeffer reached into his suitcoat pocket and pulled out a second copy of his script. Schmidt took it away. Shortly after he returned, Bonhoeffer went on the air.

Bonhoeffer, who spoke rapidly in normal conversation, delivered his radio address slowly and deliberately. He described the development of Adolf Hitler's "Führerprinzip," or "leadership principle," through which discipline and dignity would be restored by vesting authority in a single leader. This idea was tremendously attractive to young Germans who had known only the chaos of the last fifteen years. At many points in his address it seemed that Bonhoeffer was embracing the Führer principle. But at the end his words grew ominous as he warned against placing blind faith in any authority.

"For should the leader allow himself to succumb to the wishes of those he leads, who will always seek to turn him into an "idol," he concluded, "then the leader will gradually become the image of 'misleader.' This is the leader who makes an idol of himself and his office, thus mocking God."

When he finished, Bonhoeffer glanced at his watch, stood and shook hands with Schmidt, and left the broadcasting room. As he was putting on his overcoat on the ground floor, Schmidt came down the stairs hurriedly.

"Dr. Bonhoeffer," he called. "Just a moment. . . . The director said I ought to tell you . . . just so you would not be surprised . . . that unfortunately the last few sentences of your address were not broadcast. It seems you went slightly over the time allotted."

Bonhoeffer's blue eyes were icy behind his rimless glasses. "What do you mean? They turned off the microphone?"

Schmidt smiled. "I'm so sorry, Doctor. But you know radio is very precise."

FEBRUARY 27, 1933

While at a party in his honor at the apartment of Joseph Goebbels, Adolf Hitler received a call telling him that the ornate, gilded Reichstag building was in flames. The Reichstag was the historic German parliament building. "It's the Communists!" the Führer shouted. Then he stalked out into the frigid night where the buildings were silhouetted against an orange sky.

Shortly thereafter, Hitler convened a meeting in Hermann Göring's nearby office. Cabinet ministers filed in, talking excitedly. Finally Rudolf Diels, head of the Soviet Police, was ushered in to report on the initial investigation. Diels said that a Dutchman named van der Lubbe had been arrested and had confessed to lighting the fire as a protest.

Both Göring and Hitler began shouting simultaneously. "This is the beginning of a Communist uprising! Now we'll show them! Anyone who stands in our way will be mowed down!"

Diels interrupted them. The idea of an uprising was nonsense; his spies all said no Communist move was coming. Undoubtedly van der Lubbe had acted alone.

Hitler ignored Diels. "This is a cunning and well-prepared plot! But they have reckoned without us and without the German people! In their rat holes, from which they are now trying to crawl, they cannot hear the jubilation of the masses!" He ranted until Diels and everyone else fell silent.

By morning truckloads of hurriedly deputized brownshirts were breaking down doors and arresting Communists throughout the nation. Four thousand suspects were sent to newly organized concentration camps. Hitler, claiming a national emergency and demanding instantaneous action, convinced the government to suspend all constitutional rights. News broadcasts proclaimed that Hitler had miraculously saved Germany from a Communist insurrection.

In this frenzied atmosphere Adolf Hitler won his first bare majority in the March 5 elections.*

APRIL 1, 1933

The first splash of morning light struck the front door of the small hardware store as three young brownshirts, laughing and joking, began fixing a large poster to the front window. The proprietor, who was sweeping the sidewalk, came over to ask what they were doing. After a short, noisy argument he retreated into his store. He could be seen from time to time peering out the door.

The sign announced, in six-inch letters visible from across the street, that the proprietor was a Jew and requested that shoppers not patronize his business. A few curious passersby gathered on the sidewalk and watched the stormtroopers post the signs on several other storefronts.

A man dressed in dark blue working clothes came down the sidewalk and walked up to the door of the hardware store, not noticing the signs or the small crowd. Before he could enter the store, one of the brownshirts politely stopped him and explained that a national boycott of all Jewish businesses had been called by Adolf Hitler. The man looked up and around, startled to see the spectators, and hurried off. The crowd chuckled.

After three days the boycott ended. Hitler had learned what he wanted to know: no one would stand up for the Jews.

On the same day the boycott was launched, a group known as the German Christians held their first national rally. Included in their number were some widely respected theologians and church leaders. Their chosen name, which placed more emphasis on *German* than *Christian*, expressed their belief that German experiences and culture had given them a unique understanding of God.

The German Christians wanted to harmonize the church in Germany with Hitler's political movement, which was, to them, more than politics; it was the revival of hope and the force of destiny for their nation. Many of them believed the Germans were God's chosen people and Hitler the new messiah. The national revival was more vital than anything they had ever found in their faith.

---

*It is generally accepted now that the fire was set by the Nazis to give them pretext for destroying the Communist political organization.

JULY 1933

In six months Hitler had accomplished an almost unbelievable consolidation of power. He had, thanks to the Reichstag fire, imprisoned all known Communists. He had convinced the members of the Reichstag parliament to virtually suspend its own powers. He had outlawed all significant opposition parties and imprisoned many of their leaders. He had taken over, by force, all labor unions and removed all Jews from the civil service.

More significantly, however, he had done all this without arousing any substantial resistance. In January he had been head of a minority party, little liked or trusted. By July, thanks to his skillful manipulation, the majority of German citizens had fallen under his spell. Germans talked excitedly of the renewal of their country. It was no longer only his swaggering, heel-clicking brownshirts who cheered Hitler to the skies. Ordinary men and women, laborers and tradesmen, businessmen and housewives went into hysterical chants of "Heil Hitler!" when he passed through the streets, his motorcade swathed in red and black Nazi flags. He had given them hope again.

William Shirer, an American correspondent in Berlin, wrote in his diary: "I'm beginning to comprehend, I think, some of the reasons for Hitler's astounding success. Borrowing a chapter from the Roman church, he is restoring pageantry and color and mysticism to the drab lives of twentieth-century Germans. This morning's opening meeting . . . had something of the mysticism and religious fervor of an Easter or Christmas Mass in a great Gothic cathedral."

The pageant Shirer had viewed was played dozens of times in every part of Germany: an immense hall packed with citizens and soldiers . . . a sea of red and black Nazi standards swaying overhead . . . a giant golden eagle glaring down from an upper balcony . . . an orchestra playing solemn symphonic music.

The orchestra stops. A hush falls over the strangely orderly crowd and thousands of people crane their necks to see. Then a stately patriotic anthem begins and from far in the back, walking slowly down the wide central aisle, comes the Führer.

Thousands of arms snap stiffly out in salute. Thousands of eyes focus on Hitler's pale, grave face. Behind him march his closest aides—faces and names that will go down in history, recorded in blood—Göring, Goebbels, Hess, Himmler. They take their places on the raised dais under huge lights. Above them is the huge Nazi Blood Flag, stained with the blood of Nazis killed in the Munich Beer Hall Putsch.

Finally the Führer himself rises to speak. Beginning in a low, velvety voice, which makes the audience unconsciously lean forward to hear, he speaks of his love for Germany and his long struggle to restore its dignity. He describes his own humble beginnings, his injuries as a foot soldier in World War I, and the terrible injuries Germany has suffered as a result of that war. Gradually his pitch increases until he reaches a screaming crescendo. But his audience does not think his rasping shouts excessive. They are screaming with him.

JULY 14, 1933

By now Hitler had only one significant source of opposition. Not the journalists, political parties, universities, or labor unions; all these had almost completely converted to Nazism in less than six months. Instead, opposition came from a most unexpected source: the church.

Two thirds of the German population—45,000,000 people—were Protestants, primarily Lutherans, who traditionally kept their noses entirely out of politics. As a group, they were known as the German Evangelical Church. They were conservative, rural, and patriotic, and had Hitler been content to leave them alone, they undoubtedly would have supported him almost unanimously at this stage. But Hitler would allow no independent source of authority in his resurrected Germany. Everyone must answer to a single leader, the Führer. Every institution must serve the aims of the Fatherland, including the church.

Publicly, in the beginning, Hitler gave the appearance of being a religious man. A nominal Catholic, he sometimes displayed a tattered Bible and spoke of its inspiration in his life. Officially, his party platform called, rather ambiguously, for religious freedom and supported "positive Christianity." In private, however, he expressed his utter contempt for the church, particularly for the Protestants. He expected their pastors to knuckle under easily to his schemes for remolding the church, his main source of opposition. "They will betray anything for the sake of their miserable little jobs and incomes."

Early on he had negotiated an agreement with Rome that removed Roman Catholic opposition to his regime. Eager to support the spirit of the times, the twenty-eight main Protestant denominations voluntarily began work on a new constitution that would unite them under one leader according to the "Führer principle."

But Hitler was impatient; he did not want to wait for the church bureaucracy. He decided to push an obscure, obsequious naval chaplain, Ludwig Müller, into leadership of the newly united Protestant church. Despite the Führer's prestigious support, however, Müller was defeated in a May 27 election.

Hitler refused to meet the elected bishop. Instead, radio and press propaganda poured out favorable material about Müller. Then in late June Nazi government officials invaded church offices, forcibly taking over administrative positions. Müller proclaimed himself national bishop-elect.

The new officials ordered services of praise and thanksgiving for this takeover. Every church in Germany was to be decorated with Nazi flags and a proclamation read from the pulpit, stating that "all those who are concerned . . . feel deeply thankful that the state should have assumed, in addition to all its tremendous tasks, the great load and burden of reorganizing the church."

But while all Germany was being wooed to Hitler, a stubborn resistance was taking root within the church itself: the Young Reformation Movement. Martin Niemoller, Hans Jacobi, and Dietrich Bonhoeffer were among its first members. They were apolitical, and their meetings often included a resolution of loyalty to the government and, sometimes, to Adolf Hitler. But they also valued the church's independence and rejected any attempt to blend a religion of Germany with the religion of Jesus Christ.

On July 14, 1933, Hitler surprised everyone by calling a special church election to be held nine days later on July 23. The German Christians were given complete access to the state-run radio and newspapers; the Young Reformation hastily organized a slate of candidates and began feverish campaigning. Over the weekend leaflets were written and duplicated.

On Monday, July 17, the Gestapo invaded the Young Reformation offices and confiscated all 620,000 campaign leaflets.

JULY 17, 1933

The cramped offices of the Young Reformers, which just two days earlier had been a hive of activity, were ominously silent. Martin Niemoller, whose rounded face and cleft chin gave him the appearance of perpetual boyhood, paced around Bonhoeffer, Jacobi, and a young man wearing the brown shirt and Nazi armband of the SA.

"I don't see any point in appealing to underlings," Niemoller said stubbornly. "You might as well appeal to the stones in the street. I would rather go directly to Hitler. If he knew what was being done, he would put a stop to it. But I am sure they all lie to him."

"How do we get to Hitler?" Jacobi asked.

"Perhaps through President Hindenburg," said Niemoller. "We have contacts there, and he has always been sympathetic."

Bonhoeffer's impatience would have been invisible to anyone who did not recognize his mannerism of fiddling with the ring on his left hand. "That is a fine idea, Martin," he said, "but the elections are Sunday. If we have no literature we might as well go home. What else can we do, stand in the street and yell our slogans? We must go to the Gestapo now!"

The discussion seesawed until Niemoller shrugged his large shoulders and smiled. "All right, go then," he said. "But at least take Henke with you." He pointed to the young storm trooper, a hybrid rare but not unknown—a staunch Nazi who was also a Young Reformer. "They may respect his uniform more than they respect yours."

Jacobi vetoed this. "Martin, I think not. Maybe these will count as much as Henke's swastikas." He indicated the two Iron Crosses he wore, won in World War I. "At any rate, for every SA member we can produce, the German Christians can show fifty."

At Gestapo headquarters on the Albrechtstrasse, Jacobi and Bonhoeffer's demand to see Rudolf Diels, the Gestapo chief, met with opposition by several underlings. They persisted. Finally a rude, overbearing officer ushered them into Diels's presence.

To their surprise, the Gestapo chief politely invited them to sit down and said that he certainly hoped he could be of help to them. It was really not his department, but he would do what he could. He noticed Jacobi's decorations and asked about his service in the war.

But the initial cordiality was mere display. When he heard their complaint, Diels did not budge an inch.

"It seems clear to me, Pastors, that you are in the wrong. You have published scurrilous literature. You have taken a slogan that cannot be proper, 'The Program of the Evangelical Church.' You are fortunate not to have been arrested yourselves." He stood up and held out his hand, as though that closed the matter.

Neither Bonhoeffer nor Jacobi moved.

"The Führer made the explicit promise that this election would be free and secret," Bonhoeffer said. "He wanted to settle the political quarrels of our church through a fair election. Do you think confiscating all of one party's literature can be considered fair treatment? It is certainly a violation of the Führer's words."

Diels slowly took his seat again.

"Pastor, I have heard the Führer's words. He appointed me to safeguard them. He did not give you that responsibility. My officers have been very lenient with you. If it were up to me I would send you to the concentration camp now. In fact I am thinking of it. Why don't you simply leave now and go prepare your next sermon?"

"You have not answered my question," Bonhoeffer pressed him. "The state has promised a free election. How can this be considered free?"

The Gestapo leader leaned down in his chair and looked Bonhoeffer over while absentmindedly brushing off his jacket. He forced a smile. "You do not really have much respect for the state, do you, Pastor?"

"I have enough respect for the state to protest when it does wrong," Bonhoeffer snapped back.

After another silence, Diels asked, "What do you want me to do? There is a court injunction against you. Do you want me to ignore it? That would be contrary to the law."

Jacobi spoke up. "The injunction is against our slogan, not against our literature."

"But the slogan is all over your literature."

"Not all of it."

Diels agreed, finally, to let them have their literature back. The pastors, in turn, agreed to change their slogan from "Evangelical Church" to "Gospel and Church."

The parting was stiff and unfriendly; no one was satisfied.

"I assure you, Pastors," Diels said, "that I am still considering whether you are safe outside this building or whether you would be better off in the KZ.* If a single pamphlet appears, under your names or anyone else's, that insults the German Christians or that uses some slogan similar to the one you have agreed to discard, I will certainly send for you. Do not think that I lack the power to put you anywhere I want to, or that I will hesitate again."

That weekend Hitler was in Bayreuth for the annual Wagner Festival. During an interval in the program, he broadcast a message calling for the German people, in support of all he had done, to elect those forces that "as exemplified by the German Christians, have deliberately chosen to take their stand within the National Socialist State."

For Martin Niemoller that address was a lightning bolt. As a former U-boat captain from World War I and an ardent German patriot, he had

*Concentration camps.

supported Hitler. Now he heard, in disbelief, a state official telling the church whom to elect as their spiritual representatives. Niemoller would never trust Hitler again.

For others, however, the address proved that as popular as Hitler was, he could sway most church members to support anything he wanted. When the votes were tallied the next day, the German Christians had over 70 percent. Even in Niemoller's parish they took half the vote. Now, by "legal" means, the Nazis took over key positions in the church.

SEPTEMBER 1933

In September the new governing body of the German Evangelical Church met. It became known as the Brown Synod because most of the delegates wore the brown shirts of the SA. They elected Hitler's man, Müller, their bishop and passed the much-debated Aryan Paragraph, outlawing all Jews or persons married to Jews from church office. They also passed a ruling that all pastors take a loyalty loath to Hitler and his government.

Dietrich Bonhoeffer urged vehemently that all dissenting pastors resign from the church. Instead, protest formed under a new organization, the Pastors' Emergency League, led by the tireless Martin Niemoller. Within a week 2,300 pastors had signed its pledge to be bound in their preaching "only by Holy Scripture and the Confessions of the Reformation." By the end of the year members would total 6,000, approximately the same number as the German Christians.

OCTOBER 17, 1933, LONDON

Dietrich Bonhoeffer stood at the window of his new London vicarage, thoughtfully smoking a cigarette. Though located in the south London suburb of Forest Hill, the large Victorian house was surrounded by a forest of trees. He watched the dying leaves being whipped away by a strong wind and shivered in the wet English air. The room behind him, one of two he would occupy, was bare and inhospitable; clearly mice had been its most frequent residents. His furniture and his piano had yet to arrive from Germany.

Bonhoeffer had come to London to pastor two tiny German-speaking congregations and to place some distance between himself and the church struggle in Germany. Still under thirty years of age, yet often consulted for his wisdom, Bonhoeffer needed time to think and pray. He was deeply concerned with the Jewish question, and he was frustrated by the gap between his own uncompromising stand and the views of others who still thought accommodation with Hitler possible.*

Just three days before Hitler had announced that Germany was resigning from the League of Nations. Germans, for whom the League was a symbol of their World War I defeat, had rejoiced as though at a stunning martial victory. Even Martin Niemoller, to Bonhoeffer's horror, had sent Hitler a congratulatory telegram.

The Germany he had left rang with the marching and singing of tanned, fit bands of children, the Hitler Youth. Hitler was obviously preparing to violate the Versailles Treaty, which limited the size and armaments of Germany's army. Yet few Germans, including his comrades in the church struggle, saw any danger. They were stirred by their love for their nation and their faith in its God-given destiny.

Sadly, the people in England were equally unaware of the danger. They did not understand the degree to which Hitler had transformed the German nation, particularly the young people, into passionate believers. They wanted Bonhoeffer to explain what was happening in Germany, but their attention span was short. The Christians he had spoken with could not even distinguish between the German Christians and those who opposed them.

London was to give Bonhoeffer a chance to develop perspective from a distance. Yet he longed for the battle he had deliberately left. He spent hours on the phone and found excuses for returning to Berlin frequently.

NOVEMBER 12, 1933, BERLIN

Martin Niemoller was a popular preacher and the services in his newly built church in the affluent suburb of Dahlem were generally full. But this Sunday many people, including the usual Gestapo plainclothesmen, came early and waited with particular expectation. Yesterday church officials had informed Niemoller and two other leaders of the Pastors' Emergency League that they were suspended from their pastorates. Later in the day the suspension had been cancelled; some said because Hitler had ordered it.

Niemoller was very different from the introspective Bonhoeffer. Blunt to a fault, he never kept his thoughts to himself. His critics called him unreasonable and unbending.

*Often in his meditations in those days he turned to the Sermon on the Mount. A few years later his thoughts would coalesce into his book *The Cost of Discipleship.*

This Sunday marked the four-hundred-and fiftieth anniversary of Martin Luther's birth. The German Christians claimed Luther as their hero. To them the bluff, courageous, uncompromising reformer embodied the true German character. What would Niemoller say to that?

He began by welcoming this "1933 picture of Luther, which represents him as a fighter." Clearly battle lines were being drawn in the German church today. It was proper to ask, which side of the battle would Luther be on if he were here?

Niemoller acknowledged with a warm smile that behind all the German Christians' discussion of the "Luther spirit" lay a genuine admiration for Luther's "naïve unconcern, for his intrepid courage, for his tenacious steadfastness, for his straightforward and unflinching will, for his profound tenderness." Many Germans felt, said Niemoller, that Germany and its church desperately needed more of this Luther spirit if they were to renew themselves.

"But here is a grave error," Niemoller said, his clear voice ringing over the quiet congregation, "the substitution of a human hero for the message God sent through him. What a strange paradox it would be if the Devil used Luther's four hundred and fiftieth birthday to fill German minds with the delusion that they needed not the grace of God, but the courage of Martin Luther! Luther's message was always that no human qualities or human works could bring salvation—only the goodness of God."

Now Niemoller applied this to practical political issues. "One can even hear that our whole nation would do the will of God if only it had purified its species and its race!" Luther himself, Niemoller said, would certainly have fought such ideas.

"There is absolutely no sense in talking of Luther and celebrating his memory within the Protestant church if we stop at Luther's image and do not look at Him to whom Luther pointed." And Luther pointed, Niemoller reminded his listeners, to a Jew, the rabbi of Nazareth.

The next evening, as though in confirmation of Niemoller's words, 20,000 German Christians, including bishops and church officials in full regalia, gathered in the Berlin Sports Palace, a massive new building, symbolic of the Nazi resurgence in its raw modernistic architecture.

Joachim Hossenfelder, head of the German Christians and a Berlin pastor, presided in his Nazi uniform. After the usual parade of swastika-bedecked flags, a fanfare of trumpets and throaty chorus of "Now Thank

We All Our God," Hossenfelder announced that in his diocese the Aryan paragraph, dismissing all Jews from church office, was being put into effect immediately. He also announced that Niemoller and other leaders of the Pastors' Emergency League would be suspended, since their activities were entirely foreign to the true spirit of Germany. At each announcement the crowd erupted into a resounding cheer.

The main speaker of the evening was a senior Nazi official who demanded that everything un-German be purged from the church. His final admonition was that the Bible be reexamined for non-German elements: "liberation from the Old Testament, with its Jewish money morality and these stories of cattle-dealers and pimps." It also meant purging the New Testament of its Jewish elements, especially the unheroic theology of the apostle Paul with his "inferiority complex." A proud, heroic Jesus must replace the model of a "suffering servant."

His speech was interrupted again and again by applause. Not one of the bishops or church leaders stood to disagree. Instead, when the speaker had finished, resolutions were enthusiastically passed supporting his words and calling for Jewish Christians to be forced into "ghetto churches."

In the days that followed, the reports in the press of the Sports Palace rally shocked many. The Emergency League printed a protest to be read from their pulpits the next Sunday, but the proclamation was confiscated and fifty pastors who read it were dismissed from their churches.

Bishop Müller, terrified that he might lose his position as head of the national church, resigned from the German Christians. He also rescinded the Aryan paragraph. At the same time, he published volleys of orders, some illegal, some self-contradictory. He secretly arranged for the transfer of all church youth work to the leadership of the Hitler Youth. He then reinstated the Aryan paragraph and published the Muzzling Decrees, which forbade the discussion of all church issues by pastors, on pain of dismissal. Most church leaders lost all confidence in him.

In January Hitler intervened. He had hoped that Müller would unite the entire church behind the Nazi program, but Müller had failed. Now the Führer himself would meet with the leadership of the German Evangelical Church.

JANUARY 25, 1934, BERLIN

Martin Niemoller and a group of his fellow bishops waited quietly in the Reich Chancellery watching the black-uniformed SS officers marching back and forth. One of the bishops nudged Niemoller as a Nazi official passed carrying a scarlet briefcase under his arm. Niemoller recognized fat, baby-faced Hermann Göring. Truly they were near the seat of power!

Finally they were ushered into the Führer's office. Hitler rose from behind his desk and came forward to greet them. Seen closely, he was less than superhuman. He was not tall; his complexion was pale, his face almost undernourished. Only his frigid blue eyes betrayed the real man.

Hitler was about to begin the discussion when Göring burst into the room. He clicked his heels, gave the Nazi salute, and breathlessly launched into a diatribe accusing Bishop Niemoller of conspiring against Hitler. As Göring read from a paper, Niemoller recognized some of his own words, a direct quote from an innocent jest he had made less than an hour before in a telephone conversation with one of his fellow pastors from the Emergency League. The slightly garbled version presented by Göring made it sound as though Niemoller had been gloating about political maneuverings that would outsmart Hitler, the master politician.

Hitler's face flushed and he began to lecture the pastors angrily, pacing the room while they stood before him. Hitler's entire manner made them feel like criminals.

"Do you think you can pull such outrageous, backstairs politics with me? You underestimate me if you do. I am sick of being treated this way, by the church leaders of all people. What have I done to you? Only tried to make peace between all your warring factions. Peace in the church and peace with the state! And this is my reward! You obstruct me at every point and sabotage every move!"

Hitler raved on. The bishops were dumbfounded and Niemoller was horrified. The thought of a treason trial crossed his mind. How would he answer these complaints? *If only Hitler would stop his horrid tirade,* Niemoller thought. *Dear God, let him stop.*

When Hitler finally did stop, Niemoller stepped to the front of the group and tried to explain calmly that the comments had been made during a private conversation with his secretary and were a perfectly innocent joke. Niemoller went on to explain that the struggle for the church was by no means aimed against the Third Reich; it was for the sake of the nation. As a pastor his concern was that the people of Germany not be deluded or led astray.

"I will protect the German people," Hitler shouted. "You take care of the church. You pastors should worry about getting people to heaven and leave this world to me."

The shaken clergymen timidly tried to soothe Hitler's temper, assuring him that isolated expressions of political discontent indicated no overall disloyalty. They suggested that Bishop Müller simply lacked the mature qualities that a national bishop needed. For their part they were tremendously grateful for the Führer's efforts to make peace in the church. The reason for their concern was the possibility of mixing false doctrines with the true gospel.

At this the German Christian representatives spoke up and said that as far as they were concerned the whole controversy was purely church politics.

Hitler listened to their wrangling without apparent interest. He had already stated in his original tirade that he would not remove Müller.

Surprisingly, in light of his anger, Hitler did shake hands with the churchmen when they left. As he came to Niemoller, the pastor looked into the Führer's face and spoke directly and carefully. "A moment ago, Herr Hitler, you told us that you would take care of the German people. But as Christians and men of the church we too have a responsibility for the German people, laid upon us by God. Neither you nor anyone else can take that away from us."

For a moment Hitler stared at him. Then he touched Niemoller's hand and moved on without a word.

Outside, several of the clergymen accosted Niemoller. "How could you speak that way to the Führer? Don't you see that you have ruined it all?"

On the Monday after their meeting with Hitler, the Protestant bishops of Germany gathered for a meeting with National Bishop Müller. Shocked and frightened by Niemoller's behavior, they completely capitulated. They issued a statement of unconditional support for Hitler, the Third Reich, and Bishop Müller, and vowed to carry out any measures and directives he ordered.

Alarmed by Niemoller's radical leadership, two thousand members of the Pastor's Emergency League—almost a third of the group—resigned. Encouraged by this victory, Bishop Müller became more aggressive and dictatorial. He published a series of disciplinary measures, suspensions, dismissals, and retirements. He declared that from then on the church would not be governed by useless synods but by a centralized bureaucracy. He appointed a Nazi lawyer with lapsed church ties to head this administration.

MARCH 13, 1934

Seeing Müller's tactics, several church leaders who had pledged loyalty began to backtrack. Two key bishops, Wurm and Meiser, met with Hitler to complain. This time Hitler was sharply belligerent.

"Christianity will disappear from Germany just as it has in Russia," he told them. "The German race existed without Christianity for thousands of years before Christ and will continue to exist after Christianity has disappeared.

"The church must get used to the teachings about blood and race. Just as the Catholic Church couldn't prevent the earth from going around the sun, so the churches today cannot get rid of the indisputable facts connected with blood and race. If they can't recognize these, history will simply leave them behind."

Other Nazi leaders had expressed such views, but never the publicly pious Hitler. Shaken, the two bishops said if this was his view they could only look forward to being his most loyal opposition. Hitler flew into a rage.

"You are not my most loyal opposition, but traitors to the people, enemies of the Fatherland and the destroyers of Germany."

MAY 29, 1934, BARMEN, GERMANY

They met in a large church in a modern industrial town: 139 delegates in all—half pastors, half laymen—representing eighteen different German denominations. A few wore Nazi uniforms; some were state officials. Some were frightened, others elated about the statement of faith they were about to draw up as the charter of the church's resistance.

The Barmen Declaration was not a political document, and it said not a word about Hitler or Müller. Rather, it set out the theological foundations of the church for which they were prepared to suffer, and it spoke strongly and directly against the false teachings of the German Christians. The clear implication was that Hitler's elevation of the German race was anti-Christian. God had not specially revealed Himself through the German nation, blood, race, or even Hitler.

Barmen also spelled out an understanding of church and state:

The Bible tells us that according to divine arrangement the state has the responsibility to provide for justice and peace in the yet unredeemed world, in which the church also stands. . . .

We repudiate the false teaching that the state can and should expand beyond its special responsibility to become the single and total order of human life, and also thereby fulfill the commission of the church.

We repudiate the false teaching that the church can and should expand beyond its special responsibilities to take on the characteristics, functions and dignities of the state, and thereby become itself an organ of the state.

The commission of the church, in which her freedom is founded, consists in this: in place of Christ and thus in the service of His own word and work, to extend through word and sacrament the message of the free grace of God to all people.

For their expression of faith, some of those present would lose their livelihood, be imprisoned or exiled. Others would lose their lives. A great many others, however, would fail the test.

One of the results of the Barmen meeting was the organization of a group that called themselves the Confessing Church. They represented the large number of Christians within the badly divided German Evangelical Church who most opposed the policies of Hitler. Among their numbers were Niemoller and Bonhoeffer.

A month after Barmen, Hitler murdered hundreds of militant, dissident Nazis in a bloody slaughter that became known as the Röhm Purge. Even the Confessing Church made no public protest—not even Niemoller. Most members expressed thankfulness that Hitler had restrained the more violent elements among his followers.

NOVEMBER 28, 1934, LONDON

Winston Churchill stood before Parliament. He was an old man, a defanged lion, regarded sometimes with pity in the House of Commons. Even his own party would not give him a cabinet position. Still the old lion could roar.

Today his deep growl was asserting that "the strength of our national defenses, and especially of our air defense, is no longer adequate to secure . . . peace, safety, and freedom." Germany's air force, which according to the Versailles Treaty should not exist, "is rapidly approaching equality with our own" and would be fifty percent stronger by the end of 1936.

The MPs settled back into their seats with relief when Prime

Minister Stanley Baldwin, another old but more amiable man, far better liked than Churchill, flatly contradicted him. Few noticed that Baldwin carefully hedged his cheery assessment of the future with the condition, "If Germany continues to execute her air program without acceleration." And while it was true that Churchill had exaggerated, it was also true that the Secret Service had told Baldwin of Hitler's plans to surpass Britain's air force by the fall of 1936.

MARCH 10, 1935, BERLIN

Outside a cold March wind swept the sky, but inside the old brick house the coal fire burned hot. Niemoller, his collar loosened, held his youngest son, Martin, on his knee. From the kitchen came the sounds of his wife washing dishes. Two of his older children were curled in chairs by a window, reading. Niemoller's eyes began to droop.

In the midst of this sleepy Sunday afternoon a knock came at the door. When the maid answered it, Niemoller heard a voice he did not recognize. She ushered in a slim, dark man in a heavy overcoat, who introduced himself as Pastor Schollen from a small church in the countryside about fifty miles from Berlin.

Schollen seemed frightened. He declined a cup of tea and sat fidgeting and glancing around nervously until Niemoller said impatiently, "Get on with it, man! What did you come about?"

Schollen fished in his wallet and brought out a small red card, which he tried to hand to Niemoller. Niemoller waved it away, smiling. He recognized it as the membership card for the Confessing Church.

"Yes, I knew you had joined, Pastor Schollen. I recognize your name."

"I came for counsel, Brother Niemoller. Did you read the statement aloud today?"

"Yes, of course. We had a meeting with the entire congregation in the parish hall. I not only read it, I demanded that everyone make clear where they stand. We took a vote and it was passed overwhelmingly."

Schollen fidgeted, looking down at his feet, then said, "I didn't read the statement this morning because the chief of police is in my congregation. He warned me against it, told me I could lose my position. And I did not feel certain that the tactics were correct." As an afterthought he added, "None of the pastors in my valley will read it. But I told them I would go and talk to you."

Niemoller's sleepiness was gone. "Pastor Schollen, you are not the only one lacking courage. But many pastors were not afraid this morning. They read the statement and hundreds more will read it next week."

"You don't think it is too severe?" Schollen asked. "Some of the pastors thought a more reasonable tone would be more honoring to those with different views. I mean, calling it 'a new religion making idols of blood, race, nation, honor, eternal Germany.' That's quite strong."

"It is nothing less than a new religion," Niemoller said. "A new religion with a different God. Do you know what they are teaching the Hitler Youth now? They are saying that just as Jesus went through three days in the grave, Hitler spent a year in prison. But Hitler's resurrection did not take him away from earth; he stayed here to save the German people. They are teaching that to our children now! Don't you know that?"

"One hears all kinds of things. But how do you know that it is the whole picture?"

"By the time you know the whole picture they will have taken down our crosses and put up swastikas. And you and I will be in the KZ!"

A tremor shook Schollen's body. Quietly he said, "They have already put Hitler's picture next to the crucifixes in our Catholic school-rooms. One of the teachers told me."

"You see?" Niemoller said, striding to the window. "What is there to discuss?"

"But even Bodelschwingh, your old mentor, says we should wait," Schollen said. "They are talking to Hitler, and soon they will reach a reasonable solution. We are good Germans. We are thankful for what the government has done. Is it proper to be making proclamations against the government when discussions are continuing on a daily basis? I ask myself, how could I justify this to the Führer?"

"Justify yourself to the Lord Jesus!" Niemoller shouted.

"I will tell you something," Niemoller added in a lower tone. "Hitler is a coward, a coward and a bully. He will terrify you so long as you are willing to be terrified. We must stand up to him for the church of Jesus Christ. I beg of you! . . . Bodelschwingh, Meiser, Wurm . . . they think they will work out some sort of agreement with the beast. But the beast will swallow them up."

"I really must go, Pastor Niemoller," Schollen said stiffly. He had heard what he needed to hear to make up his mind. He left quickly, not looking back.

That week seven hundred pastors were arrested before they went to church to read the statement passed by the Prussian synod, which was a regional faction of the Confessing Church. German Christians were dispatched to lead the services in their churches. In some Berlin churches the congregations walked out on these substitutes after singing "A Mighty Fortress Is Our God."

Niemoller was one of those arrested. The police were polite and released him after two days. From then on, Niemoller's prayers from the pulpit included prayers for pastors in prison, in concentration camps, or under house arrest. The Gestapo came and took notes.

On the same Sunday as the arrests, the most massive military parade in decades marched through Berlin, viewed by cheering, jubilant throngs estimated at half a million. Hitler had announced that all young men would be conscripted into the growing army.

SEPTEMBER 15, 1935, NUREMBURG

Every September in the Third Reich thousands gathered at the ancient city of Nuremburg for the Nazi Party convention. From all over the nation they came, the best and most loyal Nazi farmers, students, and workers. They stayed in carefully regimented tent camps and marched in precise formations to the vast field where rallies were held. The gigantic assemblies were masterpieces of emotional orchestration, building up to the moment each night when Hitler arrived.

The tiny specks of humanity in the darkened stadium welcomed their Führer in a frenzy of awe and worship. During his two years in office, unemployment, inflation, and poverty had magically disappeared. Germans now had clean streets, orderly cities, disciplined and enthusiastic young people. They remembered the disorder and decadence of only a few years ago and were grateful. Part of their pride was in the resurgent German army; it meant the shame of World War I was erased. Germany was strong and independent again.

When the wild cheering had quieted, Hitler began to speak in his quiet, fatherly tone. This year he had reassuring words for Christians: the Nazis would never intervene against Christianity or against either the Roman Catholic or Protestant churches. This came on top of his formation, two months before, of a new government department, the Ministry of Church Affairs.

Then Hitler's voice changed to a snarl as he turned to the subject of his most implacable hatred. He had summoned the Reichstag, the almost useless Parliament, to Nuremburg just for this. He asked them to unanimously pass two laws against Jews. One took away all their rights of German citizenship. The other forbade marriages between Germans and Jews. From now on, Jews had no rights in Germany.

SEPTEMBER 23, 1935

"I can see no purpose in self-inflicted martyrdom," Bishop Meiser said to Martin Niemoller. The two men sat facing each other in a small hotel room, heatedly discussing the agenda for the gathering of the Free Synod at the Berlin-Steglitz church. This was the same body that had passed a strong antiheathenism resolution in March, but now they were greatly divided in spirit.

The radicals, led by Martin Niemoller, did not want to compromise with Hitler's new church ministry nor to approve the Nuremburg laws. Many others, such as Meiser, counseled moderation and conciliation.

"We are trying to bring peace to the church," said Meiser, "and this Jewish question can only make us seem like the greatest troublemakers in Germany."

"What does it matter how we look in Germany compared with how we look in heaven?" Niemoller replied forcefully. "We pray for our pastors when they are imprisoned. Why has no one prayed for the Jews?"

"But the business of a synod is the church. We cannot pronounce judgment on all the ills of society. Most especially we ought not to single out the one issue that the government is so sensitive about, with the foreign criticism filling the air. First things first."

"And what is the first thing you are referring to?" Niemoller asked.

"The very existence of a church free from interference!" Meiser said.

"And how are we free if we cannot pronounce judgment on the ills of society?" Niemoller asked wearily. "Tell me that."

The Free Synod ended with nothing resolved. True they had, over Bishop Meiser's opposition, asserted that everyone, including Jews, should be offered salvation. They had strongly censured congregations that refused baptism to Jews. But the matter of the general condition of Jews in Germany had been referred to a committee. The majority of pastors thought laws about Jews were a state matter. So long as the Jews' position in the church remained unrestricted, the church should not interfere.

Bonhoeffer was depressed. Back in Germany now and heading a new seminary for the Confessing Church, he had come to the conference along with several of his students, who were bitter. They were

becoming an embattled minority within an embattled minority—
the radical faction of the Confessing Church in a Germany that cared
little about the disputes of a handful of pastors and bishops.

Only Niemoller still had fire in his eyes. As he looked out over the
delegates, he issued a solemn warning: "We shall be obliged to say
more," he said, "and it may be that our mouths will only be really
opened when we have to undergo suffering ourselves."

DECEMBER 1935

Hans Kerrl, the new government minister heading Hitler's Ministry
of Church Affairs, had set up a church committee to resolve the disputes
within the German Evangelical Church. He persuaded a widely reputed
clergyman to chair it, and some of the foremost leaders of the Confessing Church agreed to cooperate—against Niemoller's adamant disapproval.

Kerrl declared all organizations of the Confessing Church illegal
and gradually, firmly, began to tighten the noose around the necks of
those who would not cooperate with his new committee. Pastors who
belonged to an illegal organization were not paid their state-supported
salaries. Seminarians from Bonhoeffer's seminary could not get pastoral appointments. Kerrl's bureaucratic harassment so blurred the
issues—they were arguing not doctrine now but salaries and pensions
and appointments—the most of the Confessing Church pastors found
cooperation easier than defiance.

In the following months the great energetic unity of Barmen began
to crack into a thousand fragments.

MARCH 7, 1936, NORFOLK, ENGLAND

Lord Lothian's twelve guests gathered around the radio after
dinner to listen to the BBC. Among them were the Astors—Waldorf, one
of the richest men in the world, and his witty, beautiful wife, Nancy, who
would later become the first woman to sit in Parliament; Thomas Jones,
secretary to the British cabinet and a close friend of the prime minister;
Thomas Inskip, a cabinet minister; and Arnold Toynbee, the famous
historian. Their host, Lord Lothian, was himself one of the most eloquent and renowned statesmen in Britain.

All were weekending in the beauty and luxury of Lothian's ancient
rose-red brick castle, Blickling Hall, with its deer park at one end and
acres of grass and woodland at the other.

Tonight, however, their pleasure was interrupted by the dry authoritative tones of the newscaster announcing that earlier that day German troops had moved into the Rhineland. Hitler had offered twenty-five years of peace based on disarmament of both sides of the border. The peace proposal was, according to the French ambassador to Germany, "as though Hitler struck his adversary across the face and said, 'I bring you proposals for peace!'"

Lord Lothian, a broad-chested, handsome man in his fifties, flicked off the radio, loosened his tie, and sat back in a heavy leather chair. "I never thought I'd hear this group so quiet," he said. "Do you think war has begun?"

"If this means war," Nancy Astor said, "it will be because of the French, not the Germans. If the Germans want to march into their own backyard, I wish them well."

"What nonsense!" said someone from the other end of the room.

"I have a suggestion," said Thomas Jones with a twinkle in his eye. "We'll form a shadow cabinet and draw up a list of suggestions. I'll call up the prime minister tomorrow morning and tell him what we think."

Toynbee enthusiastically supported the idea. He himself had recently returned from a long meeting with Hitler. "I suppose that this may well be the only drawing room in all Britain containing two men who have had a long conversation with Herr Hitler," he said. "Lord Lothian, it seems to me that the essential question is one of motive. Do you think, based on your conversation with the man, as well as with Göring, Ribbentrop, and so on, that Hitler is merely making the first of a series of expansionist movements? Or are you convinced as I am that Hitler really has no evil intentions? He certainly convinced me that he wants peace."

"Why don't we call up Winston and ask him to help us on that point?" Jones jested.

"Heavens, no!" Nancy Astor retorted. "If the real cabinet won't have him, why should the shadow?"

"Hear, hear!" said Lothian. "We can easily refer to Churchill's views on the Germans without his presence. To him the Germans are the Devil incarnate.

"Speaking of the German motives," said Lothian, folding his arms across his chest, "I would state firmly that the Germans are not fundamentally aggressive. They have been goaded into aggression by the Versailles Treaty and by the French policy of encirclement. A great nation with an ancient culture and history cannot reasonably be denied a position of equality in Europe. Yet the view of the French government, and incidentally some elements in our Foreign Office, is that they are a group of gangsters the likes of which the world has never seen."

"If we don't give them what they deserve," said Nancy Astor, "we'll have war, and we'll be the ones to blame when the entire continent is Bolshevik."

The debate carried late into the night, for this mannered, richly dressed crowd loved talking politics more than almost anything. In the morning, Jones telephoned Prime Minister Baldwin with their resolutions: the group "welcomed Hitler's declaration wholeheartedly" and thought he wanted "above all to be accepted by England as respectable"; therefore, the militarization of the Rhineland was to be treated as relatively insignificant. The chief thing was to seize on Hitler's peace proposals.

Nobody mentioned the military fact that was to be reinforced so strikingly in years to come. The Rhineland had been demilitarized at Versailles deliberately to make Germany vulnerable; without it, France and Britain lost any leverage short of war—for which the underarmed British and disorganized French were clearly unprepared.

In permitting the German troops to march into the Rhineland, both countries were betting that reason alone would persuade the Germans to behave in a civilized manner. And the elegant men and women at Blickling Hall believed in the power of reason.

AUGUST 3, 1936, BERLIN

They sat in a circle, sober-faced and quiet. In the distance they could hear the popping of fireworks and the low murmur of sound from a crowd of happy Berliners enjoying the festivities of the Olympic games. Those sounds came from a different world than the one facing these leaders of the Confessing Church.

Bonhoeffer was there, as well as Niemoller and Jacobi—the young and the middle-aged, but not one of the older bishops.

Bonhoeffer was depressed. He was thinking of yesterday, spent at the games in Olympic Stadium. He had been happy and excited.

Warm summer sun had bathed the tanned, happy crowds surrounding him. Children, their hair bleached white from hours in the sun, clutched their parents' hands and tried to see everything. I *do love my country*, Bonhoeffer had thought, *in spite of everything*.

Berlin was decorated and scrubbed clean for the games. White Olympic flags and red Nazi pennants hung from every lamppost. The ugly signs warning shoppers away from Jewish shops had disappeared overnight. Uniformed, heel-clicking troops still filled the streets, but they seemed like part of the parade.

With Bonhoeffer had been a seminarian named Schultz. Ordinarily a serious and rather dull fellow, the young man bubbled with enthusiasm. But his pleasure had turned to sadness during their parting conversation at the end of the day.

"Dr. Bonhoeffer . . . I must tell you," the young man had begun haltingly. "I am taking a parish in Hamburg. I could not refuse."

For a moment Bonhoeffer had been speechless. "Leaving the Confessing Church?"

"No, Dr. Bonhoeffer, please understand my deep respect and admiration for all that you stand for. I only think that I am called to be a pastor and there are no pastorates for those of us who will not cooperate. What is the good in preaching if you have no congregation? Where will this noncooperation lead us? We are no longer a recognized body; we have no government assistance; we cannot care for the souls in the armed forces or give religion lessons in the schools. What will become of the church if that continues? A heap of rubble!"

"Those are not your words," Bonhoeffer had instantly accused.

"No, you are right. They are Riehl's. He has convinced me that we must for the sake of Jesus Christ make use of the great opportunities the government is offering us rather than sticking to a path so narrow there is only space for one at a time."

Bonhoeffer had stared disbelievingly at him. "If you board the wrong train, Schultz, it is no use running along the corridor in the opposite direction."

Schultz's words had been like a knife. So all the teaching and all the community they had practiced at the seminary had been wasted on this man! And, Bonhoeffer wondered, on how many others? That was the question that pounded in him as he sat in the meeting. How many others?

Suddenly his reverie about the day before was broken by the words of Niemoller—"Why not read the whole memorandum, just as we sent it to Hitler?"

"We will certainly lose Meiser and others if we do that, Martin," said Jacobi. "They will say we should stick to the issues of the church and leave the politics to the state."

"The Jews are our issue!" Niemoller shot back. "And the concentration camps! We had the courage to write to Hitler. Why not read it to our congregations?"

Someone asked Bonhoeffer what he thought. He had difficulty raising himself out of his gloom.

"I think," he said slowly after a few moments of silence, "I think we must not worry what people think. We must be the church and speak as Christ. And the words of Proverbs, which some have quoted so often, remain relevant, 'Open your mouth for the dumb.'"

On August 23 only a few hundred pastors, out of perhaps 18,000, read the proclamation. The uncompromising Confessing Church was now very small.

JULY 1, 1937, BERLIN

The symbol of defiant resistance to Hitler crouched on the floor in his bathrobe, pushing a toy car. His son, Martin, only a toddler, yelped with glee.

Niemoller had arrived home late the night before, exhausted from a tour of church meetings. His eyes and gaunt face showed the strain. The screws had tightened on the Confessing Church. In the past three weeks many of the resisting leaders had been arrested. But with every arrest Niemoller's drive seemed to grow.

Downstairs the doorbell rang. The maid came to tell him that two Gestapo agents were waiting in the living room. It had become a familiar routine.

Niemoller dressed hurriedly and went downstairs. The officers shook hands politely. They had a few questions to ask him. Would he please accompany them?

A trace of sadness crossed Niemoller's face. This once, on a Saturday, he would have liked to play with his son and talk to his wife. He went to tell Else what was happening. "They say it will be brief," he said. "But only God knows, my love."

Once he was seated in the black police van, he did not bother to look out the window. He knew too well the route to police headquarters. Exhaustion settled over him and he nearly slept.

At the Alexanderplatz they took him to a large room and left him. Several hours passed inside the bustling headquarters before a tall captain entered, called Niemoller's name, and coldly told him to follow.

The officer did not take the familiar route up the stairs to the interrogation rooms. Instead, he turned in the opposite direction and led the pastor outside to a black police van.

"Are you sure?" Niemoller asked the officer. "No one has talked to me yet."

The captain just nodded. Now Niemoller was strangely afraid, and this time he looked out the window. They were not retracing the route. Eventually they reached Moabit prison, its ancient dark walls fringed with barbed wire. *You do not come here for questions*, Niemoller thought. *You come to stay.*

When they heard of Niemoller's imprisonment, many pastors felt ill-disguised satisfaction. They had, after all, warned him. Perhaps now he would not disturb them with his uncompromising speeches.

An earnest chaplain, visiting the Moabit prisoners, happened upon Niemoller. Somehow this chaplain had not heard the news of his arrest.

"But brother!" he said in shock, "What brings you here? Why are you in prison?"

"And, brother, why are you not in prison?" Niemoller replied.

In succeeding months seven hundred pastors were arrested. Most were released after a few days or weeks behind bars. Some were sent to concentration camps. Yet the vast majority of the 18,000 German Evangelical Church pastors stayed well out of trouble. The reputable Bishop Marahrens issued a statement: "The National Socialist conception of life is the national and political teaching that determines and characterizes German manhood. As such, it is obligatory upon German Christians also."

MARCH 2, 1938, MOABIT PRISON, BERLIN

It was the final day of Martin Niemoller's trial. He sat in the courtroom, awaiting the judges' verdict, dressed neatly in a dark suit, conservative wing collar, and black tie. He had lost weight but not spirit. In the front row sat his Else and his eldest daughter, Brigette. They had been apart for eight months. How wonderful even to see their faces. Perhaps tonight they would be together again.

He had been charged with "malicious and provocative criticism of the minister of Propaganda and Public Enlightenment, Dr. Goebbels, of the Minister of Education, Dr. Rust, and of the Minister of Justice, Dr. Gurtner, of a kind calculated to undermine the confidence of the people in their political leaders." Another charge dealt with his reading from the pulpit names of people the government had imprisoned.

Yet the prosecution had failed to bring out any convincing evidence of his guilt. Instead, a series of witnesses had endorsed him as a man of sterling character. Niemoller's spirits, so grim at the beginning of the trial, had been rising. Waiting for the judges to enter, he could not keep a smile from his face. He chatted and joked with his attorney and kept glancing at his wife's shining, hopeful face.

The presiding judge began to read, slowly. They had found him guilty!

As the fifteen typed pages of the judgment unfolded, however, it became clear that the conviction was merely a slap. Niemoller, the judge read, had been inspired by "completely honorable motives." He was a man of "unquestionable veracity, the type of person who has nothing whatsoever of the traitor in him." Nonetheless, he has violated the letter of the law and must be found guilty. He would be imprisoned for seven months and fined 2,000 marks. The eight months he had already served would apply, so he could be freed today. As the implication came home to him, Niemoller beamed. It was as good a verdict as he could have possibly hoped for—as good as an acquittal. So there were still honest men in Germany!

At last the judges were finished and he was able to grasp his wife's hand. "Pack our trunks," he said in her ear. "We'll have a holiday together."

"Will they really let you go?" Else asked, still uncertain of their good fortune.

"Pack our bags!" he said, looking into her eyes. "I'll be home in an hour or two."

Hitler had arranged to hear the Niemoller verdict immediately. He was furious. He remembered well meeting the pastor two years before when Niemoller had spoken so impudently.

Calling an immediate cabinet meeting, Hitler demanded a resolution that Niemoller be placed in a concentration camp.

"This man is my personal prisoner," Hitler shouted. "And that is the end of it!"

In the early hours of the morning, Martin Niemoller passed through the barbed wire of Sachsenhausen, a concentration camp of 30,000 prisoners.

11

Roots of War
(Part II)

For any government deliberately to deny to their people what must be their plainest and simplest right [to live in peace and happiness without the nightmare of war] would be to betray their trust, and to call down upon their heads the condemnation of all mankind.

I do not believe that such a government anywhere exists among civilized peoples. I am convinced that the aim of every statesman worthy of the name, to whatever country he belongs, must be the happiness of the people for whom and to whom he is responsible, and in that faith I am sure that a way can and will be found to free the world from the curse of armaments and the fears that give rise to them, and to open up a happier, and a wiser future for mankind.

—Prime Minister Neville Chamberlain, November 1937

MARCH 11, 1938, NO. 10 DOWNING STREET, LONDON

Prime Minister Neville Chamberlain gave no impression of bending to his nearly seventy years. He was a tall, hawklike man with a luxuriant mustache and a rather high opinion of himself. Perhaps he was entitled. No one in government worked harder than he.[1]

Chamberlain came from a peculiar background for a prime minister. Unlike a great many members of his cabinet, he had made a success of himself—first in running a hard-headed, family-owned manufacturing firm and later in politics—without benefit of a huge inheritance or elegant title. A further drawback might have been his religious affiliation. His family had long been Unitarians, who, because they rejected the deity of Christ, were ostracized from semiofficial Church of England channels. Yet it was that very affiliation that contributed so strongly to the Chamberlain family's dedication to public service; both his father and older brother were prominent in politics. Government was a natural vocation for those raised in Unitarian tradition, with its belief in the universal goodness of all men, growing out of a sense of duty to mankind and a deep-seated belief that reasonable, fair-minded men could work together to solve any difficulty.

Chamberlain had reached the pinnacle of power in his country, succeeding Baldwin without a struggle because no one else was comparably qualified. Now, well into his first year, he was warming to his task with all sorts of ambitious improvements in mind. If only he could keep the German issue in its proper perspective and not let the war-lovers in either country gain too much momentum.

The latter concern was on his mind today as he greeted the German ambassador, Joachim von Ribbentrop, whom he had invited to this farewell luncheon in the spacious inner rooms of his residence. Ribbentrop was a ridiculous, strutting ninny with cotton for a brain, but he was closely connected with Hitler. What a pity, Chamberlain thought, that a great nation is governed by such irrational men, driven by such illogic. If he could only make them see sense!

Chamberlain, a private man whom most thought cold and arrogant, tried to make small talk as he escorted the German ambassador among the clusters of men he was hosting; most were chatting informally and shaking hands with an easy, confident charm, as well they might. They were on the whole the most powerful men of the most powerful empire in the history of the world.

Feeling the pull of the leonine presence, Chamberlain looked over at Churchill sprawled in a chair at the other end of the table. The prime minister could never help feeling a little scornful of the man who had never made the top rank despite his long career in government and his rhetorical gift. They had worked together on previous cabinets, but he would never let Churchill serve under him. The man was too emotional, drank too much, and his tirades took up precious time. He rarely had his facts straight. Churchill, Chamberlain thought, would gladly fight

Germany tomorrow, if only to give himself a chance to make saber-rattling speeches in the House.

The lunch went well, Chamberlain thought. With elaborately feigned politeness, Ribbentrop raised the issue of Chamberlain's "White Paper on Defense" given to the House five days before.

"Why do you talk of fighting?" Ribbentrop asked. "You say that you want peace and then you talk of fighting. The Führer is a man of peace, but he is also a man of strength, and this talk of fighting for democracy he can only see as pure aggressiveness."

Only a German could have read his talk as aggressive, Chamberlain groaned inwardly. But he answered patiently and logically that his policy had always been based on a willingness to defend his nation were it necessary. "I assume that Germany's policy is the same; that is the only legitimate reason for keeping armies and navies. You may remember that I also spoke of our earnest hopes for appeasement and then disarmament."

He was not sure his words made any impression on Ribbentrop, who immediately began speaking at great length on what a peace-loving man Hitler was. Fortunately Churchill held his tongue.

After lunch Chamberlain and Ribbentrop spent another twenty minutes together as the prime minister tried to drive home his one point: he wanted to solve any difficulties Germany might face as the result of the Versailles Treaty. If he repeated that message often enough it might make its way back to Berlin.

Yet Ribbentrop persisted in babbling on about the astonishing transformation of Germany, a miracle to those who had known the bad years. "It is preposterous that the British public remains so utterly ill-informed," he complained peevishly. "Yesterday I met a mob of people shouting the most intolerable insults about Pastor Niemoller's imprisonment. I am sure they would be astonished to learn that there are twice as many people in church today as there were five years before, when Hitler came to power."

At last Chamberlain smilingly withdrew and returned to the drawing room where the other guests lingered. He was handed some telegrams to read and stopped short, bristling in disbelief. The telegrams informed him that Hitler, that morning, had delivered an ultimatum to the Austrian Chancellor. Schuschnigg was to resign his office by 2:00 P.M. and turn over the government to Seyss-Inquart, the Nazi Hitler had forced into the government just a month before. Hitler's troops were massed on the border, ready to march if Schuschnigg refused. Schuschnigg begged the British government for advice. All this had happened while he was chatting pleasantly about peace with Ribbentrop.

Chamberlain quietly asked the German ambassador for "a private word" in his office downstairs, along with Lord Halifax, England's foreign secretary. Any attempts at friendliness had disappeared into British frost as he read out the telegrams and stiffly demanded an explanation. "I want you to understand that this has the most serious implications for our relations."

Ribbentrop smiled and said he personally knew nothing about these negotiations. "Do you have any confirmation of these reports? Because I know for a fact that the Chancellor's discussions with Schuschnigg were conducted in a tremendously friendly atmosphere. I was there personally. I must say that I would think Schuschnigg's resignation would be a very positive development and a hopeful sign for a peaceful solution."

"This is intolerable behavior in a civilized nation," Halifax said, his voice loud and threatening. He called it naked aggression.

Chamberlain admitted graciously that they had no definite proof of aggression but said they had ample reasons for deep concern. "All we can ask is that you convey to Herr Hitler our sincere and ardent wish that he hold back from any rash act that would imperil our chances for a negotiated settlement."

After Ribbentrop left, Chamberlain sank into a wing chair and cut short the overexcited Halifax. "If you must, go and talk to Ribbentrop at the embassy."

Then he dictated a response to Schuschnigg, which Halifax accepted with a pinched, reluctant expression. "His Majesty's Government cannot take responsibility of advising the chancellor to take any course of action that might expose his country to dangers against which His Majesty's Government are unable to guarantee protection."

Afterward Chamberlain sat alone in his study with his dark thoughts. He would not get off to the country for a rest this weekend. His plans were spoiled. His carefully drafted message to Hitler would be buried under the necessary protests. It meant more work for him—not positive work, but preventive. Seeing Halifax in a rage had only reinforced the prime minister's conviction that he was the only one cool enough to abide the Germans' irrational behavior and make them see reason.

Late that afternoon the Austrian government, finding support from no other country, capitulated, and the German army marched unopposed across Austria's border.

Chamberlain wrote his sisters, his closest confidantes, that he took comfort in the fact that the *Anschluss* had taken place without any loss of life.

MARCH 25, 1938, CLIVEDEN

The house rose up ahead of them like a tiered wedding cake, more of a monument than a home—Cliveden, where for years Nancy Astor had gathered the wittiest and wealthiest men and women in Britain for weekend parties. Hardly anyone of significance failed to turn up at Cliveden, even the king and Gandhi. George Bernard Shaw was a frequent guest, although he usually stayed in his room, writing.

Cliveden was a comfortable weekend retreat for Prime Minister Chamberlain. Many of his cabinet spent time there, and the ceaseless political talk was so reliably conservative that the press had seized on the idea of a "Cliveden set" that was supposed to be darkly pro-German. Chamberlain found the idea amusing; as though any Cliveden set determined *his* foreign policy.

Today Nancy Astor, a short woman with a high-cheeked face that had once been beautiful, met Chamberlain and his wife at the door with one of her usual greetings. "Hello, you old windbag. Your speech was so exquisitely balanced that no one had the slightest idea where you stood."

"Thank you," he said with a smile. "I intended that."

"If you were truly part of the Cliveden set you would let Herr Hitler know where you stand by singing 'Deutschland Uber Alles' to the House."

"I'll leave that to you, Nancy, in your next speech."

"No, no, those Nazis are not my friends. If they would stop locking up Christian Scientists they might be."

Nancy Astor was a devout Christian Scientist who always had Christian Science lecturers at her weekend gatherings. Lord Astor and Lord Lothian were Christian Scientists too. Their sympathetic view of Germany was strengthened by the Christian Science doctrine that man is good, that there is no evil that the mind cannot overcome. This Chamberlain was inclined to agree with, though he was quite irreligious himself.

As they bantered, waiting for the servants—there were dozens of them at Cliveden—to hustle in the Chamberlains' luggage, other guests began drifting into the vast dark paneled entrance hall with its elaborately carved wooden columns, suits of armor, and tapestries. Chamberlain knew most of the guests, except for an American couple and an odd looking man whom he supposed was one of Nancy's ever-present Christian Science lecturers. Several people thanked him for the speech he had given in the House on Thursday. Sir Alexander Cadogan, his undersecretary of state for foreign affairs, took him aside and said that the nation had breathed a sigh of relief at stepping back from the brink.

"I don't believe we stepped back," Chamberlain said dryly. "I wanted us to avoid stepping over." He had declined before the House of Commons to guarantee that Britain would come to Czechoslovakia's aid if Germany invaded. Since Austria had been adopted into the Reich, Czechoslovakia was now vulnerable, half-surrounded by German armies.

"Yes, I liked what you said," Cadogan admitted, "about not letting others determine when we would fight."

"I have the sense," said Chamberlain, "that to draw a line in the dust is to dare Herr Hitler to cross it. I am not anxious to enter matches of daring with him. I want to convince him that he can get all that Germany is entitled to without having to fight."

The next morning Chamberlain rose early and went into the dining room where breakfast was laid out as a self-service buffet. Nancy Astor always provided every luxury and pleasure imaginable—except liquor; she was an absolute teetotaler. Nancy herself, as usual, would not join her guests until nearly noon; she was alone in her bedroom reading her Bible.

A light mist was falling as Chamberlain strolled out across the formal garden, past pieces of Italian statuary, and into one of the long lanes that led through Cliveden's forest, with views over the Thames. A solitary person, Chamberlain loved to walk. Often after a session of Parliament he would walk as many as six miles to calm himself.

He mused as he walked about the state of affairs with Germany. The subject nagged at him as though there were some detail he had neglected. Yet really things were going well. The whole country stood behind him.

But he saw clearly enough that this support might not last. Europe was an unstable mass, like snow on the mountains that even a loud shout might turn into an avalanche. He had to find the way to create stability, with little time to do it. He had to discover precisely what

Germany wanted and how to get it for them. *If only we could sit down and reason together*, he thought. *I am sure we could ease the tensions overnight.*

His thoughts grew darker, for the future was so unknown and he was a man who liked to make tidy plans.

Churchill had made one of his magnificent bursts of oratory in response to Thursday's speech. Chamberlain could still hear that deep, robust voice booming out the warning like Pompeii's town crier.

"I have watched this famous island descending incontinently, fecklessly, the stairway which leads to a dark gulf. It is a fine broad stairway at the beginning, but after a bit the carpet ends. A little farther on there are only flagstones, and a little farther on still these break beneath your feet. . . ."

Yes, Chamberlain thought, *the warning is just. Except Winston's warmongering is likely to speed our journey down.*

On his return to the house he walked through a little cemetery. Cliveden had served as a hospital during the Great War, and those who had died of their wounds were buried here under a Union Jack. It was a beautiful, melancholy spot, all moss and shadows. Standing there, he thought of his cousin Norman, the only man he had ever been truly attached to, buried in France in a much vaster cemetery than this. Nothing matters more, he thought, than avoiding war; another generation of Normans must not die.

Suddenly his melancholy lifted. He would find a way to make a lasting peace.

SEPTEMBER 12, 1938, LONDON

Chamberlain sat by a large radio cabinet at No. 10 Downing listening fretfully to the man who held the world in the palm of his hand. It was the end of the greatest Nuremburg Party Congress yet—the first to celebrate the new, expanded Germany. Now, at the climax of the week, endless squadrons of Hitler Youth, Hitler Workers, SS, army, navy, and air force had converged to hear their Führer. All over the world, in Czechoslovakia, in France, in England, and in America, men and women listened in rapt fear to the crowd's roars of "Sieg Heil!"

Chamberlain was not afraid. He was distressed. The world held its breath waiting for the words of a lunatic! How foolish. How utterly mad! How could the lives of hundreds of millions, as well as his own reputation, hang on this?

He had written his sister: "I fully realize that if eventually things go wrong . . . there will be many, including Winston, who will say that the

British government must bear the responsibility and that if only they had had the courage to tell Hitler now that, if he used force, we would at once declare war, that would have stopped him."

Now, as the prime minister listened, Hitler began his assault on Czechoslovakia, working himself into his usual snarling frenzy. Thousands standing before him responded wildly. They were primed for battle, ready to die for the honor of Germany.

The world waited, expecting Hitler to declare war. But instead, he veered onto another subject.

Listening to the distant roar, Chamberlain let out an involuntary sigh. "Not so bad as I feared," he said to himself. "Distasteful, though."

SEPTEMBER 24, 1938

Chamberlain was leaving Germany after his second visit with Adolf Hitler in ten days. On September 15 he had arrived at Hitler's Berghof headquarters for his first face-to-face encounter with the man who was shaking the world. At that time he had learned of Hitler's plans to proceed against Czechoslovakia.

Shocked at first, he had left feeling he had made an impression on the Führer. His only problem was convincing his own nation and France—as well as Czechoslovakia—to simply cede a large portion of Czechoslovakia to Nazi Germany, a portion that held large numbers of Czechs as well as Germans and also contained most of the border defenses that made Czechoslovakia a significant, if overmatched opponent for the invading German army. Chamberlain had already made up his mind that such a price was worth paying for peace.

Now the prime minister felt betrayed. He had risked his political career for the proposals given at Berchtesgaden a few days earlier. He could not understand why the Führer, when he would receive all the territory he wanted through peaceful means, insisted on using force. An immediate takeover of Czechoslovakia by German troops would be looked on as sheer aggression. All this he had said to the Führer, but Hitler was adamant.

Now that he was setting off for London, however, the prime minister had recovered some of his equilibrium. The situation did not look so utterly hopeless. He was beginning to adjust to Hitler's demands. The immediate occupation would offend democratic sensibilities, but was it worth fighting a war over?

Back in London at 5:30 that afternoon Chamberlain spoke to the cabinet.

He spoke of Hitler's anxiousness to develop better relations with Great Britain, stressing that Czechoslovakia was the last territorial claim the Führer would make. "It would be a great tragedy if we lost this opportunity of reaching an understanding with Germany. I have now established an influence with Herr Hitler. I believe he trusts me and is willing to work with me."

But the cabinet raised so many objections that Chamberlain backed off on his recommendation that they advise the Czechs to accept Hitler's plans.

A few days later the Czechs, who were given the German demands without any recommendations, rejected them in ringing terms.

SEPTEMBER 26, 1938, CLIVEDEN

Charles Lindbergh, the brave, dashing pilot who ten years before had challenged the Atlantic and won, was one of the most famous men in the world. Tall, firm, resolute, he never doubted himself for a moment. Full of his own importance in a tortured way, he hated yet needed adulation.

But Lindbergh was more than a great pilot; he had become a high priest of a new technological era. People listened to him, particularly of late.

He had spent several weeks in Germany, warmly welcomed by the Nazis, even given a medal, and had come away tremendously impressed. The democracies seemed to him tired and decadent; in Germany he found a virile masculinity and spirited commitment that resonated in his own soul.

He had also been impressed by the German air force; so much so that wherever he went he preached that no one could stand against it.*

After the terrible kidnapping and death of their son, the Lindberghs had fled America for England; today they were guests at Nancy Astor's Cliveden weekend. Anne, Lindbergh's pretty, shy, intelligent, and adoring wife, soon faded into the background when Charles and the others held forth on the possibility of war.

"I am afraid this is the beginning of the end for England," Lindbergh said sternly. "The old instincts are being summoned up for war.

---

*Lindbergh was wrong in his estimates of German air dominance. London was at the very limit of bomber range from Germany. Without bases in Holland or France it is doubtful the German air force could have done significant damage.

People are talking about 'dishonorable peace,' and so on. Nobody seems to realize that England is in no condition to fight a war."

"It's madness," Nancy Astor said in one of her wild, stabbing protests. "War will destroy Western civilization. Europe will be destroyed. Then certainly Communism will spread, for it always feeds on death like a vulture."

Lord Astor and Thomas Jones came into the room looking glum and depressed; they too had been discussing war. Jones's Welsh twinkle was gone; he looked old and haggard. "I understand that Chamberlain has sent two messages to Hitler to be delivered before he speaks tonight. The first is a last plea for more negotiations on the terms they had previously agreed on. If Hitler rejects that, he will be given the second message, a warning that if he marches into Czechoslovakia England will go to war."

"It's madness," Lady Astor said. "To destroy our civilization with our eyes open to all that we are doing."

"There are some things that are worth more than life," Jones said stiffly.

"Unquestionably!" said Lindbergh. "But that is not the case now. We would not be fighting to preserve something. Unless war is averted now there will be no one left who knows the meaning of the words *right* and *wrong*. This is no longer an affair of national pride and laws of right and wrong. It is a case of our whole civilization going under."

"I must disagree with you," Lord Astor said, his back to the fireplace. "I have supported all the prime minister has done to appease the Germans. But by now we can see that they are bent on war. We shall have to fight them, and I think it would be better to stop them now before they grow any stronger."

"Your logic may be sound, but it ought to lead you in the opposite direction," said Lindbergh, pouncing eagerly. "If we must fight—and I am not so certain as you seem to be that Hitler is bent on war—then by all means buy as much time as possible. At the moment England's defenses are so weak as to be utterly incapable of defending the nation, let alone punishing Hitler."

Astor looked around him with sad, kind eyes, but the way he gripped the fireplace betrayed his tension. "I think you have it wrong. Germany is already arming at full speed; it would be years before we could even reach her pace. So every day we wait to fight, Germany grows stronger. Furthermore, if we keep backing down to every threat Hitler makes, we will soon have no friends to fight with us."

"But don't you think that before you go to war you must have some idea of victory? You cannot separate political decision from military strategy."

"Would you simply have us surrender?" Astor asked.

"No, but avoid war at any cost!" said Lindbergh.

There was an awkward pause. Jones glanced at his watch. "The speech is about to begin," he said. "Unfortunately, the decision may be out of our hands."

The small troop gathered by the radio in the parlor included two German boys summering in England. Lady Astor had asked them to translate the speech.

Lord Astor turned on the radio and almost immediately the angry roar of the mob could be heard. It was a terrifying sound: animalistic, threatening, violent. First Goebbels spoke, his high, ranting voice interrupted by cheers, chants, and shouts. The German boys scribbled on pads of paper and shouted out brief summaries during the roaring of the crowd.

Then Hitler spoke, beginning with his usual calm and slowly catching fire as never before. His voice snarled, ripped, rasped, and cut. He returned repeatedly to "Benes." The Czech head of state, his name spoken like a curse, had become the fountain of all the hurt and harm that Germany had ever suffered.

"My patience is at an end," Hitler concluded. "The decision now lies in his hands. Peace or war . . . I have never been a coward. Now I go before my people as its first soldier. And behind me—this the world should know—there marches a different people from that of 1918. We are determined!"

Hitler had never spoken with such demonic fury. The crowd roared on and on into a single furious will, delirious with the delight of hatred.

"A terrifying speech," said Jones. "But no declaration of war. He spoke gratefully of the prime minister's efforts on behalf of peace. He also said that there would be no more territorial demands after this one."

"We have a little more time," Lindbergh said solemnly. "And with every extra day there is a little more hope."

Jones and Astor, more at ease now, were gradually swayed by Lindbergh's argument. If he was right, it would be necessary to face facts and avoid war at all costs. They agreed before they went to bed that they would dedicate the next few days to escorting Lindbergh into

the highest governmental circles they could reach. And those at Cliveden had access to some very high circles indeed.

SEPTEMBER 28, 1938, LONDON

A darkness hung over London. Trenches were being dug in every
park. Children were being herded into trains, evacuating the city that
everyone expected would be annihilated in flames within the next
twenty-four hours. Outside Parliament a grim, quiet crowd gathered.
Hitler's deadline for Czechoslovakia to accept his ultimatum had been
2:00. It was 2:50 when Chamberlain began his speech to the House of
Commons where the narrow benches were jammed.

There was not a wearier, more discouraged man in England than
the prime minister. He had not given up trying. He had sent fresh
appeals to Mussolini and Hitler, suggesting a five-party conference. But
little hope now existed.

Last night he had addressed the nation on the BBC, his voice filled
with despairing resignation, yet still incredulous that his efforts had
been in vain and that death would soon rain down on his beloved
nation.

"How horrible, fantastic, incredible it is that we should be digging
trenches and trying on gas masks here because of a quarrel in a faraway
country between people of whom we know nothing. . . .

"I have done all that one man can do to compose this
quarrel. . . . I shall not give up the hope of a peaceful solution or
abandon my efforts for peace as long as any chance for peace
remains. . . . But at this moment I see nothing further that I can
usefully do."

Wearily, dryly, he told the whole story in careful chronological
detail: of all the British government had done, of the moments of
apparent hope and the dashing of hopes, of last-minute appeals. He
spoke for over an hour, building to only one conclusion. The certainty of
war.

Then, with hardly anyone noticing, a piece of paper was handed
into the House. It moved to several ministers before John Simon, the
chancellor of the exchequer, waved it at Chamberlain. Deeply involved
in his speech, the prime minister did not immediately notice.

Simon finally got his attention and Chamberlain quickly scanned
the paper. He hesitated for a moment, then whispered to Simon, "Shall
I tell them now?" Simon vigorously nodded yes.

When Chamberlain spoke again, life had flooded into his voice. "I have now been informed by Herr Hitler that he invites me to meet him at Munich tomorrow morning. He has also invited Signor Mussolini and Monsieur Daladier . . . I need not say what my answer will be."

Someone in the back of the hall shouted, "Thank God for the prime minister."

Chamberlain continued. "We are all patriots and there can be no honorable member of this House who did not feel his heart leap that the crisis has been once more postponed to give us once more an opportunity to try what reason and goodwill and discussion will do to settle a problem which is already within sight of settlement. . . ."

Again from the back a voice boomed out, "Thank God for the prime minister." Then all were on their feet, applauding, cheering, crying, throwing papers into the air. The great fear that had gripped them all was ecstatically released.

No one, or practically no one, thought about the fact that although Hitler had invited Italy, France, and Britain to meet with him, he had not invited Czechoslovakia.

SEPTEMBER 30, 1938

"What is that noise?" Chamberlain asked.

It was morning. They had signed the agreement at 1:30 A.M., and after that he had had to endure the conference with the Czechoslovakians, who had wept.

William Strang, a top foreign office representative, strode to the window of the Regina Palace and looked out. "The street is full of people," he said. "They want to see you. Why don't you step out onto the balcony for a moment?"

Chamberlain did and found himself bathed in a warm ovation. Leaving the hotel a few minutes later, he had to press through the large, happy crowd, bronzed by the sun and still in summer clothing. He could not help smiling.

Chamberlain sat in a flowered armchair in the same apartment where Hitler, unknown to the prime minister, had only the day before vilified him to Mussolini. Today Hitler was gracious, though pale and subdued. They talked in generalities, and nothing the prime minister could say would make the Führer disagree with him.

"I trust that the Czechs will not be mad enough to reject our agreement," Chamberlain said. "But in case they do, I hope that you will do nothing which would diminish the high opinion in which you will be held throughout the world in consequence of yesterday's proceedings." Chamberlain glanced at Hitler while the translator interpreted his words. Seeing no resistance, he pressed on. "That is to say, I trust that there will be no bombardment of Prague or killing of women and children by attacks from the air."

Hitler smiled and raised his hand. "As a matter of principle," he said, "I intend to limit air action to frontline zones. I will always try to spare the civilian population and confine myself to military objectives. I hate the thought of little babies being killed by gas bombs."

Returning to the hotel, Chamberlain's car could only creep through the crowds. Men and women pressed forward from all directions, trying to shake his hand. Children threw flowers. Some women wept. All cheered.

Sitting down to lunch with Strang at the hotel, the prime minister proudly patted his breast pocket. "I've got it," he said, a visionary gleam in his narrow eyes. "It" was a brief communique that Hitler had agreed to sign. The central paragraph read, "We regard the agreement signed last night . . . as symbolic of the desire of our two peoples never to go to war with one another again."

He had the same scrap of paper in his hands when he stood, exhausted and elated, at a large open window at No. 10 Downing Street. The street below could not take another body; the cheering made it impossible to hear another sound.

All day he had been cheered—in Germany, then arriving back in England at Heston airport, and on the road all the way to Buckingham Palace where he had met with the king to accept his congratulations. Now he raised his hands until the crowd quieted enough for him to be heard.

Waving the communique, he said, "My good friends, this is the second time in our history that there has come back from Germany to Downing Street peace with honor."

The crowd roared its approval at the historic phrase that the famous statesman Disraeli had used at *his* hero's welcome sixty years before.

"I believe it is peace for our time," he concluded.

OCTOBER 5, 1938, LONDON

Winston Churchill was one of the few in all of England who understood that government's first duty was not to avoid confrontations with evil but to restrain it. As a result he was an outcast, going against the tide of opinion. He stood solemnly before the House of Commons, knowing full well the immense enthusiasm supporting Chamberlain. Nevertheless, his deep bass reverberated, full of doom.

"All is over. . . . Silent, mournful, abandoned, broken, Czechoslovakia recedes into the darkness. I do not begrudge our loyal, brave people . . . the natural, spontaneous outburst of joy and relief when they learned that the hard ordeal would no longer be required of them at the moment. . . . But they should know the truth. They should know that there has been gross neglect and deficiency in our defenses. They should know that we have sustained a great defeat without a war, the consequences of which will travel far with us. . . . They should know that we have passed an awful milestone in our history . . . the terrible words have for the time being been pronounced against the Western democracies: 'Thou art weighed in the balance and found wanting.' And do not suppose that this is the end. This is only the beginning of the reckoning."

NOVEMBER 9, 1938, CRYSTAL NIGHT

It was late afternoon when the truck lurched to a stop in front of the synagogue in the small German town. About thirty men got out, some in uniforms, others in street clothing. A red can of paint appeared and one of them began painting a huge red star on the synagogue. The others shouted insults.

A passerby, a woman carrying a bulging shopping bag, asked what the problem was. A uniformed officer explained. "The diplomat Rath, the one the Jews shot in Paris, has died. We are expressing our outrage. This is to happen all over Germany."

Just then two of the men who had run inside emerged dragging a man in a skull cap. "There's more in there," they shouted. "Go get them out." Others raced into the building. From inside came angry cries and the sharp sound of breaking glass. Shards of crystal rained down on the street from a second-story window.

The dozen or so men who still stood in the street were shouting insults at the Jewish man. Two of them held him on his knees, pressing his nose into the cobblestones. A small silent crowd had gathered, standing cautiously at a distance.

Eight more Jews were herded out, five men, one woman, and two young girls. The jeers of the men grew louder as these too were forced to kneel on the pavement. One of the men struggled against his captors. They lifted his head by the hair and banged it down on the stones. Once, twice, three times. Blood oozed between the cracks in the stones.

The woman with the shopping bag approached the knot of men holding the two girls. "Why don't you let me take these two away. They're just children."

"No, Fräulein, these are not children," one said. "They're Jews."

"What's the difference?" the woman demanded.

The man hesitated a moment. Then he pointed his chin down to the road. "You go away if you don't want to watch this. Those who interfere will only be hurt. You go away now."

When the woman hesitated, he spat out, "So you're a Jew-lover?"

She turned and crossed the street, where she continued to watch.

The Jews were formed into a rough circle; then the men took turns kicking them, yanking their hair, slapping their faces. The victims stared at their tormentors silently. They had stopped crying for mercy. One of their number already lay on the pavement, blood flowing from one of his ears.

From one of the broken windows above, a thread of smoke wandered skyward. One man pointed it out to the others. "It's burning," he cried with excitement. He seized the hair of the woman and whirled her violently around, jerking her head back. "Look you bloodsucker!" he screamed. "You Christ-killer, your synagogue is burning!"

Similar scenes were played out in almost every town in Germany.

NOVEMBER 10, 1938

The world was shaken from its post-Munich bliss. The night, which became known as Crystal Night because of the broken glass, sparked foreign protest. In Germany, however, the government announced that the extensive damage would be repaid by appropriating Jewish bank accounts. The Jews, after all, had provoked the spontaneous reaction.

Chamberlain was annoyed. He would probably have to make a statement in the House; someone was certain to raise the matter. This could well disrupt further negotiations. But he did not refer to it in his public speech that night in which he said, "Political conditions in Europe are now settling down to quieter times."

Charles Lindbergh wrote with bewilderment in his diary: "They have undoubtedly had a difficult Jewish problem, but why is it necessary to handle it so unreasonably?"

In Germany the official church said not a word. Only a tiny minority of Christians were brave enough to offer public sympathy. One lonely Catholic priest, Father Lichtenberg, led his Berlin congregation in prayer for the persecuted non-Aryans. He was imprisoned and eventually died in confinement. In Württemberg, Pastor von Jan used his sermon to warn against such violent hatred, which he said condemned the German people in the sight of God. He called for contrition, lest God allow Germany to reap the harvest they had sown. Eleven days later a screaming mob of about five hundred men dragged him from a home Bible study and beat him for two hours. He was then imprisoned.

Dietrich Bonhoeffer found himself staring again and again at Psalm 74. He underlined verse 8: "They burned every place where God was worshiped in the land," and in the margin beside it wrote, "Nov. 11, 1938." Then he underlined the verse that followed, putting an exclamation mark beside it: "We are given no miraculous signs; no prophets are left, and none of us knows how long this will be."

MARCH 15, 1939

In the frozen dawn Hitler's armed column probed its way through the thick fog that lay on the Czechoslovakian border. The proud Czech border guards did not resist, but stood and watched the tanks rumble by. Just a few hours before they had received orders from Prague not to fight.

Hitler had, through a series of manipulations and ultimatums, convinced a fractured government not to put up a pointless and bloody battle against his invasion.

In London Chamberlain was stunned. Less than a month before he had written to his sisters: "I myself am going about with a lighter heart than I have had for many a long day. All the information I get seems to point in the direction of peace. . . . I believe we have at last got on top of the dictators."

The British cabinet, meeting in emergency session, decided to offer no military aid to the nation they had "guaranteed" at Munich. Chamberlain held sway when he said that although he did "bitterly regret what has now occurred," the country should not "on that account be deflected from our course. . . . The aim of this government is now, as it always has been, to substitute the method of discussion for the method of force in the settlement of differences."

Yet they could not keep this blindfold on much longer. A few days later Chamberlain reversed himself completely, speaking long and bitterly about Hitler's broken promises. Wearily he spoke of the implications he had just begun to see and wondered aloud, "Is this, in fact, a step in the direction of an attempt to dominate the world by force?"

JULY 7, 1939, NEW YORK

Dietrich Bonhoeffer leaned on the railing of the ship looking at the jagged silhouette of Manhattan skyscrapers against the night sky. Tomorrow at 12:30, they would sail. He had been in New York for nearly a month. A month filled with frustration, anxiety, and uncertainty.

He smiled to himself and thought of how he must have confused his American hosts. Ostensibly he had come to the United States at the invitation of several professors who had made hasty arrangements under the mistaken impression that he was about to be thrown into a concentration camp. But his entire stay had been a struggle to determine why he was there. Had he fled the coming struggle in Germany? Was he afraid of what he had to do? His hosts had tried so hard to help, had welcomed him so warmly, and all he had done was smoke an endless chain of cigarettes, speak obscure and contradicting pronouncements, and scribble illegible notes to himself.

A few days ago, while still wavering, he had written in his journal: "Today I read by chance in 2 Timothy 4, 'Make every effort to come before winter,' Paul's petition to Timothy. 'Come before winter'— otherwise it might be too late. That has been in my mind all day. . . . We cannot get away from it any more. Not because we are necessary, or because we are useful (to God?), but simply because that is where our life is. . . . It is nothing pious, more like some vital urge. But God acts not only by means of pious incentives, but also through such vital stimuli. 'Come before winter'—it is no misuse of Scripture, if I accept that as having been said to me. If God gives me grace for it."

Now, at last, on the verge of returning to the darkest corner of the earth, his mind was at ease. He had not known how deeply he loved Germany and loved the church in Germany until now.

SEPTEMBER 1, 1939, BORDER BETWEEN POLAND AND GERMANY

The early morning darkness was warm and beautiful, the clear sky filled with clusters of stars. On the roads from Berlin long convoys of trucks, troop transports, tanks, and artillery moved slowly toward Poland. But here at the border nothing moved.

Suddenly a flare of light flickered through the trees; almost immediately the boom of an artillery piece followed. As if in reply, hundreds of guns up and down the border began to thunder.

The invasion of Poland was launched. World War II had begun.

Afterword

When Germany invaded Holland and France in 1940, Chamberlain's government collapsed in ignominy. Churchill became prime minister, promising "blood, toil, tears and sweat." Exhausted and sick, Chamberlain died that same year when a besieged Britain was the only democracy left in Europe.

During the war, pressure eased somewhat on the Confessing Church in Germany; the government had other worries. Besides, the most troublesome pastors were either in the army or in concentration camps. Only scattered individuals in the church protested against the wholesale annihilation of Jews, gypsies, and the mentally retarded.

Dietrich Bonhoeffer evaded the draft and continued secret activities in the resistance. In 1943 he was arrested and, just before the surrender of Germany in May 1945, was executed for his part in an attempted assassination of Adolf Hitler.

Martin Niemoller narrowly escaped execution and emerged from seven years in the concentration camps to play a significant role in the reconstruction of Germany.

It would be an overstatement to suggest that Chamberlain's inability or unwillingness to see the nature of Hitler's evil was the cause of World War II. Like all major events of history, the war was the result of a combination of powerful forces. But it is unarguable that Chamberlain and many in Britain grossly misjudged the situation on the continent. Why?

First of all, there was great revulsion in England over the senseless butchery of trench warfare in the First World War. The country had little stomach to fight again. Chamberlain himself had lost a cousin, perhaps his closest friend, in France. He never stopped grieving.

A second factor was Chamberlain himself. He had grown up in a tight-knit Unitarian family. They rejected the Christian belief in man's innate sinfulness, preferring to place faith in the innate goodness and "reasonableness" of man. Influential Britons of all backgrounds were infected by such thinking. Faith in the social sciences, in intellectual solutions to moral problems, had never been higher than in the thirties. The flourishing of Christian Science within Nancy Astor's influential circle at Cliveden was symptomatic; Christian Scientists believe that all evil is an illusion that can be eliminated by the exercise of the mind. Chamberlain, who was close to many of the Cliveden group, lived among people to whom the harshness of human evil had ceased to seem real. Hitler gave Chamberlain more than adequate evidence that he was evil, unreasonable, and bent on war. Yet the prime minister could not, would not, see it. Well-meaning, honorable, quoting Shakespeare all the way, he earned a dreadful epitaph: "He could have stopped Hitler."

And finally, the church in England failed to provide an independent moral voice for the country. They too had difficulty discerning evil except in "outmoded" policies. Much of the clergy seized on the peace issue and promoted forums like the League of Nations with such indiscriminate fervor that they seemed to believe that God Himself spoke exclusively through international gatherings. Led by Bishop William Temple, they put more faith in progressive politics and economics than in God. Churchmen were so enamored with the fledgling ecumenical movement that, to Bonhoeffer's disgust, they refused to censure the German church even after German Christians had taken control. Though a few individuals were well informed about Germany, most Christian leaders in Britain failed to see the critical moral issues unfolding there. Even though men like Dietrich Bonhoeffer made a point of appealing to them, they failed to understand what the church struggle in Germany represented and thus failed to warn against it. The church, representing the Kingdom of God, was caught up in the trendy issues of the time, surrendering its influence as an independent moral voice.

This failure of both the state and the church contributed to the disaster that befell the world. Had they acted sooner to discharge their respective duties, the Holocaust might well have been avoided.

*   *   *

On the continent the circumstances were reversed. A power-hungry maniac who masterfully played upon the passions of the masses seized the German government. From the start Hitler was determined to exceed government's ordained and delegated role. For him the state was everything, and he was its god. The Communists and the Jews, his hated targets, could offer little organized resistance, and no one spoke in their defense. In the face of Hitler's enormous popularity, all the trusted institutions of modern society utterly failed to resist. The trade unions, the Parliament, the political parties, the universities, the associations of medical doctors, scientists, and intellectuals—all were completely under Hitler's power within six months. Only the church had the independence and the institutional power to stand between Hitler and absolute totalitarianism.

Oddly, the story of the German church struggle has all but disappeared from modern historical accounts. But in contemporary writings it was cited as the single outstanding example of resistance to Hitler. The New York Times, for instance, filed approximately 1000 separate news accounts of the German church struggle from 1933 to 1937. Martin Niemoller's name was a household word.

Nazi files clearly record that the church struggle was a constant thorn in the flesh to Hitler and his aides during their early years in power. This was hardly due to the church's political vision or sophistication; rather it was a credit to the church's reliance on an ultimate authority and vision quite apart from the political order to resist Hitler's blasphemous claims, even when his political popularity was soaring. The church's authority, deeply rooted in the lives of the German people, could not be erased by a simple directive from Berlin. It was the only institution in Germany that offered any enduring or meaningful resistance.

But it was not enough. Eventually alone, divided from within, with large numbers of its membership capitulating and even supporting Hitler's schemes, the church failed to hold the state to account.

The roots of World War II were in a sense theological. In England and in Germany, the state and the church failed to fulfill their God-ordained mandates. And whenever that happens, evil triumphs.

12

Year Zero

What will we do as the earth is set loose from its sun?

—*Friedrich Nietzsche*

Six years after Hitler's troops marched into Poland, much of Europe lay in ruins. London, victim of German air power in the early years of the war, had been bombed incessantly; France, Italy, and the Netherlands had faced the cruelty of enemy occupation. The soil was red with the blood of their defenders. But it was Japan that had borne the full brunt of modern warfare: the atom bomb. Her will to fight was incinerated in the mushroom clouds that devastated Hiroshima and Nagasaki.

Sunday, September 2, 1945, as the sun climbed in the sky over Tokyo Bay, the decks of the battleship USS *Missouri* grew hot. The massive hulk of steel, the length of a football field, was the site of the formal surrender ceremony of the Axis powers to the Allies.[1]

General Jonathan Wainwright, commander of the American forces defeated in the Philippines, had been liberated only four days earlier after three years in a Manchurian prison camp; he and Percival, the British general who had surrendered Singapore, flanked General Douglas MacArthur, now supreme commander for the Allied powers. Fanning out behind them on either side were Allied admirals and generals from England, Canada, Australia, New Zealand, Russia, China, the Netherlands, and America.

In the center of the rows of khaki, medals, and ribbons stood a microphone, an old mess table covered with a thick green cloth, and two straight chairs. Surrounding them was the network of scaffolding erected for war correspondents and cameramen, now clinging to their perches, checking camera angles, and scribbling notes. The gun turrets and decks overhead were lined with sailors in sparkling white. Many held Kodaks, straining for a shot of General MacArthur.

High above it all, the Stars and Stripes snapped in the breeze, the same flag that had flown over the U.S. Capitol on the morning of December 7, 1941, when the Japanese had destroyed the American fleet in Pearl Harbor.

At 9:00 A.M., Commander Horace Byrd, the *Missouri*'s gunnery officer, cupped his hands to his mouth and shouted, "Attention all hands." The jubilant buzz of conversation quieted as the Japanese delegation approached the *Missouri*.

Eleven Japanese officials, wearing silk hats, ascots, and cutaways, climbed the ship's stairway, their faces expressionless. Several had been forced to participate in the ceremonies by the emperor himself; they had vowed to commit hara-kiri, as many of their fellow officers already had, upon their return to Tokyo.

The ceremony began with an invocation by the ship's chaplain, then the "Star Spangled Banner" blared over the public-address system. General MacArthur, wearing his familiar sun glasses and visored cap, walked briskly to the microphone. He stood erect and confident, though his hand trembled slightly as he held the sheet of notes before him.

"We are gathered here, representative of the major warring powers," he said in a strong voice, "to conclude a solemn agreement whereby peace may be restored. . . . It is my earnest hope and indeed the hope of all mankind that from this solemn occasion a better world shall emerge out of the blood and carnage of the past—a world founded upon faith and understanding—a world dedicated to the dignity of man and the fulfillment of his most cherished wish—for freedom, tolerance and justice."

Two copies of the surrender agreement lay on the table, one bound in leather for the Allies, the other bound in canvas for the Japanese. Cameras clicked everywhere as the signing began. Foreign Minister Shigemitsu sat down and fumbled with his hat and gloves, obviously bewildered. MacArthur's chief of staff showed him where to sign. Then the other Japanese officials signed the agreement, as did the nine representatives of the Allied powers. At eight minutes past nine, MacArthur sat at the table and affixed his signature to the document.

"Let us pray that peace be now restored to the world and that God will preserve it always," he announced. At that moment a steady drone in the clouds above the ship became a deafening roar, and an aerial pageant of 400 B-29s and 1,500 carrier planes swept across the sky and disappeared in the mists of Mount Fuji to the southwest.

World War II had ended.

At that dramatic moment General Douglas MacArthur spoke the first words of peace to a waiting world.

"Today the guns are silent . . . the skies no longer rain death . . . the seas bear only commerce . . . men everywhere walk upright in the sunlight. The entire world is quietly at peace. . . .

"A new era is upon us. Even the lesson of victory itself brings with it profound concern both for our future security and the survival of civilization. The destructiveness of the war potential, through progressive advances in scientific discovery, has in fact now reached a point which revises the traditional concept of war. . . .

"Men since the beginning of time have sought peace, [but] military alliances, balance of power, leagues of nations, all in turn failed, leaving the only path to be by way of the crucible of war.

"*We have had our last chance. If we do not now devise some greater and more equitable system, Armageddon will be at our door. The problem is basically theological and involves a spiritual recrudescence and improvement of human character. It must be of the spirit if we are to save the flesh.*"

*   *   *

Nineteen forty-five, "Year Zero," as one historian labeled it,* was the year of promise. Old mistakes were not to be repeated.

Douglas MacArthur was one of the few who was in a position to fully understand that the challenge of this new beginning was not primarily

---

*John Lukacs in his book 1945: *Year Zero* (Garden City: Doubleday, 1978). Lukacs explains: "Nineteen forty-five was both Year Zero and Year One. Year Zero, Jahr Null—this is what a generation of Germans called the year 1945. Year One, Year I of the Atomic Age, this is how certain intellectuals, editorialists, scientists kept referring to that year, at least for awhile." Lukacs contends that the end of a united Germany was a much more important event in 1945 than the atomic bomb.

political, military, or economic, but spiritual. The crisis was not one of organization or technology, but of character and ideas. He issued his prophetic challenge in light of two events that had already occurred, ominous portents that would shape the post-war world: the atom bomb and the accession to Stalin's demands.

The bomb MacArthur had seen. He knew that the devastating power of the atom bomb would forever change the rules of war, international politics, and the universe. Hiroshima's blackened ruins testified to the possibility of global annihilation and the ultimate destructive power of man over nature and humanity. The mushroom cloud of Armageddon would haunt future generations.

Catholic novelist Georges Bernanos, author of *The Diary of a Country Priest*, called the use of the bomb the "triumph of technique over reason."[2] Questions of justice, prudence, responsibility, and consequences were set aside in pursuit of a technique to win the war. Though the bomb hastened the end of the war, it would shape civilization's values for the remainder of the century. Just as technique had triumphed over reason, kso expediency would triumph over morality.

The second event that was to significantly shape the post–World War II world was the Allied decision to accede to Soviet demands for the return of all Russian nationals. Thus, the West was amazingly compliant; the singular goal was victory and that meant keeping Stalin happy. In 1944 hundreds of thousands who had come under Allied control during the liberation of Europe were sent back to the Soviet Union.

Sir Patrick Dean, legal advisor for the British foreign office, advised his superiors: "This is purely a question for the Soviet authorities and does not concern His Majesty's government. In due course, all those with whom the Soviet authorities desire to deal must be handed over to them, and we are not concerned with the fact that they may be shot or otherwise more harshly dealt with than they might be under English law."[3]

Again, technique superseded reason and principle at the price of an estimated one and a half million people. The forced repatriation served Stalin's death warrant on Croats, cossacks, and the other Russians who had hoped to escape Communist rule.

MacArthur realized the peril the post-war world faced. But his stirring words of warning that day in Tokyo Bay were washed away in the waves of euphoric relief that swept over victor and vanquished alike. Instead of seeking spiritual renewal, which might have established a healthy balance between the religious and the political, the post-war generation was left to thrash about in a vacuum of values.

For at that point the modern mind had already been seized by the powerful ideas of an odd prophet—a syphilitic and eventually insane German who could see into the soul of our century from the middle of the last.

In 1889 Friedrich Nietzsche told a parable:

> Have you not heard of the madman who lit a lamp in the bright morning and went to the marketplace crying ceaselessly, "I seek God! I seek God!" There were many among those standing there who didn't believe in God so he made them laugh. "Is God lost?" one of them said. "Has he gone astray like a child?" said another. "Or is he hiding? Has he gone on board ship and emigrated?" So they laughed and shouted to one another. The man sprang into their midst and looked daggers at them. "Where is God?" he cried. "I will tell you. We have killed him—you and I. We are all his killers! But how have we done this? How could we swallow up the sea? Who gave us the sponge to wipe away the horizon? What will we do as the earth is set loose from its sun?"[4]

Nietzsche's point was not that God does not exist, but that God had become irrelevant. Men and women may assert that God exists or that He does not, but it makes little difference either way. God is dead not because He doesn't exist, but because we live, play, procreate, govern, and die as though He doesn't.

The effect of this widespread notion can be seen in the despair that followed World War I, in the void that gave rise to fascism, in the militant atheism that has claimed countless lives in Russia and China, and in modern Western culture. The death of God has profound implications for individuals as well as for society and politics because it is the philosophic context in which modern governments operate.

In Western civilization God had traditionally played the role of legitimizing government. In classical and Christian political philosophy He was the author of natural law—that body of just and reasonable standards that guided human rulers and by which the ruled were bound to respect and obey those given charge over them. Even atheistic political philosophy acknowledged that the idea of God was useful: a little dose of religion would keep the masses quiet. As Napoleon said, "Religion is what keeps the poor from murdering the rich."[5]

But Nietzsche's atheism was the most radical the world had yet seen. While the old atheism had acknowledged the need for religion, the new atheism was political, activist, and jealous. One scholar observed that "atheism has become militant . . . insisting it must be believed. Atheism has felt the need to impose its views, to forbid competing visions."[6]

Nietzsche himself predicted the result of this new atheism on politics. "I am not man, I am dynamite . . . my truth is fearful; it is that in the past we called lies the truth—the devaluation of all values. . . . The concept of politics is completely taken up in a war of the spirits, all the structures of power are blown up into the air, for they are based on the lie. There will be wars of a kind that have never happened on the earth."[7]

"The devaluation of all values" is what the death of God has meant to politics. Distinctions between right and wrong, justice and injustice have become meaningless. No objective guide is left to choose between "all men are created equal" and "the weak to the wall."

In Year Zero no one could have predicted the consequences that the void at the heart of the nations would produce. But philosopher Blaise Pascal had foreseen, three centuries earlier, the chilling consequences. He argued that in a spiritual vacuum, men can pursue only two options: first, to imagine that they are gods themselves, or second, to seek satisfaction in their senses. Unknowingly, he predicted the routes that would be followed in the East and West in the aftermath of World War II.

On the surface, however, when the USS *Missouri* sailed out of Tokyo Bay, there seemed every reason for hope. Plans were being laid for a great council of nations dedicated to the dignity of man and the end of war. It would be a brave new world in which the nations of the globe could unite to seek peace and justice.

*   *   *

The United Nations complex sits on sixteen acres of New York City's choicest real estate, bordering the East River and Manhattan. The lean, immense Secretariat building rises into the sky, the sun reflecting off its window walls. Bright flags of the nations of the world fly in the breezes off the river; the most prominent is the blue and white UN flag, its two white reeds of olive branches surrounding the world.

A visitor is immediately struck by the grandeur of the building, stirred by the sight of dignitaries stepping out of black limousines to cross the massive plaza. He realizes that if this place represents the powers of the world, one might well want to see the place of worship, where the nations bow before the One under whose rule they govern.

The information personnel are bemused. "The chapel? We don't have a chapel. If there is one, I believe it's across the street."

The visitor darts across the thoroughfare, dodging New York's taxis, and successfully arrives at the opposite building's security-clearance desk.

"Well, there's a chapel here," responds the officer, "but it's not associated with the UN." He thumbs through the directory. "Oh, I see, all right, here it is. It's across the street—and tell them you're looking for the meditation room."

Again the visitor dashes across the pavement. An attendant tells him that the room is not open to the public; it's a "nonessential area," and there has been a personnel cutback. But a security guard will escort the visitor through long, crowded hallways and swinging glass doors. Again, there is the pervasive sense of weighty matters being discussed in the noble pursuit of world peace.

The guide pauses at an unmarked door. He unlocks it and gingerly pushes it open. The small room is devoid of people or decoration. The walls are stark white. There are no windows. A few wicker stools surround a large square rock at the center of the room. It is very quiet. But there is no altar, rug, vase, candle, or symbol of any type of religious worship.

Lights in the ceiling create bright spots of illumination on the front wall. One focuses on a piece of modern art: steel squares and ovals. Beyond the abstract shapes, there is nothing in those bright circles of light. They are focused on a void. And it is in that void that the visitor suddenly sees the soul of the brave new world.

13

Marxism
and
the Kingdom of God

If you will not have God (and He is a jealous God), you should pay your respects to Hitler and Stalin.

—T. S. Eliot

"**G**od remains dead," wrote Nietzsche. "How shall we, the murderers of all murderers, comfort ourselves? Must not we ourselves become gods simply to seem worthy of it?"[1] With these words Nietzsche was at once echoing Pascal's first option that "men become gods themselves" and heralding the creation of a new type of man—a heroic individualist no longer bound to a traditional "slave" morality, but creating his own rules. Such a "superman" would exercise the "will to power."

Today one-third of the world's population lives in the viselike grip of states that are the product of such gangster-statesmen who established governments that attempted to fill the vacuum of values with secular ideology or the cult of personality. The goal of these massive bureaucracies is to preside over the death of God; their system for achieving it is most often called Marxist Leninism. It carries out its policies with surgical efficiency, as millions of Christians and Jews who have passed through Communist gulags would testify. If they could. But sometimes the system performs with comic clumsiness, as I witnessed one night in Leningrad.

In February 1973 President Nixon had sent me to the Soviet Union for follow-up negotiations to the trade agreements Nixon and Leonid Brezhnev had announced at their 1973 summit. My real job, however, was to pressure the Soviets into allowing more Jews to emigrate. Their refusal to do so was imperiling trade legislation in the U.S. Congress.

After our official meetings in Moscow, my wife Patty and I were escorted on a three-day visit to Leningrad, Russia's showcase city for Western visitors.

Leningrad takes on an eerie beauty in the filtered light of the northern winter, its sprawling skyline a dazzling mix of gilded, traditional onion domes and the rich blue and pastel hues of French and Italian provincial architecture. This splendid city is the place where East and West have traditionally met—and divided.

Like all Western visitors, Patty and I eagerly walked the treasure-laden corridors of the Hermitage, one of the world's greatest art repositories; saw the famed Peter and Paul fortress, within whose massive walls have been enacted many of the turbulent events of Russian history; explored the palaces where czars of the Imperial era lived in unrivaled splendor; and visited the cathedrals of Leningrad, which reflect the Russian culture. The ecclesiastical façade of one, the Peter and Paul Lutheran Church, has been preserved, but the interior has been converted into a gigantic public swimming pool. Another, the spectacular Cathedral of Our Lady, is now a state museum exhibiting the history of religion and atheism.

The Soviet Foreign Ministry capped our visit with an evening at the Kirov Ballet for a performance of Tchaikovsky's Swan Lake. The Kirov is the crown jewel of Leningrad. The Soviets spared nothing to repair the heavy damage the building suffered during World War II, restoring its nineteenth-century elegance. During the renovation, which was completed in 1970, nearly nine hundred pounds of gold were used to gild the interior walls where five tiers of balconies sweep around the huge horseshoe-shaped hall like elegant ivory and gold rings, glistening in the blaze of massive crystal chandeliers. The sight took our breath away.

Our escort, a veteran U.S. Consulate officer, seemed pleased as we were shown to our orchestra center seats—thick, plush, sapphire-velvet chairs.

"This is very good for protocol," he whispered.

"Good for watching great ballet too," I replied.

His smile vanished. "Of course we may not see *Swan Lake*," he said. I thought he was joking. "Why not?" I asked, prepared for a quip.

"Well, we know the Soviets respect your high rank because you got these seats," he said. "And often when American VIPs come they pull a switch at the last minute and put on a dreadful atheistic propaganda piece called *Creation of the World*. I've seen it six times."

"But these people," I said, gesturing at the audience. "They're here to see *Swan Lake*. They'll be in an uproar."

"No, they won't," the consular officer replied with a smile. "This is Russia."

Sure enough, when the lights dimmed and the velvet curtain rose, it was not the opening strains of Tchaikovsky's masterpiece we heard, but the strident chords of *Creation of the World*. I watched the faces of the surrounding audience. Not a murmur, not a single expression of displeasure. Seventeen hundred people sat stoically in their seats.

It was a dreary evening indeed. The ballet was a parody on the Garden of Eden, where a buffoonlike character, God, contested with a vital, vigorous figure, Satan, for the soul of man. In the closing scene God retreated lamely, vanquished, leaving self-sufficient man living happily ever after in his earthy paradise.

The architect of this earthly paradise was Vladimir Ilyich Ulyanov, the son of Christian parents, known to history as Lenin.

Lenin, a single-minded radical, became the most successful revolutionary of the twentieth century. With the "will to power," he pursued and eliminated his enemies ruthlessly—liberals and socialists, rival Marxists, reluctant peasants and skeptical military officers, monarchists and capitalists, Jews and various other "class enemies." Above all, Lenin pursued and murdered Christians. He hated them. "There can be nothing more abominable than religion," he wrote.[2]

Lenin particularly hated seriously committed Christians. Weak Christians he could manage, but serious Christians meant nothing but trouble for a Marxist-Leninist regime. They owed allegiance to the one power greater than the totalitarian Communist state. History has borne Lenin out on this point, if not on others.

The pattern of Communist persecution of Jews and Christians is remarkably ecumenical. It has fallen on orthodox believers in Russia, Romania, Bulgaria, and the Ukraine; Roman Catholics in the Baltic Republics, Poland, Hungary, Cuba, Vietnam, and Nicaragua; Lutherans in East Germany and Czechoslovakia; Reformed Christians in Hungary and Czechoslovakia; Pentecostals, Baptists, and other evangelicals in Eastern Europe, Latin America, and Asia; house church believers in China.

In 1980 twenty-eight Marxist regimes around the world were committed to a policy of atheism, repressing and persecuting Christianity to some degree. These nations contained approximately 250 million Christians—almost one of every five Christians in the world. Those twenty-eight nations have a total population of 1.48 billion—more than a third of the world's people.[3]

Consider just a few representative reports of that persecution around the world:

—In Vietnam seventeen evangelical pastors are in jail. Some 200 churches have been closed since 1975, the year the only Protestant seminary in the country was closed.

—In the Soviet Union criminal charges are filed against Nedezhda Mativkhina for allowing a group of Christians to meet in her home. Mativkhina, a double amputee, has already served two terms in the gulag and now faces a third.[4]

—In Czechoslovakia and Hungary the police crack down on leaders of "basic communities" where Catholic adults and young people meet for Bible study and prayer.

—In China authorities "liberalize" rules covering Christians by banning Protestant house churches, restricting religious gatherings to licensed church buildings, and forbidding evangelism.*

---

*It is much more difficult to obtain accurate statistics on religious belief in China than in the Soviet Union—though there is evidence of a flourishing house-church movement, a state-controlled national Protestant church, and continuing Catholic presence. Before Mao Tse-tung's takeover in 1949, Christians were a tiny minority. Both Protestant and Catholic missionaries, however, had established a robust presence, and the 80 percent of the Chinese people who followed various folk religions seemed relatively receptive to the gospel. Indeed, the Christian churches have grown steadily in Hong Kong, Taiwan, and Macao—Chinese areas free of Communist control.

If the churches in mainland China had grown at the same rate as those in Taiwan or Hong Kong, we could have expected the Christian population of China to be 90 million by 1980. The most

—In Nicaragua dozens of Moravian pastors serving impoverished Miskito Indians on the country's Atlantic Coast are imprisoned and killed. Moravian communities are uprooted.

—In the Soviet Union dissident Anatoly Shcharansky is given 130 days in solitary for refusing to surrender his book of Psalms.

The Soviet Union has set the course that virtually all Marxist governments have followed. Before the 1917 revolution 83.4 percent of the people living in what is now the Soviet Union were identified as Christians—three quarters of them Russian Orthodox. Orthodox, Catholic, and Protestant Christians have suffered violent persecution since the revolution, except for a brief period during World War II when the regime needed the support of the churches. Since 1917, some 60 million Soviet citizens have been killed and 66 million have been sent to labor camps or imprisoned. At least half of these have been Christians.[5]

Activist theologian Reinhold Niebuhr once described Communism as "an organized evil which spreads terror and cruelty through the world."[6] And Aleksandr Solzhenitsyn, the great writer who came to faith while in prison, explains why Communists are so determined to destroy Christianity: "They flee from Christ like devils from the sign of the cross."[7]

*   *   *

Cardinal Joseph Mindszenty, the primate of Hungary, stood naked in his chilly cell in the secret-police headquarters at 60 Andrassy Street in Budapest, trembling with fear and cold as a furious agent of the state advanced on him with a rubber truncheon in one hand and a long knife in the other.

"I'll kill you," the man snarled, lashing the truncheon across the cardinal's back. "By morning I'll tear you to pieces and throw the remains of your corpse into the canal. We are the masters here now."

He prodded Mindszenty with the knife. The cardinal moved away. Another prod. And another. The cardinal moved and moved again. Soon he was running in circles. For several hours the agent drove the naked, middle-aged prelate unrelentingly around the cell like a horse in training.

optimistic private Western estimate of China's Christian population is 50 million. The official government figure is 1.8 million—a scant 200,000 more than the Christian population in 1900. Nicholas Piediscalzi, "China's New Policy on Religion," *Christian Century* (June 19–26, 1985), 613.

It was late January 1949. Cardinal Mindszenty had been enduring such tortures since his arrest the day after Christmas. Every night his Communist interrogators demanded that he confess to crimes against the state, including the preposterous charge that he had conspired with the American government to restore a Hapsburg king to the throne of Hungary. Every night Cardinal Mindszenty refused to sign the confession.

During the day the cardinal sat on a filthy couch trying to recover from the night's tortures. If he drifted into sleep, one of the jailers who sat in the room prodded him awake. At night the cycle began again.

"I was being made to feel in my soul, my body, my nerves, and my bones the power of bolshevism which was taking over the country," he later wrote.

Although his jailers may not have known it, Cardinal Mindszenty embodied, in a sense, the sufferings of an entire nation. The events that led to his imprisonment paralleled the ideological imprisonment of the Hungarian churches. The Communists had consolidated their power the summer before, in 1948, and their first target had been the churches. Two days after the new regime took control, they secularized the nation's religious schools. Party boss Matyas Rakosi pressed church leaders to submit to government control over church affairs, including requirements that priests and ministers publicly support government policies.

Bishop Lajos Ordass, the ablest leader of the Lutheran Church, refused to cooperate and was arrested and imprisoned. Bishop Laszlo Ravasz, the independent-minded head of the Hungarian Reformed Church, was forced out and replaced by a compliant theologian who thought support for Marxist Leninism was obligatory for Christians.

The chief obstacle to the Communists' plans, however, was Cardinal Mindszenty. As Catholic primate, he was the leader of the largest denomination in Hungary, a stubborn man with a record of fierce opposition to tyrants. The Nazis had jailed him during World War II. Later, as Communist power grew in Hungary, he constantly protested their abuses of human rights.

Cardinal Mindszenty was especially offended by the government's demands that the church sign a formal treaty with the state. He had watched Lenin and Stalin subdue the Orthodox Church in the Soviet Union through a campaign of terrorism, judicial persecution, and subversion. He vowed that he would not allow the same thing to happen in Hungary.

The church-state agreement in the Soviet Union gave the sate control over religious instruction, seminary education, and appointment of bishops. Bishops were called upon to give public support to government policies when their Communist masters wanted it, and all priests had to swear allegiance to the Communist government.

Significantly, the party ruthlessly forbade the church to evangelize or to provide services to the poor, elderly, sick, and needy. Thus, the church was barred from conducting any activities that would publicly testify to its members' allegiance to another King.

Party Chief Rakosi wanted to make the church in Hungary a puppet church like the one in the Soviet Union. Cardinal Mindszenty would have none of it. After months of bickering with the recalcitrant cardinal, Rakosi and his henchmen moved against the church leader.

The day after Christmas 1948, police occupied the cardinal's offices in Esztergom. Officers carrying submachine guns led Cardinal Mindszenty to a car and drove him to secret-police headquarters in Budapest. There he was subjected to torture.

Thirty-nine days after his arrest—beaten, confused, plagued with despair, and racked with fear and anxiety—the cardinal signed the confession the authorities wanted.

Later he told the harrowing account of those weeks of torture in his memoirs.[8] The mental and psychological pain were far worse than the physical deprivations and beatings, he wrote, and he was certain that the police had used drugs on him. He candidly admitted that the Communist torturers had shattered his personality, reducing him to a state where even the regime's most absurd charges began to seem plausible.

Certainly the man whom the Communists put on public trial for treason in February 1949 looked like a drugged, programed shell, reciting the lines of a memorized script. He was found guilty of treason and sentenced to life in prison.

Soon after Cardinal Mindszenty's trial, the government suppressed the Catholic Church in Hungary. Religious schools were abolished, religious instruction was outlawed, and religious orders were dissolved. Monks and nuns scattered into the population and were left to find what work they could.

In their place the government organized "peace priests" composed of ambitious collaborators and covert Communist agents. Soon these priests, many of whom led dissolute lives, controlled all the higher posts in the church. Catholics who wanted authentic pastoral care had to seek out priests who carried on their ministry in secret.

Eventually the regime got the agreement it wanted. The bishops agreed to support the government and its "peace priest" movement, and to tolerate state supervision of seminary training, clerical appointments, and other internal matters. In return, the government allowed the church to open eight schools and put the clergy on the state payroll.

The Reformed Church submitted to a similar agreement.

Thus the Communist rulers in Hungary have achieved what they consider "normal" relations with the church. Church authorities clear key appointments in advance with the government. Troublesome clerics are reassigned to the provinces. Bishops make regular expressions of support to the regime. When needed, priests and ministers read from their pulpits pastoral letters composed by the government Bureau of Religious Affairs.

Why is the conflict between the Christian church and the Marxist state so fundamental, ceaseless, and protracted?

Many in the secularized, tolerant West are offended by terms like "mortal enemies," preferring to see Communists as a particularly enthusiastic band of social reformers and the church as one of the many social institutions that must adapt to changing political circumstances. History, however, teaches a different lesson. Communism and Christianity are at odds for very good reasons.

First, Christianity and Communism are irreconcilable in their basic premises. The Christian believes that the dynamic of all history is spiritual, that its unfolding reveals God's dealings with men, that Jesus Christ is God in the flesh, and that at the end of history, He will reign over all the nations.

For Marxists, the material realm is all there is. God and the spiritual order are illusions. Mankind swims in the current of history, which progresses by economic forces from the decline of capitalism, through the dictatorship of the proletariat, to the earthly paradise of the classless society. Communists are materialists and determinists; individuals count for nothing, the collective or state for everything.

Lenin thought that those who believed in God were worse than fools. "Every man who occupies himself with the construction of a god, or merely even agrees to it, prostitutes himself in the worst way," he wrote. "For he occupies himself not with activity, but with self-contemplation and self-reflection, and tries thereby to deify his most unclean, most stupid, and most servile features and pettinesses."[9] Consequently, anyone who believes in God is not simply in error; he is mentally deranged. This is why believers in the Soviet Union are frequently judged insane and committed to mental institutions.

Second, Communism and Christianity clash because each is a religion and each is inherently expansive and evangelistic.

Marxists claim that their system is scientific, in contrast to the "superstition" of Christianity. But anyone who has visited Communist countries knows better. Marxist Leninism functions as a religion in the lives of the faithful. Communist "saints" and martyrs are revered, their utterances preserved in books and studied carefully. May Day marches and other public ceremonies are atheistic liturgies whereby unbelievers worship the superiority of unbelief.

Philosophically, Marxism is certainly a religion. It offers a comprehensive explanation of reality and claims to put adherents in touch with higher powers—namely, the inexorable laws of history. Its eschatology is millennial. At the end of the class struggle against capitalism lies the classless society where exploiters are banished, the state withers away, and man's natural goodness flows forth unobstructed. The laws of history will bring justice to the oppressed and wipe away every tear. It's a system that an atheist can put his faith in.

Lenin, Stalin, and Rakosi recognized that a renewed and purified Christianity was the only force that could move the masses as powerfully as the Marxist ideal could. They attacked it as the enemy that it was and is.

Trotsky, Tito, Mao, Ho Chi Minh, Castro—and the Sandinistas of the eighties—all the tyrants who have followed Marx have believed substantially the same thing about Christianity.

Nothing has changed. Despite his shrewd public effort to picture himself as a benign and progressive reformer, Mikhail Gorbachev adheres to this same ideology. As recently as November 1986, he described the struggle with traditional religion as "decisive and uncompromising" and called for more aggressive atheistic education.[10]

Like Lenin, Gorbachev knows who his enemies are. The greatest obstacle to the Marxist ideal of total control is the Christian faith, which is not simply a set of intellectual beliefs or weekly worship services, but involves personal submission to a King whose culture is incompatible with Lenin's. The Christian church and the Marxist state may work out an accommodation for a time, but they will always be adversaries. The very nature of each makes any lasting accommodation impossible. They are the two great contenders for the soul of mankind.

The people of Jaworzyna had had enough. For years they had petitioned the party authorities in the Silesia region of Poland for permission to build a church. Their repeated applications were denied. The men on the church-building committee tried pulling strings with higher party officials in Crakow and Warsaw. No luck. When they angrily protested the refusal, the petty bureaucrats turned a deaf ear. Now, other measures were required.

Months before, the authorities had issued a permit to build an auto-repair garage on a site near a highway. Now workers moved onto the site, erected a tall fence, and began to build the garage. The building progressed slowly over a period of two years, but no one paid much attention. The party authorities in Jaworzyna were busy men.

Then, on Sunday, February 5, 1978, the fence came down and the garage turned out to be a new church—its wide portals adorned with a picture of Our Lady of Częstochowa, the protector of Poland. Masses were celebrated until late in the evening; thousands of people came to worship and rejoice.

That spring, Cardinal Karol Wojtlya of Crakow came to Jaworzyna to dedicate the church. Soon afterward the authorities tried to close it, but hundreds of angry Poles organized a twenty-four-hour guard. The church building committee was taken to court and fined. Their clever lawyers tied the case up in procedural disputes.

Just before the May Day celebrations of the glorious triumph of Communism in Poland, the party authorities attempted to hide the church from the nearby highway by surrounding it with giant billboards bearing propaganda. The next morning the billboards lay on the ground, their messages celebrating the revolution ripped and shredded, their supports smashed. Even the cement footings had been ripped from the ground.

The wreckage lay outside the church for months. Many in Jaworzyna took it as a graphic symbol for the conflict in Poland between the church, which bears authority, and the state, which merely has power.

Joseph Stalin, who murdered millions during his twenty-nine-year reign as perhaps the most ruthless tyrant in history, once scoffed at a colleague who warned that the pope was likely to denounce one of Stalin's barbaric plans. "The pope!" sneered Stalin. "How many divisions does the pope have?"[11]

The pope's divisions were on display to the entire world in June 1979 when the former Cardinal Karol Wojtlya of Crakow, now John Paul II, visited his homeland. Ecstatic crowds gathered everywhere he went—200,000 in Warsaw, 500,000 at the shrine of the Black Madonna at Częstochowa, 1,000,000 in Crakow. Similar throngs were present at Gniezno, the first capital of Poland; at Wadowice, the pope's birthplace; and at Auschwitz and Birkenau, the sites of the infamous Nazi extermination camps. The world saw that the church possessed the soul of the Polish people and embodied the essence of Polish nationhood. By contrast, the Polish Communists who operated the machinery of the state were alien usurpers who did the bidding of Russian masters. Though he went out of his way to avoid a direct confrontation with the Communist regime, John Paul's message was widely understood by the restive Polish masses, and he lit a fuse during his triumphant nine-day visit to his homeland.

"Christ would never approve that man be considered merely as a means of production," he told workers in his old archdiocese in Mogila.[12]

At Częstochowa, he urged the government to honor "the cause of fundamental human rights, including the right to religious liberty."[13]

At Novy Targ, he told Poles to set a Christian example "even if it means risking danger."[14]

The long fuse that the pope lit exploded in July 1980 when workers at the Lenin shipyards at Gdansk went out on strike. Under the leadership of a Catholic electrician name Lech Walesa, the workers seized the shipyards and made a radical demand of the authorities: the right to organize free labor unions. Workers throughout the country walked off their jobs in sympathy. The Communist regime, discredited and despised, lost control.

By 1981 the Polish government was desperate. Millions of Poles, including many members of the Communist party, had joined the Solidarity movement. Lech Walesa was a household name around the world. Labor unrest was spreading from the cities to the rural areas. The economy was a shambles. The Red army maneuvered on Poland's eastern border. No one doubted that Soviet party boss Leonid Brezhnev would use his divisions if the pope's couldn't be curbed.

John Paul II announced that if Soviet tanks moved, he would return to stand with his countrymen. In desperation the government did the only thing it could do: it turned to the church. Cardinal Stefan Wyszynski, the primate of Poland, skillfully negotiated a deal among church, state, and Solidarity. The state would allow Solidarity freedom to organize and would loosen censorship in return for labor peace and an end to attacks on the fundamental legitimacy of the regime. The church would guarantee the arrangement.

That June, shortly after negotiating the agreement, Cardinal Wyszynski died at the age of eighty. He had been imprisoned by the Communist regime from 1953 to 1956. Now he received a state funeral that rivaled the funerals of Winston Churchhill and Charles de Gaulle for national pomp. The nation went into official mourning. The state radio played only solemn religious music. Theaters closed. Flags flew at half-staff. The president of Poland and three deputy prime ministers came to the funeral to honor the cardinal. They stood with a quarter million other Poles in Victory Square in Warsaw under a forty-three-foot-high wooden cross that proclaimed the triumph of Christianity.

Later that year, in December 1981, a reorganized Polish government imposed martial law and drove the Solidarity movement underground. That Solidarity was a religious movement no one, least of all the Soviets, can deny. In November 1981, Pravda denounced "religious fanaticism" as a grave challenge to socialism; failure to contain it, Pravda said, was at the root of the problems in Poland.[15]

Neither does anyone doubt that the currents of discontent will break out anew in the years ahead. Three times in forty years the Polish people have risen against their government and its Russian masters, each uprising triggered by Christian outrage over the brutality of the regime, its indifference to human needs, its suppression of fundamental rights, and its incessant lying. Christianity possesses the hearts of the people and shapes the Polish culture. This was evidenced at the height of the Gdansk strike when Western newspapers published front-page photos showing strikers in the Gdansk shipyards kneeling to receive communion. Such a sight was a shock to jaded, secularized eyes. Union workers in other industrialized countries are often part of the anticlerical left. In Poland the Christian workers are loyal to the church against the state.

Why is the church so much stronger in Poland than almost anywhere else in the world, certainly stronger than in Hungary and elsewhere in Eastern Europe?

The election of a Polish pope is surely a factor. So is the fact that Christianity has been firmly established in Poland for a thousand years. But a primary reason is the church's long tradition of resistance to secular power.

From 1795 to 1918 the Polish nation was divided among the Prussian, Austrian, and Russian empires, and church authorities resisted all three. In 1874 the archbishop of Poznan was imprisoned for opposing Bismarck's program of requiring religious instruction in German. The czar's plans for forced Russification in eastern Poland ran into similar opposition. From 1918 to 1939, during the period of the First Republic, the church remained independent from the Polish republic. The church also resisted the Nazi regime and suffered greatly for it. A third of the

Catholic clergy in Poland were executed by the Germans or died in concentration camps.

When the Communists imprisoned him in 1953, Cardinal Wyszynski reflected that of his seventeen seminary classmates, only he had thus far escaped being sent to German or Russian concentration camps. Cardinal Wyszynski confided a somewhat wry reflection to his diary: "Most of the priests and bishops with whom I worked had experienced prisons. Something would have been wrong if I had not experienced imprisonment. What was happening to me was very appropriate."[16]

A church with such a history, led by such tough-minded men, was ready for anything the new totalitarian state could devise. As Jacques Ellul, the French Protestant philosopher, has written, the "role of Cardinal Wyszynski after 1945 was to uphold the traditional church in the face of Communist power . . . to pressure [it] from . . . surrendering ideologically. It thus was and is the force behind Solidarity and the most powerful force in Poland today."[17]

The Polish church is one of the few in Eastern Europe to have avoided entanglement with the state. Many other church bodies allowed themselves to become closely identified with secular authorities, and in doing so, the official church in these countries lost the people. They are today mere puppets of their Communist ruler.

Ellul points out this lesson, one that the church around the world needs to remember: "Collaboration with power, whether Communist or not, is always ruinous for the church. If the church exists, if it is to have legitimacy in the eyes of the people, it must always stand erect as a counter-power to political power."[18]

Cardinal Wyszynski understood this. In prison in 1953, alone but supremely confident, he wrote a prophetic comment in his diary: "Any form of government, no matter how ruthless, will slowly cool and wane as it runs up against difficulties that the bureaucrat cannot resolve without cooperation from the people. Somehow the people must be taken into account."[19]

When the time came to reach the people, the Polish state found the church already there. It had been there for centuries.

*   *   *

The struggle between church and state has lasted for centuries in Poland. In Nicaragua it began in the early seventies when the Catholic church opposed the right-wing tyranny of the dictator Anastasio Somoza. It continues today.

Jimmy Hassan wasn't surprised when the police came for him in October 1985.

He had become national director of Campus Crusade for Christ in Nicaragua in 1982, when the revolutionary Sandinista government started serious persecution of evangelicals. Because Hassan was a lawyer and a former judge, his connections in Managua afforded him some protection. But many of his friends and co-workers had been harassed. Hassan had known it would only be a matter of time until the police came for him.

An officer at the security police headquarters held up a copy of Campus Crusade's basic literature, a small booklet called "The Four Spiritual Laws."

"Is this yours?" he snarled.

Hassan admitted it was. The officer ripped it up. Several agents shoved him in a car and drove him to Campus Crusade's Managua headquarters. There they confiscated about 2000 "Four Spiritual Laws" booklets and hundreds of books, including New Testaments and Bibles.

The next stop was the shop that did Campus Crusade's printing. There the junta's agents confiscated 50,000 copies of "The Four Spiritual Laws." They threatened the printer with jail if he ever did any more work for Hassan or Campus Crusade.

The police then locked Hassan alone in a room at the Interior Ministry.

Hassan thought of his wife and three children. He thought of the Moravian pastors in the remote Atlantic provinces of Nicaragua who had been murdered by Sandinista gangs. He thought of his evangelistic work and the churches that were growing. People were being saved despite the persecution. It gave him satisfaction to know he was being held because the Marxist authorities hated Campus Crusade's success. But he wondered whether he would ever see his family again.

The security forces released him in late afternoon, and Hassan went home. At 11:00 P.M. the agents returned with a summons to report back to the Interior Ministry the next morning.

When he got there, he was taken to a room and interrogated.

"Who is your CIA controller?" they asked.

"How much did the CIA pay you to do this work in Managua?"

"What political party do you belong to?"

"Why don't you make statements supporting the Sandinistas?"

To all the accusations Hassan replied that he was not involved in politics, that he had nothing to do with the CIA, and that he only wanted to be left in peace to preach the gospel.

The interrogators threatened him with prison. They said he would be beaten if he did not confess. Hassan took these threats seriously, but he would not budge.

Then a tall man came into the room, took out a pistol, and held it to Hassan's head.

"You have one more chance to confess," one of the agents said. "Do it now. You are a paid American agent. Tell us about it. If you don't, you'll be killed."

"My only activity is to preach the gospel," Hassan replied.

The tall man pressed the pistol against Hassan's forehead. Hassan could feel the pressure increase as the man pressed his fingers on the trigger. Harder. He pulled the trigger.

Hassan heard a click. . . . The gun was empty.

Hassan was released later that day with threats that he would be killed the next time they had to deal with him. Just before Christmas that year, the Hassan family escaped to Mexico. In exile, Jimmy spoke for other evangelicals of his country: "No matter what the threat, no matter what the conditions, no matter what the persecution, we will not stop preaching the gospel to the people of Nicaragua."[20]

In 1982, the year Jimmy Hassan took over Campus Crusade, Nicaragua's evangelicals were a minority in a Catholic country. Traditionally, they avoided politics. That meant the Protestants had little leverage in high places; most didn't know what was coming when a Marxist regime began to consolidate its power.[21]

In May the authorities began to confiscate evangelical churches, many of them in remote Atlantic provinces far from the capital and the inconvenient scrutiny of the Western press.

In August Interior Minister Borge told a mob that Protestants were collaborating with the CIA and the defeated Somoza regime.

"*Que se vayan, que se vayan.*" "Get them out. Get them out," chanted a mob of militants. They seized more Protestant churches.

At the same time the Sandinista government moved against the Catholic Church, which claims the loyalty of 80 percent of the Nicaraguan people. The revolutionary junta expelled two foreign priests who had worked with the poor for many years and accelerated a propaganda campaign against Catholic clergy and lay leaders who were critical of the regime. The Sandinistas also pressured the Catholic schools, replacing loyal Catholic teachers with Cuban-trained personnel indoctrinated in Marxist ideology. The schools were forced to adopt a new curriculum featuring crude Marxist propaganda.

Since 1982 harassment and persecution of evangelicals has continued. Officials of the Assemblies of God, the National Council of Evangelical Pastors, and other churches have been arrested and questioned. Moravian pastors working in Miskito Indian communities on Nicaragua's Atlantic Coast have been beaten and killed. Whole Miskito communities have been uprooted and resettled in areas under army control. Thousands have been murdered.

The visit of Pope John Paul II in 1983 was marked by open hostility between the Sandinista regime and the Catholic church. Government officials lined the ramp when the pope descended from his plane on his arrival in Managua. Ernesto Cardenal, a Catholic priest who continued to serve as a member of the revolutionary government despite a papal ruling that he step down, knelt to kiss the pope's ring. John Paul II angrily snatched it away, thus making dramatically clear to those watching his disapproval of priests serving in the Sandinista government.

The climax of the pope's visit came when he celebrated Mass in a public square in the center of Managua. The pope stood alone on a platform while Sandinista officials held back the huge, friendly crowd. Then they took over the front seats and, for the benefit of the grinding television cameras, shook their fists and screamed at the pope. Each time they did so he lifted his crucifix higher over his head.

The Sandinista officials were genuinely angry. John Paul II, a remarkable linguist, was conducting the Mass in the language of the Miskito Indians. Symbolically he was conveying a powerful truth: God offers grace to the people you killed. He was also indicting the Sandinistas. The crowd cheered; the protesters howled with rage. Much of the American media missed it altogether, expressing wonderment that the Pope would conduct mass in the language of a remote tribe.

In 1985 ten foreign priests were expelled from the country. In 1986 the junta expelled Fr. Bismark Carballo and Bishop Pablo Vega, president of the Nicaraguan bishops' conference. Both men were persistent critics of the Sandinista regime.

While these acts of overt pressure resemble the oppression of Christians in Eastern Europe in the fifties, in reality, Nicaragua opens a new chapter in the history of conflict between the Christian church and the Marxist state.

Most Christians, including the Catholic bishops, welcomed the 1979 revolution that toppled the corrupt regime of Anastasio Somoza. Archbishop Miguel Obando y Bravo had been a persistent and effective critic of Somoza for a decade. In fact, the revolution probably would not have triumphed without the active support of the bishops and the great mass of clergy and lay leaders.

The Marxist Sandinistas were a minority in the broad coalition that made up the revolutionary government that took over in 1979. By 1980, however, the Sandinistas had forced most of their democratic colleagues out of the governing junta by using time-honored Marxist techniques: control of the army and ruthless, single-minded pursuit of their goals, unhampered by democratic procedure. But the Sandinistas could not subdue the church. It had wisely kept a distance from the state before the Sandinistas came to power. The people were with the church.

So a new strategy emerged: the Sandinistas dressed the Communist program in Christian language and raised the "peace priests" tactics of Lenin and Hungary's Rakosi to new heights.

Four Catholic priests hold cabinet office in the Sandinista government. Sandinista officials speak of the "Kingdom of God" coming through the revolution, and many Sandinistas passionately regard themselves as members of *la iglesia popular* (the people's church)and followers of *el Dios de los pobres* (the God of the Poor). Protestant sympathizers with the Sandinista regime act through the Center for Promotion and Development. One of its leaders declared in 1982 that "it is required that we as Christians understand that biblical faith is inseparable from political militancy."[22]

The strategy was expounded by Daniel Ortega, the junta leader, in his address at Managua airport welcoming Pope John Paul II. The true Christians in Nicaragua, he said, were "basing themselves on faith corresponding to the revolution."[23]

A coalition of "revolutionary Christians," both Catholic and Protestant, expressed the same sentiments in theological terms in 1980: "The only way to love God, whom we do not see, is by contributing to the advancement of this revolutionary process in the most sensible and radical way possible," they wrote. "Only then shall we be loving our brothers, whom we do see. Therefore, we say that to be a Christian is to be a revolutionary."[24]

The vehicle for this congruence of Christianity and revolutionary politics has been liberation theology, a movement that has come to equate partisan political involvement with Christian commitment. As the Protestant liberation theologian Jose Miguez Bonino says, "Latin American theology becomes a militant theology—a partisan theology, perhaps."[25]

"Our only solution is Marxism," says Fr. Ernesto Cardenal, the Nicaraguan minister of culture and one of the four priests in the government. "The revolution and the Kingdom of heaven mentioned in the gospel are the same thing. A Christian should embrace Marxism if he wants to be with God and all men."[26] Or as a revolutionary poster put it, "Faith without revolution is dead."[27]

This line of thinking guts the gospel. If a Christian must embrace Marxism and revolution to do God's will, then something was lacking in the atonement and revelation of Jesus Christ.

One Sandinista pamphlet makes exactly that point. On the cover is a drawing of a young man in a beret, wearing a crucifix around his neck, carrying an automatic rifle in his left hand and a Molotov cocktail in his right. One section inside is titled "Jesus Christ Is Not Enough for Us." The text explains how the gospel must be supplemented by Marxism.

The paradoxical end to this hall of mirrors is the bizarre conclusion that Christians need Marxists far more than Marxists need Christians. In fact, Fr. Miguel D'Escoto, the Sandinista foreign minister, came to precisely that conclusion. Marxism, he said, is "one of the great blessings on the church. It has been the divine whip to bring it back."[28]

This new strategy is spreading throughout Latin America. It has been echoed in Cuba by the government's director of religious affairs who said, "Christians won't be free without socialism, and socialism won't be built on this continent without Christians."[29] This statement comes on the heels of the disclosure in Armando Valladeres' memoirs that for twenty-five years, Christians have been beaten and imprisoned in Castro's own gulags.

Despite co-opting and oppression, however, Catholic as well as Protestant churches continue to resist the Sandinistas. For years, church authorities denounced and opposed the tyranny of the right. Now they denounce and oppose the tyranny of the left. They resisted pressures to do the conservatives' bidding for the sake of "order, stability, and tradition." Today they resist the left's demands to identify the gospel with "equality, justice, and peace." They demonstrate the first law of survival for the church under pressure from secular authorities: Do not legitimize tyranny. Remain aloof from the enticements and threats of the secular authority. Be faithful to God alone.

These stories of the church in Hungary, Poland, and Nicaragua are just a part of the picture. They are, however, representative of the raging conflict. With rare exceptions, the church has been driven underground or made a puppet of the state in Marxist-dominated countries. At no other time in human history has so much of the world come under the dark cloud of an oppressive regime consciously determined to eliminate religious influence from culture.

But we can be grateful that the Kingdom of God does not depend on the structures of man. Though a third of the world lives under tyranny and the official "religion" of atheism, the Kingdom of God remains visible. It is visible when leaders like Jimmy Hassan and John Paul II take their stand. It is visible when ordinary people refuse to compromise what is most precious in their lives.

That was the case in the little town of Garwolin, Poland, in March 1984.[30]

The government of Polish Prime Minister Jaruzelski had ordered crucifixes removed from classroom walls, just as they had been banned in factories, hospitals, and other public institutions. Catholic bishops attacked the ban that had stirred waves of anger and resentment all across Poland. Ultimately the government relented, insisting that the law remain on the books, but agreeing not to press for removal of the crucifixes, particularly in the schoolrooms.

But one zealous Communist school administrator in Garwolin decided that the law was the law. So one evening he had seven large crucifixes removed from lecture halls where they had hung since the school's founding in the twenties.

Days later, a group of parents entered the school and hung more crosses. The administrator promptly had these taken down as well.

The next day two-thirds of the school's six hundred students staged a sit-in. When heavily armed riot police arrived, the students were forced into the streets. Then they marched, crucifixes held high, to a nearby church where they were joined by twenty-five hundred other students from nearby schools for a morning of prayer in support of the protest. Soldiers surrounded the church. But the pictures from inside of students holding crosses high above their heads flashed around the world. So did the words of the priest who delivered the message to the weeping congregation that morning.

"There is no Poland without a cross."

14

Conflict and Compromise in the West

> It is bad to live under a prince who permits nothing, but much worse to live under one who permits everything.
>
> —John Calvin

Before the War of the Crosses erupted in the streets of Poland in 1984, a similar battle had already been lost in the U.S. In 1980 the Supreme Court declared unconstitutional a Kentucky law requiring that the Ten Commandments be posted in public-school classrooms.[1]

In Poland the outcry against removal of the crucifixes led to mass defiance. The crucifixes were reinstated. But in Kentucky, when the offending commandments were taken down, the few holdouts, threatened with court action, soon capitulated.

What a repressive government could not force upon Poland was quietly accepted in an indifferent West. The Kentucky case is less important on its own merits than as a symbol of a growing movement in the courts that is narrowing the influence of religion in American life. Of the many cases, none has been more revealing—and bizarre—than one originating in the quiet Oklahoma town of Collinsville.

"Welcome to Collinsville," proclaims the sign marking the city limits where state highway 20 slices through this small Oklahoma town and slows down to fit the lifestyles of its three thousand citizens. Many of them are retired, enjoying Collinsville's grid of neat streets, the Crown Theater, Deb's Happytime Pizza, Collinsville Cablevision, and the Ranch House Café. Residents can choose from five feed-and-seed stores, eleven grocery stores, two funeral homes, and twenty-nine churches.

Collinsville's teenagers hold a somewhat dimmer view of its charms. "There's nothin' to do but get drunk and drag Main," says a young waitress at the Tastee Freez.

But in 1984 Collinsville became the focus of a national media spotlight when one of its citizens, thirty-six-year-old nurse Marian Guinn, sued her church for invasion of privacy.[2]

Marian Guinn was raised in Kansas as a southern Baptist. She married at eighteen and had a child at nineteen. Three other children followed, then a divorce. Guinn wanted to start over. In 1974 she moved to Collinsville, about twenty-five miles north of Tulsa, to live with her sister, Sue Hibbard.

Sue was active at the Collinsville Church of Christ, and Marian began attending the 110-member church with her sister. The members welcomed her. They baby-sat her children while she attended a high-school equivalency class; they provided food, clothing, and Christmas presents after Guinn moved into her own small rented house; the elders drove her to the hospital when her daughter had pneumonia. Later the church gave Guinn a car.

Guinn joined the church and was baptized. She eventually enrolled in college, then nursing school, and seemed to be getting her life together. But after a few years Marian Guinn's church attendance began to slip. Perhaps it was her school schedule; or maybe it was her romance with Pat Sharpe, part owner of Howland and Sharpe Pharmacy and former mayor of Collinsville.

Sharpe, like Marian Guinn, was divorced, and neighbors began to notice his blue-and-white Cadillac parked in her driveway late at night. In Collinsville their relationship was the juicy gossip item it might not have been in New York or Los Angeles. But to the Church of Christ leadership it was a spiritual problem. The elders felt that Guinn's relationship with Sharpe and lack of participation in the church were evidence of spiritual wavering. During the course of a conversation with one of the elders on an unrelated matter, Pat Sharpe admitted he and Marian were sleeping together.

In spite of the later assertion of Guinn's lawyer that "he was a single man. She was a single lady. And this is America," the Collinsville Church of Christ adhered to a different standard: the biblical law from the Old and New Testaments stating that sexual relations outside of marriage—fornication—is sin. They also abided by the biblical mandate that the church has a distinct responsibility "not to associate with sexually immoral people"[3] and that rebuking their sin must be public "so that the others may take warning."[4]

Church elders Ron Witten, Ted Moody, and Allen Cash met with Marian Guinn three times, praying with her and asking her to break off her relationship with Sharpe and return to the church's fellowship. Guinn tearfully refused. The elders said they would give her time to reconsider, but after a certain date they must make a public announcement urging the congregation to withdraw fellowship from her because of her lack of repentance. This was in accordance with the mandates of Matthew 18:15–17 and with the practices of the church.

At this point Guinn, a slight woman with large dark eyes, was angry and embarrassed. She scribbled a letter to the elders: "I do not want my name mentioned before the church except to tell them that I withdraw my membership immediately!" she wrote furiously. "I have never fully adopted your doctrine and never will! . . . You have no right to get up and say anything against me in church. . . . I have no choice but for all of us [herself and her children] to attend another church—another denomination where men do not set themselves up as judges for God. He does His own judging."

The elders maintained that the church was not some sort of club. Guinn had agreed to abide by its doctrine and adhere to scriptural mandates. She knew, or should have known, the consequences of her actions.

At the end of the Sunday-morning service on October 4, 1983, elder Ted Moody read a short letter to the congregation: "After much time spent in counseling, exhorting, encouraging, and prayer, we the elders of the Collinsville Church of Christ have no alternative but to lead in the withdrawing of fellowship from our sister in Christ, Marian Guinn."

Guinn accused the elders of libel. But to be libelous, the things being said have to be untrue, and Guinn acknowledged in court depositions that she was having an affair. She was content, therefore, to file a $1.3 million civil lawsuit against the church and its elders for invasion of privacy and emotional distress.

A Tulsa court took jurisdiction over the case, and in March 1984, a twelve-member jury sided with Guinn and awarded her $390,000 for her distress. One juror summed up their reasoning: "I don't see what right the church has to tell people how to live."

This is the kind of case that makes everyone mad.

Christians see within it a takeover of the church's realm by the state. After all, people don't join a church blindly, not knowing what is expected of them. And if the church can't hold its members to a biblical standard, what is it allowed to do? Become a Sunday-morning hymn-singing club? What right does the government have to prevent a church from maintaining standards of holiness, one of its primary purposes?

Meanwhile, many secularists view the elders' actions as the worst type of backwoods inquisition. Guinn's colorful Tulsa lawyer, Tommy Frasier, called the elders a "goon squad" and "the ayatollahs of Collinsville."

"It doesn't matter if she was fornicating up and down the street," Frasier declared angrily. "It doesn't give [the church] the right to stick their noses in."

One doubts that the citizens of Collinsville would agree that Guinn or anyone else has an inherent right to fornicate up and down highway 20. But Frasier's words reflect what has become a cardinal rule of American life: the right to personal autonomy.

The Guinn ruling pushes the privatization of religion to the extreme, allowing government to restrict religion to an internal matter bearing no relationship to one's behavior. It also says that the church has lost its right to define its own rules for membership.* And as Richard Neuhaus has written, "When an institution that is voluntary in membership cannot define the conditions of belonging, that institution in fact ceases to exist."[5]

But the church's principal task, as we have seen earlier, is a spiritual one—to proclaim the Good News and to cultivate holy living

---

*The government has consistently held that people not discriminate even in private organizations; but if a policy applies equally to all, it is nondiscriminatory. The Church of Christ rules applied equally to all. Guinn willingly surrendered her right to privacy when she joined the church. And while in some churches she might have been allowed to quietly resign, the particular doctrine of the Church of Christ, to which Guinn subscribed, does not permit resignation.

among its members. If a church cannot do this, it no longer has a purpose for existing.

The Guinn case is just one of the latest of assaults in the conflict between Christians and the state that have narrowed the influence of religion in American life. Others have dealt with equally sensitive issues, like religious activity on public property. The Evansville, Indiana, case is one.

At the Harper Elementary School in Evansville, teacher's aide Mary May and several Christian co-workers had met before classes every Tuesday morning since early 1981 for prayer, Bible reading, and discussion. Students were not allowed to participate. But in 1983 the principal told May and her seven fellow Christians that there were to be no more Tuesday-morning meetings—or they would all be fired.

Mary May eventually sued the board of education and the superintendent of schools, claiming that the school board had violated her First Amendment rights to free speech, free association, and the free exercise of religion. She also argued that other teachers and aides discussed politics, economics, and sports over their morning coffee before school; why couldn't she and her friends talk about God?

A school-board representative replied that impressionable elementary-school kids might see "her carry a Bible to and from a meeting in their school, even if it is before classes. To children, teachers are very strong authority figures." And, he added, school officials would be forced to make sure that no Bibles or other religious materials were left behind. "We don't want the children exposed to them," he concluded ominously.[6]

Even the right of religious organizations to insist that their employees adhere to their beliefs has been challenged, as in the much-publicized 1986 case of the Dayton Christian School. The Court ruled that it was "unlawful discriminatory practice" for any employer to refuse to hire an employee because of the religion or sex of that person.[7]

By this ruling, notes constitutional lawyer William Ball, St. John's Church, a Lutheran congregation, could not, solely on the basis of the applicant's religion, refuse to hire a pastor who was of some other religious faith; nor could St. Mary's Seminary, a Roman Catholic seminary, refuse to hire a woman as an instructor solely on the ground of her sex—in spite of the Canon Law of the Catholic Church that would forbid use of female instructors within the seminary.

A number of zoning cases have affected the right of worship in private homes. In Colorado Springs, minister Richard Blanche has been repeatedly cited for holding religious meetings in his home in violation of a city zoning ordinance. In Fairhaven, Massachusetts, local zoning officials ruled that Bible studies were home occupations and therefore prohibited under the town's property-use ordinances. In Los Angeles, officials ruled that home-occupancy regulations forbade orthodox Jews from holding prayer meetings in their homes. As civil-liberties lawyers could not help but note in a Stratford, Connecticut, case, prayer in home Bible studies is penalized while Tupperware parties enjoy the full protection of the Constitution.

More recent cases seem to reflect a determination to strip even the thin veneer of religious signs and symbols from culture.

During the spring of 1986 a last-minute decision by the Los Angeles Board of Education took God off the programs of area high-school commencements. A lawsuit filed by an area atheist successfully barred prayers, invocations, or religious observances from graduation ceremonies. Even as local schools made sure that offending prayers were removed from the programs, one principal noted, however, that students will, God forbid, occasionally mention Him during a speech. "If you happen to get a kid who's religious, they frequently thank God. That's all right. I'm not going to censor the kids' speeches."[8]

We can be grateful for that at least.

The height of hysteria was reached in a conflict involving the city seal of Zion, Illinois, which since 1902 has included a cross, dove, crown, scepter, and the words *God Reigns*. The emblem appears on the city's water tower, badges worn by public officials, and city vehicles.

Robert Sherman, director of the Illinois chapter of the American Atheists, though not a resident of Zion, was so offended by the seal on the water tower that he threatened to sue if it wasn't removed, describing the seal as the "most blatant abuse of religious symbols by a governmental unit in the history of mankind."[9]

But where religious symbols have been spared, it has been on grounds that offer little solace to the religious. The celebrated Pawtucket crèche decision is a case in point.

For forty years, one of the highlights for Pawtucket's predominantly Catholic citizenry was the annual Christmas display that included something for everyone: Santa Claus, reindeer, Christmas trees, and a crèche scene with baby Jesus, Mary and Joseph, and assorted barn animals.

The crèche was challenged, however, because it was paid for ($1,365, with another $20 a year to maintain it) by tax money; this was said to be an infringement on the separation of church and state.

In 1984 the Supreme Court, in a 5–4 decision, upheld the city's right to display the crèche—because, as Chief Justice Warren Burger expressed it, the crèche served a "legitimate secular purpose." After all, he noted, the crèche was merely "a neutral harbinger of the holiday season, useful for commercial purposes, but devoid of any inherent meaning."[10]

Burger's words are significant beyond the Pawtucket case: religion "devoid of any inherent meaning" defines that which is legally and culturally acceptable in contemporary culture.

A torrent of church-state cases, which have with rare exception been decided against the church, was unleashed by the landmark 1963 school-prayer case, Abington School District v. Schempp. Contrary to popular opinion, the most radical import of this case was not that public Bible reading or organized prayer could not be held in public schools, but the grounds on which the court made its decision. While acknowledging as historical fact that religion had been a crucial aspect of human experience, it for the first time held as conscious policy that the state must be indifferent toward all religion in any form.

This was a dramatic turnabout from the 1954 Zorach v. Clauson case, in which Justice William O. Douglas, a civil libertarian, explicitly upheld what had been the law from the nation's beginning. Douglas refused to "find in the Constitution a requirement that the government show a callous indifference to religious groups. That would be preferring those who believe in no religion over those who do believe."[11]

Two dissenting justices in Abington warned that "unilateral devotion to the concept of neutrality can lead to . . . not simply noninterference and noninvolvement with the religious which the Constitution commands, but a brooding and pervasive devotion to the secular and a passive, or even active, hostility to the religious."[12]

The dissenters were prophets. No phrase could more aptly summarize public life of the last two decades than this "brooding and pervasive devotion to the secular." Seven years after Abington the Court redefined religion. What had been in 1931 "obedience to the will of God" was now defined as "a sincere and meaningful belief which occupies in the life of its possessor a place parallel to that filled by God."[13] Thus by 1970 religious belief had become a belief in whatever one might fancy—from the Rockettes to Ramtha.

Then in 1973 came the case that aroused the deepest passions of all, Roe v. Wade.

Could Roe v. Wade—or the entire Pro-Choice Movement—have been imagined without the dominance of a "passive, or even active, hostility to the religious"? The right to life, guaranteed by the Constitution, had always been understood as a sacred right, a right that preexisted all governments, grounded in the relationship of the Creator with His creation. But as Richard Neuhaus observed, "for the first time . . . it was explicitly stated that it is possible to address these issues of ultimate importance without any reference to Judeo-Christian tradition. . . . For the first time in American jurisprudence, the Supreme Court explicitly excluded philosophy, ethics and religion as factors in its deliberation."[14] And in *Roe v. Wade*, the Court replaced the right to life and its transcendent origins with a new right, the right to privacy or individual autonomy—regardless of the expense.

The Supreme Court has thus held that great moral issues can be decided without reference to transcendent values. The decision assumes that government's sole purpose is to protect individual, personal values.

Why such a radical reversal—from a court explicitly approving religion's crucial public role to one committed to its total privatization—in just nine years? The dramatic change has been nothing short of a judicial revolution, but the reasons for the revolution are not so much legal as political and cultural. Judges, after all, don't live in cocoons—they go to church, listen to television, read magazines, belong to clubs, and talk to their families over the breakfast table.

To understand this cultural backdrop, however, we must go back to 1945, Year Zero. After fifteen years of depression and war, unemployment and rationing, Americans were determined to make up for lost time—and as the years went on, times were good.

The nation's nuclear monopoly seemed to assure security; for the first time in history nearly everyone could afford their own home; millions of returning veterans went to college on the GI bill; business boomed. Eisenhower's 1956 reelection theme, "Peace, Progress, and Prosperity," captured the mood of the nation.

Admittedly, there were undercurrents of discontent. The Korean War had not been lost, but it hadn't been won either. The "beats," led by Jack Kerouac and Allen Ginsberg, had already "dropped out" of society. In *The Lonely Crowd*, sociologist David Riesman described how self-discipline and self-motivation were being replaced by peer pressure as the primary determinant of American character. And though church attendance was up, religion was, in the words of an eminent historian, "so empty and contentless, so conformist, so utilitarian, so sentimental, so individualistic, and so self-righteous."[15]

On the surface, however, these were the best of times. The sixties began with the same confidence. A handsome young president expressed America's bravado and promised the moon. "Let every nation know, whether it wishes us well or ill, that we shall pay any price, bear any burden, meet any hardship, support any friend, oppose any foe to assure the survival and the success of liberty."[16] The future held only opportunity.

Five years later a rapid-fire series of historical events had shaken Americans' faith in their political institutions. Our vigorous young heroes were dead with the assassinations of John Kennedy, Bobby Kennedy, and Martin Luther King, Jr. Streets across the country reeked of pot and tear gas as a new generation bombed buildings, did drugs, and dodged the draft. Once again society was adrift.

The nuclear monopoly was lost when an aggressive Soviet empire acquired the bomb. An unending war in Vietnam took thousands of lives—and network television brought the carnage into American living rooms each evening. A once-popular and powerful president was forced to give up his reelection bid. Just a few years later, a White House scandal shook the confidence of the nation—and caused a disgraced president to resign in ignominy.

At the same time, a destructive philosophic trend had gripped American intellectuals. The long fuse lit by the ideas of Nietzsche, Freud, and Darwin finally set off an explosion of relativism. All moral distinctions were equally valid and equally invalid since all were equally subjective.

A bland civil religion was no match for these powerful trends. Millions felt betrayed by their leaders and resentful that the establishment had any more claim to truth than they did. Sociologist Daniel Bell argues that "the ultimate support for any social system is the acceptance by the population of a moral justification of authority."[17] Now this support was removed and all authority questioned.

These developments were most obvious in the universities, which became both centers of political activism and defenders of relativism. But just as the influence of the university was expanding, it suddenly had very little to teach. The very idea of truth had been called into question as early as 1940, when Reinhold Niebuhr warned that America was a victim of "an education adrift in relativity that doubted all values, and a degraded science that shirked the spiritual issues."[18]

Universities responded by simply changing the goal of education. Where once the object of learning had been the discovery of truth, now each student must be allowed to decide truth for himself. Dogma, not ignorance, became the enemy.

The youth culture of the universities took what they were taught to heart, developing what scholar James Hitchcock calls "a visceral sense that all forms of established authority, all rules, all demands for obedience, were inherently illegitimate."[19]

Influenced by existential writers such as Jean-Paul Sartre and Albert Camus, the generation of the sixties made autonomy its god and sought meaning in the pleasures of easy sex and hard drugs. The consequences were felt not only in private standards of morality, but in the literature and art of the times. Take for example the work of Andy Warhol, who on his death in early 1987 was hailed by *Newsweek* as "the most famous American artist of our time."[20] Warhol was responsible for the rise of "pop art" in the early sixties, gaining international fame for his two hundred Campbell soup cans, an oil painting of row after row of those familiar red and white labels.

Inspired by the mass production techniques of industrial societies, pop art deliberately denied the distinctions between high culture and popular culture. Implicitly and explicitly it asserted relativism's principal tenet that all values are equal: The distinction between bad taste and good taste is elitist; all notions of bad and good are merely one class's way of snubbing another. There are no lasting values, no timeless truths, only artifacts of the moment.

Within such an aesthetic vision there can be no room for the eternal. Shortly before his death, Warhol remarked that he always thought his tombstone should be blank. Then as an afterthought he added, "Well, actually I'd like it to say 'figment.'"[21]

In place of MacArthur's spiritual recrudescence, the post-war generation created figments: images devoid of meaning in place of objective truth. These figments set the stage for the "me decade" of the seventies and the acquisitive yuppieism of the eighties captured in one popular T-shirt and bumper-sticker slogan, "He who dies with the most toys wins."

Pascal's second option has thus become the route of western experience: Separated from God, men seek satisfaction in their senses. This is more than mindless hedonism; it is a world view in which, according to professor Allen Bloom, "the self has become the modern substitute for the soul."[22]

A 1985 study titled *Habits of the Heart* calls this attitude "utilitarian individualism," arguing that the two primary ways Americans attempt to order their lives are through "the dream of personal success" and "vivid personal feeling."[23] This was reinforced as those interviewed consistently defined their ultimate goals in terms of self-fulfillment or self-realization. Marriage was seen as an opportunity for personal development, work as a method of personal advancement, church as a means of personal fulfillment.

What this study reflects is simply the inevitable consequences of four decades of the steady erosion of absolute values. As a result we live with a massive case of schizophrenia. Outwardly, we are a religious people, but inwardly our religious beliefs make no difference in how we live. We are obsessed with self; we live, raise families, govern, and die as though God does not exist, just as Nietzsche predicted a century ago.

This cultural revolution, rendering God irrelevant, has permeated the Western media, the instrument that not only reflects, but often shapes societal attitudes. God is tolerated in the media only when He is bland enough to pose no threat. One national columnist, annoyed by what she regarded as religious zealots, wrote longingly of ancient Rome, where "the people regarded all the modes of worship as equally true, the intellectuals regarded them as equally false, and the politicians regarded them as equally useful. What a well-blessed time. . . . I think we could try to emulate the laid-back spirit it reveals."[24]

More often, however, the media reflect something less than this laid-back spirit and at times even seems infected with a "brooding and pervasive devotion to the secular—and . . . hostility to the religious," a view confining religion to a "neutral status, devoid of any inherent meaning."

One illustration was the coverage of the so-called Monkey Trial II, the December 1981 challenge to the Arkansas statute requiring that creationism be taught in schools alongside evolution. The following description of the two parties involved appeared on the front page of the December 21, 1981, *Washington Post*.[25] "The ACLU and the New York firm of Skadden Arps attacked the Arkansas law with a powerful case. Their brief is so good that there is talk of publishing it. Their witnesses gave brilliant little summaries of several fields of science, history of sciences, history and religious philosophy." Such was the enlightened plaintiff.

The witnesses defending creationism, however, were "impassioned believers, rebellious educators and scientific oddities. All but one of the creation scientists came from obscure colleges or Bible schools. The one who didn't said he believed diseases dropped from space, that evolution caused Nazism, and that insects may be more intelligent than humans but are hiding their abilities."

With whom were uninformed readers going to align themselves? The firm of Skadden Arps with its brilliant summaries or the backwoods idiots from no-name colleges who probably still make live animal sacrifices up in the hills when nobody is looking?

Though such a negative slant within news coverage appears regularly, the more common tactic is to ignore religion altogether. A few years ago the late theologian and Christian writer Francis Schaeffer approached PBS to air *How Shall We Then Live*, his film series presenting a view of history, creation, and the universe framed in the Judeo-Christian tradition. He was turned down cold; his series was "too religious."

In a slick manifesto called *Cosmos*, Carl Sagan artfully packaged his own creed: "The Cosmos is all there is, or was, or ever will be."[26] The Supreme Court's working definition of religion, "A sincere and meaningful belief which occupies in the life of its possessor a place parallel to that filled by God," would seem to identify Sagan's video treatment of the Cosmos (which he religiously capitalizes) as religious. But PBS and public-school classrooms regularly air *Cosmos*, while they shun Schaeffer's or any similar work.*

I've often encountered the same attitude in interviewers who suggest, just before we go on the air, that we steer away from religious topics. "Some people take offense, you know," said one. Another advised me it was against station policy to discuss religion on the air. Others say nothing; once we begin they simply steer the questions to the comparatively safer ground of prisons, criminal justice, or politics. They usually appear aghast when I bring the answers back to my experiences with Jesus Christ.

The print medium does the same thing. Over the years since I became a Christian, I have always deliberately explained that I have "accepted Jesus Christ." These words are invariably translated into "Colson's professed religious experience." I discovered that one major U.S. daily, as a matter of policy, will not print the two words *Jesus Christ* together; when combined, the editor says, it represents an editorial judgment.

Such reporting is not always a matter of hostility; it often reflects the reporter's lack of knowledge in spiritual matters. It can also be the result of the very nature of news itself. By definition, the media report events that are out of the ordinary—the bizarre, the hostile, the aberrant; otherwise news is not news. Thus, coverage of Christianity, when it

*In fairness it should be noted that some viewers believe there is a significant quality difference between the two film series. Still, that was not the basis of PBS's rejection of the Schaeffer series.

occurs at all, is most often the outlandish exception rather than the norm practiced by millions of Christians daily.

Consider the sensational coverage in early 1987 of Rev. Carl Thitchener, a New York minister who distributed condoms to his congregation to dramatize the AIDS crisis. Camera crews obligingly descended on his church; evening news broadcasts featured Thitchener's parishioners braying the word *condoms* as he somberly challenged them to repeat it after him. The ludicrous scene made for an entertaining close-out to the evening news, featured as a current event in the church.

What the media failed to distinguish, however, is that as a Unitarian Universalist, Thitchener is not a Christian minister. His church rejects the divinity of Christ. The media also overlooked several small details about Thitchener's life and character. Consider, for example, his police record: "Subject: male, Caucasian, 54. . . . Pled guilty to second degree assault, 1957. Convicted of exposing himself, 1958. Convicted of drunk driving, 1975. Convicted of 'Parading naked in front of Brownies,' 1982. Convicted of drunk driving, 1984."[27]

Such selective media focus is not the result of a conscious antireligious policy but is indicative of a pervasive cultural attitude, what G. K. Chesterton described as "a taboo of tact or convention, whereby we are free to say that a man does this or that because of his nationality, or his profession, or his place of residence, or his hobby, but not because of his creed about the very cosmos in which he lives."[28]

Harvard psychiatrist Robert Coles gives a poignant illustration of this taboo. He found he could write about almost any human motivation without having its authenticity questioned. But when he once wrote about a Civil-Rights worker who risked his life "out of love for Jesus," people around him considered the worker, and maybe Coles himself, to be phony.[29]*

The same disposition to dismiss religious influence pervades the field of education.

Paul Vitz, professor of psychology at New York University, examined sixty social-studies textbooks used by 87 percent of the nation's elementary-school children in a study done under the auspices of the U.S. Department of Education.[30] He looked for "primary" references to religious activity such as prayer, church attendance, or participation in religious ceremonies, as well as "secondary" references, such as citing

---

*In short, orthodox faith is treated the way homosexuality once was: it is tolerated as long as it is practiced only by consenting adults and isn't flaunted in public.

the date when a church was built. What Vitz discovered was a "total absence of any primary religious text about typical contemporary American religious life"[31] and only a few secondary pictures and passages touching upon the religious. The few direct references to historic religion centered on Amish, Catholic, Jewish, and Mormon faiths, leaving a "very curious" deletion of characteristic Protestant religious life.[32]

Religion appeared to be relevant only in remote points in history. Pictures of pilgrims and the first Thanksgiving were bountiful—without any mention of to whom thanks was being given. One mother told Vitz that her son's social-studies book made no mention of religion as part of the pilgrims' life. Her son told her that "Thanksgiving was when the pilgrims gave thanks to the Indians." When the mother called the principal of her son's suburban New York City school to point out that Thanksgiving originated when the pilgrims thanked God, the principal responded, "That's your opinion." He continued by saying that the schools could only teach what was in the books.[33]

Vitz concluded that the study suggests "a psychological motive behind the obvious censorship of religion present in these books. Those responsible for these books appear to have a deep-seated fear of any form of active contemporary Christianity, especially serious, committed Protestantism. This fear could have led the authors to deny and repress the importance of this kind of religion in American life."[34]†

This elimination of the transcendent from serious public discussion is merely a reflection of an underlying cultural revolution that has eliminated absolute values from public consciousness, thus ushering in an age of relativism. This has inevitably affected public policy, as in the court decisions discussed earlier, and it has turned our traditional notion of pluralism on its head.

Historically pluralism meant that conflicting and firmly held values could be voiced in public debate, and from such debates might emerge

†In the midst of the controversy aroused by the Vitz study, Doubleday, a major publisher, announced its decision to write God back into school textbooks. "We made a decision long before Judge Hand's decision in Alabama that you can't leave religion out of textbooks," said Herb Adams, president of Doubleday's Laidlaw Educational Publishing division, which ranks among the nation's top ten textbook publishers. "The allegation that religion had been softpedaled in textbooks is true," he added. So by the end of the year Doubleday will have prepared a supplementary book that discusses the role of religion in the development of the country. It is being designed to go along with existing history and social-studies books. Many other textbooks will be fully rewritten and revised, said Adams, but it will be a "long, long process." Adams added that the reason religion had been omitted from textbooks in the past was that publishers wanted to "avoid controversy." Evangelical Press News Service (February 6, 1987).

a consensus of values by which a community would be governed. But relativism, which insists that there are no objective truths, drives all values out of public debate, since in a pluralistic society they are "divisive." In an attempt to be neutral, we ignore all values. Columnist Joseph Sobran writes, "The prevailing notion is that the state should be neutral as to religion, and furthermore, that the best way to be neutral about it is to avoid all mention of it. By this sort of logic, nudism is the best compromise among different styles of dress. The secularist version of 'pluralism' amounts to theological nudism."[35]

This modern vision of pluralism has infiltrated nearly every branch and level of government, progressively institutionalizing the privatization of religious values. The absurd extreme to which this has taken us is illustrated by the New York law outlawing the use of children in pornography.[36] In its preamble the statute specifically states that it is not based on any moral or religious considerations. Only by making such a disclaimer did the bill's drafters believe it could withstand a court challenge that it was "religiously" motivated and thus unconstitutional.

Congressman Henry Hyde offers a personal perspective of what it means to run afoul of the secular need for control. In 1976 Congress passed the Hyde Amendment, which barred federal funding for abortion in the Medicaid program. Planned Parenthood, the American Civil Liberties Union, and other groups challenged the amendment's constitutionality, claiming that it "used the fist of government to smash the wall of separation between church and state by imposing a peculiarly religious view of when a human life begins." To prove their theory, the lawyers for these organizations asked to review Hyde's mail for expressions of religious sentiment. They also hired a private investigator who followed Hyde to a Mass for the unborn and took notes as the congressman read Scripture, took communion, and prayed. The investigator even recorded in his notebook the inscription on the cathedral's statue of St. Thomas: "I die the king's good servant, but God's first."

In an affidavit, the plaintiffs presented these observations to the court as proof of a religious conspiracy. They claimed that Hyde, as a devout Catholic, could not separate his religion from his politics and that the amendment was therefore unconstitutional. The judge threw out the affidavit, and Planned Parenthood and the ACLU finally lost their case in 1980 when the Supreme Court affirmed the amendment's constitutionality.

Though victorious, Hyde was infuriated by his opponents' tactics. "The anger I felt when they tried to disenfranchise me because of my religion stayed with me. These are dangerous people who make dangerous arguments. Some powerful members of the cultural elite in our country are so paralyzed by the fear that theistic notions might reassert themselves into the official activities of government that they will go to Gestapo lengths to inhibit such expression."[37]

This stripping away of religious import is not limited to the U.S. Europe has become a post-Christian culture in which the principal religious influence is visible in art treasures and cathedrals filled with tourists rather than worshipers. Church attendance is 4 percent in West Germany, East Germany, Scandinavia, and Austria. In France regular attendance at Mass is below 15 percent, while in Spain it has dropped to between 3 and 5 percent. And in England, site of the great nineteenth-century awakening and home of missionary movements, more people worship in mosques than in the Church of England. Regular church attendance is no more than 6 percent of the population.[38]

In fact, resistance to Christian influence has become overt. Donald Bloesch cites an official on ecclesiastic affairs in Sweden who boasted, "We are dismantling the church bit by bit and where necessary we are using economic means to do so." Denmark is presently refusing to renew the visas of evangelical missionaries, particularly from America. There are reports on the desecration of churches and Christian cemeteries in Sweden and West Germany.[39]

Perhaps one of the most fitting images of this spiritual apathy was captured years ago in Italian filmmaker Federico Fellini's award-winning film *La Dolce Vita*. The movie opens with a panorama of Rome's magnificent skyline, the grand dome of St. Peter's in the center. A helicopter carrying a large object appears in the distance. The camera zooms in; the object is a statue of Christ being hauled away from a downtown square. The camera then focuses on a group of young sunbathers who, distracted from their pleasure by the whirring blades, laugh mockingly. Why shouldn't Jesus take the bus like everyone else? The helicopter flies on to discard its outdated cargo on a trashpile, and the youngsters return to their sun worship.

Fellini filmed his blasphemous scene in 1959, but it has proved prophetic.

Many believe that religious values and liberties have fallen victim to some sinister conspiracy in which the ACLU, humanist educators, and the media meet in darkened corridors of CBS headquarters to plot the demise of religion in America.

Admittedly, the ACLU has a powerful lobby, the media are unsympathetic, and skeptics dominate college campuses. But even if such forces were organized to consciously eradicate religious values they could do little to wipe out real Christianity.

Christian values are in retreat in the West today, primarily, I believe, because of the church itself. If Christianity has failed to stem the rising tides of relativism it is because the church in many instances has lost the convicting force of the gospel message. Earlier we argued that while humanists did not understand humans, Christians did not understand Christianity. This is surely evident in post-World-War-II Christianity, which has become a religion of private comfort and blessing that fills up whatever small holes in life that pleasure, money and success have left open, what Bonhoeffer called a "god of the gaps."[40]

Television's emergence as the dominant medium of communication gave birth to the slickly marketed health-wealth-and-success gospel rampant in today's church. As Donald Bloesch notes, "I believe that technology can be harnessed in the service of the gospel, but I recognize that such a venture entails the risk of accommodating the Christian message to technological values. Utility, i.e., practical efficacy and tangible results, rather than fidelity to truth then becomes the criterion for evaluating the program of the church."[41] When asked about his affluent lifestyle in the face of a needy world, one prominent evangelist explained, "I live in one of the finest homes. I drive one of the finest, safest cars, and if a newer, safer one were to pull up in front of my door, I'd go out and say, 'I want it,' . . . God designed life for believers to be an abundant life, . . . God designed for you to live in the overflow."[42]

In addition to succumbing to this arrogant heresy, the church has allowed itself to become dangerously polarized into two camps: politicized and privatized views of faith. The problem is, neither view has anything to do with historic Christianity.

The politicization of the church in the sixties was largely the work of liberal mainline denominations whose bureaucracies issued weekly policy papers on social issues. They became so absorbed in social causes that they neglected the church's first mission and in the process suffered declining membership.* Just as their influence was waning, the

---

*As James Wall observed in the liberal *Christian Century*:
Mainline religion . . . has failed to convince the public that there is a link between its politics and its theology because, perhaps unwittingly, it has allowed religion to be confined to what David Tracy has perceptively termed the "reservation of the spirit."

political polarity was reversed, and the Christian New Right emerged as a potent force in American politics. They made the same mistake—equating the gospel with a particular partisan agenda. Many in the New Right appear ready to make politics the ultimate goal, putting politics ahead of spirituality.

Politicized religion simply reinforces the tendency toward civil religion, which was perhaps best articulated by Dwight Eisenhower who once said that American government makes no sense "unless it is founded in a deeply felt religious faith—and I don't care what it is."[43] What Eisenhower was referring to was nothing more than a generic religion—any brand will do, no-name is the best—to encourage civic duty.

On the other side is privatized faith, which divorces religious and spiritual beliefs from public actions. Like its politicized counterpart, privatized faith has a mixed heritage theologically and politically. In the nineteenth century, conservative evangelicals led the abolition campaign and progressive social reforms; in the early twentieth century, they abandoned this commitment in reaction against modernism and the so-called social gospel. Fundamentalists separated from the mainstream, leaving the world's concerns behind so they could preach the good news among the faithful.

All of this dramatically changed by the late seventies when Jerry Falwell led a fundamentalist stampede back to center stage. Ironically, liberals who had been so socially concerned were now, in reaction perhaps, arguing that faith is a private matter. Perhaps it depends on which issues are identified at any given moment as religious and moral.

This would seem the case in the 1984 presidential campaign. Democratic challenger Walter Mondale attacked President Reagan's public statements that "without God, democracy will not and cannot long endure" as "moral McCarthyism."[44]

Mondale's running mate, Geraldine Ferraro, added, "Personal religious convictions have no place in political campaigns or in dictating public policy."[45] In an interview with the New York Times, Ms. Ferraro asserted that her faith was "very, very private."[46]

. . . the political left has had a morbid fear of religion encroaching on the secular realm. This fear leads, at its extreme, to legal action if a crèche shows up on city property. Such expressions of cultural religion hardly pose a threat to the separation of church and state, but the doctrine of the left is that "religion" must not lead the public debate. Instead, it must be on call to serve only when commanded by secular leaders.

Ironically, this view of religion imposes as rigid an attitude toward societal solutions as that found on the political right. Mainline religion has for too long taken this "closed" attitude for fear of appearing to impose religious solutions in a pluralistic culture.

Governor Mario Cuomo of New York made the most eloquent defense of this privately engaging but publicly irrelevant faith during his much-publicized speech at the University of Notre Dame in 1984. As a practicing Catholic, he said, he subscribed to his church's teachings on the question of abortion. But as an officeholder in a secular society he could not impose his views on anyone else. So far, so good.

Cuomo then went on to say that he was under no obligation to advocate the views of his church or to seek a public consensus based on those views (which he confesses to be the truth of God) until there is what he calls a "prudential judgment" that could justify such a course.[47] In other words, one is under no obligation to provide leadership on moral issues. Thus, Cuomo carried privatized faith to its ultimate conclusion when he asserted that he could, while agreeing with his church, nonetheless tolerate or even support pro-choice legislation. This clever but dangerous argument gives sophistry a bad name.

Those who fear the encroachment of religion in public life can relax. Neither politicized civil religion or privatized religion is likely to impose itself on our government or social institutions, for in either case there is nothing to impose. The one holds the gospel hostage to a particular political agenda while the other is so private it refuses to have any impact on daily life in the public arena. Thus is the divided church impotent to reverse the tides of secularism.

In 1896 the Victorian-minded planners of St. John the Divine in New York city envisioned a great Episcopal cathedral that would bring glory to God. Nearly a century later, though the immense structure is still under construction, it is in use—in a way that its planners might well have regarded with dismay.[48]

St. John's Thanksgiving service has featured Japanese Shinto priests; Muslin Sufis perform biannually; Lenten services have focused on the ecological "passion of the earth" (one gathers that Christ's passion is passé). The cathedral has featured "Christa," a huge crucifix with a female Christ, and St. John's pulpit welcomes everyone from the Rev. Jesse Jackson to Norman Mailer, rabbis, imams, Buddhist monks, secular politicians, atheist scientists, and during the feast of St. Francis in October 1985, an arkload of animals received blessings from the high altar, including a llama, an elephant, and a goose.

Logistical questions such as curbing your elephant within the cathedral notwithstanding, St. John the Divine seems to have ceased to be a house of the one God of the Scriptures, and has become instead a house of many gods. Novelist Kurt Vonnegut Jr. wrote for the cathedral's centennial brochure that "the Cathedral is to this atheist . . . a suitable monument to persons of all ages and classes. I go there often to be refreshed by a sense of nonsectarian community which has the best interests of the whole planet at heart."

Underneath the main altar are seven stone chambers housing the cathedral's artists-in-residence: two painters, three photographers, a sculptor, a calligrapher, a poet, a blacksmith, and a high-wire performer. I suppose every church should have its own trapeze artist.

Dean James Morton has encountered opposition. Some Episcopalians are concerned about the menorah, Islamic prayer rug, and Shinto vases that adorn the sanctuary altar along with the crucifix. But the dean responds, "This cathedral is a place for birth Episcopalians like me who feel constricted by the notion of excluding others. What happens here—the Sufi dances, the Buddhist prayers—are serious spiritual experiences. We make God a Minnie Mouse in stature when we say these experiences profane a Christian church."

As Newsweek observed admiringly, "The eclectic dean of St. John's seems to be reaching for a theology as high and wide as the cathedral he serves."

Maybe so. Or perhaps his grand cathedral, like the United Nations meditation room, is a monument to no god at all—and thus, a fitting icon of twentieth-century Western culture.

15

The Naked Public Square

The greatest question of our time is not communism versus individualism, not Europe versus America, not even the East versus the West; it is whether men can live without God.

—Will Durant

A recent *Time* magazine cover story titled "Ethics" raised many disturbing issues: "What's wrong? Hypocrisy, betrayal and greed unsettle the nation's soul. . . . At a time of moral disarray, America seeks to rebuild a structure of values."[1]

Yet even in the midst of this long-overdue national soul-searching, the authors still hedged the issue. "Who is to decide what are the 'right' values?" wrote a professor of education. "Does ultimate moral authority lie with institutions such as church and state to codify and impose? Or, in a free society, are these matters of private conscience, with final choice belonging to the individual?"[2]

What such experts do not see is that by raising such questions, they are pointing to the answer. We live in a society in which all transcendent values have been removed and thus there is no moral standard by which anyone can say right is right and wrong is wrong.

480

What we live in is, in the memorable image of Richard Neuhaus, a naked public square.

On the surface, a value-free society sounds liberal, progressive, and enlightened. It certainly sounded that way to the generations of the sixties and early seventies—probably many of the same people now wringing their hands on the pages of *Time*. But when the public square is naked, truth and values drift with the winds of public favor and there is nothing objective to govern how we are to live together. Why should we be shocked, then, by the inevitable consequences; why should we be surprised to discover that society yields what is planted?

Why are we surprised that crime soars steadily among juveniles when parents fail to set standards of right behavior in the home, when school teachers will not offer a moral opinion in the classroom, either out of fear of litigation or because they cannot "come from a position of what is right and wrong," as one New Jersey teacher put it?[3]

Why are we horrified at the growing consequences of sexual promiscuity—including a life-threatening epidemic—when sex is treated as casually as going out for a Frosty at Wendy's?

Why are we shocked at disclosures of religious leaders bilking their ministries of millions when they've been preaching a get-rich-quick gospel all along?

Why the wonderment over the fact that, for enough dollars or sexual favors, government employees and military personnel sell out their nation's secrets? As C. S. Lewis wrote forty years ago, "We laugh at honor and are shocked to find traitors in our midst."[4]

Why is it so surprising that Wall Street yuppies make fast millions on insider information or tax fraud? Without objective values, the community or one's neighbor has no superior claim over one's own desires.

Whether we like to hear it or not, we are reaping the consequences of the decades since World War II when we have, in Solzhenitsyn's words, "forgotten God." What we have left is the reign of relativism.

As discussed in an earlier chapter, humanity cannot survive without some form of law. "The truly naked public square is at best a transitional phenomenon," wrote Richard John Neuhaus. "It is a vacuum begging to be filled."[5] Excise belief in God and you are left with only two principals: the individual and the state. In this situation, however, there is no mediating structure to generate moral values and, therefore, no counterbalance to the inevitable ambitions of the state. "The naked public square cannot remain naked, the direction is toward the state-as-church, toward totalitarianism."[6]

As we have seen, this has already occurred in Marxist nations where the death of God has created a new form of messiah—the all-powerful state whose political ideology acquires the force of religion. The same is true, though not as extreme, in the West where traditional religious influences have been excluded from public debates either by law or Chesterton's "taboo of tact or convention." As a result, government is free to make its own ultimate judgments. Hence government ideology acquires the force of religion.

The removal of the transcendent sucks meaning from the law. Without an absolute standard of moral judgment backing government "morality," where is the protection for the minorities and the powerless? "When in our public life no legal prohibition can be articulated with a force of transcendent authority, then there are no rules rooted in ultimacies that can protect the poor, the powerless and the marginal, as indeed there are now no rules protecting the unborn, and only fragile inhibitions surrounding the aged and defective."[7]

With no ultimate reference point supporting it—no just cause for obedience—law can only be enforced by the bayonet. So the state seeks more and more coercive power.

But the most dangerous consequence of the naked public square is the loss of community.

A community is a gathering of people around shared values, a commitment to one another and to common ideals and aspirations that cannot be created by government. As Arthur Schlesinger observed, "We have forgotten that constitutions work only as they reflect an actual sense of community."[8]

Without commitment to community, individual responsibility quickly erodes. One vivid illustration of this was a Princeton student's protest after President Jimmy Carter proposed reinstating the draft registration in 1977. Newspapers across the country showed the young man defiantly carrying a placard proclaiming: "Nothing is worth dying for."

To many, these words seemed an affirmation of life, the ultimate assertion of individual worth. What they fail to reckon with, however, is the reverse of that slogan: if nothing is worth dying for, is anything worth living for? A society that has no reference points beyond itself "increasingly becomes a merely contractual arrangement," says sociologist Peter Berger. The problem with that, he continues, is that human beings will not die for a social contract. And "unless people are prepared, if necessary, to die for it," a society cannot long survive.[9]

In these last twenty years of the twentieth century, we are sailing uncharted waters. Never before in the history of Western civilization has the public square been so devoid of transcendent values.

The notion of law rooted in transcendent truth, in God Himself, is not the invention of Christian fundamentalists calling naïvely for America to return to its Christian roots. The roots of American law are as much in the works of Cicero and Plato as in the Bible. But if fundamentalist are guilty of distorting American history, their critics are guilty of distorting the whole history of Western civilization.

Plato, in terms as religious as Moses or David, claimed that transcendent norms were the true foundations for civil law and order. He taught that "there exist divine moral laws, not easy to apprehend, but operating upon all mankind." He refuted the argument of some Sophists that there was no distinction between virtue and vice, and he affirmed that "God, not man, is the measure of all things."[10]

Cicero, to whom the American Founding Fathers looked for guidance, maintained that religion is indispensable to private morals and public order and that it alone provided the concord by which people could live together.[11] "True law," wrote Cicero, "is right reason in agreement with Nature; it is of universal application and everlasting; it summons to duty by its commands, and averts from wrong-doing by its prohibitions."

Augustine wrote The City of God to defend the role of Christianity as the essential element in preserving society, stating that what the pagans "did not have the strength to do out of love of country, the Christian God demands of [citizens] out of love of Himself. Thus, in a general breakdown of morality and of civic virtues, divine Authority intervened to impose frugal living, continence, friendship, justice and concord among citizens."[12] Augustine contended that without true justice emanating from a sovereign God there could never be the concord of which Cicero wrote.

During the French Revolution, Edmund Burke acknowledged that the attempt to build a secularized state was not so much irreverent as irrational. "We know, and it is our pride to know, that man is by his constitution a religious animal; that atheism is against, not only our reason, but our instincts; and that it cannot prevail long."[13]

Religion has always been a decisive factor in the shaping of the American experience. According to one modern scholar, it was the

Founding Fathers' conviction that "republican government depends for its health on values that over the not-so-long run must come from religion."[14]

John Adams believed that the *moral* order of the new nation depended on biblical religion. "If I were an atheist . . . I should believe that chance had ordered the Jews to preserve and propagate to all mankind the doctrine of a supreme, intelligent, wise, almighty sovereign of the universe, which I believe to be the great essential principle of all morality, and consequently of all civilization."[15]

Tocqueville, the shrewd observer of American democracy, maintained that "religion in America takes no direct part in the government of society, but it must be regarded as the first of their political institutions. . . . How is it possible that society should escape destruction if the moral tie is not strengthened in proportion as the political tie is relaxed? And what can be done with a people who are their own masters if they are not submissive to the Deity?"[16]

In considering such lessons from the past, historians Will and Ariel Durant cited the agnostic Joseph Renan, who in 1866 wrote, "What would we do without [Christianity]? . . . If rationalism wishes to govern the world without regard to the religious needs of the soul, the experience of the French Revolution is there to teach us the consequences of such a blunder." The Durants concluded, "There is no significant example in history before our time, of a society successfully maintaining moral life without the aid of religion."[17]

The supreme irony of our century is that in those nations that still enjoy the greatest human freedoms, this traditional role of religion is denigrated; while in nations that have fallen under the oppressor's yoke, the longing for the spiritual is keenest. In the West intellectuals widely disdain religion; in the Soviet Union they cry out for its return.

In a wave of recent articles, three popular contemporary Soviet writers, Vasily Bykov, Viktor Astafyev, and Chinghiz Aytamatov, have blamed Russia's moral degradation upon the decline of religion. "Who extinguished the light of goodness in our soul? Who blew out the lamp of our conscience, toppled it into a dark, deep pit in which we are groping, trying to find the bottom, a support and some kind of guiding light to the future?" asks Astafyev, a Christian, in *Our Contemporary*, a popular Moscow journal.[18] Though a Muslim, Aytmatov centers his writings on Christ, whom he admires as a greater influence than Mohammed. He and his fellow writers have boldly attacked Communism for creating "an all-encompassing belief" that has plunged the Russian people into a moral abyss. Bykov, winner of every Soviet literary award, declares there can be no morality without faith.[19]

Yet our twentieth century has set itself apart as the first to explicitly reject the wisdom of the ages that religion is indispensable to the concord and justice of society.

Mankind now has three choices: to remain divorced from the transcendent; to construct a rational order to preserve society without recourse to real or imagined gods; or to establish the viable influence of the Kingdom of God in the kingdoms of man.

The first option invites chaos and tyranny, as the bloodshed, repression, and nihilism of this century testify. We are then left with the second and third choices. These opposing arguments were well presented by two of the great thinkers of the twentieth century: the eminent journalist, Walter Lippmann, and Nobel laureate, Aleksandr Solzhenitsyn.

Before writing A *Preface to Morals*, Lippmann concluded that modern man could no longer embrace a simple religious faith. For Lippmann, the goal was to create a humanistic view in which "mankind, deprived of the great fictions, is to come to terms with the needs which created those fictions." For himself, Lippmann came to a rather fatalistic conclusion: "I take the humanistic view because, in the kind of world I happen to live in, I can do no other."[20] Lippmann thus set about to extract the ethical ideals of religious figures from their theological and historical context. Man in his own rational interest, he believed, could sustain a man-made religion. Some religion, even if it was a religion that denied religion, had to be followed.

On the other side of the spectrum from this religion of humanism stands Aleksandr Solzhenitsyn, a lonely and often outspoken prophet. In his 1978 Harvard commencement address, Solzhenitsyn listed a litany of woes facing the West: the loss of courage and will, the addiction to comfort, the abuse of freedom, the capitulation of intellectuals to fashionable ideas, the attitude of appeasement with evil.

The cause for all this was the humanistic view Lippmann had embraced. "The humanistic way of thinking," thundered Solzhenitsyn, "which had proclaimed itself as our guide, did not admit the existence of evil in man, nor did it see any task higher than the attainment of happiness on earth. It started modern western civilization on the dangerous trend of worshiping man and his material needs . . . gaps were left open for evil, and its drafts blow freely today."

In American democracy, said Solzhenitsyn, rights "were granted on the ground that man is God's creature. That is, freedom was given to the individual conditionally, in the assumption of his constant religious responsibility."

Solzhenitsyn lamented that two hundred years ago, as the Constitution was being written, or even fifty years ago, when Walter Lippmann was trying to preserve the husk of Western virtue, "it would have seemed quite impossible . . . that an individual be granted boundless freedom with no purpose, simply for the satisfaction of his whims. . . . The West has finally achieved the rights of man, and even to excess, but man's sense of responsibility to God and society has grown dimmer and dimmer."[21] Like MacArthur, Solzhenitsyn was saying that nothing less than spiritual renewal could save Western civilization.

If we reject the nihilism that denies all meaning and hope, we must believe human society has purpose. We are forced to choose, therefore, belief in man, faith in faith, hope in hope, and the love of love; or we must look for a point beyond ourselves to steady our balance.

The view that man in his own rational interest can sustain a man-made religion is voiced regularly on op-ed pages, on television specials, even from church pulpits. It remains fashionable because it offers a positive view of human nature, filled with hopeful optimism about man's capacities. But it ignores the ringing testimony of a century filled with terror and depravity.

If the real benefits of the Judeo-Christian ethic and influence in secular society were understood, it would be anxiously sought out, even by those who *repudiate* the Christian faith. The influence of the Kingdom of God in the public arena is good for society as a whole.

PART IV

PRESENCE
OF THE KINGDOM

16

Benefits of the Kingdom

Although church and state stand separate, the political order cannot be renewed without theological virtues working upon it . . . It is from the church that we receive our fundamental postulates of order, justice and freedom, applying them to our civil society.

—*Russell Kirk*

If Solzhenitsyn, MacArthur, and many of the great political philosophers since Cicero are right that society cannot survive without a vital religious influence, then where does this leave us? Will any religion or belief do?

No. As expressed earlier, I believe as a matter of faith *and* intellect that the Judeo-Christian religion must be that transcendent base. But—and I cannot emphasize this too strongly—even if I did not, I would still argue that Christianity is the only religious system that provides for *both* individual concerns and the ordering of a society with liberty and justice for all. A creed alone is not enough, nor is some external law code.

If Christianity were merely another creed, it would have no superior claim over Hinduism and Buddhism, for example. Or if it were merely another prescriptive order for society, it would have no advantage over Islam. Instead, Christianity alone, as taught in Scripture and announced in the Kingdom context by Jesus Christ, provides both a transcendent moral influence and a transcendent ordering of society without the repressive theocratic system of Islam.

I have already stated that humanists fail to understand human nature just as Christians fail to understand Christianity. This is particularly true when it comes to the presence of the Kingdom of God in this world. Christians tend to see their faith as either a belief system or a religious palliative for all life's ills. Secularists see it, most often, through the pejorative pen or the selective lens of the media, which portray the Christian activist as a religious Archie Bunker—a Bible-thumping bigot condemning everyone, expounding simplistically on everything from evolution to gun control, and pushing heatedly to take over the government to cram his narrow-minded agenda down society's unwilling throat. Sadly, many in the church have perpetuated this stereotype with thoughtless rhetoric and posturing.

Yet none of this bears any resemblance to true Christianity. The Kingdom of God provides unique moral imperatives that can cause men and women to rise above their natural egoism to serve the greater good. God intends His people to do this; furthermore, He commands them to influence the world through their obedience to Him, not by taking over the world through the corridors of power.

No one can be coerced into true faith, and the last people who even ought to try to do so are Christians, either individually or as members of the institutional church. As the Westminster Confession states, "God alone is Lord of conscience."[1] This conviction lies at the heart of the agreement reached by America's Founding Fathers. For them, secularists and believers alike, freedom of conscience was the first liberty guaranteed by the Constitution. This means religious liberty for all—Jew, Muslim, Christian, Hindu, Buddhist, atheist, or California bird worshiper.

The Christian, knowing that the will of the majority cannot determine truth, seeks no preferential favor for his religion from government. His confidence, instead, is that truth is found in Christ alone—and this is so no matter how many people believe it, no matter whether those in power believe it. While this may sound exclusivistic, it is this very assurance that makes (or should make, when properly understood) the Christian the most vigorous defender of human liberty. And those who resent the exclusive claims of Christianity are practicing the same intolerance they profess to resent. The essence of pluralism is, after all, that each person respects the other's right to believe in an exclusive claim to truth.

If society's well-being depends on the presence of a healthy religious influence, then, it is crucial that Christians understand their responsibilities in the kingdoms of man as mandated by the Kingdom of God. It is equally imperative that the rest of society realize the benefits those responsibilities, when properly carried out, offer them.

We are a benefit-driven society. How will this move benefit us? we ask. What benefits come with this plan? What benefits does this company offer if I take the job? It should come as welcome news to the pragmatists of the world that the Kingdom of God offers benefits no society can afford to be without.

* * *

When I was serving time for my part in the Watergate conspiracy, Al Quie, a senior congressman, offered to serve the remainder of my prison sentence if authorities would release me so I could be with my then-troubled family. Al, who later became governor of Minnesota, was a respected political leader; I was a member of the disgraced Nixon staff and a convicted felon. Al and I had not even been friends until a few months earlier when we met in a prayer group. Why would a man like Al Quie make such an offer?

The answer? Al took seriously Jesus' words: "As I have loved you, so you must love one another."[2] This commandment is a central law of the Kingdom, and Al Quie was my first encounter with it.

This law of the Kingdom is what motivates Christians to serve the good of society. Certainly it motivated Christians of the nineteenth century when they spearheaded most of our nation's significant works of mercy and moral betterment. They founded hospitals, colleges, and schools; they organized welfare assistance and fed the hungry; they campaigned to end abuses ranging from dueling to slavery. Though much of this work has now been taken over by government agencies, Christians provided the original impetus. Today, Christians still contribute the bulk of resources for private charities of compassion.

This is not to say that all good deeds are done by Christians or that all Christians do good deeds. Sacrificial deeds are often done for other than religious motives, of course. But in those instances the actions depend on an individual's personal reasons. Motive is crucial. In one instance it is an individual choice—a choice that often wavers or falters. For the Christian it is a matter of obedience to God's commandments; it is not choice, but necessity.

It is, in fact, their dual citizenship that should, as Augustine believed, make Christians the best of citizens. Not because they are more patriotic or civic-minded, but because they do out of obedience to God that which others do only if they choose or if they are forced. And their very presence in society means the presence of a community of people who live by the Law behind the law.

Even as unreligious a figure as modern educator John Dewey recognized that "the church-going classes, those who have come under the influence of evangelical Christianity . . . form the backbone of philanthropic and social interest, of social reform through political action, of passivism, of popular education. They embody and express the spirit of kindly good will towards [those] in economic disadvantage."[3]

A recent Gallup poll confirms Dewey's observations. Forty-six percent of those in the United States who describe themselves as "highly spiritually committed" work among the poor, the infirm, or the elderly—twice as many as those describing themselves as "highly uncommitted" spiritually.[4]

To accomplish works of mercy and justice, however, Christians do not rely on government, but on their own penetration of society as "salt and light." This too is in obedience to a command of God that orders them to be the "salt of the earth" and "the light of the world"[5]—the great cultural commission of the Kingdom.* In Hebrew times salt was rubbed into meat to prevent it from spoiling. In the same way the citizen of the Kingdom is "rubbed in" to society as its preservative.

Citizens of the Kingdom, therefore, form what Edmund Burke called "the little platoons," mediating structures between the individual and government that carry out works of justice, mercy, and charity.[6]

The presence of Christians in society also helps break the endless cycle of evil and violence in the world. For example, the generations-old conflicts in Northern Ireland and the Middle East thrive on hatred and bigotry, the basest of human instincts, which in turn beget violence, which begets more violence. Only forgiveness and love can break this cycle, and only the Kingdom of God orders its citizens to take such radical steps. God commands His people to forgive those who hurt or wrong them and to love their enemies.

---

*The Great Commission is Jesus' command to *preach the gospel.* "Therefore go and make disciples of all nations, baptizing them in the name of the Father and of the Son and of the Holy Spirit" (Matt. 28:19). The cultural commission, as I've called it, is to *do the gospel.* That is, to be salt and light, letting "your light shine before men, that they may see your good deeds and praise your Father in heaven" (Matt. 5:16).

Though "turning the other cheek" may sound like weakness or impractical idealism, in reality it takes raw courage and is the most powerful weapon for restoring civil tranquility—far surpassing any bayonet or legislation. No conquering army can destroy evil; at best it can suppress it. But as we will see dramatically illustrated in a later chapter, whenever men and women are reconciled by the Law of the Kingdom, evil is defeated.

In this and many other ways, the moral standards demanded of the citizen of the Kingdom of God inevitably affect the moral standards of the kingdoms of man. This is not well understood today because of the widespread view that private moral values have no bearing on public conduct. Scripture and history indicate otherwise, as do our own life experiences.[7]

Whether a politician cheats on his wife, for example, should have no bearing on his fitness for office, many say. But a broken vow is a broken vow and reveals a weakness of character. If a man or woman cannot be trusted with private moral decisions, how can he or she be trusted with moral decisions affecting the whole of society?

Moral values do affect character, and the influence of individual character has an impact on society. Not just with public officials, but in the lives of ordinary citizens. Nowhere is this more evident than in the area of criminal behavior.

Though for years conventional wisdom held that racial discrimination, economic deprivation, and environment were the chief causes of crime, leading criminologists and psychiatrists are now concluding that personal character is the single greatest determining factor in criminal behavior.

James Q. Wilson, Harvard law professor, after surveying American history and comparing religious activity with crime data during specified periods, discovered a startling correlation.

In the middle of the nineteenth century when rapid urbanization would normally lead one to expect increased crime, the level of crime actually fell. Interestingly, it was during that same period that a great spiritual awakening occurred. Thus, Wilson explains, morality took hold just as industrialization began. From the mid-1800s to 1920, despite environmental, economic, and social pressures that should have made it rise, the crime rate decreased.

Conversely, during the "good" economic years of the twenties, crime began to rise. Because, says Wilson, "the educated classes began to repudiate moral uplift, and Freud's psychological theories came into vogue." People no longer believed in restraining a child's sinful impulses; they wanted to develop his "naturally good" personality.[8]

Even more surprising, crime did not rise, as sociologists expected, during the Great Depression when, it is estimated, that 34 million men, women, and children were without any income at all—28 percent of the population.[9] Tough times seem to develop strength of character and a tendency for the populace to pull together, whereas good times leave people free to seek self-interest and satisfaction, legally or otherwise. If this correlation is valid, the soaring crime rates in today's affluent, egocentric Western culture are altogether understandable.

Correlation between religious values and public order was dramatically evident during a religious revival early in this century. The revival began in small Methodist churches in Wales and quickly spilled out into society. During New Year's week in 1905, for the first time ever there was not a single arrest for drunkenness in Swansea County, the police announced. In Cardiff the authorities reported a 40 percent decrease in the jail population while the tavern trade fell off dramatically. Prayer meetings sprang up in coal mines; stores reported stocks of Bibles sold out; dockets were cleared in criminal courts; and many police were unemployed. Stolen goods were returned to shocked store owners. One historian reported, "Cursing and profanity were so diminished that . . . a strike was provoked in the coal mines . . . so many men had given up using foul language that the pit ponies dragging the coal trucks in the mine tunnels did not understand what was being said to them and stood still, confused."[10] The revival soon spread throughout the British Isles and much of the English-speaking world. Church attendance rose, and in many areas, as in Wales, public morality was dramatically affected.

Men and women who profess allegiance to the Kingdom of God become models for the rest of society. The role of the City of God, as Augustine said, is "to inspire men and women to organize their communities in the image and likeness of the heavenly city."[11]

Nowhere in modern culture is this more crucial than in the area of the nature and origins of law. In the Kingdom of God, God is King and Lawgiver for all. This does not mean that the Old Testament's civic code should be passed by modern governments. What it does mean, as Plato and Cicero recognized, is that there are moral absolutes that must govern human behavior; there is a law rooted in truth upon which the laws of human society are based.

The presence of the Kingdom of God in society means the presence of a community of people whose lives testify to this Law behind the law. They eschew relativism, believe that some things are right, some are wrong, and adhere to universal ethical norms. The presence of such people in society, therefore, is a powerful bulwark to legal sanity.

But the Kingdom of God is more than just a model. It actually operates as a restraint on the kingdoms of man through its individuals and through its most visible manifestation, the church. For in our society the church is the chief institution with the moral authority to mediate between individuals and the government, to hold the state to account for its obligations to its citizens.

The American government was established with the understanding that such transcendent values would affect what otherwise is simply a social contract. When the state forgets or denies those values that were original conditions of the contract, in essence it abrogates its contract with its citizens. It is then that the church must take the initiative and call the state to account, for as Richard Neuhaus writes, the church is "the particular society within society that bears institutional witness to the transcendent purpose to which the society is held accountable."[12]

This is the point at which the conflict between the two kingdoms often becomes the greatest. Government by nature seeks power and will always attempt to generate its own moral legitimacy for its decisions. Inevitably, it resents any group that attempts to act as its conscience.

But as history demonstrates, and as we have already discussed, the result of government attempting to impose its own moral vision upon society or acting without the restraint of an independent conscience is tyranny. Contrary to today's popular illusion, the job of propagating moral vision belongs not to government but to other institutions of society, most notably the church. When the state oversteps the bounds of its authority, the church becomes, as we have seen in Poland, the one effective source of moral resistance. The church does this not for its own ends as an earthly institution, but for the common good.

This may well be the area most perplexing to Christians and secularists alike, for both sides are frequently confused about the right, and indeed in some cases the duty, of the church, as well as individuals within the church, to confront the state.

To understand, we must first examine what citizenship in the Kingdom really means. What must citizens of the Kingdom do to be true to their allegiances and bring the healthiest influence of the Kingdom of God to bear on the kingdoms of this world—to be true patriots in the best sense of the word?

17

Christian Patriotism

Whatever makes men good Christians, makes them good citizens.
—Daniel Webster

In the kingdoms of man, young people learn the basics of good citizenship in high-school civics courses. Immigrants attend special classes to learn their new country's laws and their civic responsibilities; they must pass a test to prove they understand their new citizenship and then must swear their allegiance. Good citizenship requires such basic duties as paying taxes, voting, serving in the military and on juries, and obeying the laws of the land.

In the Kingdom of God one learns the obligations of citizenship from the Scriptures, the ultimate source of basic Christian truth. Unfortunately, most people, churched or unchurched, are woefully ignorant in this area. Though 500 million Bibles are published in America each year—that's two for every man, woman, and child—over 100 million Americans confess they never open one. In a recent survey only 42 percent could name who gave the Sermon on the Mount.[1] (Some thought it was delivered by a person on horseback.)

If the average churchgoer is uninformed, however, one does not

496

have to look far to understand why. Church leaders have treated us to a smorgasbord of trendy theologies, pop philosophies, and religious variants of egocentric cultural values.

Recently, for example, a group of church scholars met to discuss which of Christ's words in the gospels could be accepted as authentic. Their modern critical analysis was carried out by ballot. Slips of colored paper were distributed to the group: a red slip meant the statement was authentic; pink meant probably authentic; gray meant probably not; and black meant not authentic. After intense discussion of each of Jesus' statements, participants cast their votes with the appropriate card. The Beatitudes and the Sermon on the Mount took a beating in the balloting. "Blessed are the peacemakers" was voted down; "blessed are the meek" garnered a paltry six red and pinks out of thirty votes. In the end only three of the twelve assorted woes and blessings from Matthew and Luke survived.

Such theological tomfoolery might be dismissed as too ludicrous to worry about except that this pink-slip mentality pervades the church. Orthodoxy—adherence to the historic tenets of Christianity—is under intense assault. This has been true since the Enlightenment, of course, but not until this century have so many in the church seriously argued that truth can be determined by majority vote or that the gospel should accommodate the whims of culture.

I have heard it said that reinterpreting the gospel in the context of modern culture is enlightened and progressive. Maybe some find that so, but Joseph Sobran better expresses my feelings: "It can be exalting to belong to a church that is five hundred years behind the times and sublimely indifferent to fashion; it is mortifying to belong to a church that is five minutes behind the times, huffing and puffing to catch up."[2]

Christianity rests on the belief that God is the source of truth and that He does not alter it according to the spirit of the times. When Christians sever their ties to absolute truth, relativism reigns, and the church becomes merely a religious adaptation of the culture.

Donald Bloesch maintains that modern "secularism is preparing the way for a new collectivism." He points to a historical precedent we have already looked at in some detail, the church in Germany. It was the confessing orthodox church in Germany that rose up in resistance to Hitler while "the church most infiltrated by the liberal ideology, the Enlightenment, was quickest to succumb to the beguilement of national societies."[3] Enticed by secular ideology, they saw the state as a vehicle for advancing the church.

Bloesch also points to a current illustration. In South Africa, "it can be shown that of the three Reformed churches the most liberal theologically is the most illiberal in racial attitudes, whereas the most consciously Calvinist is the most courageous in speaking out against racial injustice."[4]

The effect of preaching a false theology can be disastrous. Most attribute the fall of Jim and Tammy Bakker to greed, sexual indiscretion, or the corruption of power. These were, of course, serious contributing factors. But the root cause of their downfall was that for years the Bakkers had preached a false gospel of material advancement: If people would only trust God, He would shower blessings upon them and indulge them with all the material desires of their hearts—a religious adaptation of the prevailing "what's in it for me" mentality. Tragically, the Bakkers deluded themselves into believing their own false message. Taking a two-million-dollar-a-year salary, living in splendor, and indulging their every whim didn't seem wrong; it was "God's blessing." And millions of followers continued to support them, even after their fall, because they too wanted such blessings.

The first responsibility for the citizen of the Kingdom, then, is to understand historic Christian truth: to know Scripture and the classic fundamentals of the faith. This is not to say that Christians are to mindlessly accept whatever they are told is an orthodox creed. Honest inquiry and thoughtful examination of the evidence, I believe, are healthy and should be encouraged, for these invariably lead to firmer belief in the truth of God's revelation interpreted by the great theologians through the ages. As Chesterton said, "Dogma does not mean the absence of thought but the end [result] of thought."[5]

When Christians either lack knowledge or are insecure about what they believe, as is the case with many today, they forfeit their place in contending for theological truth, and secularism advances. This is why James Schall implores Christians "to regain their confidence in their own dogmas. . . . These are not idle speculations," he writes, "but the order of reality out of which a right order in human things alone can flow."[6] Such confidence is essential if Christians are to contend for values in culture and restore a sense of the transcendent to secular thought.

The problem is, as literary critic Harry Blamires states flatly, "there is no Christian mind."[7] By this he means that Christians have their own set of beliefs but, lacking confidence, keep them to themselves. As long as they are in a secular context, they act by secular values. When they return to the privacy of their religious enclaves where they can safely think and act in Christian terms, they do so. As a result their most fundamental beliefs never penetrate the culture. Jacques Ellul reminds us that the only way theological truth reaches the world is through the actions of laypeople in the marketplace.[8]

It is this first step of Christian citizenship in the Kingdom of God—knowledge and confidence in classical Christian truth—that enables the Christian to be a good citizen in the kingdoms of man. And it is in Scripture and classical doctrine that he or she finds the clearest expression of an individual's responsibility to both kingdoms.

On the one hand Scripture commands civil obedience—that individuals respect and live in subjection to governing authorities and pray for those in authority.[9] On the other it commands that Christians maintain their ultimate allegiance to the Kingdom of God. If there is a conflict, they are to obey God, not man.[10] That may mean holding the state to moral account through civil disobedience. This dual citizenship requires a delicate balance.

Christians who are faithful to Scripture should be patriots in the best sense of that word. They are "the salvation of the commonwealth," said Augustine, for they fulfill the highest role of citizenship.[11] Not because they are forced to or even choose to, not out of any chauvinistic motivations or allegiance to a political leader, but because they love and obey the King who is above all temporal leaders. Out of that love and obedience they live in subjection to governing authorities, love their neighbors, and promote justice. Since the state cannot legislate love, Christian citizens bring a humanizing element to civic life, helping to produce the spirit by which people do good out of compassion, not compulsion.

But Christians, at least in the United States, have all too often been confused about their biblical mandates and have therefore always had trouble with the concept of patriotism. They have vacillated between two extremes—The God-and-country, wrap-the-flag-around-the-cross mentality and the simply-passing-through mindset.

The former was illustrated a century ago by the president of Amherst College who said that the nation had achieved the "true American union, that sort of union which makes every patriot a Christian and every Christian a patriot."[12] This form of civil religion has endured as a peculiar American phenomenon supported by politicians who welcome it as a prop for the state and by Christians who see it enshrining the fulfillment of the vision of the early pilgrims.

The passing-through mindset is represented by those who believe they are simply sojourners with loyalties only in the Kingdom beyond. Patriotism has become a dirty word to them, particularly in the wake of Vietnam, and they believe it their real duty to oppose the United States in just about every endeavor on just about every front—from nuclear power to Nicaraguan policy to welfare for the homeless.

These two extremes miss the kind of patriotism Augustine had in mind. He believed that while as Christians we are commanded to love the whole world, practically speaking we cannot do so. Since we are placed as if by "divine lot" in a particular nation state, it is God's calling that we "pay special regard" to those around us in that state. We love the world by loving the specific community in which we live.[13]

C. S. Lewis likened love of country to our love for the home and community in which we were raised. It is a natural love of the place where we grew up, he said, "love of old acquaintances, of familiar sights, sounds and smells." He also pointed out, however, that in love of country, as in love of family, we don't love our spouses only when they are good. Similarly, a patriot sees the flaws of his country, acknowledges them, weeps for them, but remains faithful in love.[14]

Dr. Martin Luther King, Jr., spoke of love for his country even as he attempted to change its laws. "Whom you would change, you must first love," he said.[15]

That's the kind of tough love Christians must have for their country. To love the land faithfully, but not at the expense of suspending moral judgment. Indeed, it is the addition of that moral judgment that makes Christian patriotism responsible. "Loyalty to the civitas can safely be nurtured only if the civitas is not the object of highest loyalty," is the way Richard Neuhaus expresses it.[16]

The basic principle from Scripture is straightforward: Civil authorities are to be obeyed unless they set themselves in opposition to divine law. As Augustine put it, "An unjust law is no law at all."[17] This is the other side of Caesar's coin and can lead to civil disobedience. Practical application of this principle, however, raises perplexing questions, as we have witnessed in recent decades.

Since the sixties, civil disobedience has become a preferred method of protest. As unlikely as it may seem to some, this is an area where the Christian church has a major contribution to make in public discussion. After all, we've wrestled with this matter for two thousand years.

If Scripture does give clear principles on the matter, as I believe it does, then when is civil disobedience justified? And how is it to be carried out?

Civil disobedience is clearly justified when government attempts to take over the role of the church or allegiance due only to God. Then the Christian has not just the right but the duty to resist. The Bible gives a dramatic example of this in its account of three young Jewish exiles who were drafted into the Babylonian civil service.[18]

All citizens of Babylon were required to worship the statue of Nebuchadnezzar, the king; those who disobeyed were incinerated. Like many political leaders, power and authority were not enough for King Nebuchadnezzar; he wanted spiritual submission as well. Shadrach, Meshach, and Abednego, the young Hebrews, refused. To worship an earthly king would be the ultimate offense against their holy God.

"Our God will deliver us," they told the king when they were condemned to death for their disobedience. "But if not, we will still not worship you."[19] (It is significant to note, a point we will address later, that they were willing to pay the price for their disobedience.) The three young men were thrown into a blazing furnace. God did miraculously deliver them—something we can't always count on—and as a result the king began to worship the one true God.

Civil disobedience is also mandated when the state restricts freedom of conscience, as in the case of Peter and John, two of Jesus' disciples.

Peter and John were arrested for disturbing the peace. They were taken before the Sanhedrin, a religious body holding authority from the government of Rome, and ordered to stop preaching about Jesus. Peter and John refused.

"Judge for yourselves whether it is right in God's sight to obey you rather than God," they said. "We cannot help speaking about what we have seen and heard."[20]

Their first allegiance was to the commandment they had been given by the resurrected Christ: the Great Commission to preach the gospel first to Jerusalem, then to the rest of Judea, and then to the ends of the earth. They could not permit the authority of the government-backed Sanhedrin to usurp the authority of God Himself.

This is a very real conflict for many Christians around the world. For example, Christians in India are imprisoned for proselytizing; in Saudi

Arabia and Afghanistan they are imprisoned for even preaching the gospel. During a recent visit to the United States, a pastor from Nepal told of his imprisonment in his own country for just this offense. In conclusion he gave an excellent summary of Christian duty. "Of course I must obey my Lord and spread His Word," he said. "But even though we are persecuted, we who are Christians in Nepal pride ourselves on being the best citizens our king has. We try to be faithful to the fullest extent we can. We love our country—but we love our God more."[21]

The third justification for civil disobedience is probably the most difficult to call. It is applied when the state flagrantly ignores its divinely mandated responsibilities to preserve life and maintain order and justice. Those last words are key for Christians in deciding to disobey civil authority. Civil disobedience is never undertaken lightly or merely to create disorder. Replacing one bad situation with another is no solution, but when the state becomes an instrument of the very thing God has ordained it to restrain, the Christian must resist.

Inadequate though it was, the resistance of the German church to Hitler was a clear modern example of this necessity. In the sixties we saw it in the Civil-Rights Movement, as we do today in the Right-to-Life Movement and nonviolent resistance to Apartheid in South Africa.

When civil disobedience is justified, how is that disobedience to be carried out? When all recourse to civic obedience has been exhausted and the evil of the state is so entrenched as to be impenetrable, then the Christian may be justified (as discussed in a later chapter) in organizing to overthrow the state. First recourse, however, is always minimum resistance. Good citizens always avoid breaking just laws to protest unjust laws.

Daniel in the Old Testament exemplifies the use of the resistance necessary to accomplish the result.

Daniel was a contemporary of Shadrach, Meshach, and Abednego, another Jewish exile living in Babylon. King Nebuchadnezzar was impressed with Daniel and enlisted his service. As a member of the king's court, Daniel was required to eat from the king's table. While such delicacies were tempting, Daniel did not want to be "defiled"; that is, he did not want to break God's strict dietary laws for His people.[22] He quietly sought his superior's permission not to eat the food, and permission was granted. Daniel could have launched a hunger strike, but it was not necessary. He achieved his objectives with minimum resistance.

Where peaceful means are available, force should be avoided. Clearly, at least in a democratic society, this should be the path civil disobedience takes. A person who, for example, feels the state's action in war is immoral has the right to pursue the matter of conscientious objection (although technically our government allows that preference only to those who practice pacifism at all times, not just for what they may perceive to be right or wrong wars).

Another important principle related to civil disobedience is illustrated by the apostles Peter and John as well as the three young Hebrews: though they disobeyed authority, they showed the appropriate respect for that authority by a willingness to accept their punishment. Those who practice civil disobedience must be prepared to pay the consequences of civil disobedience.

These general principles from Scripture are clear enough; but it is often another thing to apply them to specific circumstances, as the case of a zealous and deeply devout young woman illustrates.

Joan Andrews is a slight, soft-spoken Catholic who on March 26, 1986, entered an abortion clinic for a Pro-Life sit-in and attempted to damage a suction machine used to perform abortions. She was charged and convicted of criminal mischief, burglary, and resisting arrest without violence. The prosecution asked for a one-year sentence. The judge gave her five.

Miss Andrews announced to the court. "The only way I can protest for unborn children now is by noncooperation in jail." She then dropped to the courtroom floor and refused to cooperate with prison officials at any stage of her processing. Labeled a troublemaker, she was transferred to Broward Correctional Institute, a tough maximum-security women's prison where she was placed in solitary confinement.

On one level, Joan Andrews's sentence was severe. For example, the same day she was sentenced, two men convicted as accessories to murder were sentenced by the same judge to four years. Five years for Joan Andrews's crimes is disproportionately harsh.

On the other hand, in her protest against abortion Miss Andrews violated a trespassing law. Much like the Civil-Rights Movement, today's Right-to-Life activists engage in sit-ins and deliberately violate trespassing laws as a means of attracting public attention. In Joan Andrews's case, the fear of doing nothing, of standing by while innocent lives were being taken, was greater than the fear of prison. But even if the cause is just, as I believe both Civil Rights and Right-to-Life to be, are such means of opposition appropriate?

In a free or democratic society there are legal means available to express political opposition: we can picket, petition, vote, organize, advertise, or pressure political officials. Is it right to abandon our respect for the rule of law, the foundation for public order, simply to make statements that could be made legally in other forums? Can one break a just law in the name of protesting an unjust law? Few biblical precedents are set for us, and those that are clearly deal with laws that were themselves unjust. In our day, breaking laws to make a dramatic point is the ultimate logic of terrorism, not civil disobedience.

There may be situations, however, in which one has to respond to a higher law when life itself is at stake. Many Jews and Christians during World War II refused to obey Nazi laws requiring registration of aliens. On the surface those might have seemed just laws, no different than alien registration laws on the books of most Western countries today. But the citizens disobeyed because they knew those laws were being used to identify individuals for extermination.

Rightly exercised, civil disobedience is divine obedience. But when Christians engage in such activities, it must always be to demonstrate their submissiveness to God, not their defiance of government.

Unfortunately, no neat formulas for civil disobedience exist. The citizen must seek wisdom in striking the fine balance between disobedience and respect for the law. The state, though ordained by God and thus deserving of respect, is not God. The true patriot, therefore, is not one who always obeys the law. If that were so, the sheriff enforcing Jim Crow laws or the Auschwitz guard would be the best of citizens. On the other hand disobedience can never be undertaken lightly.

Many on both the political right and left seem all too eager to defy civil authority and disrupt order to make a point on the six-o'clock news. Their causes range from preventing CIA recruiters from entering college campuses to sheltering illegal immigrants to saving California condors to censoring bookstores. Some seem temperamentally disposed to such protest, as if they get high on the thrill of civil disobedience. But as Harvard law professor Alexander Bickel warns, "Civil disobedience, like law itself, is habit-forming, and the habit it forms is destructive of law."

Good citizenship requires both discernment and courage— discernment to soberly assess the issues and to know when duty calls one to obey or disobey, and courage, in the case of the latter, to take a stand.

The citizens of the Kingdom of God should be patriots in the highest sense, loving the world by loving those in the nation in which they live because that government is ordained by God to preserve order and promote justice. Perhaps this is why John Adams wrote that a patriot must be "a religious man."[23] Christians understand the phrase "a nation under God" not as a license for blind nationalism or racial superiority but as a humbling acknowledgment that all people live under the judgment of God.

Christian patriots spend more time washing feet than waving flags. Ideally, flags should not even be thought of as symbols of military and economic might, but of the common good of the specific people a sovereign God has called them to serve.

18

Little Platoons

The greatest thing is to be found at one's post as a child of God, living each day as though it were our last, but planning as though our world might last a hundred years.

—C. S. Lewis

Ever since giving to the needy became chic in Hollywood, we've been treated to a billion-dollar bonanza of celebrity benefits. Band-Aid, the British concert to help starving children, started the aid wagons rolling. Then came 1985's Live Aid, a marathon rock concert simulcast from London and Philadelphia. This was followed by Fashion Aid, Farm Aid, and what could only be thought of as AIDS Aid. Hands Across America linked up from Los Angeles to New York to raise $100 million for domestic homelessness and hunger, while the Freedom Festival raised money for Vietnam veterans.

And then there's my favorite: Sport Aid, which began with a runner leaving Ethiopia with a torch lighted from a refugee's campfire. He jogged through several European cities. Then this tireless athlete flew to New York, torch in hand, (I wonder what he did when the "no smoking" sign came on?), where he lighted a flame in Manhattan's

United Nations Plaza, signaling the start of simultaneous 10-kilometer runs around the world. The plan, said organizer Bob Geldof, also the mastermind of Live Aid, was to raise money to fight disease and hunger in Africa.

While few of us would deny that helping starving, homeless, and needy people is a good thing, this sudden aid frenzy did raise some practical questions.

In an industry where publicity is the ticket to success, one may be excused for wondering if celebrity participation in such compassion extravaganzas is altogether altruistic. The "We Are the World" video, which has sold millions of copies, reminds us less of starving children than of the great humanitarianism of its showcase of rock idols. The goals may be worthy, but such slickly publicized charity certainly recalls biblical warnings against hiring trumpeters—or camera crews—to record one's good deeds.

We might put aside our suspicions as petty if only we knew that those in need were being helped. But are they?

The *New Republic* reports that while USA for Africa, the organization behind Live Aid, appeals for contributions to help the starving, 55 percent of its money is instead waiting to be spent on "recovery and long-term development projects," something celebrity efforts may be ill-equipped to pull off.[1]

As of early 1986, of the $92 million raised by Live Aid and Band Aid, according to *Newsweek*, only $7 million has gone to emergency relief. Another $6.5 million has been spent on trucks and ships to haul supplies; $20 million has been earmarked for projects like bridges in Chad. The rest sits in bank accounts somewhere.[2]

Even noncontroversial goals such as feeding the hungry can get bogged down in squabbles over how money and food should be distributed, or stymied at the Marxist-controlled ports of Ethiopia. Let's not kid ourselves. Just because the fans in London or Philadelphia go home satisfied does not mean that the hungry in Africa go home fed.

Rock promoter Bill Graham said of celebrity aid, "It's an incredible power, knowing on any given day you can raise a million dollars."[3] *Newsweek* observed: "Perhaps that is why Live Aid and Farm Aid were such oddly upbeat exercises in self-congratulation. An industry was celebrating its power. Far from challenging the complacency of an audience, such mega-events reinforce it. . . . Now by watching a pop-music telethon and making a donation . . . fans can enjoy vicariously a sense of moral commitment."[4]

Despite all the ballyhoo, feeding the hungry did not originate with

Live-Aid. Christians have been doing it since the church began, not for T-shirts and pop albums, but in obedience to Christ's command to care for those in need. Organizations such as World Vision, Catholic Relief Services, the Salvation Army, and millions of local churches have for generations been feeding the hungry, housing the homeless, and clothing the needy without the glamorous carrot-and-stick razzle-dazzle so recently discovered by the rich and famous. This kind of Christian patriotism also benefits society as a whole.

Jacques Ellul wrote that the answer to the big government illusion is small voluntary associations. As mentioned earlier, eighteenth-century statesman Edmund Burke described such voluntary groups as the "little platoons."[5] These are citizens—individuals or groups—who perform works of mercy and oppose injustice. They are the salt and light of which Jesus spoke.

Culture is most profoundly changed not by the efforts of huge institutions but by individual people being changed. In the process, these citizens provide the main bulwark against government's insatiable appetite for power and control, and a safeguard against the sense of impotence fostered by today's overwhelming social problems. One person can make a difference.

A few months after Bob Geldof announced the success of Live Aid, and while critics were still questioning whether food was actually arriving in the places of need, I went to Nairobi, Kenya, for a Prison Fellowship International conference. There I met a man who, though worthy of adulation, will never make the cover of Rolling Stone.

Pascal was a university professor when he was thrown into a Madagascar prison after a Marxist coup. While in prison he became a Christian.

After his release, Pascal began a small import-export company, but he kept returning to prison to preach the gospel to the men he had met there and others who had arrived since. During one such visit in early 1986, he walked past the infirmary and was shocked to see more than fifty naked corpses piled on the screened veranda, identification tags stuck between their toes.

Pascal went to the nurse. Had there been an epidemic, he asked. Of sorts, he was told. Prisoners were dying by the dozens of malnutrition.

Pascal left the prison in tears. He tried to get help to feed the starving inmates, but his own church was too poor, and there were no relief agencies to assist. So he began cooking food in his own kitchen and taking it to the prison.

Today, Pascal and his wife feed prisoners every week, paying for the food out of the earnings from their small business. Without benefit of a government agency or even a theme song, this little platoon makes all the difference for seven hundred prisoners in Madagascar.

There is no age limit for enlistment in the little platoons.

In December 1983, eleven-year-old Trevor Ferrell saw a television news report on Philadelphia's inner-city homeless. The young boy couldn't believe people actually lived on the streets. When he questioned his parents, Frank and Janet reluctantly agreed to broaden their son's sheltered horizons—and their own. They left their home in an exclusive suburb and drove downtown.

A block past city hall, they spotted an emaciated figure crumpled on a sidewalk grate. While his parents watched a bit apprehensively, Trevor got out of the car and approached the man.

"Sir," he said, "here's a blanket for you." The man stared up at Trevor at first. Then, "Thank you," he said softly. "God bless you."

That encounter altered the Ferrells' lives forever. Night after night they drove downtown, trying in small ways to help the street people. They emptied their home of extra blankets, clothing, and dozens of peanut-butter sandwiches. When others learned what they were doing, someone donated a van and volunteers charted nightly food distribution routes. To the Ferrells' surprise, "Trevor's Campaign" had begun.

Young Trevor found himself explaining what they were doing to local media, then to the nation. Pat Robertson, Merv Griffin, Mother Teresa, Ronald Reagan—all wanted to meet the small boy with the big mission. He told them simply, "It's Jesus inside of me that makes me want to do this."

But Trevor is a reluctant celebrity. He endures interviews with one eye on the door. He doesn't know why people make such a fuss over him. Is it because helping the homeless is so unusual? In that case, says his father, the more who follow Trevor's example, the better.

"Our social life has changed a lot since the campaign began," Frank says. "Our church is behind us one hundred percent; but some of our old friends don't understand why we're messing with the homeless. They just tolerate our 'eccentricities.'"

Nightly now, the blue van travels the downtown streets of Philadelphia. It stops first to deliver food to the residents of Trevor's Place, a ramshackle rooming house where some of the formerly homeless now live. Then it proceeds to feed the hungry people gathered on sidewalk grates and street corners.

Asked how these handouts can make a difference in the complex business of helping the homeless, Frank Ferrell sighs. "We're trying to meet short-term needs and figure out ways to bring long-term changes to these people's lives. Sometimes it seems like just a band-aid. But this is how we build relationships. These people become our friends and they trust us to help them in bigger ways."

Frank pauses for a moment, looking at the landscape of broken bottles and bodies. "There are plenty of struggles. But I know one thing: *giving* has made all the difference in my Christian life. I used to just read the Scriptures. Now I feel like I'm living them."

The little platoon that began with a small boy's concern makes a big difference to the homeless and hungry on the streets of Philadelphia—and to those who give as well.

Thousands of miles from the home of the Liberty Bell, a young Liberian woman operates her own little platoon in Monrovia.

Lorince Taylor had a future in management as a claims supervisor for an insurance company, but her passion was for telling people about Christ. She wanted to do it full-time. When her husband encouraged her to follow her vision, Lorince resigned her job and in September 1985 began preaching in the city marketplace and in prisons and hospitals.

Although a number of people became Christians, Lorince soon realized that their problems went beyond the spiritual. She had to do more than tell them about Jesus. This became particularly evident one day when she visited a local mental hospital and, inadvertently, arrived during a staff strike.

The halls were littered with trash and dirty food trays. No doctors or nurses were in sight. The patients lay naked on the floors in their own filth, abandoned not only by their families but by those paid to care for them.

Lorince Taylor left that building praying, "Lord, this is wrong. Help me do what I can to make it right."

Shortly thereafter Lorince went to the studios of ELTV, a national television station, and told them what she had found at the hospital.

Reporters returned to the institution with her and filmed the shocking scenes of neglect. When the report aired, viewers were outraged. Public pressure not only got the hospital cleaned up, but brought forth donations of food and clothing for the patients.

Next Lorince went to the prostitutes of Monrovia. Many were receptive to her spiritual message; they became Christians and began studying the Bible with her. But sooner or later they returned to their old livelihood. Most had four or five children to support and had no other way to survive. Prostitution was all they had ever known.

"I believe," cried one young woman, "but I can't live the Christian life. I just can't climb out of the life I'm living."

It was then that Lorince envisioned a vocational center where the women could be trained in sewing, secretarial and other skills. When a friend of mine last saw Lorince Taylor, a Liberian Christian had just donated a brand-new building to her ministry; and she had begun her center where former prostitutes and others in need can learn vocational skills.

Lorince Taylor's little platoon offers a ladder of escape to women trapped in a lifestyle that usually has no escape.

Another one-woman platoon began when Frieda Weststeyn, in the course of her volunteer work in a California prison, noticed the number of pregnant inmates in the visiting room. Curious, she asked how the women would care for their babies. The answer jolted her. Most of the children would go into foster homes, be put up for adoption, or farmed out to the inmates' families. The mothers would rarely, if ever, see their babies once they were born.

Frieda went home, talked to her husband, prayed, and decided to do something practical to help these imprisoned mothers. Soon she was caring for five babies in her own home. (The state, which had no such program of its own, did enter at that point—ironically—to restrict Frieda to care for only three children at a time.)

At this writing, two-month-old Ryan, seventeen-month-old Petey, and eight-month-old Amber live at the Weststeyn home, where schedules revolve around bottles and diapers. Three days a week, Frieda takes the babies to see their mothers in the prison.

"I stepped out in faith," Frieda says. "I have no money to jump into a full-fledged ministry, but I knew this was a need I could help with." She does receive assistance from the Department of Human Services in the form of formula, milk, cheese, and other staples. Also, after Frieda was featured on the NBC network news in 1986, people across the country send donations to help with the babies.

There are hundreds of thousands of prisoners' children, one might respond. What difference can one person make? The answer is clear to Ryan, Petey, and Amber—and their mothers.

Frieda's little platoon fulfills Augustine's view of Christian citizenship; she is loving the world by loving her particular neighbors. In her case they happen to be in prison.

Robert Lavelle's neighborhood is one of the most isolated, forgotten, and helpless communities in America—the inner city.

"People tell me, 'You're crazy, man,'" says Lavelle, "but I have to do it." He is referring to his savings and loan and real estate operations in Pittsburgh's Hill District, an area where wrecking ball, drug dealer, and welfare check are a way of life. Many of Lavelle's bank loans go to people who would be unable to obtain credit elsewhere. Though federal regulators and others have urged him to move to a "better" location, Lavelle refuses.

Dwelling House Savings and Loan goes further than financial loans, however, for Lavelle takes a personal interest in his clients. If they fall behind in payments, he visits their homes to help them figure out budgets and challenges them to set an example of financial responsibility for their children. This appeal to self-respect and accountability is the key to helping needy people, he says. It is the only way to break the cycle of their poverty. Handouts enslave people. Teaching them how to manage and extend their resources helps set them free.

Lavelle doesn't have much faith in government programs. "Government is limited in what it can do," he says. "It primarily just perpetuates itself." But "when we provide the means for the poor and minorities, the economics of their neighborhoods change from dope, numbers, prostitution, pimping, and loan-sharking to home ownership, good city services, police and garbage collections, quality schools, viable businesses, and jobs."

Lavelle, who lives within walking distance of his office, is quick to tell his clients about spiritual freedom as well, but his faith is most evident by what he does, not by what he says. "For me," he says, "being a Christian is a matter of obedience—and that means helping people in need as the Holy Spirit leads."

Lavelle explains his little platoon of upside-down banking business in terms of the Good Samaritan: the people in the inner city are lying by the roadside, wounded by economic hardship; they don't even know how to help themselves. Meanwhile, he says, there are a lot of good church people passing by on the other side. "Someone needs to stop and take a risk," he says, "and who better to do that than a banker?"

John Perkins's little platoon dramatically illustrates a similar restoration of community.

John grew up picking cotton in Mendenhall, Mississippi, for eight cents an hour. Early on, he grew frustrated with the injustice and endless cycle of poverty that fettered generations of black families in the rural south. He determined to escape.

Eventually, John beat the system by making it work for him. He and his wife, Vera May, left Mendenhall far behind for a successful business and comfortable lifestyle in California. But in 1957 John became a Christian and could no longer ignore those he had left behind. So in 1960 John and Vera May returned to Mississippi with a vision of making the Kingdom of God visible there.

John had formulated a practical basis for change, what he now calls the three Rs of community development: relocation, reconciliation, and redistribution.

First, he saw that he couldn't help people from afar. Those who want to help the poor need to *relocate* and become part of their neighborhoods. Second, from his own experience, he realized that racial, social, and economic barriers created by racial hostility in the rural south of the sixties could be broken only by the forgiveness and healing that take place through *reconciliation*; only the gospel of Christ truly provides this. And third, as he read his Bible, John saw that Christ presents a radical call for those who have, to share with those who do not. This means *redistribution* through sharing skills, technology, and educational resources.

As John, his family, and a growing platoon of individuals began to operate on these principles in Mendenhall, they formed what is now the Voice of Calvary Church. They soon began a store, a cooperative farm, nutritional and education programs. Meanwhile, the Christian community also came head to head with the injustice of racism dividing the South. In 1970 John and several others were jailed and nearly beaten to death by highway patrolmen and county sheriffs for their Civil-Rights work. Once again, John struggled with bitterness in his own life—but he was able to forgive his tormentors.

Voice of Calvary expanded, adding organized tutoring and recreation programs, an adult education program, and a health center. By 1978 the Mendenhall work had become a model of Christian development in a rural community. In keeping with another of John's most passionate commitments, it was led by those who had been trained to lead in their own community.

In 1982 John and Vera May were ready for retirement. They returned to California, anticipating a quiet life of writing and traveling. Instead, the Perkinses decided to move into a crime-and-drug-infested neighborhood in otherwise peaceful and affluent Pasadena.

John knew the same principles that had given new life and dignity to people in rural Mendenhall would apply as well in the inner city. The result is the Harambee Center, a community of Christians helping their neighbors through education, employment, nutrition, neighborhood pride, and leadership training. Harambee, the Swahili word best translated "let's get together and push," evokes the Perkinses' commitment to working together with those who need help to help themselves.

John Perkins's little platoons model the values and hopes of the Kingdom of God for the kingdoms of man. Like Lorince Taylor's work, they are based in human dignity and a view of economics designed to equip people to climb out of their condition rather than manacling them to their poverty.

Sometimes the work of the little platoons mushrooms into a movement.

One such movement began with Jerry Falwell, a man who often evokes controversy. But even those who disagree most violently with Dr. Falwell's political views have a hard time faulting his outreach ministries to women facing crisis pregnancies.

Several years ago during a press conference, a reporter asked Falwell, "What practical alternatives to abortion do pregnant girls have when they are facing an unwanted pregnancy?"

"They can have the baby," Falwell shot back.

"Do you really think it's that simple?" the young woman responded. "What are you doing for women who want to keep their babies but can't find any way to do it . . . who are young and poor and powerless? Is it enough to take a stand against abortion when you aren't doing anything to help the pregnant girls who have no other way?"⁶

Falwell couldn't forget the reporter's question, and the result was Liberty Godparent Ministries, formed in 1982. The Lynchburg, Virginia-based operation includes a crisis-pregnancy center where women can get confidential pregnancy tests and counseling; a national hotline that receives an average of 2000 calls a month; a home where thirteen-to-eighteen-year-olds can live during their pregnancy and receive health care, birth instruction, and continue their education; shepherding homes where older women can prepare for their baby's birth; and a licensed adoption agency.

Nearly 600 programs based on the Liberty Godparent concept have sprung up across the nation. Thousands of local churches and other ministries are also working in similar ways. With names like Bethany Christian Services, Samaritan Ministries, Salem Pregnancy Center, and Amnion, they mobilize Christians to speak out against abortion and to offer loving, viable alternatives that replicate Christ's care and compassion.

Another movement confronting widespread social evil is Mothers Against Drunk Driving (MADD). Started by a young mother whose teenage daughter was killed by a drunk driver, MADD has shattered complacency about alcohol and the carnage drunk drivers have created in our society. It offers services to victims through support groups and lobbies for legislatures to beef up drunk-driver laws. In a nation where a person is killed every twenty-seven minutes by a drunken driver, MADD has made a significant impact where government had made little progress.

Like the little platoons involved in MADD, who are committed to cracking down on a widespread social ill, millions of Americans have passionately campaigned against pornography. As one of the nation's least-regulated industries (earning $6 billion in 1985), pornography recognizes few standards except the increasingly perverse tastes of its clientele. Yet it prospers, despite the FBI Academy's report convincingly tracing pornography's role in fantasies prior to sex-related murders, and such statistics as those from the Michigan State Police directly linking pornography to 40 percent of its assault cases.[7]

Pornography was not an area the government had ignored. In 1984 the attorney general appointed a panel to report on the issue. A year later the Commission on Pornography surfaced from the murky world of smut, and antipornography campaigners pinned great hopes on the panel's recommendations. Working through the leverage of big government seemed the most effective way to destroy such a widespread social cancer.

The commission, which included Focus on the Family's Dr. James Dobson, strongly believed there was a connection between some pornography and violent crimes. It recommended tougher prosecution, stronger federal laws, and more vigorous enforcement of existing obscenity laws.

Even if the panel's laudable proposals make it through the tough legislative process, however, they can expect extended court challenges. As Barry Lynn of the American Civil Liberties Union boasted, "There are enough constitutional questions here [in the Meese report] to litigate for the next twenty years."[8]

As the commission was completing its report, the high-flying pornography industry suffered a major setback that caught everyone by surprise. It came from a little platoon.

When Jack Eckerd, founder of the Eckerd Drug chain, became a Christian in 1983, he called the company president and urged him to take *Playboy* and *Penthouse* magazines out of the Eckerd stores. The executive protested, telling him the magazines amounted to several million dollars a year in business. Jack Eckerd persisted. Eventually all 1,700 Eckerd drugstores stopped carrying *Playboy* and *Penthouse*. Eckerd then wrote to the directors of other retail stores and encouraged them to do the same. When his letters went unanswered, he wrote again.[9]

Meanwhile, the National Coalition Against Pornography was picketing and boycotting stores selling "adult" magazines. The pressure began to pay off. One by one, Revco, People's, Rite Aid, Dart Drug, Gray Drug, and High's Dairy Stores pulled pornography from their shelves. And finally 7-11 removed these magazines from its 4,500 stores and recommended that its 3,600 franchises do the same.

Thus, without one debate before Congress or one case entangled in the courts, the shelves of nearly 12,000 retail stores were cleared of pornography!

Playboy's lawyers, shocked at their declining circulation, charged that a letter from the Meese Commission had put coercive pressure on the stores. Maybe so. But the real impetus came from the little platoons—thousands of individuals and one courageous man who put his faith into practice in his own business.

One of my favorite little platoons is a group of prison volunteers whose names I don't even know.

It was a rainy, dismal day in February when we arrived at the Maryland prison at Jessup, but the entry area was filled with the bright lights of television cameras. Reporters scribbled notes while Maryland officials greeted us warmly. Governor Harry Hughes had even issued a proclamation for the occasion.

By the time we got to the prison chapel, it was on the verge of exploding with the excitement of more than 125 inmates and several dozen Prison Fellowship volunteers, all of whom had been participating in one of our in-prison seminars. With us was Wintley Phipps, the internationally known gospel singer who had sung only the day before for President Reagan at a prayer breakfast. When Wintley let loose in that cinder-block prison chapel, I thought the walls would come tumbling down.

Then Herman Heade gave his testimony. Herman had been converted while in a solitary-confinement cell. He had tremendous rapport with other inmates and his message was powerful, dramatic, and convincing.

The excitement continued as I challenged the men to accept Christ, then prayed with them. Afterward the inmates crowded around, hugging us and weeping.

The next day our instructor, Dick Robinson, was relieved to find all the inmates were back for the seminar's final session. He had thought the last day might be anticlimactic. Several inmates gave their impressions of the previous day.

"I really appreciated Chuck Colson's message," said one tall prisoner. "Wintley Phipps's singing stirred me beyond words, and Herman's testimony reached me right where I was at. But frankly, those things really didn't impress me as much as what happened later.

"When the celebrities and TV cameras left," he continued, "the ladies among the volunteers went into the dining hall, with all the noise and confusion, and sat at the table to have a meal with us. That's what really got to me," he concluded, his voice choked.

Wintley's singing and Herman's testimony and my sermon were all appreciated. But the most powerful message came from the volunteers who went into the crowded, dingy dining hall to share prison food with the inmates.

Celebrities don't make the difference in society. The little platoons of ordinary people living extraordinary lives do.

*   *   *

At the end of all the "feed the hungry" celebrity hoopla, when organizer Bob Geldof announced that his aid campaign's mission had been accomplished, he concluded, "It's like a shooting star . . . for once . . . something absolutely good and absolutely incorruptible came and went and worked."[10]

But shooting stars don't feed starving multitudes, and long after Hollywood has moved on to other causes, the hungry will remain.

Fortunately for the kingdoms of man, the little platoons march on.

19

The Problem of Power

It is a magician's bargain: give up our souls, get power in return. But once our souls, that is, ourselves, have been given up, the power thus conferred will not belong to us. We shall in fact be slaves and puppets of that to which we have given our souls.

—C. S. Lewis

John Naisbitt observed in Megatrends that significant movements begin from the bottom up, not the top down.[1] Truly important changes in culture begin not from officials or celebrities, but through ordinary people: the little platoons. Every person can—and should—seek to make a difference in his or her corner of the world by personally helping those in need.

Beyond this, some people, like William Wilberforce, are called to work through government structures and by political means to bring Christian influence into the culture. Those who do, however, need to be forewarned: the everyday business of politics is power, and power, as I know so well from my own experience, can be perilous for anyone.

My purpose here is not to deal exhaustively with the complex issue of power, nor could I. Entire books have been written on the subject. Yet no discussion of Christianity and politics would be complete without at least examining the dynamics of power, particularly as it affects the political arena and those who enter it.

The history of the last fifty years has validated Nietzsche's argument that man's desire to control his own destiny and to impose his will on others is the most basic human motivation. While I reject Nietzsche's atheistic cynicism, I do agree with his diagnosis of human nature. So did Christian psychiatrist Paul Tournier, who wrote, "We are moved without knowing it by an imperious will to power, which brooks no obstacles."[2]

Nietzsche's prophecy that the "will to power" would fill the twentieth-century's vacuum of values has been fulfilled. We see it on an individual level in the quest for autonomy and the shedding of all restraints. On a corporate level, it is dramatically evident in the rise of gangster leaders like Hitler and Stalin, and evident as well in the bloated growth of Western governments.

The resultant illusion—that all power resides in large institutions—is the salient characteristic of modern politics. Since power is often measured by one's prominence and ability to influence others, in today's world, politics is the most visible means to both.

Hunger for political power lures men and women from the comfort of their homes and jobs in the private sector and drives them to spend months, even years, traveling about their state or nation, subsisting on stale sandwiches, greasy chicken, and little sleep as they shout the same soul-stirring speech over and over until they are hoarse. Candidates for Congress spend several million dollars to fight for a job that pays $89,000 a year; others settle for lower-paying bureaucratic positions. Still others give huge political contributions in the hopes of acquiring even an obscure embassy appointment.

Certainly in every generation there are statesmen motivated by a genuine noblesse oblige, a sense of high calling to serve humanity. For the most part, though, it is Nietzsche's "will to power" that fuels political passions in every culture.

I've seen it up close.

Even before I was invited to become part of the White House staff in 1969, I felt a sense of guilt that many of those I had worked with in the 1968 campaign were now in government at salaries far less than my own lucrative law-practice income. And duty to country had always weighed heavily with me, the flag-waving, ex-Marine, conservative political activist.

So when the offer came, even as I made the perfunctory protests about sacrifice, interrupting my career and burdening my family, I was already packing up my office files. More than duty called me, of course.

There was glamorous protocol, the possibility of shaping headlines and history, the enticement of being part of the inner circle surrounding the president of the United States. Deep down, though I wouldn't admit it, the White House represented the pinnacle of the power I had pursued all my life.

Joining the staff nine months into the new administration had some disadvantages. One of the first visible yardsticks of power is size and placement of office, and the best offices were already taken. I was given an inside suite a long way down the hall from the president's working office in the stately Old Executive Office Building. Also I reported not to the president, but to Bob Haldeman, his hard-nosed chief of staff. Not an auspicious beginning.

Within months, circumstances worked in my favor. An aide left, and everyone played musical offices. With a little fast footwork I maneuvered my way across the hall to an office commanding an impressive view of the South Lawn. From there I edged my way down the corridor toward the seat of power.

Within a short time my brusque get-it-done-at-all-costs approach won Nixon's favor, and I began to work directly with him. With that kind of clout I had little difficulty rearranging several secret-service agents and secretaries so I could occupy the office immediately next to the president's.

Though the evidence of my change in status was visible in the attitude of my visitors when they realized that the president himself was just on the other side of the wall, the move was symbolic of something much more important. It meant I had passed an invisible divide. I was now *inside*. A Newsweek feature article heralded my arrival with the news that I was now on the top of every Washington hostess's guest list (ironic, since I never attended parties) and that the mere mention of my name "makes the tensions come in like sheet rain."[3] In Washington that means power.

In the political arena one of the most important attributes of power is its visibility. So we went to great lengths to protect our territory or prerogatives.

One Sunday in June 1971 the White House faced a sudden crisis: the New York Times published the "Pentagon Papers," the highly classified documents stolen by Daniel Ellsberg, a one-time Johnson-administration official turned antiwar activist. Mr. Nixon feared that our secret negotiations with the North Vietnamese would be exposed. For two days meetings went on around the clock, with the president, egged on by Henry Kissinger, barking angry orders to the Pentagon, the Justice

Department, and his staff. (One such order led to my involvement in smearing Ellsberg, for which I later pleaded guilty and went to prison.)

At 8:00 on Tuesday evening the president phoned me with his latest instructions. "Chuck, I want you to call Lyndon Johnson. You explain to him that I'm taking all the heat for this. These are *his* administration's papers—now, the least he can do is make some public statement supporting us. I mean, that will help us with the Democrats at least. You know what I mean? Now, just let Henry know and then you call Johnson. Understand?"

"Yes, sir," I replied.

"Good, good," said Nixon. "You get it done, and don't bother to call me back. I'm going to bed early."

Dutifully following orders, I called Kissinger first. The national security adviser, who admittedly had had a bad day, was outraged.

"If anyone is to call former President Johnson, it is me," he insisted, his accent thickening with his resolve.

Nothing I said made any difference, so I played my trump. "But the president ordered *me*, Henry," I said.

"Then I will call the president, and he will reverse that order," Kissinger replied.

In our power game Kissinger had checked me. The president had been up most of the night before; he needed sleep. Besides, he shouldn't have to bother with such squabbles. Kissinger knew this and he knew that I knew it. I hesitated a moment, then folded.

"Okay, Henry. Let's agree that neither of us will call until morning. Then we'll ask the president when we see him at the eight o'clock meeting."

"Good, Chuck. That is very good," he answered.

"But now you promise me," I added quickly, "that you won't bother him about it tonight."

"You have my word, Chuck," Kissinger said somberly.

The heat of our exchange left no doubt in my mind that the call to Johnson was important to Kissinger. Perhaps he feared that my making the call would indicate he was losing his influence or that I was taking responsibility for national security affairs. Whatever his thinking, I wasn't surprised at the White House operator's reply when I called ten minutes later to ask if anyone had phoned the president. "Oh, yes, sir," she replied. "Dr. Kissinger called him ten minutes ago."

Later that night Kissinger placed the call to Lyndon Johnson. Maintaining the appearance of power is also paramount, even when the reality is inconsequential.

On Nixon's last presidential trip abroad, in June 1974, he was accompanied by two senior aides, Al Haig and Ron Ziegler, both of whom were vying for top position. The trip, begun in the Soviet Union and including stops in Iran and Israel, was a vain last-ditch effort to divert attention away from the president's political crisis. By that time everyone knew Mr. Nixon couldn't survive the public clamor more than another month or two; his entire administration was about to collapse. Even so, the advance team was equipped with tape measures and meticulous instructions to insure that in all sleeping accommodations Mr. Ziegler's bed and General Haig's bed would be equidistant from the president's.

The pursuit of power affects entire governments or regions, as well as individuals. Those in office use their power to keep themselves in office. This is an accepted tradition in most Western democracies. In every American election since the forties the party in power has used grants and federal aid programs for political advantage. Truman won his upset victory in 1948 by doling out federal funds to struggling farmers and openly courting special-interest groups. Eisenhower judiciously announced grants in key states during the 1956 campaign. In the Kennedy and Johnson years a special White House office monitored election-year grants, and party fund-raisers notified defense contractors of impending contracts. Administrations since have adopted similar practices.

We were certainly not to be outdone in the Nixon years. I recall one incident from early 1972 when Bob Haldeman and I met with the president one morning to discuss reelection campaign strategy and schedules. We couldn't know at that point that Nixon would win in a record landslide. The polls showed him dead even with his expected opponent, Senator Edmund Muskie from Maine. Even though Nixon had only token primary opposition, I raised the question of visits to key primary states.

Haldeman chuckled. "No worry about the two big ones, New Hampshire and California. The Chinese and Russians will take care of those for us." Nixon laughed.

When I looked from one to the other in bewilderment, Haldeman delighted in detailing the tour de force he had arranged. Nixon's trip to China, he explained, was deliberately scheduled one week before the first primary in New Hampshire. Live coverage would dominate prime time for a week. Nixon would then receive a hero's welcome home, just days before the New Hampshire voters went to the polls.

The summit in Moscow, Haldeman continued, would spotlight the first strategic-arms agreement ever signed on live television from inside the Kremlin. It was timed to transpire one week before the all-important California primary. The president would fly home on Air Force One, take a helicopter from Andrews Air Force base to the Capitol. There he would address a joint session of Congress—all televised live on prime time, just four days before millions of Californians cast their votes. Haldeman had arranged which network reporters would be included. History had been scheduled according to the Nielsen ratings.

Nixon leaned back in his chair, took a long, deliberate puff on his Meerschaum pipe, and grinned. "Not bad, is it, Chuck? The Democrats won't even be able to buy time on TV."

"No, sir, not bad," I replied with open admiration. Even foreign policy was fair game.

There are not isolated examples, of course. All governments use the reality as well as the façade of power to maintain their own power. In democratic structures the process is somewhat subtle, but in regimes where there are few moral restraints, power is wielded shamelessly. We call it totalitarianism. George Orwell captured this in one of the most riveting scenes of his classic 1984.

The book's central character, a hapless fellow named Winston, defies the state. He is eventually tracked down and tortured by the chief party functionary, O'Brien. As O'Brien administers massive electrical jolts to Winston's squirming body, he abandons all pretense and shrieks into Winston's ear, "The party seeks power entirely for its own sake . . . we are interested only in power . . . the object of power is power."[4]

Stalin rose to power by systematically murdering those who stood in his way; he then maintained his power by slaughtering millions. Hitler executed all potential threats to the Third Reich—even his own SA—then consolidated his power grip on Germany with a regime of terror. Recent tyrants, such as Idi Amin and the Cambodian Communists, have done the same.

One of the most startling commentaries on this century is the fact that millions more have died at the hands of their own governments that in wars with other nations—all to preserve someone's power.

*   *   *

In The Masters, British novelist C. P. Snow tells the story of a man who chooses not to be king but kingmaker, the ultimate achievement power affords.[5] Snow might well have been writing about me.

I entered government believing that public office was a trust, a duty. Gradually, imperceptibly, I began to view it as a holy crusade; the future of the republic, or so I rationalized, depended upon the president's continuation in office. But whether I acknowledged it or not, equally important was the fact that my own power depended on it.

While power may begin as a means to an end, it soon becomes, as O'Brien screamed in Winston's ear, the end itself. Having witnessed Watergate from the inside, I can attest to the wisdom of Lord Acton's well-known adage: Power corrupts; absolute power corrupts absolutely.

It is crucial to note, however, that it is power that corrupts, not power that is corrupt. It is like electricity. When properly handled, electricity provides light and energy; when mishandled it destroys. God has given power to the state to be used to restrain evil and maintain order. It is the use of power, whether for personal gain or for the state's ordained function, that is at issue.

The problem of power is not limited to public officials, of course. It affects all human relationships, from the domineering parent to the bullying boss to the manipulative spouse to the pastor who plays God. It is also wielded effectively by the seemingly weak who manipulate others to gain their own ends. The temptation to abuse power confronts everyone, including people in positions of spiritual authority.

The much-publicized corruption of some television evangelists can easily be traced to an inability to handle power. It's a heady business to run worldwide ministries, multimillion dollar television shows, or wealthy amphitheater churches. Leaders who rise to prominence in the religious world are placed on the precarious pedestal of Christian celebrity. When the celebrity is magnified a million times over by the electron tube, the dangers of falling increase dramatically.

Take the case of Jim and Tammy Bakker. When I first visited their ministry in 1976, their shoestring operation was housed in an old building. They were, I was convinced, sincerely concerned with reaching others with the Good News. A year later I was invited to their new, modern facilities and was immediately struck by the change in their demeanor. I did not return. I witnessed the same phenomenon with one of the country's most popular daytime interviewers. The first time I was a guest on his show, before he had begun to soar in the ratings game, the interviewer was humble, keenly interested in the subject, well-prepared, and congenial. Two years later, when this man had become the sensation of the television world, he breezed into the room flanked by obsequious aides, was woefully unconcerned with

526 KINGDOMS IN CONFLICT

what his guests had to say, and was arrogant and rude on the air—to the delight of his audience.

It's ludicrous for any Christian to believe that he or she is the worthy object of public worship; it would be like the donkey carrying Jesus into Jerusalem believing the crowds were cheering and laying down their garments for him. But the perks and public adoration accompanying television exposure are enough to inflate nearly anyone's ego. This leads to the self-indulgent use of power some have dubbed the "Imelda Marcos syndrome," which reasons, "because I'm in this position, I have a right to do whatever I want," with total selfishness and disregard for others. Power is like saltwater; the more you drink the thirstier you get.

The lure of power can separate the most resolute of Christians from the true nature of Christian leadership, which is service to others. It's difficult to stand on a pedestal and wash the feet of those below.

It was this very temptation of power that led to the first sin. Eve was tempted to eat from the tree of knowledge to be like God and acquire power reserved for Him. "The sin of the Garden was the sin of power," says Quaker writer Richard Foster.[6]

Power has been one of Satan's most effective tools from the beginning, perhaps because he lusts for it so himself. Milton wrote of Lucifer in *Paradise Lost*, "To reign is worth ambition, though in hell. Better to reign in hell than serve in heaven."[7]

In the process of announcing the Kingdom and offering redemption from the Fall, Jesus Christ turned conventional views of power upside down. When His disciples argued over who was the greatest, Jesus rebuked them. "The greatest among you should be like the youngest, and the one who rules like the one who serves," he said.[8] Imagine the impact His statement would make in the back rooms of American politicians or in the carpeted boardrooms of big business—or, sadly, in some religious councils.

Jesus was as good as His words. He washed His own followers' dusty feet, a chore reserved for the lowliest servant of first-century Palestine. A king serving the mundane physical needs of His subjects? Incomprehensible. Yet servant leadership is the heart of Christ's teaching. "Whoever wants to be first must be slave of all."[9]

His was a revolutionary message to the class-conscious culture of the first century, where position and privilege were entrenched, evidenced by the Pharisees with their reserved seats in the synagogue, by masters ruling slaves, and by men dominating women. It is no less revolutionary today in the class-conscious cultures of the East and West where power, money, fame, and influence are idolized in various forms.

The Christian understanding of power is that it is found most often in weakness. This paradox has been a thorn in the flesh of tyrants. The Judeo-Christian teaching that man is vulnerable to the temptations of power has also caused democracies and free nations to build restraints and balances of power into their structures.

Clearly this is what motivated the revolutionaries in England to guarantee a Parliament independent of the monarchy. And in America the Founding Fathers, influenced by Judeo-Christian teaching about the vulnerability of man, wisely adopted the principle of the separation of powers. Within the government, power was diffused through a system of checks and balances so no one branch could dominate another. The Founders also assumed that the religious value system, evidenced through the separate institution of the church, would be the most powerful brake on the natural avarice of government. As Tocqueville observed, "Religion in America takes no direct part in the government or society but it must, nevertheless, be regarded as the foremost of the political institutions of that country."[10]

The most important restraint on power, however, is a healthy understanding of its true source. When power in the conventional sense is relinquished, one discovers a much deeper power.

Prisoners often discover this, as did Jerry Levin and Aleksandr Solzhenitsyn. In his memoirs of the gulag, Solzhenitsyn wrote that as long as he was trying to maintain some pitiful degree of worldly power in his situation—control of food, clothing, schedule—he was constantly under the heel of his captors. But after his conversion, when he accepted and surrendered to his utter powerlessness, then he became free of even his captors' power. Perhaps this is why Boris Pasternak once wrote that the only place one can be free in a communist society is in prison.

The apostle Paul said, "My power is made perfect in weakness," and concluded, "When I am weak, then I am strong."[11] And throughout Scripture God reveals a special compassion for the powerless: widows, orphans, prisoners, and aliens. Though the message of the Kingdom of God offers salvation for all who repent and believe, God does not conceal His disdain for those who repent and believe, God does not conceal His disdain for those so enamored of their own power that they refuse to worship Him or to acknowledge His delight in the humble.

A culture that exalts power and celebrity, that worships success, dismisses such words as nonsense. Strong individuals rely on their own resources—which will never, ultimately speaking, be enough—but the so-called weak person knows his or her own limits and needs, and thus depends wholly on God. Perhaps this is why God so often confounds the wisdom of the world by accomplishing His purposes through the powerless and His most powerful work through human weakness.

I first learned this in prison. When the frustration of my helplessness seemed greatest, I discovered God's grace was more than sufficient. And after my imprisonment I could look back and see how God used my powerlessness for His purposes. What He has chosen for my most significant witness was not my triumphs or victories, but my defeat.

Similarly, Prison Fellowship's work in the prisons has been effective not because of any power we may have as an organization, but because of the powerlessness of those we serve. During an unforgettable trip to Peru in 1984, for example, I visited Lurigancho, the largest prison in the world. There seven thousand inmates, including a number of terrorists, were crowded in abysmal conditions; hatred, hostility, and despair seeped out of the cellblocks. Yet within the darkness of Lurigancho is a thriving Christian community—men who have found Christ and experienced renewed hearts and minds.

After visiting with these brothers, I went directly from the prison to meet with a number of government officials in downtown Lima. Covered with prison dust and marked with the sweaty embraces of Christian prisoners, I addressed these officials at the highest level of government—and they listened intently.

Had I gone to Peru specifically to meet with the key government leadership, I would have likely been stymied. They wanted to meet me not because of any power or influence I had, but because of our work in the prisons. They knew that in the chaos of Lurigancho, Prison Fellowship was doing something to bring healing and restoration. Therefore, they were eager to listen to our recommendations, ready to discuss a biblical view of justice and prison issues. Whatever authority I had in speaking to these powerful men came not from my power but from serving the powerless. I have experienced this in country after country. It is the paradox of real power.

*   *   *

Nothing distinguishes the kingdoms of man from the Kingdom of God more than their diametrically opposed views of the exercise of power. One seeks to control people, the other to serve people; one promotes self, the other prostrates self; one seeks prestige and position, the other lifts up the lowly and despised.

It is crucial for Christians to understand this difference. For through this upside-down view of power, the Kingdom of God can play a special role in the affairs of the world.

As citizens of the Kingdom today practice this view of power, they are setting an example for their neighbors by modeling servanthood and exposing the illusions power creates.

But how does this paradoxical view of power apply to the Christian who is in a position of influence and control? Sociologist Tony Campolo, drawing on the classic work of Max Weber, offers helpful guidance through the distinctions he draws between power and authority. Power involves the use of coercive force to make others yield to one's wishes even against their own will. Authority is achieved—or is conferred upon one—by virtue of character that others are motivated to follow willingly.[12]

Therefore, the citizen of the Kingdom should seek authority that comes from his or her own spiritual strength. Never for self-advantage, but for the benefit of others.

This does not mean that the Christian can't use power. In positions of leadership, especially in government institutions to which God had specifically granted the power of the sword, the Christian can do so in good conscience. But the Christian uses power with a different motive and in different ways: not to impose his or her personal will over others but to preserve God's plan for order and justice for all.

Those who accept the biblical view of servant leadership treat power as a humbling delegation from God, not as a right to control others.

Moses offers a great role model. Though he had awesome power and responsibility as the leader of two million Israelites, he was described in Scripture as "a very humble man, more humble than anyone else on the face of the earth."[13] He led by serving—intervening before God on his people's behalf, seeking God's forgiveness for their rebellion and caring for their needs above his own.

The challenge for the Christian in a position of influence is to follow the example of Moses rather than fulfill Nietzsche's prophecy concerning the will to power. In doing so the citizen of the Kingdom has an opportunity to offer light to a world often shrouded by the dark pretensions of a devastating succession of power-mad tyrants.

20

Christians in Politics

Who's to say religion and politics shouldn't mix? Whose Bible are they reading anyway?

—*Archbishop Desmond Tutu*

Frequently I'm asked whether I would have participated in Watergate if I had been a Christian when I worked in the White House. The implication is that Christians are immune to corruption.

I'm always tempted to say, "Of course not." But that's self-righteous nonsense. While Christians know that their faith requires high standards of righteousness, they are human and often capitulate to the same temptations as anyone else. In fact, Christians may well face more problems than others when they become involved in the political process.

How does a Christian deal with the inherent divided loyalties: duty to God and duty to the national interest? Can a Christian successfully avoid the subtle snares of power? Can a Christian make the compromises necessary for the everyday business of politics?

What about the question of candor, for example? At times national security may well require not only concealing the truth, but lying. When

I was in the White House, we went to elaborate lengths to conceal essential secret negotiations. Henry Kissinger had a bad cold when he visited Pakistan in 1971—or so we told the press. Actually he had been flown to Bejing to conduct clandestine meetings in preparation for Mr. Nixon's historic visit to China.

Or take the day Nixon announced a major troop withdrawal in Vietnam. He immediately ordered Kissinger to bring Soviet Ambassador Dobrynin to a secret meeting room in the White House basement. "Henry," he roared, "You shake him up. Tell him not to believe these news stories. We're only pulling out a few troops—and if the Russians don't back off in sending supplies to Hanoi, we'll bomb the daylights out of that city. Tell him the president is uncontrollable, a madman— that he'll do anything. Let's keep them off balance." That such meetings took place was flatly denied in order to protect the lives of the withdrawing troops.

President Reagan did the same thing in 1983. When reporters asked about a rumored invasion of Grenada, official White House spokesmen dismissed such questions as "preposterous." Actually, troops were at that moment disembarking on the island's beaches. A "no comment" to the press, however, would have been tantamount to a "yes"—an admission that would have endangered lives.

In these days of delicate international tensions and the instant communications ability of an almost omnipresent press, such deceit is a common instrument of foreign policy. The press even accept it. In a 1987 *Newsweek* interview, crack ABC interviewer Ted Koppel acknowledged that government officials must be "prepared to mislead and . . . sometimes even to lie."[1]

Deliberate lies, the corruption of power, compromise with ideological opponents, temptations on all sides—these appear to be the mechanisms of modern government. Should the Christian circumvent the messy business of politics altogether?

The answer must be an emphatic no. As Robert L. Dabney wrote, "Every Christian . . . whether law-maker or law executor or voter, should carry his Christian conscience, enlightened by God's Word, into his political duty. We must ask less what party caucuses and leaders dictate, and more what duty dictates."[2]

There are at least three compelling reasons Christians must be involved in politics and government. First, as citizens of the nation-state, Christians have the same civic duties all citizens have: to serve on juries, to pay taxes, to vote, to support candidates they think are best qualified. They are commanded to pray for and respect governing authorities. (For years many Christian fundamentalists shunned the "sinful" political process, even to the extent of not voting. Whatever else may be said about it, the Moral Majority performed a valuable public service in bringing these citizens back into the mainstream.)

Second, as citizens of the Kingdom of God they are to bring God's standards of righteousness and justice to bear on the kingdoms of this world. This is the cultural commission discussed earlier. As former Michigan state senator and college professor Stephen Monsma says, Christian political involvement has the "potential to move the political system away from . . . the brokering of the self-interest of powerful persons and groups into a renewed concern for the public interest."[3]

Third, Christians have an obligation to bring transcendent moral values into the public debate. All law implicitly involves morality; the popular idea that "you can't legislate morality" is a myth. Morality is legislated every day from the vantage point of one value system or another. The question is not whether we will legislate morality, but whose morality we will legislate.

Law is but a body of rules regulating human behavior; it establishes, from the view of the state, the rightness or wrongness of human behavior. Most laws, therefore, have moral implications. Statutes prohibiting murder, mandates for seat belts, or regulations for industrial safety are all designed to protect human life—a reflection of the particular moral view that values the dignity and worth of human life. And efficacy doesn't affect morality. If in America we have more homicides per capita than in any other country, it's not reason to repeal the laws making murder a crime.

The common argument against the legislation of morality is Prohibition, which conjures up such caricatures as Billy Sunday waving a chair over his head and Carrie Nation chopping up whiskey barrels. The church has taken an undeserved bad rap for this. No one entity imposed Prohibition; it was voted in by a clear majority after a lengthy national debate.

Admittedly, over the years of its existence Prohibition became increasingly difficult to enforce; it encouraged organized crime and ultimately led to widespread disrespect for the law. Eventually the costs outweighed the benefits.

But was it morally justified? Certainly one's personal decision to drink alcohol is a private matter. When millions do it to such excess that public safety is endangered, however, it becomes a public concern. That was the case in the pre-Prohibition era. Thousands reported to their factory jobs under the influence and were maimed or killed by the heavy industrial machines then being introduced in the American economy. The tavern trade spawned prostitution rings at a time when, like AIDS today, there was no cure for the raging epidemic of venereal disease.

Though many write off Prohibition as a complete failure, the facts are that industrial safety improved dramatically as per capita drinking, particularly among working people, dropped precipitously, and the VD epidemic slowed. Not until 1970 did per capita consumption of alcohol again reach pre-Prohibition levels.[4]

With one person being killed every twenty-seven minutes in the U.S. by a drunk driver and the majority of crimes being committed by people under the influence of drugs or alcohol, can anyone really argue realistically today that moral issues are not matters of public interest?

The real issue for Christians is not whether they should be involved in politics or contend for laws that affect moral behavior. The question is how.

*   *   *

On an individual level, political involvement for the Christian entails not only voting and other basic responsibilities of citizenship, but dealing directly with political issues, particularly where justice and human dignity are at stake. A friend of mine, a prominent attorney in Ecuador, experienced this firsthand.

Dr. Jorge Crespo has always been an activist. For years he was an attorney for labor unions, fighting for justice and humane working conditions for Ecuador's laborers. Later he ran unsuccessfully for the presidency of his country. Then, after meeting with Prison Fellowship's South American regional director, Javier Bustamante, he agreed to consider prison ministry, even though he had always seen prisons as places where delinquents—and some clients—ended up.

But as soon as Dr. Crespo walked the cellblocks of a Quito prison, he felt "a deep sensation of pain, something like an echo of the pain of the prisoners. Since we are made in His image, we have been given His compassion toward our neighbor," he explained.

So Dr. Crespo became president of Prison Fellowship Ecuador. As he investigated prison conditions, he uncovered, to his horror, instances of cruelty, deprivation, and misery. In one prison twenty prisoners were wedged into a cell the size of a small bedroom. In another inmates received less care than animals; their food budget was less than that of the officers' guard dogs. In most women's prisons, children were incarcerated along with their mothers. In some cases they were being used as pawns in child prostitution rings to make profits for their parents, the prison guards, or both.

There were also reports of inhumane treatment. Some prisoners had confessed to crimes of which they were innocent in order to escape such measures.

Dr. Crespo and his colleagues documented their case, then began to educate the public through press, radio, and television. They sent letters to the prison wardens with copies to the minister of government; they met with ministers of social rehabilitation and justice. Their campaign was not without personal sacrifice and political risk.

Finally, they approached the tribunal overseeing constitutional enforcement, a governmental committee safeguarding Ecuador's provisions for human rights.

Crespo spent two hours testifying about the despicable prison conditions as well as the inhumane treatment of inmates and those who had been detained for crimes but not yet proven guilty.

The justices were shocked. Never before had such ugly topics been addressed in their ornate chambers. At the conclusion, the vice-president leaned forward to Dr. Crespo. "You have come here as Christians," he said, "and what you have done today is truly Christian."

As a result of Dr. Crespo's boldness, a series of reforms have been adopted in Ecuador. He has also organized a group of Christian police officers who are working to assure humane police investigation that does not rely on brutality.

Dr. Crespo is seeing slow but deliberate progress in the prisons.

The political and personal risks have been worth it, he says. "To act as Christians we have to stand against injustice, and with prophetic voice talk courageously about truth, justice, fear, love. We ought not to bear infamy or atrocities. I believe a Christian who will remain silent is not a Christian."

Activist Christians like Jorge Crespo who work as private citizens to address problems within the structures of government do so, as Stephen Monsma has written, "not as moral busybodies who are seeking to foist their morals onto all of society by the force of law, but as those who have a passion for justice, as those who respect all persons as unique image bearers of God and who therefore seek to treat them with justice."[5]

*   *   *

But many others are called to make a Christian witness from positions within government itself. After all, as men like William Wilberforce or the great nineteenth-century social reformer, Lord Shaftesbury, clearly illustrate, Christians who are politicians can bear a biblical witness on political structures, just as they do in medicine, law, business, labor, education, the arts, or any other walk of life. Augustine called God-fearing rulers "blessings bestowed . . . upon mankind."[6] They exhibit this in their moral witness and their willingness to stand up for unpopular causes, even if such causes benefit society more than their own political careers.

U.S. Senators Nunn of Georgia and Armstrong of Colorado attended a Bible study several years ago on the topic of restitution as a biblical means of punishment. The two leaders later examined the federal statutes and discovered that restitution was only vaguely mentioned. Even though "lock 'em up" legislation was in political vogue, the two men, both committed Christians, sponsored legislation to set new standards for sentencing: prison for dangerous offenders, but tax-dollar-saving alternative punishments, such as work and restitution programs, for nondangerous offenders. In 1983 the bill was adopted, after heated debate, as a resolution of the Congress and later was used as model legislation by several states.

Christians can also bring mercy, compassion, and friendship to those in the cutthroat business of politics.

After his resignation Mr. Nixon withdrew to isolation behind the walls of his San Clemente compound. For nearly a year, as he struggled to recover from both the deep emotional wounds of Watergate and life-threatening phlebitis, Mr. Nixon saw only his family and a few close friends. No one, other than gloating reporters, tried to visit him.

No one, that is, except one man who had opposed Mr. Nixon as vigorously as anyone in the Senate. Without fanfare, Mark Hatfield, an evangelical Christian, traveled twice to San Clemente. His reason? Simply, as he told me later, "to let Mr. Nixon know that someone loved him."

Sometimes even minor things can have a significant ripple effect in the everyday business of government. Concerned about the pressures government service puts on congressional families, Congressmen Frank Wolf and Dan Coats hosted a series of receptions to show James Dobson's excellent family-counseling films. More than a hundred members and their spouses attended; several later sought counseling help. Through Coats and Wolf the films were also shown to the Joint Chiefs of Staff and Pentagon officials, who have since made them available for use in military training programs.

Christians in public office are motivated by something more than popularity or self-interest, something that frees them from being held hostage to political expediency. Their motivation to pursue what is right, in obedience to God, also gives them a source of wisdom and confidence beyond their own abilities. Michael Alison, member of Parliament and Prime Minister Thatcher's senior parliamentary aide, offers a clear example.

After his Christian conversion at Oxford in the forties, Michael Alison initially planned to go into the ministry. But his keen interest in politics—and a desire to serve his nation—led him to change vocational directions. Elected to Parliament in 1964, he quietly earned his way from the back bench to leadership.

In 1979 Michael was named minister of state for Northern Ireland, a responsibility that included administration of Ulster's notorious prisons. Then, in the late fall of 1980, young Catholic terrorists in Belfast's Maze prison began to starve themselves to death in protest of British rule in Northern Ireland. By Christmas the first prisoner had gone nearly two months without food and was near death. Worldwide attention focused on Belfast. Would the British government allow this young inmate to die, or would they force-feed him once he slipped into a final coma?

The prison doctor came to Michael Alison for the decision. It was, of course, a Hobson's choice. To force-feed the protester would cause riots among the Irish Republican Army faithful; to let him die would be callous.

Michael had been praying for weeks for wisdom in the horrible situation. "Go to the prisoner's fellow hunger strikers," he told the doctor. "Ask them to make the decision." The other protesters could not have their brother's death on their consciences, but in the process of putting him on life-support equipment, they saw the inconsistency of their own position. The hunger strike ended, the crisis averted.*

But while being biblically motivated and informed may give wisdom, it does not necessarily assure political success. In this arena Christians in politics are often at a disadvantage.

In the self-aggrandizing world of politics, Michael Alison is an anomaly. He seems more comfortable helping his adversary to his feet than cutting him down in debate. Though one of the most powerful men in British government, he has the unpolitical knack of blending into the background of any crowded political gathering.

---

*By the time of a second IRA hunger strike several months later, the protesters hardened their resolve, and ten of their comrades starved to death.

His unconventional attitude begins early in the day with his morning devotional. "If I was consumed with politics," he explains, "my first priority would be the morning newspapers, not the Bible." But Michael's first priority is not his political career; it is his relationship with God.

Because of that, though Michael is conscientious in his work, his first ambition is not for the continued pursuit of position. He spurns political infighting and places a higher premium on trust than power. Of his role as Prime Minister Thatcher's assistant, he says he is one of the few people she knows she can take for granted. "That's the highest compliment I could hope for in my role."

This servantlike attitude is so diametrically opposed to society's that it can easily be mistaken for weakness. In reality it gives a greater strength. The Christian in a position of power is not enslaved by that position—and thus the Christian has tremendous freedom to follow the dictates of conscience, not the fickle winds of self-interest.

But Christians are also exposed to greater struggles of conscience. They are honor bound to be the best statesmen they can be, as well as the best Christians they can be. These competing allegiances caused British writer Harry Blamires to conclude that perhaps "a good Christian [can] be a good politician . . . but it is probably quite impossible for a good Christian to be a highly successful politician."[7]

Blamires may well have been referring to some of the dilemmas mentioned at the beginning of this chapter. Foremost is the issue of divided allegiances between God and the state. When there is a conflict of loyalty, the sincere Christian must obey God. Yet the politician's oath of office is to uphold the laws of the state.

The prevailing American view that faith is something private with no effect on public responsibility was first put forth by John Kennedy in a dramatic speech to the Houston Ministerial Association in the 1960 campaign. Protestants feared that Kennedy, a Catholic, would be bound by the dictates of the Roman church. So Kennedy pulled off a political masterstroke when he told the Texas ministers, mostly Baptists, that "whatever issue may come before me as president, if I'm elected . . . I will make my decision in accordance . . . with what my conscience tells me to be in the national interest, and without regard to outside religious pressure or dictate. And no power or threat of punishment could cause me to decide otherwise."[8]

Kennedey's message, which brought the house down, was a key to his election. But it set a precedent that has now become part of established American political wisdom: One's religious convictions must have no effect on one's public decisions.

But consider Kennedy's words: "No power . . . could cause me to decide otherwise." Not God? Though Kennedy's approach was enormously popular, it was also a renunciation of any influence his religion might have. He subsumed his church responsibility under his patriotism—or his candidacy.*

What else can a public official do? you may ask. The officeholder in a free society cannot *impose* personal views on the electorate; the democratic process must be respected in a pluralistic society. That is true.

Some go on to conclude, however, that the Christian officeholder is thus free, in the name of political prudence, to support or accept the majority will when it is contrary to Christian teaching (a view eloquently espoused by Governor Mario Cuomo in his 1984 Notre Dame address). Religious conviction is thereby reduced to a private matter; the social implications of the gospel are simply ignored. And as we have seen, the results of such privatization can be dangerous to society as a whole.

Another position, often taken in reaction to the Kennedy-Cuomo view, is represented by the fictional President Hopkins of our prologue, who was prepared to thrust his own theological view on an unsuspecting nation. This view, articulated by some in political debate today, argues that a Christian politician should use his position to speak for God.

But such reasoning has no place in a pluralistic society and would, if carried out, make the frightening conclusion of Hopkins's fictional scenario entirely plausible. In his case the issue was not a conflict between human rights or human life and state policy, areas where a Christian leader must take a stand. Rather, it was a question of biblical prophecy, whose fulfillment is the responsibility of God, not man. Hopkins presumptuously, if unconsciously, played God.

Hopkins was also confused about the duty of government. As God's servant, his sworn task was to preserve order, promote justice,

*By contrast, Hilaire Belloc stood for election in 1906 in the British Parliament. As a Roman Catholic, he knew he would have to struggle to overcome religious prejudices, so he decided to confront the issue head-on. In his first campaign speech, he stood at the rostrum with a rosary in his hand and said, "I am a Catholic. As far as possible I go to Mass every day. As far as possible I kneel down and tell these beads every day. If you reject me on account of my religion, I shall thank God that He has spared me the indignity of being your representative." He was elected. From *The Little, Brown Book of Anecdotes* (Boston: Little, Brown, 1985), 50.

and restrain evil, which in this case meant acting decisively to prevent war in a volatile international situation. Richard Neuhaus writes, "To gain public office and take an oath before God to maintain the constitutional order, and then to use that office as a tool for advancing one's reading of Bible prophecy is an act of hubris, treachery, treason and deceit."[9]

Both views—privatized faith and using political power to play God—are deeply flawed. This brings us full circle: Is it possible for a devout Christian to serve in public office without compromising either his or her conscience or constituency?

It is possible. But only if the Christian officeholder understands several key truths. First, a government official must not play God; one's duty is to facilitate government's ordained role of preserving order and justice, not to use government to accomplish the goals of the church. Second, the Christian must respect the rights of all religious groups and insure that government protects every citizen's freedom of conscience.

There is an alternative to the imposition of religious values or the passive acceptance of majority opinion, a principle that pays both pluralism and conscience their due. Christian politicians must do all in their power to make clear, public arguments on issues of moral and political importance, to persuade rather than coerce. A recent Vatican statement put it this way: "Politicians must commit themselves through their interventions upon public opinion, to securing in society the widest possible consensus on . . . essential points (matters concerning human rights, human life, or the institution of the family)."[10]

A third concern brings us back to the question posed at the outset of this chapter. What about the Christian responsibility in an age where national leaders in the nuclear age do not—perhaps, cannot—be entirely candid in public pronouncements? Consider the dilemma posed by the Reagan administration's disinformation campaign designed to unsettle the government of Mohammar Khadaffi—a murderous tyrant imperiling any number of nations. Confronted with this question, Secretary of State George Shultz defended the government's actions by quoting Winston Churchill: "In times of war, the truth is so precious, it must be attended by a bodyguard of lies."[11]

The pressures of nuclear-age diplomacy create conscience-wrenching agony for sincere Christians in office. Yet the Bible offers some surprising principles, citing Rahab, a prostitute, as one of the great heroes of the faith. Why? Rahab's place in history was established by the fact that she lied to protect Hebrew spies. Similarly, concentration-camp survivor Corrie Ten Boom lied to the Nazis to protect the Jews she was hiding. Most Christians today would likely do the same, for in this cruel and complex world, a lesser evil may be required to prevent a greater one. A Christian in public office may be placed in a similar situation, say, to save the lives of hostages. If the situation forced the Christian to lie against his or her conscience, the Christian should resign.

*   *   *

So far we have considered only laymen. But what about priests or ministers in public office, a question made timely by the presidential candidacies of the Reverends Pat Robertson and Jesse Jackson?

Before Constantine's Christianizing of the Roman empire, all Christians were advised to avoid civil office because of the idolatrous emperor worship it demanded. (In some instances that concern is as relevant today as it was in ancient Rome.)

Even after Constantine, church policy restricted members of the clergy from holding office on the grounds that civil office would inevitably prevent their giving full attention to their ecclesiastical concerns.*

At one point in England's history, the government prohibited ordained ministers from holding office. The American colonists wrote similar prohibitions into several state constitutions, which remained in effect until 1978, when the U.S. Supreme Court struck down the Tennessee restrictions as a violation of a minister's First Amendment right.[12]

Despite the Tennessee case and the fact that the U.S. Constitution contains no such prohibition, the tradition remains strong. Few clergy have held major offices in Western democracies.

In the Catholic church, Pope John Paul's rejection of the tiara of temporal authority was a clear signal: ecclesiastical goals would not be sought through political means. Thus it was consistent that John Paul II in 1980 ordered priests out of secular office entirely. Five-term Congressman Robert Drinan, a Jesuit priest and outspoken liberal, quietly resigned.

---

*There were few exceptions over the centuries; when they were made, it was to protect religious liberty, as, for example, when anti-Catholic legislation was being enacted in Hungary; the priests were released to engage in politics "for the sake of safeguarding religion or promoting the common good."

In Nicaragua, however, three priests defied the papal order. This has been a major cause of the rift not only within the church, but it has compromised the integrity of the church. Those priests may say they are acting in a civil capacity but can they really disavow responsibility for the expulsion of missionaries, restriction on the free press, including *Iglesia*, the official Catholic newspaper?

The cleric in public office can hardly avoid such double-mindedness. And presenting two faces to the world inevitably damages the work that should be of primary concern: the witness of the church.

Regardless of one's stand on abortion, for example, no one could seriously imagine Sister Agnes Mary Mansour as commissioner of Health and Welfare in Michigan, supervising state-funded abortions while in conscience maintaining her vows to a church that forbids abortion. Definitions of integrity have been stretched in recent years, but not that far.

Any priest or minister who feels called to seek public office should, as a citizen, be free to undertake that vocation. But doing so means that he must leave the pulpit, resigning all ecclesiastical functions. He must make it clear that he is acting as a private citizen seeking office to fulfill civic, not spiritual goals. (In many denominations, however, the priestly office cannot actually be resigned.)

But if the clergy should not hold office, should the institutional church be silent on political issues? This is perhaps the most sensitive question of all.

As we've noted earlier, the church acts as the conscience of society. Christopher Dawson notes that Christianity is "the soul of Western civilization. And when the soul is gone, the body putrefies."[13] So the church must address moral issues in society and measure public actions by biblical standards of justice and righteousness.

But there are pitfalls. One of the greatest is the tendency Christians have to believe that because the Bible is "on their side" they can speak with authority on every issue. Many church bureaucracies have succumbed to this temptation in recent decades, spewing out position papers on everything from public toilet facilities to nuclear war. The New Right has engaged in such excesses with its scorecards covering the gamut of issues from trade legislation to the Panama Canal. When Christians use the broad brush, they become simply another political interest group, pontificating on matters about which they are often woefully uninformed.

A case in point was the U.S. Catholic bishops' position paper on nuclear war. It hardly seems necessary to convene a conference to announce that it is a moral issue to unleash weapons that would annihilate millions. The bishops did, however, and they went on to conclude that the deterrent posture of the United States was unsatisfactory from a moral point of view.[14]

That could be true—particularly if one realizes that our missiles are aimed at Soviet cities, just as Soviet missiles are aimed at U.S. cities. But deterrence itself is not immoral by definition; deterrence is impeding another nation's hostile act. The existence of a nuclear weapon (as with a policeman's gun) may prevent a much greater evil.

Any moral analysis must take into account the complexity of modern nuclear strategy and the actual efficacy of deterrence. To determine this, one cannot simply consider just numbers of bombs or throw-weight, but targeting studies and the whole range of strategic options; what would remain after a surprise attack; what defenses neutralize attacking missiles; what would the communications capacity be, and the like. Ironically, the country that renounces a first strike (the more moral position, as the bishops would no doubt agree) has need for a much larger deterrent capability (which the bishops decry as immoral). The logical consequences of their paper is a Catch-22.

While the bishops certainly could have commented on the immorality of unleashing nuclear war, they simply didn't have all the facts necessary to render an authoritative judgment beyond that. This was summed up by a University of Chicago professor who agreed personally with the bishops' position, but concluded that they could not determine whether deterrence was immoral because such judgment depended on facts "which are secret—and thus, unknown to the bishops."[15]

Russell Kirk, a Catholic layman himself, has described the delegates to such conferences as "utopians . . . wondrously unaware of the limits of politics."[16] Certainly the heated controversy resulting from the bishops' attempt to formulate United States defense policy called their own competence into question far more than the government's. After attending a conference in which religious leaders addressed issues on every imaginable question of policy, most about which the church demonstrably lacked expertise, Kirk mused that he would "as soon go to a bartender for medical advice as to a church secretary for political wisdom."[17]

Poland's Catholic bishops seem to have understood the need to deal with issues within their particular competence better perhaps than their U.S. counterparts. When the Polish government engaged in one of its periodic purges of political dissidents in 1985, the bishops quickly condemned the persecution. A clear issue of human rights was at stake, and the moral question was unambiguous. They added, however, that "the Church is not and does not, want to be a political force [but it] has the right to give moral assessments, even in questions of political affairs when the basic rights of the individual or the salvation of the soul demands it."[18]

The Polish bishops understood the restraints imposed on the church when it speaks as the church. This is a crucial distinction. It is one thing for an individual Christian to address whatever issue his or her conscience dictates, but the church as a body, which purports to speak God's truth, should speak only to those matters in which fidelity to holy Scripture itself makes it necessary to speak out: Issues where human life or dignity, religious liberty, or justice are involved. Even then, the church should claim no superior wisdom except in those areas where it is uniquely able to bring biblically informed truth to the debate.* An excellent example, one that stands in distinct contrast to the pastoral letter on nuclear policy, was the 1987 Vatican statement on human life and biomedical ethics. It spoke forthrightly to a clear biblical issue on which the church has special competence and about which the secular world was grossly confused. It has been perhaps the single most useful document issued thus far to clarify moral questions in the growing debate over reproductive technology.

Politics is not the church's first calling. Evangelism, administering the sacraments, providing discipleship, fellowship, teaching the Word, and exhorting its members to holy living are the heartbeat of the church. When it addresses political issues, the church must not do so at the risk of weakening its primary mission. As mainline churches discovered in the sixties, the faster they churned out partisan statements, the faster they emptied their pews.

*Russell Kirk quotes Renee Divismay Williamson at length in Kirk's classic article, "Promises and Perils of 'Christian Politics'," Intercollegiate Review (Fall/Winter 1982), 13, to clarify these difficult questions.

There are controversial issues in which the principle is unmistakable and the command of the hour comes through loud and clear. On these issues the church must make pronouncements. . . .

But there are other general issues in which facts and motives are mixed, consequences contradict the principles involved and equally dedicated and knowledgeable Christians disagree. In these cases the church should remain silent, letting individual Christians and Christian groups decide for themselves what Christian witness means. . . . For the church to sponsor a political party, engage in lobbying, form coalitions with secular pressure groups and become entangled in the decisions of private business corporations, would be to take a position on precisely those issues in which the religious significance is unclear, ambiguous or non-existent.

And while the Christian citizens can afford to be as partisan as they wish, Christian pastors cannot. If they are, they may soon discover they have compromised both their own witness and that of their church.

An extreme example was the case of the bishop who presided at the May 1987 funeral of former CIA Director William Casey. Because President Reagan, former President Nixon, and a host of other government officials were in the congregation, the bishop used the occasion to attack U.S. foreign policy in Central America, for which the deceased Mr. Casey was an outspoken proponent. It was in such deplorably bad taste that the incident, reported worldwide, resulted in an adverse reaction not against U.S. policy, but against the church. Grieving families should receive spiritual comfort, not a political harangue against their loved one's views.

Admittedly a fine line exists here. It is clearly partisan for a pastor to stand in a pulpit and endorse a particular candidate, as some clergymen endorsed Jimmy Carter in 1980, and others endorsed Ronald Reagan 1984. But what about Cardinal O'Connor's statement in the same campaign that a Catholic could not in conscience vote for a candidate who supported abortion? His remarks were reported as a partisan rebuke of the views of two of his New York parishioners, Governor Mario Cuomo and vice-presidential candidate Geraldine Ferraro. Admittedly, the cardinal's timing made his remarks suspect, but they could also be regarded as no more than a statement of elementary logic. Since the Catholic church believes that the taking of unborn lives violates God's law, could a Catholic in conscience logically vote for one who willfully violated that law? While I believe an open pulpit endorsement of a candidate is improper, I also feel that—if made responsibly from the right motivations—a cleric's statement that Christians should not support candidates who reject basic human rights is justified.

Within these limits, then, we can conclude that Christians, both individually and institutionally, have a duty, for the good of society as a whole, to bring the values of the Kingdom of God to bear within the kingdoms of man.

It is fair to say, however, that Christians have not done a particularly good job at this task. Often they have terrified their secular neighbors, who see Christian political activists as either backwoods bigots or religious ayatollahs attempting to assault them with Bible verses or religious magisteriums. In a pluralistic society it is not only wrong but unwise for Christians to shake their Bibles and arrogantly assert that "God says . . ." That is the quickest way for Christians, a distinct minority in civil affairs, to lose their case altogether.

Instead, positions should be argued on their merits. If the case is sound, a majority can be persuaded; that's the way democracies and free nations are supposed to work.

I'm often asked to meet with government officials concerned with criminal-justice policies. They are frustrated. The more prisons are built—at great expense—the more the crime rate goes up. So whenever I suggest restitution as an inexpensive and effective alternative to prison for nonviolent offenders, politicians are receptive. But only after I have cited the facts of the position (for instance, only one tenth of the cost of incarceration is statistically effective in reducing recidivism) do I explain that the source of restitution was God's law prescribed to Moses at Sinai.[19]

Christians are to do their duty as best they can. But even when they feel that they are making no difference, that they are failing to bring Christian values to the public arena, success is not the criterion. Faithfulness is. For in the end, Christians have the assurance that even the most difficult political situations are in the hands of a sovereign God.

This assurance comes from the teaching of Christ. Jesus likened the Kingdom to the humble act of a farmer sowing seeds. The farmer tills the soil, but the seeds sprout and grow because of a power beyond the farmer's control.

What Jesus was saying is that Christians are to do their part, of course, as best as they are able, but the manifestation of the Kingdom comes through God's power, not theirs. I saw this firsthand over a six-year span in one of the toughest penitentiaries in America. It all began with one of the most frightening days I've spent in any prison.

21

Signs of the Kingdom

He also said, "This is what the kingdom of God is like. A man scatters seed on the ground. Night and day, whether he sleeps or gets up, the seed sprouts and grows, though he does not know how. . . . The kingdom of God is like . . . a mustard seed, which is the smallest seed you plant in the ground. Yet when planted, it grows and becomes the largest of all garden plants."
—Mark 4:26–27, 30–32

They called it the "Concrete Mama," the nearly one-hundred-year-old patchwork of brick and concrete surrounded by thirty-foot walls set amid the beautiful hilly country of Washington State. Mama wasn't beautiful inside, however—not on the October morning in 1979 when I first visited there.

The state penitentiary at Walla Walla, considered one of the toughest prisons in America, had been cited by an inspection report of the American Corrections Association as overcrowded, filthy, and out of control. The inmates carried knives; homosexuals and drug pushers in silk shirts roamed the cellblocks; an inmate biker gang ran roughshod over underpaid and ill-trained guards as well as the other inmates. Walla Walla was, in the words of a longtime California warden, "Simply the worst prison in the U.S."

Four months before our visit a guard had been killed, and Walla Walla had been locked down ever since. That meant the prisoners were confined to their cells for twenty-three out of every twenty-four hours. Fifty-eight guards had gone on strike during the lockdown; most had subsequently been fired. Morale was miserable.

"When were the men released from lockdown?" I asked the officer at the gate, privately wondering who in my office had managed this kind of scheduling.

"Yesterday," he said, straightening his visored cap and squinting into the sun. "But don't worry. Riot police are standing by."

As I was digesting that heartwarming piece of information, the assistant warden, a former Jesuit priest, arrived at the gatehouse. "Glad you're here, Mr. Colson," he said cheerily. (I wasn't sure I was.)

"What's it like inside?" I asked.

He shrugged. "Tense, I guess. I don't really know. I don't get into the yard much. Whatever you can do I'm sure will help, though."

Unaccompanied by guards, we toured the concrete prison yard, and the cellblocks confirmed that the ACA had not exaggerated the conditions. The filth and overcrowding were incredible, and the tension in the air was as palpable as the concrete. The two thousand men in Walla Walla were angry.

At the moment their anger was directed at something that had happened during lockdown, senior chaplain Jerry Jacobson told me. The one relief from the sterile cement world inside the walls had been a grass playing field in the center of the compound. There, the inmates could lounge on the grass and play football. But when the men had been released from lockdown the day before, they discovered that their field had been covered by tons of concrete.

Officials said it had been done for security reasons; the men hid weapons in the grass. Valid or not, the fact was that the prison was now solid concrete. And to make it even worse, during the days the men had been locked in, the concrete pad had absorbed the heat of the hot autumn days. In every way Walla Walla was heated to the boiling point.

Chaplain Jacobson accompanied me on my tour, including a visit to the dungeonlike basement cellblock containing the more than ninety men in protective custody. These were inmates who could not be mixed with the rest of the prison population: informers, psychopaths, and sex offenders. As we completed the tour, a crackling loudspeaker invited all inmates to the auditorium to hear me speak immediately after lunch.

The auditorium was a cavernous room that seated a thousand men.

The acoustics were terrible, but the only other meeting place was the chapel, and no one would attend if it was held there, since the chapel was used chiefly as a meeting place for homosexuals.

At 2:00 Jerry introduced me. In front of 850 empty chairs and 150 pairs of unresponsive eyes, I told how Prison Fellowship began, using lines that never failed to produce laughter. There was stony silence.

Two older inmates stared intently from the front row. Both sat erect, arms folded across their chests with an air of authority. I concentrated on them as I concluded my talk.

Later, as I walked across the yard to leave, consoling myself that at least there had been no trouble, I heard a gruff voice call my name. I turned and saw the two inmates from the front row. The first, a man in his forties with graying hair, stuck out his hand.

"I'm Don Dennis. We've been talking, and we believe you," he said without expression.

The other inmate slapped me on the back. "Yeah," he said, grinning, "you're one helluva guy."

"We'll do everything we can to help you guys," I said, grabbing their hands. I didn't realize then what that promise would mean.

The following week I asked George Soltau, Prison Fellowship's most experienced instructor, to conduct two Bible-study seminars at Walla Walla.

When George arrived at the penitentiary, the chief of security told him that he expected a blood bath any day. So George didn't know what to expect as he went to the private meeting that inmate Don Dennis had requested. With Dennis were six young prisoners who had long sentences, nothing to lose, and were ready, as Don put it, to "blow this place." George's palms were moist as he shook hands with each of the men.

From them George learned what we had not known the week before. After my sermon, inmate leaders had called off a riot they had planned. Six guards had been targeted for murder; there had even been talk of taking me hostage. Instead, the inmates had decided they could trust us and would seek our help in working out their grievances.

George was face-to-face with the kind of hatred and anger that leads men to kill. People's lives were in his hands. One misstep and the pent-up fury of the four-month lockdown would be unleashed.

George conducted a series of intense meetings with convict groups. When he learned that there had been no communication between inmates and prison officials for eighteen months, he approached the warden, who promised he would consider meeting with inmate leaders.

That promise at least bought time. When George returned to Walla Walla a week later, there was a glimmer of hope. The inmate power bases—the lifers, the bikers, the native Americans, the Hispanics, and others—who were almost perpetually at war with each other were at least, for the moment, talking. Two men had become Christians in George's seminar, and they, along with Don Dennis, were gradually taking some leadership. Several guards who had been charged with brutality had been dismissed, and the warden was still promising to meet with the prisoners.

Over the next few months, George Soltau and Al Elliott, another Prison Fellowship staffer, shuttled in and out of Walla Walla, meeting with prison officials and convict leaders. Progress was slow, but violence was at a minimum. One night, however, frustrations erupted. Several men slashed their wrists and barricaded themselves in their cells to protest conditions.

Al Elliott was called to the scene. He stood alone outside the barricaded cells and pleaded with the men. Pools of blood gathered on the concrete floor. As Al talked, one man surrendered, then another, and finally the whole group. Medics rushed in with gurneys and plasma.

Later Al was in the mess hall when a chant began at several corner tables. The noise grew louder, echoing off the high ceilings. Al climbed on top of his table and shouted, trying to make himself heard above the clamor. Gradually the voices subsided.

"Don't blow this thing," he begged. "The politicians are beginning to listen, finally. But you'll lose it all if there's bloodshed. Chuck Colson has been called to address the state legislature about the situation." At that, there was a loud roar of approval.

Two Christian politicians, Bob Utter, chief justice of the Washington State Supreme Court, and Skeeter Ellis, a newly elected Republican representative, had proposed that I speak to the Republican caucus committee about the conditions at the prison. When I laid out the hard facts of what I had seen at Walla Walla and what needed to be done, the legislators seemed interested, even receptive.

Later that day I gave the same message to an equally responsive Democratic caucus, and shortly thereafter the House passed a resolution vowing to deal with conditions at Walla Walla. This had no legal effect but signaled to the inmates that those in power were listening.

Justice Utter then organized a committee of prominent Christians to work with the legislators who were developing model legislation. My associate, attorney Dan Van Ness, now president of Justice Fellowship,* and a Christian attorney in Seattle named Skip Li proposed several significant amendments, which were incorporated in the reform package. After his election Governor John Spellman appointed Amos Reed, a committed Christian, to head the state corrections system. Amos immediately backed the proposed bill.

Meanwhile, a federal court was nearing a decision on an inmate lawsuit complaining of conditions at Walla Walla. Indications were that the case would go against the state.

These developments electrified the atmosphere at the prison. "Someone has finally heard us," an inmate told Al Elliott, choking back his tears.

During those months I also met with representatives from each of the ruling inmate gangs. Al warned me that they were a tough and unusual bunch of characters. *They can't be any more unusual than anyone else I've met in Walla Walla*, I thought. I was mistaken.

At the first meeting they were waiting for me, shoulder-to-shoulder in a tight semicircle, at the bikers' club headquarters, a small, bare-walled room with one barred window. One by one I greeted them, some of the toughest inmates I'd ever seen. Their leader, Bobby, had black hair hanging over a leather headstrap adorned with badges; a bushy beard flowed down the front of his leather jacket.

"Bobby," I said as I gripped his tattooed hand, "I'm here to help you."

His response was a nod and a grunt.

The next inmate wore elaborate eye makeup and deep red lipstick. He took my hand limply and said in a high-pitched voice, "Thank you, Mr. Colson." My eyes widened with shock; this was Bobby's cellmate, a transvestite and leader of the "Queens." Walla Walla had its

---

*Justice Fellowship was incorporated in 1983 as the criminal justice affiliate of Prison Fellowship Ministries. As a national volunteer organization, Justice Fellowship works to make federal and state criminal justice systems more consistent with biblical teaching on justice and righteousness. It promotes restorative punishments, such as restitution and community service, based on the conviction that crime is primarily an offense against a victim rather than the state. For further information contact Justice Fellowship, P.O. Box 17181, Washington, D.C., 20041.

own rules, its own code for survival. The inmates' hard eyes defied me to pass judgment.

In May 1980 the U.S. District Court ruled that Walla Walla had violated the constitutional prohibition against "cruel and unusual punishment." Trial testimony had produced a litany of horrors: an inmate sodomized by a guard, another whose leg had to be amputated because gangrene was neglected, a third held naked in isolation for four days. But what proved decisive was the startlingly honest admission under oath of warden James Spaulding. His prison, he said, ought to be "closed down." It was simply beyond saving.

The inmates were jubilant. Help might finally be coming.

George and Al cut back their Walla Walla trips to once a month. Even the guards seemed to breathe easier as the court order transferred inmates to other prisons and relieved the overcrowding.

But the transferred inmates created dangerous overcrowding at the other prisons, and by the end of the year bloody riots erupted. One inmate was killed, twenty-five were injured, and there was $2 million in property damage. The tension affected the entire prison system, and officials imposed new restrictions at Walla Walla.

By early 1981, despite the best efforts of inmate leaders to prevent it, Walla Walla was again seething. A gang burned a prison office building. The warden threw the troublemakers, along with several inmate leaders who had had nothing to do with the riot, into segregation. The arbitrary order infuriated the inmates, who retaliated with a work strike. Their one demand was the removal of warden Jim Spaulding.

Spaulding ordered another lockdown, and I returned to Walla Walla.

"Visit the hole," one inmate whispered to me. "But don't announce it. Just walk in." I followed his advice.

When the guards grudgingly swung open the heavy steel gate of B tier of segregation, I immediately stepped back. A foul mist hung in the air, giving an eerie glow in the dim overhead lights. Piles of rotting food and human excrement littered the floor. I had to force myself forward.

At the first cell the inmate rubbed his eyes. "You Colson?" he asked. Not even waiting for a reply, he continued listlessly, "What can you do?" as if my answer couldn't matter anymore. *Maybe he's right*, I thought.

I asked his name. It sounded familiar I said.

"No." He shook his head. "You might have heard the name, but it's my brother. He hung himself in here last week. Just couldn't take no more after a year."

"A year!" I exclaimed.

"Man, that ain't nothin'." He shook his head again. "Some dudes been in here like two and three years."

Once outside I bent over, my hands on my knees, almost retching as I gulped the cold air of the prison yard. My face was hot, flushed with anger. How could human beings be allowed to live in such degradation? I made my way to Warden Spaulding's office.

Jim Spaulding was a decent and intelligent man, seemingly unflappable. But like his predecessors he had wrestled with the beast of Walla Walla and lost.

"Jim," I said, "you have to clean up segregation. Today. Use fire hoses or whatever it takes, but that swill has got to go."

"Wait a minute," he snapped. "What can I do? They throw everything at the officers. I can't order my men to clean it up."

"Have you been in that place?" I asked.

He shook his head.

The next day I held a press conference at which I described Walla Walla's segregation unit in detail. Spaulding fired back in the press, saying that the inmates "wouldn't let the staff clean the building." But soon thereafter, after a state investigation, Jim Spaulding was transferred.

Amos Reed, the corrections chief, began courting the Washington legislature to overhaul the criminal-justice system in the state. Justice Utter's committee continued to mobilize public support, and the court ruled in the inmates' favor and appointed a liaison to oversee the situation.

In the spring of 1981, almost two years after the Walla Walla lockdown began, the Washington state legislature passed the first in a series of reforms. A sentencing commission established a policy to put nonviolent offenders in alternative programs. Early-release plans relieved overcrowding, and several million dollars were allocated to clean up and refurbish Walla Walla.

*   *   *

Easter morning 1985 I returned to Walla Walla. From the road approaching the gatehouse, nothing seemed to have changed. Concrete Mama still loomed on the hilltop, as forbidding as it had looked nearly six years earlier.

The new warden, Larry Kinchloe, met us at the gate. "Wait until you see this place," he said enthusiastically.

Our first service was in the protective-custody wing. The floors were scrubbed clean, most of the cells newly painted, and recreation areas had been constructed in every block. It was still a prison, cold and sterile, but it had been miraculously—if that's a fair term to apply to a building—transformed. The prison population was stable, conditions were decent, and alternative programs were beginning. The reform legislation was working, and millions of state tax dollars were being saved.

The service for the maximum-security unit was held in the brand-new chapel, and I stood at the door greeting the men as they crowded in. I recognized some I had met years before as angry, hostile convicts; by their open faces and enthusiastic greetings, I realized they were now brothers in Christ.

Then came one vibrant, middle-aged inmate surrounded by a cluster of friends. "Remember me?" he grinned and grabbed my hand. I struggled for recognition. "Don't blame you," he laughed, stroking his clean-shaven chin. "I'm Bobby."

It was Bobby, the boss biker who had lived with the transvestite. He was a Christian now and sat through the service with a broad smile on his face, holding a well-worn Bible.

I watched in amazement, realizing that it was not just an institution that had been transformed. The story of Walla Walla was more than legislation and fresh prison paint, important as those changes were. It was the story of transformed lives.

Easter weekend at Walla Walla ended with a fitting postscript, yet another sign of the Kingdom at work. Fred, a young man with a heroin habit and a robbery record, had done time at Walla Walla. The family of one of his robbery victims had prayed for him for years, visited him in prison, and eventually led him to Christ. During a subsequent parole hearing, Fred had confessed to additional crimes of which he had not been convicted, explaining to the startled parole board that as a Christian, he felt he could not do otherwise.

Fred's original conviction was overturned; he was released from prison and began to rebuild his life. He became active in a local church and got involved in a Christian ex-prisoner fellowship while awaiting his retrial.

As it happened, Fred's case was scheduled to be heard on Easter Monday. The Seattle Superior Court was filled with friends, family, and supporters who had already testified on his behalf. Fred had freely confessed his guilt; and now he told Judge Francis Holman that he was prepared to accept whatever punishment the judge deemed appropriate. For in any event, said Fred, "I am ready to go back to prison and serve Jesus Christ in there."

The judge leaned back in his tall leather chair and ticked off a long list of possible sentences. There was an awkward, drawn-out silence.

Then Judge Holman pounded his gavel. Ten years on each count of robbery—suspended. Fred would be free on probation, providing he would continue in a drug-treatment program and make restitution to his victims at 150 percent of their loss, or $2,200. He looked down at Fred again, his face still solemn: "We send you on your way with best wishes."

For a moment no one moved. Then Fred's pastor jumped to his feet and gestured to the packed courtroom. "Let's sing it!" he shouted.

A reporter for the *Seattle Times* captured what came next: "Everyone stood up, little old ladies in spring dresses, ex-cons, girls in jeans, men in business suits, a biker with his motorcycle jacket and helmet, prison guards—and they began to sing: 'Praise God from whom all blessings flow. . . .'"[1]

Officials later said that it was the first time a Seattle Superior Court case had ever closed with the Doxology.

As I flew back home after that glorious Easter weekend in Washington State, I was exuberant. I have to confess I was thrilled at Prison Fellowship's involvement in the changes at Walla Walla, in the transformed lives of men like Bobby and Fred. Sending out a puffy fund-raising letter about the story was a tempting idea; the first lines were already beginning to form in my mind.

But as I started to put words on paper I was stopped by the sudden realization that I couldn't definitively say how the changes had come about at Walla Walla or who was responsible. Certainly George Soltau and Al Elliott had risked their lives going in there in the early days when the situation was red hot. Don Dennis, Bobby the Biker, and others played a vital role in convincing angry cons to talk with bitter guards and exhausted administrators. And then there was the work of Christian lawyers, legislators, and politicians: men like Amos Reed, Bob Utter, Skip Li, Skeeter Ellis, Dan Van Ness.

But the real transforming miracle at Walla Walla had been accomplished not by the efforts of all these people, but by the unseen work of the hand of God. I suddenly saw on the page before me the words of Christ—that the signs of the Kingdom of God are like a man planting a seed. We do our part; but then God makes the seed—or the prison reform—grow.

And so I threw away my fund-raising letter, and the words of the Doxology from that Seattle courtroom filled my mind: "Praise God, from whom all blessings flow." For it is God who produces the signs of His Kingdom on this earth. We are merely the instruments.

We need to constantly be reminded that our efforts, vital as they are, will never bring utopia to this earth. Walla Walla, after all, is still bleak; it is still a prison filled with the angry, desperate, broken lives of those who seem unable to live in society. But it *has* changed. Because of God's power, not ours, Walla Walla is a "concrete" example of the Kingdom of God transforming places of hopelessness in the kingdoms of man. Justice and hope can now be found where there was once only inequity and despair.

Should Christians get involved in political issues and social reform?

Can anyone look at the story of Walla Walla and believe otherwise?

22

Perils of Politics

Christian faith may work wonders if it moves the minds and hearts of an increasing number of men and women. But if professed Christians forsake heaven as their destination and come to fancy that the state . . . may be converted into the terrestrial paradise—why they are less wise men than Marx.
—*Russell Kirk*

Christians in politics can make a difference—as Justice Utter, Skeeter Ellis, and others in Washington State illustrate. But these men were only part of the Walla Walla story. Private citizens, church groups, the courts, wardens, even inmates all had a hand in the process. Man planted, and God, using many people, brought in the crop.

But in recent years many Christians have urged a more direct approach for bringing needed social change: simply elect Christians to political office. One spokesman has even suggested a religious version of affirmative action; if, for example, 24 percent of the people are born again, then at least 24 percent of the officeholders should be born again. Others have argued that Christians should "take dominion" over government, with those in public office speaking "for God as well as for the American people."[1]

On the surface this shortcut might seem to some an appealing answer to America's declining morality. It is, however, simplistic and dangerous triumphalism. To suggest that electing Christians to public office will solve all public ills is not only presumptuous and theologically questionable, it is also untrue.

Today's misspent enthusiasm for political solutions to the moral problems of our culture arises from a distorted view of both politics and spirituality—too low a view of the power of a sovereign God and too high a view of the ability of man. The idea that human systems, reformed by Christian influence, pave the road to the Kingdom—or at least, to revival—has the same utopian ring that one finds in Marxist literature. It also ignores the consistent lesson of history that shows that laws are most often reformed as a result of powerful spiritual movements. I know of no case where a spiritual movement was achieved by passing laws.

In addition, history puts the lie to the notion that just because one is devout one will be a just and wise ruler. Take the nineteenth-century leader who forged a unified Germany from a cluster of minor states. Otto von Bismarck-Schönhausen was a committed Christian who regularly read the Bible, spoke openly of his devotion to God, and claimed divine guidance in response to prayer. "If I were no longer a Christian, I would not serve the king another hour," he once declared.[2]

Yet Bismarck was also the ruthless architect of *Deutschland Uber Alles* (Germany Over All), a chauvinistic worldview that laid the foundation for two world wars. Historians describe Bismarck as a Machiavellian master of political duplicity who specialized in blood and iron.

As we have said earlier, power can be just as corrupting—or confusing—to the Christian as to the non-Christian. And the results in some ways are more horrible when power corrupts men or women who believe they have a divine mandate. Their injustices are then committed in God's name. This is why an eminent conservative historian has suggested that "religious claims in politics should vary inversely with the power or prospects for power one has."[3]

It's a fair distinction: Prophets should make religious claims. Political leaders should not—otherwise they can become ayatollahs.

So the first test for public office should not be a spiritual one. The celebrated claim that "the ability to hear from God should be the number one qualification for the U.S. presidency"[4] is dangerously misguided.

Politicians, like those in any other specialized field, should be selected on the basis of their qualifications and abilities *as well as* on their moral character. Even in Israel's theocracy, Jethro advised Moses to select "capable men . . . who fear God" to help in governing the Jewish nation.[5]

Jethro's advice makes sense. If terrorists were to take control of an airport, would we want policemen who were merely devout Christians handling the situation, or would we choose those who had specialized training in hostage negotiations? Luther had it right when he said he would rather be ruled by a competent Turk than an incompetent Christian.

The triumphalist mindset also fails to make the crucial distinction between a Christian's function as a private citizen and as an office-holder. As private citizens, Christians are free to advocate their Christian view in any and every form. In America that is a fundamental constitutional right. Christian citizens should be activists about their faith, striving by their witness to "Christianize" their culture—not by the force of the sword, but by the force of their ideas.

But Christians elected to public office acquire a different set of responsibilities. Now they hold the power of the sword, which God has placed with government to preserve order and maintain justice. Now they act not for themselves but for all whom they serve. For this reason they cannot use their office to evangelistically "Christianize" their culture. Their duty is to ensure justice and religious liberty for all citizens of all beliefs.

This does not mean they can compromise their faith or their first allegiance to God; they should speak freely of their Christian faith and witness Christian values in their lives. But they cannot use their offices to seek a favored position for Christianity or the church.

A Christian writer has summed this up well: "The 'Christian state' is one that gives no special public privilege to Christian citizens but seeks justice for all as a matter of principle."[6]

At the turn of the century a towering Dutch theologian, Abraham Kuyper, was elected prime minister of the Netherlands. His opponents voiced fears of theocratic oppression. Instead, his administration was a model of tolerance and public pluralism as Kuyper affirmed proportional representation, that the legitimate rights of all be fully represented.[7]

If Christians today understood this distinction between the role of the private Christian citizen and the Christian in government, they might sound less like medieval crusaders. If secularists understood correctly the nature of Christian public duty they would not fear, but welcome responsible Christian political involvement.

But Christians should not unwarily plunge into the political marsh-lands, thinking they will drain the swamp.

There are traps. I know; I used to set them.

My first assignment as President Nixon's special counsel was to develop strategies for his 1972 reelection. A tough task. He had been elected by only a small margin in the three-way 1968 election against Hubert Humphrey and George Wallace. Not only was the Republican party a minority, but Nixon had inherited an unpopular war and a hostile press. Added to this, he himself projected something less than a charismatic presence for the television image-makers just beginning to dominate politics.

I studied the political classics, particularly the strategy devised by Clark Clifford for Harry Truman in the 1948 election. I learned that Clifford had curried the favor of disparate special-interest groups, one by one, assembling voting blocs into a surprise majority.

My first memorandum to the president outlined a similar strategy: write off the minorities, but reach out to traditional supporters in business and farm groups; pick off some conservative labor unions; cultivate Southern evangelicals; build a new coalition among Catholic, blue-collar voters of the Northeast and Midwest. I labeled it the "Middle America Plan," later dubbed the "Silent Majority Strategy." It was cynical, pragmatic, and good politics, designed to exploit whatever allies would let us cultivate them.

Nixon loved it. The memo was returned a few days later with his markings all over the margins: "Right. . . . Do it. . . . I agree." It became one of the key documents for the political strategy of Mr. Nixon's presidency.

Setting out to put it into practice, I began by inviting key leaders to the White House, following a scenario staged for maximum benefit.

First, they dined with me in the executive dining room located in the basement of the West Wing. I would escort my guests past saluting guards, down a long corridor lined with dramatic photographs of the president in action, then pause at the door to the dining room, pointing to another door to the right. "That's the situation room," I'd say in hushed tones. They all knew of the legendary super-secret national-security nerve center. The very words conjured up images of map-covered walls, whirring computers, and a bevy of generals studying the movements of Soviet aircraft. (Actually, it was then nothing more than a large, crowded office with some communications equipment and old charts on the wall; the real command centers had been moved to the Pentagon after World War II.)

The executive dining room was paneled in rich, hand-rubbed mahogany, lined with a waiting row of red-jacketed Navy stewards. Seated at the dozen tables, huddled in conversation, would be most of the cabinet and senior staff.

The dramatic effect overwhelmed even the staunchest adversary. One union leader, a lifelong Democrat who had never been to the White House before, blurted out during our first lunch together that he'd be available to help in any campaign. A Chicago alderman strong in the Polish neighborhoods signed up on the spot.

Those who needed more prodding were treated to a walk upstairs after lunch. If the president was out, I'd usher them reverently through the Oval Office; if Mr. Nixon was there, I'd ask (always by prearrangement) if my visitor would like to meet the president. His chin would drop as I led him in the side door, cut almost unnoticeably into the wall, and remarked casually, "Oh, Mr. President. I was just having lunch with Jim here. Could we say hello?"

Nixon was a master at the game. He always gave his dazzled visitor gold-plated cuff links with the presidential seal. The person would be overwhelmed as he left, almost bowing, not more than sixty seconds later. It's not easy to resist the allure of the Oval Office.

I took all kinds of groups to see the president, from friendly cattlemen to sophisticated educators enraged over budget cuts or the Vietnam war. It was always the same. In the reception room they would rehearse their angry lines and reassure one another, "I'll tell him what's going on. He's got to do something."

When the aide came to escort us in, they'd set their jaws and march toward the door. But once it swung open, the aide announcing, "The president will see you," it was as if they had suddenly sniffed some intoxicating fragrance. Most became almost self-conscious about even stepping on the plush blue carpet on which was sculpted the Great Seal of the United States. And Mr. Nixon's voice and presence—like any president's—filled the room.

Invariably, the lions of the waiting room became the lambs of the Oval Office. No one ever showed outward hostility. Most, except the labor leaders, forgot their best-rehearsed lines. They nodded when the president spoke, and in those rare instances when they disagreed, they did so apologetically, assuring the president that they personally respected his opinion.

Ironically, none were more compliant than the religious leaders. Of all people, they should have been the most aware of the sinful nature of man and the least overwhelmed by pomp and protocol. But theological knowledge sometimes wilts in the face of worldly power.

I frequently scheduled meetings for evangelical groups, denominational councils, and individual religious leaders. Henry Kissinger's briefings in the Roosevelt Room across the hall from the Oval Office were always a big hit.

The weekly church services Nixon scheduled most Sundays for the East Room provided great opportunities as well. To select the preacher, we determined who would give us the greatest impact— politically, that is, not spiritually. At the time I was a nominal Christian at best and had no way to judge the spiritual. And there were always two hundred or more seats to be filled, tickets that were like keys to the political kingdom.

Then there were invitations to social functions and state dinners. I was allowed a quota for every event and filled it with those whose support we coveted most. It is difficult to resist the allure of that most regal of events, the state dinner, held in honor of visiting world leaders. Each of the twelve tables seated ten of the most influential people in America—Supreme Court justices, senators, ambassadors, film stars, cabinet members—and my targets for political support.

One instance I recall illustrates just how well the system works. We needed several electoral-rich Northeastern and Midwestern states to win the 1972 election—or so we thought. So one spring day I called a prominent Christian leader whose influence was particularly great in that region and invited him for a private dinner cruise with the president.

As we arrived at the Washington Navy Yard, sailors in white dress uniforms lined the gangway at attention and saluted as the three of us boarded the presidential yacht, *Sequoia*. Its mahogany sides and brass fittings sparkled as the grand old vessel eased away from its dock.

The Washington skyline faded into the distance, and the president escorted us to dinner in the main salon. White House china, silver, and crystal appointed the starched white tablecloth; stewards scurried back and forth serving chateaubriand and the vintage La Fête Rothschild.

The dinner discussion was as impressive as the food. When our guest mustered the courage to raise points of concern to the religious community, Mr. Nixon showed an amazing grasp of even the intricate details of those issues (as a dutiful aide, I had briefed him thoroughly that afternoon). Every now and then he would stop and say, "Chuck, I want this done. This man is right. You order the attorney general to take care of that tomorrow morning." Then he would resume the conversation.

It wasn't all sham, of course. The president meant what he said, and we even thought some of the things might be accomplished. But whatever else happened, that religious leader was convinced that Richard Nixon was on his side.

Before we arrived at Mount Vernon, the president led us to the foredeck and stood at attention as the colors were retired, his hand over his heart. Our guest did the same. When the bugle had faded, we docked; a waiting Marine helicopter took our new friend back to the airport, and another returned Mr. Nixon and me to the White House lawn.

It would be wrong to suggest that this leader was unduly influenced; but even such a wise, honorable, and religious man could not help but be impressed by the trappings of power. He got what he wanted—the president's ear on certain key issues. And we got what we wanted.

Nixon's prominent public friendship with this leader sent a powerful signal to millions of voters. That fall we carried more than 58 percent of the vote in many Northeastern and Midwestern precincts that had never before voted for a Republican.

This is not to suggest that the Nixon White House was engaged in a sinister conspiracy to corrupt the church. It is simply the way political systems work. People in power use power to keep themselves in power. Even if they are genuinely interested in a special-interest group's agenda—or naturally disposed to their position—they will work that relationship for everything they can get out of it.

In totalitarian regimes some officials are so unscrupulous as to feign religious interest simply to ensnare Christians. In Nicaragua, Interior Minister Thomas Borge maintains two offices. When he is receiving churchmen or American visitors, he sits in a Bible-laden office adorned with crucifixes. When he meets with government officials or visitors from socialist nations, he occupies an office displaying Marxist slogans and pictures of such revolutionary heroes as Marx, Engels, and Lenin.

I'm not advocating that religious groups or leaders boycott the White House or the palaces and parliaments of the world. That's where the political action is, and Christians need to influence policies for justice and righteousness. That is in the best biblical tradition of

Jeremiah, Amos, Micah, Daniel, and a host of others—though many prophets clearly preferred the desert to the palace.

But Christians (and others as well) need to do so with eyes open, aware of the snares. C. S. Lewis wrote that "the demon inherent in every [political] party is at all times ready enough to disguise himself as the Holy Ghost."[8] Tolstoy made a similar point: "Governments, to have a rational foundation for the control of the masses, are obliged to pretend that they are professing the highest religious teachings known to man."[9]

Consider several of the most dangerous pitfalls awaiting the unwary.

The first is that the church will become just another special-interest group.

When President Reagan was challenged by the press during the 1980 campaign for mixing religion and politics by attending a meeting of Religious Right activists, he responded that the church was like any other special-interest group, after all—like a union, for example.[11] Reagan was refreshingly candid, but dead wrong.

The church is not and must never allow itself to become just another special-interest group lined up at the public trough. For in doing so, as one contemporary scholar observes, it would "sacrifice its claim to objective ethical concern which [is the church's] chief political as well as moral resource."[11]

Tocqueville warned that if the church were to become a mere interest group, it would then be measured and honored according to political and not moral criteria.[12] The great strength of the American church, he believed, was that it was not linked to a partisan cause. By way of contrast, he pointed out that in Europe people "reject the clergy less because they are representatives of God than because they are friends of authority."[13]

A second danger is that politics can be like the proverbial tar baby. Christian leaders who are courted by political forces may soon begin to overestimate their own importance. The head of one large international relief agency mistakenly came to believe that heads of state welcomed him because of who he was rather than what he represented. It wasn't long before his work and his personal life failed to measure up to his delusions of power. He left his family and was eventually removed from his position—after doing great harm to the cause he had served for much of his life.

A side effect of this delusion is that rather than lose their access to political influence, some church leaders have surrendered their independence. "If I speak out against this policy," they reason, "I won't get invited to dinner and my chances to minister will be cut off." While such rationalizing is understandable, the result is exactly the opposite; they keep their place but lose their voice and thus any possibility of holding government to moral account.

In this way the gospel becomes hostage to the political fortunes of a particular movement. This is the third and perhaps most dangerous snare. Both liberals and conservatives have made this mistake of aligning their spiritual goals with a particular political agenda.

One Christian New Right leader, when asked what would happen if the Democrats won the 1988 U.S. election, said, "I don't know what will happen to us."[14] After the 1980 election, a Methodist bishop wrote, "The blame [for Reagan's victory] ought not to be placed on all the vigor of the Right, but maybe on the weakness of saints." A better day will come, he said, "If the people of faith will be strengthened by defeat and address themselves to the new agenda which is upon us."[15] The implication was clear: if you disagreed with the bishop's partisan politics, you were not among "the people of faith."

Several years ago a prominent leader of a large Christian mission visited a Third World nation ruled by an authoritarian leader. The leader was friendly to the U.S. and held a regal dinner party at the palace honoring the mission executive. The awestruck visitor publicly and effusively praised the head of state. Months later when that head of state was deposed, the Christian's mission work in that country was deposed right along with him.

Inevitably, this kind of political alignment compromises the gospel. James Schall writes, "All successful Christian social theory in the immediate future must be based on this truth: that religion be not made an instrument of political ideology."[16]

Because it tempts one to water down the truth of the gospel, ideological alignment, whether on the left or right, accelerates the church's secularization.[17] When the church aligns itself politically, it gives priority to the compromises and temporal successes of the political world rather than its Christian confession of eternal truth. And when the church gives up its rightful place as the conscience of the culture, the consequences for society can be horrific.

As we've seen, many German churches in the thirties allied themselves with the new nationalistic movement. One churchman even described the Nazis as a "gift and miracle of God."[18] It was the *confessing* church, not the politically-minded church, which retained its orthodoxy and thus resisted the evils of Hitler's state.

Today's liberation theologians have fallen into this trap, putting ideology ahead of orthodoxy. It began, as did many Christian political movements, with noble intentions. Righteously outraged at injustices to the poor in so-called Christian cultures, priests and church workers began to organize communities for action. So far, so good.

But as those organizations failed to solve problems, frustrations grew; attacks on structures became more strident.

When Christians put economic issues ahead of spiritual salvation, they are embracing economic determinism; it is then but a short step to revolutionary politics, Marxism, and the fatal mistake of believing the Kingdom of God can be ushered in by political means, as Father Ernesto Cardenal, a Nicaraguan government official, well illustrates: "A world of perfect communism is the Kingdom of God on earth."[19]

Does all this mean that Christians cannot work with political groups? Certainly not. In fact, often Christians must work with coalitions of like-minded people who have different motivations. But as Donald Bloesch has pointed out, "In order to maintain their Christian identity they must inwardly detach themselves from the motivations and ultimate goals of their ideological colleagues."[20]

In World War II, for example, a devout Christian might have fought to stop the evil of Nazism and the Holocaust because he believed God commanded that the state is to restrain evil. Next to him in the same foxhole might have been a soldier fighting solely for national pride or honor. Both would have been shooting at the same enemy, but for different reasons.

Today Christians may find themselves suspect—I have experienced this myself—to the very people on whose side they are fighting. But that is the price they must pay to preserve their independence and not be beholden to any political ideological alignment.

Only a church free of any outside domination can be the conscience of society and, as Washington pastor Myron Augsburger has written, "hold government morally accountable before God to live up to its own claims."[21] And as the amazing events in the next chapter demonstrate, when the church faithfully fulfills this role, even the most determined of tyrants topple.

23

People Power

Justice without mercy is tyranny, and mercy without justice is weakness. Justice without love is pure socialism, and love without justice is baloney.
—Jaime Cardinal Sin, speaking at
a Prison Fellowship International
conference in Nairobi, Kenya, 1986

A small Filipino man with penetrating brown eyes stared, unbelievingly, at his prison door's cool, smooth surface. It was 1972. Moments before, the door had crashed shut on him with metallic finality. It felt like a bad dream. Never before had he been in prison. In fact, until that day he had expected to become the next president of the Philippines.

It seemed impossible—ridiculous, really. Benigno Aquino was the boy wonder of Philippine politics—mayor of a large town at twenty-two, governor of a province at twenty-eight, at thirty-five elected senator, the youngest ever. Now he measured the entire extent of his freedom in two or three paces. He sat on his bunk and thought, and as the day passed into night he continued to sit there. For the first time in his life he had nothing else to do—nothing.

Son of a wealthy family, this charismatic, gregarious politician suddenly found himself stripped of everything that had propped up his ego. All his plans, his friends, his busy schedule, all his carefully cultivated followers were gone, replaced by the sheer loneliness and boredom of the prison cell and the venomous hostility of his guards. He kept waiting for Marcos to send for him, to offer a deal. Surely he could not simply leave him to rot in prison!

Half a year went by before Aquino was even questioned or confronted with any charges. Then a trumped-up murder case was brought, and a rigged military court condemned him to death. This too was a bad dream, for the real reason for his imprisonment was President Ferdinand Marcos's greed for power. With his two-term limit as president due to expire in 1973, Marcos had declared martial law, granting himself almost unlimited powers. He had thrown Aquino and other political opponents into prison. Marcos intended never to leave office—and so was determined never to let a popular Aquino out to challenge him.

Prison had, for Aquino, the same bewildering effect it has held for so many others. He lost all sense of direction and perspective. He became bitter not only at Marcos, but at the world, even at God. He hated everyone and his prison guards goaded him on. They sometimes put his dinner plate on the ground and let a mongrel dog wolf part of it down; then, kicking the dog aside, they gave what was left to Aquino. He lost forty pounds. He suffered two heart attacks. When he was not longing for revenge, he wanted to die.

His mother, deeply concerned, sent him a book, the memoirs of another prisoner. It was my story—*Born Again*.

At first Aquino looked at it with little appetite. Watergate was poorly understood outside America. Nonetheless, there were similarities in our careers. So Aquino read the book—and it touched him.

He read how I too had lost everything and entered the disorienting, mocking maze of prison. But God had shown me that such losses were not in vain as I found my true life in Christ.

Aquino began to search for the meaning I had found. A voracious reader, he pored over the Bible and other Christian books. He found great inspiration in a little classic, *The Imitation of Christ* by Thomas à Kempis. He was surprised to discover in reading the works of an early Filipino hero, José Rizal, that the same book had motivated his life and struggle for his country.

One night Aquino knelt in his jail cell and gave his life to Jesus Christ. Overcome with grief for his anger toward God, he begged forgiveness. His viewpoints, his life, most of all his bitterness—all changed. He had a sense that his life had suddenly moved into a different channel with another purpose.

As Jaime Cardinal Sin of the Philippines has said, it is hard for our doubting hearts to believe that spiritual power—which is peaceful, prayerful, humane, forgiving, willing to suffer on the side of the poor and oppressed—can change society. We know the gospel affects the lives of individuals, but can it make an impact on institutions and governments, where the heartless realities of power pierce like a knife? It is hard to fathom this.[1]

Nevertheless, it can happen. It does happen. One can never quite calculate how one conversion like Benigno Aquino's in a lowly prison cell may set in motion a train of events to shake a nation.

I met Benigno Aquino in 1980—a chance encounter, seemingly, on an airplane. He reached out to grasp my arm as we boarded the plane. "You're Mr. Colson," he exclaimed. "I must talk with you." Since we were blocking the aisle I offered him the empty seat next to mine. "I can't believe I am meeting you," he said. "I wanted to die in prison until I read your book." I knew when we had completed our flight, I had another Christian brother.

After eight years in prison Aquino had been released by Marcos under then President Carter's prodding. The grounds were humanitarian—he needed triple-bypass surgery. Aquino survived the heart operation and took a fellowship at Harvard. Marcos would not let him return to his own country.

Robert Shaplen, a foreign correspondent who had known Aquino for many years, wrote for the *New Yorker* magazine, "At fifty, he seemed to have acquired a new maturity, and, though he also retained his natural ebullience, a relative serenity that he had never had before. Some of his friends felt he had undergone something like religious conversion as a result of his years in prison. . . ."[2]

Indeed he had. Yet that conversion took away none of his heartfelt concern for his nation. Ninoy, as his friends called him, vowed he would one day return to the Philippines. If he could run for office he believed he would be president. If Marcos threw him in prison, then he would be president of Prison Fellowship. "If I'm killed, I'll be with Jesus," he told me, smiling.

Marcos was using martial law as a cover while he raped the country. He and his business cronies were bleeding the nation dry, making huge profits through monopoly powers and putting the money into New York real estate and Swiss banks. Meanwhile, half the working population could not find jobs. The ugly scabs of slums, many without running water or flush toilets, spread across Manila and other cities.

Marxist guerrillas were quickly gaining ground, and the military, riven by corruption, seemed unable to stop them. They found it easier to savage poor peasants than to fight the Communists. Things had reached the point where anyone who helped the poor was under suspicion. Filipino army units arrested, killed, and tortured even Catholic priests and nuns who had chosen to work with the desperately poor. A few Catholics had, it is true, taken the side of the Marxists, but the vast majority simply ministered in the name of Jesus to those in need. Between the Marxist insurgency and the Marcos dictatorship, there was little room in the middle.

Aquino knew Marcos's ruthless side—he had, after all, suffered in solitary confinement. He also thought he knew of a better side; he believed he might reason with him to restore free elections. So in the summer of 1983 he decided, after much soul searching, to leave comfortable Cambridge and return home.

Shortly before leaving, Aquino testified at a congressional subcommittee: "It is true, one can fight hatred with a greater hatred, but . . . it is more effective to fight hatred with greater Christian love. . . . I have decided to pursue my freedom struggle through the path of nonviolence, fully cognizant that this may be the longer and the more arduous road. . . . Only I will suffer solitary confinement once again, and possibly death. . . . But by taking the road of revolution, how many lives, other than mine, will have to be sacrificed?"[3]

It was August 21, 1983. Benigno Aquino rose in Taiwan at 5:00 A.M. after only four hours of sleep. His first act was prayer. He then called his wife Cory, still in Massachusetts. She read the Bible to him over the phone. He spoke briefly to each of his five children, and tears spilled down his cheeks. After hanging up he sat down and wrote each child a letter. "The one regret I have," he told his brother-in-law who was traveling with him, "is that Cory has had to suffer so much."

Though Aquino had tried to keep his flight to Manila a mystery to the government, the plane was jammed with journalists. Filipino passengers, startled to find themselves flying with a celebrity, mobbed him. One woman repeatedly kissed him while news cameras clicked and Aquino squirmed uncomfortably. He gave a series of interviews to the journalists on board. The mood was celebration. Aquino hoped to lead a march of 20,000 supporters to Marcos's lush Malacalang Palace.

Eventually, when the plane began its descent, the cabin sobered. Aquino went into the bathroom, removed the shirt to his cream-colored safari suit, and grimly put on a bulletproof vest.

Back in his seat he thoughtfully removed his watch and handed it to his brother-in-law. "I just want you to have it," he said. Then he sat quietly as the plane landed. His lips moved in silent prayer.

The airliner eased to a stop at the gate and the jetway crawled out to clamp its mouth to the door. Journalists and passengers pressed their foreheads to the windows, watching for signs of trouble. Suddenly they saw a blue van pull up, and a contingent of uniformed soldiers carrying automatic weapons leaped out and circled the plane. Some of the passengers had stood up ready to deplane, but now a voice over the intercom asked them to be seated. "They're coming!" someone sang out from a window seat.

Three khaki-clad soldiers entered the cabin. Blinded by television lights and the commotion of photographers fighting for a good angle, they pushed down the aisle looking about them. The first soldier missed Aquino altogether, walking past his seat. But the second soldier, wearing sunglasses, recognized him and stopped. The third soldier leaned over, and Aquino smilingly took his hand. They exchanged a few words in Tagalog.

The soldiers slowly led Aquino through the crush to the front of the plane. Behind them came a sea of journalists, pushing, shouting. The jetway was jammed; no one could hear or see over the crush of bodies and the noisy confusion.

The soldiers escorted Aquino out of the plane door. But as soon as they turned the corner into the jetway, one of them opened the service door leading to a set of stairs descending to the tarmac below. The soldiers pushed Aquino through and slammed the door shut behind them. A soldier's body blocked the door window. Left inside, cameramen shouted, pushing and banging against the door. Nine seconds later, above the frantic noise, a shot rang out. People screamed, cursed. Then three more shots. Then a burst of automatic rifle fire.

At the foot of the stairs, sprawled on the pavement face down, his arms akimko and blood oozing from his mouth, lay Aquino. He was dead, shot in the back of the head.

Two million people walked in the rain to his funeral. Soft warm drops from a gray sky glazed their faces, but they seemed not to notice. For hours they streamed through Manila streets, a seemingly endless mass of dazed people, moving as if by memory. Some wept. Some carried banners. But on the whole they were frighteningly silent.

Few Filipinos gave any credence to the military's story that a Communist-hired gunman had penetrated the tight airport security and shot Aquino, then died himself in a hail of soldier's bullets. They believed that their government had reached a new low; it had murdered, in cold blood and in front of the world, a man who had come in peace. It was an act so callous that it shocked many into action who had until then accepted corruption and violence with a cynical shrug.

Cardinal Sin gave an eloquent, moving sermon to those who found space in the crowded Santo Domingo Church. Among them was the frail-looking, grave woman who had read the Bible to Aquino on the day of his death: Cory Aquino. Privately Sin predicted, "This is the beginning, when people will be opening their eyes."

A few weeks later the government organized a rally in the affluent Makati district of Manila. No one quite knew why Marcos staged these affairs; the organizers sometimes slept through the speeches, and the crowds had to be bussed in from distant suburbs where ward leaders could round up, at ten to twenty pesos a head, enough people with nothing to do. But this time the utterly unexpected happened. From the glass and chrome skyscrapers of the Philippines Wall Street poured tens of thousands of officer workers. They had not been paid to attend, but then they were not cheering for Marcos. They carried hurriedly scrawled banners: "I love Ninoy," "Ninoy our Hero," "Justice for Aquino—Justice for all," "Who Killed our Hero?" The air rained colored paper and computer tapes. It was an unprecedented, spontaneous outburst of outrage and—yes, unmistakably—of joy. No one had ever seen anything like it in the Philippines—People Power. Aquino's death had awakened them.

Jaime Sin is a heavy-set, jovial man with a face as round as a wheel, a deep infectious laugh, and a rich sense of humor. He was appointed cardinal in 1983, the same year that Aquino died.

In 1984 the *New York Times* referred to Sin as the most popular man in the Philippines. He is certainly a lovable character and a remarkable preacher, but his popularity was due to more than that. The Philippines was disintegrating, its deep tradition of democracy degraded by a government that made less and less pretense of justice. Aquino's murder brought a wave of grief and revulsion.

Marcos himself was rumored to be desperately sick; it was not clear who ran the government on any given day. Communist guerrillas grew in strength. Yet the moderate opposition was a rats nest of infighting. Among this confusion only Sin and the Christian church he represented had credibility and moral authority.

Sin refused to serve on the official government commission investigating Aquino's murder, for he felt sure the commission would be a tool in the hands of the government. Instead he poured his energies into preaching the demands and privileges of the Kingdom of God. He sent pastoral letters criticizing the government for human-rights abuses; these were read in every Roman Catholic church in the Philippines. Yet Sin made clear that he did not speak for opposition politicians. He spoke for God.

He saw his role as a spiritual, not a political leader. Sin had been studying the Book of Chronicles. He saw in the account of Israel's corrupt leaders a parallel with the grief his own nation was enduring. *When God wants to punish a people*, he reasoned, *He gives them unjust rulers. Like Marcos.* So the answer is for the people to repent, turn from their ways, be converted, and seek God.

Among the lush green islands Sin preached to legions of poor farmers as well as the stylishly dressed elite. His simple message took root. His battle cry was "Cor," which means "heart"—an acronym: C for conversion, the changed life created through repentance and forgiveness from God. O stood for the offering of obedient lives to God—for true conversion had to make a difference in behavior. R stood for reparation—for the "making right" required of true repentance. Sin called Filipinos to prayer and fasting. Bible studies and prayer groups spread, even in the military. As Sin told one visiting reporter, "You will see our churches filled up. There is no space even on weekdays. . . . They are complaining to God. They are bringing their sadness before the altar of God."

Throughout the Philippines people felt that change was coming. But along with hope there was much fear. People did not know how change would come or with how much blood.

Cardinal Sin walked through the familiar halls of Malacalang Palace wondering just what he would say to Marcos. A glance at the velvet upholstery, the mahogany paneling, the rich heavy curtains reminded Sin that this world was well insulated from the climate of change he sensed throughout the Philippines. The ostentatious style smelled of money and privilege. What words would cut through the confidence of Marcos's political and business cronies?

Sin had talked to Marcos many times, to no avail. Marcos often promised to change or to investigate abuses. Then he would proceed to do the opposite of what he had promised. A crisis was coming for the Philippines. Sin felt it.

Marcos stood respectfully in welcome, though he seemed to totter slightly on his feet. His handshake was weak; his face looked gray and puffy. Nonetheless he was the familiar man: shrewd, genial, talkative, sidestepping questions when it suited him. Marcos was known even by those who hated him as the smartest, shrewdest politician in Philippine history. It was very difficult to be sure where truth ended and fiction began with Marcos. It was not certain Marcos knew or cared.

"The reason I have come," Cardinal Sin said when the pleasantries were done, "is this, Mr. President. Your term of office is due to end next year. Why are you calling for a snap election?"

Marcos had announced elections to be held early in February, just two months away. It was not clear why. The U.S. had been pressing him, but why do it on such short notice? Did he realize how unpopular he had become? Why run when he was so sick? Sin had come to try to understand what he was up to.

Marcos smiled at Sin. "I want to have a fresh mandate from the people," he said.

"It is very dangerous for you to call a snap election," Sin said. "You may lose. You will be forced to step down."

Marcos kept a smile stuck on his mouth, but his bland, puffy face looked as warm as a cobra's. "You think that you understand politics, which they never taught you in seminary. So you interfere. When you should support your government in its struggle against Communists, you instead disturb the peace by criticizing. But you do not understand the way things are done. I cannot lose an election to an opposition that is hopelessly divided. They will tear each other to pieces."

The two men stared frostily at each other. Sin was angry—at

Marcos's insolent words and at his disregard for his own people's needs. He only cared about power, not the good he could have done with power. And he was so seemingly confident that he could control, through political maneuvers, the people's will.

Sin spoke slowly: "Sir, I will unite the opposition in order that there may be a fair election."

The two maintained a fierce stare. Did Marcos feel a slight pull of panic underneath his expressionless mask? Did he have a hint of what Sin could unleash? He gave no sign of it.

Sin stood. "Good-bye," he said. "And may the Lord come down to protect our people." Without a handshake he turned and left, his red robe swirling behind him, Marcos still in his chair.

Sin, in anger, had crossed a line. Until that time he had been very careful not to marry the church to the opposition. He had maintained the careful role of a church leader in the political realm: that of conscience, of reconciliation, of proclaiming God's good promises. But part of the risk of politics is that emotions become involved.

Sin was convinced only one person could unite the squabbling opposition: Cory Aquino, the quiet, self-effacing widow of the slain Ninoy. Sin knew her well. He knew of her deep Christian faith. She alone could raise the level of opposition above mere politics to a moral plane. She alone could ride on the wave of emotion that her husband's assassination had begun two and a half years before.

But she claimed no political aspirations. Sin met with her several times, urging her to stand for the presidency. She always said no. Then one day, after a huge worship service celebrated in Manila's Luneta Park, which six million people attended, Sin returned home to find Cory Aquino waiting for him.

She was the opposite of Marcos; disinterested in appearances, she wore no makeup, and her simple dress was yellow, her husband's favorite color. Yellow had become the symbol of those seeking to carry out the work he had begun.

"Why are you here?" Sin asked mildly.

"I have decided to run," she said quietly.

"Cory, under what political party? Who will be your running mate?"

"I will run alone," she said.

Sin knew that without a political organization her campaign would be hopeless. "Don't do that," he said. "You cannot organize a political party now. There is too little time. You run under UNIDO, with Laurel as your vice-president. Will you do that?"

"But Laurel is planning to run himself."

"I will get him to agree if you accept him first."

After a few moments of quiet reflection, Aquino said simply, "Yes, yes, I will run with him."

Sin's face broke into a wide and sunny smile. "God bless you. Out of your weakness this great man will come down. He has been insulting you, saying that women are only good for the bedroom. So you will win."

She fell to her knees in front of him, her hands clasped together, and Sin leaned down slightly to place his hand on her head and give his blessing. "I bless you and you will win." Cardinal Sin had now consciously crossed the line—to stay.

The Philippine election was remarkable for two reasons. The first was the outpouring of emotion that accompanied Cory Aquino wherever she went. Her motorcade was perpetually late because of the chanting crowds jamming the roads, the people swarming alongside her begging for a scrap of conversation or a handshake. She did not seem to care about the schedule: she always took time to talk to the lowliest person. Her campaign soon stood for more than a political faction; it became a festival of democracy. And it was accompanied by a great deal of prayer. Sin's preaching of repentance and conversion had made a deep impact on the nation, and now it bore fruit.

Democracy is not prescribed in the Bible, and Christians can and do live under other political systems. But Christians can hardly fail to love democracy, because of all systems it best assures human dignity, the essence of our creation in God's image.

Such a love for democracy was plain in the Philippines: in the cordons of nuns wrapping their arms around the aluminum ballot boxes as though they were protecting human life; in the crowds of fervent poll watchers, often from church groups; in the computer operators who walked off their vote-counting jobs because they saw the discrepancy between their count and the officially released results, and who were rushed to a nearby church for protection from the police. The enthusiasm, the tears, the confrontations all reflected a tremendous will for government of the people and for the people. Cory Aquino, in her calm, firm, common-sense manner—just the opposite of a glib, polished professional politician—seemed to embody democracy. She was a housewife pressed into politics by the need of her nation.

The other exceptional aspect of the election was the sheer cynicism and brutality of Marcos's party. They made very little attempt to hide what they were doing from foreign reporters, so American television audiences were shocked to witness ballot boxes stolen at gunpoint, votes purchased like potatoes, thousands of voters driven away from polling places by armed thugs. Filipinos were unable to see such reports; the state-controlled news calmly reported that everything was normal, that there were only scattered reports of fraud. But millions of Filipinos personally witnessed the election being stolen.

Sin had seen it coming and had issued a statement two weeks before: "If a candidate wins by cheating, he can only be forgiven by God if he renounces the office he has obtained by fraud. There will be no divine forgiveness for this act of injustice without a previous decision to repay the damage done."[4]

But apparently God's forgiveness was unimportant to those ruling the Philippines. They rigged the vote. All the passion for democracy and all the prayers of the people had not stopped them.

On February 14, one week after the election, the Marcos dominated National Assembly laid all doubts about their objectivity to rest by proclaiming Ferdinand Marcos the electoral winner. Public anger and frustration was mounting and the danger of it erupting grew more likely each day. Aquino called a protesting political rally for the sixteenth, a Sunday. Small knots of marchers gathered at different points in the vast city of Manila, converging from all directions on Manila's downtown Luneta Park.

Many wore yellow T-shirts in memory of the slain Benigno Aquino. Yellow headbands proclaimed, "I love Ninoy." Marchers carried signs and banners and chanted, "Cory, Cory." The procession gradually grew as it entered the main city arteries. Supporters poured out of apartments, slums, churches. They did not stroll; they dog-trotted along, swinging their elbows. Mothers, children, old wizened men—it seemed as though half of Manila was marching, singing, chanting. The air of celebration that had marked Aquino's campaign had hardened into a tougher sense of determination.

Well over a million people reached the park together. Elbow to elbow they sang "Bayan Ko," the haunting, emotive melody of Philippine independence:

Even birds who freely fly
When caged will struggle to escape.
What more of a country endowed with nobility,
Would she not strive to break free?
The Philippines, my cherished land,
My home of sorrow and tears,
Always I dream to see you truly free.

Now, with such a mass of humanity together, the cry, "Cory, Cory" seemed to saturate the air, the ground. Many wept.

This was the kind of crowd a politician might dream of. They would march anywhere, do anything, on command.

Yet Cory Aquino stood in front of the vast assemblage spread like a colored mosaic at her feet and spoke in her calm, rational, head-librarian manner. She did not send them to storm Malacalang Palace—though they would have gone. She asked them for a day of prayer.

She also called for a series of nonviolent protests—boycotting certain banks and businesses owned by Marcos cronies and setting up a "noise barrage" every evening after she spoke on the Catholic radio station. They were to do this patiently until the government conceded. "You have given a lot to the country," she said, "but in the coming days you will have to give more. We thought election day was the day of our redemption, but it proved the start of our further struggle."

A young Catholic bishop read a statement issued by the bishops two days before: "The people have spoken. Or tried to. Despite the obstacles thrown in the way of their speaking freely, we the bishops believe what they attempted to say is clear enough. In our considered judgment the polls were unparalleled in the fraudulence of their conduct."

The church leaders supported nonviolent civil disobedience. "A government that assumes or maintains power through fraudulent means has no moral basis," they said. "If it does not of itself freely correct the evil it has inflicted on the people, then it is our serious moral obligation as a people to make it do so." Nonetheless they warned against "the enormous sin of fratricidal strife."

Some American reporters left the rally shaking their heads. How could this nonviolent, prayerful approach make a revolution?

During that tense, rumor-filled week, it seemed the reporters might be correct. Marcos might ride it out. He controlled the guns, after all.

Marcos did not, however, entirely control the men who carried the guns. Secret meetings were held, mainly by younger officers. They discussed the possibility of announcing their loyalty to Aquino whom they considered the duly elected president. A plan was hurriedly formed in consultation with the minister of defense, Juan Ponce Enrile.

The officers were a group who, years before, had begun questioning orders to make arrests without legal evidence or to use torture in interrogations. Their military training had given them no basis for judging how to respond to such orders. When was it right, if ever, for a military officer to refuse to obey?

The search for answers had led them to Christ. They began holding Bible classes and prayer meetings. As they studied the Bible their sense of moral outrage grew. They began demanding change and became known as the Reform Group.

Benigno Aquino's murder heightened their awareness that more than politics was at stake. Perhaps they intuitively grasped that the dignity of the individual, created in the image of God, was on trial. Now, with the election stolen, they felt it impossible to remain loyal to Marcos.

But Marcos discovered their plans to desert him and late Friday began to move loyal military units into position. By Saturday morning a watchful Enrile knew something was going on; he had reports of troops ferried into Manila. While eating a late breakfast with his daughter, Enrile received a warning telephone call from another cabinet minister. He suddenly realized that he would be arrested soon along with many others. He had to react within hours or face possible death.

They could flee the city. Or they could take a stand within Manila and appeal for popular support. There was no time to think through all the implications of the choices. Enrile elected to stay and at about 3:00 P.M. helicptered into the ministry of defense headquarters at Camp Aguinaldo on the edge of town. Only a few hundred troops were on duty. It was virtually defenseless.

Enrile's first action was to call his wife. He asked her to reach Cardinal Sin and appeal to him for help.

At 6:30 that night, as darkness settled over Manila, Enrile and a much-respected general, Fidel Ramos, held a press conference in Camp Aguinaldo. Radio Veritas, the Catholic station, covered it live. Enrile explained their decision: "We can no longer support Marcos as our commander-in-chief—because of our honest belief that he did not receive the people's mandate in the election. I believe in my heart and mind that Mrs. Aquino was duly elected president of the Philippines. . . . We will never surrender, and if we are assaulted, we will all die together."

Death seemed a real possibility. Though they had stretched a thin defense force around the camp's perimeter, they were sitting ducks. As military men, they knew that they could be quickly overwhelmed by superior forces. They could only hope that somehow, something would turn in their favor.

At 9:00 that night it did. Sin's familiar warm voice suddenly came on Radio Veritas. He ordered all nuns into their chapels where they were to pray continuously until God delivered the Philippines. Then he spoke to *all* Christians. "Go to Camp Crame and Camp Aguinaldo. Lend your support to Enrile and Ramos. Protect them and bring them food: they have nothing to eat."

Within thirty minutes two million people were on the streets. Unarmed, often gathered as church groups, they simply waited, listening to their radios, praying and singing through the long night. No one had told them how to carry out their unprecedented assignment to protect soldiers.

Catholic believers provided the impetus for this mass movement; but they were joined in the streets by Protestants. CONFES, an evangelical Protestant group formed to push for an honest election, was one of the earliest groups to make its way to the gates of the military camps. There, with barbed-wire fences for their backdrop, they organized into shifts for the vigil. They read Scripture, sang hymns, made signs. Everyone felt the tension. This was a protest that could end in blood.

The next day Marcos's troops began to come. One long column of tanks and trucks carried a regiment of marines, headed by a muscular, bronzed general, one of Marcos's strongest supporters. In the midday heat the tanks ground noisily over the Manila streets toward the camps. Thousands of civilians crowded around, shouting, beckoning. Some of the crowd began hurriedly pushing cars and buses into a major intersection ahead of the tanks. A barricade of dozens of vehicles forced the convoy to a temporary halt.

Groups of marines armed with automatic rifles leaped out of the trucks and jogged to the front. They took up menacing positions, guns ready. The general came forward with his bullhorn and ordered the people to disperse. The huge milling crowd, composed largely of women and children, instead moved closer. Some held out crosses;

others offered flowers. Still others were praying. An old woman in a wheelchair cried out for the soldiers; kill her if they must, but not their own people.

The soldiers did not know what to do. None of these rebels threw anything at them or even insulted them. Apparently they had no fear. Could they shoot?

"We're all Filipinos!" shouted one woman. "What are you doing? Don't kill us!"

One slender, brave woman pushed her way between two bewildered soldiers right up to the general. She threw her arms around him, calling his name. "You have a wife and children too! Don't do it! Don't kill us in the name of a dictator."

The general gently pushed her away. For some time he nervously surveyed the masses of people in front of him. Finally, he ceremoniously took off his bulletproof vest. "We don't want to kill civilians," he told one of his aides. "Our quarrel is with Enrile and Ramos."

He climbed on top of a tank and with his bullhorn told the people that the tanks would have to pass. "We will not hurt you. We have orders to enter Camp Aguinaldo."

"No, no!" people cried. Many threw themselves to their knees and began praying out loud. The general ordered his men to start the tanks. The people prayed louder above the roaring engines. The tanks jerked forward, their treads creaking and clattering. There were high screams of horror; men held their heads, anticipating the moment when the first bodies would be crushed. But just as the lead tank reached the first kneeling bodies—many of them priests and nuns—it stopped. For just a moment there was virtual silence. Then the crowd let out a prolonged cheer.

The top of the tank opened and a helmeted, bemused soldier poked his head out, looked around at the masses of happy people, and shrugged his shoulders, as though to say, "What can we do about this?"

By Monday morning there were dozens of such tanks on the streets all around the military camps, stopped not by antitank missiles but by the bodies of praying Filipinos. Young soldiers sprawled on top of their beached vehicles eating food offered by the people who had stopped them.

On Tuesday Marcos fled the country, defeated.

*   *   *

Benigno Aquino was felled by an assassin's bullet. But what he represented could not be destroyed. In two and one half years Marcos was gone and Aquino's wife was president. Miraculously it was a blood-less transition.

The problems of the Philippines were not solved overnight—and its political future remains clouded. Communist insurgents continue to try to achieve with bullets what the Filipino people have rejected with their ballots. And Cory Aquino's first year in office was shaky at best; this simple housewife with faith of iron, narrowly survived several coup attempts while she grappled to get control of a government that had been almost wholly corrupt.

I met with Cory Aquino in her office on the very weekend in November 1986 that she was to depart for her first trip to Japan. The press worldwide was speculating that her now defiant defense minister, Juan Enrile, would take over in her absence. Manila was abuzz with rumors. The young man who met me at the airport to drive me to Mrs. Aquino's office suggested I also visit Enrile: "He'll be president next week."

But Cory Aquino was at perfect peace. "I didn't seek this," she told me, "and I only want to serve my people. I simply have to put my trust in the Lord." Then she explained that she had given Cardinal Sin full instructions on what to say to the people if she were "unable to do so myself." I had the impression she could face death as resolutely as had her husband.

The next morning I went to Cardinal Sin's residence. We had met earlier when he addressed our International Conference in Nairobi—and we had become fast friends. I was delighted to discover at the chancery that the bishop had several months earlier instructed his entire staff to read Born Again. Several told me they had.

The cardinal, wearing a huge smile, swung open his door. "Welcome to the House of Sin, dear brother," he chuckled, enveloping me in a massive embrace.

During our conversation I expressed concern over the expected coup. Sin leaned back in his chair, rolled his eyes upward, and put both hands up, palms out. "There will be no coup, praise God," he said. Then with a mischievous expression he told me that he had met with Enrile the night before. "I've taken care of that, now you can do your part," he said, grinning. "You preach to those businessmen tonight from the Scripture." I was that evening to address a thousand conservative evangelicals at a major dinner. Many of them had been Enrile sympathizers. "You tell them to be born again—and pray for those in authority, for their Christian president."

There was no coup. Nearly a year after the revolution Jaime Cardinal Sin remained the most powerful individual in the Philippines.

*   *   *

Regardless of the future of Philippine politics, the February revolution will be remembered as the most remarkable church-state confrontation in this century. The contrast with Nazi Germany in the thirties is striking. In Germany the church was institutionalized and lacked evangelical fervor and the emotional support of the populace; so Hitler could strike fast and dismember it before it could collect itself for opposition. In the Philippines, on the other hand, the church was strong, the masses were powerful, conversions were sweeping the islands, Benigno Aquino was a powerful martyr, and there was never any doubt that the remarkable Cardinal Sin was in charge. So in the Philippines the church prevailed, withdrawing its moral legitimization for a corrupt, repressive regime; it succeeded in holding the state "morally accountable before God to live up to its own claims," as one prominent pastor put it.[5]

But the church went further than simply withdrawing its support. It was the chief instrument in the overthrow of Marcos. In an earlier chapter we discussed an individual's right to disobey the state, but this story raises even more difficult questions as to the role of Christians as a body—the church. What are the grounds for disobedience? What form may it take? And what about the role of the clergy, which, as discussed in previous chapters, is called to preach the Good News, minister to the church, not form opposition political parties. And in the light of Scripture, can Christians actively advocate and participate in political revolutions? The apostle Paul does not equivocate in his instructions to the Romans. God has ordained government to preserve order; Paul offers no exception because even a bad government is a better alternative than no government—which results in chaos.

But Paul also says that government's authority is from God; it is a delegation. Therefore, governments—all governments—whether they acknowledge it or not, rule under God. But does God give an unrestricted delegation? Certainly not. As Jesus made clear with the coin, there are two realms—and Caesar is not to usurp what belongs to God. Any government that violates the law that is higher than its own is

exceeding the legitimate authority God has granted.* As Dietrich Bonhoeffer put it, "If government persistently and arbitrarily violates its
assigned task, then the divine mandate lapses."[6]

In that case the state becomes evil incarnate, as in Nazi Germany.
Instead of acting as God's instrument for preserving life and order, it
does the reverse, destroying life and order.

Then the church must resist. Though as argued earlier, the church's
primary function is evangelization and ministering to spiritual needs;
as the principal visible manifestation of the Kingdom of God, it must be
the conscience of society, the instrument of moral accountability. Richard Neuhaus eloquently wrote that "the church can and should subject
to moral questioning every political agenda or cause, thus keeping the
entirety of human politics under the transcendent judgment of God."[7]

The real question then is not whether to resist, but how. The same
principle applies with the individual Christian. Earlier I cited the example of Daniel's refusing the king's choice food: Use the minimum
resistance necessary to achieve the result.

The church's first duty then would be to publicly expose the state's
immorality. Though I have argued that the clergy should avoid parti-
sanship, it is not partisan to speak against unjust war—as the British
bishops did against their own government bombing of civilian targets
in World War II—corruption, oppression, the deprivation of civil liberties, or the taking of innocent lives.

As a second step the church should refuse to have any part in the
state's immorality. When New York barred discrimination against hiring
active homosexuals by private agencies that had city contracts, the
church faced a serious dilemma: Lose vital financial support or violate
clear, biblical teaching. To their everlasting credit the Salvation Army
forfeited $4.5 million in state contracts; Augdath Israel Temple,
$513,000; and the Catholic Archdiocese of New York, $72 million.

But what if speeches and sermons and noncooperation fail to deter
the state? The church must take the next more severe measure of
resistance lest its words be rendered hollow. In the abolition campaign
the church used internal discipline and external pressure. The great

---

*One eminent authority cautions that in interpreting Paul's word in Romans, a distinction must be
made between government and nation. Government must always be respected, otherwise anarchy results; but the nation may attempt to venerate a culture or race. Donald Bloesch writes,
"When the state is made to serve the aspirations of race or nation instead of the cause of justice for
all, it becomes a demonic state warranting resistance and rejection by the Christian faith." Donald
Bloesch, *Crumbling Foundations* (Grand Rapids, Mich.: Zondervan, 1984), 183.

evangelist Charles Finney refused communion to slave-holders. Others organized the underground railroad and rescued fugitive slaves from prison. Many ministers broke the law, were arrested, and some imprisoned.

But the state's evil, even as egregious as slavery, does not give an unrestricted license to disobey any law; only the unjust law can properly be disobeyed. While active resistance may succeed, as it did with slavery and the Civil-Rights Movement, it may not, however, be enough in the face of the raw power modern totalitarian states have achieved. So what does the Christian do when all peaceable means fail? Is revolution ever justified?

Scottish reformation theologians like John Knox and Samuel Rutherford believed they could be, advocating the right of Christians to rise up against ungodly rulers. Many ministers in the colonies agreed as well; when they preached that the people had the authority to resist the king when the king violated God's commands, they were setting the stage for the American Revolution. After dumping tea in Boston Harbor the next step of resistance was the musket. A Boston preacher said that for a people to "arise unanimously and resist their prince, even to dethrone him, is not criminal but a reasonable way of vindicating their liberties and just rights."[8] John Adams observed, "The revolution was in the minds and hearts of the people, a change in their religious sentiments of their duties and obligations."[9]

Some Christian activists today loosely call for a new American Revolution just as the young radical youth movements did in the sixties. But as history reveals, revolution most often results, after the bodies are buried, in one form of tyranny replacing another. G. K. Chesterton summed it up well: "The real case against revolution is this: That there always seems to be much more to be said against the old regime than in favor of the new regime."[10]

So for the Christian, revolution is never to be lightly regarded. It is the most extreme form of disobedience. It could only be contemplated on the same justification as a just war; that is, that there must be a better alternative as a result of the revolution. Its advantages must outweigh the suffering, and the evil employed in the revolution must prevent a far greater evil than the status quo. This was the reasoning that caused Albert Einstein to abandon his pacifism in the face of Hitler's rise to power. "To prevent the greater evil, it is necessary that the lesser—the hated military—be accepted for the time being," Einstein contended.[11] It was this reasoning that caused Bonhoeffer to participate in the plot to assassinate Hitler.

For Christians to justify participation in revolution, therefore, they would have to be convinced that the state had become totally opposed to the purposes of God for the state and there was no other recourse to prevent massive evil.*

In the light of this, then, what about the Philippines? What lessons are to be drawn from it?

Though commonly called the February Revolution, it is, I believe, a misnomer. It was not the overflow of an existing order, rather the replacement of a corrupt ruler, one who was clinging to power, in fact, by fraud and deceit, having reversed the outcome of a legitimate election. And the anti-Marcos forces were unarmed, engaging throughout in peaceful protest.

So what happened in the Philippines was more like a coup, removing an unlawful leader. Mrs. Aquino was following the will of a democratic electorate that had been thwarted by Marcos's tyranny. She was not overthrowing, but rather restoring and fulfilling a system that had been in place since 1946.

But regardless of whether it was properly labeled a revolution, did the church have grounds to take the leadership it did? When I was in Manila in late 1986 I talked with businessmen and politicians, both conservative and liberal. The conclusion was unanimous: If Marcos had remained in power the Philippines would have collapsed and fallen into the hands of Communist insurgents. Those I talked to believed that justified the revolution; but that alone would not be a basis for the church to act.

Nor would Mrs. Marcos's 3,500 pairs of shoes or the incredible greed of Marcos, who stashed away billions in U.S. and Swiss banks while half the populace was unemployed and starving.

While no one could ever develop a rigid formula, it seems to me that the combination of the Marcos regime's refusal to allow free elections, the suspension of civil liberties, the massive corruption of the governmental process, the trampling of human rights, and Marcos's own blasphemous, at times messianic pretensions, gave the church a mandate to act. Cardinal Sin acted heroically in mobilizing the church to say no to evil.

---

*The Exodus from Egypt is often cited as a model for political action by liberation theologians, but they ignore the fact that in the Exodus, God did not overthrow the political system in Egypt. He extracted His own people from that system, taking them to Mount Sinai that they might worship Him.

And in the first stage his approach was entirely biblical. By preaching repentance and conversion, he encouraged outbreaks of spiritual revival all across the Philippine islands. He called people to pray for their country.

But when Sin stared down Marcos, in the passion of the moment, he crossed an invisible divide. He did not just denounce raw injustice. He married the church to an opposition political movement. And when he created the UNIDO ticket, convincing Salvador Laurel to run with Cory Aquino, he momentarily left the sanctuary and entered the back rooms of power-brokering politics. For this he was immediately chastised by the Vatican and disciplined again in early 1987.

Sin later acknowledged his excess, issuing orders that all clergy would remain out of partisan, political camps. He also announced he would stay "in the background." I know Cardinal Sin; and I can only hope that while he will keep his word not to step over the line, he will not fail to keep the church a vital instrument for holding government to moral account.

A courageous cardinal, the Philippine church, and two million ordinary citizens opened a crack of light in the dark canopy that envelops so much of planet earth. Through their civil disobedience and resistance to evil, the Kingdom of God has been made visible.

The late Francis Schaeffer once wrote, "If there is no place for civil disobedience, then the government has been made autonomous, and as such, it has been put in the place of the living God."[12]

The belief that government is autonomous, the ultimate repository of power, the solution to all of society's ills, is the greatest imposter of the twentieth century. As the next chapter demonstrates, Christians and the church have no higher calling than to expose it by every legitimate means.

24

The Political Illusion

Governments are composed of persons who meet occasionally in a hall to make speeches and to write resolutions; of men studying papers at desks, receiving and answering letters and memoranda, listening to advice and giving it, hearing complaints and claims and replying to them; of clerks manipulating more papers; of inspectors, tax collectors, policemen, and soldiers. These officials have to be fed, and often they overeat. They would often rather go fishing, or make love, or do anything than shuffle their papers. They have to sleep. They suffer from indigestion and asthma, bile and palpitation, become bored, tired, careless, and have nervous headaches. They know what they happen to learn, they are aware of what they happen to observe, they can imagine what they happen to be interested in, they can accomplish only what they can command or persuade an unseen multitude to do.

—Walter Lippmann

What is so remarkable about the story of the Philippines is that millions of people believed more in the power of prayer than in the power of politics; they believed that the message "repent, be converted, and trust in Jesus" could topple even an authoritarian leader. They believed their deliverance was spiritual.

Such belief runs counter to the myth that all human problems are political and solvable by all-powerful human institutions. An extreme example was the prominent New Right leader who declared in 1985, after Congress failed to pass his legislative agenda, "The only way to have a genuine spiritual revival is to have legislative reform. . . . I think we have been legislated out of the possibility of a spiritual revival."[1] Evidently, the work of the Kingdom of God had been defeated by a majority vote in the kingdoms of man.

I'm sure that individual didn't mean to deny the sovereignty of God, but his statement insinuates that nothing can be accomplished except through government. Jacques Ellul could well have been describing this leader when he wrote that politics has become "the supreme religion of the age."[2]

This political illusion springs from a diminishing belief in God and the growth of big government. What people once expected from the Almighty, they now expect from the almighty bureaucracy. That's a bad trade for anyone; but for the Christian, it's rank idolatry.

The media encourage the illusion. Stories of spiritual conversion, growth, and revival don't make good thirty-second new spots. While the everyday actions of ordinary citizens lack headline punch, politics offers confrontation, controversy, and scandal.* News coverage gravitates to political power centers, exalting the momentary, assuring suspense. The public waits expectantly for the next installment in the unfolding political soap opera.

On one level media and government are natural antagonists; on another they are natural allies, depending on each other for their influence. News organizations concentrate their resources in political capitals; governments gear their policies and decisions for primetime audiences. The media spotlight politics and politics feeds the media. Because the illusion serves those with the power to perpetuate it, neither side cares to expose it.

The 1972 summit meetings between the Soviet Union and the United States provide a good illustration. All agreements had been reached before Mr. Nixon's arrival in Moscow; there was nothing further to be negotiated or discussed. The president, in fact, was so bored that he resorted to calling me in Washington every night to discuss domestic affairs—at length.

---

*When religion does make the cover of *Time* or a spot on the network news, it is usually the result of scandal, as with the extraordinary coverage of Jim and Tammy Bakker. That's not a complaint; it's simply the way the news business works, which in turn is merely satisfying the public appetite.

Though all the summit events were ceremonial, television cameras covered every one. Anchormen gave breathless blow-by-blow accounts of the five-day proceedings. To the viewer back home, world peace hung in the balance. (White House officials did everything possible to encourage that impression.) So as the world watched anxiously, the two leaders met, discussed the weather in Moscow, and signed already confirmed documents.

The 1985 Reagan-Gorbachev summit in Geneva followed an identical format—except there were no prearranged agreements to be signed. More than three thousand journalists pounded the pavements of the beautiful Swiss city, desperate for something to film. Some, in a daring exposure of East-West competition, compared the fashions of Mrs. Gorbachev and Mrs. Reagan. Others analyzed Mrs. Reagan's anti-drug campaigns and Mrs. Gorbachev's interest in schoolchildren. Some cameramen shot footage of each other. A few gave up and went out for fondue.

In a rare moment, one network anchorman questioned whether the Geneva meetings actually warranted such coverage. Such a question treads perilously close to heresy. News is big business, after all, with hundreds of millions of dollars riding on Nielsen ratings. Network personalities hold multimillion dollar contracts, and they, as well as many print journalists, enjoy the handsome rewards of celebrity. Even in nations with public-owned media, the illusion guarantees power, privilege, and access to the elite. These are not willingly surrendered.

This unwavering focus heightens both the promise and expectation of what government can do. Political rhetoric, therefore, must offer panaceas to all human ills. Can anyone recall a major candidate who did not claim he could solve any problem if elected?

President Gerald Ford and his opponent Jimmy Carter, for example, devoted an entire debate in the 1976 campaign to the question of who would balance the budget first. Ford insisted he would do so by 1979; the best Carter could promise was 1981.[3] In reality, of course, both men must have known that more than 80 percent of the federal budget—entitlement programs and other congreessionally mandated outlays—was beyond their control. Neither candidate could have balanced the budget.

But politicians have little choice. Modern technology has reduced all issues to their lowest common denominator. Since there is no time to explain the complexities of the budget process, and since instant perceptions shape voter attitudes, politicians can do no more than create appealing visual impressions.

In his memoirs, former Budget Director David Stockman chided Reagan aides Baker and Meese for being more interested in the evening network news than in government policy. But perhaps they were more realistic. Policy has no meaning apart from how it is perceived, and that perception is heavily influenced by newscasters.

That is why Lyndon Johnson obsessively watched three evening news programs simultaneously on a three-console television set. He knew public reaction to the televised portrayal of Vietnam would influence opinion far more than battlefield strategies. He was right: the outcome of that war was decided in American living rooms.

To maintain the illusion, government attempts to shape, even manipulate public perceptions. One of my White House assignments was to do just that. I chaired a committee of White House staff who worked full time studying daily news briefings, monitoring public reactions to presidential speeches, taking daily polls, and feeding positive information to friendly reporters. Often we aggressively tried to manipulate public opinion.

For example, immediately after every presidential speech, I would unleash a small army of assistants who would call key leaders in every walk of life. We might make five hundred calls, each following the same script: "The president asked me to call to find out what you thought of his announced policy. . . ." The reactions would be collated, typed, and within hours a report surveying the opinions of hundreds of leaders would be in the president's hands. We got helpful information, but we also influenced public reactions toward acceptance of our policy. To be told that the president wanted one's opinion flattered even the cynics. Those called rarely offered a critical reply; most could hardly wait to call their friends and casually mention that "by the way, the president just called" to ask their opinion.

Our efforts were at times singularly successful. During the weekend of August 15, 1971, President Nixon was closeted at Camp David with his key economic advisors. The economy was sluggish, the trade deficit rising, and both unemployment and inflation were approaching what were then unacceptable levels of 5 percent. Something had to be done. Nixon was trailing in the polls with only fifteen months until the election.

On Sunday morning the president decided on a bold stroke recommended by Treasury Secretary John Connally: wage and price controls, and closing the gold window, thus allowing the dollar to float in world markets.

I was stunned—but at the same time impressed with Mr. Nixon's boldness. For his entire political career the president had opposed economic controls; to make them work would require a massive bureaucracy. Other advisors were equally shocked, some predicting that the stock market would plummet. On one thing we all agreed: Mr. Nixon was taking the biggest gamble of his presidency. The policy's success would depend entirely on the public reaction—especially the stock market.

At 8:00 that evening the president announced his "new economic policy" on national television.* Even the news commentators were caught off guard. But before the president's speech was over, I was on the phone to the heads of the ten largest brokerage firms in the country. I knew most of them, and I knew how the pack mentality worked.

The first call was to an old friend. He thought the bottom might drop out of the market. I assured him he was wrong, that I had talked to five other brokerage firm heads and all were bullish.

Each call followed the same pattern, and by 9:30 I had spoken with the opinion leaders of Wall Street. Though most were unenthusiastic at the outset, they were quickly converted when told that everyone else expected the market to soar.

The next day it did—up 32.93 points, the largest single one-day rise in its history to that point. The media immediately declared the president's policy "the Nixon Rally," and as public support grew, the controls, mostly voluntary, succeeded—at least well enough to perk up the flagging economy just ahead of the 1972 election. It would have failed disastrously had the market turned down. (If I had not gone to prison for my part in Watergate, perhaps I should have for manipulating the stock market—not for personal but political profit. Such maneuvers, unfortunately, are not uncommon in the age of the political illusion.)

This manipulation of public attitudes by politicians is not a peculiarly American phenomenon. In the seventies President Nicolae Ceausescu of Romania, though a pragmatic and often ruthless ruler, was frequently photographed at the scene of fires or disasters. In deference to the media age, other Communist leaders, most recently Gorbachev and Castro, have carefully cultivated favorable public images. Castro even agreed to extensive interviews with compliant American broad-

---

*We didn't discover until later—and to our considerable embarrassment—that the term *new economic policy* was not original. Lenin had first coined the phrase for his 1921 Plan.

casters to clean up his image in the U.S. Even in totalitarian societies the illusion has power.

With government policy so dependent on public reaction, it's little wonder that the celebrity syndrome has become such a major force in Western politics. During the debate on the farm bill of 1985, for example, a parade of farm groups, agricultural experts, and government officials appeared before the House committee. The press found little to cover. No one was excited and the bill was mired in committee.

So the committee chairman scheduled actresses Jane Fonda, Sissy Spacek, and Jessica Lange to testify. All three networks covered the hearings. The chairman later gushed, "I knew everyone would pay attention when they came."[4] The bill was whisked through committee and was passed by the House.

What are the qualifications of these stars? None had agricultural expertise. But in a fitting tribute to the media age, all three had *played* farm women in recent films. Celebrities, as *Time* film critic Richard Schickel has observed, have become "the chief agents of moral change in America."[5]

The subtle danger of all this manipulation is that people no longer view their own circumstances as reality. Only what appears in print and on the screen is real. As Ellul puts it, "The man of the present day does not believe in his own experiences, his own judgment and his own thought. . . . In his eyes, a fact becomes true when he has read an account of it in the paper and he measures the importance by the size of the headlines."[6]

The individual gradually loses all sense of continuity. Whether a policy is good or bad, a success or failure, is of no account; all that matters is the emotion its instant image induces. No one remembers from one day to the next. On a Monday a president can say that "the Russians blinked." Everyone is happy. The next day it is disclosed the Russians didn't blink—we did—but no one remembers. So on to the next night.

The process is mesmerizing. Images pile on images, day after day, anesthetizing the public so they feel individually impotent and that all power resides in images they see on their television screens.* This eventually erodes their own sense of political responsibility and makes them easy prey to the appetite of an authoritarian state. Ellul believes

---

*This point is developed at length by Neil Postman in his masterful book *Amusing Ourselves to Death: Public Discourse in the Age of Show Business* (New York: Viking, 1985).

that that consequence is irresistible. Jewish philosopher Hannah Arendt would agree, writing that the chief characteristic of tyranny is isolation of the individual, denying him access to the public realm "where he would show himself, see and be seen, hear and be heard."[7]

"Even democracies need institutions and agencies through which the individual can resist the tendency of all central governments to grow larger, stronger, and more domineering."[8] For the only thing that stands between the multitudes and totalitarianism, says Ellul, are the mediating structures of society: families, small groups of citizens, churches, voluntary associations that are independent of and resistant to the collective state.

Long before the age of instant media, Tocqueville made the same point that if the American experiment were to succeed, it would require the continued help of voluntary associations.[9]

Of all these independent institutions, the church should be the one best able to expose the political illusion. For the message of a transcendent reality is a resounding warning against the futility of seeking immortality from the instruments and institutions of this life. Mastery of nature through technology has given modern man the illusion that he has mastered life itself. The message of the Kingdom is that only God is master of life, and attempts to create alternatives to His rule are futile.

Hannah Arendt, who spent much of her life studying man's attempts to construct his social and political environment, has pointed out how Western society first learned this painful lesson: "The fall of the Roman Empire plainly demonstrated that no work of mortal hands can be immortal, and it was accompanied by the rise of the Christian gospel of an everlasting individual life to its position as the exclusive religion of Western mankind. Both together made any striving for an earthly immortality futile and unnecessary."[10]

My own experiences have repeatedly confirmed this truth, one incident in particular left an indelible impression. It happened in Colombia, South America, in the spring of 1984 while I was visiting Prison Fellowship ministry leaders there.

Immediately after speaking to the inmates in the central prison in Bogotá, I was taken to meet the minister of justice. Several Prison Fellowship Colombia board members were with me. It was late in the day, and the minister had a packed schedule. His announced crackdown on drug traffickers was all over the front pages that day. His aide suggested that I be brief, and I assured him we would confine our visit to five minutes.

Minister Rodrigo Lara Bonilla was a handsome young man with intense, penetrating eyes. He bounded up from his chair to shake our hands and invited me to describe Prison Fellowship's ministry. His English was flawless, so I spoke rapidly. Five minutes into the meeting I thanked him for his courtesy, particularly for allowing me to visit his country's prisons, and I prepared to leave.

He leaned forward. "You've been in the prisons?" he asked. "What do you think of them?"

Did he not know what rat holes his prisons were? I wondered. *Should I be politic or tell him the truth?*

I blurted out, "They're dreadful, sir."

"Hah!" He slammed his palm on the polished table. "You are right; they are pigsties, unfit for humans. Corrupt too. The inmates pay more for food than people on the street."

I was startled. Bonilla had a reputation as a reformer; he was leading a massive assault on the biggest industry in Colombia, the drug traffic. But never had I heard an official be so critical of his own department.

"What do you think we should do?" he asked.

I outlined the reforms Prison Fellowship has advocated in many countries. Bonilla's mind was razor sharp, and he frequently interrupted with questions. Our discussion went on for about a half hour.

Then he leaned back in his chair. "Finally," he sighed, "I've met people who understand the problem. Will Prison Fellowship work with me, Mr. Colson? Send me someone who can help straighten out these holes."

I promised to send an expert to Colombia the next month.

Bonilla then summoned an aide, instructing him that the ministry was to extend full cooperation to Prison Fellowship. We would have open access to the prisons.

After we had photographs taken together, Bonilla embraced me. It was spontaneous, as if to seal our covenant to join together to clean up the horrors of Colombia's prisons. I gave him a Spanish edition of my book, *Life Sentence*, which he said he would read.

Outside the office, our Colombia directors were jubilant. "This man is the second most powerful man in the government, expected to be elected president in the next election," one said enthusiastically. Another exclaimed, "With his backing Prison Fellowship will be able to do anything!"

Two hours later I arrived at the penthouse apartment of one of Bogotá's leading businessmen, where I was to speak at a dinner gathering of business leaders and government officials. My host greeted me at the door, ashen faced. "Have you heard the news?" he asked. I shook my head.

He told me Rodrigo Lara Bonilla had been assassinated, shot to death by two gunmen—agents of the drug lords—as he was driven home from his office. I had been the minister's last appointment.

That night the president of Colombia declared the country in a state of siege. We were fortunate to get to the airport the next morning to catch our scheduled flight to the U.S. On the front page of the Bogotá newspaper was a grisly picture of the blood-spattered interior of Bonilla's Mercedes. On the seat, covered with shattered glass, was the copy of *Life Sentence*.

I was horrified at the death of this vigorous and brilliant young leader, saddened by the loss of a new friend. I was also sobered as I remembered our enthusiasm the day before. We had talked as if Bonilla's endorsement would assure Prison Fellowship's success.

A year later, in spite of the loss of this dynamic leader, we found that the ministry was actually flourishing, with more seminars going on in Colombian prisons than ever before. Though we had lost a friend and ally in a position of influence, the work of the Kingdom of God is not dependent on power in the kingdoms of man. "It is better to take refuge in the Lord than to trust in princes," wrote the psalmist.[11] Political kingdoms may rise and fall—but the Kingdom of God goes on forever.

Modern history is replete with similar lessons about the futility of putting ultimate trust in much-vaunted political systems. A greedy tyrant is overthrown in Nicaragua; the idealist replacing him promises liberation and hope for the oppressed. The people are jubilant. But in a short time the liberator becomes the oppressor himself, resplendent in his $3,500 designer glasses. When autocracy is replaced by bureaucracy, only the icons change.

Ideology, which in so many parts of the world has replaced true religion, is powerless as well. As Ellul points out, the promised utopias of the twentieth century, either Marxist or Fascist, are doomed because they accept the essential premises of current civilization and move with its lines of internal development: "Thus, utilizing what this world itself offers them, they become its slaves, although they think they are transforming it."[12] Even massive weapons of destruction fail to assure anything for today's mightiest governments. Wars reach no permanent solutions; there is no such thing as a lasting peace or, as Americans so fondly believed, "a war to end all wars." Terrorists stalk the globe, and governments can do little to stop them.

Wars proliferate; political solutions fail; frustrations rise. Yet we continue to look to governments to resolve problems beyond their capability. The illusion persists.

Nowhere is that more evident than in one troubled corner of the world. But even there, in the midst of carnage, violence, and hatred, the example of a few people offers hope, pointing the way for civilization to emerge from its darkness.

25

The Indestructible Kingdom

That which man builds man destroys, but the city of God is built by God and cannot be destroyed by man.

—*Augustine*

Before my first visit to Northern Ireland in 1977 I stopped in England. Perhaps I could gain insight into Ulster by discussing her problems with British politicians.[1]

In London my friend Michael Alison arranged a dinner for us with a number of the members of Parliament. As we convened in an elegant Westminster dining room, a page stepped through a side door, formally announcing, "Gentlemen, the Speaker."

With that, George Thomas strode into the room. He was a short, feisty Welshman, bubbling over with enthusiastic good humor. In his

This chapter is based on accounts of actual events in the day-to-day struggle of Northern Ireland; all the participants are real people; and the stories are told with their permission. In a few instances, however, events have been consolidated and chronology reconstructed somewhat for purposes of clarity.

black knickers, white lace shirt, and powdered wig, he looked like he had emerged straight from the pages of *Punch*.

The beef Wellington matched the excellence of the conversation; seated next to George Thomas, I enjoyed myself immensely. After dessert I was asked to speak. I told the MPs about my conversion and responded to a number of questions. As the evening drew to a close, I said, "I've been answering questions all evening, gentlemen. Now I think it's only fair that we do a turnabout and I ask you one.

"I'm going to Belfast tomorrow for a series of meetings. Perhaps you could give me some insights into government policy and Ulster's political solutions." I paused. "What are the answers to the struggles in Northern Ireland?"

Several MPs glanced at each other; others toyed with their silverware. George Thomas grinned and then spoke for the group.

"That's easy," he said. "There is no answer in Northern Ireland."

*   *   *

Northern Ireland. A small nation with less than two million people. Yet scarcely a week goes by without a bombing, a shooting, or a riot. Between 1969 and 1987 several thousand people were killed and more than 26,000 injured in what the people of Northern Ireland euphemistically call "the Troubles."

The troubles are centuries old and result from the clash between two deeply rooted traditions: the Roman Catholics who make up 40 percent of the population, and the Protestants who make up the other 60 percent. The Catholics tend to be Republicans who want Northern Ireland's six counties united with the Republic of Ireland and free of Great Britain's control. Protestants tend to be Loyalists, determined to keep their British allegiance.

The struggle is more political—a contest for power—than religious, however. As one wag put it, the combatants are Catholic atheists on one side and Protestant atheists on the other. And so deep is the conflict that it cannot be resolved by new political parties, British troops, or even the impassioned pleas of those who have suffered the most—the families of the slain.

Belfast, Northern Ireland's capital, lies between the chill waters of Belfast Lough and Lough Neagh. It is a gray industrial city of crowded nineteenth-century houses. Viewed from the air, the great shipbuilding cranes on the River Lagan stand like giant croquet wickets in the sea of gray and brick-red roofs. Smoke rises from tall chimneys nearby and blends with the low-hanging clouds that so often blanket the city.

In downtown Belfast nearly every block contains bomb-blackened, boarded-up buildings. Police stations of the Royal Ulster Constabulary are fortresses rolled in barbed wire, their thick, high walls tented with steel mesh to guard against the terrorists' habit of lobbing homemade bombs over the walls. Army vans filled with British soldiers are everywhere.

Yet the wartime setting is incongruous. Belfast is still a place of laughter, and the people are hospitable, friendly, and a bit apologetic about their country's reputation.

"Surely we're not as bad as you've heard we are?" a shopkeeper inquires anxiously. "We don't shoot strangers—just each other."

"Well, what do you think of the Troubles?" a cab driver asks. And when you apologize for not really understanding the complexity of the conflict, he responds cheerfully, "We don't understand it either."

Most would agree, however, that the modern struggle began in August 1969 when British troops marched onto the streets of Belfast and Londonderry, or Derry, as Republicans call the ancient walled city in the north of Ulster.

At that time unrest over civil rights and bottled-up bitterness had exploded into widespread rioting that the British government believed could be quelled only by a military presence. The soldiers' presence added to the tension. Sectarian shootings dominated the headlines, and the troops were targets of booby traps, ambushes, and bombings. The Protestant-controlled government, meeting at Stormont, the official government chambers, could do nothing.

Then came Bloody Sunday: January 30, 1972. British soldiers, attempting to break up a civil-rights rally in Londonderry, shot and killed thirteen demonstrators.

By mid-February retaliatory bombs were exploding in Northern Ireland at the rate of four a day. Those who survived each new blast lived in terror of the next. Citizens sometimes paid dearly just by going about their daily business, as did the six shoppers who died—and the 147 who were wounded—the day the Irish Republican Army, or IRA, left a gelignite bomb in a parked car in a busy Belfast shopping district.

Fifty-four days after Bloody Sunday, the Stormont government fell. British Prime Minister Heath declared Northern Ireland incapable of handling its own affairs and imposed direct rule from Westminster.

Since then there have been more than 2,600 bloody deaths in

Ulster. One out of every twenty households has felt the pain of either death or injury from the incessant shootings and bombings.

It isn't the grim statistics that tell the story of Northern Ireland, however. It is the lives of those who live, work, and survive there.

PEARL AND KAREN . . .

It was a Saturday evening in Belfast, September 25, 1982. As twenty-year-old Karen McKeown drove her mother, Pearl, home from a special service at their Protestant church, she was still humming the song the choir had sung: "I will enter into His courts with praise." Mother and daughter talked about Karen's classes at Queen's University, Pearl's early shift the next morning at the hospital, the contact lens Karen had lost.

Pearl watched Karen, thinking her daughter had never looked prettier. Her dark hair was glossy and thick with a determined curl that Karen spent much of her energy trying to tame. Her new white sweater and skirt set off her dark eyes and pale complexion beautifully. *She has so much ahead of her*, Pearl thought proudly.

Karen dropped off her mother at home, waved good-bye, and headed back to the church to help clean up for Sunday services. She pulled into the church parking lot, got out, and was locking the car when a young man appeared by her side.

"I want you to know that I'm going to shoot you," he said, placing a heavy pistol against the base of Karen's neck.

He pulled the trigger.

The bullet ripped into Karen's neck and tore through her spinal column. She collapsed to the concrete, bleeding and paralyzed, unable to breathe. Her assailant ran away into the night.

Friends in the church heard the crack of the gun and called the ambulance, which took Karen to the Royal Victoria Hospital. By the time Pearl and John McKeown arrived, their daughter was fighting for her life in intensive care.

Pearl refused to believe that Karen was the latest victim in Belfast's endless violence. Only as she sat day after day by her daughter's bedside did the full implication dawn.

Karen could still communicate, and Pearl would lean close to her face as she mouthed her words. It was through those words that Pearl learned the answers to the bloody bitterness of Northern Ireland.

One afternoon when she arrived to visit, she found Karen propped up on several crisp white hospital pillows with tubes coming out of her throat, nose, and arms. Machines, screens, and dials monitored her every breath.

Karen's eyes brightened when she saw her mother. "Mum," she mouthed, "could you squeeze my hands?"

Pearl gripped the slender fingers.

Karen's eyes fell. "I can't feel anything," she said. After a pause she continued, "But it doesn't matter. The only thing that matters is that we trust the Lord and never give the Devil a victory."

The inverted glass container of an intravenous tube was dripping a solution into Karen's veins, and the drug made her sleepy. Her eyelids batted a few times; then she drifted into sleep.

Pearl sat down in the armchair next to the bed, bowed her head, and wept. A few minutes later she looked up and discovered Karen awake again. "Mum," she whispered, "you think you have troubles. But just think about the troubles *his* mum has.

"When he said he was going to shoot me, I thought he was one of the boys from church, and I laughed," Karen continued. "It was as if the Lord put His arms around me. When I hit the ground I was still laughing."

Late that evening at home Pearl went into Karen's cluttered room and picked up her thick leather Bible. It had been a Christmas gift a year and a half earlier and was already worn, its pages marked with Karen's notes and underlinings. Pearl looked at the inside cover page where Karen had written, "To be a brave disciple is to be a bondslave to Jesus Christ, and to find that His service is perfect freedom."

In the Book of Job she found more notes. "This is not an explanation but an inspiration. Job's soul was a battleground without his knowledge. Could this be the reason for suffering today? In all cases, God is supreme and just. The Devil functions within God's purpose." Karen's underlining clotted the chapters of the short book. "Though he slay me, yet will I hope in Him. . . . You will lie down, and no one will make you afraid."

Pearl's eyes filled with tears. Here in her daughter's strong, square script were notes that clearly prefigured what had happened. *If this is how Karen views suffering,* Pearl thought, *then this is how I must see what has happened to her.*

Meanwhile, the forensic results came back from the crime lab; the bullet taken from Karen's neck was from the same gun used to assassinate a prominent attorney. The gun could be traced to the INLA, the Irish National Liberation Army, a Catholic terrorist organization.

The next day Pearl went home, tired and frustrated, to pick up the mail before returning to Karen's bedside. A thin white envelope fell out of the stack of get-well cards and letters. The handwriting was unfamiliar. Her eyes went to the return address: Her Majesty's Prison, Magilligan.

She slit the envelope and unfolded the sheet inside. The writer explained that he had heard about Karen's attack through a Bible study in his prison. He was, he said, an ex-INLA prisoner who had become a Christian. He was no longer a member of the organization responsible for Karen's attack, but he wanted to ask Mrs. McKeown's forgiveness and permission to pray for Karen. Would she mind?

Pearl stared at the letter in her hand. The signature read "Liam McCloskey." She thought about her daughter's peaceful face, about the underlined verses in her Bible, and about her forgiving spirit and absolute trust in Christ. She realized Karen would welcome this man's request.

Pearl jotted a quick note to Liam McCloskey, enclosing an old photograph of Karen and telling him a little about her daughter and her faith.

LIAM . . .

Liam McCloskey had not always been part of a Bible-study group praying for Protestant victims of terrorism. For much of his violent young life he had been a member of the Irish National Liberation Army, an impatient, Marxist offshoot of the IRA—the same INLA that would later shoot Karen McKeown. But he had been changed unalterably during one of the most notorious chapters of Northern Ireland's troubled history.

In December 1977 Liam had been convicted of armed hijacking and robbery offenses. At the time he was in his early twenties—a freckled young man with reddish brown hair and a quick, whimsical laugh.

Liam began his ten-year sentence at Belfast's Maze Prison, the highest-security prison in the world, where the immense perimeter was rolled with huge coils of razor wire that could slit a man's skin in an instant. Its eight steel and concrete H-blocks were a forbidding reminder of both the desperation of those in the Maze and the determination of their captors. Though a good part of the prison population were deemed "ODCs"—Ordinary Decent Criminals—the Maze was packed with those convicted of terrorist offenses.

Liam shared a cell with Kevin Lynch, a childhood friend who now shared the same political goals. Inmates like Liam and Kevin had at one time been given a political-prisoner status, but in 1976 the British government had rescinded that designation, preferring not to allow paramilitaries—Protestant or Catholic—special privileges. Ever since, the paramilitaries had been trying to get the status reinstated.

They had started with blanket protests, during which the inmates refused to wear prison clothes. When this failed, they began what was called the dirty protest.

Prisoners on dirty protest refused to wash, refused to wear clothing, refused to leave their cells. They sat on the concrete floor, covered only by a blanket with a ragged hole cut out for the head. They smeared their excrement on the walls and rinsed their hands in their own urine. Their hair and beards grew long and knotted, streaked with filth. Uneaten food molded in the corners of their cells.

Though the men inside grew accustomed to the incredible stench, officers often vomited and fainted. Visitors were nonexistent. Periodically the inmates were forcibly washed down with firehoses and moved to new cells while the old ones were cleansed and repainted. Then the cycle began again.

As the level of filth increased in the cellblock, so did the level of frustration. The inmates had broken the glass out of the narrow cell windows so they could smear excrement on the walls outside their cells. Orderlies used high-powered firehoses to clean the walls.

Liam would wait until they had rolled up the hoses; then he would put his waste out. One morning as he was about to do so, an orderly came past his window. On an impulse Liam threw the filth at him. The man turned his face away just in time, but it struck his shoulder, hair, and the side of his head.

Liam got down from the window and waited for the warders. It wasn't long before he heard the sound of heavy boots. The door opened, and he was told to put on a pair of pants. Then he was marched down the hall.

He was told to face the wall, then instructed to turn around. As he did so, an orderly hit him in the face. When he fell to the ground in a ball, a sea of fists and boots punched and kicked him. He was then taken to the punishment block where orderlies washed him down with scrubbing brushes. A bristle from one of the brushes entered his ear, opening an old wound from childhood.

Liam continued on the dirty protest for years, with periodic washings. By Christmas Eve 1980 the protest had accomplished nothing. Liam began to pray for inner strength and to read the Bible. Yet outwardly he seemed as deeply committed to his political cause as ever. "I was trying to walk with God and Republicanism at the same time," he says. "But there appeared to be more and more contradictions between the two."

GLADYS . . .

While Liam McCloskey sat in his own filth on Christmas Eve 1980, Miss Gladys Blackburne was having her tea in a small Belfast flat and preparing to visit the Maze Prison. A retired schoolteacher in her midsixties, Miss Blackburne was an inch shy of five feet, with gently curled gray hair, sensible shoes, and a determined way about her.

In August 1969, when civil unrest erupted in Northern Ireland, Gladys Blackburne took her country's situation personally.

"I was desperately ashamed," she says. "The whole world was watching, and here in our land the name of Jesus was being dragged in the gutter. I wept and asked God to show me what I could do to honor His name."

Since then, Gladys had been doing what she believed God told her to do: to be the best citizen she could in her small troubled nation and to show the love of Christ to soldiers, as she was already doing with children, students, and other groups. That love was desperately needed. The soldiers were rotated out of Northern Ireland every few months; service there was too stressful for them to last much longer than that.

Whether they accepted her message or not, the soldiers loved Miss Blackburne. She had access to every army post in Northern Ireland, and when she wanted to visit soldiers in the field or injured men in the hospital, the army gladly gave her a lift. It was not unusual for Gladys to step out of a helicopter or an army lorry, handbag firmly in her grasp, and march off for a day of visiting soldiers.

She was also approved for a position on the Maze Prison Board of Visitors, a citizens' group set up to monitor the prison and report any irregularities or abuses. As such, she had access to any part of the prison, day or night.

On this Christmas Eve Miss Blackburne prayed about how God would have her celebrate the birth of His Son. *I must do something as near as possible to what Jesus did when He left His home in glory and was born in a Bethlehem stable,* she thought.

A stable, she repeated to herself. *Does God want me to go to the dirty protest where the cells smell like stables?* I can't do that. But Gladys Blackburne was not a person to take God's direction lightly. So she put on her coat and gloves, and prayed for the grace to be able to handle what she would find at the Maze.

She hitched a ride to the prison and cleared the laborious security checks at the main gate. Before she went to the cells of the dirty protesters, however, a prison officer took her aside.

"There's a Protestant lad in a different wing asking a lot of questions about Christianity," he said. "Why don't you visit him first?"

CHIPS . . .

Chips McCurry was sitting on the edge of his bunk, head down, when his heavy cell door swung open. A Protestant paramilitary, Chips had been committed to terrorism since he was twelve years old—with the IRA murdered his father.

When he was sixteen he had joined the Ulster Volunteer Force, an illegal paramilitary organization passionately opposed to Republican attempts to bring about a unified Ireland. He was bent on inflicting as much pain as his family had suffered. But on February 19, 1976, when he carried out his first order, it was to assassinate a fellow Protestant suspected of spying within UVF ranks. Chips was convicted of murder and sent to the Maze.

He was by then a thin, solemn young man with wire-rimmed glasses and thick curly hair already flecked with gray. After several months in prison his exposure to Catholic inmates made him realize that families on both sides had been fractured by the violence. *There has to be an answer*, he thought. *It's a political situation. There must be a political solution.*

Chips began reading everything he could get his hands on—first a flirtation with fascism, then a stint as a Marxist. He studied smuggled guerrilla-warfare manuals, hoping to start a full-scale revolution when he got out.

His political search ended in disillusionment. Politics didn't offer any real answers. Perhaps religion did. *If there is a God*, he thought, *and if there is a hell, then I'm surely heading toward it. But there are so many different religions. These Christians can't have a monopoly on truth. If I ever come across the truth, then I'll follow it.*

So Chips began a new search, questioning both inmates and officers he knew were Christians. They, in turn, began to pray for him. Tracts arrived mysteriously in his cell. He threw them all away. His search for truth was philosophical and abstract. He wasn't looking for any kind of personal faith.

When Gladys Blackburne entered his cell on Christmas Eve, Chips recognized her. He had often seen her in the prison and knew, like most of the other inmates, that "if you don't want to hear the gospel, then you'd better run when you see Miss Blackburne coming."

But there was nowhere to run. Miss Blackburne took the chair at the small desk directly opposite Chip's cot and asked if she could read some Scriptures. Chips prepared himself for a recitation of the Christmas story. Instead, Miss Blackburne opened her Bible to Luke 23, the account of the Crucifixion. She stopped when she came to the words of the thief on the cross: "'Lord, remember me when you come into your kingdom.'"

"Now who was this thief calling 'Lord?'" Miss Blackburne asked Chips, her pale blue eyes looking intently into his. "Here was a man who had had a crown of thorns thrust into His head. Here was a man who was spat upon, stripped, beaten, whipped, and so disfigured He was unrecognizable. Does that look like a Lord to you? But this thief called Him 'Lord'—because Jesus was still Lord on the cross."

Chips' eyes fell. He didn't know quite why, but Gladys Blackburne's words made him aware of all the hatred and bitterness that had consumed him for years. For the first time he caught a glimpse of a connection between Christ's death and himself. *Christ was perfect*, Chips thought. *And I am full of evil—the sin He had to die for.*

He looked at the small woman. "How do I become a Christian?" he asked.

"You need to accept Christ as Lord, just like the thief on the cross," she said. "You need to turn away from your sins and believe that He died for them. And you need to confess Him as Lord to others."

Confess Christ as Lord? Chips hesitated. He had taunted enough Christians himself to know how hard that was in prison.

Miss Blackburne didn't push it. "Let me show you one more verse," she said. "Then I need to go visit some other friends." She flipped the pages of her worn New Testament and read him John 6:37: "'He who comes to me I will in no wise cast out.'"

"If you come to Christ," she said, "He will never let you go."

After Miss Blackburne left, Chips McCurry sat in his cell thinking. Finally, late that night, he knelt by his cot and committed his life to Jesus Christ. He had seen the self-perpetuating emptiness of violence and the impotence of political philosophy. He realized he had finally met the Truth.

The next morning, Christmas Day 1980, Chips woke early. A cold gray light pierced the thick concrete slates of his cell. His first thought was, I'm not really a Christian.

Then he remembered Miss Blackburne's words: "If you come to Christ, He will never let you go."

At the usual time Chips was released from his cell to go to the canteen for breakfast; there he smiled broadly as he stirred sugar into his tea. The man across the small table glared at him.

"What're you smilin' about?" he growled. "No one smiles in prison on Christmas morning."

Here I go, Chips thought. Aloud he said, "I've become a Christian."

The man exploded, his kindest incrimination being to call Chips a phony.

"Just wait and see," Chips told the man.

LIAM . . .

That same Christmas morning, the Catholic prisoners in the Maze were preparing for their final protest. The dirty protests had achieved nothing; paramilitaries were still denied political status. In pursuit of their objectives, the IRA leaders determined to turn the violence upon themselves.

Hunger strikes had been a revered form of protest for IRA faithful since the turn of the century. To threaten death by starvation was an act of defiance that could not be ignored—or so the IRA leaders thought.

A hunger strike held that fall had already ended in failure, however; no one died and no demands were met. So the IRA asked for volunteers to begin a new strike—to the death. One hundred of the Maze's seven hundred Catholic paramilitaries volunteered.

Liam McCloskey was one of those men.

At first Liam had wanted nothing to do with the hunger strikes, since he was questioning his political allegiance anyway. Then Liam's cellmate, Kevin, signed up for the strike. In spite of a knot of fear within him, Liam signed up as well.

Bobby Sands, leader of the Catholic inmates, was to begin the fast in early March. Shouting through his cell door to the others on the wing, he said there was a strong possibility he would die. But if he did, Sands said, it could be enough to "light the flame of freedom in the Irish people's hearts that would lead to British withdrawal and a Socialist Ireland."

Though attention to the hunger strike grew slowly, a county election in which Bobby Sands was elected to Parliament on April 9,

1981, gave it the boost it needed to capture the interest of the world press. Liam hoped the publicity would save Bobby's life, but it was not to be.

> Death [came] at last to convicted IRA Terrorist and Hunger Striker Robert (Bobby) Gerard Sands, 27, by virtue of his own will. His earthly remains were little more than a husk after a 66-day fast in the H-block section of Northern Ireland's Maze Prison. . . .
> As the clanging of garbage can lids announced the news of Sands' death, gangs of Catholic youths once again rampaged through the streets, despite calls from the IRA itself for calm as the organization prepared its martyr's farewell. . . . One youngster blew himself up as he tried to plant a crudely made bomb . . . a Belfast policeman was shot to death. . . . Heavy police protection was given to scores of British Members of Parliament.
> Sands' fatal hunger strike now appears to be only the prelude to a sustained movement by other Maze prisoners. . . . One senior Whitehall official repeated the government's refusal to compromise with the prisoners or to propose any solutions to the deeper problems in the near term. The situation was, he said, evoking centuries of bitterness, "a classic Irish tragedy from which at the moment there seems no escape." The desperate death of Bobby Sands appears to be the start of a new chapter in just such a prolonged and dangerous tragedy.[2]

Then came Kevin's turn to strike. Liam was racked with doubts and questions. He refused to believe that his cellmate would die. Yet it had become apparent that the British government was digging in on the issue and that there was little hope of a solution. Liam also wrestled with the fact that he was next on the list. His fear of death made him hesitant, along with his own changing views and growing faith. *Since I have doubts about the rights and wrongs of killing,* he thought, *I won't be any good to Republicanism. And since I haven't fully accepted the Word of God, I'm no good to Him either. Better that I die than someone who would be of use to the movement.*

Kevin died. *My own hunger strike,* Liam thought, *will be my last act as a Republican, one way or another. Live or die.*

> Even when the end is not far off, there are some lighter moments. Only days before he died, Kevin Lynch asked his family to bring him some cigars. He lay there, his body emaciated, his voice a whisper, blowing smoke toward the ceiling.[3]

Liam began the strike on August 3, 1981, a Monday morning.

> Hundreds of families . . . live in dread of the sudden news that their sons have volunteered to starve. When the name of the

latest hunger volunteer, Liam McCloskey, 25, was announced last week, his |family| protested to the IRA that their son had a chronic ear infection that could cause early death. They dared to express their indignation.[4]

During the first two weeks of the strike, Liam's main problems were coldness and an almost overwhelming desire to eat one last pea, chip, or bean just to taste food again. Food was blown out of proportion in his mind.

> But after two weeks, the war of nerves becomes irrelevant. The trays keep arriving, but by now the prisoners have lost their craving for food. The stomach cramps and pains recede and eventually disappear. The prisoners concentrate instead on their daily five pints of water. Now their only concern is whether they can hold down the water without retching. A small bowl of salt is provided for each prisoner, and he can sprinkle in as much as he wants. When the hunger strikes are far along, the prisoners ask for carbonated water and the British grant the request.
> This is the world of the zealots, where Irish youth are willing to starve themselves for their cause of driving the British out of Northern Ireland. It is an astounding kind of sacrifice—a brutal, lingering death, full of hatred and martyrdom, so fanatical and Irish. The moment one striker dies, 50 volunteer to take his place.[5]

After four weeks, Liam was moved to the prison hospital. On his forty-second day of the strike, August 14, 1981, his eyes began to roll uncontrollably back and forth and he began to vomit green digestive fluid. Within a few days the vomiting eased, but August 17 Liam was totally blind.

> At 42 days, almost exactly, a nightmarish experience occurs. . . . They are struck by something called nystagmus, a loss of muscular control due to severe vitamin deficiency. If they look sideways, their eyes begin to gyrate wildly and uncontrollably, first horizontally and then vertically. The prisoners struggle to stare straight forward, even cupping their hands against the sides of their heads, but they cannot help themselves. . . .
> Now the end is not far off. Their speech is slurred, and they try not to talk because the sound of their own voices echoes in their heads. Their hearing is failing and visitors have to shout during normal conversations. They are slowly going blind. Even their sense of smell is failing.[6]

Liam began to pray. *There has to be a God*, he thought. *Life makes no sense without one.* He thought back on twenty-five years of life with nothing to show for it. *Can I go before God with nothing but a self-centered life of striving after sex, drink, and good times? And what about my involvement in Republicanism?*

If I had continued as I was outside of prison, he thought, *I would have taken life for that cause. Who was I that I should appoint myself judge, jury, and executioner of any man?*

Will my life even show up as a dot on eternity? he wondered. *Here I am, about to throw it all away for Ireland, like countless others who are prepared to do evil for Ireland or Ulster or Britain.*

By this time the hunger strike was falling apart. Ten men had died; one protester was taken off the strike by his mother, another by his wife. Liam's resolve weakened. Yet he felt he had to keep going for the sake of his fellow prisoners. He also decided it would better to die than to live blind. Still, he prayed the prayer that had haunted him since he began the strike: "Not mine, but Thy will be done."

By August 26, his fifty-fourth day on the strike, Liam knew he would be in a final coma in a day or two. How great it would be to walk through a field of grass, to smell flowers, to see the waves lapping on the seashore. His thoughts were hazy and dreamlike.

DAVID . . .

While Liam McCloskey lay dying in the Maze, a Protestant inmate in a prison on the other side of Belfast knelt in prayer for him. Yet anyone who knew David Hamilton would have said it most unlikely that he would pray for the recovery of a Catholic terrorist, for David had spent most of his life trying to eliminate enemies like Liam. His hatred of Catholics had started young.

David had grown up in Rathcoole, the largest government housing project in Europe, a product of a late-fifties Belfast slum-clearance program that moved the urban working class into the suburbs. Yet even with its bare concrete row houses and its maze of high-rise flats, Rathcoole was still a place where children played together happily.

David was one of those children, a sturdy Protestant boy with thick dark hair and startling blue eyes. He thrived on being "one of the boys," and in those days that meant playing football every afternoon with a gang his own age, including Catholic boys like Bobby Sands who lived just down the block—the same Bobby Sands who would later starve himself to death in the Maze.

But after the summer of 1969, when David was twelve years old, being one of the boys meant something else entirely. Suddenly the difference in religious beliefs mattered, and the Protestants, who made up roughly 60 percent of Rathcoole, let their unwanted neighbors know. Within months, thousands of Catholic families had fled to the Falls or Divas Flats or other places in the city where the Catholics were in control and the Protestants had moved out.

One afternoon David stole a ride into Belfast on the back of a lorry. On a downtown corner he spied Tom, an old friend he used to play with in Rathcoole every Sunday after Tom came home from Mass. Tom's family had moved away from Rathcoole some months ago and this was the first time David had seen his friend since then.

David raised his arm and yelled, "Hello, Tom."

Tom, who was standing with several other lads, looked at David like he had never seen him before. "Get away from me, you Orange bastard," he screamed, shaking his fist and letting loose a string of profanity. The other boys joined in.

David stared for a moment, then turned away, his heart pumping with anger and shame. From that moment on, his lighthearted spirit was replaced by a growing bitterness. Soon all Catholics were suspect; they were all probably members of the IRA, David thought.

We aren't doing enough to fight back, he thought. He had no faith in the British security forces, but he had observed the power of the street gangs in Rathcoole. Security came in aggression and numbers. So when the Ulster Volunteer Force came recruiting, David was one of the first of the boys in his gang to enlist. He was fifteen.

So David went from football to automatic weapons. He became an expert at robbing banks and post offices.

When he was seventeen, David was arrested for his paramilitary activities. While awaiting trial and sentencing, he was held at Long Kesh, an old air-force base near Belfast where prisoners lived in war-time Nissen huts grouped into compounds. Long Kesh was a graduate school in terrorism for David.

One evening several of the prisoners, agitated by the home brew they were drinking (made by fermenting bits of fruit kept hidden from the officers), seized a man they suspected of being an informer. It was Charlie, a likable fellow David had just been talking to that afternoon. As Charlie pleaded his innocence, they held a mock court-martial, found him guilty, and pronounced sentence. Death.

Later that night, Charlie was murdered.

Despite his terrorist involvement, David had never seen murder before. He was scared. He had never been religious, but he began to pray desperately. He hated prison. He hated being separated from his family and his girlfriend. And now he was frightened of the violence. He promised God he would attend church every Sunday—the ultimate sacrifice—if God would just get him out of Long Kesh.

Shortly thereafter, his case came before the court and he was sentenced to five years in prison.

So much for praying, David thought.

But late that night as he lay in the solitary-confinement cell where just-sentenced prisoners were held, he spotted a bit of writing high in the corner of the white concrete wall next to his bunk. It was a name, written in precise block letters: Charlie—his friend who had been murdered.

There are worse fates than prison, David thought. *Charlie would gladly trade places with me now. Maybe God hasn't given me such a bad deal after all.*

But David wasn't ready to think much about God. If God did exist, He had nothing to do with the flesh-and-blood struggles of Northern Ireland. *All that church stuff's no use to me,* he thought. *I'm just a bad egg, and if I go to hell, I go to hell.*

So when he was unexpectedly released from prison, with a warning from the judge to stay out of paramilitary organizations, David ignored the warning. He married his girlfriend Roberta and promised her he wouldn't get involved with UVF again, though he had no intention of keeping his word.

One Friday evening David was showing a few of his mates how to assemble automatic weapons while Roberta was out shopping with her mother. They had gun parts spread all over the kitchen table, when suddenly the back door creaked open, and his wife and mother-in-law stood in the doorway.

His wife's eyes filled with tears of rage. "You promised!" she screamed. She turned and ran out the door, her mother close behind her. David didn't see her for a week. When she returned, nothing was said about the UVF. It had become an acknowledged reality but a closed subject.

Sometimes, however, his involvement could not be ignored. Like the night David and Roberta were sitting in a Chinese restaurant in Belfast eating chicken chow mein and three hooded IRA men stormed in the front door. In the sudden silence that followed their entrance, David threw down his tea cup and told Roberta to take cover under the table.

"It's me they want," he said.

He slid out of the booth, crashed past tables of terrified diners and through the double doors to the kitchen, shoving cooks and waiters aside in his effort to reach the back door. Behind him, he could hear people screaming as the gunmen followed.

David cursed when he reached the backdoor, a fortress of bolts and chains. He ripped them apart, tore the door open, and fled. As he scrambled up an outside wall and over the top, the gunmen began firing. The last thing he heard was his would-be assassins cursing their aim.

Then in 1978 the reality of David's paramilitary involvement burst into their lives again. David and dozens of other UVF men were arrested in their homes at 4:00 one morning in a police sweep. David ended up in the Crumlin Road Prison where he had spent the thoughtful night after Charlie's death several years earlier.

Months later an utterly alien thought entered David's mind: *Become a Christian*. David had been working in the prison laundry with a man named Trevor who was an outspoken Christian. David knew from listening to Trevor that becoming a Christian meant making a lot of changes. For starters, it would mean giving up the UVF, drinking, violence, and chasing women—the things that made his life meaningful.

He discarded the thought, but it kept returning. The next morning in the laundry he said, "Trevor, I'm thinking about becoming a Christian."

All that day while Trevor worked double time, David sat on a pile of towels reading gospel tracts. The other inmates taunted him.

"Thinkin' about becoming a member of the God squad?" they shouted.

By suppertime, David had made his decision. He returned to his cell and knelt to pray for the first time since childhood.

"If you want this life," he told God simply, "it's yours."

The next day he approached an IRA prisoner. The two men had never spoken but had come to blows one day in the laundry.

"I've become a Christian," David told the man.

"What are you tellin' me for?" the inmate sneered.

David looked him in the eye. "I figure that's as good a reason as any to start talkin' to you," he said.

In the days that followed David was shocked to find that God had taken away his hatred of IRA men. He joined a prayer group, and several of the members were former Catholic paramilitaries, now Christians. David still considered himself "a good Prod," but he found himself accepting Catholics as people, not faceless enemies.

Seeing years of hatred eradicated gave David new vigor and

certainly about God's miraculous power in situations humanly impossible to resolve.

An IRA man serving time for three murders spoke to him one day. "I've been watchin' you," he said. "You must be the happiest man in this prison."

"That I am," David said. "I know God."

"How can you say that?" the other man sputtered.

David told how he had seen God work in his life and explained the gospel. The IRA man prayed to receive Christ, and he and David hugged there in the prison cell.

*   *   *

While such reconciliation was taking place between Protestants and Catholics within prison walls, the violence on the streets of Belfast was reaching spectacular proportions. It even extended across the Irish Sea to the British Parliament.

Airey M. S. Neave had been a Tory member of Parliament for twenty-five years. In 1976 Margaret Thatcher had appointed Neave to her shadow cabinet as spokesman for the affairs of Northern Ireland. Though he was consequently a natural target for terrorist violence, Neave had always firmly stated that British troops should remain in the strife-torn land.

Northern Ireland was not much on Neave's mind on the chill afternoon of March 30, 1979, as he prepared to leave the Parliament buildings in London. Mrs. Thatcher was to formally open her campaign the next day, and Neave had been planning election strategy for months. He was tired.

As usual, he had left his blue Vauxhall in the five-story underground parking garage beneath the heavily guarded government buildings. He got into the car and slowly accelerated up the long ramp leading to the street with its famous silhouettes.

Less than fifty yards from Big Ben, Neave's car exploded. In the deadly stillness that followed, staff and members of Parliament came running from the House of Commons. A British reporter was one of the first to arrive. He wrote:

> The car was swollen like a balloon by the force of the blast. There was glass everywhere. The driver was still in his seat—almost standing—his face bloody and blackened. He was unrecognizable. His gray pinstripe trousers and black jacket were torn and ragged. I

thought he looked dead, but a policeman who felt his pulse shouted, "He's still alive." Blood was running from the car and there was glass and mangled pieces of metal thrown up above the ramp into the yard."[7]

Airey Neave died forty minutes later.

That evening, telephones rang at Dublin newspaper offices. "We have a message for the British government," said a husky Irish voice. "Before you decide to have a general election, you had better state that you have decided not to stay in Ireland."

The next day Scotland Yard announced that both the Provisional IRA and the Irish National Liberation Army had claimed responsibility for the killing. Both claims were under investigation.

Protestant terrorists were not to be outdone by Catholic terrorists, as one of Belfast's most shocking murders proved.

Mervyn and Rosaleen McDonald, a young Catholic couple, lived on a Belfast street called Longlands Road. Though not politically active, the McDonalds had Republican ties. Rosaleen's father was a member of the political wing of the official faction of the IRA; Mervyn drank in a Republican bar. Those were reasons enough for them to be on a Protestant paramilitary death list.

One warm, hazy evening Mervyn was sitting at the kitchen table having dinner while Rosaleen watched the local television news in the main room. She held baby Margaret in her arms; two-and-a-half-year-old Seamus sat next to her on the sofa.

A white Austin pulled slowly up to the curb outside beyond the McDonalds' tall hedge. One man remained at the wheel; the other two got out. One had on a long overcoat.

The men knocked on the door and Rosaleen answered. "We're from the New Lodge. Is your husband in?" said one of the men. Thinking they were friends of her husband's family, who had connections on New Lodge Road, Rosaleen motioned them in.

Hearing strange voices, Mervyn got up from the dinner table and came to the doorway. As he did so, the man with the overcoat ripped a submachine gun from behind his back and fired at Mervyn, blowing off part of his face.

Clutching her baby, Rosaleen screamed, "Why us?"

The gunman turned toward her, tore the baby from her arms, pushed Rosaleen toward the sofa, and fired into her back. She fell in a pool of blood, while her children cried hysterically on the sofa.

The assassins left the house nonchalantly, climbed into the white Austin, and drove back to their base in Rathcoole. They agreed that their mission had been a success.

A neighbor found the McDonalds. Mervyn had been killed instantly; Rosaleen died four hours later—two more statistics in Northern Ireland's bitter toll.[8]

*   *   *

LIAM . . .

When Liam McCloskey woke on Saturday morning, August 27, 1981, the fifty-fifth day of his hunger strike, he was considerably weaker. He was blind; his hearing was going.

His mother arrived. As soon as Liam went into a coma, she told him tearfully, she would have him fed intravenously. But by then it would be too late; his blindness would be permanent. She pleaded with him to end the strike before it was too late, since she was going to take him off it anyway.

Even in his weakened state, Liam was coherent enough to understand how supremely unfair he was being. His mother could not carry the responsibility for his death—or his blindness—on her conscience. He was trapped. He decided to end the strike.

"As I made that decision," he said later, "tears streamed out of my eyes. Tears of relief, tears of frustration, tears of sadness, tears of joy. I received a vitamin injection almost immediately and soon after some milk to drink.

"Waves of guilt washed over me as I sat eating, thinking about the men still on the hunger strike. So when the strike ended the Saturday of that week, I was a happy man. Even though it had ended in failure, no more would die that slow, lingering death."

Sectarian tensions were at their highest level since the early 1970s, when the region hovered on the verge of civil war. At the source of Ulster's new troubles is an apparent shift in IRA tactics. Having failed to win political concessions with hunger strikes, which disintegrated in the face of Prime Minister Margaret Thatcher's unyielding resistance and an erosion of support from families of participating prisoners (ten of whom died this year), the IRA has returned to the gun and stepped up its campaign of terror.

During the past three weeks, twelve people have been killed in Northern Ireland, including the 17-year-old son of an Ulster Defense Regiment solider, and an 18-year-old Catholic youth who was shot as he walked home on the night of Bradford's murder. [The Rev. Robert Bradford, a Protestant member of Parliament and an evangelical Christian, was assassinated by IRA gunmen on November 17, 1981.] The IRA has also launched a series of bomb attacks in Britain. Four bombs have exploded in London during the past six weeks, killing three people.[9]

Liam's eyesight began to return, then his equilibrium. In the prison hospital he learned to walk again, rebuilding leg muscles deteriorated by the fast. He also began to think about resigning from the INLA.

"I was ripping myself apart inside," he says, "thinking about the men who had died, thinking about God, and the truths I had begun to discover on hunger strike.

"The first decision was to stop walking the way of Republicanism and the way of Jesus at the same time. It was impossible to walk both; one must override the other. I had to choose.

"I had reached the crossroads of life, and I took the way of Jesus. I found the rest I had long sought. Things became clearer in my mind. The Bible was no longer a book, but the way to God. I began to realize that God loved me and I loved God."

After Liam left the hospital, he was moved to a special H-block in the Maze for former protesters. He kept putting off his letter of resignation to the INLA, until one night he saw a television interview with the father of a young boy killed by an IRA bomb. The man said he forgave those who had planted the bomb and asked that no one retaliate.

There is a truly Christian man, thought Liam. *A beam of light in the darkness that engulfs this land. With people like that here, we are not beyond hope.*

He requested a transfer to Magilligan Prison, and it was granted. The night before he left he wrote his resignation to the INLA.

"As I left the Maze," says Liam, "it felt like a cloud lifting from me. I had left behind much of my old self in that place." He was finally ready to submit entirely to God, to pray with conviction, "Thy will be done."

As he was taken by van to Magilligan, he noticed the beauty of the countryside, and a wave of sadness swept over him. *People are dying together rather than living together to enjoy the land that God has given us all.*

Ready to be a force for reconciliation, Liam sought bold ways to show it. He decided to begin by breaking the stark lines of segregation between Protestants and Catholics in Magilligan Prison.

One place that segregation was already broken was in the Monday afternoon Bible study of Dr. Bill Holley, who later became one of Prison Fellowship's most faithful volunteers. His study was a proving ground for the unity to be found in Christ. Muscled inmates sporting "God & Ulster" tattoos up and down both arms shared Bibles with prisoners tattooed with "God & Ireland."

Several members of Dr. Holley's study had spent time in the Maze. Liam even became friends with UVF men and with Gerry, a former IRA man and now an outspoken Christian.

JIMMY . . .

Another man who ended up in Dr. Holley's Bible study had traveled many of the same roads as the other prisoners. Short and muscular, with even white teeth and fine brown hair, Jimmy Gibson had gotten involved with the Protestant paramilitaries and was now in prison for attempted murder.

When he arrived at Magilligan, Jimmy wanted nothing to do with Christianity. He thought there probably was a God, but he certainly wanted nothing to do with Him. Certainly not with the things he was planning to do when he got out of prison. Retaliation against Catholic paramilitaries headed his list.

Jimmy respected the Christians at Magilligan, however. They weren't wishy-washy about their faith. He watched several of them closely—not only fellow Protestants, but Catholics like Gerry and Liam McCloskey, the slight, freckled prisoner who walked with a limp. Jimmy knew Liam had spent fifty-five days on a hunger strike; he also knew Liam had resigned from the INLA and become some sort of religious fanatic.

One day as Jimmy and two other Loyalist prisoners sat down for dinner, Liam limped toward their table, tray in hand. Jimmy's cellmate nodded at Liam.

"That's okay," he said. "You can sit here."

Jimmy kicked his mate under the table and felt his face grow hot. Liam sat down, said his grace, and took a forkful of beans. Excluding the prayer, the rest of the table followed suit.

The invisible line segregating Catholics from Protestants had been crossed.

Jimmy wasn't prepared to start a hunger strike of his own, so he continued to come to meals, despite the fact that Liam McCloskey did too—and his usual place was right next to Jimmy.

Slowly, as months went by, Jimmy began to see Liam as a person, not just a former hunger striker turned religious fanatic. Finally, one day Jimmy addressed him for the first time.

"What are you going to do to the other side when you get out?"

"Nothing," Liam responded.

I *don't believe it*, Jimmy thought to himself. He knew he couldn't give up the revenge he was plotting against his enemies.

Jimmy's inner turmoil continued to build until he knew he had to become a Christian. To tell God, "I reject You," would only mean God would reject him.

Finally Jimmy glumly told God he would give his life to Him. Later he went to Dr. Holley's Bible study. Liam, Gerry, and his other sworn enemies were jubilant, slapping him on the back and laughing. Jimmy was quiet—embarrassed—possibly the most miserable convert in Northern Ireland.

But the misery of his conversion didn't alter its veracity. Jimmy had thought it all through; he was ready to obey God's Word whatever it took. He hadn't come to Christianity to feel good; he came because it was true. He began speaking to Catholics and prison guards, whom he had hated equally. He began reading his Bible and telling others about his faith. He began learning how to forgive and seek reconciliation rather than plot revenge.

LIAM AND JIMMY . . .

One autumn evening as the men in the Magilligan Bible study met for prayer, a young girl named Karen McKeown headed their list. Dr. Holley had told them the week before about the young Protestant girl who had been shot by the INLA. Their prayer list always contained victims of the Troubles, but Liam had felt a special responsibility for Karen's suffering. He had written to her mother.

"I heard from Mrs. McKeown," Liam said, passing Karen's picture around the circle. "I haven't been able to stop thinking about her."

The group bowed their heads and joined hands. Then, one by one, the former terrorists—Catholic and Protestant—prayed for Karen McKeown and her family, asking that God heal this latest young victim of Belfast's violence.

Liam closed the prayer with the words he had first prayed during his months on the hunger strike. "Not ours, Lord, but Thy will be done."

PEARL AND KAREN . . .

By the end of her second week in the hospital, Karen slept a little more each day. Pearl treasured the moments she was awake. By the third week, meningitis set in, and Karen slipped into a coma.

Then, early one morning while the rain fell outside the hospital windows, Pearl watched her daughter die.

Shortly after that, another letter arrived from Liam McCloskey.

"Pearl, we make strange friends in this troubled land. It is to the glory of God and He who makes it possible. Remember John 8:51, 'And I tell you most solemnly. Whoever keeps My Word will never see death.' Karen has left us, and even though it was no choice of mine, yet you can make a conscious decision in your own mind to see it as a gift of God. Your beautiful daughter to our beautiful Father who knows best. Surely the peace of Christ will be yours."

In the summer of 1983 Prison Fellowship conducted its first international conference in Belfast, Northern Ireland. At a time when travelers were passing up the troubled country, we decided it was a fitting backdrop for the theme of our conference: "In Christ, Reconciliation."

The work of Christians like Dr. Bill Holley and Gladys Blackburne and the reality of Christ in the lives of former terrorists clearly portrayed the power of God to bring unity. The struggles of Belfast represented the unresolved conflicts throughout our world. Northern Ireland illustrated both the hope and the desperate needs.

The highlight of the conference came one evening during a meeting open to the public. Hundreds of townspeople—both Protestant and Catholic—streamed into Queen's University's elegant Whitlow Hall, donated for the occasion. Clearly our ministry in Northern Ireland's prisons had captured the interest of many of Ulster's citizens.

Liam McCloskey and Jimmy Gibson had been furloughed from prison to be with us for the week. Their presence, more than anything else, evidenced the reconciling nature of the gospel. That evening, each told how he had come to know Christ. Liam concluded by putting his thin arm around Jimmy's muscular shoulders.

"My hope is to believe that God is changing the hearts of men like myself and Jimmy," Liam said. "That's the only hope I have for peace in Northern Ireland. Before, if I had seen Jimmy on the street, I would have shot him. Now he's my brother in Christ. I would die for him."

As members of the audience murmured in disbelief, James McIlroy, director of Prison Fellowship for Northern Ireland, took the microphone.

"There's a woman I'd like you to meet," he said, motioning to someone in the back row. A lithe, energetic woman began to thread her way toward the front.

As she did, James briefly told the story of Pearl and Karen McKeown; of Karen's death at the hands of an INLA gunman; of Pearl's friendship through the mail with Liam, the former INLA terrorist; how Pearl and Liam had grown to love one another as mother and son, though they had never met.

Pearl climbed the stage steps and walked slowly toward Liam, arms outstretched. They hugged. Then Pearl held Liam's hand as she tearfully explained how Karen's death had been to God's glory.

"Liam told me his prayer is now that of St. Francis," she said. "'Lord, make me an instrument of your peace. Where there is hatred, let me sow love. Where there is injury, pardon. Where there is death, life. Where despair, hope. Where there is darkness, light. Where there is sadness, joy.'

"And Liam *has* been God's instrument of peace to me," she concluded in a choked voice. "For he is the one who has showed me how to love God again."

By now tears glistened in many eyes as the audience strained to capture the incredible tableau: the two former terrorists, Catholic and Protestant, once sworn enemies, now standing together as brothers in Christ; the bereaved Protestant mother and the Catholic terrorist, holding hands.

Such is the reconciling power of God in Northern Ireland.

* * *

But widespread peace in Northern Ireland is as remote as ever. Bombs and bullets continue to fly. Political solutions continue to fail. And death tolls of civilians, paramilitaries, soldiers, and police continue to mount. Yet this seemingly endless cycle is weakened a little every time someone seeks peace rather than war, forgiveness rather than retribution, love rather than hate.

What is the answer to the troubles of Northern Ireland? Nothing in its chaotic history suggests there are political answers. George Thomas was right that night at our dinner in London: politically speaking, "There is no answer in Northern Ireland." But when every political effort of men and their institutions has been frustrated, when the kingdoms of man are utterly impotent, it is then that the power of the Kingdom of God, in all its glory, breaks into the dark stream of history. And it is the citizens of the Kingdom of God who carry that light into the darkness—

which cannot overcome it. Thus these Christians of Northern Ireland—and many others—continue the witness of the indestructible Kingdom in the midst of their nation's chaos.

Pearl McKeown works as a nursing assistant and serves as a Prison Fellowship volunteer, sharing her message of forgiveness and reconciliation with those who are imprisoned as well as those bound up in hatred outside prison walls.

Liam McCloskey was released from prison in late 1983 and now lives quietly in Derry near his family. He works on a farm owned by Columba House, a Catholic outreach to those in need.

Gladys Blackburne has now passed the age of seventy and is thus no longer eligible to serve as a member of the Maze Prison Board of Visitors. She contents herself with visits to British soldiers at their Northern Ireland outposts. She has confided to friends that she would like the following epitaph on her tombstone: "She did what she could—Mark 14:8."

David Hamilton, released from prison in 1983, is now assistant director for Prison Fellowship of Northern Ireland. He spends much of his time counseling ex-prisoners and urging young men to seek Christ rather than drift into violence as "one of the boys."

Jimmy Gibson, released in late 1983, works at a Belfast YMCA, teaching teenage boys carpentry skills. He also occasionally speaks to community groups, telling about the Carpenter who changed his life from one of revenge to reconciliation.

Chips McCurry, released from prison in 1985, is now studying at Baptist College in conjunction with Queen's University. When a BBC radio program interviewed Chips and an ex-IRA man together, Chips told the story of his conversion. Gladys Blackburne happened to hear the broadcast and was thrilled; until then, she had not known the results of her Christmas Eve visit with him in 1980.

Perhaps it is Chips who best articulates the problems—and the solution—for Northern Ireland.

"I spent almost ten years in prison. I saw guys fighting, dying for God and Ulster. Or for God and Ireland. What would happen if either side got what they wanted? You see that politics can't bring any lasting solutions.

"The only thing that will make any lasting peace, the only things that will bridge the gulf between the Catholics and the Protestants here is for people to give up violence and learn forgiveness. The only way that can possibly happen is through Jesus Christ."

Epilogue

The light shines in the darkness, and the darkness has not overcome it.
            —John 1:5[RSV]

It is said that as Winston Churchill lay critically ill, he reflected on conditions in the world he had so heroically helped rescue. "There is no hope," he sighed. "There is no hope." And with that despairing observation, the great leader died.

Churchill's words might well have been describing the tragedy of Northern Ireland; though on the surface a religious war, it is in reality a long-standing struggle for political and economic power. Indeed, political and economic solutions there have failed.

But Ireland is only one of the seemingly hopeless political situations of our world today. Consider Lebanon. Once a beautiful seaside land of pine trees and fragrant flowers, today it reeks of death. The blood of Jews and Christians and Muslims runs together through the gutters of Beirut.

Or Sri Lanka, an island paradise once called the place where people always smile. Few smile there today amid the terror of Tamil bombs. Or the peasants of Nicaragua, caught in a crossfire of ideology,

623

money, helicopters, and guns. Their chickens and produce are taken one day by pillaging Sandinista soldiers, stolen the next by marauding Contras. Or consider the fact that hardly a Cambodian has not lost a son or brother, wife or mother, in the most massive genocide since the Holocaust: Three million people murdered by their own government.

Millions live under the repression of South Africa's apartheid, which strips black, colored, and white of their dignity. Political options promise only more chaos, and when the seething cauldron of bitterness boils over, Communist revolutionaries will be standing by, ready to offer collectivist salvation for a tired and turbulent land.

Over half the world lives under the ultimate result of such "salvation." Millions in this century have been condemned to live—bound, gagged, and tortured—and die in the gulag. And today's much-heralded *glasnost* is little more than a public-relations campaign; the deadly face of Communism remains the same.

But in the other half of the world, which lives ostensibly in freedom, millions are enslaved by more subtle rulers. In the inner cities of America a generation is in bondage to the rule of drugs and poverty; many see crime as their only way out and end up in the wasteland of America's prisons. Meanwhile more affluent Americans embrace the false gods of materialism, hedonism, egoism. And man's basest passions have unleashed a plague called AIDs, which now holds millions hostage.

And hovering over all of planet earth is the mushroom cloud, the same gray ghost that Douglas MacArthur saw that day in 1945 when he warned the world it had but one last chance. The cloud seems darker and more ominous when tanks roll in Eastern Europe or Central America, in Southeast Asia or Africa, when vessels in the Persian Gulf patrol at full alert. At other times it seems to recede. Yet it is always a heartbeat away.

In this latter part of the twentieth century, a great irony persists. Technology has given man power he has never known before; giant institutions offer panaceas for all human ills. But never has man seemed less able to devise political strategies to produce order and harmony among people. The more powerful the institution appears, the more impotent it is. The proudest pretensions of the strongest nations are mocked by a single bomb-laden terrorist truck. Belfast, Beirut, Central America, South Africa, Cambodia, Korea, Chad, and forty other places like them are but open sores on the body politic, reminding us that even in this age of technological wonders, modern governments have devised nothing to cure the unbridled passions of man.

Is there no hope? Were Churchill's dying words the epitaph for our age?

Like any author, I would like to end this book on a triumphant note, announcing that ultimate peace and harmony can be achieved through human efforts. But that utopian illusion is shattered by the splintered history of the human race. Governments rise; even the most powerful fall. The battle for people's hearts and minds will continue.

Where then is hope? It is in the fact that the Kingdom of God has come to earth—the Kingdom announced by Jesus Christ in that obscure Nazareth synagogue two thousand years ago. It is a Kingdom that comes not in a temporary takeover of political structures, but in the lasting takeover of the human heart by the rule of a holy God.

Certainly, as I hope this book has shown, the fact that God reigns can be manifest through political means, whenever the citizens of the Kingdom of God bring His light to bear on the institutions of the kingdoms of man. But His rule is even more powerfully evident in ordinary, individual lives, in the breaking of cycles of violence and evil, in the paradoxical power of forgiveness, in the actions of those little platoons who live by the transcendent values of the Kingdom of God in the midst of the kingdoms of this world, loving their God and loving their neighbor.

Thus in the midst of the dark and habitual chaos of earth, a light penetrates the darkness. It cannot be extinguished; it is the light of the Kingdom of God. His Kingdom *has* come, in His people today, and it is yet to come as well, in the great consummation of human history. While the battle rages on planet earth, we can take heart—not in the fleeting fortunes of men or nations, but rather in the promise so beautifully captured in Handel's *Messiah*.

Stop. Listen. Over the din of the conflict, if you listen carefully, you will hear the chorus echoing in the distance: "The kingdom of this world has become the kingdom of our Lord and of His Christ."

Listen. For in that glorious refrain is man's one hope.

Let us then . . . . rejoice that we see around us at every hand the decay of the institutions and instruments of power, see intimations of empires falling to pieces, money in total disarray, dictators and parliamentarians alike nonplussed by the confusion and conflicts which encompass them. For it is precisely when every earthly hope has been explored and found wanting, when every possibility of help from earthly sources has been sought and is not forthcoming, when every recourse this world offers, moral as well as material, has been explored to no effect, when in the shivering cold the last faggot has been thrown on the fire and in the gathering darkness every glimmer of light has finally flickered out, it's then that Christ's hand reaches out, sure and firm. Then Christ's words bring their inexpressible comfort, then His light shines brightest, abolishing the darkness forever. So finding in everything only deception and nothingness, the soul is constrained to have recourse to God Himself and to rest content with Him.[1]

With Gratitude

If this book accomplishes nothing more than to cause readers to turn to Richard John Neuhaus's *Naked Public Square*, I shall consider my labors well rewarded. Of the thirty or more books I studied in preparation for writing *Kingdoms in Conflict*, Neuhaus's work was second only to Augustine's classic *The City of God*. I am thus deeply indebted to Richard. My prayer is that what I have written will in some way contribute to his heroic struggle to defend religious values in Western culture.

I'm also indebted to esteemed theologian Dr. Carl F. H. Henry, my beloved friend, for both his various writings on church and state issues and for his critique of this manuscript. When I asked Carl for his counsel, the publisher's deadline was imminent and he was leaving in twelve hours for an extended teaching trip. I was astonished to discover the entire manuscript in my office the next day, thoroughly reviewed. With characteristic generosity and devotion, he had simply stayed up all night to read it.

I'm also profoundly grateful to Jacques Ellul, the French sociologist and critic, for his many prophetic works, most significantly *The Political Illusion* and *The Presence of the Kingdom*. These are classic commentaries on our times and, in what is in itself a sad commentary on our times, are out of print. Also of tremendous importance was Donald Bloesch's *Crumbling Foundations*.

Paul Johnson's *Modern Times* was a great inspiration as well. If my writing has aroused in the reader's mind a desire to know more of the philosophical undercurrents of this century, I could recommend nothing more highly than this insightful, provocative critique.

In the "For Further Reading" section, I've listed other contemporary writers and their works that greatly assisted me in the reference section to follow, in the hope that readers will go deeper into the complex and crucial issues of church, state, and the Kingdom of God.

As with *Loving God*, this book was the result of a team effort: My wonderfully gifted editorial associate, Ellen Santilli Vaughn, who assisted with certain chapters of *Loving God*, was this time my colleague in the fullest sense, as the title page properly acknowledges. It is a joy to work closely with one who combines keen editorial skills with such an uplifting Christian spirit.

Kenneth Myers, editor of *This World: A Journal of Religion and Public Life*, provided research help with early drafts and wise theological counsel throughout. So did David Coffin, a doctoral candidate at Westminster Theological Seminary and head of Berea Ministries.

Tim Stafford, another *Loving God* collaborator, provided tremendous assistance with the Prologue, the material on the Philippines, and particularly with his fascinating research and reporting of the events leading up to World War II.

My very talented friend Jim Manney, editor of *New Covenant Magazine*, provided outstanding research for the Christianity and Marxism material. My research assistant, Michael Gerson, did a brilliant job, providing provocative research and well-reasoned drafts. Elizabeth Leahy, director of the Prison Fellowship Information Center, gave invaluable and exhaustive help, excavating mounds of obscure sources and cites—without ever losing her smile.

But the most important member of the team was my editor, Judith Markham. Judith edited *Loving God*; and, in spite of the pain an editor's surgery causes any writer, we ended up good friends. I also gained enormous admiration for Judith's ability—her availability was the deciding factor in my selection of a publisher. She did not disappoint me. Judith Markham is, in my opinion, the master craftsman of her trade.

I was enormously helped as well by my extremely competent executive secretary, Grace McCrane, who tamed this manuscript through, in some cases, ten or more drafts, offering important suggestions and helpful additions throughout. She was assisted with typing of early drafts by Patti Perkins. I am grateful as well to Margaret Shannon, who provided the idea and initial research for the Cliveden material, as well as to Jim Park, Prison Fellowship Oklahoma area director, for his research into Collinsville.

In addition to Carl Henry, Richard Neuhaus, and theologian Arthur Lindsley, several of my Prison Fellowship colleagues read and critiqued the manuscript. I'm particularly grateful to Dan Van Ness, president of Justice Fellowship, and his colleague David Coolidge, who as a church-state student himself, offered excellent and insightful suggestions throughout. I'm indebted as well to Prison Fellowship president Gordon Loux, who from the beginning of our ministry has been my closest confidant and friend. A word of thanks is also due to Ron Nikkel, executive director of Prison Fellowship International, for his consistent encouragement, and to Fellowship Communications president Nelson Keener and my executive assistant, Jim Jewell, for their help with contract matters and book promotion.

The support of my family, especially Patty, the helpmate God has given me, proved indispensable to this book. Five months before the deadline I was hospitalized for major surgery. Patty and my daughter, Emily Colson Boehme, were faithfully at my side during the month I spent in the hospital; my sons Wendell and Chris also came from great distances to offer encouragement, as did my mother and stepfather. I wonder if I would have made it without them.

Patty then nursed me through two months of recovery only to lose me to long days—and nights—as I labored over this manuscript. There are far easier callings than to be married to those who periodically feel compelled to take pen in hand; but without Patty's consistent encouragement, *Kingdoms in Conflict* could not have been written.

Finally, my gratitude to all those in Prison Fellowship who encourage and support me; to the teachers who have given so unstintingly of their time; and to the readers of my books who frequently encourage me with their letters. And of course most important, my eternal gratitude goes to the One who guides my hand across the page. May this book glorify Him in every way.

Charles W. Colson
June 20, 1987
P.O. Box 17500
Washington, D.C. 20041

Notes

CHAPTER 1

1. Paul Vitz, *Psychology as Religion: The Cult of Self-Worship* (Grand Rapids, Mich.: Eerdmans, 1977), 114. Quoted in Donald G. Bloesch, *Crumbling Foundations* (Grand Rapids, Mich.: Zondervan, 1984), 67.

2. Justice William O. Douglas's opinion in *Zorach v. Clauson*, 343 U.S. 306 (April 28, 1952) is cited in Robert T. Miller and Ronald B. Flowers, *Toward Benevolent Neutrality: Church, State, and the Supreme Court*, rev. ed. (Waco, Texas: Markham Press Fund, 1977), 327.

3. Jack Kroll "The Most Famous Artist," *Newsweek* (March 9, 1987), 64.

4. Justice Goldberg's dissenting opinion in *Abington Township School District v. Schempp*, 374 U.S. 203 (June 17, 1963) is cited in Miller and Flowers, *Toward Benevolent Neutrality*, 372.

5. Walter Shapiro, "Politics and the Pulpit," *Newsweek* (September 17, 1984), 24.

6. Ronald Reagan speech at an ecumenical prayer breakfast in Dallas Texas is quoted in Jeremiah O'Leary, "Reagan Declares that Faith Has Key Role in Political Life," *Washington Times* (August 24, 1984).

7. Shapiro, "Politics and the Pulpit," 24.

8. Mario M. Cuomo, "Religious Belief and Public Morality: A Catholic Governor's Perspective," a paper presented to the Department of Theology at the University of Notre Dame (September 13, 1984), 12.

9. *New York Times* (April 10, 1983). Quoted in a speech given by Stephen V. Monsma, "The Promises and Pitfalls of Evangelical Political Involvement," (October 17, 1986).

10. Will Durant, *Caesar and Christ: A History of Roman Civilization from Its Beginnings to* A.D. 337 (New York: Simon and Schuster, 1944), 164.

11. St. Augustine, *City of God* (Garden City, N.Y.: Image/Doubleday, 1958), 88.

12. *London Times* editorial: "Evil in the Air," (May 12, 1983), 15A

13. Quoted in Richard John Neuhaus, *The Naked Public Square* (Grand Rapids, Mich.: Eerdmans, 1984), 95.

14. Quoted in Neuhaus, *Naked Public Square*, 115.

15. Adam Michnik, *Letters from Prison and Other Essays* (Berkeley, Calif.: University of California Press, 1986). Quoted in Norman Davies, "True to Himself and His Homeland," *New York Times Book Review* (October 5, 1986).
16. Vernon J. Bourke, "Introduction," in St. Augustine, *City of God*, 9–10.
17. "Indian Leader Urges Gandhi to 'Stamp Out' Missionaries," *Presbyterian Journal* (November 20, 1985), 6.

CHAPTER 2

1. This chapter is based on several studies of Hemingway's life, the most helpful of which were John Killinger, *Hemingway and the Dead Gods* (Lexington, Ky.: The University of Kentucky Press, 1960), and A. E. Hotchner, *Papa Hemingway: The Ecstasy and Sorrow* (New York: Quill, 1983).
2. "Hero of the Code," *Time* (July 14, 1961), 87.
3. Killinger, *Hemingway and the Dead Gods*, 69.
4. Maurice Natanson, "Jean-Paul Sartre's Philosophy of Freedom," *Social Research*, XIX (September 1952), 378.
5. E. L. Allen, *The Self and Its Hazards: A Guide to the Thought of Karl Jaspers* (London: Hodder and Stoughton, 1953), 7.

CHAPTER 3

1. The information in this chapter is based on news reports and an interview with Jerry and Sis Levin conducted by Ellen Santilli Vaughn (April 9, 1987).

CHAPTER 4

1. Quoted in R. C. Sproul, *If There Is a God, Why Are There Atheists?* (Minneapolis: Dimension Books, 1978), 48.
2. Harry Blamires, *The Christian Mind* (Ann Arbor, Mich.: Servant Books, 1963), 44.
3. Carl Sagan, *Cosmos* (New York: Random House, 1980), 4.
4. Eugene Mallove, "Gravity: Is the Force that Makes the Apple Fall the Clue to Creation?" *Washington Post* (March 3, 1985), C-1-a.
5. Bertrand Russell, *The Autobiography of Bertrand Russell*, a letter to Lady Ottoline Morrell dated August 11, 1918 (Boston: Little, Brown, 1968), 121.
6. Quoted in Joseph Frank, *Dostoyevsky: Years of Ordeal* (Princeton, N.J.: Princeton University Press, 1983), 159.
7. Jeremiah 22:16.
8. Paul Johnson, "A Historian Looks at Jesus," unpublished speech (1986).
9. "Conversation with an Author: Mortimer J. Adler, Author of *How to Think About God*," *Book Digest Magazine* (September 1980).

CHAPTER 5

1. Aleksandr I. Solzhenitsyn, *The Cancer Ward* (New York: Dell, 1968).
2. Paul Johnson, "The Necessity for Christianity," *Truth*, 1:1 (1985), 2.
3. Peter Singer, "Sanctity of Life or Quality of Life?" *Pediatrics* (July 1983), 129.
4. Quoted in Thomas Molnar, *Utopia: The Perennial Heresy* (London: Tom Stacey, 1972), 4.
5. William Golding, *The Lord of the Flies* (New York: Wide View/Paragrees Books, 1954).
6. E. L. Epstein, "Notes on *Lord of the Flies*," in Golding, *Lord of the Flies*, 186.
7. Armando Valladares, *Against All Hope* (New York: Knopf, 1986), 4.
8. Valladares, *Against All Hope*, 135.
9. Paul Johnson, *Modern Times: The World from the Twenties to the Eighties* (New York: Harper & Row, 1983), 11.
10. Charles Murray, "No, Welfare Really Isn't the Problem," *Public Interest* (Summer 1986), 10.
11. Leszek Kolakowski, "The Idolatry of Politics," *New Republic* (June 16, 1986), 29–36.

12. Quoted in James V. Schall, *Christianity and Politics* (Boston: St. Paul Editions, 1981), 295.

13. Molnar, *Utopia*, 7.

CHAPTER 6

1. Luke 4:18, in which Jesus quotes Isaiah 61:1–2. The story that follows is related in Luke 4:20–30.

2. Matthew 6:33.

3. St. Augustine, *The Confessions of St. Augustine*, translated and edited by J. G. Pilkington (New York: Liveright, 1943), 1.

4. Acts 16:30.

5. Edmund Clowney, "The Politics of the Kingdom," *Westminster Theological Journal* 41 (Spring 1979), 302.

CHAPTER 7

1. Paul Johnson, "The Family as an Emblem of Freedom," *Emblem of Freedom: The American Family in the 1980s*, edited by Carl A. Anderson and William J. Gribbon (Durham, N.C.: Carolina Academic Press, 1981), 23.

2. Beth Brophy, "Children Under Stress," *U.S. News and World Report* (October 27, 1986), 58.

3. Paul C. Vitz, *Censorship: Evidence of Bias in Our Children's Textbooks* (Ann Arbor, Mich.: Servant Books, 1986), 37–38.

4. Stanton E. Samenow, *Inside the Criminal Mind* (New York: New York Times Book Co., 1984).

5. James Q. Wilson and Richard J. Herrnstein, *Crime and Human Nature* (New York: Simon and Schuster, 1985).

6. Carl F. H. Henry: "The Modern Flight from the Family," *The Emblem of Freedom, the American Family in the 1980s*, edited by Carl A. Anderson and William J. Gribbon (Durham, N.C.: North Carolina Academic Press, 1981), 46.

7. Romans 13:4.

8. 1 Peter 2:14.

9. Quoted in Michael Harrington, *The Politics at God's Funeral* (New York: Penguin, 1983), 107.

10. Jay Marcellus Kik, *Church and State in the New Testament* (Grand Rapids, Mich.: Baker, 1962), 20.

11. Exodus 18:13.

12. Exodus 18:15–16.

13. 1 Timothy 2:2.

14. Robert Nisbet, *The Quest for Community* (New York: Oxford University Press, 1953).

15. Robert L. Saucy, *The Church in God's Program* (Chicago: Moody Press, 1972), 91.

16. Floyd Filson, *Jesus Christ the Risen Lord* (Nashville: Abingdon Press, 1956), 253.

17. Jacques Ellul, *The Presence of the Kingdom* (New York: Seabury Press, 1948/1967), 47.

18. Pope John Paul II, "Opening Address at Puebla" (1979). In *The Pope and Revolution: John Paul II Confronts Liberation Theology*, edited by Quintin L. Quade (Washington, D.C.: Ethics and Public Policy Center, 1982).

19. Edmund Clowney, "The Politics of the Kingdom," *Westminster Theological Journal* 41:2 (Spring 1979), 306.

20. Clowney, "Politics of the Kingdom," 307.

CHAPTER 8

1. This chapter was based on a number of studies of Wilberforce's life and the fight for the abolition of the slave trade in England. Several of the most helpful sources were: Robin Furneaux, *William Wilberforce* (London: Hamilton, 1974); John Pollock, *Wilberforce*

(New York: St. Martin's Press, 1978); William Wilberforce, *Real Christianity*, a modern edition edited by James Houston (Portland: Multnomah, 1982); Ernest Marshall Howse, *Saints in Politics: The Clapham Sect* (Unwin, 1974); Garth Lean, *God's Politician: William Wilberforce's Struggle* (London: Darton, Longman and Todd, 1980).

CHAPTER 9

1. Acts 17:6–7.
2. F. F. Bruce, *The Spreading Flame: The Rise and Progress of Christianity from Its First Beginnings to the Conversion of the English* (Grand Rapids, Mich.: Eerdmans, 1958), 293.
3. Etienne Gilson's "Foreword," quoting Fustel de Coulanges, in St. Augustine, *The City of God* (New York: Image/Doubleday, 1958), 15.
4. Alexis de Tocqueville, *The Old Regime and the French Revolution*, translated by Stuart Gilbert (Garden City: Doubleday/Anchor Books, 1955), 149.
5. Tocqueville, *The Old Regime and the French Revolution*, 149.
6. Romans 13:5, 7.
7. Edmund Clowney, "The Politics of the Kingdom," *Westminster Theological Journal* (Spring 1979), 306.
8. Harold J. Berman, "Atheism and Christianity in the Soviet Union," in *Freedom and Faith: The Impact of Law on Religious Liberty*, edited by Lynn R. Buzzard (Westchester, Ill.: Crossway Books, 1982), 127–43.
9. William Blake, "And Did Those Feet," *The Norton Anthology of Poetry*, 3rd ed. (New York: W. W. Norton, 1983), 266.
10. Richard John Neuhaus, *The Naked Public Square* (Grand Rapids, Mich.: Eerdmans, 1984), 231.
11. Patricia Hynds, a Maryknoll lay missionary, was quoted in an article by Juan Tamayo, *Miami Herald* (March 6, 1983).
12. Oscar Cullman, *The State in the New Testament* (New York: Scribner's, 1956), 91.
13. Hugh T. Kerr, ed., *Compendium of Luther's Theology* (Philadelphia: Westminster Press, 1966), 218.
14. Carl F. H. Henry, "The Gospel for the Rest of Our Century," *Christianity Today* (January 17, 1986), 25–I.
15. Quoted in Neuhaus, *Naked Public Square*, 61.
16. "James Madison's Memorial and Remonstrance, 1785," in Edwin S. Gaustad, ed., *A Documentary History of Religion in America: Vol. I* (Grand Rapids, Mich.: Eerdmans, 1982), 262–63.
17. Quoted in A. James Reichley, *Religion in American Public Life* (Washington, D.C.: The Brookings Institute, 1985), 105.
18. Reichley, *Religion in American Public Life*, 360.

CHAPTER 10

1. The following sources were particularly useful in the research of this chapter: Eberhard Bethge, *Dietrich Bonhoeffer* (New York: Harper & Row, 1977); John Conway, *The Nazi Persecution of the Churches* (New York: Basic Books, 1968); Arthur C. Cochrane, *The Church's Confession Under Hitler* (Allison Park, Penn.: Pickwick, 1977); Richard Gutteridge, *Open Thy Mouth for the Dumb! The German Evangelical Church and the Jews* (New York: Barnes and Noble, 1976); Dietmar Schmidt, *Pastor Niemoller* (New York: Doubleday, 1959); William Shirer, *A Berlin Diary* (New York: Knopf, 1941).

CHAPTER 11

1. This chapter is based on a number of studies on England and the thirties, including: Neville Chamberlain, *In Search of Peace* (Salem, N.H.: Ayer, facsimile of 1939 edition); Keith Middlemas, *The Strategy of Appeasement: The British Government and Germany, 1937–1939* (New York: Times Books, 1972); John W. Wheeler-Bennett, *Munich: Prologue to*

Tragedy (Duell, 1962); David Dilks, *Neville Chamberlain* (New York: Cambridge University Press, 1984); Martin Gilbert and Richard Gott, *The Appeasers* (Boston: Houghton Mifflin, 1963).

CHAPTER 12

1. Many of the historical details in this chapter are taken from William Manchester, *American Caesar: Douglas MacArthur 1880–1964* (Boston: Little, Brown, 1978). See especially chapter 7, "At High Port," for additional information.
2. Quoted in John Lukacs, *1945: Year Zero* (Garden City: Doubleday, 1978), 239.
3. Paul Johnson, *Modern Times: The World from the Twenties to the Eighties* (New York: Harper & Row, 1983), 430.
4. Friedrich Nietzsche, *The Gay Science*, as quoted in Michael Harrington, *The Politics at God's Funeral* (New York: Penguin Books, 1983), 85.
5. Quoted in Robert Byrne, *The Other 637 Best Things Anybody Ever Said* (New York: Fawcett Crest, 1984), 6.
6. James V. Schall, *Christianity and Politics* (Boston: St. Paul Editions, 1981), 102.
7. Harrington, *The Politics at God's Funeral*, 85.

CHAPTER 13

1. Walter Kaufmann, ed. and trans., *The Portable Nietzsche* (New York: Penguin Books, 1954), 95.
2. Paul Johnson, *Modern Times: The World from the Twenties to the Eighties* (New York: Harper & Row, 1983), 50.
3. Patrick Egan, "Christians Under Communism," *Pastoral Renewal* (January 1984), 72–74.
4. Evangelical Press News Service (September 26, 1986).
5. Egan, "Christians Under Communism."
6. Richard N. Ostling, "The Definitive Reinhold Neibuhr," *Time* (January 20, 1986), 71.
7. Aleksandr I. Solzhenitsyn, *The Gulag Archipelago: Book II* (New York: Harper & Row, 1974), 374.
8. Joseph Mindszenty, *Mindszenty* (New York: Macmillan, 1974).
9. Quoted in George Seldes, *Great Thoughts* (New York: Ballantine, 1985), 241
10. Evangelical Press News Service (December 19, 1986), 13, quoting a speech made in Tashkent, USSR, on November 24, 1986.
11. Seldes, *Great Thoughts*, 397.
12. "Christ Would Never Approve that Man Be Considered Merely as a Means of Production," *New York Times* (June 10, 1979), 1:6.
13. "Urged the Government to Honor the Cause of Fundamental Human Rights, Including the Right to Religious Liberty," *New York Times* (June 6, 1979), 1:3.
14. "Told Poles to Set a Christian Example Even If It Means Risking Danger," *New York Times* (June 7, 1979), 8:1.
15. Evangelical Press News Service (November 21, 1981).
16. Stefan Wyszynski, *The Freedom Within: The Prison Notes of Stefan Cardinal Wyszynski* (New York: Harcourt Brace Jovanovich, 1982), 12.
17. Jacques Ellul, "Lech Walesa and the Social Force of Christianity," *Kattalagete* (June 1982), 5.
18. Ellul, "Lech Walesa and the Social Force of Christianity," 6.
19. Wyszynski, *The Freedom Within*, 26.
20. Beth Spring, "Campus Crusade Director Describes Government Harassment of Evangelicals," *Christianity Today* (February 7, 1986), 52–53. Most of the details concerning Jimmy Hassan were drawn from this article.
21. The information on Nicaragua was drawn from Humberto Belli, *Breaking Faith: The Sandinista Revolution and Its Impact on Freedom and Christian Faith in Nicaragua* (Westchester, Ill.: Crossway Books, 1985).

22. Benjamin Cortes quoted in Belli, *Breaking Faith*, 158.

23. Belli, *Breaking Faith*, 212.

24. Belli, *Breaking Faith*, 156.

25. Belli, *Breaking Faith*, 152.

26. Belli, *Breaking Faith*, 161.

27. Belli, *Breaking Faith*, 162.

28. Belli, *Breaking Faith*, 161.

29. José Felipe Corneado, quoted in "Cuba: A New Attitude," *Christianity Today* (September 5, 1986), 4, International News Section.

30. The story of Poland's school children and the crucifixes was gathered from articles in the following issues of the *New York Times*: (March 8, 1984), I, 15:1; (March 9, 1984), I, I:3; (March 10, 1984), I, 24:1; (March 11, 1984), I, 3:4; (March 14, 1984); I, 1:1, (March 15, 1984), I, 4:3.

CHAPTER 14

1. *Stone v. Graham*, 449 U.S. 39 (1980), cited in Robert T. Miller and Ronald B. Flowers, *Toward Benevolent Neutrality: Church, State, and the Supreme Court*, rev. ed. (Waco, Tex.: Markham Press Fund, 1977), 327.

2. Material regarding the Marian Guinn case was taken from a wide variety of new stories and wire reports, a transcript of a CBS "60 Minutes" interview (April 22, 1984), and a number of articles, including Lynn Buzzard, "Is Church Discipline an Invasion of Privacy?" *Christianity Today* (November 9, 1984), 37–39; and "Marian and the Elders," *Time* (March 26, 1984).

3. 1 Corinthians 5:9.

4. 1 Timothy 5:20.

5. Richard John Neuhaus, *The Naked Public Square*, (Grand Rapids, Mich.: Eerdmans, 1984), 142.

6. Nat Hentoff, "Religion on School Property," *Washington Post* (November 1, 1984), A-25.

7. The information from the Dayton Christian School case was taken from William Bentley, "Secularism: Tidal Wave of Repression," in *Freedom and Faith*, edited by Lynn R. Buzzard (Westchester, Ill.: Crossway Books, 1982).

8. Dorothey Korber, "No Adverse Reaction to Prayer Ban," from an undated California newspaper clipping.

9. Jonathan Kalstrom, "Fire and Brimstone: An Atheist Takes on Small Town America," *Liberty* (January/February 1987), 22–25; and NFD *Journal* (August 1986), 14.

10. *New York Times* (March 6, 1984), II, 6:1.

11. *Zorach v. Clauson*, 343 U.S. 306 (April 28, 1952). Cited in Miller and Flowers, *Toward Benevolent Neutrality*, 327.

12. *Abington Township School District v. Schempp*, 374 U.S. 203 (June 17, 1963). Cited in Miller and Flowers, *Toward Benevolent Neutrality*, 372.

13. *United States v. Seeger* (no. 50); *United States v. Jakobson* (no. 51); *Peter v. United States* (no. 29) 380 U.S. 163 (March 8, 1965). Cited in Miller and Flowers, *Toward Benevolent Neutrality*, 177.

14. Richard John Neuhaus, "Moral Leadership in Post-Secular America," *Imprimis*, 2:7 (July 1982), 3.

15. Will Herberg, *Protestant, Catholic, Jew: An Essay in American Religious Sociology* (Chicago: University of Chicago Press, 1983), 269.

16. John F. Kennedy, "For the Freedom of Man," inaugural address, Washington, D.C., January 20, 1961. Quoted in *Vital Speeches of the Day*, February 1, 1961.

17. Daniel Bell, *The Cultural Contradictions of Capitalism* (New York: Basic Books, 1978), 77.

18. Quoted in James Hitchcock, *What Is Secular Humanism?* (Ann Arbor, Mich.: Servant Books, 1982), 66.

19. Hitchcock, What Is Secular Humanism? 66.

20. Jack Kroll, "The Most Famous Artist," Newsweek (March 9, 1987), 64.

21. Kroll, "The Most Famous Artist," 64.

22. Quoted in David Brock, "A Philosopher Hurls Down a Stinging Moral Gauntlet," Insight (May 11, 1987), 12.

23. Robert N. Bellah, et al., Habits of the Heart: Individualism and Commitment in American Life (New York: Harper & Row, 1985), 281.

24. Meg Greenfield, "The Grinches vs. the Creche," Newsweek (December 24, 1984), 72.

25. "Creation Trial: Less Circus, More Law," Washington Post (December 21, 1981), A-3-b.

26. Carl Sagan, Cosmos (New York: Random House, 1980), 4.

27. "The Week," National Review (May 8, 1987), 16.

28. G. K. Chesterton, The End of the Armistice (New York: Sheed and Ward, 1936), 121–22.

29. Quoted in Martin E. Marty, "A Profile of Norman Lear: Another Pilgrim's Progress," Christian Century (January 21, 1987), 57.

30. Paul C. Vitz, Censorship: Evidence of Bias in Our Children's Textbooks (Ann Arbor, Mich.: Servant Books, 1986).

31. Vitz, Censorship, 15.

32. Vitz, Censorship, 16.

33. Vitz, Censorship, 3.

34. Vitz, Censorship, 16.

35. Joseph Sobran, "Pensees: Notes for the Reactionary of Tomorrow," National Review (December 31, 1985), 48.

36. Richard John Neuhaus, The Naked Public Square, Christianity Today (October 5, 1984), 32.

37. Henry Hyde, For Every Idle Silence (Ann Arbor, Mich.: Servant Books, 1985), 12–13.

38. Donald G. Bloesch, Crumbling Foundations (Grand Rapids, Mich.: Zondervan, 1984), 83–84.

39. Bloesch, Crumbling Foundations, 57.

40. Quoted in Neuhaus, Naked Public Square, 260.

41. Bloesch, Crumbling Foundations, 19.

42. "Persecution Next Step—Roberts," Washington Times (April 6, 1987).

43. Quoted in Sydney E. Ahlstrom, A Religious History of the American People (New Haven, Conn.: Yale University Press, 1972), 954.

44. Walter Shapiro, "Politics and the Pulpit," Newsweek (September 17, 1984), 24.

45. New York Times (August 14, 1984), A-21.

46. New York Times (August 14, 1984), A-21.

47. Mario M. Cuomo, "Religious Belief and Public Morality: A Catholic Governor's Perspective," a paper presented to the Dept. of Theology at the University of Notre Dame (September 13, 1984).

48. The information and citations concerning St. John the Divine Cathedral are drawn from Kenneth L. Woodward and Deborah Witherspoon, "The Awakening of a Cathedral," Newsweek (June 16, 1986), 59–60.

CHAPTER 15

1. Walter Shapiro, "Ethics: What's Wrong?" Time (May 25, 1987), 14.

2. Ezra Bowen, "Ethics: Looking to Its Roots," Time (May 25, 1987), 26.

3. Elwood McQuaid, "Lying as a Lifestyle," Moody Monthly (July/August 1987), 8.

4. C. S. Lewis, The Abolition of Man (New York: Macmillan, 1974), 35.

5. Richard John Neuhaus, The Naked Public Square (Grand Rapids, Mich.: Eerdmans, 1984), 86.

6. Neuhaus, Naked Public Square, 89.

7. Neuhaus, Naked Public Square, 153.

8. Arthur Schlesinger, *The Vital Center* (New York: Houghton Mifflin, 1962), 188. Quoted in Neuhaus, *Naked Public Square*, 91.

9. Peter L. Berger, "Religion in Post-Protestant America," *Commentary* 81:5 (May 1986), 44.

10. Russell Kirk, *The Roots of American Order* (LaSalle, Ill.: Open Court, 1974), 81.

11. Will Durant, *Caesar and Christ: A History of Roman Civilization from Its Beginnings to* A.D. 337 (New York: Simon and Schuster, 1944), 164.

12. Etienne Gilson, "Foreword," in St. Augustine, *The City of God* (New York: Image/Doubleday, 1958), 19.

13. Edmund Burke, *Reflections on the Revolution in France*. Quoted in *The Portable Conservative Reader* (New York: Penguin, 1982), 27.

14. A. James Reichley, *Religion in American Public Life* (Washington, D.C.: Brookings Institute, 1986), 9.

15. Kirk, *Roots of American Order*, 17.

16. Quoted in Sydney E. Ahlstrom, *A Religious History of the American People* (New Haven, Conn.: Yale University Press, 1972), 386.

17. Will and Ariel Durant, *The Lessons of History* (New York: Simon and Schuster, 1968), 50.

18. Boris Rumer, "Soviet Writers Decry Loss of Spiritual Values in Society," *Christian Science Monitor* (October 7, 1986), 1.

19. Rumer, "Soviet Writers Decry Loss of Spiritual Values in Society," 1.

20. Walter Lippmann, *A Preface to Morals* (New York: Time, 1929), 134.

21. Aleksandr I. Solzhenitsyn, *A World Split Apart: Commencement Address Delivered at Harvard University, June 8, 1978* (New York: Harper & Row, 1978), 49.

CHAPTER 16

1. *Westminster Confession of Faith*, XX, 2.

2. John 13:34.

3. Quoted in Richard John Neuhaus, *The Naked Public Square* (Grand Rapids, Mich.: Eerdmans, 1984), 178.

4. *The Religion and Society Report*, 3:9 (September 1986), 5.

5. Matthew 5:13–14.

6. Quoted in George F. Will, *Statecraft as Soulcraft: What Government Does* (New York: Simon and Schuster, 1983), 129.

7. See Matthew 25:14–30 and Luke 16:10–31 for discussion of this issue.

8. James Q. Wilson, "Crime and American Culture," *The Public Interest* 70 (Winter 1983), 22.

9. Paul Johnson, *Modern Times: The World from the Twenties to the Eighties* (New York: Harper & Row, 1983), 246–47.

10. Edwin J. Orr, *The Flaming Tongue: The Impact of 20th Century Revivals* (Chicago, Ill.: Moody Press, 1973), 17–18.

11. Etienne Gilson, "Foreword," in St. Augustine, *The City of God* (New York: Image/Doubleday, 1958), 32.

12. Neuhaus, *Naked Public Square*.

CHAPTER 17

1. "Jesus Christ in the Lives of Americans Today," a poll conducted by the Gallup Organization, Inc., for the Robert H. Schuller Ministries (February 1983), 12.

2. Joseph Sobran, "Pensees: Notes for the Reactionary of Tomorrow," *National Review* (December 31, 1985), 50.

3. Donald Bloesch, *Crumbling Foundations* (Grand Rapids, Mich.: Zondervan, 1984), 38.

4. Bloesch, *Crumbling Foundations*, 73.

5. G. K. Chesterton, *The Victorian Age in English Literature* (New York: Holt, 1913), 43.

6. James V. Schall, "The Altar as the Throne," in Stanley Atkins and Theodore McConnell, eds., *Churches on the Wrong Road* (Chicago: Regnery, 1986), 231–32.
7. Harry Blamires, *The Christian Mind* (Ann Arbor, Mich.: Servant Books, 1963/1978), 3.
8. Jacques Ellul, *Presence in the Kingdom* (New York: Seabury Press, 1948/1967), 119.
9. Romans 13:1; 1 Timothy 2:2.
10. Acts 5:29.
11. St. Augustine, *City of God* (Garden City, N.Y.: Image/Doubleday, 1958).
12. Quoted in Richard John Neuhaus, *The Naked Public Square* (Grand Rapids, Mich.: Eerdmans, 1984), 209.
13. St. Augustine, *City of God*.
14. C. S. Lewis, *The Four Loves* (New York: Harcourt, Brace, World, 1960), 41.
15. Quoted in Neuhaus, *Naked Public Square*, 237.
16. Neuhaus, *Naked Public Square*, 75.
17. Quoted in Lynn Buzzard and Paula Campbell, *Holy Disobedience: When Christians Must Resist the State* (Ann Arbor, Mich.: Servant Books, 1984), 123.
18. Daniel 1–3.
19. Paraphrase of Daniel 3:16–18.
20. Acts 4:19–20.
21. Charles Mendies, in an interview with Ellen Santilli Vaughn (September 1986).
22. Daniel 1:8.
23. Quoted in A. James Reichley, *Religion in American Public Life* (Washington, D.C.: Brookings Institute, 1986), 104.

CHAPTER 18
1. Mickey Kaus, *New Republic* (February 24, 1986), 16.
2. *Newsweek* (February 10, 1986), 7, graph.
3. "Brother Can You Spare a Song?" *Newsweek* (October 28, 1985), 95.
4. "Brother Can You Spare a Song?" 95.
5. Quoted in George F. Will, *Statecraft as Soulcraft: What Government Does* (New York: Simon and Schuster, 1983), 129.
6. Jerry Falwell, *If I Should Die Before I Wake* (Nashville: Thomas Nelson, 1986), 10–11.
7. Cited in March Bell, "A Justice Department Commission is Escalating the War Over Pornography," *Eternity* (May 1986), 15–21.
8. "ACLU Reports, Deplores Antipornography Drive," *Washington Post* (February 24, 1986), A-12.
9. This story is told in more detail in Jack Eckerd, *Finding the Right Prescription* (Old Tappan, N.J.: Revell, 1987).
10. Quoted in "Personalities " section of *Philadelphia* Inquirer.

CHAPTER 19
1. John Naisbitt, *Megatrends: Ten New Directions Transforming Our Lives* (New York: Warner Books, 1983).
2. Paul Tournier, *The Violence Within*. Quoted in Cheryl Forbes, *The Religion of Power* (Grand Rapids, Mich.: Zondervan, 1983), 17.
3. *Newsweek* (September 6, 1971), 16.
4. George Orwell, *1984* (New York: New American Library, 1961), 217.
5. C. P. Snow, *The Masters* (New York: Scribner's, 1982).
6. Richard J. Foster, *Money, Sex and Power* (New York: Harper & Row, 1985), 175.
7. John Milton, *Paradise Lost and Paradise Regained* (New York: New American Library, 1968), 54.
8. Luke 22:26.
9. Mark 10:44.

10. Quoted in Sydney E. Ahlstrom, *A Religious History of the American People* (New Haven, Conn.: Yale University Press, 1972), 386.

11. 2 Corinthians 12:9–10.

12. Anthony Campolo, *The Power Delusion* (Wheaton, Ill.: Victor Brooks, 1984).

13. Numbers 12:3.

CHAPTER 20

1. "America's Question and Answer Man," *Newsweek* (June 15, 1987), 56.

2. Robert L. Dabney, *Discussions*, vol. 2, edited by C. R. Vaughan (Harrisburg, Virginia: Sprinkle Publications, 1982), 408.

3. Stephen Monsma, "The Promises and Pitfalls of Evangelical Political Involvement," a speech (October 17, 1986), 9.

4. Andrew Sinclair, *Prohibition: The Era of Excess* (Boston: Little, Brown, 1962).

5. Monsma, "The Promises and Pitfalls of Evangelical Political Involvement," 15–16.

6. St. Augustine, *City of God*, (Garden City, N.Y.: Image/Doubleday, 1958), 88.

7. Harry Blamires, *The Christian Mind* (London: S.P.C.K., 1963), 25.

8. Vernon Grounds, "Crosscurrents," *Moody Monthly* (July/August 1986), 80.

9. Personal letter from Richard John Neuhaus (June 8, 1987).

10. "Vatican Statement on Respect for Human Life in Its Origins and on the Dignity of Procreation: A Reply to Certain Questions of the Day" (1987), 37.

11. Quoted in Joseph Laitin, "Web of Lies," *Washington Post* (October 5, 1986), C-6.

12. *McDaniel vs. Paty*, 435 U.S. 618.

13. "Christopher Dawson: His Interpretation of History," *Modern Age* (Summer 1979), 263.

14. U.S. Bishops' paper on nuclear war, *The Challenge of Peace: God's Promise and Our Response* (May 3, 1983), from the National Conference of Catholic Bishops is discussed in William McNeal, *New York Times* (December 26, 1982), E-3.

15. McNeal, *New York Times* (December 26, 1982), E-3.

16. Russell Kirk, "Promises and Perils of 'Christian Politics'," *Intercollegiate Review* (Fall/Winter 1982), 15.

17. Kirk, "Promises and Perils of 'Christian Politics'," 23.

18. Roman Catholic Polish bishops' statement (June 23, 1985).

19. Exodus 21–22.

CHAPTER 21

1. Richard W. Larsen, "A One-Eyed Angel," *Seattle Times* (April 14, 1985).

CHAPTER 22

1. Quoted in *Christianity Today* (September 5, 1986), 54.

2. Vernon Grounds, "Authentic Piety," *The Other Side* 21:7 (October 1985), 56–57.

3. George Marsden, *Reformed Journal* (November 1986), 3.

4. Quoted in *Christianity Today* (September 5, 1986), 54.

5. Exodus 18:21.

6. James Skillen, "The Bible, Politics and Democracy," a speech delivered at Wheaton College (November 7–8, 1985), 5.

7. McKendree Langley, *The Practice of Political Spirituality* (Jordan Station, Ontario, Canada: Paideia Press, 1984).

8. C. S. Lewis, *God in the Dock* (Grand Rapids, Mich.: Eerdmans, 1970), 198.

9. Quoted by Colman McCarthy, "For Bennett, A Failing Grade in History," *Washington Post* (September 22, 1985), G-8.

10. Interviews with Ronald Reagan after his meeting with the Religious Roundtable in Dallas (August 22, 1980).

11. A. James Reichley, *Wall Street Journal* (November 25, 1985), 28.

12. Quoted in *Journal of Law and Religion*, 2:1 (1984), 71.
13. "Keeping the Church Doors Open," *Christianity Today* (March 21, 1986), 14.
14. *Time* (September 2, 1985), 58.
15. Kent R. Hill, "Religion and the Common Good: In Defense of Pluralism," *This World* 83 (Spring 1987), 83.
16. James V. Schall, "The Altar as the Throne," in Stanley Atkins and Theodore McConnell, eds., *Churches on the Wrong Road* (Chicago: Regnery, 1986), 233.
17. Donald Bloesch, *Crumbling Foundations* (Grand Rapids: Mich.: Zondervan, 1984), 39.
18. Bloesch, *Crumbling Foundations*, 40.
19. Richard Wurmbrand, *Marx and Satan* (Chicago: Crossway, 1986), appendix.
20. Bloesch, *Crumbling Foundations*, 39.
21. Myron Augsburger, *Christianity Today* (January 17, 1986), 21–I.

CHAPTER 23

1. Jaime Cardinal Sin, from a press conference of the Prison Fellowship International Triennial Symposium in Nairobi, Kenya (August 3, 1986).
2. Robert Shaplan, "Letter from the Philippines," *New Yorker* (February 2, 1985), 61.
3. Benigno Aquino, testimony before the House Foreign Affairs Committee (June 20, 1983).
4. Jaime Cardinal Sin, "A Call to Conscience," a pastoral letter (January 1986).
5. Myron Augsburger, *Christianity Today* (January 17, 1986), 21–I.
6. Quoted in Lynn Buzzard and Paula Campbell, *Holy Disobedience: When Christians Must Resist the State* (Ann Arbor, Mich.: Servant Books, 1984), 142.
7. Richard John Neuhaus, *Religion and Society Report* 3:6 (June 1986), 2.
8. Jonathan Mayhew, *A Discourse Concerning Limited Resistance and Non-Resistance* (Boston, 1750).
9. Buzzard and Campbell, *Holy Disobedience*, 58–59.
10. G. K. Chesterton, *Sidelights on New London and Newer New York*, (New York: Dodd and Mead, 1932), 191.
11. Quoted in David R. Weber, *Civil Disobedience in American History* (Ithaca, N.Y.: Cornell University Press, 1978), 244.
12. Francis Schaeffer, *The Complete Works of Francis A. Schaeffer: A Christian Worldview*, vol. 5 (Westchester, Ill.: Crossway, 1981), 491.

CHAPTER 24

1. "Leaders of the Christian Right Announce Their Next Step," *Christianity Today* (December 13, 1985), 65.
2. Jacques Ellul, *The New Demons* (New York: Seabury Press, 1975), 167.
3. *Time* (November 1, 1976), 20.
4. "The Farm Act," *Washington Post* (May 7, 1985), B-1; and "Actresses Appeal for Aid to Farmers," *New York Times* (May 7, 1985), 8.
5. Richard Schickel, *Intimate Strangers: The Culture of Celebrity* (New York: Doubleday, 1985).
6. Jacques Ellul, *The Presence of the Kingdom* (New York: Seabury Press, 1948/1967), 100.
7. Quoted in Parker J. Palmer, *Company of Strangers: Christians and the Renewal of America's Public Life* (New York: Crossroads Publishing, 1981), 80.
8. Alexis de Tocqueville, quoted in Palmer, *Company of Strangers*.
9. Tocqueville, *Democracy in America*. Cited in Arendt, *Company of Strangers*, 80.
10. Quoted in Palmer, *Company of Strangers*.
11. Psalm 118:9.
12. Ellul, *Presence of the Kingdom*, 35.

CHAPTER 25

1. The information in this chapter is based on interviews conducted by Ellen Santilli Vaughn (April 1986).

2. George Russell, "Shadow of a Gunman," *Time* (May 18, 1981), 52–54.

3. Robert Ajemian, "Ready to Die in the Maze," *Time* (August 17, 1981), 48.

4. Ajemian, "Ready to Die in the Maze," 47.

5. Ajemian, "Ready to Die in the Maze," 46.

6. Ajemian, "Ready to Die in the Maze," 47.

7. *New York Times* (March 31, 1979), 1.

8. Based on an account in Jack Holland, *Too Long a Sacrifice* (New York: Dodd and Mead, 1981), 84–89.

9. Guy Garcia, "Edging Toward the Abyss," *Time* (November 30, 1981), 58.

EPILOGUE

1. Malcolm Muggeridge, *The End of Christendom* (Grand Rapids, Mich.: Eerdmans, 1980), 56.

For Further Reading

I would like to acknowledge the following works, which were especially useful in the research and preparation of this book. This is by no means intended to be an exhaustive bibliography on the issues of church and state, religion and politics—but readers will find these sources useful in their own further study.

St. Augustine. *The Confessions, The City of God, and On Christian Doctrine.* Chicago: University of Chicago, Great Books Series, Encyclopedia Britannica, 1952.

Belli, Humberto. *Breaking Faith: The Sandinista Revolution and Its Impact on Freedom and Christian Faith in Nicaragua.* Westchester, Ill.: Crossway, 1985.

Berger, Peter. "Religion in Post-Protestant America." *Commentary* 81:5 (May 1986).

————. *The Sacred Canopy.* Garden City, N.Y.: Anchor, 1968.

Blamires, Harry. *The Christian Mind.* Ann Arbor, Mich.: Servant, 1963.

Bloesch, Donald. *Crumbling Foundations.* Grand Rapids, Mich.: Zondervan, 1984.

Bright, John. *The Kingdom of God.* Nashville: Abingdon, 1953.

Buzzard, Lynn, and Paula Campbell. *Holy Disobedience: When Christians Must Resist the State.* Ann Arbor: Servant, 1984.

Campolo, Anthony. *The Power Delusion.* Wheaton, Ill.: Victor, 1983.

Christianity Today Institute. For its extraordinarily useful summary of *The Christian as Citizen.* Christianity Today, 1985.

Clowney, Edmund, "The Politics of the Kingdom." *Westminster Theological Journal* 41 (Spring 1979).

Cullman, Oscar. *The State in the New Testament.* New York: Scribner's, 1956.

Durant, Will and Ariel Durant. *The Lessons of History*. New York: Simon and Schuster, 1968.

Ellul, Jacques. *The Presence of the Kingdom*. New York: Seabury, 1948/1967.

————. *The New Demons*. New York: Seabury, 1975.

————. *The Political Illusion*. Translated by Konrad Keller. New York: Vintage, 1972.

Forbes, Cheryl. *The Religion of Power*. Grand Rapids, Mich.: Zondervan, 1983.

Herberg, Will. *Protestant, Catholic, Jew: An Essay in American Religious Sociology*. Chicago: University of Chicago, 1983.

Johnson, Paul. *Modern Times: The World from the Twenties to the Eighties*. New York: Harper & Row, 1983.

Jones, E. Stanley. *The Unshakable Kingdom and the Unchanging Person*. Nashville: Abingdon, 1972.

Kik, J. Marcellus. *The Story of Two Kingdoms*. New York: Nelson, 1963.

Kirk, Russell. "Promises and Perils of 'Christian Politics'." *Intercollegiate Review* (Fall/Winter 1982).

————. "Religion in the Civil Social Order." *Modern Age* (Fall 1984).

————. *The Roots of American Order*. LaSalle, Ill.: Open Court, 1974.

Mott Stephen, *Biblical Ethics and Social Change*. New York: Oxford University, 1982.

Neuhaus, Richard John. *The Naked Public Square*. Grand Rapids, Mich.: Eerdmans, 1984.

————. *Unsecular America*. Grand Rapids, Mich.: Eerdmans, 1986.

Reichley, A. James. *Religion in American Public Life*. Washington, D.C.: Brookings Institute, 1985.

Runner, Evan. Especially his "Preface" to McKendree R. Langley, *The Practice of Political Spirituality*. Jordan Station, Ontario: Paideia, 1984.

Schaeffer, Francis. *How Should We Then Live?* Old Tappan, N.J.: Revell, 1976.

Schall, James V. "The Altar as the Throne." *Churches on the Wrong Road*. Chicago: Regnery, 1986.

————. *Christianity and Politics*. Boston: St. Paul Editions, 1981.

Skillen, James. "The Bible, Politics and Democracy: What Does Biblical Obedience Entail for American Political Thought?" In *The Bible, Politics and Democracy*. Edited by *Richard John Neuhaus*. Grand Rapids: Eerdmans, 1987.

Sproul, R. C. *If There Is a God, Why Are There Atheists?* Minneapolis: Dimensions, 1978.

————. *Classical Apologetics*. Grand Rapids, Mich.: Zondervan, 1984.

Valladares, Armando. *Against All Hope*. New York: Knopf, 1986.

Vos, Gerhardus. *Biblical Theology: Old and New Testaments*. Grand Rapids, Mich.: Eerdmans, 1984.

Wood, James E., Jr. *Nationhood and the Kingdom*. Nashville: Broadman, 1977.

Index Kingdoms in Conflict

CHARLES W. COLSON received his bachelor's degree from Brown University and his law degree from George Washington University. From 1969 to 1973 he served as special counsel to President Richard M. Nixon. He pleaded guilty to offenses related to Watergate in 1974 and served seven months in prison. He is now Chairman of Prison Fellowship, a Washington, D.C.–based organization that he founded in 1976. Colson is the author of three best-sellers, *Born Again*, *Life Sentence*, and *Loving God*, and is also a frequent contributor to magazines and journals. All Mr. Colson's speaking fees and book royalties are donated to further the work of Prison Fellowship Ministries.

ELLEN SANTILLI VAUGHN, a native of Washingotn, D.C., received her bachelor's degree from the University of Richmond and her master's in English literature from Georgetown University. She serves as Editorial Director for Prison Fellowship Ministries and has worked as an editor and writer with Charles Colson since 1980. She and her husband, Lee, live in Wayne, Pennsylvania.